James M. Shirley
2-23-84

CONTEMPORARY OPERATIONS MANAGEMENT

THOMAS M. COOK
American Airlines, Inc.

ROBERT A. RUSSELL
The University of Tulsa

CONTEMPORARY OPERATIONS MANAGEMENT

text and cases

2nd edition

Prentice-Hall, Inc., Englewood Cliffs, New Jersey 07632

Library of Congress Cataloging in Publication Data

COOK, THOMAS M.,
    Contemporary operations management.

    Includes bibliographies and index.
      1. Management—Mathematical models. 2. Management
science. 3. Production management—Mathematical models.
I. Russell, Robert A.,   II. Title.
HD30.25.C66 1984   658.4'034   83-19162
ISBN 0-13-170449-4

Editorial/production supervision
  and interior design: Linda C. Mason
Cover design: Diane Saxe
Manufacturing buyer: Ed O'Dougherty

Printed in the United States of America

10 9 8 7 6 5 4 3 2 1

ISBN 0-13-170449-4

Prentice-Hall International, Inc., *London*
Prentice-Hall of Australia Pty. Limited, *Sydney*
Editora Prentice-Hall do Brasil, Ltda., *Rio de Janeiro*
Prentice-Hall Canada Inc., *Toronto*
Prentice-Hall of India Private Limited, *New Delhi*
Prentice-Hall of Japan, Inc., *Tokyo*
Prentice-Hall of Southeast Asia Pte. Ltd., *Singapore*
Whitehall Books Limited, *Wellington, New Zealand*

CONTENTS

PREFACE

This book is designed for use in a semester or quarter course that introduces the student to the field of operations/production management. The book is aimed at the business or engineering student who will most likely pursue a career in an organization requiring some managerial ability and decision-making skill. The level of the text is appropriate for an introductory course at the graduate or undergraduate level.

One of the objectives in the text was to select those topics that are considered to be in the mainstream of the POM area. It has been designed with AACSB guidelines in mind and should satisfy text requirements for introductory courses in production/operations management or applied quantitative methods.

The mathematical level of the book is purposely kept low in order to make the material readable for both the student and the layman. A course in college algebra or finite mathematics is sufficient mathematical preparation. In Chapter 2 on linear programming, the simplex method and more mathematical material have been placed in an appendix at the end of the chapter and may be skipped without loss of continuity. Although the mathematical level of the book is relatively low, the book is decision-oriented and devotes significant time to the explanation of quantitative methods that are of particular use to operations managers; the limitations of these methods are discussed, as well as their utility.

A special effort is made in this text to bridge the gap between the theory and the practice of operations management. Numerous references to successful applications are made throughout the chapters of the text. Particularly relevant applications from the literature are briefly described as small cases or scenarios. Harvard-type cases are presented at the end of the book and may be used as assignments or the basis for discussion. These cases should stimulate student interest and help the student develop a more realistic view of POM problems. Case discussions and solutions are provided in the instructor's manual.

The format of the chapters has been designed to facilitate the learning of both descriptive and analytical material. Key concepts and words are italicized in the text (these are defined in the glossary at the end of the book), and each chapter contains a summary and set of review questions. In addition, several solved problems are presented at the end of each chapter to further illustrate the application of various methods and concepts. An ample number of unsolved problems and review questions are included with each chapter, along with answers to selected problems at the end of the book.

The book is divided into five parts. The first section is an introduction to the POM area. The second contains a description of three quantitative tools—linear programming, simulation, and queuing theory—that are especially helpful to the operations manager in his decision-making role. The third section is concerned with the design of the productive system. Topics such as plant location, facility layout, process design, and job design are discussed in this section. The fourth and fifth parts address the problems inherent in operating and controlling an ongoing productive system. Important topics in these sections are forecasting, aggregate planning, inventory control systems, material requirements planning, scheduling, and quality assurance.

In the second edition, a significant effort was made to insure that the material is current. New material on productivity such as the use of CAD/CAM and robotics has been included. Japanese innovations such as quality circles have been added to the appropriate chapters. In addition, the pedagogy of the text has been enhanced with hundreds of minor modifications, many new figures, and fifty percent more end of chapter problems and new cases. In short, the second edition does not represent a major departure from the first edition but we believe it is more current and significantly improved pedagocially.

Several people have been extremely helpful to us at various stages of this project. We would like to thank the reviewers, whose comments and suggestions led to an improved manuscript: Prof. F. J. Brewerton, Middle Tennessee State University, Prof. David M. Dougherty, University of Texas at El Paso, Prof. Douglas A. Eluers, University of North Carolina at Chapel Hill, Prof. William N. Ledbetter, Auburn University, Prof. Jugoslav, S. Milutinovich, Temple University, Prof. Richard G. Newman, Indiana University Northwest.

We would also like to thank the staff at Prentice-Hall for its assistance, particularly Production Editor Linda Mason. We would like to thank our typists Judy Tillery and Dianne Mooty who did an outstanding job preparing the manuscript.

Finally, we would like to thank our families for their understanding and encouragement during the course of this project.

THOMAS M. COOK
ROBERT A. RUSSELL

CONTEMPORARY OPERATIONS MANAGEMENT

1

INTRODUCTION TO OPERATIONS MANAGEMENT

Brief historical overview
The nature of operations management
   designing
   scheduling
   operating
   control
A systems approach
Decision making
   models
   heuristics
   management information systems (MIS)
Productivity
   productivity growth problem
   reasons for productivity growth decline
   solutions to productivity problem
   Japanese connection
Operations management in action
   scheduling policies for surgical patients
   development of annual operating plan
   for plywood manufacture
   inventory control system

The importance of studying the management of *productive systems* can be estimated by considering the importance of productive systems in the world today. It is through these systems that we come to have our food, shelter, durable and nondurable goods, health care, education, and general standard of living. The quality of their productive systems is one main difference between highly industrialized countries and underdeveloped countries.

Civilizations have progressed hand in hand with their productive systems. Humanity has gone from hunting and tilling the ground to houses with two-car garages and the landing of men on the moon. Since the turn of the century, the productivity output per man-hour has increased by about 600 percent. Science and technology have laid the foundations for our rapid progress, but along with science and technology has emerged a discipline called *operations management*. This discipline is relatively new and consists of scientific principles, concepts, and techniques for managing productive systems. It is our purpose in this introductory textbook to study the salient topics in operations management.

In spite of tremendous progress (at an increasing rate), there is a pressing need to further understand and use effective principles in managing productive systems. One look at our modern world and its growing population, resource shortages, pollution–environmental problems, high product demand, and unstable world economies substantiates the need for effective management. This need extends not only to manufacturing industries, but also to service, governmental, and agricultural industries.

Before we turn to what operations management is all about in the modern sense, let's look at a brief history of and some of the earlier contributions to the management of productive systems.

BRIEF HISTORICAL OVERVIEW

The earliest signs of people using thought processes to aid productivity date back to the development of crude tools, and the banding together to hunt and grow food. Much further up the scale of evolution we find the amazing construction of the Egyptian pyramids, around 2500 B.C. The building of these huge monuments obviously required the management of vast resources and people. Other interesting architectural accomplishments include the Greek Parthenon, the Roman aqueducts and roads, and the Great Wall of China; all of these occurred before 100 B.C.

During the Middle Ages, little growth in technological achievement took place. However, at the end of the fourteenth century, Heinrich von Wyck developed the mechanical clock; some historians claim that it is the clock rather than the wheel or steam engine that has played the most important role in the industrial age. And early in the fifteenth century, the Venetian shipbuilders seem to have used a type of assembly-line process in the outfitting of ships, and instituted standardization in key parts of ships.

The real roots of what we call operations management did not begin to develop until the Industrial Revolution. This period is characterized by the emergence of the factory system (with its advantages and disadvantages) and greatly increased productivity. In 1764, James Watt improved the steam engine to the extent that it could be used as a source of power in industry. Shortly thereafter, in 1776, Scottish economist Adam Smith wrote his book, *The Wealth of Nations*, in which he advocated division of labor. In his observations regarding the manufacture of straight pins, he noted three economic advantages of such division: (1) development of dexterity upon repetitive performance of a single task, (2) time savings owing to less changeover effort, and (3) likely development of machines that simplify work and increase worker productivity. Smith's book laid the foundation for modern work simplification methods, but it also helped create some monotonous jobs that are very limited in scope.

In 1832, an English mathematician and genius, Charles Babbage, wrote his milestone treatise, *On Economy of Machines and Manufactures*. In his book, Babbage recommended scientific methods in analyzing business problems. He agreed with Smith concerning the division of labor, but he further proposed skill differential in wages—that not all workers be paid the same amount; but rather be paid on the basis of the skill required to do the job.

Around the turn of the century, Frederick Taylor formally advocated a scientific approach to the problems of manufacturing. He formalized some of the ideas Babbage had espoused and focused mainly on work standards and wage incentives. He demonstrated that scientifically conceived work standards and wage incentives could improve productivity. Taylor wanted to replace old work methods with the development of a science for each element of work. His ideas, which came to be known as scientific management theory, were not popular with everyone, especially in the case of labor unions. However, Taylor's ideas made a revolutionary impact, and he was to be known as the father of scientific management. His efforts were largely responsible for developing industrial engineering as a profession. Modern fields most affected by Taylor's early efforts include methods engineering and work measurement, human engineering, and personnel.

Henry Gantt, a contemporary of Taylor's, refined the content of early scientific management by bringing into consideration the human aspect of management's attitude toward labor. He espoused the importance of the personnel department to the scientific approach to management. Perhaps his greatest contribution, however, was his scheduling system for loading jobs on machines. Basically a recording procedure, Gantt's system was devised to minimize job completion delays; it permitted machine loadings to be planned months in advance. Other contemporaries of Taylor were Frank and Lillian Gilbreth, who pioneered time and motion study and industrial psychology.

In 1913, Henry Ford introduced the first moving assembly line for automobiles. The innovation allowed cars to be produced about eight times faster than before, and high levels of output fueled consumerism in the U.S. economy. In 1915, F.W. Harris published a simple lot-size formula that constituted the basis for inventory control for several decades and still finds wide use today.

During the twenties and thirties, most of the contributions to operations management were quantitative in nature. A.K. Erlang developed formulas to predict waiting times for callers using automatic telephone exchanges. His work founded modern waiting-line analysis, or queuing theory (see Chapter 4). Statistical quality control methods were introduced by Walter Shewhart in 1931, and L.H.C. Tippett developed statistical sampling to determine standard work times in 1934. Aside from these developments in statistics during the thirties, the well-known Hawthorne experiments were carried out to determine the effects of environmental changes on the work output of employees at a Western Electric plant. Their surprising results were that workers responded more to mere changes in their environment rather than to the nature of those changes. For example, increasing the lighting or temperature raised output, but so did returning all environmental conditions to their original state. These results tended to refute the scientific management theories and led to schools of thought founded more on human behavioral theories, such as human relations.

During World War II, the British organized a team of talented people, called "Blackett's Circus," ranging from mathematicians and physicists to physiologists and army officers, to study the military and logistics problems facing Great Britain during the war. This interdisciplinary scientific approach to operations-type problems was successful in British military efforts and soon spread to the U.S. military. Such a scientific team approach, using mathematical models and techniques, became known as *operations research* (also called *management science*), and its applications soon spread to business.

Operations research/management science is a sister discipline that provides many of the quantitative tools for use in operations management and other functional areas of business. In 1947, George Dantzig helped develop linear programming (see Chapter 2), and, along with the development of high-speed computers, this brought about a modeling and systems type of approach to business problems. At the beginning of the fifties, a new era had begun in much the same way that scientific management had emerged at the beginning of the century. Rapid progress was made in the fifties with computer hardware, data processing, and mathematical solution techniques. Operations research/management science and industrial engineering were rapidly becoming a profession, but production/operations management had not yet "come into its own." Most of the research focused upon well-defined operational problems for which an analytical solution could be found.

In the late fifties and early sixties, some books and articles began to appear that dealt specifically with production management as opposed to industrial engineering or mathematical programming. Earlier courses in production management dealt with such topics as plant layout, process design, time and motion studies, aggregate planning, inventory, and quality control. Meanwhile, the practice of production management was becoming recognized as a profession in itself, and much progress was being made in the use of the computer to solve production problems. Commercial computer programming packages became available from major computer manufacturers for areas like scheduling, inventory control, plant location, and forecasting. The founding of the American Production and Inventory Control Society (APICS) in 1957 did much to advance the practice of production and inventory management, as well as the status of production management as a profession.

The late sixties to the eighties, the current era, has been characterized by the systems approach and an attitude toward solving real management problems more than narrow mathematical problems. The discipline is now usually called operations management rather than production management, as it applies also to the management of operations outside the factory. Many of the planning, scheduling, and controlling methods are now applied to service and nonmanufacturing organizations, operations management is now recognized as a profession in itself, and a student pursuing such a career is often known as a student of POM (production/operations management).

The modern *systems approach* requires the organization to consider its decisions in relation to the whole of the organization and its environment. Implementing the true systems approach is somewhat difficult, since it requires management to consider higher-order and lower-order implications of any decision. The current practice of operations management does not always employ a true systems approach, although some efforts such as materials requirements planning systems (see Chapter 11) come very close. The current era is characterized by very rapid data processing and the increasing trend to the use of machines for power and computation. Further progress in incorporating human or behavioral considerations and a more thorough or pervasive use of the systems approach should characterize future advancements in the field of operations management.

THE NATURE OF OPERATIONS MANAGEMENT

The brief history in the preceding section outlines how people have greatly increased their ability to produce goods and services. A productive system is the mechanism by which goods and services are created. Operations management, quite simply is the management of productive systems.

We must stress the fact that operations management goes well beyond the manufacturing operations of assembly and fabrication. Productive systems also include the operation of banks; city, state, and federal government agencies; hospitals; public utilities; school systems; insurance companies; retail department stores; and so on. We shall see that many of the basic principles of operations management can be applied to both manufacturing and service organizations.

The management of both service and manufacturing organizations can be unified by viewing a productive system as one that transforms inputs into outputs. Figure 1-1 illustrates a basic diagram of a productive system.

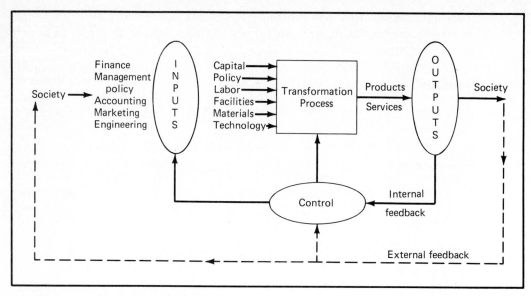

FIGURE 1-1   Diagram of Productive System

We may define operations management more formally as the management of a productive system that transforms inputs into outputs. The responsibility of the operations manager can be seen in Figure 1-1 as the area between inputs and outputs. The operations manager, whether the official title is production manager, or vice-president of operations, or whatever, must follow the policies set by top management and work cooperatively with other organizational functions such as finance, marketing, and engineering. The manager has some control over the inputs, such as labor, use of capital, facilities, and available technology, and the primary concern is management of the transformation process to create quality products or services efficiently. Listed in Table 1-1 are some systems that typify the transformation process for both products and services.

You might have learned in your first management course that management functions in general involve planning, organizing, staffing, direction, and control. These same functions apply to the operations manager. There are also several important functions that apply specifically to the management of the transformation process of any productive system. These four basic functions are designing, scheduling, operating, and control.

Designing

Designing the transformation process involves basic issues such as equipment selection, type of process, and work-flow patterns. Transformation processes are usually either continuous, intermittent, or "one-shot" projects. Continuous processes are generally highly specialized to produce one type of product or service. Associated

Table 1-1   Systems Transformation Processes

TYPE OF SYSTEM	MAIN INPUTS	COMPONENTS	FUNCTION	MAIN OUTPUT
Automobile plant	Steel, parts	Assembly line, equipment, workers	Assembly of autos	Automobiles
Hospital	Patients	Doctors, nurses, equipment, supplies	Health care	Healthy people
Insurance claims office	Claims, phone calls	Claims agents	Rejecting, accepting, settling claims	Settled claims
University	Students	Professors, books, facilities	Imparting knowledge and information	Educated students
Computer center	Jobs to be processed	Programmers, CPU, peripheral equipment	Processing of computer jobs	Processed jobs

equipment is usually of a special-purpose type with little flexibility. Intermittent processes are more general and utilize a variety of multipurpose equipment. Classical examples of continuous, intermittent, and project processes are automobile assembly lines, job shops, and building construction respectively. The choice of the best type of process is dictated by economical considerations and volume of output desired. Other design factors include the layout of the facility and pattern of work flow to achieve a smooth flow of output.

Scheduling

After a process is designed, it must be scheduled to produce the desired product or service at the right time. Scheduling can be broken down into long-range and short-range planning. In long-range scheduling, forecasts of future demand are obtained and aggregate plans are devised to estimate needed amounts of manpower, capacity, and materials. Long-range scheduling involves the tentative scheduling of future activities to meet future demand. It requires the planning of manpower and materials to have them available at the right time and the right place to transform the inputs to the desired outputs. Much attention is given to this type of scheduling in Chapter 11 on materials requirements planning (MRP). Another type of scheduling involves the management of projects over time and utilizes the PERT/CPM method to pinpoint bottleneck activities and avoid delays. Short-range scheduling gets down to the micro level of weekly or daily operations. It involves sequencing activities such as jobs through machines, vehicles through routes, and patients through a hospital. In Chapter 12 we will examine systematic methods for scheduling.

Operating

Operating the transformation process is closely related to scheduling. But whereas scheduling refers to a type of planning prior to execution, operating often refers to the actual implementation of the transformation procedures. Effective operation requires the ability to react to last-minute changes and unexpected delays in planned schedules. The operating phase also involves longer-range decision activities not pertaining to scheduling, such as purchasing, implementing market strategies, and process redesign.

Control

The control function is graphically depicted in Figure 1-1. It involves the monitoring of the transformation process to ensure a quality end product or service. The control mechanism usually consists of some means of measuring the product or service before its completion; people and automated machines are both used. Often, computers are used to monitor inventory levels and can signal an out-of-stock or backorder situation. Machines also exist to measure chemical processes such as the octane rating of various gasolines. Another type of feedback can occur externally to the firm, from society. However, the purpose of quality control (see Chapter 13) is to help ensure an acceptable product or service before it reaches the customer.

We have taken a brief look at the basic functions of managing a production system. We have mentioned some of the primary responsibilities of the operations manager, but certainly not all of them. Table 1-2 further delineates the major responsibilities associated with managing a productive system.

Table 1-2   Major Responsibilities of the Operations Manager

DESIGN	*SCHEDULING*
1. Product design	1. Aggregate planning
2. Job and process design	2. Scheduling manpower levels
3. Capital equipment selection	3. Project management
4. Setting labor standards	4. Timing inventory replenishments
5. Developing labor skills	5. Routing and sequencing
6. Plant location and layout	6. Job-shop scheduling

OPERATING	*CONTROL*
1. Purchasing	1. Quality control
2. Forecasting requirements	2. Inventory control policies
3. Process redesign	3. Monitoring of production processes
4. Operation of transformation process	4. Cost control
5. Maintenance	5. Resource allocation

A SYSTEMS APPROACH

Operations managers must all be involved with the basic functions of designing, scheduling, operating, and controlling. The managerial approach that is used in performing these four functions can and does vary widely. An underlying philosophy of this text (and most others) is that a systems approach is the most effective approach to operations management decision problems.

The word *system* is much used in our society. We hear of computer systems, solar systems, and political systems. In the broad definition of general systems theory, a system is a whole comprising interrelated parts intended to accomplish a specific objective. Thus, a computer system is made up of hardware components such as the central processor unit, card reader, disk drives, and tape drives, and software components such as the operating system software and compiler programs. These components interact to accomplish the objective of processing computer jobs.

Organizations, too, conform to our definition of a system. The operations manager, for example, is concerned with human/machine systems comprising components such as machinery, departments, divisions, and individual people. The main thrust of the systems approach is to broadly define problems that when solved yield benefits that are in line with the highest order and overall goals of the organization.

Failure to use the systems approach can sometimes yield good results for a component of the system, but not for the system as a whole. For example, suppose the inventory division of an organization is experiencing higher-than-average inventory levels and costs. Reducing inventory levels may reduce costs in the inventory division but may reduce sales for marketing and cause unemployment on the production line; this may not be consistent with the goals of the organization as a whole. This is called suboptimization rather than optimization of the organization goals.

Traditional approaches to operations management viewed the organizational boundaries of the firm as being relatively fixed. The basic idea was for each department of the organization to do its job as well as possible, but apart from other departments. This approach can lead to optimization of departmental goals but suboptimization of the goals of the organization as a whole.

In order to optimize the goals of the organization, the systems approach requires the inclusion of all factors relevant to the problem. In the example above, we would require input from not only inventory but also marketing and personnel. The modern systems approach cuts across departmental and divisional lines. It recognizes the interdependence of the various functions of an organization. Decisions made by operations managers have an effect on the engineering, marketing, and finance functions of the organization. Likewise, decisions made in these departments can have significant impact on the productive function.

The systems approach calls for an integration of the goals, policies, and decisions of the separate functions of the organization. This blend of viewpoints will result in an integrated decision that leads to the best overall good of the firm as perceived by management. Figure 1-2 depicts the synthesis of input and output between the various organizational departments and integrated decisions.

The systems approach, although the most effective, is not always the easiest approach to implement. It requires cooperation between departments and an examination of perhaps more alternatives than does a traditional approach. It may also require the resolution of conflict between departments whose objectives are not in complete agreement. Such decisions often require common sense and the subjective judgment of management. There is never a guarantee that the resulting decisions will always be perfect; in the business world, decisions are too complex and contingencies too prevalent. However, the use of the systems approach will lead to a systematic way to reach the goals of the organization and balance between departments.

Just as a systems approach helps us to have a balanced perspective concerning an organization's components, it also helps us to view the organization as a component, or subsystem, of the environment in which it exists. Figure 1-3 depicts the productive system as a subsystem of the organization and its environment.

Systems methodology is very broad and applicable to other endeavors in addition to operations management. It is particularly valuable in decision structuring or decision-making endeavors such as business and economic policy of quantitative decision making.

DECISION MAKING

All decision problems can be classified as either (1) strategic, (2) tactical, or (3) operational.

Strategic problems involve the establishment of organizational goals and objectives. These kinds of problems generally affect the organization as a whole and entail decisions that have long-term impact on the organization. Strategic decision making is usually the role of top management, but operations management is often involved in the design phases. For example, decisions regarding product mix, plant locations, and the degree of automation are all strategic decisions.

Tactical decisions generally involve not the organization as a whole but rather some component or subsystem. Tactical decisions deal with means of implementing strategic decisions. Operations managers must make hundreds of tactical decisions in their managerial careers. Examples of tactical decisions are allocation of resources such as raw materials and capital, yearly manpower levels, selection of equipment, and process redesign or improvement.

Operational decisions are concerned most with efficiency of performance and deal with an even more limited subsystem of the organization, such as an inventory department or machine shop. Thousands of operational decisions must be made yearly by the operations manager and perhaps foremen or first-line management.

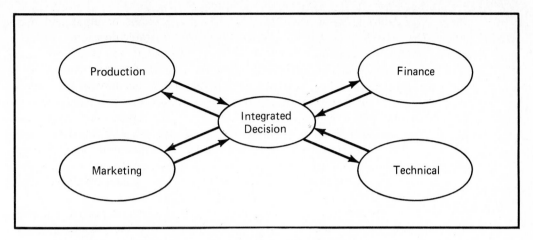

FIGURE 1-2   Integrated Decisions through the Systems Approach

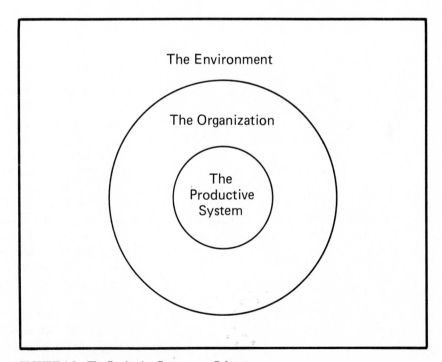

FIGURE 1-3   The Productive System as a Subsystem

Operational decisions involve a wide range of activities, from scheduling of day-to-day activities to pricing and production levels. The main concern of operational decisions is the performance of specific jobs in a timely and cost-efficient manner.

Given the systems approach as the general structure for decision making, we can distinguish between decision alternatives as affecting system effectiveness or system efficiency. Starr defines strategic decisions as affecting the organization as a whole and thus affecting system effectiveness.[1] Tactical and operational decisions affect only various subsystems and hence system efficiency. Obviously, system effectiveness is more important than system efficiency. Decisions to improve system efficiency should not be made at the expense of system effectiveness. However, given a high level of system effectiveness, it is desirable to achieve system efficiency as well.

There are several ways for the operations manager to arrive at decisions for strategic, tactical, or operational problems. He can use his subjective judgment, mathematical decision models, or heuristic decision methods. The appropriate choice of methods depends upon the nature of the decision problem. One of the main purposes of this text is to familiarize you with effective approaches to various decision-making problems.

An important factor in any decision problem pertains to the amount of risk or uncertainty underlying the problem. Figure 1-4 illustrates the range of risk in decision making. Deterministic problems are those in which all information regarding the problem is known with certainty. Stochastic problems involve more risk, as only a probability distribution is known. In decision problems under uncertainty, little or nothing is known about the decision environment. To illustrate these three types of problems, let's consider a simplified decision problem for an inventory manager who has to place an order at the beginning of each month to replenish stock. In a deterministic problem, he would know next month's demand with certainty, so he could order exactly that amount. In a stochastic problem, he would not know next month's demand, but he would know the probability distribution of demand; for instance, the demand may be normally distributed with a mean of 250 units. Last, under uncertainty, he would have little or no idea what the next month's

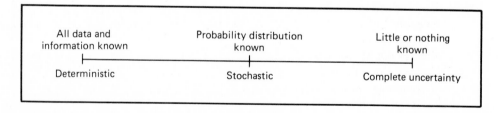

FIGURE 1-4   Continuum of Uncertainty in Decision Problems

---

[1]M.K. Starr, *Production Management: Systems and Synthesis* (Englewood Cliffs, N.J.: Prentice-Hall, 1972).

demand would be or how much to order. Most decision problems are neither completely deterministic or completely uncertain.

For decision problems that are completely deterministic, objective decision methods have been most helpful in achieving an effective solution. Tactical and operational as well as some strategic problems have been solved successfully by objective means such as mathematical models and heuristics. Earlier efforts with objective methods tended to focus on simple, well-defined problems in which efficiency was the prime consideration. More recently, however, attention has begun to focus on more general operations management problems and system effectiveness. Nevertheless, as decision problems become more complex and less clearly defined, and as multiple objectives are considered, then the decision maker's own personal judgment becomes more involved in the final decision.

Models

Models can be very useful in making objective decisions about decision problems in general. Model development and solution have been a key development in the discipline of operations research/management science. Many of these models and problem-solving techniques are applicable to operations management problems.

A *model* is a representation or an abstraction of an object or a particular real-world phenomenon. A good model accurately displays the key properties of the entity it represents. Models are used in many disciplines besides operations management; economics and engineering are two other areas that make extensive use of them. The purpose in using a model is to gain specific information about and general insight into the phenomenon it represents. By using models, it is possible to investigate certain cause-and-effect relationships and the interaction between key variables.

In operations management, the primary models of interest are mathematical models. We can use equations and algebraic relationships to express certain managerial goals and physical constraints. Consider, for example, a production scheduling problem in which many possible products can be selected and scheduled for production. The human mind could probably find an acceptable production schedule, but a good model solved by an optimization technique can usually achieve a 10–15 percent better solution. Models also offer the capability of exploring various alternatives. Given an accurate model of a productive system, we can solve it many different times in order to determine the effects of changing various inputs. This type of *sensitivity analysis* is extremely useful and allows management to ask "what-if" questions. For instance, if management was uncertain about the availability of a certain raw material, it could input several different raw-material levels to this model and obtain production schedules and estimated profits in each case.

Models can thus be especially helpful in the decision-making process, but management must realize their limitations and the fact that a solution is usually a good starting point but not necessarily the final answer.

Heuristics

Models can be an effective tool for decision making, but in some cases a model cannot be constructed, or its solution is too cumbersome and impractical. Many decision problems in operations management are complex and involve many interacting variables and relationships; this is particularly true in the area of scheduling. Heuristics have been devised as a simple means to determine effective objective solutions to problems. A *heuristic* is a method or rule of thumb that determines good but not necessarily optimal solutions to a problem. Heuristics are widespread in operations management, and we shall consider several throughout this book.

As an example, consider a cargo-loading problem in which the load placed on a truck is to have maximum value. There are 99 cartons of various volumes and values, but not all the cartons will fit in the truck simultaneously. Which cartons should be loaded? Let's consider two heuristic decision rules:

Heuristic 1:   Load cartons in decreasing order of value.
Heuristic 2:   Load cartons in decreasing order of value per volume.

The first heuristic simply loads those cartons having highest value first. The second heuristic is usually more effective, as it considers not only the value but the volume of the cartons.

Neither heuristic would guarantee an optimal solution. But an important analogy can be made here. Management is usually practical-minded and is interested in getting an effective solution quickly and then proceeding to the next important problem. Sometimes an additional 5 percent improvement offered by an exact model or optimization procedure is not worth the additional time and effort.

Most decision problems encountered by operations managers are still resolved by human judgment. As mathematical techniques and heuristics improve and become more widespread, we can expect progressive operations managers to turn more to these approaches; however, there are still situations in which the human mind is superior to quantitative techniques. Managers must deal with not only people and behavioral considerations, but multiple and sometimes conflicting goals of the organization. These kinds of decisions seem to be predominant in managerial activities. Research is in progress on multiple-criteria decision making. Perhaps with further advancements in this area, management will have some objective quantitative methods that will prove useful in a much wider range of real-world decision problems.

Management Information Systems (MIS)

Recent progress in operations management can be partially attributed to the systems approach and the use of scientific decision methods. But a factor that has perhaps been utilized even more by practicing operations managers is a *management information system*. No matter what decision method is used, accurate and timely information is critical to effective managerial decision making; each of the phases of designing, scheduling, operating, and controlling requires the collection, processing, and presentation of data. Computer-assisted planning and control extend the abilities of management to perform these important functions.

A management information system (MIS) is a means of collecting, storing, and processing data so that they are useful for decision making. The system consists of the personnel and the computer hardware and software necessary to process the data, and it serves the purpose of converting raw data to timely, usable information for management. The MIS manipulates the data or statistically summarizes them so that a more accurate scientific decision process can be used. Even though information systems do not generate decisions, they do automate many routine tasks and provide quantitative data for evaluation.

Management information systems can support all three levels of managerial planning. However, operations problems are characterized by frequent repetition of planning, making this area more attractive for computer support than strategic planning, which occurs less frequently.

There are many important examples of information systems used in operations management. They are perhaps most widely used in the management of inventory. In many firms, it is important to have immediate access to the inventory status of various items. With a computer-based information system, it is possible to continuously monitor inventory transactions. We shall see in Chapter 11 that information systems are an indispensable part of MRP for management of inventories subject to dependent demand.

Forecasting and other planning activities are aided by the accurate and sometimes voluminous historical data that can be stored and manipulated with a computer-based information system. This same type of data can be easily converted to a form that is acceptable to computerized planning models. The control function of the operations manager is also aided by a computer-based information system, since such a system makes it possible to monitor system performance continuously rather than periodically.

Management information systems that contain a model base to support decision making are called decision support systems (DSS). This advanced type of information system is aimed at relatively unstructured problems that can be aided by rapid access to data bases and computerized problem-solving techniques. As this type of system is on the leading edge of technology, few applications have been reported in the POM area. However, financial planning and forecasting are common DSS application areas and we can expect future POM contributions in the areas of production planning, resource allocation, distribution, and scheduling.

PRODUCTIVITY

Productivity is a measure of how efficiently we can convert labor and materials (resources) into finished goods and services. Traditionally productivity has been measured in terms of labor productivity; that is, output divided by labor input. For example, labor productivity for the United States as a whole is calculated as:

$$\text{Labor productivity} = \frac{\text{GNP}}{\text{labor hours}}$$

A more accurate measure of productivity might include capital as well as labor. This total productivity measure for the United States is calculated as:

$$\text{Total productivity} = \frac{\text{GNP}}{\text{labor} + \text{capital}}$$

Productivity measures are also available for industries, organizations, and even individuals. However, no productivity measure has been developed that is totally accepted or accurate. Issues involving quality, nontangible services, value, and customer satisfaction are rarely included in productivity measures.

Productivity Growth Problem

The United States is the most productive country in the world. However, the rate of productivity growth has slowed appreciably and currently lags behind many of the prominent industrialized nations. This decline in U.S. productivity growth is a recent phenomenon. After World War II U.S. productivity growth averaged just under 3 percent per year. This trend continued into the sixties and then declined to approximately 2 percent from the midsixties to the midseventies. Since 1977 U.S. productivity growth in the private business sector has been minuscule, actually dropping in some years and averaging approximately .1 percent for the five-year period.

Table 1-3 illustrates the rate of labor productivity growth for the U.S. compared to other industrialized countries from 1960 to 1977. It is apparent from Table 1-3 that Japan and other industrialized countries have achieved a higher rate of productivity growth than the United States.

The consequences of reduced productivity growth are far reaching. National productivity affects the nation's ability to compete effectively in foreign markets and

Table 1-3   International Indexes of Labor Productivity (1967 base year)

YEAR	U.S.	JAPAN	UNITED KINGDOM	WEST GERMANY	FRANCE
1960	78.8	52.6	76.8	66.4	68.7
1964	94.8	75.9	89.7	84.5	83.7
1967	100.0	100.0	100.0	100.0	100.0
1970	104.5	146.5	108.6	116.1	121.2
1973	119.4	179.0	126.3	136.6	143.7
1977	126.9	206.6	126.6	169.6	171.6

SOURCE: U.S. Department of Labor.

has a direct impact on the standard of living. For example, consider the U.S. automobile industry. The number of auto workers rose by 15 percent between 1957 and 1976, but the number of cars and trucks they built rose by 75 percent. Wages and benefits, adjusted for inflation, more than doubled. Translated into standard-of-living increases for consumers, this meant that a median income family had to work $4\frac{1}{2}$ months to buy a car in 1977, as opposed to $7\frac{1}{2}$ months in 1957.

Reasons for Productivity Growth Decline

There have been many reasons stated for the decline in U.S. productivity growth. Some of these reasons are widely accepted and others are somewhat controversial. The list of reasons extends well beyond operations management and into the domains of economics, social issues, and politics. Since the early seventies, the U.S. has been beset by an oil embargo, inflation, and high interest rates. But, are these factors the cause or the result of other causes which have affected productivity?

Purported causes of the slowdown in U.S. productivity growth can be found in many sources; productivity decline is a highly visible topic. Two interesting sources include an article by McConnell[2] and a special issue of *Business Week*.[3] Listed below are some reasons given for the productivity decline. As some of the reasons are controversial, you will need to assess the relative merit of each position.

Economic Reasons

1. Decline in the capital to labor ratio—work force has expanded more rapidly than the capital stock.

2. Change in composition of labor force—the proportion of young workers with less experience and skill has been increasing.

3. Shift in labor from agriculture to industry—the exodus from farms to more productive industrial jobs has slowed down thus inhibiting productivity increases.

4. Progress in technology—research and development spending has decreased from a peak of 3 percent of GNP in 1964 to 2.1 percent in 1977.

5. Increased expenditures on environmental and worker protection has accounted for one-tenth to one-fifth of the productivity decline.

6. Unproductive military sector—military production is a deterrent but wasteful and without true economic use.

7. Decline in savings—Americans save only 3–4 percent of their income. Japanese save approximately 20 percent and have a better capital stock from which to finance capital acquisitions and modernization of equipment.

---

[2] C.R. McConnell, "Why Is U.S. Productivity Slowing Down?" *Harvard Business Review*, March–April 1979, pp. 36–60.

[3] "The Reindustrialization of America," *Business Week*, Special Issue, June 30, 1980, pp. 56–144.

8. Transition towards more service industries in the economy—productivity gains are more easily achieved in manufacturing than in service industries. The U.S. economy is becoming increasingly service oriented.

Social Reasons

1. Alienated work force—workers' aspirations and educational levels have increased but levels of jobs have not kept pace. There is frustration with the bureaucratization and segmentation of work processes.

2. Emergence of social person—an attitude is emerging that a person is not merely an economic creature but one who is concerned with the quality of life in general.

3. Decline in American work ethic—some claim that Americans do not want to work as hard as the Japanese do, and that there is too much expectation of "entitlement."

Business and Government Reasons

1. Outdated plants and equipment—this is true, for example, in the steel industry where some of the modern Japanese plants are more productive.

2. Overemphasis on short-term profits—lack of risk taking and failure to plan for long-term corporate success.

3. Excess government regulation and intervention—American business has been more restricted than international competition.

4. Lack of coherent national policy—the federal government has not developed consistent policies with respect to regulations, pollution standards, and imports and exports. This uncertainty makes it difficult for American business to carefully plan and evaluate corporate strategies.

Solutions to Productivity Problem

There probably is no single or simple cure to the productivity problem just as there is no simple answer for the general economic malaise. Certainly, attempts to address and alleviate some of the 15 problems or reasons listed above would be helpful. Efforts have been made to encourage savings, and accelerated depreciation allowances have been aimed at stimulating investments in new plants and equipment. In some cases the necessity of having various governmental regulations has been examined carefully. Perhaps more importantly, companies and industries have begun to realize that there is a productivity problem and have begun to address the issue. Efforts by the various levels of management and workers have yielded productivity gains in some instances. Focusing productivity studies at an industry or at individual companies falls under the purview of production and operations management. Thus, the discipline that we address in this book is often the logical home of applied productivity improvement efforts. Not everything that we study in the chapters ahead deals with productivity, but many of the topics can lead directly to improved productivity, and some, such as computer-aided design and computer-aided manufacturing (CAD/CAM), and robotics, reflect the most current advances.

Japanese Connection

At one time the phrase "made in Japan" connoted a cheap and shoddy piece of workmanship. This is no longer the case; in fact in many instances "made in Japan" implies superior quality. Since World War II the Japanese have come a long way and are recognized as one of the most productive countries in the industrialized world, with the third largest GNP. Part of their secret of success has been the borrowing and adapting of many ideas originally developed in the U.S. For example, statistical quality control ideas developed by Deming have been widely adopted in Japanese manufacturing. Various management theories have been studied by the Japanese and implemented in their management philosophies.

Through their efforts, the Japanese have become international leaders in the production of automobiles, steel, and electrical appliances. The tide has turned and now the U.S. has begun to study the productivity success of the Japanese. Teams of experts have gone to Japan in hopes of importing some of the successful Japanese methods. The most significant Japanese accomplishments seem to be in the areas of manufacturing processes, company–employee relationships, and quality control. The KANBAN production system which Toyota uses in car manufacturing is an example which is being studied for possible implementation in the U.S.[4] However, it is not clear that such a method can be successful here. Perhaps the ideas which are having the most impact on U.S. productivity involve labor relations. The cooperative spirit of the Japanese has led to a proposed new type of organization called a type Z organization.[5] The concepts are seminal at this time, but point in a direction which might be appropriate for a changing American society.

Lastly, the Japanese have had a significant impact on quality control methods with their initiation of QC circles or quality control groups. These are groups in which the workers themselves organize to make suggestions about more productive or more quality conscious ways of doing their jobs. We shall describe QC circles in Chapter 13 of this book when we examine the topic of quality control.

OPERATIONS MANAGEMENT IN ACTION

Thus far in this chapter, we have tried to convey what operations management is all about and its key characteristics. At this point, it seems best to show you some real-world scenarios of successful operations management applications. Many possible examples exist in manufacturing and service industries, and in the private and public sectors. We have chosen the following three applications because they are representative of modern scientific approaches and because they report their results.

---

[4]D.O. Nellemann and L.F. Smith, "Just-in-Time vs. Just-in-Case Production/Inventory Systems Concepts Borrowed Back from Japan," *Production and Inventory Management*, 23, no. 2 (1982), 12–21.

[5]W. Ouchi and A. Jæger, "Type Z Organization: Stability in the Midst of Mobility," *Academy of Management Review*, 3(April 1978), 305–314.

Scheduling Policies for Surgical Patients[6]

Rising medical costs, limited facility space, and increasing pressure for surgical-suite utilization caused the Deaconess Hospital in St. Louis, Missouri, to review it policies for scheduling patients through its surgical suite (capacity five patients) and recovery room (capacity twelve patients). The hospital had been using a random-input policy for scheduling patients for surgery. A team of researchers suggested a computer simulation approach to scientifically study different queueing decision rules for scheduling patients. It was not allowable to experiment with different schedules using actual patients, and the simulation approach permitted the testing of different policies on the computer without affecting hospital functions.

Not all patients require a recovery room after surgery, so data had to be collected regarding the statistical distribution of types of surgery, their times, and the patient's duration of stay (if any) in the recovery room. The GPSS simulation language was used to write a simulator that could analyze five different scheduling rules for the 27 patients that needed to be scheduled each day. The scheduling had to allow for certain priorities, such as the fact that a patient needing the recovery room must always have a bed available.

Each of the five patient scheduling rules was used by the simulator on a previous 103-day schedule involving 2,781 patients. It was found that significant improvement could be obtained by using any of the four new scheduling rules. In particular, one scheduling rule, which was based on scheduling those patients requiring the longest surgery first, offered the following improvements: higher operating- and recovery-room utilization rates, increased patient load in the recovery room during a shorter day, and more timely completion of the surgical and recovery schedule. Additionally, the average length of workday in the recovery room was reduced 21 percent, allowing the reduction of manpower requirements of one registered nurse and one operating-room technician. The $17,000-a-year cost savings more than outweighed the cost of the simulator and scheduling.

These improvements were found using very simple scheduling rules; the Deaconess Hospital planned to adopt the one scheduling rule while continuing to investigate other scientific scheduling approaches.

Development of Annual Operating Plan
for Plywood Manufacture[7]

Prior to 1967, Canadian Forest Products Ltd. based its plywood production choices on past experience, gut feel, and intuition. In 1967, rising costs prompted the company to consider a linear programming approach to its production plan.

---

[6]N.K. Kwak, P.J. Kuzdrall, and H. Schmitz, "The GPSS Simulation of Scheduling Policies for Surgical Patients," *Management Science*, 22 (May 1976), 982–89.

[7]D.B. Kotak, "Application of Linear Programming to Plywood Manufacture," *Interfaces*, 7 (November 1976), 56–68.

The plywood production process is more complicated than you might think. There are seven grades of peelable logs available, from five sources, which can be peeled into four veneer thicknesses (140 possible combinations). Peeling results in veneers of four thicknesses, two species, and twelve grades (96 combinations). Plywood can be made into ten thicknesses, twelve grades, three widths, and five lengths, and may be sold in two separate markets (3,600 possible combinations). Also, the production process involves four different lathes, seven dryers, and five presses!

The company decided that its objective was to maximize contribution margin (= Sales income − Wood costs). A linear programming model was developed that included input from raw materials, production, sales, and the different operating strategies. The computer output from the model, then, is the basis for the annual operating plan, the detailing of most profitable products and annual targets for raw materials, and production and sales by item, grade, and market.

The annual plan is implemented by scheduling on a biweekly basis. The biweekly schedule is then implemented in turn on a day-to-day basis by scheduling the mill on a daily and shift basis. Since changes in sales, production, and costs do occur, actual production and inventories are monitored against the targets specified by the annual operating plan. The daily tracking and biweekly performance reports show how well the annual plan is being implemented. However, the plan is not a gospel, and whenever market and operating conditions change significantly, the operations plan is revised by reoptimizing the LP model with new data.

As a result of using the scientific approach, the contribution margin of the Plywood and Hardboard Division has increased by an average of $1 million per year between 1970 and 1975 as compared to the base year, 1969.

Inventory Control System[8]

Finally, let's consider the inventory problem faced by a large food distributor in St. Louis, Missouri. The company's objective was to more effectively manage the coordinated inventory of several branch warehouses. The purpose of the branch, or satellite warehouses was to increase the firm's competitive advantage by offering quick delivery times to customers. The satellite warehouses were managed by a centralized inventory control group whose objective was to maintain adequate levels of inventories to provide good customer service at least cost.

Prior to a new approach in 1968, the inventory manager's policy was to restock each major warehouse once a week. The manager reviewed each inventory item daily and ordered approximately a two-month supply of any product for which the current level was below one month's estimated sales. In an effort to improve upon

---

[8]J. Bishop, Jr., "Experience with a Successful System for Forecasting and Inventory Control," *Operations Research*, 22 (November–December 1974), 1224–31.

the manual inventory system, the company decided to computerize certain tasks such as inventory forms and, at the same time, to investigate other possible changes.

Other improvements in inventory policy were slow to evolve, however, because management tended to be skeptical about radically innovative management science techniques. One of the first changes was the development of a more accurate procedure for forecasting each satellite warehouse's transactions. An exponential smoothing procedure was used to forecast sales; then, based on these sales forecasts, new reorder points and order quantities were calculated by means of inventory control models. Daily ordering reports were generated by the computer, which provided relevant data for each product. Included in the report were suggested order quantities. However, the report had a unique feature: It allowed management to override the computer on any items whose inventory levels were below the reorder point. Thus, management had the option of accepting the computerized order quantities or suggesting order quantities of its own. This manual override feature turned out to be the key to implementing the scientific approach successfully. It gave management an awareness of its participation in, and essential control over, decision-making processes. Initially, management was reluctant to accept the computer output, and it countermanded 80 percent of the computer's decisions. A year later, however, confidence was gained, and overridden output had dropped to 10 percent.

Several other reports were generated for the firm, including a monthly out-of-stock analysis and a final report that summarized the month's transactions and the status of satellite warehouse operations. The new approach was successful in that manual errors were reduced by 75 percent, inventories by 30 percent, and out-of-stock situations by 25 percent. The first-year return on investment was approximately 150 percent, all development costs included.

The experience was so positive that the firm undertook further systematic investigations. The second phase included a computer simulation model of the inventory system. With the aid of the simulation model, the firm studied different inventory policies, review periods, and levels of the production-planning horizon. The practice of modern operations management has become an ongoing function in this firm.

REVIEW QUESTIONS

1. In your opinion, what has been the single most important event in the advancement of operations management?
2. What are some of the characteristics of the modern approach to operations management?
3. Paraphrase the definition of operations management in your own words.
4. Characterize the inputs, components, and outputs of the transformation process of systems such as (a) a bank, (b) book publishing, (c) a football team, (d) a job shop.

5. What are the four basic functions of the operations manager?

6. Briefly explain the nature of the systems approach.

7. Differentiate between decision making under deterministic conditions, stochastic conditions, and uncertainty.

8. What is the primary benefit of using models in the analysis of a problem?

9. What is a heuristic? Give an example of one.

10. What is an MIS? How have these systems improved the practice of operations management?

11. List any application you have seen that you would consider operations management in action.

12. Distinguish between system effectiveness and system efficiency.

13. Characterize strategic, tactical, and operational decision problems.

14. In your opinion, what are the five most important reasons for the decline in U.S. productivity growth?

15. List three suggestions for increasing the rate of productivity growth.

16. In what areas of production have the Japanese achieved international leadership?

REFERENCES

BUFFA, E.S., *Operations Management: The Management of Productive Systems*. New York: John Wiley, 1976.

CHASE, R.B., and H.J. AQUILANO, *Production and Operations Management*. 3rd ed. Homewood, Ill.: Richard D. Irwin, 1981.

DRAKE, A.W., R.L. KEENEY, and P.M. MORSE, eds., *Analysis of Public Systems*. Cambridge, Mass.: M.I.T. Press, 1972.

EASTON, A., *Complex Managerial Decisions Involving Multiple Objectives*. New York: John Wiley, 1973.

GEORGE, CLAUDE S., *The History of Management Thought*. Englewood Cliffs, N.J.: Prentice-Hall, 1968.

JOHNSON, R.A., F.E. KAST, and J.E. ROSENZWEIG, *The Theory and Management of Systems*. New York: McGraw-Hill, 1967.

MCCONNELL, C.R., "Why Is U.S. Productivity Slowing Down?" *Harvard Business Review*, March–April 1979, pp. 36–60.

OLSEN, R.A., *Manufacturing Management: A Quantitative Approach*. Scranton, Pa.: International Textbook, 1968.

STARR, M.K., *Production Management: Systems and Synthesis*. Englewood Cliffs, N.J.: Prentice-Hall, 1980.

VOLLMAN, T.E., *Operations Management: A Systems Model-Building Approach*. Reading, Mass.: Addison-Wesley, 1973.

2

LINEAR PROGRAMMING

Areas of application
   production applications
   government and nonmanufacturing applications
Nature of linear models
   assumptions of linear programming
Formulating LP models
   product-mix and capacity planning example
   R & D budget allocation example
   the graphical method of solution
A linear distribution model
   the VAM heuristic for solving transportation problems
Network models in operations management
Summary
Supplement to Chapter 2
   the simplex method
   minimization problems and other types of constraints
   after the solution, then what?
   computer output of LP solutions

In this chapter we begin our study of quantitative methods of particular importance to operations managers. First we shall study linear programming, its methodology, and its applications to operations management. In Chapter 3 we will examine the extremely useful tool of computer simulation, and in Chapter 4 we will study queuing theory and its usefulness in analyzing waiting lines.

Of all the quantitative tools available to the operations manager, *linear programming* is one of the most widely used. It is primarily concerned with the determination of the best allocation of scarce resources. Thus, it can be used to allocate limited resources such as capital or raw materials among competing alternatives in order to maximize the objectives of a particular enterprise. Linear programming is not limited to allocation problems however; it has many applications in scheduling and distribution functions. These applications are extensive not only in production and nonmanufacturing industries, but also in government agencies and companies in the public sector.

Linear programming is just one technique in the more general area of mathematical programming. Mathematical programming is concerned with the development of modeling and solution procedures for the purpose of maximizing the extent to which the goals and objectives of the decision maker are realized. Special linearity conditions must hold before a general mathematical programming problem is actually an LP problem; we shall examine these conditions later in the chapter.

Despite the implication of its name, LP has little to do with computer programming. In LP, the word *programming* is related to planning. Specifically, it refers to modeling a problem and subsequently solving it by mathematical techniques. As we shall see, LP is very similar to setting up and solving a system of linear equations.

Even though LP is quite different from computer programming, computer development has played an integral part in the successful application of LP. Real-world LP problems often involve hundreds of variables and equations. These problems would be impossible to solve without a high-speed computer.

Linear programming has numerous applications to the production and operations functions. In a survey sent to the directors of production/operations at roughly half of *Fortune's* top 500 companies, we found that 95 percent of those responding used LP to some extent in managing their operations. Undoubtedly, smaller companies use LP less. In some cases, it is not needed; in other cases, managers may not understand LP or realize its potential.

AREAS OF APPLICATION

Linear programming has applications in a wide range of disciplines, from economic theory to the social sciences. Industrial, agricultural, and military applications are the most extensive. In this section, we focus on a small portion of applications that are relevant to operations management. Linear programming is usually not the only means used in solving the following problems, but is an effective tool to use in the decision-making process.

Production Applications

Capacity Planning and Product Mix.   Given a finite productive capacity and several products or services, LP can be used to determine which combination of products or services to offer in order to maximize profit and stay within the limits of available capacity.

Blending.   In blending problems, the objective is to determine the combination of raw ingredients that will result in a satisfactory end product and minimize costs. Examples of blending problems are the blending of petroleum products, mixing of cattle feed, mixing of meats to make sausage, and mixing of paint.

Production Scheduling.   This problem involves the determination of a production schedule that meets demand subject to fluctuations. The objective is to meet demand and yet maintain reasonable inventory levels and employment levels, while minimizing the overall costs of production and inventory.

Manpower Planning.   LP can be used to make decisions for departmental staffing requirements for a given period of time. It has also been used to evaluate long-range hiring, promotion, and retirement schemes, as well as proposed compensation schemes[1] and the assignment of salesmen to territories.

Physical Distribution.   Distributing products from plants to warehouses or customer demand points has been one of the more fruitful areas of application of LP. The objective is to meet demand while minimizing transportation costs. Models have also been developed to minimize the combined cost of production and distribution.

Aggregate Planning.   Aggregate planning or scheduling involves the determination of minimum-cost production levels for several months into the future. Changing demand rates require decisions aimed at minimizing the costs of varying production rates, varying work-force levels, inventory, overtime, and subcontracting.

Process Control.   The operation of various processes that generate scrap can be aided by LP models that help to minimize waste. Examples are the cutting of stock paper, fabric materials, and steel parts to fill various orders.

---

[1]Richard C. Grinold, "Input Policies for a Longitudinal Manpower Flow Model," *Management Science*, 22 (1976), 570–75.

Government and Nonmanufacturing Applications

Agriculture.   Among the agricultural applications of linear programming have been land allocation and animal diet problems.[2] LP can be used to determine the allocation of land areas to crops in order to minimize costs or maximize profits and meet certain crop requirements. It can be applied to diet problems, both animal and human, in order to meet nutritional requirements at minimal cost.

Environmental Protection.   Linear programming has been used to analyze alternatives for handling liquid waste material in order to satisfy antipollution requirements. LP has also been used as a tool in the analysis of paper recycling,[3] air cleaner design,[4] and analysis of alternative energy policies.[5]

Urban Development.   More recently, LP has been used to analyze public expenditure planning,[6] school busing, and drug control. Political redistricting and financial analysis of new community development processes have also been tackled with LP.[7]

Facilities Location.   Location analysis by linear programming includes the location of public parks and recreation areas within communities,[8] of hospitals, ambulance depots,[9] nuclear power plants,[10] telephone exchanges, and warehouses for centralized distribution.

---

[2]D.F. Lyons and V.A. Dodd, "The Mix-Feed Problem," *Operational Research* (Amsterdam: North-Holland Publishing, 1975); V.E. Smith, "A Diet Model with Protein Quality Variable," *Management Science*, February 1974, pp. 971–80.

[3]C.R. Glassey and V.K. Gupta, "A Linear Programming Analysis of Paper Recycling," *Management Science*, December 1974, pp. 392–408.

[4]S. Advani, "A Linear Programming Approach to Air Cleaner Design," *Operations Research*, March–April 1974, pp. 295–97.

[5]W. Marcuse, L. Bodin, E. Cherniavsky, and Yasuko Sanborn, "A Dynamic Time Dependent Model for the Analysis of Alternative Energy Policies," *Operational Research* (Amsterdam: North-Holland Publishing, 1975).

[6]M. Feldstein and Harold Luft, "Distributional Constraints in Public Expenditure Planning," *Management Science*, August 1973, pp. 1414–22.

[7]R.L. Heroux and W.A. Wallace, "Linear Programming and Financial Analysis of the New Community Development Process," *Management Science*, April 1973, pp. 857–72.

[8]C. Revelle, D. Marks, and J. Liebman, "An Analysis of Private and Public Sector Location Models," *Management Science*, 16 (1970), 692–707.

[9]E. Savas, "Simulation and Cost-Effectiveness of New York's Emergency Ambulance Service," *Management Science*, 15 (1969), B608–27.

[10]R. Dutton, G. Hinman, and C.B. Millham, "The Optimal Location of Nuclear Power Facilities in the Pacific Northwest," *Operations Research*, May–June 1974, pp. 478–87.

NATURE OF LINEAR MODELS

We have presented a smattering of LP applications. Let us now focus on the nature of a linear model, what it is, and how to formulate it. Linearity is a very simple relationship between variables. To be precise, any linear expression is of the form:

$$a_1 x_1 + a_2 x_2 + \cdots + a_n x_n$$

where the a_i represent coefficients and the x_i represent variables. A linear model is constructed from linear expressions. A linear expression called the *objective function* represents the goal or objective to be achieved; for example, the objective function may represent profit maximization or cost minimization. The remainder of any LP model is made up of *constraints*; these constraints are linear expressions that mathematically state the limited resource availability, various conditions, policies, or technical specifications.

The canonical form of an LP model is as follows:

2.1   Maximize (or Minimize) $c_1 x_1 + c_2 x_2 + \cdots + c_n x_n$

subject to the restrictions: $a_{11} x_1 + a_{12} x_2 + \cdots + a_{1n} x_n \leq b_1$

$$a_{21} x_1 + a_{22} x_2 + \cdots + a_{2n} x_n \leq b_2$$

2.2

$$\vdots$$

$$a_{m1} x_1 + a_{m2} x_2 + \cdots + a_{mn} x_n \leq b_m$$

2.3   and $x_1 \geq 0, x_2 \geq 0, \ldots, x_n \geq 0$

Any problem whose mathematical formulation fits this general model is an LP problem. The expression 2.1 is the objective function, inequalities 2.2 are the constraints, and the inequalities 2.3 are called nonnegativity conditions; they prevent the variables from assuming negative values. We should note that the constraints need not be stated with just less-than-or-equal-to ($\leq$) signs, but may also be stated with equalities ($=$), or greater-than-or-equal-to ($\geq$) signs.

The x_j variables in the general model above are decision variables; that is, they are variables whose values are determined when the LP model is solved. Their values provide the answers that are being sought in the LP analysis. In order to determine the values of the decision variables, the LP model needs data. The objective function coefficients c_j, the constraint coefficients a_{ij}, and the right-hand-side coefficients b_i are parameters of the model. The particular values of the parameters determine the final solution to the decision variables.

Not all mathematical models fit the general form of expressions 2.1–2.3. Any mathematical model not of this form is called a nonlinear model. Operations management applications also exist for nonlinear models, but, owing to their limited use and relatively complex nature, they are considered in advanced courses. In order for linear programming to be applicable to any mathematical model, the following conditions must hold.

Assumptions of Linear Programming

1. The objective function and constraints must be linear. This implies that the variables' values are additive. Thus, 2 units of profit contribution from decision variable x_1 and 3 units of profit contribution from decision variable x_3 must add together to contribute 5 units to profit. Linearity also implies proportionality. If variable x_2 requires 2 hours of labor, then 2 units of x_2 require 4 hours. The last implication of linearity is that the decision variables are divisible. Fractional values such as $3\frac{3}{4}$ or 4.78 must be acceptable in the final solution. If whole-number solutions are required, we must resort to a mathematical programming technique called integer programming.
2. The parameters of the model must be known or accurately estimated. Numerical values must be provided for each parameter.

FORMULATING LP MODELS

In formulating any mathematical model, the decision maker is attempting to represent the essence of some problem in terms of relationships between symbols; in linear models, these relationships are all linear. Model building is more an art than a science; thus, formulating accurate models depends greatly upon the decision maker's own ingenuity and experience. Formulation is the most critical aspect of an LP analysis, for once the model is *correctly* formulated, it can be solved readily on a computer. The following guidelines serve as an aid in the formulation process:

1. Understand the problem.
2. Identify the decision variables (i.e., those variables whose values, if found, would solve the problem).
3. Choose a numerical measure of effectiveness for the objective function.
4. Represent this measure of effectiveness as a linear expression involving the decision variables.
5. Identify and represent all constraints as linear expressions involving the decision variables.
6. Collect data or make appropriate estimations for all parameters of the model.

We illustrate these guidelines in the following LP formulations.

Product-Mix and Capacity Planning Example

The Electrovox Company is a relatively new firm that manufactures CB radios. It currently manufactures a deluxe hi-gain unit and a standard model; Electrovox has the facilities to produce either the deluxe or the standard model, or a combination of both. Since production resources are limited, it is critical that the firm produce the appropriate number of deluxe and standard models. The deluxe unit sells for $150 and contributes $50 to profit; the standard unit sells for $100 and contributes $20 to profit. There are only three production resources that limit the production quantities, and the production requirements of the two CB radios are summarized in Table 2-1.

Table 2-1

PRODUCT	HI-GAIN TRANSISTORS	ASSEMBLY HOURS	INSPECTION HOURS
Hi-gain	1	4	1
Standard	0	1.2	.5

Additionally, there are 40 hi-gain transistors, 240 assembly hours, and 81 inspection hours available on a daily basis. We shall assume that the firm can sell all the components it can produce and that plant equipment and labor skills are interchangeable between hi-gain and standard units.

Defining the Decision Variables and Objective Function. Assuming that we understand the problem, the next step is to define the decision variables. What is the Electrovox Company trying to decide? Specifically, how many hi-gain and how many standard CB radios should it produce? To answer the basic question, let x_1 equal the number of standard units to be produced daily, and let x_2 equal the number of hi-gain radios to be produced each day. Since x_1 and x_2 contribute $20 and $50 to profit, respectively, we may state the objective function as:

$$\text{Maximize } 20x_1 + 50x_2$$

Constructing the Constraints. The production process is limited only by the daily limitation of hi-gain transistors, assembly man-hours, and inspection man-hours. Thus we will have three constraints, one for each of the scarce resources.

The limited supply of hi-gain transistors will affect only the production of hi-gain CBs. Thus, the first constraint limits the production of hi-gain CBs to 40 per day and is stated as $x_2 \leq 40$.

Both CBs require assembly time; thus, the assembly-time constraint must ensure that the combined assembly time of both units not exceed 240 hours. This may be expressed as $1.2x_1 + 4x_2 \leq 240$. Similarly, the inspection-time constraint is stated as $.50x_1 + 1x_2 \leq 81$. Since it is impossible to produce a negative number of CB radios, we impose the nonnegativity conditions $x_1, x_2 \geq 0$. The final LP formulation is thus:

$$\text{Maximize } 20x_1 + 50x_2$$

$$\text{subject to:} \qquad x_2 \leq 40$$

$$1.2x_1 + 4x_2 \leq 240$$

$$.50x_1 + 1x_2 \leq 81$$

$$x_1, x_2 \geq 0$$

R & D Budget Allocation Example

The Viscus Oil Company must decide how to allocate its budget for energy research and development. The government grants certain tax breaks if the company invests funds in research concerned with energy conservation. However, the government stipulates that at least 60 percent of the funds must be funneled into research for automobile efficiency. Viscus has a $1 million budget for energy research and development this year; the research proposal data are shown in Table 2-2.

Table 2-2

PROJECT	MANAGEMENT POLICY ON UPPER LIMIT OF EXPENDITURES ($)	FORECASTED RETURN ON INVESTMENT (%)
Methanol fuel research	400,000	4.0
Electrically operated cars	200,000	0.1
Emission reduction	400,000	3.0
Solar cells	300,000	2.0
Windmills	200,000	1.0

Assuming that Viscus wants to maximize return on its investment and yet receive the government tax break, let us formulate the problem as an LP model.

The decision variables should reflect the question management is asking; that is, How much should we invest in each research alternative? Therefore, let x_1 = Amount invested in methanol fuel research, x_2 = Amount invested in electrically operated cars, x_3 = Amount applied toward emission reduction, x_4 = Amount allocated to solar cells, and x_5 = Amount invested in windmills.

The objective function should measure return on investment and is stated as:

$$\text{Maximize } 4.0x_1 + .1x_2 + 3.0x_3 + 2.0x_4 + 1.0x_5$$

One constraint is the budget limit itself. Thus, the total spent must not exceed $1 million, or:

$$x_1 + x_2 + x_3 + x_4 + x_5 \leq 1,000,000$$

Furthermore, at least $600,000 must be spent on research for automobile efficiency:

$$x_1 + x_2 + x_3 \geq 600,000$$

Finally, management has limited the expenditures on any single project:

$$x_1 \leq 400,000$$
$$x_2 \leq 200,000$$
$$x_3 \leq 400,000$$
$$x_4 \leq 300,000$$
$$x_5 \leq 200,000$$

Since it is impossible to allocate negative dollars in this case, the nonnegativity conditions also apply:

$$x_1, x_2, x_3, x_4, x_5 \geq 0$$

The Graphical Method of Solution

Thus far we have examined the applications of linear programming and the formulation of linear models. The next consideration is how to solve these linear models in order to obtain specific values for the decision variables. In this section we shall look at the graphical method of solution; it is particularly useful in yielding insight into the nature of LP problems. The graphical method is not useful, however, for obtaining the solution to real-world LP problems; the method cannot handle more than three variables, since we cannot graph in more than three dimensions. In actual applications, LP problems are solved by the *simplex method* on a computer. The simplex method is discussed in the supplement at the end of this chapter.

The graphical method of solution simply involves plotting each of a problem's constraints to form a region of possible solutions. We then examine this region to select the best alternative. Let's return to the Electrovox product-mix example and solve it by the graphical method. Recall that the objective is to produce the appropriate number of hi-gain and standard CBs in order to maximize profit. The model we formulated is:

Maximize $20x_1 + 50x_2$ profit

subject to: $x_2 \leq 40$ transistor availability

$1.2x_1 + 4x_2 \leq 240$ assembly time

$.5x_1 + 1x_2 \leq 81$ inspection time

$x_1, x_2 \geq 0$

The first step in the graphical method is to plot the constraints on a graph. Since the Electrovox constraints are inequalities rather than equations, their graphs are regions rather than lines. However, the easiest way to graph an inequality is first to graph it as an equality, then simply shade in the appropriate area.

The first constraint, $x_2 \leq 40$, can be located on the graph by first locating its x_1 and x_2 intercepts on the x_1 and x_2 axes respectively. Treating the constraint as an equation ($x_2 = 40$), we find that the x_2 intercept is 40 and the x_1 intercept does not exist. Thus, the graph of $x_2 = 40$ is parallel to the x_1 axis. The inequality $x_2 \leq 40$ is graphed from $x_2 = 40$ by simply observing on which side of the line the origin $(0,0)$ is located. Substituting $x_1 = 0$ and $x_2 = 0$ into the inequality $x_2 \leq 40$, we find that $0 < 40$, and the origin is thus included in the inequality. The graph of $x_2 \leq 40$ is the region established by the line $x_2 = 40$ and the shaded area in Figure 2-1. Notice that

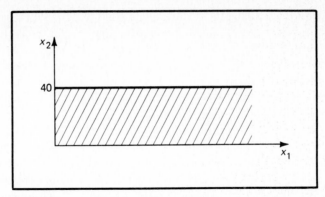

FIGURE 2-1   **Graph of Inequality $x_2 \leq 40$**

the nonnegativity conditions restrict the shaded area in Figure 2-1 to the first quadrant.

In the second constraint, we determine the x_1 intercept by letting $x_2 = 0$ and solving $1.2x_1 + 4(0) = 240$, from which we obtain $x_1 = 200$. Setting $x_1 = 0$, we obtain the x_2 intercept by solving $1.2(0) + 4x_2 = 240$; thus we have $x_2 = 60$. Plotting the third constraint in a similar manner and shading the appropriate regions, we obtain the total region of possible solutions in Figure 2-2.

Any proposed production quantities for the Electrovox problem are possible only if they fall in the shaded area in Figure 2-2. Any point (x_1, x_2) that satisfies all

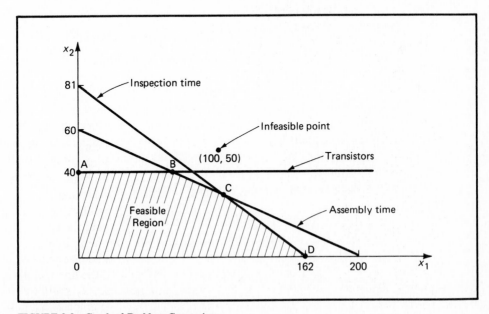

FIGURE 2-2   **Graph of Problem Constraints**

constraints, including the nonnegativity conditions, is said to be feasible. The shaded area in Figure 2-2 is called the feasible region. For example, suppose Electrovox wants to produce $x_1 = 100$ standard and $x_2 = 20$ hi-gain CBs. This solution satisfies all three constraints, falls in the feasible region, and is feasible. On the other hand, the production of $x_1 = 100$ and $x_2 = 50$ violates the third constraint and falls outside the feasible region, as illustrated in Figure 2-2. Thus, the point $(100, 50)$ is infeasible.

In solving the Electrovox problem, we want the most profitable product mix. An optimal solution is a feasible solution that also achieves the best possible value for the objective function. If we are trying to increase profit, then an optimal solution maximizes profit. Similarly, if we are reducing costs, an optimal solution is a feasible solution that minimizes costs. The goal of an LP solution procedure is to find the optimal solution to the formulated model.

In determining the optimal solution, we may restrict our search to the feasible region. The feasible region, however, contains an infinite number of points. Fortunately, a fundamental result from linear programming theory restricts our search to a finite number of points. The extreme-point theorem states that if an optimal solution exists, then at least one such optimal solution must be an extreme-point solution. By an extreme point we mean a vertex or corner point of the feasible region. From the theorem we can conclude that one of the extreme points 0, A, B, C, or D of Figure 2-2 is the optimal solution.

We could find the optimal solution by determining the coordinates of each extreme point and substituting into the objective function to find the highest value. However, we can use the objective function as a measuring device to avoid evaluating all extreme points. Let P = profit; then we wish to maximize $P = 20x_1 + 50x_2$. The objective function is now in the form of a linear equation. If we let $P = \$2,000$, we can plot the graph of $20x_1 + 50x_2 = 2,000$. Doing this, we get the result shown in Figure 2-3.

Any point on the line $20x_1 + 50x_2 = 2,000$ within the feasible region will yield a profit of $\$2,000$. Letting $P = \$3,000$, we obtain a different isoprofit line in Figure 2-3. Moving the isoprofit lines toward the northeast increases the profit. Moving the isoprofit lines as far as possible (and remaining in the feasible region) intersects the point C. Thus, the point C is the optimum solution to the Electrovox problem.

How does the point C yield the optimum? This is answered by determining the x_1 and x_2 coordinate values associated with the point C. Since C occurs at the intersection of the two lines $1.2x_1 + 4x_2 = 240$ and $.5x_1 + 1x_2 = 81$, we can solve these two linear equations simultaneously to obtain x_1 and x_2.

$$
\begin{array}{rcr}
1.2x_1 + 4x_2 & = & 240 \\
-2.0x_1 - 4x_2 & = & -324 \\
\hline
-.8x_1 \qquad\quad & = & -84 \\
x_1 & = & 105
\end{array}
$$

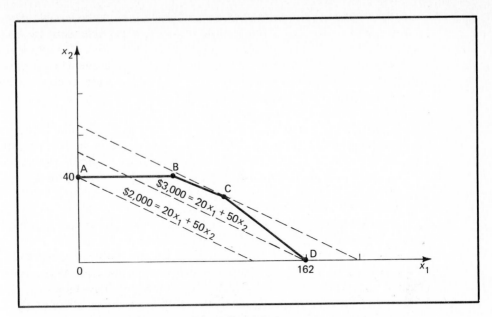

FIGURE 2-3   Graph of Profit Lines and Optimal Solutions

Substituting 105 for x_1 in the first equation, we obtain $x_2 = [240 - 1.2(105)]/4 =$ 28.5. Thus, the optimal product mix is to produce 105 standard and 28.5 hi-gain units each day. The profit associated with the optimal solution is $20(105) + 50(28.5)$ = \$3,525 per day.

Notice that the optimal LP solution calls for the production of 28.5 hi-gain units per day. We can interpret this as the production of 28 whole units and half of another unit that is to be finished the next day. This solution reflects the divisibility assumption of LP. If we want integer solutions, then we must round off or resort to integer programming. However, rounding off LP solutions does not necessarily yield optimal or even feasible solutions.

A LINEAR DISTRIBUTION MODEL

The graphical method illustrates the solution of the general LP model. Some LP models are designed for solving special classes of problems. In particular, LP has probably been most widely applied in the distribution aspect of operations management. These applications have generated specially structured LP models that, although solvable by general methods, are usually solved by techniques that exploit the special properties of the models; the end result is a much more efficient solution procedure.

Table 2-3 Data for Electrovox Distribution Problems

FROM \ TO	WAREHOUSE				
	NEW YORK	CHICAGO	DALLAS	SAN FRANCISCO	SUPPLY
Plant:					
Washington, D.C.	$ .80	$ .90	$1.10	$1.60	50
Denver	1.20	.70	.50	.80	80
Los Angeles	1.40	1.00	.60	.70	120
Demand	90	70	40	50	250

To illustrate the use of LP in distribution-type problems, let us consider the distribution problem faced by the East of the Rockies Region of Shell Oil Co.[11] Since approximately 20 percent of Shell's revenues go to pay for transportation costs, efficient distribution is critical. Figure 2-4 illustrates the Shell distribution problem. Shell's problem is relatively complex; basically, it is to distribute three products among four refineries and a large number of transshipment points and terminals. To further complicate the model, Shell has a choice among three different modes of transportation (pipelines, barges, and tankers).

The resulting LP model has 1,050 decision variables and 575 total constraints. The model operates in the IBM 370 series using IBM's MPSX as the LP programming code. A well-designed report generator offers more then ten optional reports, depending upon the system goals and different users. Even though the LP model is fairly large, its computer solution on an IBM 370/168 costs only $20 to $30 in daytime and $15 to $20 at night. Thus, the LP model is a cost-effective means of improving Shell's distribution efforts, as its benefits outweigh its costs.

We now focus on a much simpler distribution model that is probably the most widely used specially structured LP model. It is called the Hitchcock Koopmans transportation model, and it is concerned with determining the least-cost means of distributing from origins to destinations.

To illustrate the transportation problem, let's consider the distribution problem of the Electrovox Company. Electrovox is very progressive and has already used LP to determine its optimal product mix. The company is now faced with the problem of how to distribute its electrical components from plants to regional warehouses. Electrovox has plants located in Washington, D.C.; Denver; and Los Angeles. Regional warehouses are located in New York, Chicago, Dallas, and San Francisco (see Figure 2-5). This month, the company has available 50 units in Washington, 80 units in Denver, and 120 units in Los Angeles. In order to meet predicted demand, Electrovox must ship 90 units to New York, 70 to Chicago, 40 to Dallas, and 50 to San Francisco. Relevant per-unit transportation costs for each component, as well as demand-and-supply data, are given in Table 2-3. Electrovox

---

[11]T.K. Zierer, W.A. Mitchell, and T.R. White, "Practical Applications of Linear Programming to Shell's Distribution Problems," *Interfaces*, 6, no. 4 (August 1976), 13–26.

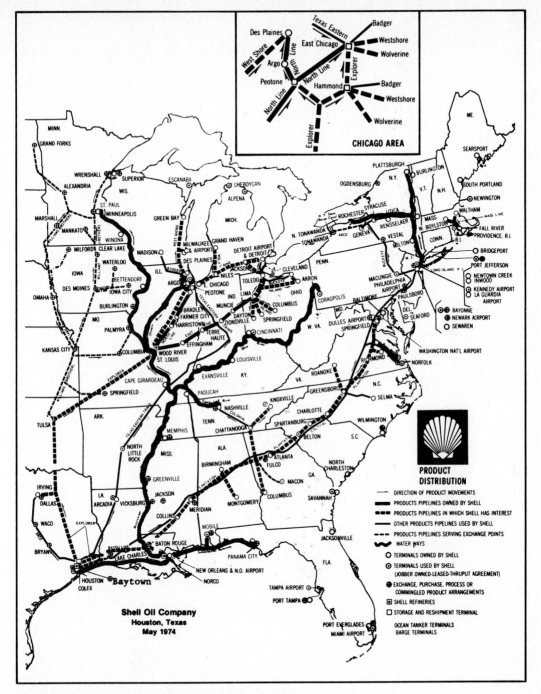

FIGURE 2-4   Shell's East of the Rockies Distribution Problem

SOURCE: T.K. Zierer, W.A. Mitchell, and T.R. White, "Practical Applications of Linear Programming to Shell's Distribution Problems," *Interfaces*, 6, no. 4 (August 1976), 13–26.

wants to determine the shipping pattern that meets all demand at minimum transportation cost.

The Electrovox distribution problem is actually an LP problem. To formulate it, let x_{ij} denote the amount to be shipped from plant i to warehouse j, where $i = 1, 2, 3$, and $j = 1, 2, 3, 4$. In this notation, x_{23} represents the number of units to be shipped from Denver to Dallas. Notice that the first subscript refers to the row (plant) in Table 2-3 and the second subscript refers to the column (warehouse). The problem may be formulated as:

Minimize
$$.8x_{11} + .9x_{12} + 1.1x_{13} + 1.6x_{14} + 1.2x_{21} + .7x_{22} + .5x_{23} + .8x_{24}$$
$$+ 1.4x_{31} + 1.0x_{32} + .6x_{33} + .7x_{34}$$

subject to:
$$x_{11} + x_{12} + x_{13} + x_{14} = 50$$
$$x_{21} + x_{22} + x_{23} + x_{24} = 80$$
$$x_{31} + x_{32} + x_{33} + x_{34} = 120$$
$$x_{11} + x_{21} + x_{31} = 90$$
$$x_{12} + x_{22} + x_{32} = 70$$
$$x_{13} + x_{23} + x_{33} = 40$$
$$x_{14} + x_{24} + x_{34} = 50$$
$$x_{ij} \geq 0; \, i = 1, 2, 3; \, j = 1, 2, 3, 4$$

The foregoing model may be solved directly by the general simplex method, as explained in the supplement to this chapter. However, streamlined simplex procedures are available that offer special computational benefits. Charnes and Cooper developed the stepping-stone method, which was one of the first specialized simplex procedures for transportation problems. Later, Dantzig developed the *modified distribution* (or MODI) *method*, which remains the best approach for solving transportation problems. Computational researchers have further refined the MODI method so that really significant computational savings can be achieved. For instance, transportation problems that have 1,000 plants and 1,000 warehouses (that is, 1 million decision variables) have been solved in 17 seconds or so on a CDC 6600 computer. Problems of this size are not even solvable without using special-purpose algorithms.

We can generalize the 3-by-4 transportation model above to m origins by n destinations. Special-purpose algorithms such as the MODI method can be used to optimize transportation problems. These optimization procedures are quite efficient, readily available, and would normally be used to solve transportation-type problems in actual practice. However, in this chapter we solve them by using a more intuitive approach, called a *heuristic*. A heuristic is a rule of thumb that may be used to obtain a good but not necessarily optimal solution to a problem. Heuristics do not

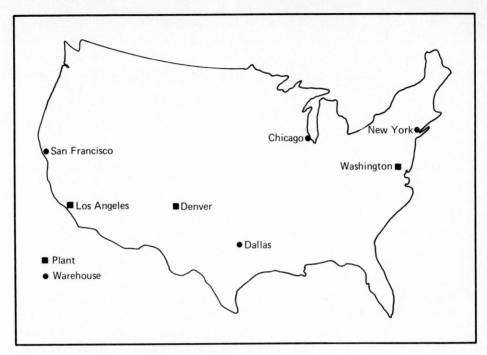

FIGURE 2-5   Location of Plants and Warehouses for Electrovox

SOURCE: Thomas M. Cook and Robert A. Russell, *Introduction to Management Science* 2/e (Englewood Cliffs, N.J.: Prentice-Hall, 1981). Reprinted with permission.

guarantee an optimal solution, but good heuristics are usually within 10 percent of optimality. The advantage of heuristics is that they are usually much faster than optimization procedures and can sometimes be solved by hand without using a computer. Also, heuristics are often used for complex problems when no optimization method exists.

The VAM Heuristic for Solving Transportation Problems

Vogel's Approximation Method (VAM) is an effective heuristic for finding near-optimal solutions to transportation problems. It is an interesting heuristic that can be applied to problems other than transportation problems. To explain the VAM heuristic, we shall need a transportation tableau. This type of table is helpful in solving transportation-type problems. Table 2-4 illustrates a transportation tableau for the Electrovox problem. Usually, the sources are listed as rows in the tableau, and the destinations are columns. The available supply for each source is listed in the far-right column, and the required demands at each destination are summarized in the bottom row. The per-unit transportation cost for shipping from source to destination is found in the upper left-hand corner of the square in the row associated with the source and the column associated with the destination. For example, the per-unit transportation cost from the L.A. source to the Chicago destination is $1.00. The twelve squares (or cells) formed by the three sources and four destinations correspond to direct routes over which shipments can be made. In any feasible solution, the sum of the shipments across any row must not exceed the supply available, and the sum of the shipments down any column must satisfy the demand required.

The basic idea in VAM is to avoid shipments that have a high cost. VAM looks at the opportunity cost of not assigning to the minimum-cost cell in a row or column of the transportation tableau. This is conservatively estimated to be the difference in costs between the lowest- and next-lowest-cost cells in that particular row or column. It then assigns to the minimum-cost cell in the row or column having the highest potential opportunity loss. If we view the opportunity cost as a possible penalty, the idea is to avoid a high penalty. This assignment, then, avoids incurring the highest opportunity loss. The details of VAM are presented as follows:

1. For each row, calculate the potential opportunity loss as the difference between the minimum-cost cell and the next-lowest-cost cell in that row.
2. For each column, calculate the potential opportunity loss as the difference between the minimum-cost cell and the next-lowest-cost cell in that column.
3. Find the highest potential opportunity loss from among all rows and columns, and find the minimum-cost cell associated with that row or column. If a tie exists in opportunity losses among rows and columns, then break the tie arbitrarily.
4. Allocate the maximum possible amount of supply to the minimum-cost cell in step 3. This will delete a row or column. Reduce the supplies and demands appropriately.
5. If a row has been deleted, recalculate the column opportunity losses. If a column has been deleted, recalculate the row opportunity losses.
6. If all allocations have been made, stop. Otherwise, begin another iteration by returning to step 3.

Table 2-4   Transportation Tableau for Electrovox

FROM \ TO	NEW YORK	CHICAGO	DALLAS	SAN FRANCISCO	SUPPLY
Washington, D.C.	.8	.9	1.1	1.6	50
Denver	1.2	.7	.5	.8	80
Los Angeles	1.4	1.0	.6	.7	120
Demand	90	70	40	50	250

We illustrate the VAM procedure by applying it to the Electrovox distribution problem. The VAM heuristic begins by calculating the potential opportunity losses of not assigning to the lowest-cost cell in each row and column. The beginning calculations are shown in Table 2-5. The highest opportunity loss is .4, which is associated with column 1. This means that if we do not ship in the least-cost cell having cost $.80 per unit, we will have to ship in a cell having a cost of at least $.40 per unit more. In fact, the additional cost will be either $.40 or $.60 per unit. Thus, we allocate all the supply possible, which is 50 units, to cell 1, 1, having the minimum cost of $.80. The supply for row 1 is exhausted, so we cross out the remaining cells in row 1 as a reminder that these costs are no longer usable in calculating opportunity losses.

In Table 2-6, we recalculate the column opportunity losses and illustrate the next iteration. The highest opportunity loss is now .3 and is associated with column 2. Thus, we allocate all that we can to the lowest-cost cell 2, 2; this allocation is 70 units, which is all the demand that is required in column 2. We adjust the supplies and demands, delete column 2 by crossing out its remaining cells, and update the row opportunity losses in Table 2-7. This time, the largest opportunity loss is .3, which is associated with row 2. Allocating the available ten units deletes row 2 and leaves only row 3 with available supply. Three more iterations are required to reach the final VAM solution. The final tableau is shown in Table 2-8.

The cost of the VAM solution is found by multiplying each shipment by its per-unit transportation cost. The distribution cost of the VAM solution is .8(50) + .7(70) + .5(10) + 1.4(40) + .6(30) + .7(50) = $203. The final distribution pattern is shown in Figure 2-6.

In this example, the total supply and demand are equal. In situations where supply exceeds demand, some supply will be left unshipped at some plant(s). Likewise, if demand exceeds supply, some demand will have to go unsatisfied; in either case, VAM can be used to determine a low-cost distribution pattern.

Table 2-5   Initial VAM Calculations for Electrovox

ROW OPPORTUNITY COST	From \ To	New York	Chicago	Dallas	San Francisco	Supply
	COLUMN OPPORTUNITY COSTS	.4	.2	.1	.1	
.1	Washington, D.C.	.8 | 50	~~.9~~	~~1.1~~	~~1.6~~	~~50~~
.2	Denver	1.2	.7	.5	.8	80
.1	Los Angeles	1.4	1.0	.6	.7	120
	Demand	~~90~~ 40	70	40	50	250

Table 2-6   Second Iteration for VAM

ROW OPPORTUNITY COSTS	From \ To	New York	Chicago	Dallas	San Francisco	Supply
	COLUMN OPPORTUNITY COSTS	~~.4~~ .2	~~.2~~ .3	.1	.1	
~~.1~~	Washington, D.C.	.8 | 50	~~.9~~	~~1.1~~	~~1.6~~	~~50~~
.2	Denver	1.2	.7 | 70	.5	.8	~~80~~ 10
.1	Los Angeles	1.4	~~1.0~~	.6	.7	120
	Demand	~~90~~ 40	~~70~~	40	50	250

Table 2-7   Third Iteration for VAM

ROW OPPORTUNITY COSTS	From \ To	New York	Chicago	Dallas	San Francisco	Supply
	COLUMN OPPORTUNITY COSTS	~~.4~~ .2	~~.2~~ ~~.3~~	.1	.1	
~~.1~~	Washington, D.C.	.8 | 50	~~.9~~	~~1.1~~	~~1.6~~	~~50~~
.3 ~~.2~~	Denver	~~1.2~~	.7 | 70	.5 | 10	~~.8~~	~~80~~ ~~10~~
.1	Los Angeles	1.4	~~1.0~~	.6	.7	120
	Demand	~~90~~ 40	~~70~~	~~40~~ 30	50	250

Table 2-8   Final Solution for VAM

ROW OPPORTUNITY COSTS	From \ To	New York	Chicago	Dallas	San Francisco	Supply
	COLUMN OPPORTUNITY COSTS	~~.4~~ ~~.2~~ 0	~~.2~~ ~~.3~~	~~.1~~ 0	~~.1~~ 0	
~~.1~~	Washington, D.C.	.8 | 50	.9	1.1	1.6	~~50~~
~~.3~~ ~~.2~~	Denver	1.2	.7 | 70	.5 | 10	.8	~~80~~ ~~10~~
~~.7~~ ~~.1~~	Los Angeles	1.4 | 40	1.0	.6 | 30	.7 | 50	~~120~~ ~~90~~ 40
	Demand	~~90~~ 40	~~70~~	~~40~~ 30	~~50~~	250

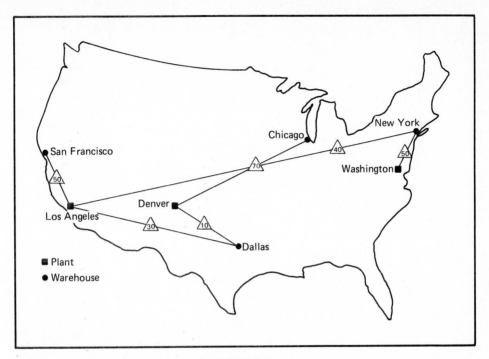

FIGURE 2-6   Final Distribution Pattern for VAM Solution

NETWORK MODELS IN OPERATIONS MANAGEMENT

Transportation models fall into a broader class of problems called network models. A *network* is a collection of nodes or points connected by links. Figure 2-7 depicts a network representation of the final VAM solution to the Electrovox problem.

Networks enjoy many applications in operations management because of the many situations they can accurately represent. Many problems can be represented as a collection of nodes connected by links. Most operations management applications of networks are in distribution and scheduling. However, network analysis is used in such areas as communications networks, transportation systems, water systems analysis, information theory, cybernetics, and project planning and control. In addition to their widespread applicability, network models constitute one of the few categories of mathematical models that is amenable to really large-scale analysis. Network models involving thousands—in some cases millions—of variables are solvable using some of the large computers.

We will run across network-type models further on in the text. Transportation models have further application in production scheduling, warehouse location, and aggregate planning. We will also consider PERT, a network approach to scheduling and controlling projects.

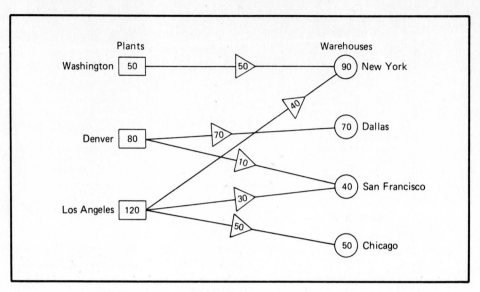

FIGURE 2-7   Network Representation of VAM Electrovox Solution

SUMMARY

Linear programming is an important operations management tool that has many applications, ranging from production scheduling to political redistricting. In spite of its power, we should be aware of the assumptions and limitations of LP, for it is not an appropriate tool for the majority of operations management problems.

In order for linear programming to be applicable to a particular decision problem, all relationships should be linear, with data obtainable and known with certainty. In other words, it must be possible to completely specify the conditions of the problem. Unfortunately, many operations management problems are not clear-cut and involve many factors that cannot be quantified in a linear model. The manager needs to know that LP can be an effective tool for a restricted class of problems; it can provide valuable input to the decision process, but is not an end in itself.

The graphical method is useful for illustrating the simplex method and how to solve LP problems. The simplex method and a computer are required for solving real-world LP problems.

The transportation model is a special LP model that is quite useful in analyzing distribution problems; it is a versatile model that has other applications, such as scheduling and aggregate planning. Its special structure facilitates the use of special-purpose algorithms in order to solve transportation problems more efficiently.

In the supplement to this chapter, we study the details of the simplex method and look at sensitivity analysis, which is very helpful in further analyzing the problem after an optimal solution has been obtained. The postoptimality phase of linear programming can be the most important to the manager. Sensitivity analysis can help answer various types of "what-if" questions. It can also be used to provide a range of alternative solutions, which is more helpful than a single solution, especially in today's dynamic and constantly changing business environment.

SOLVED PROBLEMS

Problem Statement

The Superstar Rent-A-Car Co. is interested in cutting gasoline costs for its fleet of cars. It has decided to use a blend of premium and regular gasoline to achieve the minimal required octane rating of 91 for the cars. Premium gas has an octane rating of 95; regular has a rating of 88. Premium gas costs $.80 per gallon, and regular is $.70. The company's storage tanks can hold 6,000 gallons this month, and the distributor can supply only 3,000 gallons of premium. How many gallons of premium and regular should Superstar Co. purchase in order to minimize costs (assuming it wants to fill its tank)?

Solution

First, we need to formulate the problem and then solve it graphically. The decision variables should answer the purchasing question. Therefore, let $x_1 = $ No. of gallons of premium to purchase, and $x_2 = $ No. of gallons of regular.

Objective function:

$$\text{Min } C = .80x_1 + .70x_2$$

s.t. constraints: $x_1 + x_2 = 6,000$ storage capacity

$$x_1 \leq 3,000 \quad \text{availability of premium}$$

$$4x_1 - 3x_2 \geq 0 \quad \text{weighted average of octane ratings}$$

$$x_1, x_2 \geq 0$$

The third constraint is obtained by forming the weighted average of octane ratings, $\dfrac{95x_1 + 88x_2}{x_1 + x_2} \geq 91$, and clearing terms, yielding $95x_1 + 88x_2 \geq 91x_1 + 91x_2$.

    The first constraint is an equation, and we first obtain the x_1 and x_2 intercepts. Both intercepts are 6,000, and the graph of the constraint is a straight line. Note that

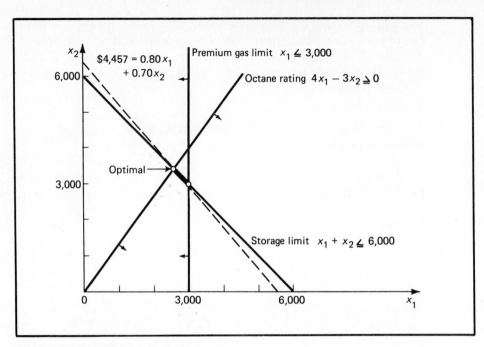

Graphical Solution of Rent-A-Car Problem

since this constraint is only a line, the feasible region will be a line segment and not an area of the plane.

The second constraint has an x_1 intercept of 3,000 and no x_2 intercept. Thus, the graph of $x_1 = 3,000$ is a vertical line.

The third constraint passes through the origin and also the point 3, 4. Plotting all three constraints, we obtain the graph of the feasible region. Notice that the feasible region consists of only the thicker portion of the line segment $x_1 + x_2 = 6,000$. The slope of the objective function is found from $.70x_2 = C - .80x_1$, or $x_2 = C/.70 - 1.14x_1$. Thus, the slope is -1.14, and for every 1.14-unit decrease in x_2 there is a 1-unit increase in x_1. The dashed isocost line passes through the point of the feasible region, which occurs at the intersection of the lines $x_1 + x_2 = 6,000$ and $4x_1 - 3x_2 = 0$. Solving these two equations simultaneously, we get:

$$x_1 + x_2 = 6,000 \qquad 4x_1 + 4x_2 = 24,000$$

$$\underline{4x_1 - 3x_2 = 0} \qquad \rightarrow \underline{-4x_1 + 3x_2 = 0}$$

$$7x_2 = 24,000, \text{ or } x_2 = 3,428.6$$

$$\therefore x_1 = 2,571.4$$

The minimal cost associated with this solution is $.80(2,571.4) + $.70(3,428.6) = $4,457.14.

Problem Statement

The Yuba Manufacturing Co. is planning its aggregate production levels for the last quarter of the year and would like to minimize the combined cost of production and inventory. Production capacities for October, November, and December are 6,000, 6,000, and 4,000 respectively. The demand for the firm's product is expected to be 3,000, 7,000, and 5,000 during the last quarter. Given that per-piece production cost is $3.00 and storage cost per month is $1.00, find a low-cost production/inventory schedule.

Solution

The formulation of this problem can be a linear programming model, but it's even simpler as a transportation-type model. Let the plant capacity each month represent the supplies available, and the demand each month represent the demand at a "destination." We have the following 3 × 3 transportation model:

OCT. DEMAND	*NOV. DEMAND*	*DEC. DEMAND*	
3	4	5	6,000 Oct. capacity
M	3	4	6,000 Nov. capacity
M	M	3	4,000 Dec. capacity
3,000	7,000	5,000	

The cell in the first row, first column, represents October production for October demand. The cell in the first row, second column, represents October production for November demand. Notice that the cost increases by $1.00 for each month the unit is stored. The Ms represent infinite costs in inadmissible cells.

We can obtain an effective heuristic (not necessarily optimal) solution by using the VAM heuristic. The sequence of VAM calculations is shown below. Ties between largest opportunity costs are broken arbitrarily. The solution stipulates that in October, Yuba should produce 3,000 units for October demand and 3,000 units for storage to meet November demand. Likewise, November production would include 4,000 units for November demand and 1,000 units for storage. In December, Yuba should produce 4,000 units as partial fulfillment of December demand.

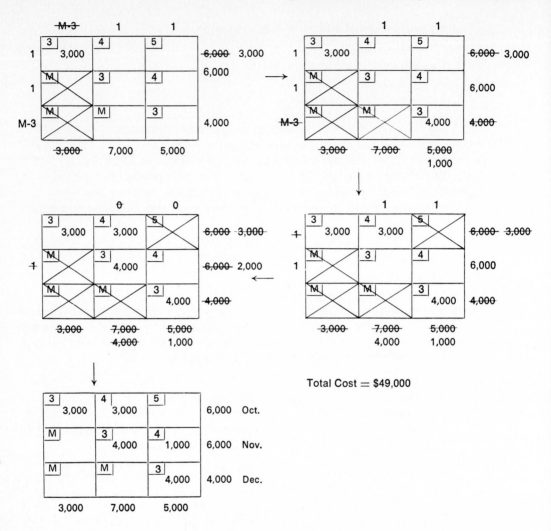

Total Cost = $49,000

<hr/>
REVIEW QUESTIONS

1. What are some applications of linear programming in the area of production, government, and nonmanufacturing operations?
2. What specific properties must be satisfied in order for a mathematical model to be solvable by linear programming?
3. What are some of the limitations of linear programming?
4. What does every optimal LP solution correspond to geometrically?
5. Explain why the transportation model is a part of the category of network models.

6. What are the advantages and disadvantages of using heuristics rather than optimization procedures to solve transportation problems?

7. Can you name some applications of transportation models other than distribution of a commodity from plant to market?

8. Briefly discuss the idea underlying VAM.

*9. Explain how to minimize rather than maximize an objective function in LP.

*10. What is a shadow price?

*11. Discuss the kinds of questions management can answer in performing sensitivity analysis.

PROBLEMS

1. *Product Mix.* The Ace Manufacturing Company produces two lines of its product, the super and the regular. Resource requirements for production are given in the following table:

PRODUCT LINE	PROFIT CONTRI- BUTION	ASSEMBLY TIME (HR.)	PAINT TIME (HR.)	INSPEC- TION TIME (HR.)
Regular	50	1.2	.8	.2
Super	75	1.6	.9	.2

There are 1,600 hours of assembly man-hours available per week, 700 hours of paint time, and 300 hours of inspection time. Regular customers will demand at least 150 units of the regular line and 90 of the super. Formulate an LP model that will determine the optimal product mix on a weekly basis.

2. *Blending.* A farmer would like to determine what quantities of various grains to feed his cattle in order to meet minimum nutritional requirements at lowest cost. He is considering the use of corn, barley, oats, and wheat. The following table relates the relevant dietary information per pounds of grain:

NUTRIENT	CORN	BARLEY	OATS	WHEAT	MINIMUM DAILY REQUIREMENTS
Protein	10	9	11	8	20 mg.
Calcium	50	45	58	50	70 mg.
Iron	9	8	7	10	12 mg.
Calories	1,000	800	850	9,000	4,000
Cost / lb.	$ .55	.47	.45	.52	

Formulate an LP model to determine the dietary mix that minimizes cost.

---

*These questions to be answered after studying the supplement to this chapter.

3. *Machine Loading*. Jiffy Job Shop would like to try a quantitative approach to its machine-loading problem. There are three machines in the shop, and they produce five different products. Each machine has an 8-hour time availability each working day. Today they have a demand of 6, 3, 2, 1, and 5 for products 1 through 5 respectively. The following table gives relevant cost and production time data:

PRODUCT / MACHINE	COST OF PRODUCING ONE UNIT OF PRODUCT j ON MACHINE i					TIME REQUIRED (IN HRS.) TO PRODUCE ONE UNIT OF PRODUCT j ON MACHINE i				
	1	2	3	4	5	1	2	3	4	5
1	12	10	13	9	8	1	.8	1.5	.5	.6
2	7	6	12	11	9	1.5	.9	.7	.4	.9
3	14	8	5	3	2	1.2	1.1	.9	.8	.5

Formulate an LP model to determine the amount of product j to be allocated for production on machine i.

4. *Purchasing*. McKisson Co. purchases two components for the assembly of their block-and-tackle sets. A total of four suppliers are available that can supply the components. However, each supplier has a different per-unit purchase price, distribution cost, and available supply. Purchase prices and freight costs are given in the table. Additionally, suppliers 1, 2, 3, and 4 have the capacity to supply 2,000, 3,000, 4,000, and 4,000 components, respectively. (Their production capacity is equally taxed by either component.) McKisson has a demand of 5,000 units for component 1 and 6,000 units for component 2. How many units of each component should McKisson order from each supplier in order to minimize costs?

Purchase Price

	SUPPLIER 1	SUPPLIER 2	SUPPLIER 3	SUPPLIER 4
Component 1	$5	$7	$6	$4
Component 2	8	8	9	7

Freight Cost

	SUPPLIER 1	SUPPLIER 2	SUPPLIER 3	SUPPLIER 4
Component 1	$1.65	$1.25	$ .95	$1.10
Component 2	1.75	1.35	1.10	1.15

5. *Production and Inventory Planning*. The Coldman Company has a production planning problem. Management wants to plan production for the ensuing year

so as to minimize the combined cost of production and inventory storage costs. In each quarter of the year, demand is anticipated to be 65, 80, 135, and 75, respectively. The product can be manufactured during regular time at a cost of $16 per unit produced, or during overtime at a cost of $20 per unit. The table gives data pertinent to production capacities. The cost of carrying one unit in inventory per quarter is $2. The inventory level at the beginning of the first quarter is zero. Formulate an LP model to minimize the production plus storage costs for the year.

Capacities (units)

QUARTER	REGULAR TIME	OVERTIME	QUARTERLY DEMAND
1	80	10	65
2	90	10	80
3	95	20	135
4	70	10	75

6. Solve the following problem graphically:

$$\text{Maximize} \quad 6x_1 + 8x_2$$
$$\text{subject to:} \quad x_1 \leq 12$$
$$x_2 \leq 10$$
$$2x_1 + 3x_2 \leq 36$$
$$x_1, x_2 \geq 0$$

7. Solve the following minimization problem by the graphical method:

$$\text{Minimize } x_1 + x_2$$
$$\text{subject to:} \quad x_2 \geq 2$$
$$2x_1 - x_2 \geq 0$$
$$3x_1 + 2x_2 \leq 12$$
$$x_1, x_2 \geq 0$$

8. *Blending.* The Slik Oil Company produces two lines of motor oils and a special engine additive called motor honey. All three products are produced by blending two components. These components contribute various properties, including viscosity. The viscosity in the product is proportional to the viscosities of the blending components.

BLENDING COMPONENT	VISCOSITY	COST / BARREL	AVAILABILITY
Component 1	20	$ 6.50	10,000 barrels / wk.
Component 2	60	11.00	4,000 barrels / wk.

PRODUCT	VISCOSITY REQUIRED	REVENUE / BARREL
30 W oil	30	$ 8.00
40 W oil	40	9.00
Motor honey	50	12.00

Assuming no limitation on the demand, determine how many barrels of each oil product Slik should produce each week.

9. *Transportation.* The P & R company distributes its product from three plants to four regionally located warehouses. The monthly supplies and demands, along with per-unit transportation costs, are given as:

FROM \ TO	WAREHOUSE 1	WAREHOUSE 2	WAREHOUSE 3	WAREHOUSE 4	SUPPLY
Plant 1	2	12	6	10	20
Plant 2	14	6	2	12	10
Plant 3	18	8	10	8	25
Demand	11	13	17	14	55

Use Vogel's Approximation Method to find a feasible shipping pattern and total transportation cost.

10. *Distribution.* The Continental Trailer Rental Co. has a problem in trying to relocate rented trailers. Currently, the supply exceeds the demand, and the firm needs to relocate trailers at minimum transportation cost. Currently, there are surplus trailers at locations 1, 2, 3, and 4, while trailers are demanded at locations 5, 6, and 7. The relevant data are:

	LOCATION						
	1	2	3	4	5	6	7
Surplus trailers	6	7	8	3			
Demanded trailers					5	4	9

Cost per Trailer Transported

TO FROM	5	6	7
1	8	11	8
2	12	10	6
3	15	7	9
4	12	12	7

Determine an effective relocation of trailers.

11. *Production/Product Mix.* A manufacturer of office equipment would like to optimize the company's product mix. Currently, the firm produces desks, chairs, tables, and filing cabinets. Each product's resource requirements are given in the table. The desks, chairs, tables, and cabinets contribute $150, $45, $100, and $40 to profit, respectively. The minimum monthly demand requirements are 75 desks, 120 chairs, 100 tables, and 50 filing cabinets. Additionally, management does not want the number of filing cabinets to exceed 10 percent of the total number of items produced. Formulate as an LP model.

PRODUCT	WOOD (BOARD FT.)	PLASTIC (SQ. FT.)	STEEL ALLOYS (LB.)	ADMINISTRATIVE WORKER HOURS
Desks	0	6	9	2.5
Chairs	3	1	1	1.2
Tables	5	2	2	2.2
Cabinets	0	0	15	1.9
AVAILABILITY	1,000	1,200	1,000	1,500

12. *Production and Distribution.* Consider a variation of the distribution problem of Chapter 2. In this problem, it is necessary to address production, as well as transportation, costs in the transportation model. Assume that two plants have production capacities of 2,600 and 1,800 respectively. The three warehouses have demands of 1,500, 2,000, and 900. The product is produced at plant 1 at a per-unit cost of $1.50, whereas the per-unit cost at plant 2 is $2. Transportation costs are given in the table. Set up and solve a transportation model that determines the amount to produce at each plant and the resulting shipping pattern.

	TO WAREHOUSE			
FROM PLANT	1	2	3	SUPPLY
1	$.30	$.50	$.80	2,600
2	$.70	$.20	$.40	1,800
DEMAND	1,500	2,000	900	4,400

13. *Production Scheduling/Inventory Storage.* The American Products Corporation must decide on its production schedule for the next four months. It has contracted to supply a special part for the months of October, November, December, and January at the rates of 12,000, 10,000, 15,000, and 17,000 units respectively. American can produce each part at a cost of $6 during regular time or $9 during overtime. Each month, American has a production capacity of 10,000 units during regular time and 6,000 units during overtime. The part can be stored at a cost of $2 per month; however, there is zero inventory on hand at the beginning of October, and there must be zero inventory at the end of January. American can thus overproduce in some months and store the excess to help meet future demand in other months. Construct a transportation model (tableau) to solve American's production scheduling/inventory storage problem. *Hint:* Define the sources as the modes of production in each month, and define the destinations as the demand required during each month.

14. *Production Scheduling.* The Akron Tire Company currently produces four lines of tires: the economy, glass-belted, snow tire, and the steel radial. Recent recessionary trends have caused a decline in demand, and the company is laying off workers and discontinuing its third shift.

   The problem it faces is that of rescheduling production during the first and second shifts for the remaining quarter of the year. The production process primarily involves the use of vulcanization, fabrication, and plastometer machines. However, the limiting resource in production is the availability of machine hours on the vulcanization machines. The economy, glass-belted, snow tire, and steel radial require 4, 5, 5, and 7 hours respectively, of vulcanizing time.

   The sales manager has forecast the expected sales for each of the four tires in the last quarter of the year. These estimates are shown in the following table:

Forecast Sales

MONTH	ECONOMY	GLASS-BELTED	SNOW TIRE	STEEL RADIAL
October	8,000	19,000	4,000	7,000
November	7,000	19,000	15,000	7,000
December	6,000	18,000	17,000	7,000

   The production capacity in terms of vulcanizing hours available is expressed by month and shift in the next table:

Available Vulcanizing Hours

MONTH	SHIFT 1	SHIFT 2
October	110,000	100,000
November	130,000	120,000
December	115,000	116,000

The labor cost of operating the vulcanizing machines is $10 per hour during the first shift. The shift differential requires that the wages be $12 per hour during the second shift. The other relevant cost is storage: It costs $4 per month to store a tire, regardless of its type. Note that it will be necessary to store some tires in the problem, as there is not enough labor available during December to meet December demand.

Assuming that the company wishes to produce exactly as many tires as the sales manager has forecast, formulate an LP model to determine a production schedule that will meet demand at minimum total cost.

*15. *Product Mix.* The Green Country Lumber Company produces two wood products: interior wood paneling and plywood. The resource requirements for each product are provided in the table. Assuming that production time is limited to 4,000 hours per week, determine the product mix that will maximize Green Country's profit.

WOOD PRODUCT	PRODUCTION TIME PER SQ. YD. (HR.)	DEMAND	PROFIT CONTRIBUTION PER SQ. YD.
Plywood	.025	At least 6,000 sq. yd. per week	$.30
Paneling	.040	At most 4,000 sq. yd. per week	.45

*16. Solve by the simplex method:

$$\text{Maximize } 8x_1 + 7x_2$$
$$\text{subject to: } 3x_1 + 4x_2 \leq 15$$
$$7x_1 + 5x_2 \leq 20$$
$$x_1, x_2 \geq 0$$

*17. *Inventory/Purchasing.* A stereo mail-order warehouse has 8,000 feet available for storage of loudspeakers. The jumbo speakers cost $295 each and require 4 square feet of space; the midsize speakers cost $110 and require 3 square feet of space; and the economy speakers cost $58 and require 1 square foot of space. The demand for the jumbo speakers is, at most, 20 per month. The wholesaler has $10,000 to invest in loudspeakers this month. Assuming that the jumbo speakers contribute $105 to profit, the midsize contribute $50, and

---

*From material in supplement to this chapter.

the economy contribute $28, how many units of each type should the whole-saler buy and stock?

*18. Use the simplex method to solve the following problem:

$$\text{Maximize } 3x_1 + 5x_2 + 4x_3$$

$$\text{subject to:} \qquad x_2 + 2x_3 \leq 6$$

$$3x_1 + 2x_2 + x_3 \leq 24$$

$$x_1 + x_2 + x_3 \leq 12$$

$$x_1, x_2, x_3 \geq 0$$

*19. The optimal simplex tableau for a maximization problem with all ($\leq$) con-straints is given by:

c_b	BASIC	c_j 4 x_1	2 x_2	0 s_1	0 s_2	0 s_3	SOLUTION
2	x_2	0	1	1	-1	0	4
4	x_1	1	0	$-\frac{1}{4}$	$\frac{3}{4}$	0	3
0	s_3	0	0	2	-4	1	8
$c_j - z_j$		0	0	-1	-1	0	20

a. What is the optimal solution?
b. What are the shadow prices?
c. Suppose the resources could be obtained at no cost. Which right-hand side would you recommend for expansion, and why?
d. Which of the three resources are being fully utilized?

*20. Solve problem 6 by the simplex method.

*21. Transform the following problem to standard form by making all constraints equations:

$$\text{Min } 13x_1 + 17x_2$$

$$\text{s.t.:} \qquad x_1 + x_2 \geq 1{,}700$$

$$3x_1 - 4x_2 = 0$$

$$x_1, x_2 \geq 0$$

---

*From material in supplement to this chapter.

*22. Listed below is the formulation and optimal computer solution to the Ace Manufacturing Company of problem 1. Let:

$$x_1 = \text{units of regular produced}$$
$$x_2 = \text{units of super produced}$$

Maximize $50x_1 + 75x_2$

subject to: $1.2x_1 + 1.6x_2 \le 1{,}600$ assembly

$.8x_1 + .9x_2 \le 700$ paint

$.2x_1 + .2x_2 \le 300$ inspection

$x_1 \qquad\quad \ge 150$ regular demand

$x_2 \ge 90$ super demand

a. What is the optimal solution and associated profit?
b. What are the marginal values of the resources at optimality?
c. Ace Manufacturing is faced with declining profit contribution in the face of inflation and would like to know the effect of declining profit on the optimal product mix. From the computer printout, determine the range over which

```
ACE MANUFACTURING COMPANY

THE ORIGINAL COEFFICIENTS OF THE CONSTRAINTS
            CODE 0 ==> <OR= CONSTRAINT
            CODE 1 ==> >OR= CONSTRAINT
               CODE 2 ==> = CONSTRAINT

  CODE CONSTANT   A(I,1)   A(I,2)
1    0   1600.00    1.20     1.60
2    0    700.00     .80      .90
3    0    300.00     .20      .20
4    1    150.00    1.00      .00
5    1     90.00     .00     1.00

THE COEFFICIENTS IN THE ORIGINAL OBJECTIVE FUNCTION TO BE MAXIMIZED ARE:
            50.00    75.00

OPTION SELECTED == PRINT SENSITIVITY ANALYSIS

BASIC SOLUTION    4
   S( 1)=   388.888672
   S( 5)=   554.444336
   S( 3)=   141.111160
   X( 1)=   150.000000
   X( 2)=   644.444336

CURRENT VALUE OF OBJECTIVE FUNCTION IS      55833.32

     THE LAST BASIC FEASIBLE SOLUTION IS OPTIMAL
       OPTIMAL VALUE OF THE ORIGINAL OBJECTIVE FUNCTION IS      55833.32
CONSTRAINT      SHADOW PRICE
       1          .0000
       2        83.3333
       3          .0000
       4       -16.6667
       5          .0000
```

---

*From material in supplement to this chapter.

```
                    ACE MANUFACTURING COMPANY
                  *** SENSITIVITY ANALYSIS ***

                  OBJECTIVE FUNCTION RANGING

                                                      * RANGE *
  VARIABLE        DECREASE          INCREASE        MINIMUM          MAXIMUM
   X( 1)         NO LIMIT           16.6667        NO LIMIT          66.6667
   X( 2)          18.7500          NO LIMIT         56.2500         NO LIMIT



                  RIGHT HAND SIDE RANGING

                                                      * RANGE *
  CONSTRAINT      DECREASE          INCREASE        MINIMUM          MAXIMUM
     1            388.8887          NO LIMIT       1211.1113         NO LIMIT
     2            499.0000          218.7500        201.0000         918.7500
     3            141.1112          NO LIMIT        158.8888         NO LIMIT
     4            150.0000          623.7498           .0000         773.7498
     5            NO LIMIT          554.4443        NO LIMIT         644.4443
```

the profit contributions of the regular and super products can vary before the current product mix is no longer optimal.

d. Over what range can each of the right-hand-side coefficients vary while maintaining the optimality of the current product mix?

───────────────── **SUPPLEMENT TO CHAPTER 2** ─────────────────

THE SIMPLEX METHOD

You may have discovered in Chapter 2 that it is impossible to use the graphical method of solution on problems that are at all complex. The greatest importance of the graphical method is as an aid to understanding the simplex method. We will discuss the simplex method in its basic form here. For large-scale, real-world applications of LP, more sophisticated variants of the simplex method are actually used; however, the principles are essentially the same.

The simplex method is similar to solving a system of linear equations. In fact, the simplex method does solve a system of equations, and the solution derived not only solves the equations but also optimizes an objective function. In this sense, the simplex method is a straightforward generalization of various methods for solving a system of equations.

The simplex method is an iterative technique. That is, it establishes an initial feasible solution, then repeats the solution process, making successive improvements, until the optimal solution is found. It is sometimes referred to as an adjacent extreme-point solution procedure, because it generally begins at an extreme point of the feasible region, then successively evaluates adjacent extreme points until the one representing the optimal solution is found.

Simplex Procedures

In order to use the simplex method, it is necessary to state all the constraints as equations rather than inequalities. Mathematically, it is easier to solve systems of equations than systems of inequalities. Therefore, we shall have to convert less-than-or-equal-to and greater-than-or-equal-to constraints into equations. First we shall learn how to convert $\leq$ constraints.

Suppose we have the constraint $x_1 + x_2 \leq 5$. We may convert this inequality to an equation by adding an additional variable, called a slack variable. Thus we have $x_1 + x_2 + s_1 = 5$, where $s_1 \geq 0$. A slack variable, as the name implies, represents unused resources. In the foregoing equation, if $x_1 = 2$ and $x_2 = 1$, then s_1 must equal 2. Thus, $x_1 + x_2 < 5$, and s_1 represents two units of the right-hand-side resource that are left over.

Notationally, we distinguish between slack and decision variables. The x_i represent decision variables and refer to actual activities; the s_i denote slack variables that represent unused capacity.

Let us refer back to the Electrovox problem of Chapter 2 in order to illustrate converting $\leq$ constraints to equations. Recall that the objective is to produce the appropriate number of hi-gain and standard CBs in order to maximize profit. Suppose that management has been able to procure additional hi-gain transistors, so that the constraint limiting transistor availability to 40 units per day no longer applies. Thus, the Electrovox problem (after dropping the transistor constraint) is written in standard form as:

$$\text{Maximize} \quad 20x_1 + 50x_2 + 0s_1 + 0s_2$$

$$\text{s.t.:} \quad 1.2\,x_1 + 4x_2 + s_1 \qquad\quad = 240$$

$$.5x_1 + 1x_2 \qquad\quad + s_2 = 81$$

$$x_1, x_2, s_1, s_2 \geq 0$$

We have thus transformed a system of inequalities into a system of equations ready to be solved by the simplex method. Notice that the slack variables are given an objective-function coefficient of zero.

The simplex method is concerned only with solutions that geometrically correspond to extreme points of the feasible region. These extreme-point solutions are also called basic feasible solutions. A complete mathematical definition of basic solutions is beyond the scope of this text. For our purposes, it will be sufficient to observe that a basic solution has exactly as many variables in solution as there are equations. Thus, a system of m equations in n unknowns will have m variables in solution for any basic solution. For example, the Electrovox problem above will have two variables in solution, since there are two constraint equations. This will leave two variables nonbasic or out of solution at a value of zero. The simplex method determines which two of the four variables are most profitable.

Basic Steps in the Simplex Procedure

Let us take a closer look at the computational steps involved with the simplex method. In successively examining adjacent extreme points, the simplex method continually finds improved solutions. That is, it only examines points that are not only feasible but yield at least as good a value in the objective function as the previous point. In short, the simplex method encompasses the following basic steps:

1. An initial basic feasible solution is established.
2. An optimality check is next performed to determine whether the solution is optimal yet. If the solution is optimal, stop, for no further calculations are needed. However, if the solution is not optimal, a new variable must be found that will improve the solution. This new entering variable is always a nonbasic variable whose value is currently zero.
3. The value of the entering variable is increased until the value of some basic variable is forced down to zero. This basic variable is called the leaving variable.
4. The entering variable now takes the place of the leaving variable; at any iteration, there are only m variables that are in the solution. The next step is to update all relevant information required in the simplex procedure. This updating process is called pivoting. After updating, the procedure returns to step 2.

The Simplex Tableau

Each repetition of steps 2 through 4 is called an iteration in the simplex method. The computer can execute such iterations by merely storing the appropriate information and then operating on it whenever it is needed. When you execute the simplex method by hand, the calculations are more conveniently dealt with in tabular form. This table is called a simplex tableau; the form of the starting tableau for the Electrovox problem is shown in Tableau 2-1.

Tableau 2-1   Initial Simplex Tableau for Electrovox

Objective function coefficients ⟶ c_j

			c_j	20	50	0	0	
	c_B	*BASIC VARIABLE*		x_1	x_2	s_1	s_2	*SOLUTION*
	0	s_1		1.2	4	1	0	240
	0	s_2		.5	1	0	1	81
		z_j		0	0	0	0	
Relative costs ⟶		$c_j - z_j$		20	50	0	0	0

Total profit

The tableau shows the coefficients of the constraint equations as well as other useful information.

The c_j row at the top of the tableau shows the coefficients of the respective variables in the objective function. The next row down simply labels the various columns. The next two rows consist of the coefficients of the two constraint equations of the Electrovox problem. The bottom row of the tableau is very important, for this row indicates whether the solution is optimal. The $c_j - z_j$ numbers in the last row are called opportunity or relative costs. They indicate the per-unit increase in the value of the objective function for every unit of variable x_j brought into the solution. The z_j numbers represent the amount of profit that is lost for each unit of variable x_j that is brought into solution.

Looking next at the columns of Tableau 2-1, the c_B numbers at the far left are the objective-function coefficients of the basic variables. They are currently all 0, as the slack variables in the initial solution all have 0 objective-function coefficients. The next column, labeled "Basic Variable," lists those variables that are in solution at this particular iteration. The last column on the far right gives us the solution values of each basic variable. In Tableau 2-1, we can see that the values of s_1 and s_2 are 240 and 81 respectively. The last entry in the solution column represents the total profit of the solution.

The Basic Steps Applied

Step 1: Establish Initial Basic Feasible Solution. To complete the initial tableau requires no calculation (except possibly the z_j values). The tableau always contains as many basic variables as there are constraints. To determine which variables are in the initial solution, we scan the original column of coefficients of the constraints in standard form and pick those variables that have a $+1$ coefficient and all other coefficients of 0. These starting variables are always either slack variables or artificial variables, which we shall discuss later. Setting up the initial tableau completes the first step of the simplex method.

Step 2: Check Solution for Optimality. In the lower right-hand corner of the initial Electrovox tableau (Tableau 2-1), the profit of the current solution is 0. This is because only slack variables are in solution. The solution column indicates that $s_2 = 81$—that is, we have 81 hours of inspection time left over—and s_1 is equal to 240. In the tableau, the decision variables x_1 and x_2 are nonbasic and equal to zero; thus, we are producing nothing and, consequently, making zero profit.

The $c_j - z_j$ opportunity costs indicate whether the current solution is optimal or not. In this case, they indicate that it is not optimal, because they are not all less than or equal to zero.

The z_j's represent the amount of profit that is given up for each unit of variable x_j that enters the solution. The c_j's indicate the amount of profit gained for each unit of x_j brought into solution. The $c_j - z_j$, then, represents the net profit for bringing x_j into solution. Thus, we can improve our profit by bringing in either x_1 or x_2. Normally, you will choose the variable whose $c_j - z_j$ is largest. This choice of entering variable gives the fastest rate of improvement, although not necessarily the greatest degree of improvement. Hence, x_2 is chosen as the entering variable.

The z_j's can be calculated by observing how much of each of the current basic variables must be given up in order for x_j to have its value increased and enter the solution. The coefficients in the column of the tableau that are directly under any variable x_j are called substitution rates or substitution coefficients. They indicate how much of the current solution must be changed for every unit of x_j brought into solution. Thus, from Tableau 2-1 we can see that if one unit of x_2 enters the solution (that is, if one hi-gain is produced), then we must give up four units of assembly slack and one unit of inspection slack time.

Furthermore, each of the two basic variables s_1 and s_2 is worth zero. It costs nothing to give them up! Thus, each $z_j = 0$. Each $c_j - z_j$ for the nonbasic variables is calculated:

$$c_1 - z_1 = 20 - [0(1.2) + 0(.5)] = 20$$
$$c_2 - z_2 = 50 - [0(4) + 0(1)] = 50$$

The $c_j - z_j$ for all basic variables is always zero.

For every unit of x_1 brought into solution, we can increase profits by 20; for every unit of x_2, we can increase profits by 50. Therefore, because when we are maximizing, we normally bring in the nonbasic variable that has the largest $c_j - z_j$ value, x_2 now enters the solution.

Step 3: Increase Value of Entering Variable Until Some Basic Variable Reaches Zero. Since only m variables can be basic (in this case, $m = 2$), we must now determine a variable to leave the basis. Our resources are limited; so increasing the value of x_2 forces at least some of the other basic variables to decrease in value. We must be careful not to increase x_2 so much that some basic variable becomes negative. Happily, there is a simple test to determine which variable should leave the solution and how much of x_2 should enter. This *ratio test* consists of dividing each number in the solution column by its associated coefficient in the column under x_2. This ratio is formed only for those rows in which the coefficient under x_2 is positive. Negative and zero coefficients are excluded. Hence, for row 1, we form the ratio 240/4, and for row 2, 81/1. As is shown in Tableau 2-2, we get 60 and 81, respectively. The row that has the smallest ratio shows the variable to leave the solution. Since row 1 has the smallest ratio, s_1 leaves the solution.

Step 4: Bring New Variable into Solution and Revise Tableau for New Iteration. In the last basic step of the simplex method, we must bring x_2 into the solution and revise all the numbers in the tableau so that we may return to step 2 and begin a new iteration. The procedure used to do this is called pivoting. All rows in the tableau, including the $c_j - z_j$, are updated by this procedure. After the initial tableau, we shall dispense with the z_j row at the bottom of the tableau. There are two steps to the pivoting process. In one step, we update the pivot row; this is the row in which the minimum ratio occurred. In the other step, we update all remaining rows.

Tableau 2-2   Illustration of Ratio Test and Pivot Selection

C_B	BASIC VARIABLE	x_1	x_2	s_1	s_2	SOLUTION	Ratio
	c_j	20	50	0	0		
0	s_1	1.2	④	1	0	240	240/4
0	s_2	.5	1	0	1	81	81/1
	$c_j - z_j$	20	50	0	0	0	

The number in the tableau that occurs at the intersection of the leaving row and the entering column is called the pivot element. In Tableau 2-2, the circled number is the pivot element, and the arrows indicate the entering column and leaving row. The entire pivot row is updated by dividing all entries in the pivot row by the pivot element. Thus, we divide the pivot row by 4 yielding 1.2/4   4/4   1/4   0/4   240/4. Tableau 2-3 shows the partially completed tableau.

For every row other than the pivot row, we can update by using the formula:

$$\text{New row} = \text{Old row} - \text{Pivot intersection number} \times \text{New pivot row}$$

where the pivot intersection number is the number in the row that is in the pivot column. To demonstrate the formula, let's update the remaining rows in the tableau:

$$
\begin{aligned}
\text{New row 2} = \quad & (.5 \quad 1 \quad 0 \quad 1 \quad 81) \\
& -(1)(.3 \quad 1 \quad .25 \quad 0 \quad 60) \\
\hline
= \quad & .2 \quad 0 \quad -.25 \quad 1 \quad 21
\end{aligned}
$$

$$
\begin{aligned}
\text{New } c_j - z_j \text{ row} = \quad & (20 \quad 50 \quad 0 \quad 0) \\
& -(50)(.3 \quad 1 \quad .25 \quad 0) \\
\hline
= \quad & 5 \quad 0 \quad -12.5 \quad 0
\end{aligned}
$$

Tableau 2-3   First Iteration with Pivot Row Updated

C_B	BASIC VARIABLES	x_1	x_2	s_1	s_2	SOLUTION
	c_j	20	50	0	0	
50	x_2	.3	1	.25	0	60
0	s_2					
	$c_j - z_j$					

Tableau 2-4   Updated Tableau After First Iteration

c_j		20	50	0	0		
c_B	BASIC VARIABLES	x_1	x_2	s_1	s_2	SOLUTION	min. ratio
50	x_2	.3	1	.25	0	60	60/.3
0	s_2	②	0	−.25	1	21	21/.2
	$c_j - z_j$	5	0	−12.5	0	3,000	

In Tableau 2-4, the completed tableau for the second solution is presented. The current solution value in the lower right-hand side of the tableau is calculated by taking the c_B column times the solution column to yield: Profit = 50(60) + 0(21) = 3,000.

The pivoting process merely involves multiplying one equation by a constant and adding it to another equation. However, certain rules involving elementary row operations are observed so that the solution to the updated system of equations is the same as the original LP model. Thus, the rows in Tableau 2-4 still represent equations.

Returning to our calculations, we can see that the second solution in Tableau 2-4 is not optimal, since $c_1 - z_1 = 5$. Thus, x_1 will be the entering variable, and the leaving variable is calculated by forming the minimum ratios 60/.3 and 21/.2. Row 2 yields the minimum ratio, and s_2 becomes the leaving variable. Thus, .2 becomes the pivot element.

In updating the rows of the tableau, we first calculate the new pivot row:

$$\left(\frac{.2}{.2} \quad \frac{0}{.2} \quad \frac{-.25}{.2} \quad \frac{1}{.2} \quad \frac{21}{.2} \right)$$
$$= (1 \quad 0 \quad -1.25 \quad 5 \quad 105)$$

The remaining rows are updated:

$$\text{New row 1} = (.3 \quad 1 \quad .25 \quad 0 \quad 60)$$
$$-(.3)(1 \quad 0 \quad -1.25 \quad 5 \quad 105)$$
$$= \ 0 \quad 1 \quad .625 \quad -1.5 \quad 28.5$$

$$\text{New } c_j - z_j \text{ row} = \ (5 \quad 0 \quad -12.5 \quad 0)$$
$$(-5)(1 \quad 0 \quad -12.5 \quad 5)$$
$$= \ 0 \quad 0 \quad -6.25 \quad -25$$

Tableau 2-5   Optimal Tableau for Electrovox Problem

C_B	BASIC VARIABLES	x_1	x_2	s_1	s_2	SOLUTION
	c_j	20	50	0	0	
50	x_2	0	1	.625	-1.5	28.5
20	x_1	1	0	-1.25	5	105
	$c_j - z_j$	0	0	-6.25	-25	3,525

The new solution value is $50(28.5) + 20(105) = 3{,}525$, which is optimal. The updated tableau is shown in Tableau 2-5.

The tableau indicates optimality, since all solution values are nonnegative and all $c_j - z_j$ are less than or equal to zero, which indicates that no higher profit can be achieved. The feasibility of the solution may be checked by substituting this tableau's value back into the original constraints of the model.

From Tableau 2-5, we can see that variables x_2 and x_1 are in the final solution at values 28.5 and 105, respectively. This corresponds to real conditions of producing 28.5 hi-gain sets and 105 standard sets. The optimal profit is found in the lower right-hand corner at a value of $3,525. This solution is precisely the same as that determined by the graphical method.

Which of the two resources is being fully utilized? From the optimal tableau, we can see that slack variables s_1 and s_2 are nonbasic and therefore have zero value. Consequently, there is no surplus assembly or inspection time, and these two resources are being fully utilized.

MINIMIZATION PROBLEMS AND OTHER TYPES OF CONSTRAINTS

So far, we have examined only maximization problems and constraints that were less-than-or-equal-to ($\leq$) type constraints. In LP analysis, it is necessary to handle minimization and equality ($=$), as well as greater-than-or-equal-to constraints ($\geq$).

There are two approaches we can use to solve a minimization problem. First, we can formulate the minimization problem, then change the signs of all coefficients in the objective function and solve the problem as a maximization problem. The resulting values of the decision variables will be correct, and changing the sign of the final objective function value yields the correct value. Many computer codes only maximize (or minimize), and the decision maker must sometimes use this reversing trick to solve an LP problem on the computer.

Another approach to minimization involves changing the simplex solution procedure. Again, the alteration is simple; it involves only a change in the selection criterion for the entering variable. Instead of picking the variable with the most positive $c_j - z_j$ to enter the solution, we simply pick the variable with the most negative $c_j - z_j$. The minimization terminates when all $c_j - z_j \geq 0$.

In solving either minimization or maximization problems, it is often necessary to include = and $\geq$ type constraints. The problem with these constraints is in determining a starting feasible solution for the simplex method. For example, if we have the constraint $3x_1 + 5x_2 = 12$, then it is already in equation form. But what are the beginning values of the basic variables? To obtain an easy starting solution, we use an artificial variable, A_1, to obtain

$$3x_1 + 5x_2 + A_1 = 12$$

Now we can begin the simplex method with $A_1 = 12$ in the initial solution. In order for the final solution to be feasible, A_1 must equal zero. Thus, we must drive the artificial variables to zero value in the final solution. There is more than one way to do this; we can assign the artificial variables an arbitrarily low objective-function coefficient for a maximization problem or an arbitrarily high value for a minimization problem. Alternatively, we could solve the LP problem in two phases, the first of which is to drive the artificial variables to zero value.

The conversion procedure to $\geq$ type constraints involves subtracting a slack and adding an artificial. Thus, $3x_1 + 5x_2 \geq 12$ becomes:

$$3x_1 + 5x_2 - s_1 + A_1 = 12$$

Some commercial LP codes make these transformations for the user; others do not. Failure to drive all artificial variables to zero value in any LP problem means that the problem has no feasible solution; that is, it is impossible to find decision variable values that satisfy all the constraints. In this case, the analyst must remodel the problem to arrive at a feasible solution.

AFTER THE SOLUTION, THEN WHAT?

Some may argue that there is no such thing as a single optimum solution to a real-world LP problem. They may say that data are not precise or that parameters of the model are continually changing and possibly changing the optimal solution. They are probably right.

It is very seldom that an LP problem is analyzed and only one solution is derived. Management usually wants to try different parameter values in order to estimate or anticipate possible changes in the optimal solution. Some models are relatively insensitive to changes in parameters, whereas other are quite sensitive to even small changes. A formal analysis that explores these effects on the optimal solution is called postoptimality or *sensitivity analysis*. In some cases, it can be more important than the single optimum solution itself. Sensitivity analysis allows the decision maker to ask "what-if"–type questions, such as, "What if prices rise?"

"What if our supply of resource A decreases?" or "What if we develop that new product?"

Some information that is helpful in sensitivity analysis is obtainable from the final simplex tableau. The numbers, called *shadow prices*, measure the marginal value of the right-hand-side resources at optimality; these shadow prices are valid as long as the same basic variables remain in solution. Thus, shadow prices can be used to estimate the value of gaining or losing particular resources. To illustrate, let us consider the final solution to the Electrovox problem, which is in Tableau 2-5. One shadow price is associated with each constraint; thus, there are two shadow prices in this problem. These two shadow prices can be found by looking in the $c_j - z_j$ row under the two variables that were in solution initially. In this case, s_1 and s_2 comprised the initial solution, and the shadow prices are $y_1 = 6.25$ and $y_2 = 25$. These are obtained from changing the signs in the $c_j - z_j$ row under s_1 and s_2. $y_1 = 6.25$ means that an additional unit of assembly time is worth \$6.25. The shadow price for inspection is $y_2 = 25.0$. If you were operations manager and were going to expand one of these two departments, which would you choose? The shadow prices tell us that each hour of assembly that we could obtain is worth \$6.25, and each additional hour of inspection is worth \$25.00. These values are gross, not net, for they do not include the cost of obtaining these resources.

There are several other types of sensitivity analysis that can be performed. These include:

1. Right-hand-side ranging—to see how much an r.h.s. value can be increased or decreased before the basis changes.
2. Changes in objective-function coefficients—exploring how much we can increase or decrease an objective-function coefficient before the basis changes.
3. Adding a new variable—determining whether it is worthwhile to introduce a new variable or product into the solution and, if so, determining the new solution.
4. Adding a new constraint—determining the feasibility of a constraint that has been added—if feasible, obtaining a new solution.
5. Changes in constraint coefficients—exploring how changes in constraint coefficients affect the feasibility or optimality of the problem.

In some cases, LP computer software packages contain options that allow the analyst to select and output various sensitivity analysis options. In the next section we illustrate a typical LP computer printout.

COMPUTER OUTPUT OF LP SOLUTIONS

Shown on page 68 is a computer solution to the Electrovox problem. The data concerning the constraints and objective function are printed out first so the user can verify the accuracy of the input. Next the basic variables and their values are printed along with the optimal objective-function value. The shadow prices are then listed for each constraint followed by two types of sensitivity analysis. Objective-function ranging explores how much each decision variable's objective-function coefficient could vary before the current solution becomes suboptimal. In the Electrovox printout, the profit of variable x_1 can vary between \$15 and \$25 without destroying the optimality of the current solution. If the profit for x_1 were to exceed \$25, then the solution would change and we would produce only x_1 rather than a combination of x_1 and x_2.

```
ELECTROVOX COMPUTER SOLUTION

    THE ORIGINAL COEFFICIENTS OF THE CONSTRAINTS

            CODE 0 ==> <OR= CONSTRAINT
             CODE 1 ==> >OR= CONSTRAINT
              CODE 2 ==>   = CONSTRAINT


   CODE CONSTANT  A(I,1)  A(I,2)

1   0    240.00    1.20    4.00

2   0     81.00     .50    1.00


    THE COEFFICIENTS IN THE ORIGINAL OBJECTIVE FUNCTION TO BE MAXIMIZED ARE:
                20.00   50.00


    OPTION SELECTED -- PRINT SENSITIVITY ANALYSIS


    BASIC SOLUTION   3

      X( 2)=     28.500000
      X( 1)=    105.000000

    CURRENT VALUE OF OBJECTIVE FUNCTION IS      3525.00


       THE LAST BASIC FEASIBLE SOLUTION IS OPTIMAL
        OPTIMAL VALUE OF THE ORIGINAL OBJECTIVE FUNCTION IS      3525.00
     CONSTRAINT    SHADOW PRICE

          1            6.2500
          2           25.0000
                     ELECTROVOX COMPUTER SOLUTION

            *** SENSITIVITY ANALYSIS ***


                 OBJECTIVE FUNCTION RANGING

                                                      * RANGE *
      VARIABLE      DECREASE        INCREASE        MINIMUM         MAXIMUM

       X( 1)         5.0000          5.0000         15.0000         25.0000
       X( 2)        10.0000         16.6667         40.0000         66.6667



                  RIGHT HAND SIDE RANGING

                                                      * RANGE *
     CONSTRAINT     DECREASE        INCREASE        MINIMUM         MAXIMUM

          1         45.6000         84.0000        194.4000        324.0000
          2         21.0000         19.0000         60.0000        100.0000
```

The final sensitivity analysis printout shows the right-hand-side ranging analysis. This tells us how much a given r.h.s. coefficient can change (while holding all others constant) before the current optimal solution becomes infeasible. For example, constraint 1 currently has a r.h.s. coefficient of 240. According to the printout, this value could range from 194.4 to 324 before the current solution becomes infeasible. This type of analysis is useful in the face of changing resource availabilities.

_____ **SOLVED PROBLEMS** _____

Problem Statement

Solve the following problem by the simplex method:

$$\text{Max } 2x_1 + 3x_2$$

$$\text{s.t.: } x_1 + 2x_2 \le 6$$

$$3x_1 + x_2 \le 8$$

$$x_1, x_2 \ge 0$$

Solution

First we must convert the 2×2 problem to standard form:

$$\text{Max } 2x_1 + 3x_2 + 0s_1 + 0s_2$$

$$\text{s.t.: } x_1 + 2x_2 + s_1 \qquad = 6$$

$$3x_1 + x_2 \qquad + s_2 = 8$$

$$x_1, x_2, s_1, s_2 \ge 0$$

Entering the slack variables first, we obtain the initial tableau:

	c_j	2	3	0	0		
c_B	BASIC VARIABLES	x_1	x_2	s_1	s_2	SOLUTION	Ratio
0	s_1	1	②	1	0	6	6/2
0	s_2	3	1	0	1	8	8/1
	$c_j - z_j$	2	3	0	0	0	

$\uparrow$

c_j		2	3	0	0		
c_B	BASIC VARIABLES	x_1	x_2	s_1	s_2	SOLUTION	Ratio
3	x_2	1/2	1	1/2	0	3	$3/\frac{1}{2}$
0	s_2	(5/2)	0	−1/2	1	5	$5/\frac{5}{2}$
	$c_j - z_j$	1/2	0	−3/2	0	9	

c_j		2	3	0	0	
c_B	BASIC VARIABLES	x_1	x_2	s_1	s_2	SOLUTION
3	x_2	0	1	3/5	−1/5	2
2	x_1	1	0	−1/5	2/5	2
	$c_j - z_j$	0	0	−7/5	−1/5	10

The optimal solution is to produce two units of x_1 and x_2 with a total profit of 10.

Problem Statement

Convert the following problem to standard form (all equations):

$$\text{Min } 14x_1 + 9x_2 + 11x_3$$
$$\text{s.t.: } x_1 + x_2 + x_3 = 400$$
$$2x_1 + x_2 + 3x_3 \leq 1{,}000$$
$$7x_1 - 5x_2 + 8x_3 \geq 100$$
$$x_1, x_2,\ x_3 \geq 0$$

Solution

Using the appropriate slack and artificial variables, we convert to equations in the following manner:

$$\text{Min } 14x_1 + 9x_2 + 11x_3 + 0s_1 + 0s_2 + MA_1 + MA_2$$
$$\text{s.t.: } x_1 + x_2 + x_3 + A_1 = 400$$
$$2x_1 + 3x_2 + 3x_3 + s_1 = 1{,}000$$
$$7x_1 - 5x_2 + 8x_3 - s_2 + A_2 = 100$$
$$x_1, x_2, x_3, s_1, s_2, A_1, A_2 \geq 0$$

The M objective-function coefficients of the artificial variables A_1 and A_2 represent very large penalty numbers. Their purpose is to ensure that no artificial variable will appear in any optimal solution. If we were maximizing, the objective-function coefficients would be a $-M$.

REFERENCES

ADVANI, S., "A Linear Programming Approach to Air Cleaner Design," *Operations Research*, March–April 1974, pp. 295–97.

CHARNES, ABRAHAM, and W.W. COOPER, *Management Models and Industrial Applications of Linear Programming*. New York: John Wiley, 1961.

DAELLENBACH, HANS G., and EARL J. BELL, *User's Guide to Linear Programming*. Englewood Cliffs, N.J.: Prentice-Hall, 1970.

DANTZIG, GEORGE B., *Linear Programming and Extensions*. Princeton, N.J.: Princeton University Press, 1963.

DUTTON, R., G. HINMAN, and C.B. MILLHAM, "The Optimal Location of Nuclear Power Facilities in the Pacific Northwest," *Operations Research*, May–June 1974, pp. 478–87.

FELDSTEIN, M., and HAROLD LUFT, "Distributional Constraints in Public Expenditure Planning," *Management Science*, August 1973, pp. 1414–22.

GASS, SAUL I., *Illustrated Guide to Linear Programming*. New York: McGraw-Hill, 1970.

GLASSEY, C.R., and V.K. GUPTA, "A Linear Programming Analysis of Paper Recycling," *Management Science*, December 1974, pp. 392–408.

GRINOLD, RICHARD C., "Input Policies for a Longitudinal Manpower Flow Model," *Management Science*, 22 (1976), 570–75.

HEROUS, R.L., and W.A. WALLACE, "Linear Programming and Financial Analysis of the New Community Development Process," *Management Science*, April 1973, pp. 857–72.

LEE, SANG M., *Linear Optimization for Management*. New York: Petrocelli/Charter, 1976.

LYONS, D.F., and V.A. DODD, "The Mix-Feed Problem," *Operational Research*. Amsterdam: North-Holland Publishing, 1975.

MARCUSE, W., L. BODIN, E. CHERNIAVSKY, and YASUKO SANBORN, "A Dynamic Time Dependent Model for the Analysis of Alternative Energy Policies," *Operational Research*. Amsterdam: North-Holland Publishing, 1975.

NAYLOR, THOMAS H., EUGENE T. BYRNE, and JOHN M. VERNON, *Introduction to Linear Programming: Methods and Cases*. Belmont, Calif.: Wadsworth, 1971.

REVELLE, C., D. MARKS, and J. LIEBMAN, "An Analysis of Private and Public Sector Location Models," *Management Science*, 16 (1970), 692–707.

SAVAS, E., "Simulation and Cost-Effectiveness of New York's Emergency Ambulance Service," *Management Science*, 15 (1969), B608–27.

SMITH, V.E., "A Diet Model with Protein Quality Variable," *Management Science*, February 1974, pp. 971–80.

ZIERER, T.K., W.A. MITCHELL, and T.R. WHITE, "Practical Applications of Linear Programming to Shell's Distribution Problems," *Interfaces*, 6, no. 4 (August 1976), 13–26.

3

COMPUTER SIMULATION

INTRODUCTION

In this chapter, we describe computer simulation, which is often referred to as *Monte Carlo simulation*. In general, simulation is a descriptive, rather than an optimization technique that involves developing a model of some real phenomenon and then performing experiments on that model. This broad definition applies to types of simulation other than computer simulation. A spacecraft simulator, a wind tunnel, a model airplane, and an analog simulation of some continuous process are all examples of simulations that differ fundamentally from the computer simulation to be discussed in this chapter. To be more specific, computer simulation is a numerical technique that involves modeling a stochastic system on a digital computer with the intention of predicting the system's behavior.

A simulation model serves the manager in much the same way as a laboratory serves the physical scientist. By making changes in the various parameters of a simulation model, a manager can observe the results of the simulation and infer how different configurations of the real system would behave under various circumstances.

Reasons for Using Simulation

The many reasons why a manager uses simulation to solve a problem can be clustered into two major categories.

First, experimentation with the real system may be impractical or impossible. A hospital administrator may have difficulty justifying experimenting with the real coronary-care unit to determine the optimal number of beds and the best medical-team configuration, whereas experimentation on a surrogate system, a computer simulation model, would be totally acceptable.

Second, the real system may be too complex to permit mathematical representation or model solution. Often, if experimentation with the real system is impractical, an alternative would be to develop a mathematical model of the system or problem in question. Many times however, the real system is too complex to model or solve mathematically, and simulation is used as the tool of last resort.

Simulation Applications

Computer simulation is probably the most generally useful quantitative technique used by the operations manager. Its major utility is its ability to solve a wide range of operational problems. The following list represents a small sample of successful applications.

Health-Care Applications.   Simulation has been used to predict the effect of various physician mixes on the utilization of hospital resources, and to plan the configuration of emergency rooms, coronary-care units, and other hospital facilities. Staffing of nursing stations, primary-care teams, and scheduling operations and admission are all problems that have been attacked using computer simulation. Even the optimal location of ambulances has been examined using simulation.

Urban Applications.   Cities have used simulation to solve some of their most pressing problems—problems such as police dispatching and beat design, the planning and design of transit systems, evaluation of operating alternatives at airports, planning for snow emergencies and garbage collection, the location of emergency vehicles, long-range financial planning, and many more.

Industrial Applications.   Manufacturing organizations have used simulation to schedule their productive process, make inventory policy decisions, design productive systems, determine machine maintenance schedules, design distribution systems, and even test the effects of increased production on the operation of an overhead crane.

Financial Applications.   The rapid growth in the use of simulation as a financial planning tool is evidenced by the more than 25 financial modeling software packages currently available commercially. All kinds of pro forma statements are produced using financial simulation packages. Portfolio selection models are common, as are capital budgeting models.

Military Applications.   Large-scale military battles, as well as individual weapon systems, have been simulated to aid in the design both of weapon systems and of strategic and tactical operations.

Agricultural Applications.   Simulation has been used to make decisions concerning equipment on a sugar plantation, to predict the effects of various policy alternatives on the Venezuelan cattle industry, and to aid in the design of regional grain collection, handling, and distribution in Canada.

Table 3-1 provides a more exhaustive list of simulation applications.

Manual Simulation

In order to give you some understanding of the technique of computer simulation, let's analyze a very simple problem. Two new ship-docking facilities are being finished this year, and a decision must be made regarding how many tugs will be necessary to service ships wishing to dock. Using data from similar ports and a great deal of subjective judgment, the time between ship arrivals is assumed to be distributed as shown in Table 3-2. Time spent at the dock is estimated in a similar

Table 3-1   Real-World Applications of Simulation

Air Traffic Control	Maintenance Scheduling
Aircraft Ground Traffic Control	Facility Layout
Airport Design	Financial Forecasting
Emergency Vehicle Location	Pro Forma Financial Statements
Assembly Line Balancing	Harbor Design
Bank Teller Scheduling	Factory Design
Grocery Store Clerk Scheduling	Parking Facility Design
Inventory Control	Baggage Handling
Data Network Design	Airport Manning
Voice Network Design	Railroad Scheduling
Computer System Design	Traffic Control
Job Shop Scheduling	Water Resource Development
Distribution System Design	Petrochemical Process Design
Warehouse Location	Library Design
Vehicle Routing	Information System Design
Emergency Room Design	Airline Passenger Demand
Hospital Design	Tool Crib Manning
Bus Scheduling	Flight Crew Scheduling
Airline Operations	Union Contract Negotiations

Table 3-2   Ship Interarrival Time Distribution

TIME BETWEEN SHIP ARRIVALS	PROBABILITY
1 hour	.30
2 hours	.25
3 hours	.15
4 hours	.15
5 hours	.05
6 hours	.05
7 hours	.05
	1.00

Table 3-3   Unloading Time Distribution

UNLOADING TIME	PROBABILITY
1 hour	.05
2 hours	.15
3 hours	.20
4 hours	.25
5 hours	.30
6 hours	.05
	1.00

manner; that probability distribution is shown in Table 3-3. Tugging time is fairly constant at one hour per tug, and ships are taken on a first-come, first-served basis, with ships being tugged to sea having priority over those being tugged to port.

The flow of a ship through the port facility is shown in Figure 3-1. Notice that a tug is needed first to tow the ship to the berth, and it is then released while the ship is unloaded. Once the ship is ready to leave the berth, a tug is needed to tow the ship into the open water.

The first step in developing the simulation is to develop a way of generating the two stochastic variables in the system: ship arrival times and unloading times. This is done using numbers from a uniform distribution whose parameters are 0 and 1.

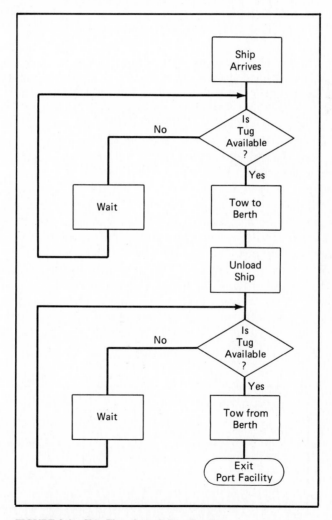

FIGURE 3-1 Ship Flow through Port Facility

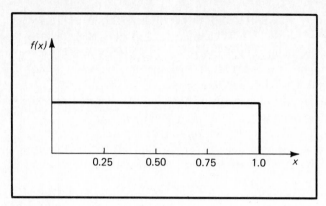

FIGURE 3-2   Uniform Distribution

Remember that a uniform probability distribution is one in which the random variable is defined over a range from a to b. If the parameters of the uniform distribution are 0 and 1, then random $P(x \leq .25)$, for example, is equal to 0.25, and $P(.25 \leq x \leq .75) = .5$. Figure 3-2 depicts the uniform distribution in graphic form.

The process of generating stochastic variables is basic to computer simulation. As shown in Figure 3-3, it is accomplished by defining a function that relates a uniformly distributed random variable to a random variable distributed in another manner. Remember that once this function, known as a *process generator*, has been developed, it is easy to sample from a uniform distribution and transform that uniformly distributed random variate into an arrival time or an unloading time. In our problem, both stochastic variables are treated as discrete variables. The function describing arrival times and unloading times can be found by defining the cumulative probability distributions of the two variables and relating that distribution to a uniform random variable between 0 and 1. Because a number chosen from a uniform distribution with parameters 0 and 1 will fall in the range of 0 to .3, 30 percent of the time approximately 30 percent of the ships generated according to the function described in Table 3-4 will arrive one hour after the preceding ship. Similarly, approximately 15 percent of the arrivals will come just four hours after the preceding ship.

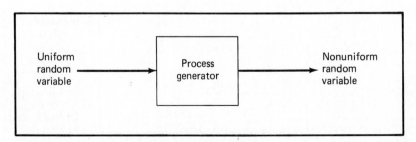

FIGURE 3-3   Schematic of Process Generator

Table 3-4 Ship Interarrival Time Generating Function

UNIFORM RANDOM VARIABLE	TIME BETWEEN ARRIVALS
.00 – .30	1 hour
.30 – .55	2 hours
.55 – .70	3 hours
.70 – .85	4 hours
.85 – .90	5 hours
.90 – .95	6 hours
.95 – 1.00	7 hours

Generation of unloading times is accomplished in a similar manner. If a random number is chosen between 0 and .05, the generated unloading time is one hour. If the random number is between .4 and .65, the generated unloading time is four hours. See Table 3-5 for the unloading time generating function.

You must remember, however, that we are describing a random process, and it would take a large number of ship arrivals for these percentages to be considered very accurate. In other words, if only 50 arrivals were generated, it would not be unreasonable for 12 to 13 ships to take three hours to unload even though the expected number of ships taking three hours to unload is 10 (.2 times 50).

Having defined the system and the process generators, we are now ready to simulate the harbor operation. First, we must decide what experiments we are interested in running. For the sake of illustration, let's run two experiments, one with one tug and the other with two tugs. The critical output variable from the simulator is the average time spent by a ship waiting for a tug. Let's simulate 48 hours and assume an around-the-clock operation. Let us also assume that the random numbers needed to generate ship arrivals are chosen from the random numbers in Table 3-6, starting in the upper left-hand corner. Random numbers to generate unloading times are chosen from the same table, starting in the upper right-hand corner. In a computer simulation, these random numbers would be generated by a random-number generating function and not chosen from a table.

Looking at Table 3-7, because the random number .445282 falls between .3 and .55, the first ship is simulated to arrive two hours into the simulated time period. The next ship arrives only one hour later, because its random number, .066257, falls

Table 3-5 Unloading Time Generating Function

UNIFORM RANDOM VARIABLE	UNLOADING TIME
.00 – .05	1 hour
.05 – .20	2 hours
.20 – .40	3 hours
.40 – .65	4 hours
.65 – .95	5 hours
.95 – 1.00	6 hours

Table 3-6 Random-Number Table

.445282	.353333	.112460	.494758	.956412	.285648	.106182
.066257	.441906	.055118	.353555	.625270	.569627	.790333
.615352	.579120	.936548	.407208	.014319	.421038	.397360
.594821	.992685	.602720	.682154	.668440	.871255	.211575
.428152	.664736	.135047	.827656	.750516	.054190	.570499
.935282	.477204	.445679	.379244	.264349	.172899	.658255
.393437	.436322	.077000	.535109	.517650	.289920	.080668
.874724	.522334	.261491	.867939	.854214	.313831	.195065
.345906	.319852	.805962	.957102	.488950	.319787	.518168
.230927	.722047	.253941	.025220	.865850	.968126	.016103
.383484	.155976	.484498	.503207	.658759	.423696	.613343
.866792	.680668	.282878	.571261	.881661	.148613	.956734
.402887	.806714	.214300	.025378	.223563	.112981	.665817
.978072	.876081	.453834	.838279	.945164	.126478	.252390
.376035	.984704	.523906	.281099	.971441	.298754	.049552
.608526	.205187	.754386	.679630	.288311	.613193	.084362
.987430	.165323	.105069	.142509	.909431	.174001	.859131
.588776	.800478	.503880	.818984	.378979	.903020	.007307
.916667	.434235	.355410	.224342	.147361	.865086	.864270
.399848	.620655	.125302	.165914	.867769	.713384	.470383
.401840	.177596	.449017	.095737	.533275	.338016	.228617
.329558	.919797	.552755	.038363	.255378	.187000	.823605
.258627	.139314	.508244	.795636	.199622	.037007	.425445
.219602	.488609	.955238	.333945	.406528	.433665	.943236
.786436	.049489	.489014	.488679	.530948	.787576	.946926
.593372	.037899	.887044	.981170	.903624	.591212	.414656
.167034	.270299	.118483	.278210	.602910	.113570	.255230
.509250	.758433	.967347	.978183	.162974	.174195	.578402
.902657	.210320	.138008	.935174	.368968	.797242	.462741
.601267	.442931	.246182	.490711	.728634	.955403	.174712
.449643	.125448	.705902	.106384	.285185	.753657	.955278
.948750	.094997	.031238	.332454	.713580	.289390	.314123
.280228	.854264	.603533	.932821	.165132	.595403	.086226
.158733	.176363	.629582	.190230	.475139	.138766	.556342
.089161	.527890	.364889	.438324	.345949	.130772	.671094
.849617	.057854	.700570	.682735	.791279	.603053	.496812
.553393	.849053	.113780	.041200	.223180	.968275	.801036
.091737	.341098	.220956	.255856	.546529	.976471	.940064
.852144	.652287	.244428	.595987	.376065	.892506	.970457
.790186	.007002	.930339	.519015	.741036	.775080	.981155
.911208	.636852	.620241	.989783	.356524	.231102	.177894
.987448	.323640	.054813	.416119	.003391	.275281	.621161
.249438	.906181	.192145	.997242	.254147	.549703	.010896
.118046	.610211	.598851	.101210	.217602	.394718	.409892
.906891	.752321	.351903	.340528	.876046	.191524	.264726
.864643	.805323	.050154	.053020	.866732	.723211	.538683
.723195	.491027	.437407	.205195	.294510	.920305	.871236
.944672	.826904	.459380	.314145	.750449	.675389	.298291
.711250	.582876	.096009	.330172	.116949	.730150	.328360
.398807	.437603	.036349	.279671	.350884	.588266	.371640

Table 3-7 Harbor Simulation, One-Tug Configuration

SHIP NO.	RANDOM NO.	ARRIVAL TIME IN HOURS	TIME WHEN TUG WAS ENGAGED (TO BERTH)	ARRIVAL TIME AT BERTH	RANDOM NO.	TIME UNLOADING IS FINISHED	TIME WHEN TUG WAS ENGAGED (FROM BERTH)	TIME TUG WAS RELEASED	TIME SPENT WAITING
1	.445282	2	2	3	.106182	5	5	6	0
2	.066257	3	3	4	.790333	9	9	10	0
3	.615352	6	6	7	.397360	10	10	11	0
4	.594821	9	11	12	.211575	15	15	16	2
5	.428152	11	12	13	.570499	17	17	18	1
6	.935282	17	18	19	.658255	24	24	25	1
7	.393437	19	19	20	.080668	22	22	23	0
8	.874724	24	25	26	.195065	28	28	29	1
9	.345906	26	26	27	.518168	31	31	32	0
10	.230927	27	27	28	.016103	29	29	30	0
11	.383484	29	30	31	.613343	35	35	36	1
12	.866792	34	34	35	.956734	41	41	42	0
13	.402887	36	36	37	.665817	42	42	43	0
14	.978072	43	43	44	.252390	47	47	48	0
15	.376035	45	45	46	.049552	47	48	49	1
16	.608526	48	49	50	.084362	52	52	53	1

Table 3-8 Harbor Simulation, Two-Tug Configuration

SHIP NO.	RANDOM NO.	ARRIVAL TIME IN HOURS	TIME WHEN TUG WAS ENGAGED (TO BERTH)	ARRIVAL TIME AT BERTH	RANDOM NO.	TIME UNLOADING IS FINISHED	TIME WHEN TUG WAS ENGAGED (FROM BERTH)	TIME TUG WAS RELEASED	TIME SPENT WAITING
1	.445282	2	2	3	.106182	5	5	6	0
2	.066257	3	3	4	.790333	9	9	10	0
3	.615352	6	6	7	.397360	10	10	11	0
4	.594821	9	9	10	.211575	13	13	14	0
5	.428152	11	11	12	.570499	16	16	17	0
6	.935282	17	17	18	.658255	23	23	24	0
7	.393437	19	19	20	.080668	22	22	23	0
8	.874724	24	24	25	.195065	27	27	28	0
9	.345906	26	26	27	.518168	31	31	32	0
10	.230927	27	27	28	.016103	29	29	30	0
11	.383484	29	29	30	.613343	35	35	36	0
12	.866792	34	34	35	.956734	41	41	42	0
13	.402887	36	36	37	.665817	41	41	42	0
14	.978072	43	43	44	.252390	47	47	48	0
15	.376035	45	45	46	.049552	47	47	48	0
16	.608526	48	48	49	.084362	51	51	52	0

between 0 and .3. Since a tug is available at two hours into the simulation, it is assigned immediately to the first ship, and one hour later the ship is ready for unloading. Unloading time for ship number 1 is generated at two hours, because .106182 is between .05 and .20. The one tug is assigned to ship 2 immediately after servicing ship 1 but is idle for an hour waiting for ship 1 to be unloaded. To make sure you understand how the simulation is working, you should verify the numbers in Tables 3-7 and 3-8.

Upon examination of Tables 3-7 and 3-8, it is apparent that if the object were to minimize ship waiting time, then two tugs should be employed, since the average waiting time is reduced from .5 hours (Hours spent waiting/No. of ships) to 0 hours. If, however, the objective is to minimize the cost of waiting plus the cost of operating the port, then costs of waiting and the cost of operating a tug would have to be determined.

Figure 3-4 is a listing of a GPSS computer program that simulates the harbor problem. The experiments described in Tables 3-7 and 3-8 were run on the computer for a simulated time of 4800 hours instead of 48 hours. It took a medium-sized third-generation computer less than 5 CPU seconds to simulate 4800 hours of harbor operation. The GPSS program took less than one hour to write and debug. During

```
       1       FUNCTION    RN1,D7
     .3,1/.55,2/.7,3/.85,4/.9,5/.95,6/1.0,7
       2       FUNCTION    RN1,D6
     .05,1/.2,2/.4,3/.65,4/.95,5/1.0,6
       TUG     STORAGE     1
       BERTH   STORAGE     2
               SIMULATE
     1         GENERATE    FN1
     2         QUEUE       TUGLN
     3         ENTER       TUG
     4         DEPART      TUGLN
     5         ADVANCE     1
     6         LEAVE       TUG
     7         ENTER       BERTH
     8         ADVANCE     FN2
     9         LEAVE       BERTH
    10         QUEUE       TUGLN
    11         ENTER       TUG
    12         DEPART      TUGLN
    13         ADVANCE     1
    14         LEAVE       TUG
    15         TERMINATE
    16         GENERATE    4800
    17         TERMINATE   1
               START       1
               END
```

FIGURE 3-4   GPSS Simulation Model—Harbor Problem

Table 3-9   Harbor Simulation Results

	TOTAL NUMBER OF SHIPS GENERATED	AVERAGE TUG UTILIZATION	AVERAGE BERTH UTILIZATION	AVERAGE TIME SPENT WAITING FOR A TUG
1-Tug Configuration	1,745	.727	.676	1.172 hours
2-Tug Configuration	1,745	.363	.671	.03 hour

that simulated time 1748 ships arrived at the port facility. A summary of the results of the two experiments is shown in Table 3-9. Although the correlation between the manual and computer simulations is quite close for the two-tug configuration, the computer simulation of the one-tug configuration gives an average waiting time of more than twice that given by the manual simulation. It should be clear that the reason we include an example of a manual simulation in this chapter is to give you a deeper understanding of what computer simulation is, not to suggest that real problems are solved using manual simulation.

STEPS IN A SIMULATION STUDY

The harbor situation introduced you to simulation as an idea and as a technique. In the rest of this chapter, we shall reinforce this intuitive understanding by describing the various stages or tasks in a simulation study. First you formulate the problem, then collect and analyze the data. Then you formulate a model, submit it to the computer for processing, and analyze the results. Figure 3-5 depicts the steps of a simulation study.

Problem Formulation

You can't arrive at the right answer if you are working on the wrong problem. Therefore, the first step is to formulate the problem properly. Often the manager has only a vague idea of what the problem is. This vague idea must be translated into an explicit, written statement of the objectives of the study. The explicit original statement of the problem should not be considered sacrosanct, however, for this reason: As the simulation study progresses, the simulator becomes more knowledgeable about the system being simulated and about the objectives of the organization. Consequently, it is sometimes necessary to modify the objectives as the nature of the problem becomes clearer. Usually, the statement of objectives takes the form of questions to be answered, hypotheses to be tested, and effects to be estimated. Obviously, it is also necessary to identify the criteria to be used to evaluate these questions. In the harbor situation, the problem was simply how many tugs should be employed, and the evaluation criteria should probably be the cost of ships waiting and the cost of providing the tug service.

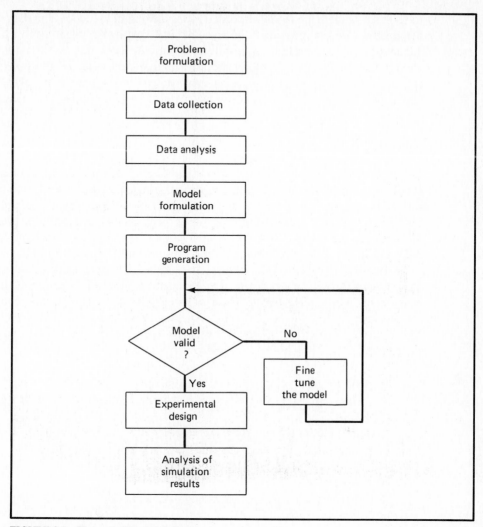

FIGURE 3-5   Phases in Simulation Study

Data Collection

The second task, and possibly the most time-consuming step in a simulation study, is the job of collecting data. Quantitative data are necessary for several reasons. First, data are required to describe the system being simulated. If you don't understand the real system thoroughly, it isn't very likely that you will simulate the system properly. Second, data must be gathered as the foundation for generating the various stochastic variables in the system. For example, in the harbor system, real data concerning arrivals and unloading times were gathered and analyzed to determine the proper probability distributions and their parameters. Finally, data are necessary to test and validate the model. In order to use a simulation model to make decisions, the decision maker must be confident that the real-world phenomenon has been adequately and accurately represented. Often, the best way to accomplish this validation is to compare simulator output with historical data. To adequately model the harbor situation, data concerning arrivals, tow times, unloading times, waiting costs, tug costs, tug downtime, and other variables would need to be collected.

Data Analysis

Once the data have been collected, they must be analyzed and the proper generating functions must be developed. In the harbor example, the stochastic variables—ship arrival times and unloading times—were generated using cumulative probability distributions. These were estimated subjectively. Actually, subjective probability distributions are somewhat atypical; probability distributions based on empirical data usually yield more reliable simulation results and thus are preferable.

Two basic tasks must be accomplished in order to generate random variables. First, the raw data of a stochastic variable must be analyzed to determine how that random variable is distributed. Then, a function must be derived to generate the stochastic variable, using a uniformly distributed random number between 0 and 1. The following procedure is typically used to determine how a random variable is distributed:

1. The data are grouped into a frequency distribution.
2. This frequency distribution is depicted graphically as either a histogram or a frequency polygon.
3. From the shape of the histogram, a probability distribution is hypothesized.
4. Probability distribution parameters are estimated using sample statistics.
5. The hypothesis is tested, using one of several nonparametric statistical tests such as the *chi-square* or *Kolomogorov-Smirnov test*.
6. If the hypothesis is rejected, distribution parameters can be changed slightly, and the new hypothesis tested.
7. If no known probability distribution can be found to fit the sample data, the simulator is often forced to use the cumulative probability distribution of the sample data.

The next step in analyzing the data is to develop the functions necessary to generate a nonuniformly distributed random variable from a uniform random number between 0 and 1. If the random variable is discrete, it is easy to use the cumulative probability distribution, as we did in the manual simulation of the harbor.

To derive a generating function for continuous random variables, you must use the integral calculus, but the basic idea is the same. The object is to define the stochastic variable in terms of a uniformly distributed random number. For example, the process generator for a random variable distributed according to a negative exponential distribution is:

$$x = -\frac{1}{\lambda}\ln(r)$$

where $\qquad$ x = an exponentially distributed random variable

$\qquad\qquad$ r = uniform random number between 0 and 1

$\qquad\qquad$ $\dfrac{1}{\lambda}$ = mean of the distribution

$\qquad\qquad$ ln = natural logarithm

Formulate the Model

A simulation model is an abstraction—usually mathematical—of some real phenomenon or system. Model building is a very difficult step in the simulation process, because the model builder must strike a balance between model realism and the cost of developing that model. If a crucial variable or functional relationship is omitted, the model does not accurately predict the behavior of the real system. If the model is too close to the real-world system, it can easily be too expensive to collect data for, or to program and execute. The goal of the model builder is to build a model that adequately describes the real system at a minimum cost of human and computer resources. You can imagine that model building is an art rather than a science.

Write and Test the Program

To solve a real problem using simulation, the computer is an absolute necessity. The computer language you use is, therefore, a matter of some consequence.

Computer programming languages can actually be thought of in a hierarchy. The assembler languages of the various computer manufacturers are at the lowest level, and they are almost never used in simulation studies for several reasons. First, they are machine-dependent, which means that an assembler language program will not run on a machine other than the model for which it was created. An IBM 370 assembler language program, for example, can only be run on an IBM 360 or IBM 370 series computer. Secondly, it is excessively complex to write a simulation program in assembler language. An assembler program to simulate the harbor problem might take as many as 10,000 assembler language instructions and as long as 200 hours to write and debug.

Compiler languages, the next level of programming languages, are often used for simulation. FORTRAN, BASIC, PL1, and ALGOL are the most popular computer languages used for this purpose. Compiler languages are machine-independent, and because they are more sophisticated than assembler languages, a programmer has far less detail to be concerned with; so the programming effort is

reduced. To simulate the harbor problem might take 300–400 FORTRAN statements and 30–40 hours programming time.

Special-purpose simulation languages, such as SIMSCRIPT, GPSS, SLAM II,
and GASP, simplify programming even more. As mentioned earlier in this chapter, a
GPSS program for the harbor problem took only 24 statements and less than one
hour to program and debug. The reason for the reduction in programming effort
with a simulation language like GPSS is that each GPSS statement or block can be
thought of as a FORTRAN subroutine (a small program in itself); and such things
as the simulation clock and next-event logic are preprogrammed into the GPSS
software. An additional benefit is that the probability of creating a valid program is
increased.

Why, then, are most simulators written in compiler languages such as
FORTRAN and BASIC? One reason is that special-purpose simulation languages
such as GPSS and SIMSCRIPT are not as widely available as the compiler
languages. All but the very smallest computers have FORTRAN, COBOL, or
BASIC compilers in their software packages. Often, a simulation language such as
GPSS is not used because the person conducting the simulation study does not know
a special-purpose language and is unwilling to invest the time needed to learn one.
Clearly, an organization that uses simulation techniques to aid in its decision process
should consider acquiring a simulation processor such as GPSS or SIMSCRIPT, and
then train its staff in the use of the simulation language.

Validating the Simulation Model

Perhaps the most difficult step in a simulation study is validating the simulation
model. It is foolish to use simulation results in the decision-making process unless
you are quite confident that the simulation model represents the real-world situation
accurately. Absolute validation is probably unattainable, but it is possible to gain
confidence in a simulation model by making certain verifications.

Program Testing. One aspect of a simulation that must be validated is
whether the programmer has instructed the computer properly. It is possible that a
simulation model is valid as designed but invalid as implemented on the computer.
Standard program-testing techniques should be employed to ensure congruence
between simulator design and simulator program. These techniques include manual
calculations, program traces, and so on. It is necessary to verify the absence of
programming errors when you are validating a simulation, but this step alone is not
sufficient. The program can be perfect and the simulation model still be totally
invalid.

Variable Generation Test. Earlier in this chapter, we mentioned that nonparametric goodness-of-fit tests could be applied to hypotheses concerning the
distributions of the various stochastic variables. These same tests should be applied

to the output from the various generating functions to ensure that the real-world variables and simulated variables are distributed in the same manner. For example, if the interarrival time in a real queuing system is normally distributed with a mean of five minutes and a standard deviation of two minutes, then the random variable of interarrival times being generated in the simulation program should also be normally distributed with $\mu = 5$ and $\sigma = 2$.

Subjective Validation. The design as well as the output of the simulation model ought to be reviewed by the people who are most familiar with the real system. This subjective validation should properly be done by people not directly involved in the simulation study.

Historical Validation. If the simulator is designed to simulate an existing system, it is often possible to simulate the system as it is currently configured and then compare actual historical data to simulation output. For example, if the real system is a harbor operation, vital statistics such as the average waiting time of a vessel and the average time a vessel spends in the harbor should be compared to the distribution of various output variables. The absence of significant differences between simulated results and historical results may tend to validate the simulator; but it does not guarantee that the simulator will accurately predict the behavior of the real system under different conditions.

Confidence in the validity of a simulation model is crucial to the successful use of simulation. For this reason, no stone should be left unturned when performing the validation step of a simulation study.

Experimental Design

Once a simulation model has been implemented and validated, it can be used for its original purpose, experimentation. Simulation, you will recall, is a means of providing information necessary for decision making when a real-world system cannot be sufficiently manipulated. A simulation model synthetically gathers the information necessary to describe the system under study. The object is to gather the information necessary for decision making—at the lowest possible cost. Usually, real-world experiments are more costly than simulation experiments, and thus one can experiment with a greater number of alternatives when using a simulation model. For example, if the system under study is a harbor and the decision variables are the number of tugs and the number of berths, management can experiment with many combinations of decision variables to determine the optimal harbor configuration using simulation. If, however, experiments were made on the real system, far fewer alternatives could be evaluated.

The questions of the length of simulation runs, initialization periods, sample sizes, and optimization procedures are beyond the scope of this text. Many of the answers are contained in the traditional literature concerning experimental design.

Analysis of Simulation Results

If the simulation model is valid and the simulation experiments have been designed properly, analysis of simulation output is fairly straightforward. Often, certain statistical techniques, such as analysis of variance, can be helpful in analyzing simulation results.

WHEN TO SIMULATE

Once the problem has been formulated, the manager must decide whether or not to attempt to solve the problem using computer simulation. This decision process is depicted in Figure 3-6.

As we said earlier, the problem should be formulated explicitly in terms of hypotheses to be tested and questions to be answered. After the problem has been formulated, a solution technique other than simulation is often judged to be more appropriate. The important point is that choosing a solution methodology must succeed, not precede, the problem-formulation phase of any scientific study. If an analytical technique or model is available or can be adapted to the problem, it should probably be used. If an analytical technique such as classical inventory theory, which is discussed in Chapter 10, or queuing theory, discussed in Chapter 4, cannot be applied, then the manager must make the decision between simulating and making an intuitive, seat-of-the-pants decision. This judgment, in turn, depends on the nature of the individual decision. In other words, is the decision important enough to justify the estimated cost of developing, validating, and experimenting with a simulation model?

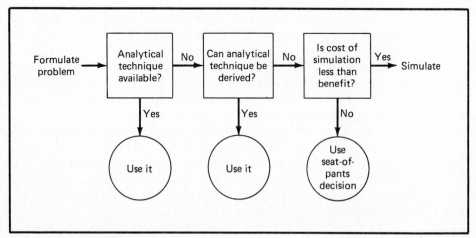

FIGURE 3-6   When to Simulate

Advantages of Simulation

In deciding whether or not to simulate, the manager must weigh the advantages of the technique.

1. The greatest advantage is that simulation allows the manager to model complex and dynamic phenomena that otherwise could not be dealt with in a scientific way.

2. Simulation permits experimentation that might be impossible or infeasible otherwise. "What-if"–questions can be asked using simulation.

3. By simulating the system, management gains valuable insight into the system and into the relative importance of the different variables.

4. Simulation allows for the compression of real time. To predict the behavior of a system over the period of a year may take only a few seconds or minutes using computer simulation.

5. Simulation is often used to test a proposed analytical solution.

6. To comprehend the basic concept of simulation does not require a sophisticated mathematical background and, consequently, managers are more likely to use simulation as a decision-making tool.

Disadvantages of Simulation

Naturally, there are some significant disadvantages to using simulation to solve operational problems.

1. Simulation is not an optimization technique. Typically, different system configurations are experimented with to find a good, but *not* guaranteed best, solution.

2. Simulation is an expensive way to solve a problem. In addition to the cost of building and validating a simulation model, experimentation using computer simulation can be quite costly.

3. Because of the nature of simulation, sampling error exists in all output from simulation models. Of course, this sampling error can be reduced by increasing the sample size or by lengthening the computer run time.

4. A real disadvantage is that simulation is often misused because many people who are qualified to write a simulation program are not qualified to perform a total simulation study. In other words, many programmers do not possess the necessary statistical background.

5. Possibly the most serious shortcoming of simulation is that it is a tool of solution evaluation and thus does not generate problem solutions. Therefore, the decision maker has to develop proposed solutions; then, simulation can be used to test the relative desirability of those solutions.

The Future of Simulation

At the beginning of this chapter, we indicated that simulation was widely used in the management of a wide variety of operations. There are four major reasons why computer simulation will continue to expand into almost every imaginable area of application.

1. Simulation is probably the most powerful of management science techniques, because many different kinds of problems can be solved using simulation.
2. The cost of computing has been decreasing and will continue to do so at a very rapid rate.
3. Simulation languages will continue to evolve and, indeed, to be invented, thus making it less expensive and less time-consuming to solve problems by means of this technique.
4. Finally, as more managers are made aware of the power of simulation as a tool for the decision-making process, the more popular simulation will become.

SUMMARY

Computer simulation is probably the most potent, most flexible, and consequently one of the most common quantitative tools used today to solve operational problems. Computer simulation is to the social scientist what a laboratory is to the chemist or physicist. Its major contribution is that it allows the decision maker to predict the behavior of a system under various circumstances and configurations.

The application of simulation to the solution of operational problems is on a steep growth trend. Simulation is being applied to a rapidly increasing variety of problems, mainly because of its ability to model complex and dynamic systems that could otherwise not be modeled. Another reason for the recent explosion in simulation applications is that the major disadvantages of simulation, cost and the unavailability of necessary data, are being mitigated by the rapid advances that have been made and are being made in computer hardware and software technology.

SOLVED PROBLEMS

Problem Statement

A car-wash chain is planning to build another car-wash facility and is trying to decide how many stalls to build. Past experience has shown that the time between arriving customers is exponentially distributed. The mean of the distribution depends on the traffic count per hour going by the facility. Based on city traffic engineering data, the mean time between arrivals is estimated to be ten minutes. The time required to wash a car is ten minutes and constant. Also, it has been established that people generally do not get in line if there are more than two cars waiting. If management wants to build a facility such that there is a low probability of losing customers because of the length of the line but at the same time doesn't want to overbuild, how many stalls should be built? Simulate for eight hours, or 480 minutes.

Solution

The process generator for the exponential distribution is:

$$x = -\frac{1}{\lambda}\ln(r)$$

Therefore, in order to calculate the time between arrivals, merely substitute the random number into the function above. For example:

$$r = .494$$
$$x = -10\ln(.494)$$
$$= (-10)(-.7052)$$
$$= 7.052, \text{ rounded to 7 minutes}$$

The time until the next arrival is $7 + x$. Let

$$r = .353$$

then,

$$x = -10\ln(.353)$$
$$= (-10)(-1.04)$$
$$= 10 \text{ minutes rounded}$$

Therefore, the second customer arrives at 17 minutes into the simulation. Tables 3-10 and 3-11 keep track of the system as simulated time progresses.

  If management were to use the simulation to make a decision concerning the number of stalls, the profit lost from customers' not stopping would have to be weighed against the cost of the second stall. Another important statistic might be the average time a customer spent waiting. Obviously, the prudent operations manager would run the simulation for more than eight hours, so that the sampling error inherent in a simulation study could be significantly reduced.

Table 3-10   Car Wash Simulation – 1 Stall

RANDOM NO.	TIME OF ARRIVAL	TIME IN	TIME OUT	NO. IN LINE	LOST CUSTOMER?
.494	7	7	17	0	No
.353	17	17	27	0	No
.407	26	27	37	0	No
.682	30	37	47	0	No
.827	32	47	57	1	No
.379	42	57	67	1	No
.535	48	67	77	1	No
.867	49	—	—	2	Yes
.957	49	—	—	2	Yes
.025	86	86	96	0	No
.503	93	96	106	0	No
.571	99	106	116	0	No
.025	136	136	146	0	No
.838	138	146	156	0	No
.281	151	156	166	0	No
.679	155	166	176	1	No
.142	175	176	186	0	No
.818	177	186	196	0	No
.224	192	196	206	0	No
.165	210	210	220	0	No
.095	234	234	244	0	No
.038	267	267	277	0	No
.795	269	277	287	0	No
.333	280	287	297	0	No
.488	287	297	307	0	No
.911	288	307	317	0	No
.278	301	317	327	1	No
.978	301	—	—	2	Yes
.935	302	—	—	2	Yes
.490	309	327	337	1	No
.106	331	337	347	0	No
.332	342	347	357	0	No
.932	343	357	367	1	No
.190	360	367	377	0	No
.438	368	377	387	0	No
.682	372	387	397	1	No
.041	404	404	414	0	No
.255	418	418	428	0	No
.595	423	428	438	0	No
.519	430	438	448	0	No
.989	430	448	458	1	No
.416	439	458	468	1	No
.997	439	—	—	2	Yes
.101	462	468	478	0	No
.340	473	478	488	0	No
.053	502	—	—		

Table 3-11 Car Wash Simulation – 2 Stalls

RANDOM NO.	TIME OF ARRIVAL	STALL NO.	TIME IN	TIME OUT	NO. IN LINE	LOST CUSTOMER?
.494	7	1	7	17	0	No
.353	17	1	17	27	0	No
.407	26	2	26	36	0	No
.682	30	1	30	40	0	No
.827	32	2	36	46	0	No
.379	42	1	42	52	0	No
.535	48	2	48	58	0	No
.867	49	1	52	62	0	No
.957	49	2	58	68	0	No
.025	86	1	86	96	0	No
.503	93	2	93	103	0	No
.571	99	1	99	109	0	No
.025	136	1	136	146	0	No
.838	138	2	138	148	0	No
.281	151	1	151	161	0	No
.679	155	2	155	165	0	No
.142	175	1	175	185	0	No
.818	177	2	177	187	0	No
.224	192	1	192	202	0	No
.165	210	1	210	220	0	No
.095	234	1	234	244	0	No
.038	267	1	267	277	0	No
.795	269	2	269	279	0	No
.333	280	1	280	290	0	No
.488	287	2	287	297	0	No
.911	288	1	290	300	0	No
.278	301	1	301	311	0	No
.978	301	2	301	311	0	No
.935	302	1	311	321	0	No
.490	309	2	311	321	1	No
.106	331	1	331	341	0	No
.332	342	1	342	352	0	No
.932	343	2	343	353	0	No
.190	360	1	360	370	0	No
.438	368	2	368	378	0	No
.682	372	1	372	382	0	No
.041	404	1	404	414	0	No
.255	418	1	418	428	0	No
.595	423	2	423	433	0	No
.519	430	1	430	440	0	No
.989	430	2	433	443	0	No
.416	439	1	440	450	0	No
.997	439	2	443	453	0	No
.101	462	1	463	473	0	No
.340	473	1	474	484	0	No
.053	502					

---------------------------- **REVIEW QUESTIONS** ----------------------------

1. Define *computer simulation*.
2. How does simulation differ from LP?
3. Discuss two major reasons for using simulation for solving decision problems.
4. Why is a computer necessary when simulating a real system?
5. What are the major phases in a simulation study?
6. What is a process generator?
7. What are uniform random numbers used for in simulation?
8. Why aren't assembler languages used to code simulation models?
9. Why is FORTRAN the most popular language used for simulation?
10. Why should one use a special-purpose simulation language?
11. List two advantages GPSS has over FORTRAN as a simulation language.
12. Why is validation an important step in any simulation study?
13. How does historical validation differ from subjective validation?
14. List three advantages of using simulation.
15. List three disadvantages of using simulation.
16. Why is the application of simulation likely to increase significantly in the near future?

---------------------------- **PROBLEMS** ----------------------------

1. The Page Milk Company has a large gallon-bottling machine that occasionally breaks down due to bearing failure. The machine has two bearings of this type. In order for one of the bearings to be replaced, the machine must be shut down. This machine shutdown costs the company approximately $30 per hour. The bearings are relatively inexpensive, at $5 per bearing. At present, a bearing is replaced only when it fails. The time between bearing failures is distributed as shown here:

HOURS BETWEEN BEARING FAILURES (1 REPLACEMENT BEARING)	PROBABILITY
20	.05
40	.07
60	.13
70	.35
80	.30
90	.07
100	.03
	1.00

The time it takes to replace a bearing is fairly deterministic at one hour. An employee has suggested that, since it is as easy to replace both bearings as one, the company should try a new policy of replacing both bearings when either one fails. Limited experience with similar bearings has yielded the following probability distribution of bearing failures when both bearings are replaced:

HOURS BETWEEN BEARING FAILURES (2 REPLACEMENT BEARINGS)	PROBABILITY
40	.05
75	.10
100	.15
125	.25
150	.20
180	.15
200	.10
	1.00

Use manual or computer simulation to solve this policy problem. If you simulate manually, simulate for the period of one month. Assume a 24-hour workday and a 7-day workweek.

2. The Checkmate Barbershop now has only one barber. Business is quite good, and the proprietor is trying to decide whether to hire an additional barber. Customers arrive at the barbershop at a rate of three per hour (interarrival times are distributed exponentially, with a mean of 20 minutes). The time it takes to give a haircut is exponentially distributed, with a mean of 15 minutes. The barber has noticed that when two customers are waiting for a haircut, a new customer generally will not join the queue. Haircuts cost $4, and a new barber would cost the shop $100 per week plus $1 for each haircut. Use simulation to help in the decision of whether or not to hire the additional barber.

3. Dr. Williams has the appointment schedule shown in the following table. Based on his past experiences, Dr. Williams's estimate of arrival times is:

Dr. Williams's Appointment Schedule

APPOINTMENT TIME	PATIENT	EXPECTED APPOINTMENT DURATION
9:00	Dupont	30
9:15	Austin	20
9:45	Stratman	20
10:00	Rief	30
10:30	Lawrence	20
11:00	Cook	30
11:30	Suess	20
11:45	Collins	30

10% chance of a patient arriving 15 minutes early
20% chance of a patient arriving 5 minutes early
45% chance of a patient arriving on time
15% chance of a patient arriving 10 minutes late
5% chance of a patient arriving 20 minutes late
5% chance of a patient failing to arrive

The duration of each patient's appointment is a stochastic variable that, from past experience, is estimated to be distributed as follows:

10% chance that it will take 80% of the expected time
15% chance that it will take 90% of the expected time
40% chance that it will take 100% of the expected time
25% chance that it will take 110% of the expected time
5% chance that it will take 120% of the expected time
5% chance that it will take 130% of the expected time

Dr. Williams is due in surgery at 1:30 P.M. and must leave the office by 12:15 in order to make it. Dr. Williams would like to know the probability of his not having to cancel any appointments and being on time for surgery. Assume Dr. Williams gets to the office at 9:00 and sees patients on a first-come, first-served basis. Use manual or computer simulation to answer Dr. Williams's question. If you simulate manually, simulate five mornings.

4. A ski shop carries a particularly popular pair of skis that sells for $150 and wishes to know how many pairs to order and when to order. Demand is not known with certainty (see the following table). Lead time is seven days. The cost of the skis, which depends on the quantity ordered, is shown in the second table. It costs $25 to place an order, and a stockout is assumed to cost $25 per unit. Cost of carrying inventory is 20% of the value of inventory per year (.055% per day).

Historical Frequency of Demand

DEMAND PER DAY	NO. OF OBSERVATIONS
0	20
1	26
2	41
3	50
4	38
5	13
6	8
7	3
8	1
	200

Price Schedule

ORDER	PRICE PER PAIR OF SKIS
Less than 25	$100
25 or more	95
50 or more	90
100 or more	80

   a. Simulate the following two inventory policies for one month (assume a 30-day month and a beginning inventory of 15 pairs with no skis on order).
      i. Order 15 pairs when inventory reaches 10 pairs.
      ii. Order 25 pairs when inventory reaches 20 pairs.
   b. Which of the policies above is better? Explain.
   c. What other experiments should be run?

5. The owner of a large laundromat is considering the opening of a second store. The location he has in mind can accommodate 20 washers and 10 dryers. At peak times, he has found time between arrivals to be exponentially distributed with a mean of 10 minutes. The number of washers used by one customer is random and distributed according to the table.

NUMBER OF WASHERS	RELATIVE FREQUENCY
1	.20
2	.35
3	.20
4	.15
5	.05
6	.03
7	.01
8	.01
	1.00

Dryers can accommodate two loads of washing. Both washers and dryers take 30 minutes. The owner has found that in order for him to make a profit, the washers must be operated at 40% capacity during peak hours. Simulate manually for two hours. Should the new laundromat be installed at the proposed location? Assume that there are five customers waiting when the doors are opened for business.

6. Consider a parts department in an auto dealership. At the present time, one clerk operates the parts department, but the owner-manager of the dealership has noticed rather long lines of mechanics waiting for parts. Interarrival times

of mechanics are exponentially distributed with a mean of six minutes. Service times are also exponential with a mean of five minutes. By simulating 25 arrivals, analyze the desirability of adding a second parts clerk.

7. A machine shop has two machine centers. Jobs arrive at the shop according to the following distribution:

NO. OF JOBS PER 8-HOUR DAY	RELATIVE FREQUENCY
0	.40
1	.20
2	.20
3	.10
4	.05
5	.05
	1.00

A given job can take one of the following four possible paths through the machine shop, with the indicated relative frequencies:

Machine Center 1 only—25%
Machine Center 2 only—10%
Machine Center 1, then Machine Center 2—50%
Machine Center 2, then Machine Center 1—15%

Amounts of time required for jobs on each machine center range according to the following probability distributions:

Machine Center 1

TIME IN HOURS	RELATIVE FREQUENCY
1	.10
2	.10
3	.15
4	.20
5	.10
6	.10
7	.08
8	.07
9	.07
10	.03
	1.00

Machine Center 2

TIME IN HOURS	RELATIVE FREQUENCY
1	.10
2	.15
3	.20
4	.20
5	.15
6	.10
7	.03
8	.03
9	.02
10	.02
	1.00

Simulate the machine shop for ten 8-hour days using the following machine-loading rules:

a. First come, first served.

b. Priority based on the amount of processing time left for the job. For example, if two jobs are waiting for machine center 2, and one has 5 hours of processing left and the other has 7 hours left, the job with 5 hours left would have priority.

8. The AAA Health Insurance Company is concerned with its cash outflows on a weekly basis. AAA is being considered for a large group policy. If AAA wins the contract and insures the group, the daily frequency of claims is estimated as follows:

NUMBER OF CLAIMS	RELATIVE FREQUENCY
0	.05
1	.06
2	.08
3	.10
4	.33
5	.14
6	.11
7	.07
8	.04
9	.02
	1.00

The probability distribution of the cost of each claim has been estimated using historical data. The probability distribution is as follows:

COST PER CLAIM	PROBABILITY
$800	.30
900	.24
1,000	.22
1,100	.18
1,200	.06
	1.00

a. Manually simulate 7 days to estimate weekly cash outflow.
b. Write a program that will output a frequency distribution of monthly cash outflows.

9. A newsstand proprietor is trying to decide how many copies of a weekly news magazine to stock. The magazines sell for $1 and he purchases them for $.60. If he has old magazines at the end of the week, they must be discarded and the proprietor loses his total purchase cost. The demand distribution for the magazines is reflected shown in the table.

NUMBER OF MAGAZINES	PROBABILITY
50	.10
55	.15
60	.20
65	.30
70	.15
75	.10
	1.00

Use simulation to determine the number of magazines to be purchased for sale at the newsstand.

10. Although other factors affect the yield per acre, the amount of rain is the most significant factor in the growing of corn on an Iowa farm. The per-acre yield can be estimated by the following regression equation:

$$y = 35x + 50$$

where y = yield per acre

x = monthly rainfall (inches)

The monthly rainfall for the growing season is distributed as reflected in the following table. Estimate the mean of yield per acre by simulating 10 growing seasons.

AVERAGE MONTHLY RAINFALL	PROBABILITY
1.0	.08
1.5	.10
2.0	.15
2.5	.21
3.0	.20
3.5	.12
4.0	.08
4.5	.03
5.0	.02
6.0	.01
	1.00

11. Consider the project information shown in the following table.

TASK	IMMEDIATE PREDECESSOR	EXPECTED TIME IN WEEKS
A	—	5
B	A	4
C	A	3
D	B	4
E	C	5
F	D	2
G	E	3

a. Simulate the completion of this project 10 times to estimate the probability distribution of project completion times. Assume an exponential distribution for each task time.

b. Write a simple program to perform the simulation and simulate the project completion 1000 times.

_____ **REFERENCES** _____

FISHMAN, GEORGE S., *Concepts and Methods in Discrete Event Digital Simulation.* New York: John Wiley, 1973.

GORDON, GEOFFREY, *System Simulation*, 2/e. Englewood Cliffs, N.J.: Prentice-Hall, 1978.

LAW, AVERILL M. and W. DAVID KELTON, *Simulation Modeling and Analysis.* New York: McGraw-Hill, 1982.

MARTIN, FRANCIS F., *Computer Modeling and Simulation*. New York: John Wiley, 1968.

MEIER, ROBERT C., WILLIAM T. NEWELL, and HAROLD L. PAZER, *Simulation in Business and Economics*. Englewood Cliffs, N.J.: Prentice-Hall, 1969.

MIZE, JOE H. and J. GRADY COX, *Essentials of Simulation*. Englewood Cliffs, N.J.: Prentice-Hall, 1968.

NAYLOR, THOMAS H., JOSEPH L. BALINTFY, DONALD S. BURDICK, and KONG CHU, *Computer Simulation Techniques*. New York: John Wiley, 1966.

PRITSKER, ALAN B. and CLAUDE DENNIS PEGDEN, *Introduction to Simulation and SLAM*. New York: John Wiley, 1979.

SCHMIDT, J.W. and R.E. TAYLOR, *Simulation and Analysis of Industrial Systems*. Homewood, Ill.: Richard D. Irwin, 1970.

SCHRIBER, THOMAS J., *Simulation Using GPSS*. New York: John Wiley, 1974.

SHANNON, ROBERT E., *Systems Simulation: The Art and Science*. Englewood Cliffs, N.J.: Prentice-Hall, 1975.

WATSON, HUGH J., *Computer Simulation in Business*. New York: John Wiley, 1981.

4

QUEUING THEORY

INTRODUCTION

Queuing theory is a branch of operations research that enables the operations manager to describe the behavior of systems that involve waiting lines. For example, the decision maker charged with the responsibility of designing a ski resort could utilize queuing theory to decide on the location, number, and type of ski lifts, and the location and number of beginner, intermediate, and advanced ski runs. The objective in designing the skiing system would be to balance the cost of construction and operation of the system with the cost of waiting experienced by those staying at the resort. Queuing theory could yield the expected waiting times for the various lifts, as well as the expected lengths of the lines, utilization of facilities, and so on.

Successful applications of queuing theory can easily be found in the management science literature. For example, in an issue of *Interfaces*, several students reported using elementary queuing models to assist a bank in making a decision on how to expand its drive-in facilities.[1] Two basic options were available: a "robo-window" system (remote tellers connected by pneumatic tubes to customer cars), and a traditional expansion of the current system that involved 8-foot-by-8-foot teller stations located on a traffic lane. The major concern of bank management was the quality of customer service and not the relative costs of the two alternatives. Data were gathered concerning arrivals and service times, and the appropriate queuing model was used to determine the distribution of waiting time. As shown in Figure 4-1, the final configuration of the drive-in banking system included the addition of two robo-windows. Bank management testifies that the system was built based on the study and that waiting times for customers had been predicted with a high degree of accuracy.

Queuing theory is often used by the manager of operations to schedule production and services. Its role in production and service scheduling is discussed in more detail in Chapter 12.

Queuing theory is different in nature from linear programming, which is treated in Chapter 2. Queuing theory does not find optimal solutions. Rather, it uses elements of statistics and mathematics for the construction of models that describe the important descriptive statistics of a queuing system. This statistical description then becomes part of the data upon which optimization decisions are based. The queuing-system descriptive statistics include such factors as expected waiting time of the calling units, expected length of the line, and percentage of idle time for the *service facility* (the source of goods or services for which the calling units wait).

---

[1] B.L. Foote, "A Queuing Case Study of Drive-In Banking," *Interfaces*, 6, no. 4 (August 1976), 31–37.

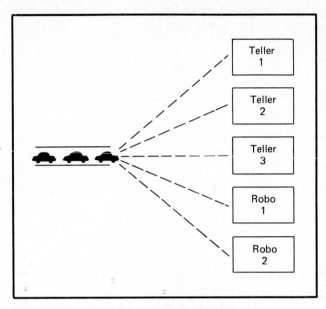

FIGURE 4-1 Approved Drive-in Banking System

When queuing theory is applied, management's objective is usually to minimize two kinds of costs: those associated with providing service and those associated with waiting time. After queuing theory has generated its statistical interpretation of the queuing system, the analyst assesses the various costs of providing service versus the costs of customer waiting in order to design the system that best meets the objectives of the organization.

Operations managers deal with many types of queuing problems. A small sample of queuing applications is shown in Table 4-1.

Table 4-1 Queuing Applications

SYSTEM	CALLING UNITS	SERVERS
Toll road	Automobiles, trucks, etc.	Toll booth
Machine shop	Jobs	Machine centers
Machine shop	Machines	Repairmen
Doctor's office	Patients	Nurse, doctor, lab, etc.
Computer system	Jobs, programs, messages	Computer
Class registration	Students	Student advisers
Ski resort	Skiers	Ski lifts
Harbor	Ships	Tugs, port facilities
Criminal court	Cases	Trial
Restaurant	Customers, orders	Tables, waiters, kitchen
Telephone	Callers	Switching equipment
Auto body shop	Wrecked automobiles	Body repair area, painting area
Professor's office	Students	Professor

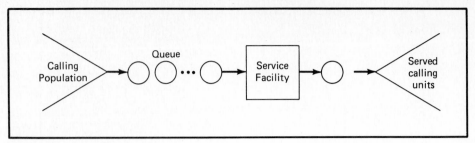

FIGURE 4-2   Queuing System

THE QUEUING SYSTEM

As you can see in Figure 4-2, there are four parts of any queuing system—the calling population, the queue, the service facility, and the served calling units. Three of these entities have certain properties and characteristics that must be considered before appropriate modeling schemes can be formulated. We shall describe the calling population, the queue, and the service facility in some detail. In general, served calling units merely leave, or exit, the system.

The Calling Population

As shown in Figure 4-3, the *calling population*, often referred to as the *input source*, has three characteristics that are important to consider when deciding on what type of queuing model to apply:

1. The size of the calling population
2. The pattern of arrivals at the queuing system
3. The attitude of the calling units

Size of the Calling Population.   This factor has a dramatic effect on the choice of queuing models. (Compare the number of alternatives associated with infinite versus finite calling populations in Figure 4-4.) Queuing systems in which the calling population can be considered *infinite* in size are generally more likely to be amenable to analytical modeling. Examples of infinite calling populations in queuing systems are cars on a toll road and patients at the emergency room of a hospital. It is much more difficult to derive queuing models that can be applied to systems in which the calling populations are very limited. Examples of *finite*, or *limited-source*, *queuing systems* would include three in-house computers that must be serviced by a customer

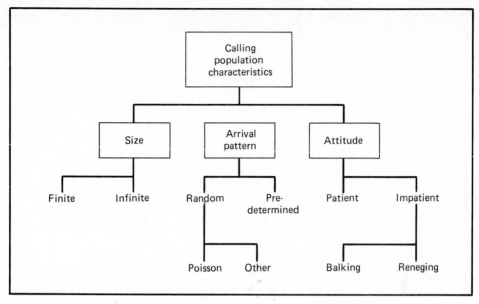

FIGURE 4-3   Calling Population Characteristics

engineer if they break down, and students who may take advantage of a professor's office hours for help in a specific course.

   The key to determining whether you can assume an infinite calling population is whether the probability of an arrival is significantly changed when a member or members of the population are receiving service and thus cannot arrive to the system. If there are only three calling units in a calling population and one is receiving service, the probability of another arrival is significantly reduced, because the size of the calling population is cut by 33.3 percent.

   Pattern of Arrivals.   Calling units arrive at the queuing system either according to some predetermined schedule or in a random fashion. If arrivals are scheduled, as are patients at a dentist's office, analytical queuing models are usually inappropriate. If arrivals are random, it is necessary to determine the probability distribution of the time between arrivals. It has been shown mathematically that if the probability density function of the interarrival times is exponential, calling units arrive according to a so-called *Poisson process*. Poisson arrivals are very common in queuing systems. They generally exist in situations where the number of arrivals is independent of how many arrivals have occurred in previous time intervals. This basic property states that the conditional probability of any future event depends only on the present state of the system and is independent of previous states of the system. The *Poisson probability density function* gives the probability of *k* arrivals in a

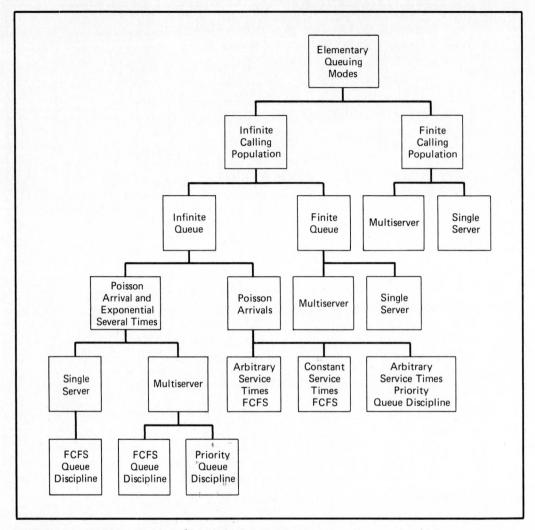

FIGURE 4-4 A Representative Sample of Elementary Queuing Models

given time period. The mathematical form of the Poisson probability function is:

$$P(x = k) = e^{-m}m^k/k! \qquad \text{for } m > 0; \qquad k = 0, 1, 2 \ldots$$

where

  e = the base of natural logarithms with a value approximately equal to 2.71828
  m = mean number of events occurring in a given time period
  k = number of events

Although many queuing systems have random arrivals that behave according to a Poisson process, it is possible for the interarrival times to be distributed in a nonexponential fashion. Therefore, it is necessary to determine the distribution and parameters of the interarrival time distribution statistically before deciding on how to approach any queuing problem.

Attitude of the Calling Units. The final characteristic of the calling population that must be considered is the attitude of the calling unit. In other words, can you assume that a calling unit will enter the queuing system regardless of the status of the system? For example, would everybody who wants to buy gas at a particular service station stop at that station if there were 15 cars waiting for service? Then, too, can you assume that a calling unit will remain in the system until served? A customer may tire of waiting and leave. Generally, most analytical queuing models assume a very patient calling unit.

The Queue

The Property of Queue Length. This characteristic of queues is related in a sense to calling-population size and, sometimes, to calling-population attitude. In applying models, the queue is characterized by its maximum length, which can be *limited* or *unlimited*. Limitation is usually attributable either to customer attitude or to the space available for the queue. There are few choices for queuing models that have finite queues. Generally, if you can assume that calling units join the queue regardless of its length, the probability of applying an analytical queuing model is greatly increased.

The Service Facility

As depicted in Figure 4-5, the three basic properties of the service facility that we must analyze are:

1. The structure of the queuing system
2. The distribution of service times
3. The service discipline

Queuing-System Structure. This characteristic is classified in part as single-phase or multiphase. A *single-phase* system is one in which the calling unit receives service from only one type of server. A pay telephone, for example, is a single-phase queuing system. A *multiphase* system exists when the calling unit must obtain the services of several different types of server. Imagine a freighter pulling into the harbor to unload its cargo: First, that freighter must obtain the services of a tugboat;

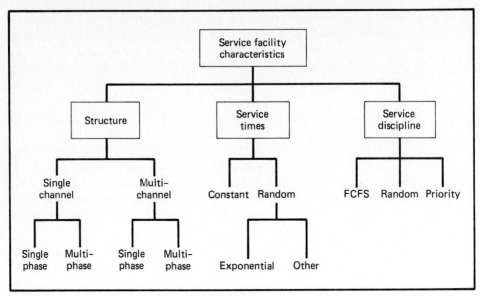

FIGURE 4-5   **Characteristics of the Service Facility**

then it must obtain a berth; then it must be unloaded; and after it is unloaded, the tug's services are needed again for the freighter's return to the open water.

In addition to multiphase versus single-phase structure, queuing systems can also be described as single-channel or multichannel. A *single-channel* system is a system with only one server. A *multichannel* system, on the other hand, has more than one server performing the same service. A drive-in bank facility is a single-channel system when there is only one teller on duty and a multichannel system when more than one teller is working. Obviously, queuing systems can represent any combination of phases and channels. An example of a multiphase, multichannel system is a harbor that has more than one tug and more than one berth. Figure 4-6 depicts schematics of several different queuing structures.

The great majority of queuing models are single-phase models. It is possible, nonetheless, to view a multiphase system as separate single-phase systems in which the output from one server becomes the input for another server.

Distribution of Service Times.   Service times can be constant or random in nature. If service time is a random variable, it is necessary for the analyst to determine how that random variable is distributed. In many cases, service times are exponentially distributed; when this is the case, the probability of finding an applicable model is increased.

As you can see in Figure 4-7, if service times are exponentially distributed, the probability of relatively long service times is small. For example, the length of telephone calls has been shown to be exponentially distributed.

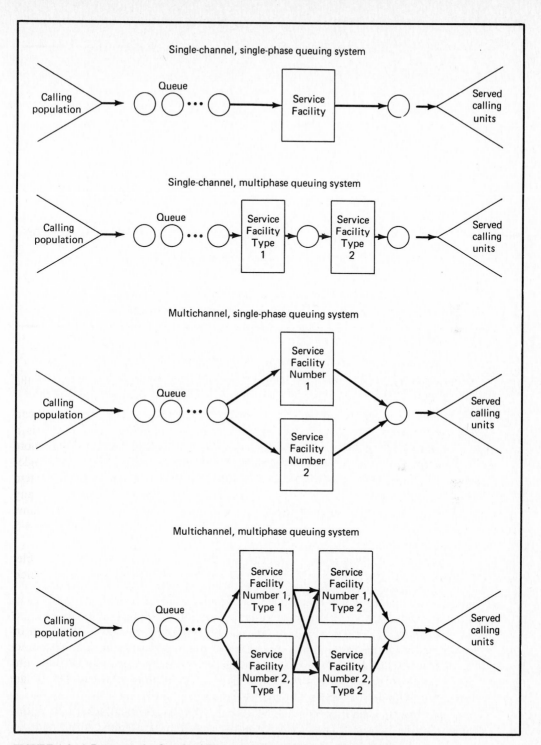

FIGURE 4-6 A Representative Sample of Elementary Queuing-System Characteristics

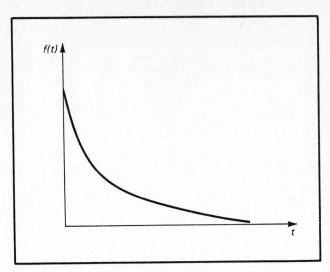

FIGURE 4-7   Graph of $f(t) = \mu e^{-\mu t}$ (**Exponential Distribution**)

The important point is that you should not make assumptions concerning either the service times of the various servers in the system or, equally important, the arrival pattern of calling units without using the appropriate nonparametric statistical tests.

Service Discipline. This characteristic is the decision rule that determines which calling unit in the queuing system receives service. A service discipline (or *queue discipline*, as it is sometimes called), can be classified in one of three ways:

1. First come, first served (FCFS)
2. Priority
3. Random

Most queuing systems that involve people operate with FCFS service discipline, even though it has been shown to be somewhat inefficient, simply because people usually do not tolerate other systems. Priority disciplines can be divided into two categories—preemptive priority and nonpreemptive priority. Preemptive priority disciplines allow calling units that arrive at the queuing system to replace units already receiving service. For example, consider an emergency room of a hospital when only one doctor is on duty. Obviously, if, at the time a critically ill patient arrives, that doctor is treating a patient whose condition is not critical, the patient who was being served is preempted, because a calling unit with a higher priority has arrived at the system.

Nonpreemptive priority simply causes the units in the queue to be arranged so that when a service facility becomes available, the calling unit with the highest priority receives service first. There is no displacement of units in service. Computer systems frequently use priority scheduling.

It is also possible for a queuing system to have no formal queue discipline, in which case the server selects calling units at random. Random selection often exists at the candy and popcorn counter in a movie theater or at European ski resorts.

Descriptive Statistics of a Queuing System

Now that we have described certain properties of its major components—the calling population, the queue, and the service facility—you should have a good notion of the nature of the queuing system itself. Before we go on to the specific subject of queuing models, you should be aware that almost all such mathematical models reveal information about the operating characteristics of a queuing system in a *steady state*.

As depicted in Figure 4-8, a steady-state condition exists when a system's behavior is not a function of time. Typically, a queuing system goes through a stage, called the *transient stage*, in which queuing statistics do not reflect the long-term expected values. This stage often occurs at a system's "start." For example, when a grocery store opens its doors in the morning, no customers are present in the system; therefore, there is a period of time when a statistic such as the expected time spent waiting in line would be understated. Following the transient stage is the *steady-state stage*, in which system behavior is not affected by time.

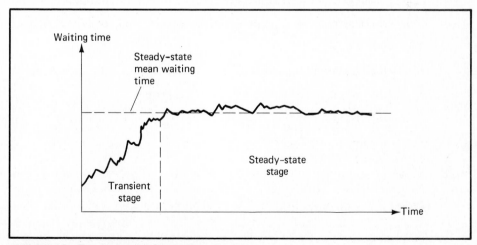

FIGURE 4-8   Transient versus Steady-State Conditioning

ELEMENTARY QUEUING MODELS

In this section, we define some of the queuing models you first saw in Figure 4-4, and show the functions that describe various queuing statistics. Because the mathematics necessary to derive most queuing models is beyond the scope of this text, we have omitted model derivations. The emphasis, instead, is on identifying the assumptions of each model and on explaining how these models are used.

Notation and Definitions

In order to help you understand the specific queuing statistics that are available from most queuing models, we must first define certain queuing terms and introduce a limited amount of notation. You should become familiar with the following list of notations and definitions before you read further in this chapter:

L_q = expected or mean length of the queue (number of calling units in the queue)

L_s = expected number of calling units in the system (number in the queue plus number being served)

W_q = expected or mean time spent waiting in line

W_s = expected or mean time spent in the system (including waiting time and service time)

λ = mean arrival rate (number of calling units per unit of time)

μ = mean service rate (number of calling units served per unit of time)

$1/\mu$ = mean service time for a calling unit

s = the number of parallel (equivalent) service facilities in the system

$P(n)$ = the probability of having n units in the system

ρ = server utilization factor (that is, the proportion of time the server can be expected to be busy)

Models That Have an Infinite Calling Population

All queuing models can be classified as either infinite-source models or finite-source models. Infinite-source models are much more numerous and varied than models with finite calling populations. All queuing statistics given are steady-state statistics.

The Basic Single-Server Model.   The assumptions of this model are:

1. Poisson arrival process
2. Exponential service times
3. Single server
4. FCFS service discipline
5. Infinite source
6. Infinite queue

The functions necessary to calculate the queuing statistics for the basic single-server model are given below:

$$P(0) = 1 - (\lambda/\mu)$$
$$P(n) = P(0)(\lambda/\mu)^n$$
$$\rho = \lambda/\mu$$
$$L_s = \lambda/(\mu - \lambda)$$
$$L_q = \lambda^2/[\mu(\mu - \lambda)]$$
$$W_s = 1/(\mu - \lambda)$$
$$W_q = \lambda/[\mu(\mu - \lambda)]$$

Example: The production supervisor of a large factory has decided to locate an additional tool crib geographically removed from the existing tool crib, so that production workers will have to spend less time walking to get tools. The plans are to make the tool crib a one-man operation, and the production supervisor would like to know the expected queuing statistics. From data gathered at the main tool crib, it is believed that employees will arrive at the new one at a rate of 20 per hour, and it takes an average of two minutes to service a tool request. Arrivals are believed to be Poisson and service times are exponentially distributed. First, it is necessary to determine the units of time for λ and μ. Obviously, λ and μ must be expressed in the same time units. Let's choose hours. Therefore, $\lambda = 20$ employees per hour, and $\mu = 30$ employees per hour.

The probability of an empty system is:

$$P(0) = 1 - \lambda/\mu = 1 - 20/30$$
$$= 1/3$$

The expected utilization of the tool crib is:

$$\rho = \lambda/\mu = 2/3 = .667$$

The number of employees expected to be waiting and in the process of being served is:

$$L_s = \lambda/(\mu - \lambda)$$
$$= 20/10$$
$$= 2 \text{ employees}$$

The number of workers expected to be waiting for service is:

$$L_q = \lambda^2/[\mu(\mu - \lambda)]$$
$$= 20^2/[30(30 - 20)]$$
$$= 400/300$$
$$= 1.33 \text{ workers}$$

The time an employee is expected to spend getting a tool, not counting walking time, is:

$$W_s = 1/(\mu - \lambda)$$
$$= 1/(30 - 20)$$
$$= .1 \text{ hours}$$
$$= 6 \text{ minutes}$$

The time an employee is expected to spend waiting, not counting service time, is:

$$W_q = \lambda/[\mu(\mu - \lambda)]$$
$$= 20/[30(30 - 20)]$$
$$= 20/300$$
$$= .0667 \text{ hours}$$
$$= 4 \text{ minutes}$$

Multiserver Model with Poisson Arrivals and Exponential Service Times.   The assumptions of this model are identical to those of the basic single-server model described previously, except that the number of servers is assumed to be greater than 1. There is an additional assumption: All servers have the same rate of service. Formulae for the basic queuing statistics are given below. The mean service rate μ in the following model refers to each server's service rate.

$$P(0) = \cfrac{1}{\displaystyle\sum_{n=0}^{s-1} \frac{(\lambda/\mu)^n}{n!} + \frac{(\lambda/\mu)^s}{s!}\left(1 - \frac{\lambda}{s\mu}\right)^{-1}}$$

$$P(n) = \frac{(\lambda/\mu)^n}{n!}P(0) \qquad \text{for } 0 \le n \le s$$

$$= \frac{(\lambda/\mu)^n}{s!\,s^{n-s}}P(0) \qquad \text{for } n \ge s$$

$$\rho = \lambda/s\mu \qquad \text{(assuming each server has the same mean}$$
$$\text{service rate of units per time period)}$$

$$L_q = \frac{P(0)(\lambda/\mu)^s\rho}{s!\,(1-\rho)^2}$$

$$W_q = L_q/\lambda$$

$$W_s = W_q + (1/\mu)$$

$$L_s = L_q + (\lambda/\mu)$$

Because $P(0)$ is difficult to calculate without making an error, tables such as Table 4-2 are often used to find the probability of an empty queuing system.

Example: Because tool-crib clerks earn considerably less than skilled workers, the production supervisor in the previous example would like to analyze the effect of hiring two clerks for the proposed new tool crib. Remember, λ is expected to be 20 employees per hour, and service time is expected to be two minutes. In order to help the production supervisor make a decision concerning the staffing of the tool crib, we must analyze the queuing system using two clerks and compare the pertinent descriptive statistics. Although not all queuing statistics are important to the production supervisor, we will calculate them for illustration purposes.

The probability of an empty system is:

$$P(0) = \cfrac{1}{\displaystyle\sum_{n=0}^{1} \frac{(20/30)^n}{n!} + \frac{(20/30)^2}{2!}\left(1 - \frac{20}{60}\right)^{-1}}$$

$$= \cfrac{1}{\dfrac{(20/30)^0}{0!} + \dfrac{(20/30)^1}{1!} + \dfrac{(20/30)^2}{2!}\left(1 - \dfrac{20}{60}\right)^{-1}}$$

$$= \frac{1}{1 + 2/3 + (2/9)(3/2)}$$

$$= \frac{1}{1 + 2/3 + 1/3}$$

$$= \frac{1}{2} = .50$$

$P(0)$ can also be found in Table 4-2. Because, $\lambda/s\mu = .33$, it is necessary to interpolate between .32 and .34.

The average utilization of the tool-crib personnel is:

$$\rho = \lambda/s\mu$$
$$= \frac{20}{(2)(30)}$$
$$= .333$$

The number of workers expected to stand in line is:

$$L_q = \frac{P(0)(\lambda/\mu)^s\rho}{s!\,(1-\rho)^2}$$
$$= \frac{(.5)(2/3)^2 1/3}{2!\,(1-1/3)^2}$$
$$= 1/12 \text{ workers}$$

The expected waiting time is:

$$W_q = L_q/\lambda$$
$$= \frac{1/12}{20}$$
$$= .00417 \text{ hours}$$
$$= .25 \text{ minutes}$$

The total time an employee can be expected to stay at the tool crib is:

$$W_s = W_q + 1/\mu$$
$$= .25 + 2.0$$
$$= 2.25 \text{ minutes}$$

The expected number of workers standing in line and being served at any one time is:

$$L_s = L_q + \lambda/\mu$$
$$= .25 + 20/30$$
$$= .9167 \text{ workers}$$

Now, back to the production manager's problem: whether to staff the new tool crib with one or two clerks. The pertinent queuing statistic is expected waiting time. Expected waiting time for the single-server case was 4 minutes as opposed to .25

Table 4-2 Multiserver Poisson-Exponential Queuing System: Probability that the System is Idle, ρ_0

	NUMBER OF CHANNELS, s								
$\dfrac{\lambda}{s\mu}$	2	3	4	5	6	7	8	10	15
.02	.9608	.9418	.9231	.9048	.8869	.8694	.85214	.81873	.74082
.04	.9231	.8869	.8521	.8187	.7866	.7558	.72615	.67032	.54881
.06	.8868	.8353	.7866	.7408	.6977	.6570	.61878	.54881	.40657
.08	.8519	.7866	.7261	.6703	.6188	.5712	.52729	.44933	.30119
.10	.8182	.7407	.6703	.6065	.5488	.4966	.44933	.36788	.22313
.12	.7857	.6975	.6188	.5488	.4868	.4317	.38289	.30119	.16530
.14	.7544	.6568	.5712	.4966	.4317	.3753	.32628	.24660	.12246
.16	.7241	.6184	.5272	.4493	.3829	.3263	.27804	.20190	.09072
.18	.6949	.5821	.4866	.4065	.3396	.2837	.23693	.16530	.06721
.20	.6667	.5479	.4491	.3678	.3012	.2466	.20189	.13534	.04979
.22	.6393	.5157	.4145	.3328	.2671	.2144	.17204	.11080	.03688
.24	.6129	.4852	.3824	.3011	.2369	.1864	.14660	.09072	.02732
.26	.5873	.4564	.3528	.2723	.2101	.1620	.12492	.07427	.02024
.28	.5625	.4292	.3255	.2463	.1863	.1408	.10645	.06081	.01500
.30	.5385	.4035	.3002	.2228	.1652	.1224	.09070	.04978	.01111
.32	.5152	.3791	.2768	.2014	.1464	.1064	.07728	.04076	.00823
.34	.4925	.3561	.2551	.1821	.1298	.0925	.06584	.03337	.00610
.36	.4706	.3343	.2351	.1646	.1151	.0804	.05609	.02732	.00452
.38	.4493	.3137	.2165	.1487	.1020	.0698	.04778	.02236	.00335
.40	.4286	.2941	.1993	.1343	.0903	.0606	.04069	.01830	.00248
.42	.4085	.2756	.1834	.1213	.0800	.0527	.03465	.01498	.00184
.44	.3889	.2580	.1686	.1094	.0708	.0457	.02950	.01226	.00136
.46	.3699	.2414	.1549	.0987	.0626	.0397	.02511	.01003	.00101
.48	.3514	.2255	.1422	.0889	.0554	.0344	.02136	.00820	.00075
.50	.3333	.2105	.1304	.0801	.049	.0298	.01816	.00671	.00055
.52	.3158	.1963	.1195	.0721	.0432	.0259	.01544	.00548	.00041
.54	.2987	.1827	.1094	.0648	.0831	.0224	.01311	.00448	.00030
.56	.2821	.1699	.0999	.0581	.0336	.0194	.01113	.00366	.00022
.58	.2658	.1576	.0912	.0521	.0296	.0167	.00943	.00298	.00017
.60	.2500	.1460	.0831	.0466	.0260	.0144	.00799	.00243	.00012
.62	.2346	.1349	.0755	.0417	.0228	.0124	.00675	.00198	.00009
.64	.2195	.1244	.0685	.0372	.0200	.0107	.00570	.00161	.00007
.66	.2048	.1143	.0619	.0330	.0175	.0092	.00480	.00131	.00005
.68	.1905	.1048	.0559	.0293	.0152	.0079	.00404	.00106	.00004
.70	.1765	.0957	.0502	.0259	.0132	.0067	.00338	.00085	.00003
.72	.1628	.0870	.0450	.0228	.0114	.0057	.00283	.00069	.00002
.74	.1494	.0788	.0401	.0200	.0099	.0048	.00235	.00055	.00001
.76	.1364	.0709	.0355	.0174	.0085	.0041	.00195	.00044	
.78	.1236	.0634	.0313	.0151	.0072	.0034	.00160	.00035	
.80	.1111	.0562	.0273	.013	.0061	.0028	.00131	.00028	
.82	.0989	.0493	.0236	.0111	.0051	.0023	.00106	.00022	
.84	.0870	.0428	.0202	.0093	.0042	.0019	.00085	.00017	
.86	.0753	.0366	.0170	.0077	.0035	.0015	.00067	.00013	
.88	.0638	.0306	.0140	.0063	.0028	.0012	.00052	.00010	
.90	.0526	.0249	.0113	.0050	.0021	.0009	.00039	.00007	
.92	.0417	.0195	.0087	.0038	.0016	.0007	.00028	.00005	
.94	.0309	.0143	.0063	.0027	.0011	.0005	.00019	.00003	
.96	.0204	.0093	.0040	.0017	.0007	.0003	.00012	.00002	
.98	.0101	.0045	.0019	.0008	.0003	.0001	.00005	.00001	

SOURCE: Donald R. Plane and Gary A. Kochenberger, *Operations Research For Managerial Decisions*, (Homewood, Ill.: Richard D. Irwin, Inc., © 1972), pp. 196–97.

minutes for the tool crib with two clerks. The per-worker difference in expected waiting time is, therefore, 3.75 minutes. If we expect 20 workers per hour, then the per-hour working time lost owing to having one tool crib clerk rather than two is 75 minutes [(20)(3.75)]. If tool-crib clerks make less money per hour than does the average worker, the production manager might be well advised to employ two tool clerks even though expected utilization (33.3 percent) is quite low.

Single-Server Model with Arbitrary Service Times.   If the analyst has determined that arrivals to the system are Poisson-distributed but cannot accept the hypothesis that service times are exponentially distributed, it is quite possible that a valid model does exist. Specifically, the assumptions of this model are:

1. Poisson arrival process
2. Infinite calling population
3. Infinite queue
4. FCFS queue discipline
5. Single server
6. The distribution of service time is unknown, but it has a mean, $1/\mu$, and a variance, σ^2. These parameters are known.

The steady-state results are:

$$L_q = \left(\lambda^2\sigma^2 + \rho^2\right)/\left[2(1 - \rho)\right]$$

$$\rho = \lambda/\mu$$

$$L_s = \rho + L_q$$

$$W_q = L_q/\lambda$$

$$W_s = W_q + (1/\mu)$$

$$P(0) = 1 - \rho$$

It is interesting to note that as σ^2 increases, L_q, L_s, W_q, and W_s all increase. This means that the performance of the queuing system is not dependent solely on mean service time but on the variance in service time as well. Consequently, a server with a higher mean service time may still be the more productive if it is also the more consistent.

When service times are constant, as might be the case in a process such as a car wash, the foregoing model can be applied. The only difference is that the variance σ^2

is equal to zero. Therefore, $L_q = \rho^2/[2(1 - \rho)]$. The other relationships remain unchanged.

    Example: A saving and loan association is opening a branch in a nearby suburb. This branch is expected to need one savings counselor, but management wants to have descriptive queuing statistics to confirm an intuition that only one savings counselor is actually necessary. Plans are to transfer one savings counselor from the main office. Data concerning this particular counselor's time spent with a customer have been collected, but goodness-of-fit tests indicate that these service times are not exponentially distributed. It is further assumed that the mean service time is 15 minutes and the standard deviation in service time is 10 minutes. Customers are expected to arrive in a Poisson manner at a rate of two per hour.

$$\lambda = 2 \text{ customers per hour}$$
$$\mu = 4 \text{ customers per hour}$$
$$\sigma^2 = 1/36 \text{ hour}^2$$
$$L_q = \frac{(4)\ (1/36) + (1/2)^2}{2\ [1 - (1/2)]}$$
$$= .36 \text{ customers}$$
$$\rho = 2/4$$
$$= 1/2$$
$$L_s = 1/2 + .36$$
$$= .86 \text{ customers}$$
$$W_q = .36/2$$
$$= .18 \text{ hours}$$
$$= 10.8 \text{ minutes}$$
$$W_s = .18 + 1/4$$
$$= .43 \text{ hours}$$
$$= 25.8 \text{ minutes}$$
$$P(0) = 1 - 1/2$$
$$= 1/2$$

    The foregoing queuing statistics suggest that either the savings and loan customers are going to have to be very patient or the firm will lose savings customers if it carries out its plan to have only one savings counselor.

    Example: The manager of a small, coin-operated car wash is thinking about adding a vacuum cleaner to the business so that customers can vacuum the insides of their automobiles. Service time for the vacuum is constant at five minutes, and arrivals are Poisson at a rate of ten per hour. For this example, assume an infinite queue and calling population. Before investing in the vacuum, the manager wishes to know what to expect with respect to customers waiting to use it.

$$\lambda = 10 \text{ customers per hour}$$
$$1/\mu = 1/12 \text{ hour per customer}$$
$$\sigma^2 = 0$$
$$\mu = 12 \text{ customers per hour}$$
$$\rho = 5/6$$
$$= .833$$
$$L_q = \frac{(5/6)^2}{2(1/6)}$$
$$= 2.08 \text{ customers}$$
$$L_s = 5/6 + 25/12$$
$$= 2.92 \text{ customers}$$
$$W_q = \frac{25/12}{10}$$
$$= .208 \text{ hours}$$
$$= 12 \text{ minutes}$$
$$W_s = 12 + 5$$
$$= 17 \text{ minutes}$$

With these results, the manager might want to seriously consider two vacuums, because the probability of a customer's joining the queue when there are two or more cars waiting is low.

Single-Server Model with a Finite Queue.   Often, queue length constitutes a constraint on the queuing system. If queue length is limited either by customer attitude or by the physical facilities, it is not possible to use any of the models previously described. The model we present in this section has assumptions identical to the first basic single-server model we developed in this chapter, except that the restriction of an infinite queue length can be dropped. The steady-state results that have been derived are as follows:

$$P(0) = \frac{1 - (\lambda/\mu)}{1 - (\lambda/\mu)^{M+1}}$$

where M = maximum number of calling units in the system and the
                maximum queue length is $M - 1$

$$P(n) = P(0)(\lambda/\mu)^n \qquad \text{for } n = 0, 1, \ldots M$$

$$L_s = \frac{\lambda/\mu}{1 - (\lambda/\mu)} - \frac{(M + 1)(\lambda/\mu)^{M+1}}{1 - (\lambda/\mu)^{M+1}}$$

$$L_q = L_s + P(0) - 1$$

$$W_q = \frac{L_q}{\lambda[1 - P(M)]}$$

$$W_s = W_q + 1/\mu$$

Example: Consider a one-chair barbershop. At the present location, a barber has, on the average, ten customers per day. The average haircut takes 20 minutes. Cutting time has been shown to be exponentially distributed. It has been this barber's experience that customers do not wait for a haircut if two people are already waiting. A move to a new location is possible. The new location would probably increase the number of customers per day to 15. What are the queuing statistics for the proposed new location?

$$\lambda = 15 \text{ customers per day}$$
$$\mu = 24 \text{ customers per day}$$

The probability of no one's being in the shop is:

$$P(0) = \frac{1 - \frac{15}{24}}{1 - \left(\frac{15}{24}\right)^4}$$

$$= \frac{.375}{.847}$$

$$= .443$$

The expected number of customers in the shop is:

$$L_s = \frac{\frac{15}{24}}{1 - \frac{15}{24}} - \frac{(4)\left(\frac{15}{24}\right)^4}{1 - \left(\frac{15}{24}\right)^4}$$

$$= \frac{.624}{.375} - \frac{.610}{.847}$$

$$= .947 \text{ customers}$$

The expected number of customers waiting for a haircut is:

$$L_q = .947 + .443 - 1 = .390 \text{ customers}$$

The probability of two people waiting, hence turning away customers, is:

$$P(3) = (.443) \cdot \left(\frac{15}{24}\right)^3$$

$$= .108$$

The expected waiting time is:

$$W_q = \frac{.390}{15(1 - .108)}$$

$$= .029 \text{ days}$$

$$= 13.92 \text{ minutes}$$

The total expected time for a customer to get a haircut is:

$$W_s = 13.92 + 20$$
$$= 33.92 \text{ minutes}$$

Model That Has a Finite Calling Population

In some queuing systems, the size of the calling population is so small that to assume it to be infinite would seriously degrade the usefulness of a queuing model. Some results that have been derived for a limited-source model are presented in this section. The model described next assumes a Poisson arrival process and exponentially distributed service times. It can be applied to a multiserver queuing system or a single-server system whose queue discipline is FCFS. The steady-state descriptive statistics are:

$$P(0) = \cfrac{1}{\left[\displaystyle\sum_{n=0}^{s-1} \frac{N!}{(N-n)!\,n!} \left(\frac{\lambda}{\mu}\right)^n + \sum_{n=s}^{N} \frac{N!}{(N-n)!\,s!\,s^{n-s}} \left(\frac{\lambda}{\mu}\right)^n \right]}$$

where

N = the number of calling units in the calling population

λ = mean arrival rate for each individual unit

$$P(n) = \begin{cases} P(0)\dfrac{N!}{(N-n)!\,n!}\left(\dfrac{\lambda}{\mu}\right)^n & \text{for } 0 \le n \le s \\[2ex] P(0)\dfrac{N!}{(N-n)!\,s!\,s^{n-s}}\left(\dfrac{\lambda}{\mu}\right)^n & \text{for } s \le n \le N \\[2ex] 0 & \text{for } n > N \end{cases}$$

$$L_s = \sum_{n=1}^{N} nP(n)$$

$$W_s = L_s/\lambda_e$$

where
$$\lambda_e = \lambda(N - L_s)$$

$$W_q = W_s - (1/\mu)$$
$$L_q = \lambda_e W_q$$

Example: In a certain manufacturing facility are three large, numerically controlled (NC) milling machines. These three machines are repaired by two repair technicians. Each NC machine breaks down in a Poisson manner on the average of every four hours. Repair times are exponentially distributed, with a mean of three hours. Determine the steady-state queuing statistics. Let's choose hours as our unit of time. Therefore:

$$\lambda = .25 \text{ per hour} \quad \text{and}$$
$$\mu = .33 \text{ per hour}$$

The probability of all machines being operational is:

$$P(0) =$$

$$\frac{1}{\left[\dfrac{3!}{(3-0)!\,0!} \left(\dfrac{25}{33} \right)^0 + \dfrac{3!}{(3-1)!\,1!} \left(\dfrac{25}{33} \right)^1 + \dfrac{3!}{(3-2)!\,2!\,2^0} \left(\dfrac{25}{33} \right)^2 + \dfrac{3!}{(3-3)!\,2!\,2^1} \left(\dfrac{25}{33} \right)^3 \right]}$$

$$= .177095$$

The probability of one machine being down is:

$$P(1) = .177095 \left(\frac{3!}{2!\,1!} \right) \left(\frac{25}{33} \right)^1$$
$$= .402489$$

The probability of two machines being down is:

$$P(2) = .177095 \left(\frac{3!}{1!\,2!} \right) \left(\frac{25}{33} \right)^2$$
$$= .304916$$

The probability of all three machines being down at one time is:

$$P(3) = .177095 \left(\frac{3!}{0!\,2!\,2^1} \right) \left(\frac{25}{33} \right)^3$$
$$= .115498$$

The expected number of NC machines broken is:

$$L_s = .402489 + 2(.304916) + 3(.115498)$$
$$= 1.3588 \text{ NC milling machines}$$

The effective arrival rate is:

$$\lambda_e = (.25)(3 - 1.3588)$$
$$= .4103 \text{ breakdowns per hour}$$

The expected total time it takes for a machine to become operational is:

$$W_s = 1.3588/.4103$$
$$= 3.31172 \text{ hours}$$

The expected time spent waiting for a repair technician is:

$$W_q = 3.31172 - 3.0$$
$$= .31172 \text{ hours}$$
$$= 18.7 \text{ minutes}$$

The number of NC machines expected to be waiting in line is:

$$L_q = (.4103)(.31172)$$
$$= .127899 \text{ NC machines}$$

An economic analysis of this queuing system would be possible, since the cost of waiting could conceivably be computed, as could the cost of additional repairmen. Consequently, the queuing model could be used to make a very rational decision regarding the optimal number of repairmen.

APPLICATION OF QUEUING THEORY

So far in this chapter, we have described the structure and characteristics of queuing systems and have defined several representative queuing models. By now, it is obvious to you that before a queuing model can be applied, the actual queuing system must be carefully analyzed.

Such an analysis of the queuing system should include the identification and verification of the system characteristics we described earlier. Once the system has been analyzed, the analyst must identify the decision variables. In simple queuing systems, these variables are usually the number of servers and, often, the type of server. The queue discipline often constitutes another controllable variable. Having identified decision variables, each of which is generally discrete in nature, the analyst must determine the criteria for a good set of decision variables. These criteria are usually economic in nature. The cost of the queuing system must be weighed against the waiting time of the calling units.

Two approaches to the problem of applying queuing theory to making decisions are common. One approach is to explicitly define the cost of one calling unit waiting one unit of time and then minimize an objective function such as:

$$Z = C_q + C_w$$

where

$$C_q = \text{cost of the queuing system}$$
$$C_w = \text{cost of waiting}$$

As shown in Figure 4-9, the cost of operating the queuing system and the cost of waiting are in direct opposition to each other. As the cost of the system increases, the waiting time is typically decreased. If the cost function depicted in Figure 4-9 can be explicitly defined, then finding the best solution to the queuing problem is fairly easy.

If you are trying to decide on how many teller windows to have open in a bank, or how many checkout counters to have open in a supermarket, the loss of goodwill caused by long lines and long waits is difficult to measure. If, however, you are trying to decide on the number of repairmen to have available to fix your productive machinery, these costs can be reasonably estimated.

The second approach to applying queuing theory is to seek to minimize a cost function subject to a set of constraints about the line length and expected waiting times. Although this approach is not as clear-cut or objective as explicitly estimating the cost of waiting, it is often more acceptable to management.

Once the queuing system has been analyzed and the criteria for decision making have been defined, the analyst must decide on the solution methodology. Either an analytical queuing model, such as one of the models presented in this chapter, can be applied, or a computer simulation model can be written. The advantages of using an analytical model as opposed to a simulation model are computational efficiency and the absence of sampling error. Although queuing theory has advanced considerably in recent years and many models have been derived, real-world queuing systems often do not have a mathematical counterpart. Rather than force a real queuing system to fit a mathematical model by simplifying the assumptions about system properties, one should use computer simulation. This

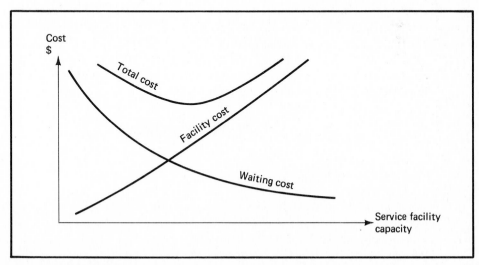

FIGURE 4-9   Queuing System Costs

relatively new tool was discussed in detail in the preceding chapter. In addition to having the flexibility to model any queuing system, simulation is not restricted to a few steady-state operating characteristics. For example, the frequency distribution of waiting times can be determined, not just the mean or expected value of waiting time.

Regardless of whether an analytical or simulation model is used to evaluate the different sets of decision variables, you should realize that determining the "best" set of decision variables is a trial-and-error process. Queuing theory is not an optimization technique; it is a descriptive tool.

SUMMARY

Queuing systems exist everywhere in the real world, and queuing theory can play an important role in the design of systems involving waiting lines and the scheduling of many services. The importance of *properly* applying analytical queuing models cannot be overstated. In order to avoid misapplication, system properties must be carefully analyzed before an appropriate model can be selected.

We have examined only a small fraction of the queuing models that have been derived, but you should realize that there is a large probability that an analytical queuing model that fits the real-world system you are interested in may not exist and may be impossible to derive mathematically. If such is the case, simulation is often used to analyze queuing systems that are too complex to be described using an analytical queuing model.

When analyzing queuing systems, it is important to understand that queuing theory, like computer simulation, is a descriptive tool that yields expected operating characteristics of the queuing system under differing configurations. Decision variables such as queue discipline, number of servers, speed of the server, and so on, must be supplied to the model and are not output from the model. Typically, the output from queuing models becomes an input to a judgmental decision concerning the configuration of the queuing system.

SOLVED PROBLEMS

Problem Statement

The city council of a small town has decided to build a tennis court in the central park. An average of ten sets of players are expected to arrive per 12-hour day. Playing time is exponentially distributed, with a mean of one hour. Arrivals are Poisson. What are the expected queuing statistics, assuming the basic single-server model?

Solution

If we let hours be the time unit,

$$\lambda = 10/12 \text{ arrival per hour}$$
$$\mu = 1 \text{ departure per hour}$$

The probability of no one using the tennis court is:

$$P(0) = 1 - \frac{\lambda}{\mu} = 2/12 = .1667$$

The expected utilization of the tennis court is:

$$\rho = \frac{\lambda}{\mu} = 10/12 = .8333$$

The number of groups expected to be waiting for a court is:

$$L_q = \frac{\lambda^2}{[\mu(\mu - \lambda)]} = \frac{(10/12)^2}{1(1 - 10/12)} = 4.167 \text{ groups}$$

The number of groups expected to be waiting and playing tennis is:

$$L_s = \frac{\lambda}{\mu - \lambda} = \frac{10/12}{2/12} = 5 \text{ groups}$$

Expected waiting time is:

$$W_q = \frac{\lambda}{\mu(\mu - \lambda)} = \frac{10/12}{2/12} = 5 \text{ hours}$$

The expected time for waiting and playing is:

$$W_s = \frac{1}{\mu - \lambda} = \frac{1}{2/12} = 6 \text{ hours}$$

Problem Statement

Given the steady-state queuing statistics found in the preceding example, the city council wants to investigate the effect of building two tennis courts rather than one.

Solution

$$\lambda = \frac{10}{12} \qquad \mu = 1 \qquad s = 2$$

The probability of empty tennis courts is:

$$P(0) = \cfrac{1}{\displaystyle\sum_{n=0}^{s-1} \frac{(\lambda/\mu)^n}{n!} + \frac{(\lambda/\mu)^s}{s!}\left(1 - \frac{\lambda}{s\mu}\right)^{-1}}$$

$$= \cfrac{1}{\dfrac{\left(\dfrac{10}{12}\right)^0}{0!} + \dfrac{\left(\dfrac{10}{12}\right)^1}{1!} + \dfrac{\left(\dfrac{10}{12}\right)^2}{2!}\left(1 - \dfrac{\dfrac{10}{12}}{2}\right)^{-1}}$$

$$= \frac{1}{1.83 + .59523}$$

$$= \frac{1}{2.425} = .4123$$

The average utilization of the tennis courts is:

$$\rho = \frac{\lambda}{s\mu} = \frac{10/12}{2} = .4167$$

The number of groups expected to be waiting for a court is:

$$L_q = \frac{P(0)(\lambda/\mu)^s \rho}{s!\,(1 - \rho)^2}$$

$$= \frac{(.4123)\left(\dfrac{10}{12}\right)^2 (.4167)}{2!\,(1 - .4167)^2}$$

$$= \frac{.1193}{.6805}$$

$$= .1753 \text{ groups}$$

The number of groups expected to be waiting and playing is:

$$L_s = L_q + \frac{\lambda}{\mu}$$

$$= .1753 + 10/12$$

$$= 1.009 \text{ groups}$$

The expected waiting time is:

$$W_q = L_q/\lambda$$

$$= \frac{.1753}{10/12}$$

$$= .21 \text{ hours, or } 12.6 \text{ minutes}$$

The average time spent playing and waiting is:

$$W_s = W_q + \frac{1}{\mu}$$

$$= 12.6 \text{ minutes} + 60 \text{ minutes}$$

$$= 72.6 \text{ minutes}$$

Problem Statement

If the assumption about exponential service times is dropped from the single-tennis-court problem and the variance is $1/2$ hour^2, what would the queuing statistics be? Remember, $\lambda = .8333$ groups per hour, and $\mu = 1$ group per hour.

Solution

The expected length of the queue is:

$$L_q = \frac{\lambda^2 \sigma^2 + \rho^2}{2(1 - \rho)}$$

$$L_q = \frac{(.8333^2)\left(\frac{1}{2}\right)^2 + .8333^2}{2(1 - .8333)}$$

$$= 3.1242 \text{ groups waiting}$$

The expected utilization of the tennis courts is:

$$\rho = \lambda/\mu$$

$$= \frac{10/12}{1} = .8333$$

The average number of groups playing and waiting is:

$$L_s = \rho + L_q$$

$$= .8333 + 3.1242$$

$$= 3.9575 \text{ groups}$$

The average waiting time is:

$$W_q = L_q/\lambda$$

$$= 3.1242/.8333$$

$$= 3.7492 \text{ hours}$$

The average time spent waiting and playing is:

$$W_s = W_q + 1/\mu$$
$$= 3.7492 + 1$$
$$= 4.7492 \text{ hours}$$

Finally, the probability of the court's not being used is:

$$P(0) = 1 - \rho$$
$$= 1 - .8333$$
$$= .1667$$

Problem Statement

Because of budget restrictions, city managers feel that only one tennis court can be built at the present time. Someone has suggested limiting play to one hour for each group in order to reduce waiting time and lines. How would this suggestion change the queuing statistics?

Solution

With the limitation of one hour playing time, the problem reduces to a single-server model with constant service times. The expected queuing statistics are as follows.
    The expected utilization of the court remains:

$$\rho = \lambda/\mu = .8333$$

The average number of groups waiting to play is:

$$L_q = \frac{\rho^2}{2(1 - \rho)}$$
$$= \frac{.8333^2}{2(1 - .8333)}$$
$$= 2.08 \text{ groups}$$

The average number of groups playing and waiting is:

$$L_s = \rho + L_q$$
$$= .8333 + 2.08$$
$$= 2.9133 \text{ groups}$$

The average waiting time is:

$$W_q = L_q/\lambda$$
$$= 2.08/.8333$$
$$= 2.496 \text{ hours}$$

The average time spent playing and waiting is:

$$W_s = W_q + 1/\mu$$
$$= 2.496 + 1$$
$$= 3.496 \text{ hours}$$

Therefore, it looks as though some improvement can be made by restricting play to one hour.

Problem Statement

One member of the city council has challenged the validity of the assumption of an infinite queue. He contends that people will not wait for the court if two groups are already waiting. What effect does the omission of the infinite queue have on the queuing statistics?

Solution

The maximum number of calling units in the system is 3. The probability of the tennis court's being idle is:

$$P(0) = \frac{1 - \lambda/\mu}{1 - (\lambda/\mu)^{M+1}}$$
$$P(0) = \frac{1 - .8333}{1 - (.8333)^4}$$
$$= .3219$$

The probability of the court's being used but no line is:

$$P(1) = P(0)(\lambda/\mu)^1$$
$$= (.3219)(.8333)$$
$$= .2682$$

The probability of one group waiting is:

$$P(2) = (.3219)(.8333)^2$$
$$= .2235$$

The probability of two groups waiting, or the probability of a group arriving and not staying, is:

$$P(3) = (.3219)(.8333)^3$$
$$= .1863$$

The expected number of groups playing and waiting is:

$$L_s = \frac{\lambda/\mu}{(1 - \lambda/\mu)} - \frac{(M + 1)(\lambda/\mu)^{M+1}}{1 - (\lambda/\mu)^{M+1}}$$

$$= \frac{.8333}{1 - .8333} - \frac{(3 + 1)(.8333)^4}{1 - (.8333)^4}$$

$$= 4.9988 - 3.7246$$
$$= 1.2742 \text{ groups}$$

The expected number of groups waiting is:

$$L_q = L_s + P(0) - 1$$
$$= 1.2742 + .3219 - 1$$
$$= .5961$$

The expected time spent waiting is:

$$W_q = \frac{L_q}{\lambda[1 - P(M)]}$$

$$= \frac{.5961}{.8333(1 - .1863)}$$

$$= .8791 \text{ hours}$$

The expected time spent waiting and playing is:

$$W_s = W_q + 1/\mu$$
$$= .8791 + 1$$
$$= 1.8791 \text{ hours}$$

REVIEW QUESTIONS

---

1. Define what is meant by the term *queuing theory*.
2. How does queuing theory differ from linear programming?
3. What are the two major costs involved in any queuing system?

4. What are the basic elements of the queuing system?

5. What characteristics of the calling population must be analyzed when applying a queuing model to a real queuing system?

6. What three basic properties of the service facility must be analyzed when applying queuing models?

7. What is meant by steady-state queuing statistics?

8. Explain two basic approaches used in applying queuing theory to decision making.

9. How would you classify the structure of a hospital's emergency room?

10. What is meant by queue discipline?

PROBLEMS

---

1. Analyze the following queuing systems by describing their various system properties:
   a. Barber shop
   b. Bank
   c. Machine repairmen
   d. Traffic light
   e. Grocery-store checkout counter
   f. Tugs in a harbor
   g. Airport runway
   h. Computer system
   i. Hospital emergency room
   j. Gas station
   k. Car wash
   l. Tool crib
   m. Laundromat

2. A large domestic airline employs one reservation clerk in a local office during the day. The reservation clerk has suggested that another clerk be hired so that customers calling for reservations will not have to wait an inordinate amount of time. Management has decided that the average customer should not have to wait more than two minutes. In order to study the desirability of adding another reservation clerk, a study was done to determine the distribution of arrival times and service times. Calls arrived in a Poisson manner on the average of 30 per hour. The time it took to make a reservation was exponentially distributed with a mean of 1.5 minutes. Given the company's policy of an average waiting time of less than two minutes, what should the manager of the local office do with regard to hiring an additional reservation clerk?

3. The Toll Road Authority wants to know how many toll booths to design into its Main Road exit. Naturally, an objective is to minimize cost, but there is also a stipulation that the expected line length during peak hours should not exceed five cars. From data taken from other toll-road exits, it has been determined that interarrival times and service times are exponentially distributed. The peak arrival rate is expected to be ten cars per minute. The average service time is 15 seconds. How many toll booths should be designed into the system?

4. At Disneyland, plans are being made to install a new ride. Management would like to get a feel for the length of lines and the expected waiting times for this ride so that a decision can be made on whether to have one or two such installations. People arrive in a Poisson manner, but the time the ride takes is constant. Estimates are that people will arrive at a rate of one every two minutes. The ride takes 1.75 minutes. Analyze the queuing system.

5. The local supermarket has the policy that checks are cashed by the store manager only. Customers wishing to cash checks arrive in a Poisson manner at an average rate of 45 customers per hour. The manager takes, on the average, one minute to cash a check. This service time has been shown to be exponentially distributed.
   a. Compute the percentage of time that the manager spends cashing checks.
   b. Compute the average time a customer is expected to wait.
   c. Compute the number of customers waiting to get checks cashed.
   d. Compute the probability of the manager's attending to some other function, assuming that check cashing is the manager's first priority.
   e. Explain to the manager how you would analyze the effect of adding the assistant manager to the check-cashing function.

6. Two lawyers are in partnership. Each lawyer has a secretary. Jobs arrive for each secretary in a Poisson manner at a rate of three per hour, on the average. It takes either secretary an average of 15 minutes to accomplish each individual job. This service time is exponentially distributed.
   a. Assuming that each secretary does only the work of one lawyer, what is the expected waiting time for each job?
   b. What would be the effect of pooling the secretaries?

7. A certain computer company has five identical computers. Each machine fails on the average of ten times per week, and it takes a customer engineer an average of 2.5 hours to fix a machine. Historical data indicate a Poisson arrival process and exponential service times. Because of serious scheduling consequences, management does not want a machine down for more than three hours. For this reason, it has been decided that expected waiting time should not exceed $\frac{1}{2}$ hour. Assume the facility operates 24 hours per day and seven days per week.

    a. What are the expected times a machine will have to wait with one customer engineer on duty? With two customer engineers on duty?

    b. What is your recommendation to management?

    c. What options do you think management has in addition to increasing the number of customer engineers?

8. An administrator at a small hospital is contemplating a relocation of the hospital's X-ray facility. Currently, the X-ray department is so located that only two patients can be waiting for the X-ray machine at one time, with the result that emergency patients are sent back to emergency and inpatients sent back to their rooms. The potential new location would double the amount of waiting space available. Arrivals at X-ray occur in a Poisson manner at a rate of six per hour. On the average, it takes about eight minutes to service an X-ray request. These service times have been shown to be exponential. Analyze the administrator's decision problem, using queuing theory.

9. Ships arrive at a harbor in a Poisson fashion at a rate of five per 8-hour day. It takes the one tug servicing the harbor an average of one hour per ship. Tugging has been shown to be normally distributed with a standard deviation of four minutes. Compute the steady-state queuing statistics for the harbor tug operation.

10. A free one-doctor outpatient clinic of a hospital takes patients without appointments from 1:00 to 5:00 in the afternoon. Patients arrive according to a Poisson process at a rate of five per hour. Service times are exponential, with a mean of ten minutes. Patients are taken on a first-come, first-served basis. Apply the appropriate queuing model and calculate pertinent queuing statistics. What assumptions did you make about the outpatient clinic?

11. Can employing two doctors be justified, in your judgment, for the outpatient clinic described in problem 10?

12. A one-pump service station has room for only two cars waiting. Cars arrive at the station in a Poisson manner at a rate of ten cars per hour. It takes, on the average, four minutes to service a customer. These times are thought to be exponential. What are the expected queuing statistics for the service station? What specifically are the assumptions of your queuing model?

13. A flying club is contemplating the construction of its own private airport. Plans are to build one landing strip. Demand for the landing strip is estimated by club members to be seven planes per hour. Landing times are known to be normally distributed, with a mean of five minutes and standard deviation of two minutes. If arrivals are assumed to be Poisson, what are the expected queuing statistics?

14. The manager of a large department store has noticed long customer lines in the catalog sales department. At present, the department has two clerks. The manager has asked you to do a study and recommend changes in the system to decrease customer waiting time and the length of the lines. You have collected arrival and service time data and have found that arrivals are Poisson-distributed and service times are exponentially distributed. Customers arrive at an average rate of 20 per hour, and the average catalog sale takes five minutes. Analyze the problem and make your recommendation to the store manager.

15. Consider a tool crib in a large factory. At the present time, one worker operates the tool crib, but the vice-president of production has noticed rather long lines of workers waiting for tools. Factory employees arrive to the tool crib at a rate of 25 per hour. Service times are exponential, with a mean of two minutes. The arrival process is Poisson. Analyze the desirability of adding a second tool crib clerk.

———————————————————— **REFERENCES** ————————————————————

CHASE, R.B., and H.J. AQUILANO, *Production and Operations Management.* 3rd ed. Homewood, Ill.: Richard D. Irwin, 1981.

COX, DAVID R., and WALTER L. SMITH, *Queues.* Agincourt, Ont.: Methuen Publications, 1961.

HILLIER, FREDERICK S., and GERALD J. LIEBERMAN, *Introduction to Operations Research*, 3rd ed. San Francisco: Holden-Day, Inc., 1980.

MORSE, PHILIP M., *Queues, Inventories and Maintenance.* New York: John Wiley, 1958.

SAATY, THOMAS L., *Elements of Queuing Theory.* New York: McGraw-Hill, 1961.

TAHA, HAMDY A., *Operations Research: An Introduction.* New York: Macmillan, 1982.

TRUEMAN, RICHARD E., *Quantitative Methods for Decision Making in Business.* New York: Holt, Rinehart & Winston, 1981.

5

PROCESS DESIGN AND FACILITIES LAYOUT

In Chapter 1, we viewed operations management as the management of an operational system in which inputs are transformed into outputs. In this chapter, we explore the design of the transformation process that converts inputs to outputs. The effective design of the transformation process is critical to the subsequent operation and control of the operational system.

Examples of transformation processes are common in service as well as manufacturing industries. Process design at General Motors assembly plants involves the design of a system that will convert raw materials to automobiles; process design at hospitals relates to the transformation of sick patients to healthy ones; and process design at universities involves the design of curricula and faculty to convert entering students to knowledgeable graduates. Even though manufacturing process design tends to be more complicated technically than service process design, certain similarities exist between the two.

Process design many involve a completely new design for a new product or service, or a redesign of an existing procedure. In either case, the design must completely specify the equipment that is to be used, the technical procedures, and the type of personnel. A poor design can result in higher production costs and future design adjustments, as well as uncompetitive levels of services. Large capital outlays are often required in obtaining the equipment necessary for process design. Thus, the need for an effective design is apparent.

The research and engineering phases of process design entail a great deal of creative art. There are few quantitative models that can be used to generate an effective process. A knowledge of the latest scientific and technological advancements is important, but the general experience and firsthand knowledge of the process designer is an indispensable ingredient for successful design. Communication and information exchange between the process designer and operating management must take place to ensure a design that is not only technically correct but flexible and economically sound. Effective design is an ongoing procedure in which technical improvements or new products dictate a frequent reexamination of current processes.

Historically, the criteria by which process design has been measured are productivity and economic considerations such as cost minimization. Since the early days of the Industrial Revolution and Taylor's scientific management heyday, a mechanistic point of view has greatly influenced the nature of process and job design. The principles of division of labor, automation, and specialization have been applied to the design of man–machine systems. These principles, coupled with technological advancements, have enabled man to increase his productivity by over 600 percent since the turn of the century.

These principles, however, do not remain the sole means of structuring modern man-machine systems in order to accomplish goals or work tasks. The harmonious

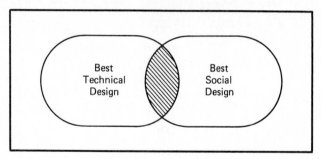

FIGURE 5-1   Effective Process Design Incorporates Technical and Social Needs

interworkings of men, machines, and physical facilities are recognized now as depending on certain human needs and values as well as automation and economic criteria. A new sociotechnical school of thought calls for the incorporation of human and social-system needs as well as technological considerations in process and job design. However, the best technical design devoid of human considerations or the best social-system design may not in either case represent the best overall design. Figure 5-1 illustrates the notion that a best overall design must incorporate technical and social needs.

The recognition of certain psychological job requirements was evident earlier in the job enlargement and job enrichment schools of thought. These approaches to job and process design will be further discussed in the next chapter. The sociotechnologists feel that a systems perspective that views both technical and social factors improves the designs suggested by both the job enrichment and job enlargement approaches. Contrasting examples of designs based on automation and psychological factors, respectively, are the U.S. auto industry and the Volvo plant in Sweden. U.S. auto manufacturing is a highly technical assembly-line production process that is largely influenced by productivity. The Volvo plant in Kalmar, Sweden, has undertaken significant changes whereby a team of 15 to 25 workers now assembles an entire automobile. So far, productivity has remained approximately the same, but worker absenteeism is down significantly. It may be several more years before the success of the Volvo experiment can be measured. One thing is certain, the operations manager of the future will have to make decisions regarding the tradeoffs between mechanistic designs and worker sociopsychological needs or preferences.

In the remainder of this chapter, we shall examine product design as a necessary input to process design. Next, we shall consider some of the important aspects of process design and some of the latest developments such as CAD/CAM and robotics. Even though process design is primarily a creative art, there are certain principles that apply. Closely tied to the process design problem is the plant or facilities layout problem. In this chapter, we study both product- and process-oriented layout problems. In particular, we will focus on assembly-line balancing and effective computer programs to aid in the layout design.

PRODUCT DESIGN

Product design serves as an input to process design and in many cases dictates the nature of the process design. The responsibility for product design usually lies with the marketing and engineering groups within a firm. However, these groups must interact with process designers in order to ensure the production feasibility, maintenance, and reliability of the final product. The marketing function generally initiates the search for a new product, and estimates consumer needs. Several alternatives may be considered, and a market analysis may be carried out to forecast sales and set pricing policies. Given a desired end product, it is necessary to determine the feasibility of actually producing the item. Preliminary decisions must be made regarding product attributes such as reliability, maintainability, and service life. If the "product" is actually a service, then decisions regarding quality, speed, cost, and reliability of the service are required. Product specifications are also key inputs to the associated process design. For example, food weights or volumes would be important specifications in the processed-foods industries, whereas blueprints and metallurgical constraints may be important for a manufacturing operation.

Preliminary product design requires an information exchange between the product and process designers. It must be established whether the firm currently has the capability of producing a given product. If not, then production capability must be obtained from an outside source, or else process research and development must be undertaken. Cost estimates for various process alternatives must be determined, and if R & D is involved, interaction between R & D and the product development group must take place. If an acceptable design can be created that will satisfy product specifications and cost limitations, then the final product design stage is entered. See Figure 5-2 for an illustration of the simplified steps of product design.

In the final design stage, potential shortcomings of the product should be reduced through the analysis of prototype models. The final product should be sound from the standpoint of both the production engineer and the consumer. The final design itself will include complete technical or physical specifications, required components, and assembly or "gozinto" charts. In some cases, a product testing program is initiated during the final design stage. Sample usage or test marketing may reveal minor modifications in the design phase that would improve the final product.

Purchasing: Make-or-Buy Decisions

A key issue in product design is whether to produce required materials in-house or buy from outside suppliers. This decision usually rests with the purchasing department or materials manager in conjunction with design personnel. The purchasing function is becoming an increasingly important aspect of operations management as prices escalate and material resources become more scarce. Total purchases by a manufacturing firm sometimes add up to 75 percent of sales revenues.

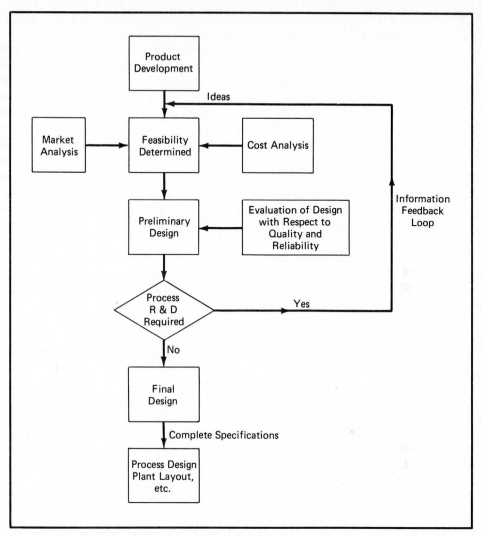

FIGURE 5-2   Simplified Diagram for Product Development

Design and production personnel must supply the purchasing department with accurate information concerning the materials needs of new products and quality changes in current products. The production process depends on purchasing to supply the required materials at the right time. It is important to avoid shortages and the disruption of the production process. In addition to supplying materials for production, purchasing departments are responsible for buying required services and paying the proper prices.

Effective operations management requires close cooperation not only between production and marketing and engineering, but also with purchasing. Purchasing and production design should work together to achieve standardization and product simplification. Costs can be reduced by minimizing the variety of items purchased and the differences between items. An accurate estimate of monthly or annual materials requirements can sometimes enable purchasing to utilize quantity discounts by buying larger quantities. Also, blanket purchase orders can sometimes be set up to secure a certain price while receiving shipments on an "as-needed" basis. Purchasing should also be aware of market prices and materials availabilities to ensure smooth and cost-effective production. If the product design personnel are also well informed, new products will be more likely to incorporate widely available materials with lower overall costs.

Joint decisions between purchasing and design must sometimes be made as to whether a particular item should be made or bought. Such decisions may be made primarily on the basis of economic feasibility; however, noneconomic factors should also be considered. For example, patents or legal restrictions may prevent a company from manufacturing certain parts. Also, the desire to have more direct control over the quality and availability of parts may force certain firms to produce in-house. Seasonal fluctuations may call for making the part during times of low demand in order to use idle facilities, and buying the part during times when there is high competition for in-house productive resources.

Many make-or-buy decisions can also be analyzed on an economic basis. What costs can be avoided if the part is bought instead of produced? What increased production costs are incurred if the part is produced in-house? One standard type of analysis involves the use of a breakeven chart to compare the fixed and variable costs of producing versus buying the specific item. Assuming a linear purchase cost (no quantity discounts), the purchase costs are related to volume of parts ordered. Line A in Figure 5-3 reflects a proportional increase in costs per increase in volume. To produce in-house, however, usually involves a fixed cost that reflects a cost for productive resources committed to producing the particular product. Fixed costs include machine setup costs and other start-up costs. Assuming that the variable or

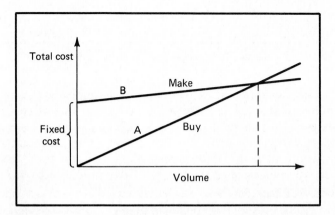

FIGURE 5-3   Breakeven Analysis for Particular Product

per-piece manufacturing cost is linear, we obtain line B in Figure 5-3. The variable cost is normally less than the purchase cost of the part, but the fixed-cost component must be "covered" before it is profitable to produce in-house. As the graph in Figure 5-3 suggests, a certain volume of output is required before it would be profitable to produce in-house. This volume is precisely where lines A and B cross. Expected volumes less than the breakeven point would economically favor buying, whereas volumes greater than the breakeven point would favor producing in-house. The economic factors should be ranked with noneconomic factors for the final decision.

PROCESS DESIGN

Process design has already been touched upon as a necessary forethought in the product design stage. Specifically, however, process design involves choice of processing system, specific equipment to be used, and choice of work flow. We assume at this point that the technology exists to produce the desired product and that the projected process costs are within economic reason. These questions should be answered during the product design stage.

Choice of Processing System

There are two basic types of processing systems: the intermittent or job-shop type of system, and the continuous or assembly-line type. In the intermittent system, general-purpose machines are grouped by their inherent function. The intermittent system is capable of operating on many different types of jobs at any one time. No single product has demand that is high enough to warrant continuous processing. Particular jobs may be in process at several different times during a week or month. Some examples of intermittent-type processing systems are job shops, hospital emergency rooms, insurance claim processing, restaurant kitchens, and computer systems.

Continuous or assembly-line-type processing systems are characterized by a high volume of output. Generally, a single product is processed continually by a group of special-purpose machines that are designed for a specific function and have little or no productive capability outside that function. Continuous-type processing systems are typical in automobile manufacturing, appliance manufacturing, petroleum and chemical processing, electronics industries, and many situations in which a high volume of a standardized product is desired. The advantages of continuous systems are primarily higher output and greater product consistency. Disadvantages include a greater initial investment required and lack of flexibility to accommodate product changes.

Some productive systems occur in a mixed form of the intermittent and continuous type. For example, one stage of a plant may fabricate component parts, with machines such as lathes, drill presses, and milling machines grouped together for this purpose. On the other hand, a continuous assembly-line operation may be used to assemble the parts into a final product. Even though the plant may comprise several mixed systems, each production stage usually falls into either the intermittent or continuous category. The final decision as to the type of system to be used in the entire plant or in a single stage depends upon several factors, such as output level, space restrictions, labor costs, capital investment costs, materials-handling costs, and the maintenance and reliability of the equipment. These factors, along with human and social factors, form the basis for the final decision as to the nature of the productive system.

Equipment Selection and Work Flow

Once the nature of the processing system has been determined, the remaining aspects of process design relate to the selection of specific equipment and the choice of work-flow patterns through the selected machines. In selecting equipment, whether it is special-purpose or general-purpose, a primary consideration is cost minimization. Factors such as initial capital cost, fixed and variable operating costs, and depreciation schedules are relevant. A thorough financial analysis is wise in making most capital investments. The major steps in a capital budgeting process include the generation of alternatives, estimation of costs and benefits, and finally the selection of alternatives. Several methods exist for selecting the most effective alternative. The one probably used most by practitioners is the payback method, in which the number of years required to recover the initial investment is calculated. A more effective procedure, which considers the time value of money, is the present-value method, in which future cash flows are discounted to the present and then compared to the cost of the investment. Ratios of benefits to costs can then be used to rank various alternatives. Finally, linear and 0-1 integer programming models can be used to apply an optimization approach to the capital budgeting decision process. These mathematical approaches would be useful primarily when many alternatives exist and several restrictions or constraints apply.

In addition to the financial aspects, other factors management should consider include:

1. Precision and engineering tolerances of output
2. Speed of operation
3. Flexibility in product input and output
4. Maintenance and reliability
5. Availability of replacement parts
6. Safety
7. Level of skill required of operator

Following the selection of equipment, one of the last considerations in process design is the flow of the product or parts through the productive system. Process flow is normally given some thought in earlier design stages, such as initial product design and capacity planning. It is difficult to determine appropriate equipment and output volume limitations without some idea of the flow of work through the system. In work-flow analysis, we begin to leave the physical design aspects of the transformation process and focus more on the means by which the product is processed. Work-flow analysis then overlaps with process planning, which phases in the daily operations aspects of production.

Process-flow choices deserve careful consideration, because they can affect the size of waiting lines at various facilities, storage area requirements, and the needed amount of in-process inventory required for smooth production. Continuous systems with more standard operations are easier to analyze than intermittent systems with widely differing job mixes. In job shops, some products require a unique flow routing, and thus it is difficult to estimate future process flows. The most common type of decision aids used in process planning is schematic charts. The nature of the product to be processed must be known before flow process charts can be used. The charts are a visual illustration of the logical sequence of a process and thus provide a means of examining and improving the process. An *assembly chart* shows the component parts of a product, the sequence of assembly, and the materials for flow pattern. Figure 5-4 illustrates an assembly chart for an energy economizer unit for commercial water-heating systems.

The assembly chart is more useful for preliminary design plans prior to manufacture. *Operation process charts* are more complete and are used to plan the exact manufacturing processes. The operation process charts specify tolerances, location and sizes of holes to be drilled for each part, and so on. Figure 5-5 illustrates a more detailed operation process chart for the economizer of Figure 5-4. This information, along with demand quantities, can be used to assign equipment and determine the sequence of operations in the process.

A common goal in the design of work flow is to avoid delays and the necessity for storage operations, as these are nonproductive stages. Intermittent processes, because of the lack of standardization, have more delays in production and transportation. Continuous processes often have fixed flows that are governed by assembly lines or overhead conveyor systems. In the plant layout section of this chapter, we shall examine some procedures for minimizing transportation and production delays. Also, in Chapter 12 on scheduling, we will study sequencing rules that aid in minimizing processing time and maximizing output from the system.

In both continuous and intermittent systems, the choice of materials-handling equipment can affect both the cost and the efficiency of transporting raw materials, parts, and finished products. We have already mentioned some common fixed materials-handling systems, such as conveyor systems. In intermittent systems as well as some continuous systems, variable-path equipment such as forklift trucks, hand trucks, electric trucks, and overhead cranes play an important part in transportation. The final selection hinges upon the type of product to be moved, layout of the plant, and costs. A financial analysis is recommended for selection of any capital equipment. Some of the more progressive production firms have implemented computer-assisted materials-handling systems. For example, at American Airlines,

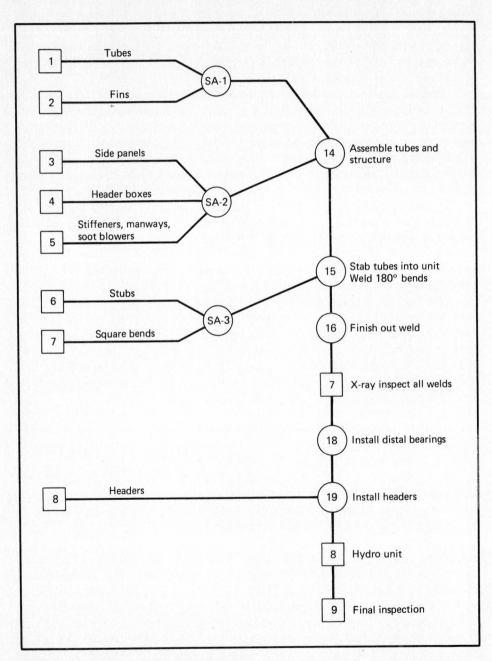

FIGURE 5-4   Assembly Chart for Fuel Economizer

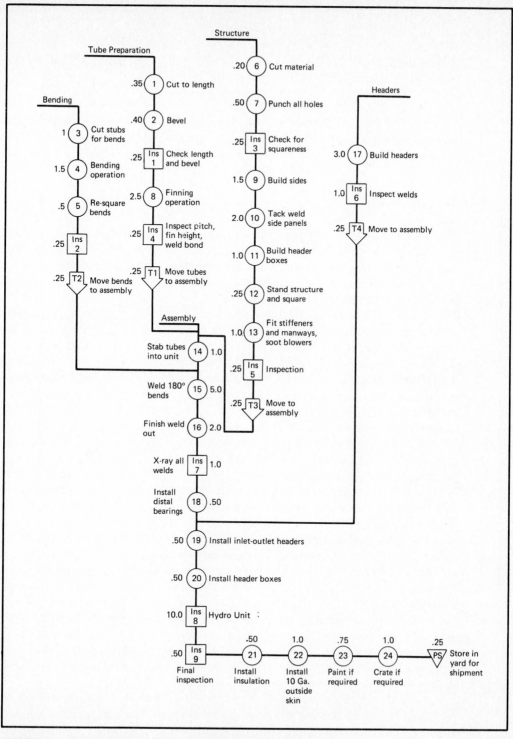

FIGURE 5-5 Operation Process Chart, Kentube Retromiser Fuel Economizer

SOURCE: Kentube Division, Tranter, Inc., Tulsa, Oklahoma.

they have developed the DOCS (Distribution Operational Control System) for moving small to moderate-sized parts from the warehouse to the main production shop. Parts are requested in the shop by personnel who present an ID badge for clearance on a remote computer terminal processor (RTP). The message for a specified number of parts is sent immediately to a computer-directed remote vehicle processor (RVP), or "auto-picker," which automatically selects the correct shelf in the warehouse and, with the aid of a human operator, loads the required parts in a pneumatic tube system that transports the parts in a matter of minutes.

Process Design Example

We have concentrated primarily on the process design of productive systems rather than service systems. Let us now consider the process design of a computer time-sharing system. We assume that the computer facilities are to be offered to interested users on a commercial basis. The objective is to design a system that will maximize job throughput and thus revenue.

Clearly, the technology exists (from many computer companies) to design a commercial time-sharing system. Assuming that the computer hardware is not already available, it will be necessary to purchase or lease a computer central processing unit and required peripheral equipment such as magnetic tape drives, central memory storage units, and disk drives for storage of user files and operating system software. The purchase-or-lease decision should be analyzed carefully, since sophisticated computer equipment costs millions of dollars and new technology renders some systems obsolete in relatively short periods of time. The choice of computer make and model depends not only on cost considerations but also such factors as systems support personnel and compatible software packages offered by the vendor. Capacity decisions regarding the speed of the CPU and size of the core memory will affect the nature of the service offered. Smaller capacity will limit not only the number of users who can process jobs on the system simultaneously, but also the size of any particular job a user can run on the system.

For large time-sharing systems, a front-end processor may be used to edit line control and to schedule messages between user and computer. Smaller systems can do without a front-end processor but must supply a time-sharing port for each user. The nature of the computing service to be offered will also be affected by the types of computer programs or software capability maintained by the time-sharing service. For example, the service may provide scientific programs for aid in solving problems in the physical sciences. Software packages for linear programming and many of the techniques covered in this course may also be offered, along with certain data-processing functions. Each of the services, however, incurs an additional cost for the system.

Once the computer hardware and supporting software have been selected, the remaining decisions concern the flow of jobs through the system. The computer job-flow problem is similar to the intermittent job-shop production problem, in that many jobs will possess unique characteristics. To improve throughput, most time-sharing systems process small jobs, requiring little CPU time and little memory, ahead of larger jobs. Really huge jobs are usually processed at night or at other non-prime-time hours. However, priorities can be built into the computer scheduling of jobs.

Given the hardware, software, and job-flow patterns, the computer time-sharing service is designed. However, later changes in user needs or demand pattern will require a redesign of certain aspects of the system. This is consistent with the notion that good process design is an ongoing activity.

CAD / CAM AND ROBOTICS

New challenges and the desire for improved productivity have dictated the increased utilization of computers in design and manufacturing. A partial answer to these challenges has resulted in CAD (computer-aided design) and CAM (computer-aided manufacturing). Today CAD/CAM is finding a wide range of applications and is freeing designers from tedious, time-consuming chores that have little to do with technical ingenuity. According to the National Science Foundation Center for Productivity, "CAD/CAM has more potential to radically increase productivity than any development since electricity."[1] This new computer-based technology is being rapidly assimilated and whereas only 10 percent of U.S. companies used CAD/CAM in 1980, projections are that at least 30 percent of manufacturers will use some form of CAD/CAM by 1985.

Computer-aided design (CAD) has thrived on the developments in computer graphics. CAD consists mainly of five distinct functional areas: geometric modeling, analysis, testing, drafting, and documentation. Most CAD systems only handle a few of these functions with drafting probably being the most common. Figure 5-6 illustrates a CAD computer graphic.

Computer-aided manufacturing (CAM) has traditionally lagged behind CAD technology but developmental work is aimed at closing the gap. Developments for systems in CAM are in four main areas: numerical control (N/C), process planning, factory management, and robotics. Probably the most mature of CAM technologies is numerical control. N/C refers to the technique of controlling machine tools with prerecorded, coded information. These automated machines drill, cut, punch, mill, turn, bend, and form raw materials into finished parts. The more advanced N/C systems control the machine by a dedicated minicomputer with N/C instructions stored in its memory; this is called direct numerical control (DNC).

Process planning considers the sequence of production steps required to make a part from start to finish. In many low-volume intermittent types of operations the frequent changes in part-routing and machine operations are far from an optimal

---

[1] P. Link, "CAD/CAM: A Much Needed Overview," *Production and Inventory Management Review*, October 1982, pp. 40–44.

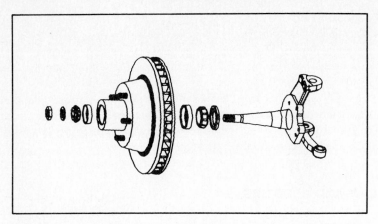

FIGURE 5-6 CAD Provides Visual Introspection to the Potential End Product

SOURCE: *P & IM Review*. Photo courtesy of Applicon, a division of Schlumberger
Technology Corporation.

work-flow sequence. Computer-assisted planning is seen as a promising approach for
increasing productivity and smoothing work flow by standardization of process
operations, tools, materials, and techniques.

The CAM factory-management function ties together the other CAM areas to
coordinate operations of an entire factory from master production scheduling to
shipping and distribution. Computers now perform various management tasks such
as order entry, capacity planning, inventory control, and production scheduling.
This is typical in material requirements planning (MRP). More advanced factory
management systems will not only control material movements, but will also
monitor and direct the factory events that make the parts. In such a system, process
definitions and master schedules will be stored in the computer and feedback data
will be received from the manufacturing processes and operators. The factory-
management system will analyze the data and determine the required time and
location of all production-related events. Output from this analysis will initiate job
changes, machine setups, job starts, and adjustments in the production plan, as well
as predicted failures with correction priorities and options.

Robotics

Robotics, or the use of industrial robots or automated manipulator arms, is the most
rapidly advancing area of CAM. Robots are used to perform a variety of material-
handling functions in CAM systems. Robots can handle materials that are too hot or
dangerous for humans and can perform many tasks with more precision. They are
well suited to repetitive tasks such as welding and spray painting automobiles,
appliances, and other high-volume items. They also can be used to perform very
precise operations in electronics manufacturing. Figure 5-7 illustrates an industrial
robot.

FIGURE 5-7   Swedish Asea Robot Sprays Aluminum Coating in Boeing Military Airplane Co. Laboratory

SOURCE: *P & IM Review*. Photo courtesy of Cincinnati Milacron Marketing Company.

Robots range in price from $10,000 to $150,000, yet experts estimate the cost per hour to buy and maintain them is about $5 compared to the current average rate of $15 per hour for an auto worker.[2] Their potential benefits for productivity are undeniable; for example, in a completely automated system, a second shift could be added at nominal additional cost. However, operations managers should be aware of the system-wide changes and risks involved with implementation.

Robot technology tends to displace workers rather abruptly, in some cases eliminating skill categories or whole segments of work forces. In some cases jobs are created for computer programming and maintenance of robots, but the prospect of eliminating major classes of jobs is likely to cause a great deal of labor union resistance. The Japanese have a much higher proportion of robots in their manufacturing systems. One of the reasons given is that the Japanese (in some of the larger companies such as Toyota) have a lifetime employment provision that tends to eliminate hostility to new technology.

It appears that robots are a certainty in the progress of automation and manufacturing. Manufacturing strategy will be drastically affected by their introduction. Future operations managers will have to consider the human aspect and carefully plan personnel matters in order to bring about a smooth integration of robots into the manufacturing system.

---

[2] K. Jenkins and A. Raedels, "The Robot Revolution: Strategic Consideration for Managers," *Production and Inventory Management*, 23, no. 3 (1982), 107–16.

LAYOUT DESIGN

Layout problems occur in a variety of enterprises—manufacturing plants, job shops, computer systems, fast-food restaurants, offices, and retail department stores, to name just a few. The basic nature of the layout design affects the efficiency with which the system can operate. For example, layout in a retail store can affect not only the capacity of the system relative to customers, but also the salability of various items. In this section we address some of the guidelines and techniques for layout design.

Layout is a continuation of process design. Layout decisions are closely tied to the earlier process design decisions regarding type of equipment, work flow, and choice of materials-handling systems. These earlier decisions depended on a tentative plan for the layout of the physical facility. Final decisions regarding layout may require some changes in earlier design choices. The entire process is an iterative process in which information and details gained at later stages of design are fed back to the earlier stages to arrive at a more effective and compatible system.

The layout decision concerns the most effective placement or arrangement of components within the productive or service system. These components may include machines, aisles, desks, conveyor systems, and sources of inventory. The objective may be to maximize output, minimize inventory costs, or minimize transportation delays between work stations. The overall objective may include some combination of these goals; in any case, the objectives must be clearly understood before layout decisions are made. The needed capacity of the system must also be estimated. Capacity decisions should reflect future capacity needs as well as those of the present. It is less costly to design a system once than to redesign it several times to accommodate future changes in product or service demand. For this reason, a good layout should be adaptable to accommodate variations in existing products or future developments of new products. A flexible design would also be able to respond to technological improvements in processes and equipment.

Another major consideration involves the building or site where the layout is to be located. A new building can be designed for any capacity or layout configuration. An existing building actually constrains the nature of the layout, although remodeling can provide additional space or configuration alternatives. Once the layout planner has studied the aforementioned details, he must select from a particular layout format. The two major formats we study in this chapter are product layout and process layout. We now turn to the basic issues involved in these types of layout.

Product Layout

Product layout is a type of layout in which the components are arranged according to the production stages of a particular product. The nature of the production steps of the product dictate the form of the layout; the components and work stations are devoted exclusively to the production of the single product. The equipment is special-purpose and the process is relatively inflexible. The degree of specialization required in product layout often necessitates a high fixed cost. A high volume of output is a characteristic of product layout, because it is necessary to cover the fixed cost of the special-purpose equipment. Product layout is typified in the automobile industry, appliance manufacturing, food processing, and chemical processing.

Product layout is not always capital-intensive. Sometimes it involves labor-intensive assembly lines; in this case, workers assemble the product in a sequence of work stations, and the final product emerges from the final station. Product layout, whether it is capital- or labor-intensive, is usually simpler than process layout. The layout decisions are mostly defined by the required production stages of the product to be produced. Once the special-purpose equipment is selected, little discretion is left as to the location of the equipment and work stations; these decisions are partly determined by the technological aspects of the production process. Graphic aids, such as two- or three-dimensional replicas, can be used to help in planning the layout.

Assembly-line Balancing. The most challenging aspect of product layout is the achievement of a smooth product flow through the production process. The problem of smoothing the assembly process and minimizing worker or machine idle time is called the *assembly-line balancing* problem. Once the general form of the line has been established, it is necessary to break the line into work stations and determine the work content of each station. At this point, the process design problem has shifted from the macro aspects of the overall problem to the micro aspects of individual work-station content. Line balancing is really more of a scheduling problem than a layout problem; however, determining the number of work stations required can affect the layout of the line.

In line balancing, we have to divide the work to be done along the line into work elements. Work elements are small tasks that must be performed on every component passing through the line. Associated with each work element is an estimated or standard time that represents an average time required by most people or processes to complete the work element. (More will be said in Chapter 6 on establishing these standard times.)

Given the work elements and their standard times, we must group the work elements into work stations. Usually, a work station is assigned to one worker; however, more than one worker may be assigned. The problem is called a line-balancing problem, since the basic idea is to balance the work load between work stations. In line balancing, the objective is usually to (1) determine the minimum number of work stations required, given a specified cycle time; or (2) determine the minimum cycle time, given a specified number of work stations. The *cycle time* is the length of time between completed products coming off the line; it is also the length of time that the partially completed product is available at each work station. Normally, the desired level of output will determine the needed cycle time and hence the minimum number of work stations in objective 1. However, both objectives are usually considered in a line-balancing analysis. Minimizing the number of work

Table 5-1   Assembly Tasks, Times, and Precedence Relationships for Accusound Speaker of Figure 5-8

TASK	PERFORMANCE TIME IN SECONDS	DESCRIPTION	TASK THAT MUST PRECEDE
a	48	Wrap wire for voice coil	—
b	6	Position spider	a
c	12	Center spider in voice coil	b
d	22	Cement paper cone to surround	—
e	16	Fasten voice coil to paper cone	c, d
f	21	Attach cone and surround to frame	c, e
g	6	Position magnet and voice coil assembly	f
h	9	Tighten nut and bolt on magnet	g
i	12	Drill four 5-mm holes in frame	—
j	20	Solder lead wires to terminals	g, i
k	35	Test frequency response in anechoic chamber	h, j
	$\overline{207}$ Total seconds		

stations is basically a layout problem, whereas determining the minimum cycle time is more of a scheduling problem.

Given the work elements and their standard times, line balancing requires that the precedence relationships between work elements be specified. *Precedence relationships* specify which work elements must precede others in order to successfully assemble the product.

To illustrate the line balancing problem, let us consider that of the Accusound Company. In Table 5-1, we present the work elements, times, and precedence relationships for the Accusound standard bookshelf speaker. The assembly data presented in Table 5-1 can be further illustrated through the use of a precedence graph as shown in Figure 5-8. The precedence graph visually depicts the precedence

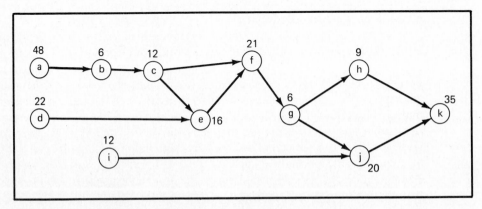

FIGURE 5-8   Precedence Graph for Accusound Speakers

relationships between work elements. Thus we can see from Figure 5-8 that tasks *c* and *e* must be completed before task *f* can be started.

In order to perform a line balancing analysis, we need to know the desired cycle time. Suppose management has forecasted a demand of 400 bookshelf speakers per day. Given an eight-hour workday, this means that the company must produce 50 speakers per hour. Thus, the available cycle time is calculated as:

$$\text{Cycle time } C = \frac{60 \text{ sec./min.} \times 480 \text{ min.}}{400 \text{ speakers}} = \frac{28,800}{400} = 72 \text{ seconds}$$

If Accusound can produce a speaker very 72 seconds, the desired output of 400 speakers per eight-hour day can be realized.

If only one worker is used to assemble the speaker, then the least amount of time in which a speaker could be produced is 207 seconds, the total time of all tasks. This assumes that no extra time is required for operator tool changing or additional movements. Obviously, to produce a speaker in 72 seconds or less, Accusound needs more than one work station. To calculate the theoretical minimum number of work stations required to output 50 speakers per hour, we can calculate SMIN, the theoretical minimum, as:

$$\text{SMIN} = T/C = 207/72 = 2.875 \approx 3$$

where T denotes the total of all work-element times, and the value of SMIN is rounded up to the next whole number. SMIN represents only a theoretical minimum; owing to precedence relationships, the actual minimum number of work stations may exceed SMIN.

Assuming that the minimal number of work stations has been achieved, the next objective is to maintain the cycle time and distribute work loads evenly throughout the work stations. An ideally balanced line would assign the exact same total of task performance times to each work station. In the Accusound balance problem, a perfectly balanced line would consist of three work stations each having the same total work time, say, 69 seconds. However, perfectly balanced lines rarely (if ever) exist in practice.

The line balancing problem is a combinatorial problem, in that many possible sequences exist for assigning tasks to work stations. If we let N = the total number of tasks to be performed, then without precedence relationships there are $N!$ possible ways to sequence the N steps. Precedence relationships reduce the possible number of feasible sequences to approximately $N!/2^p$, where p denotes the number of precedence relationships. In the Accusound example of Figure 5-8, there are 11 tasks and 12 precedence relationships, for approximately $11!/2^{12} =$ 39,916,800/4,096 = 9,745 possible sequences. For large-scale line balancing problems, the number of possible sequences becomes astronomically large. A systematic procedure is clearly needed to determine a good sequence that effectively balances the line.

Table 5-2 Ranked Weights of Tasks

TASK	TIME OF TASK PLUS FOLLOWING TASKS
a	173
d	129
b	125
c	119
e	107
f	91
g	70
i	67
j	55
h	44
k	35

Computational studies have shown that the dynamic programming approach of Held, Karp, and Sharesian, and the biased sampling approach of Arcus, are currently the most effective methods for balancing assembly lines.[3] However, both these techniques require significant amounts of computer computation. One relatively effective procedure, which is also easy to calculate, is the rank positional weight technique by Helgeson and Birnie.[4] This technique assigns each task a "weight" based on the sum of the time to perform that task plus the performance times of all the tasks that follow it in the precedence chart. The rule may be stated as: *Assign those tasks with the largest weights first, taking into account allowable cycle time and precedence constraints.* Thus, the ranked positional weight procedure assigns the tasks with the largest weights to the first work station (in conjunction with precedence relationships) until the sum of task times fills the cycle time. The remaining tasks are assigned in order of descending weights to work stations 2, 3, and so on.

To illustrate the procedure, let's apply it to the Accusound line balancing problem. Referring to Figure 5-8, we can add up the performance times of all tasks and their successors. These resulting "weights" are shown in Table 5-2. Allocating tasks according to the ranked positional weight rule, we obtain the work-station assignments shown in Table 5-3.

Notice at work station 2 in Table 5-3 that tasks i and j could not follow g, since the total time assigned to work station 2 would then exceed the cycle time of $C = 72$ seconds. The work-station configuration would appear as the sequence of steps shown in Figure 5-9.

---

[3]M. Held, R.M. Karp, and R. Sharesian, "Assembly-Line Balancing: Dynamic Programming with Precedence Constraints," *Operations Research*, 11, no. 3 (May–June 1963); A.L. Arcus, "COMSOAL: A Computer Method for Sequencing Operations for Assembly Lines," *International Journal of Production Research*, 4, no. 4 (1966).

[4]W.B. Helgeson and D.P. Birnie, "Assembly Line Balancing Using the Ranked Positional Weight Technique," *Journal of Industrial Engineering*, 12, no. 6 (November–December 1961).

Table 5-3 Ranked Positional Weight Assignments of Tasks to Work Stations

	TASK	TASK TIME	REMAINING FEASIBLE TASK WITH HIGHEST RANK
Work station 1 {	a	48	d
	d	22	—
		70 total	
	b	6	c
	c	12	e
Work station 2 {	e	16	f
	f	21	g
	g	6	h
	h	9	—
		70 total	
	i	12	j
Work station 3 {	j	20	k
	k	35	—
		67 total	

The actual cycle time achieved for the Accusound balancing problem is $C = 70$ seconds. This is the largest total performance time at any one station. Under ideal conditions, an Accusound speaker would roll off the assembly line every 70 seconds.

One measure of the balance of an assembly line is called the balance delay factor. This factor measures the percentage of idle time along the line. From Figure 5-9 we can see that work station 3 is idle three seconds for every speaker produced. If we let $\sum_{i=1}^{N} t_i$ denote the sum of all the task performance times and n the total number of work stations, then the balance delay factor is calculated as:

$$\text{Balance delay } d = 100 \times \frac{n \times C - \sum_{i=1}^{N} t_i}{n \times C}$$

In the Accusound example, the balance delay is:

$$d = 100 \times \frac{3 \times 70 - 207}{3 \times 70} = 100 \times \frac{210 - 207}{210} = 1.43\%$$

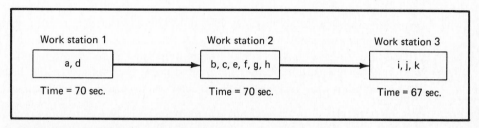

FIGURE 5-9 **Work-Station Layout Along Line**

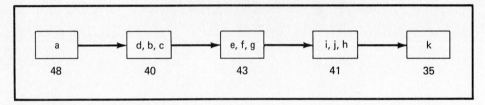

FIGURE 5-10   Line Layout with Cycle Time *C* = 48

Any delay percentage under 10 percent is considered a relatively good balance. The balance delay factor depends upon not only the technique used to balance the line, but also the specified cycle time. Some cycle times will have a higher balance delay factor even when the line is optimally balanced. For example, if Accusound wants to produce 600 speakers a day, the required cycle time is 48 seconds. Rebalancing the line with *C* = 48, we obtain a 5-station layout as in Figure 5-10. In this solution by the ranked positional weight technique, we obtain an actual cycle time of 48 seconds and a balance delay of:

$$d = 100 \times \frac{5 \times 48 - 207}{5 \times 48} = 100 \times \frac{240 - 207}{240} = 13.75\%$$

Each station except the first will have a significant amount of idle time.

Further Considerations.   Line balancing problems involving people will undoubtedly incur operator or worker variability. The actual task performance times will vary somewhat between operators and by the same operator at different points in time. Thus, the idea of a perfectly balanced line is never a reality. One implication of operator variability is the need for in-process inventory. If the line is semipaced and the input of one station depends upon the output of the preceding one, a slow output may cause the next station to wait unnecessarily unless some in-process inventory exists to keep the next station busy. Determining an appropriate amount of in-process inventory to maintain is difficult, but computer simulation can be used as a tool in analyzing this problem. For example, the production line could be simulated with various levels of in-process inventory, and the level that provided the most production output for the cost of inventory would be selected.

Some factors in actual practice may prove to be more important to output than balance in the line. In a paced line, in which work is paced by a conveyor or machine, Conrad has found that the critical factor was how long the part or work piece was available to the operator. He found that if parts were fixed to the moving line, the operator would occasionally miss the part and reduce output. Full line capacity was utilized, however, when parts were allowed to form queues or waiting lines at the work station. Under these conditions, the operator could balance his short cycle against his high long cycles to achieve the desired average output.[5]

---

[5]R. Conrad and B.A. Hille, "Comparison of Paced and Unpaced Performance at a Packing Task," *Occupational Psychology*, 20, no. 1 (January 1955), 15–28.

A final consideration in line balancing concerns the human element. Thus far, the product layout analysis has been from a mechanistic point of view. The sociotechnical aspects of production lines sometimes create the problem of a choice between achieving high output and worker morale or satisfaction. Monotonous assembly-line jobs can sometimes be made more satisfying by enlarging the scope of the job at each station. This process requires that the cycle time be increased. One possible solution is to employ multiple production lines. Thus, a single line with cycle time of $C = 48$ would be equivalent to two lines with $C = 96$, or three lines with $C = 144$. Multiple lines obviously require a different layout and may impose different restrictions in terms of work flow and materials handling. One benefit of multiple lines is that the longer cycle time generally allows greater flexibility in assigning tasks to work stations, and consequently a better balance delay. Also, reliability may be improved, in that the breakdown of a single machine or line will not affect production along the other lines. The operating flexibility of multiple lines may be further backed by human considerations. What good is a theoretically balanced line if absenteeism is high or workers are on strike?

Process Layout

Process layout is characteristic of intermittent systems just as product layout is more common in continuous systems. In process layout, no one product dominates the layout scheme. Department or work areas are grouped together according to similarity of function. Thus, in a job shop, a deburring machine might be located near a drilling machine, and in a hospital, the nursery might be located near the labor/delivery room. The objective in locating manufacturing departments is to minimize materials-handling costs or transportation costs. In office layout, the objective may be to minimize cost-weighted employee trips between departments. A similar application in engineering office layout may attempt to locate close together work areas that have a high number of face-to-face contacts over a period of time.

Whether the process layout problem involves a manufacturing, hospital, or office system, the idea is to locate departments relative to each other in order to optimize a chosen criterion. Since intermittent systems are not restricted to fixed paths, the layout of departments must strive to be effective for the overall combination of departmental interactions. Thus, the best relative location of departments may be excellent or good for some paths in the system but poor for some others. What we need is a systematic procedure to help achieve the best overall locations.

Several quantitative models have been developed to aid in the layout decision process. Some of these are available as computer programs and have been used many times in practice. However, these quantitative models have their limitations and quite often have to be improved by human refinements on the part of the layout designer. Practical aids such as two- and three-dimensional scale models are also helpful in arriving at an effective layout. With the aid of templates or three-dimen-

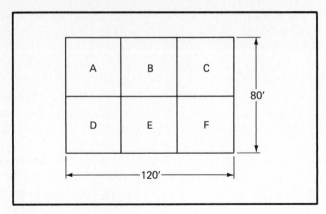

FIGURE 5-11   Hospital Floor Plan

sional scale models, the designer can experiment with various layouts without actually implementing them.

To gain further insight into the nature of process layout, let's consider the following example, in which we want to arrange six hospital departments. Figure 5-11 depicts an idealized hospital floor plan in which each department is assumed to have the same dimensions. Our objective is to assign six departments to the six locations so as to minimize the sum of the products of distance and number of patient trips. Table 5-4 displays the average number of patient trips per week between the departments. This type of data could be determined from existing hospital records or collected over a period of time. If the hospital was not yet built, the interdepartmental traffic data would have to be estimated.

One objective in our layout could be to minimize the number of nonadjacent departments. However, it seems more meaningful to weight the distance of patient trips between departments by the frequency of those trips. Measuring the distances between the centers of the respective department areas, we obtain the distance matrix in Table 5-5.

Table 5-4   Patient Trips per Week

FROM DEPARTMENT		TO					
		OB/GYN 1	NURSERY 2	X-RAY 3	LAB 4	OR 5	ICU/CCU 6
OB/GYN	1		80	10	20	15	
Nursery	2	95		5	10		
X-ray	3		15		100		8
Lab	4	20		90		25	
OR	5		20				40
ICU/CCU	6		35		60		

Table 5-5 Distances Between Department Areas

	A	B	C	D	E	F
A	—	40	80	40	57	90
B	40	—	40	57	40	57
C	80	40	—	90	57	40
D	40	57	90	—	40	80
E	57	40	57	40	—	40
F	90	57	40	80	40	—

We can use the numbers in Tables 5-4 and 5-5 to calculate a weighted distance or "cost" for each assignment of departments to locations. These weighted distances are the distances between areas, weighted by the traffic flow between departments. For example, suppose we assign departments 1 and 2 (OB/GYN and Nursery) to areas A and B respectively. The distance between A and B is 40 feet, the traffic flow from department 1 to department 2 is 80 patients per week, and the traffic flow from department 2 to department 1 is 95 per week. Thus, the weighted distance is:

$$\text{Weighted distance} = \text{Distance} \times \text{Total traffic flow}$$
$$= 40 \times (80 + 95)$$
$$= 40 \times 175$$
$$= 7,000$$

Using weighted distances emphasizes the importance of placing departments with a large amount of traffic close together. With this reasoning, it would seem from Table 5-4 that departments 1 and 2 should be close together, as well as 3 and 4, and 5 and 6. Thus, a layout designer may come up with the layout as presented in Figure 5-12.

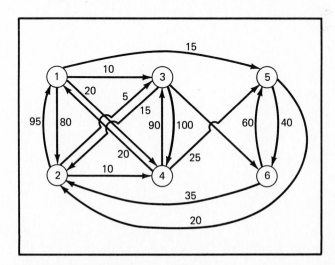

FIGURE 5-12   Flow Graph of Initial Solution

The complex interactions between departmental distance and traffic flow make it difficult to visualize further improvement in the layout. Fortunately, quantitative models are available to aid in this decision process.

CRAFT. Computational studies have shown that one of the most effective tools is the CRAFT algorithm. CRAFT stands for Computerized Relative Allocation of Facilities Technique. CRAFT is a heuristic algorithm that was developed by G.C. Armour and E.S. Buffa.[6] Being a heuristic, CRAFT does not guarantee an optimal layout but generally yields an effective solution. The CRAFT algorithm requires a starting layout from which it tries to make improvements by exchanging the locations of two (or three) departments. For each possible exchange, the computer program calculates the net change in total weighted distance. The best exchange is kept at each trial and serves as the starting point for the next trial of exchanges. The procedure terminates when no two (or three) departmental exchanges yield a reduction in total weighted distance.

Let us apply the CRAFT heuristic to the hospital layout problem. Since there are six departments, there are 6! = 720 possible arrangements. Limiting the exchanges to only pairwise exchanges greatly reduces the number of arrangements to 15. For brevity, let's consider only pairwise exchanges of the first department with all other departments. This yields the six possible layouts shown in Table 5-6. The initial assignment of Figure 5-12 is shown with a total weighted distance of 30,501. This was obtained by computing the distance times total flow between departments. Given six departments taken two at a time, there are $\binom{6}{2} = \dfrac{6!}{4!2!} = 15$ pairs of weighted distances to calculate. These are broken down as:

DEPARTMENT PAIRS	WEIGHTED DISTANCE	
1 – 3	400	
1 – 5	1,200	
1 – 2	7,000	
1 – 4	2,280	
1 – 6	0	
3 – 5	0	
3 – 2	1,140	
3 – 4	7,600	
3 – 6	456	
5 – 2	1,800	
5 – 4	1,425	
5 – 6	4,000	
2 – 4	400	
2 – 6	2,800	
4 – 6	0	
	30,501	Total

[6]G.C. Armour and E.S. Buffa, "A Heuristic Algorithm and Simulation Approach to Relative Location of Facilities," *Management Science*, 9, no. 1 (1963), 294–309.

Table 5-6

AREA	A	B	C	D	E	F	TOTAL WEIGHTED DISTANCE
Assigned	1	3	5	2	4	6	30,501
departments	3	1	5	2	4	6	33,550
	5	3	1	2	4	6	43,251
	2	3	5	1	4	6	30,121
	4	3	5	2	1	6	30,731
	6	3	5	2	4	1	37,055

The fourth pair of exchanges yields a slight improvement in total weighted distance. The location of 2–A, 3–B, 5–C, 1–D, 4–E, and 6–F yields a weighted distance of 30,121. This arrangement is depicted in Figure 5-13. Whether or not this solution is optimal is not yet established. The CRAFT heuristic would proceed with another trial of paired exchanges, and so on until no improvement was found. But another improved solution, if found, still may not be optimal. Generally, however, it will be better than a manually derived layout. The vast number of calculations for even moderate-sized problems dictates the use of a computer for the CRAFT algorithm

The actual CRAFT computer program can solve layout problems with up to 40 departments. The program requires an initial feasible layout from which it tries to make improvements. Unlike those in our simple example, the departments can be of different sizes, and they can be specified as fixed in a particular location. This feature of the program is very useful in evaluating layouts where some of the departments are already established. Some sample computer output from the CRAFT computer program is shown in Figure 5-14.

Other computerized layout techniques have also been developed. ALDEP and CORELAP use preference ratings instead of weighted distances between the centers of locations as the goal to be achieved. Both techniques utilize subjective managerial preferences as to the importance that locations be close together. In some cases, it may be advantageous to incorporate subjective preferences, but in several different studies, CRAFT has proved to be the most effective tool for generating layouts that achieve low materials-handling or departmental interaction costs.

Although useful, CRAFT is not without limitations. It assumes that distances between departments are always measured from the centers, and sometimes it will

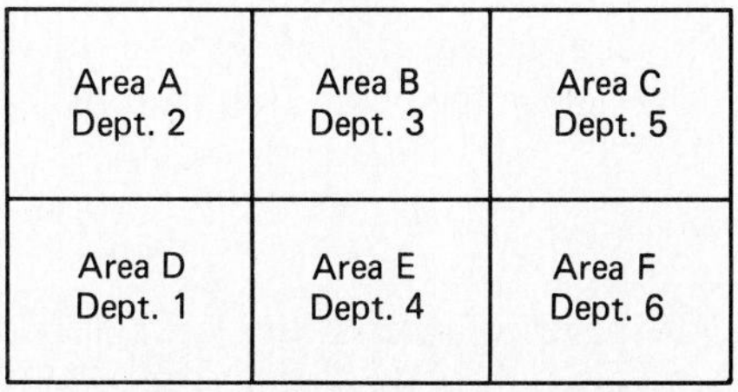

Area A Dept. 2	Area B Dept. 3	Area C Dept. 5
Area D Dept. 1	Area E Dept. 4	Area F Dept. 6

FIGURE 5-13   Improved Solution Layout

```
       1  2  3  4  5  6  7  8  9 10 11 12 13 14 15 16 17 18
  1    A  A  A  A  B  B  B  B  B  B  B  E  E  E  D  D  D  D
  2    A        A  B                 B  E     E  D        D
  3    A  A  A  A  B  B  B  B  B  B  B  E     E  D        D
  4    I  I  I  I  I  I  E  E  E  E  E  E  E     E  D  D  D  D
  5    I              I  E                 E  G  G  G  G  G
  6    I              I  E           E  E  G              G
  7    I              I  E           E  G  G              G
  8    I              I  E           E  G                 G
  9    I              I  E  E  E  E  E     E  G           G
 10    I              I  C  C  C  C  E  E  E  G           G
 11    I              I  C        C  C  E  E  G           G
 12    I              I  C        C  E  E  G              G
 13    I              I  C           C  E  E  G  G  G  G  G
 14    I              I  C  C  C  C  C  E  E  G  G  H  H  H
 15    I  I  I  I  I  I  I  I  I  I  I  I  I  I  H        H
 16    I  F  F  F  F  F  F  F  F  F  H  H  H  H  H  H     H
 17    F  F                       F  H                 H
 18    F                          F  H                 H
 19    F  F  F  F  F  F  F  F  F  F  H  H  H  H  H  H     H
 20    J  J  J  J  J  J  J  J  J  J  J  J  J  J  J  H     H
 21    J                                      J  H     H
 22    J  J  J  J  J  J  J  J  J  J  J  J  J  J  J  H  H  H  H

TOTAL COST: 1847.90
```

FIGURE 5-14   Final Output from CRAFT for an Engineering-Office Layout

SOURCE: E.S. Buffa, *Modern Production Management*, 4/e (New York: John Wiley, 1973).

produce oddly shaped departments (although of the appropriate square footage). CRAFT also assumes that cost varies linearly with distance. Thus, solutions generated by CRAFT serve mainly as input to the final decision process. The layout designer has the freedom and insight to refine the computer-generated layout that is restricted by assumptions. This designer will need to consider restrictions on the locations of heavy equipment, nearness of transportation means to receiving facilities, limited access to various departments, and the confines of the facility if it already exists. The final layout should thus be the product of not only an objective analysis but also human refinements and, in some cases, managerial preferences.

SUMMARY

In this chapter, we have considered the basic issue of process design and facilities layout. We have focused upon the series of decisions that must be made in order to effectively design the transformation process. From product design to process design, an information feedback loop is necessary in order for tentative designs to be refined into final designs. The cost of appropriate forethought is far less than the potential costs of future redesigns.

We considered the macro aspects of process design, such as choice of equipment and work flow, as well as the micro aspects pertaining to the tasks at individual work stations. We have also taken a look at the latest technological developments such as CAD/CAM and robotics.

Facilities layout is a continuation of process design. In both product and process layout, computerized models are available to aid in the planning process. Although valuable, these computer models have their limitations, and potential users should be aware of the assumptions and limitations. Final layouts result from a blend of subjective and objective inputs.

Many of the design problems we have considered depend upon the creative insight and experience of the designer more than on a quantitative decision model. However, certain principles do exist as guidelines for design and layout problems. Most of the principles extend to service industries as well as manufacturing industries. Service industries are characterized by simpler technologies than manufacturing industries, and hence their design problems require less technical expertise.

The systems approach is the most effective approach to any type of decision problem. In process design and facilities layout, the systems approach involves the incorporation of sociotechnical as well as economic considerations. Current productive systems are dominated by economic criteria, but future systems will need to be designed with adequate consideration given to worker satisfaction and the meaningfulness of jobs.

SOLVED PROBLEMS

Problem Statement

Telcomp Co. is getting ready to produce a new line of cathode-ray-tube (CRT) computer terminals. A decision is needed on whether to produce the power supply or to purchase it from an outside supplier. The per-piece manufacturing cost would be about $47 per unit after a fixed cost of $18,000. Purchase price of the power supply is $65. Telcomp anticipates sales of 2,000 units over the next two years. How should the firm proceed?

Solution

Since variable costs appear to be proportional to units made or purchased, we can apply a breakeven analysis. The graph below shows the costs for the volume considered. For a volume of 2,000 units, the nondiscounted cost of producing the power supply is $112,000, whereas the cost of purchasing is $130,000. If Telcomp has the available production capacity and no other production alternatives are more profitable, it should produce the power-supply unit.

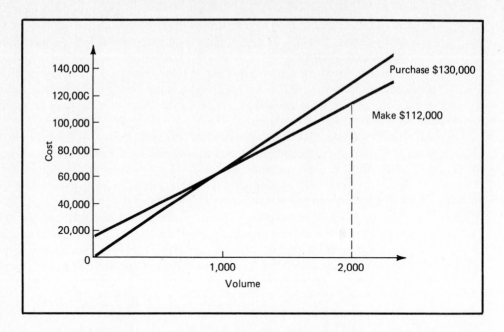

Problem Statement

A Chicago toy manufacturer produces a toy with the following precedence graph. The times associated with the tasks are in minutes.

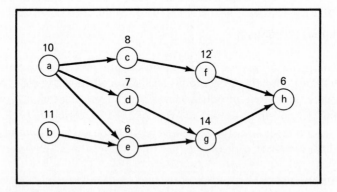

1. What is the minimum cycle time?
2. How many of these toys could the company make per 8-hour (480-min.) workday with one assembly line?
3. Given a cycle time of 20 minutes, find the minimum number of work stations and balance the line.

Solution

1. Since the maximum task time is 14 minutes, the minimum cycle time possible is 14 minutes.

2. Given one assembly line and a desired cycle time of 14 minutes, the number of toys produced per day would be:

$$\frac{\text{time available}}{\text{cycle time}} = \frac{480}{14} = 34.28 \approx 34 \text{ toys per day}$$

3. The minimum number of work stations needed is:

$$\text{SMIN} = T/C = 74/20 = 3.7 \approx 4$$

Using the ranked positional weight heuristic, we obtain the following assignment of tasks to work stations:

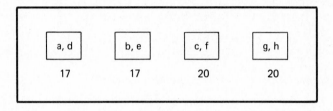

The balance delay d is only:

$$100 \times \frac{4 \times 20 - 74}{4 \times 20} = 7.5\%$$

Problem Statement

Consider a CRAFT heuristic that exchanged the location of departments three at a time. How many possible exchanges are there for 50 departments?

Solution

Taking 50 things three at a time, we obtain:

$$C_3^{50} = \binom{50}{3} = \frac{50!}{3!47!} = \frac{50 \cdot 49 \cdot 48}{3 \cdot 2 \cdot 1} = 19,600 \text{ possible exchanges}$$

Problem Statement

Figby Co. is a manufacturing concern with six main departments. The plant is broken into six main areas, as shown below.

Area 1	Area 2	Area 3
Area 4	Area 5	Area 6

The work flow between departments is shown in the following table:

			TO			
FROM	A	B	C	D	E	F
A			6	5	2	
B					3	6
C	4				7	1
D	3				8	
E		5				4
F		7	2			

How should the departments be arranged?

Solution

The main objective is usually to arrange the departments so that departments having traffic flow between them are adjacent or as close as possible. The following arrangement was obtained by inspection, but it is very effective, since all departments with flow between them are adjacent.

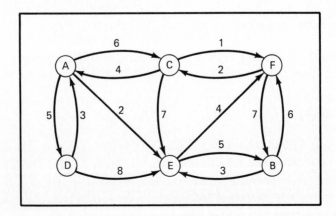

_____ **REVIEW QUESTIONS** _____

1. What are some differences in process design between manufacturing and service industries?
2. What are some primary considerations in product design?
3. Why is it important to have an information feedback exchange between product and process design?
4. Briefly explain the sociotechnical view of process design.
5. What are the two basic types of processing systems?
6. Explain the difference between assembly and operation process charts.
7. What are the relevant factors in a make-or-buy decision?
8. How is facilities layout a continuation of process design?
9. What are two basic layout formats, and what are the likely objectives of each?
10. What conditions should exist in order for an assembly line to be justified?
11. Under which of the following conditions would you expect a worker to perform best on an assembly line? (a) Work pieces are spaced 5 feet apart on a paced line moving 5 feet per minute; or (b) work pieces are space $2\frac{1}{2}$ feet apart on a paced line moving $2\frac{1}{2}$ feet per minute.
12. How can you enlarge the scope of jobs on assembly lines?
13. What computerized procedures are available for process layout? How do they differ?
14. Explain how assembly-line balancing and process layout are combinatorial problems.
15. Why is a heuristic used for large-scale process layout problems?
16. What are some limitations of the CRAFT algorithm for process layout?
17. What are the five functional areas of CAD?
18. What are the four main areas in CAM?
19. List two advantages and two disadvantages of using robots in a production system.

_____ **PROBLEMS** _____

1. Construct an assembly chart for a pair of eyeglasses.

2. What process design problems would you expect in the following?
   a. Bank
   b. Cafeteria
   c. Hospital emergency room

3. A valve is needed to complete a particular subassembly. The Ajax Company is trying to decide whether to make the valve or buy it from an outside supplier. The valve would cost $10 from an outside supplier and $5 to produce in-house. If the fixed costs of producing the valve are $2,000 and the expected demand for the valves is 500, what should the company do?

4. Suppose that in problem 3, the demand for valves is not really certain. Management estimates that there is a 40% chance of needing 300 valves and a 60% chance of needing 600 valves. How would you approach the problem?

5. The purchasing department of Haley Manufacturing Co. is trying to decide whether to make or buy a blower motor for its new line of gas furnaces. A purchased unit would cost $110, whereas Haley could make one for $70. Assuming that the fixed costs of gearing up for production of the motor are $15,000, how large would total demand have to be in order to justify manufacturing the motor?

6. Maxwell Supply Co. orders a particular product on a monthly basis. Orders are placed at the beginning of the month and arrive at the end of the month for sale in the following month. The firm has no problem selling all available units, but its small warehouse limits storage to 120 units of the product. The firm is trying to decide on a purchasing strategy for the next quarter. Purchase and selling prices vary each month and are shown below:

MONTH	PURCHASE PRICE BEGINNING OF MONTH	SELLING PRICE DURING MONTH
Jan.	70	78
Feb.	75	80
Mar.	80	95

Fifty units of inventory are on hand before January, and none is desired after March. Formulate a linear programming model to determine how many units to buy and sell in each month in order to maximize profits.

7. Balance the Accusound speaker problem of Figure 5-8 for a cycle time of $C = 90$ seconds.

8. Solve the following line balancing problem for a cycle time of $C = 15$.

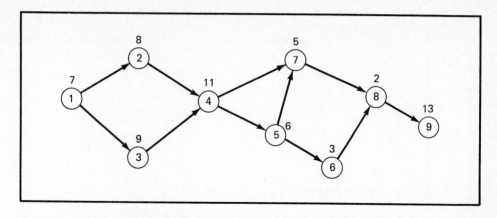

9. Consider the hospital layout problem of Table 5-4. See if you can find a layout with a lower total weighted distance than 30,121.

10. The Hartwell Electronics Co. wants to produce a microprocessor, with the work broken down into the following steps:

TASK	PERFORMANCE TIME IN SECONDS	IMMEDIATE PREDECESSORS
1	18	—
2	10	1
3	9	1
4	7	2
5	12	2, 3
6	14	4, 5
	70 sec.	

a. If Hartwell would like to produce 1,000 microprocessors per day, what is the maximum allowable cycle time?
b. What is the theoretical minimum number of work stations required?
c. Balance the line.
d. Calculate the balance delay.

11. For a large layout problem with 25 departments, how many possible combinations of layouts are there if we consider exchanging locations only a pair at a time? three at a time?

12. Use the CRAFT heuristic rule to solve the following process layout problem. Assume the objective is to minimize total weighted distance.
Assume that the initial layout is D–1, B–2, C–3, and A–4.

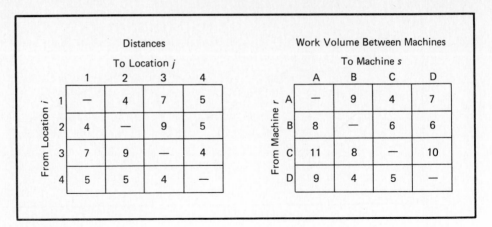

13. Develop your own solution to the layout problem presented in problem 12. Use trial and error or your own method.

14. Consider the following initial layout for six departments:

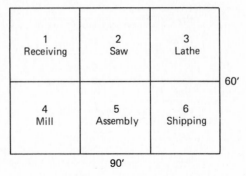

Below is the average interdepartmental load summary for one month:

			TO			
FROM		*REC. 1*	*SAW 2*	*LATHE 3*	*MILL 4*	*ASS. 5*	*SHIP 6*
Receiving	1		300	50	50		
Saw	2			150	100	50	
Lathe	3				250	150	
Mill	4					300	100
Assembly	5						300
Shipping	6						

Each department is 30′ × 30′ in size; estimate the distance between locations and try to find a better layout that will minimize weighted total distance between departments. Use the CRAFT heuristic.

15. Without using the CRAFT heuristic, develop you own solution to the layout example in problem 14.

16. The nodes shown below represent the centers of eight different locations in a plant. The letters represent departments and the areas represent traffic loads between departments. An initial layout is shown. Perform an operations sequence analysis to improve the layout. That is, rearrange the departments at the nodes so that departments with traffic between them are closer together.

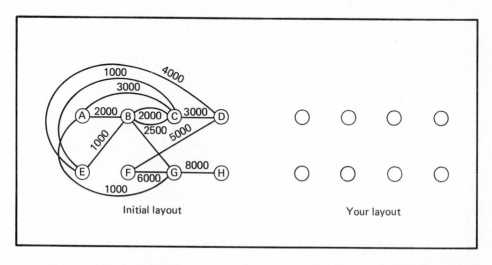

17. Suppose that the layout developed in problem 16 is to be housed in a 100′ by 50′ building. Listed below are the square footages required of each department. Using your solution to problem 16, design the departmental physical dimensions so that they will fit in the 100′ × 50′ building. Assume all rooms are rectangular in shape.

Department	Sq. Ft.
A	1500
B	1250
C	1250
D	1000
E	1250
F	750
G	2000
H	1000

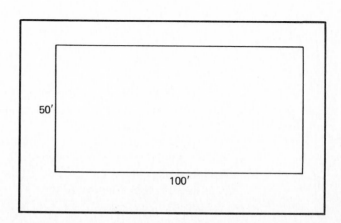

18. Listed below are the task performance times and precedence relationships for an assembled product.

TASK	PERFORMANCE TIME IN MINUTES	TASKS THAT MUST PRECEDE
A	6	—
B	12	A
C	14	A
D	10	A
E	4	A
F	8	B, C
G	10	C
H	9	D
I	6	E, F, G, H

a) Draw the precedence graph.
b) Assuming a cycle time of 14 minutes, determine the minimum number of work stations and balance the line using the ranked positional weight technique.
c) Repeat part b with a cycle time of 20 minutes.
d) Compute the balance delay efficiency of the two solutions in b and c.

19. Assume that the tasks listed below must be performed in alphabetical order.

TASK	PERFORMANCE TIME IN MINUTES
A	3
B	6
C	4
D	8
E	7
F	3
G	2
H	5

a) What is the maximum possible output per 8-hour day?
b) How many work stations will be required for the maximum output in part a?
c) What is the bottleneck operation in part a?
d) Balance the line with a cycle time of 10 minutes.
e) Assuming one operator at each work station in part d, what is the projected total idle time per 8-hour day?

REFERENCES

ARCUS, A.L., "COMSOAL: A Computer Method for Sequencing Operations for Assembly Lines," *International Journal of Production Research*, 4, no. 4 (1966).

ARMOUR, G.C., and E.S. BUFFA, "A Heuristic Algorithm and Simulation Approach to Relative Location of Facilities," *Management Science*, 9, no. 1 (1963), 294–309.

BUFFA, E.S., G.C. ARMOUR, and T.E. VOLLMANN, "Allocating Facilities with CRAFT," *Harvard Business Review*, 42, no. 2 (March–April 1964), 136–59.

CONRAD, R., and B.A. HILLE, "Comparison of Paced and Unpaced Performance at a Packing Task," *Occupational Psychology*, 20, no. 1 (January 1955), 15–28.

COOK, THOMAS M., "Job Scheduling in a Multiprogrammed Computer," *Proceedings of the 1974 Winter Simulation Conference*, vol. 2, 675–87.

DAVIS, L.D., and E.L. TRIST, "Improving the Quality of Work Life: Experience of the Socio-Technical Approach," in *Work in America*. Cambridge, Mass.: M.I.T. Press, June 1972.

ENGLESTAD, P.H., "Socio-Technical Approach to Problems of Process Control," in *Design of Jobs*, eds. L.E. Davis and J.C. Taylor. Middlesex, England: Penguin Books, 1972.

FRANCIS, R.L., AND J.A. WHITE, *Facility Layout and Location: An Analytical Approach*. Englewood Cliffs, N.J.: Prentice-Hall, 1974.

HELD, M., R.M. KARP, and R. SHARESIAN, "Assembly-Line Balancing: Dynamic Programming with Precedence Constraints," *Operations Research*, 11, no. 3 (May–June 1963).

HELGESON, W.B., and D.P. BERNIE, "Assembly Line Balancing Using the Ranked Positional Weight Technique," *Journal of Industrial Engineering*, 12, no. 6 (November–December 1961).

JENKINS, K., and A. RAEDELS, "The Robot Revolution: Strategic Consideration for Managers," *Production and Inventory Management*, 23 no. 3, 1982.

RITZMAN, L.P., "The Efficiency of Computer Algorithms for Plant Layout," *Management Science*, 18, no. 5 (January 1972), 240–48.

TARAMAN, K. ed., *CAD/CAM: Meeting Today's Productivity Challenge*, Computer and Automated Systems Association of SME, 1980.

6

JOB DESIGN AND WORK MEASUREMENT

INTRODUCTION

As stated in the preceding chapter, one of the primary design functions of management is the designing of the man–machine system that is to be used in the transformation process. As depicted in Figure 6-1, the nature of man–machine systems has been evolving since primitive times. Not too many years ago, human beings performed the majority of the work in most man–machine systems. Today, except in some of the less-developed countries of the world, the human work role is changing. In today's sociotechnical system, people are called upon to do less physical labor and perform more of a machine-supervisory role.

Obviously, in many man–machine systems, people still perform the dominant work role. One could cite many sectors of a modern economy in which machines still perform only as an aid, helping people perform a work function. For example, the construction industry remains a labor-intensive industry where machines are employed to do the demanding physical tasks, but people still play a dominant role. The health-care industry employs many sophisticated machines but remains a labor-intensive industry. At the other extreme are process control plants, such as oil refineries, which employ only a few people for the purpose of supervising the machines that actually do the work.

Herbert Simon predicted in 1960 that in 25 years the technology would exist for machines to perform any and all tasks in an organization. Although Simon may have missed his prediction by a few years, it is clear that sometime in the relatively near future, technology will have advanced to the stage he predicted. Does this mean that wide-scale unemployment will exist? Does it mean that people will be replaced by machines as soon as it is technically feasible? The answer to these questions is obviously no. Today, it is technically feasible to accomplish many human tasks with machines, but for many of these tasks, it is not yet economically feasible to replace a

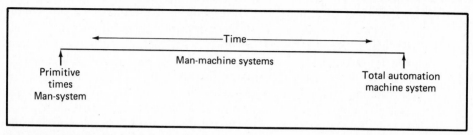

FIGURE 6-1 Evolution of Work

person with a machine. Because the human role in the transformation process will remain critical for many years, it is important to study job design and work measurement in an effort to design a more efficient and humanely satisfying productive system.

Job design is simply the structuring of work activities for an individual or a team. Good job designs must answer the following job-related questions:

- What work is to be performed?
- Who is to perform the work?
- Where is the work to be done?
- When is the work to be done?
- Why is the job necessary?
- How should the work be accomplished?

The majority of this chapter is devoted to answering these questions.

For organizational purposes, we divide job design into two basic elements, a human element and a work element. Important human factors relating to job design include physiological considerations, social considerations, and psychological considerations. In studying the work element of a job, the questions of what is to be done, how it is to be accomplished, and how the work is to be measured are all important considerations.

THE HUMAN ELEMENT IN JOB DESIGN

When discussing the human element in job design, it is convenient to organize the discussion into two sections, physiological or physical considerations and psychosociological considerations. Both areas are extremely important to the sound design of any job in an organization.

Physiological / Physical Considerations

Generally, machines have been shown to have definite comparative advantage over human beings when it comes to tasks that involve applying a great amount of force, doing repetitive tasks, and storing and processing data. It does not follow, however, that these types of tasks are consistently assigned to machines to perform. On the contrary, millions of people are employed to do jobs that machines could do better. Therefore, determining the physical and physiological limitations with respect to a job is an important segment of the job design function. If a job is designed that is physically impossible for a person to perform consistently well, then the psychological and social considerations of the job design have little meaning. In other words, the physical and physiological considerations help define the feasible region of the appropriate job design.

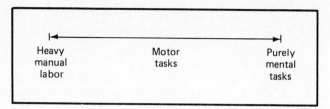

FIGURE 6-2   Work Continuum

One way of describing work would be to identify a continuum of work as shown in Figure 6-2. Regardless of whether the task involves the strenuous use of large muscles or the use of small muscles, or is purely mental in nature, there are limits concerning fatigue within which a job must be constrained. Work physiology aids the job designer by identifying the physiological limits of a job. These limits are identified by developing physiological indexes such as heartbeat rate, perspiration rate, body temperature, and oxygen-consumption rate. The basic methodology for a work physiology study is depicted in the flow chart in Figure 6-3. Let us illustrate, using an example.

The job being designed is that of lifting hot sheets of aluminum coming off the assembly line and stacking them. Different configurations would have two or three

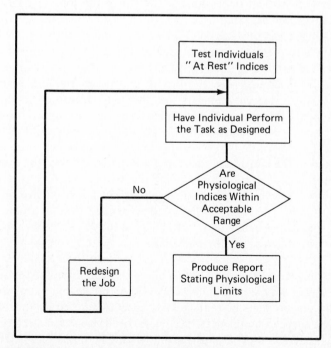

FIGURE 6-3   Flow Chart of a Work-Physiology Study

people on each side of the sheets of aluminum. Other decision variables are how many extra workers to employ for relieving purposes. The first step would be to test average workers to find their physiological indexes, such as heartbeat at rest and calorie consumption per minute. Then, take the four-person configuration with one extra person and perform the job for a period of time with the proper measuring instruments. If this configuration showed that the work load was too demanding, other configurations could be tried until the job came within normally accepted physiological limits.

Although most of the research of work physiology has been concerned with strenuous jobs using large muscle groups, the same principle of finding the physiological limits of a job can be followed for less strenuous tasks. The difference is in the measurement of fatigue. In some instances, other physiological indexes can be used; in other instances, it is necessary to observe the individual and infer that fatigue has set in when response rates fall or error rates increase.

Often, the physiological limits of a job depend on the environment in which the job is to be performed. If workers are asked to do a strenuous task in a non-air conditioned plant where temperatures sometimes exceed 100°, they can't be expected to do as much work as if the plant had a constant temperature of 75°. Similarly, the expectations of output from a design engineer should increase when he or she is provided with a private office, free from distractions.

It should be obvious that analyzing the environment in which a job must be done is of critical importance in designing the job. The job designer should ask questions such as, What is the best physical environment in which to accomplish this task? Is the best physical environment economically feasible? What compromises can be made in the environmental setting? Given an environment, what are the physiological constraints of the job?

To illustrate, take the job of a worker banding together bales of scrap aluminum in the cast house of an aluminum factory. The air in the cast house is dusty, the lighting is poor, the temperature ranges from 95° to 110°, the humidity is high, and so is the noise level. The job designer might have decided that the optimal environment would be a well-lighted, air-conditioned room, but the machine is located in the cast house and those are the conditions that exist there. A fan might be installed as a compromise, but the adverse conditions would be only slightly improved. Other changes in the environment might require an unacceptable capital expenditure. Therefore, all the job designer can hope to accomplish from a physical standpoint is to define an acceptable pace for the workers so that they will have time to recover from physiological fatigue.

Since Congress passed the Occupational Safety and Health Act (OSHA) in 1970, many operations managers have less flexibility in designing jobs. Jobs that are considered unsafe from an accident viewpoint or that entail environmental hazards under the law must be redesigned to meet safety and health standards.

Failure to meet safety and health standards can result in fines or occasionally a court order to suspend operations. It should be noted that OSHA does not eliminate the possibility of accidents on the job or guarantee that workers are safe from all environmental hazards. Rather, the legislation attempts to reduce the probability of an industrial accident and reduce the level of air or noise pollution to acceptable levels.

Psychological Considerations

In the preceding chapter, we described a relatively new school of thought that defines the productive system as a sociotechnical system that has social and technical subsystems. Historically, the productive system has been largely thought of as a technical system, and consequently, the designers of processes and jobs have used productivity and economic considerations as the primary criteria in the design process. With productivity as the yardstick for success, jobs have become more and more specialized.

Jobs that had been accomplished by one master craftsman have now been divided into many small work elements to be done by many workers with significantly lower skill levels. The job depicted in Figure 6-4, might now be accomplished by as many as 15 workers because of job specialization.

In the late eighteenth century, Adam Smith articulated three major advantages of the division of labor. First, he stated, the worker develops a higher level of skill when a task is performed repetitively. Second, time is saved that is normally lost when a worker changes from performing one task to performing another. Finally, as men or women specialize in specific tasks or work elements, they will develop tools and machines to aid in the performance of, or to completely perform, the task. The results of the principle of division of labor have been impressive. Indeed, our present high standard of living is the direct result of mass production.

Since the early 1930s, operations managers and researchers in the field of management have proposed another goal for the design of processes and jobs: job

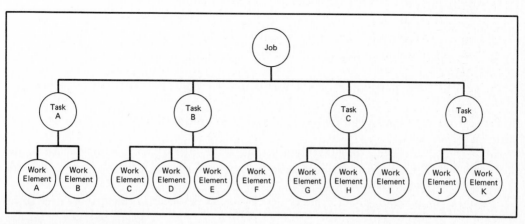

FIGURE 6-4   Job Specialization

satisfaction. A recent movement in the management literature, the job enlargement movement, proposes a reversal in the trend of increased specialization of labor. Advocates of job enlargement feel that specialization has been carried too far and that the trend toward specialization must be reversed for the good of society as well as for the good of the worker.

Job enlargement involves adjusting or enlarging a job in one or two dimensions. Horizontal job enlargement usually means a greater variety of tasks for the worker. A keypuncher's job might be enlarged horizontally by increasing the number of applications to be punched by a single operator. In other words, an operator who had been keypunching only payroll data from one source document could be given other applications with other source documents, thus increasing the scope of his or her job. Vertical job enlargement, often referred to as job enrichment, refers to giving the worker increased responsibility with respect to a given task. If the keypunch operator were involved in the design of the source document he or she was punching from and was responsible for the verifying operation, the job would have been enlarged vertically in two aspects.

There are many advantages and disadvantages of job enlargement, both to productivity and to the worker. First, the advantages of job enlargement to productivity, or the technical side of the sociotechnical system, often include the following:

- Increased quality of the good or service that is produced
- Decreased absenteeism
- Decreased tardiness
- Decreased turnover of personnel
- Fewer labor grievances

The disadvantages of job enlargement to productivity include:

- Lower productivity, due to less repetitive work
- Higher training costs, due to increased skill levels and responsibility
- Higher wages, due to the increased difficulty of finding suitable replacements
- Higher recruiting and hiring costs

The advantages of job enlargement to the individual worker often include:

- Increased gratification from the work itself, due to increase in variety and responsibility
- Increased control over the work flow, which often decreases frustration and fatigue
- Increased opportunity to affect the productive system through developing new work methods
- Increased growth opportunities, so that an individual's organizational role can be expanded
- Decreased boredom, caused by less repetition of tasks

- Increased social benefits, due to necessary change in the layout of the work area and the increased contact with other workers
- Decreased localized muscle fatigue, due to less repetitive tasks

What are advantages to some workers are disadvantages to others, owing to the variability in personalities and the psychosociological needs an individual requires from his work. In other words, some workers would list increased responsibility as an advantage of job enlargement, whereas others, with different utility functions, would list it as a disadvantage. Other commonly accepted worker advantages, like increased mental effort required or increased educational background, are disadvantages to those without a surplus of mental capacity or education.

One might ask, What is wrong with viewing the productive system from a purely technological point of view if giant strides in productivity have resulted historically from such a strategy? The answer lies in how the objectives of productive organization are defined. If the sole objective of the productive system is production, then any concession made to the goals of the coexisting social system must be rationalized by their positive effect on production. Although many have tried to justify the concepts and ideas of job enlargement and job enrichment by alluding to increases in productivity and other economic measures, to date no study has conclusively shown that increased productivity results from the job enlargement process. There have been many reports describing a job enlargement or job enrichment process that conclude that subsequent increases in productivity and product quality have resulted. Unfortunately, these studies have almost universally suffered from inadequate experimental design that invalidates the cause-and-effect relationship, making it impossible to say that increased production wasn't caused by some factor other than the simple enlargement of the job. Therefore, at present the jury is still out, and there are many who feel that job enlargement has a detrimental effect on productivity and that its only justification is in terms of job satisfaction on the part of the individual worker. The unanswered questions are:

- Is the law of diminishing returns applicable to the continuing increase in specialization?
- Is there a point at which continued increase in specialization has a detrimental effect on production?
- Have we as an industrialized nation passed the point of diminishing returns in many industrial and service organizations?

As we approach the job design function of the operations manager, however, we must reconcile the goals of the sociotechnical system we are working within. Earlier in this chapter, we said that the goals and objectives of the technical systems differ dramatically from the goals of the social system present in an organization. If we assume that the goals of the social system are relevant goals of the organization, then it is not necessary to justify all job design decisions in terms of increased productivity. Changes in existing jobs or the design of new jobs can be made considering the human in the man–machine system as an individual and not merely a factor of production. His or her goals, self-actualization needs, social needs, and the like should be seriously considered during the job design process. Tradeoffs between productivity and human needs must be made. Merely optimizing either the technical system or the social system is an unsatisfactory answer to the job design problem.

THE WORK ELEMENT IN JOB DESIGN

The remaining portion of this chapter deals with work methods and work measurement techniques. Historically, work methods have been considered the domain of the worker. No one told the eighteenth-century blacksmith precisely how to accomplish a given task. As the trend toward specialization of jobs continued, many jobs and work methods have been designed by experts in methods engineering or methods analysis. Today, it is common for input concerning work methods to come from specialists in methods engineering as well as from the workers themselves. Regardless of who performs the analysis, the primary goal remains increased efficiency through either decreased cost or increased productivity.

Work Methods

Tools. In the detailed definition of work methods, the analyst has a number of tools at his or her disposal. In this section, we describe the most commonly used tools and indicate their sphere of application. Then the major steps taken in a methods improvement study will be described.

Regardless of the type of job being analyzed, the analyst can take advantage of the numerous principles of motion study that have evolved over many years. An excellent list of motion-study principles can be found in *Motion and Time Study* by Ralph M. Barnes[1]. Mr. Barnes categorizes his principles into the following three categories.

- Use of the human body–Examples include:
  - Use two hands and strive to begin as well as complete the motions at the same time
  - Momentum should be used to assist the worker
  - Smooth continuous motions are preferable to motions involving sudden and sharp changes in direction

  Eye fixations should be minimized and as close together as possible.
- Arrangement of the work place–Examples include:
  - All tools and materials should have a permanent place
  - Tools and materials should be placed close to the point of use

---

[1] Barnes, Ralph M., *Motion and Time Study: Design and Measurement of Work* 6th edition (New York: John Wiley & Sons, Inc., 1968) p. 220.

–Gravity feed bins should be used to deliver material when possible

–The height of the work place should permit either standing or sitting with good posture.

- Design of Tools and Equipment–Examples include:

  –A jig, fixture or a foot-operated device should relieve the hands where possible.

  –Tools and materials should be prepositioned when possible

  –Levers, cross bars, and hand wheels should be located to minimize the change in the worker's body position and maximize the mechanical advantage.

In addition to these principles of motion economy, there exist various charting techniques that are extremely valuable when properly applied to work methods design. The various charts are used under different conditions and circumstances, and as we describe the different types of charts, the appropriate application areas are indicated.

Flow diagrams and process charts similar to those found in Figures 6-5 and 6-6 are helpful in eliminating or combining unnecessary steps, shortening transportation distances, or identifying unnecessary delays in a productive process. Once the present mode of operation has been documented using a flow diagram or process chart or both, questions such as the following can be asked to improve the existing design:

What work is to be performed? Is it necessary? Can it be refined?

Who is to perform the work? Can others perform the work who are less skilled or less experienced?

Where is the work to be done? Can it be done elsewhere?

When is the work to be done? Can it be done earlier or later?

Why is the individual job element necessary? Can it be eliminated? Can it be combined?

How is the work being done? Are there alternatives?

An operations chart divides the functions of each hand into components of reach, grasp, transport, position, and so on. As shown in Figure 6-7, each hand is analyzed in parallel often on a time scale so that the manner in which the hands work together can be analyzed. Operations charts are primarily used to analyze tasks that have short cycles and are of a repetitive nature.

If the task were a repetitive, short-cycle task that had a high volume, it might be economically feasible to analyze it using a micromotion study, in which the task is filmed using a high-speed camera and then each frame of film is analyzed to develop a simo (simultaneous motion) chart. The major difference between an operations chart and a simo chart is the level of detail and the relative costs. For many low- to medium-volume applications, a simo chart cannot be shown to be cost-effective. See Figure 6-8 for an example of a simo chart.

When both the man and machine components of the man–machine system are important parts of the task being studied, man–machine charts are often a useful

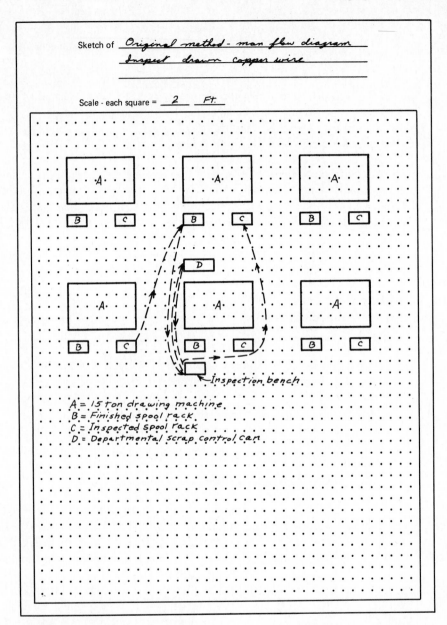

FIGURE 6-5   Example of Flow Diagram

SOURCE: Marvin E. Mundel, *Motion and Time Study*, 4th edition (Englewood Cliffs, New Jersey: Prentice-Hall, Inc., 1970).

Type of chart	PROCESS CHART – MAN ANALYSIS	

Method __ORIGINAL__   Machine no. __D-GROUP__

Operation __INSPECT DRAWN COPPER WIRE__   Operation no. __I-3__

                                   Part no. __⌒__

Part name __ALL DRAWN COPPER__   Chart by __C.W. Mc.__

Operator __SIMON GREEN__   Date charted __6/4/__

DIST.	SYMBOL	DESCRIPTION
24'	○	To next finished spool
	○	Take spool
24'	○	To inspection bench
	○	Place spool on bench
	○	Strip and cut outer layer which is always damaged in drawing
15'	○	To scrap container
	○	Dispose of scrap
15'	○	To inspection table
	○	Cut 2' from end, then 2" sample from 2' piece
	◇	O.D. with box micrometer
	○	Pick up spool
24'	○	To machine's "inspection" rack
	○	Place spool

SUMMARY	
○	7
□	0
◇	1
○	5
▽	0
Dist.	102' AVG.

FIGURE 6-6   Example of Process Chart

SOURCE: Marvin E. Mundel, *Motion and Time Study*, 4th edition (Englewood Cliffs, New Jersey: Prentice-Hall, Inc., 1970).

RIGHT AND LEFT HAND OPERATION CHART — Page 1 of 2

Improved _____ Method _____
Assembly _____ Operation _____
Hand-hole Cover Part _____
R. Allen Operator _____

Bench Mach. No. _____
a-321 Opr. No. _____
GG Part No. _____
W.H. Chart by _____
3/4 Date _____

Left hand description			Right hand description
1. To bolt			To bolt
2. Pick up bolt			Pick up bolt
3. To work area			To work area
4. Assem. bolt to jig			Assem. bolt to jig
5. To washer			To washer
6. Pick up washer			Pick up washer
7. To assembly			To assembly
8. Assem. washer			Assem. washer
9. To cover plate			To cover plate
10. Pick up plate			Pick up plate
11. To assembly			To assembly
12. Assem. Plate			Assem. plate
13. To bar			To bar
14. Pick up bar			Pick up bar
15. To assembly			To assembly
16. Fit and spin on			Fit and spin on
17. To cotter pin.			To cotter pin
18. Pick up cotter			Pick up cotter
19. To right side assem.			To right side assem.
20. Right s			Assem cotter

RIGHT AND LEFT HAND OPERATION CHART — Page 2 of 2

Improved _____ Method _____
Assembly _____ Operation _____
Hand-hole Cover Part _____
R. Allen Operator _____

Bench Mach. No. _____
a-321 Opr. No. _____
GG Part No. _____
W.H. Chart by _____
3/4 Date _____

Left hand description			Right hand description
1. To left side assem.			To left side assem.
2. Assem. cotter			Left side assem.
3. Left side assem.			To pliers
4.			Pick up pliers
5.			To assembly
6.			Bend left cotter
7. To right side assem.			To right side assem.
8. Right side assem.			Bend right cotter
9. For right hand			To aside pliers
10.			Place pliers
11. To left assembly			To right assembly
12. Pick up assem.			Pick up assem.
13. To finished parts			To finished parts
14. Place assembly			Place assembly
15.			
16.			
17.			
18.			
19.			
20.			

FIGURE 6-7 Example of an Operations Chart

SOURCE: Marvin E. Mundel, *Motion and Time Study*, 4th edition (Englewood Cliffs, New Jersey: Prentice-Hall, Inc., 1970).

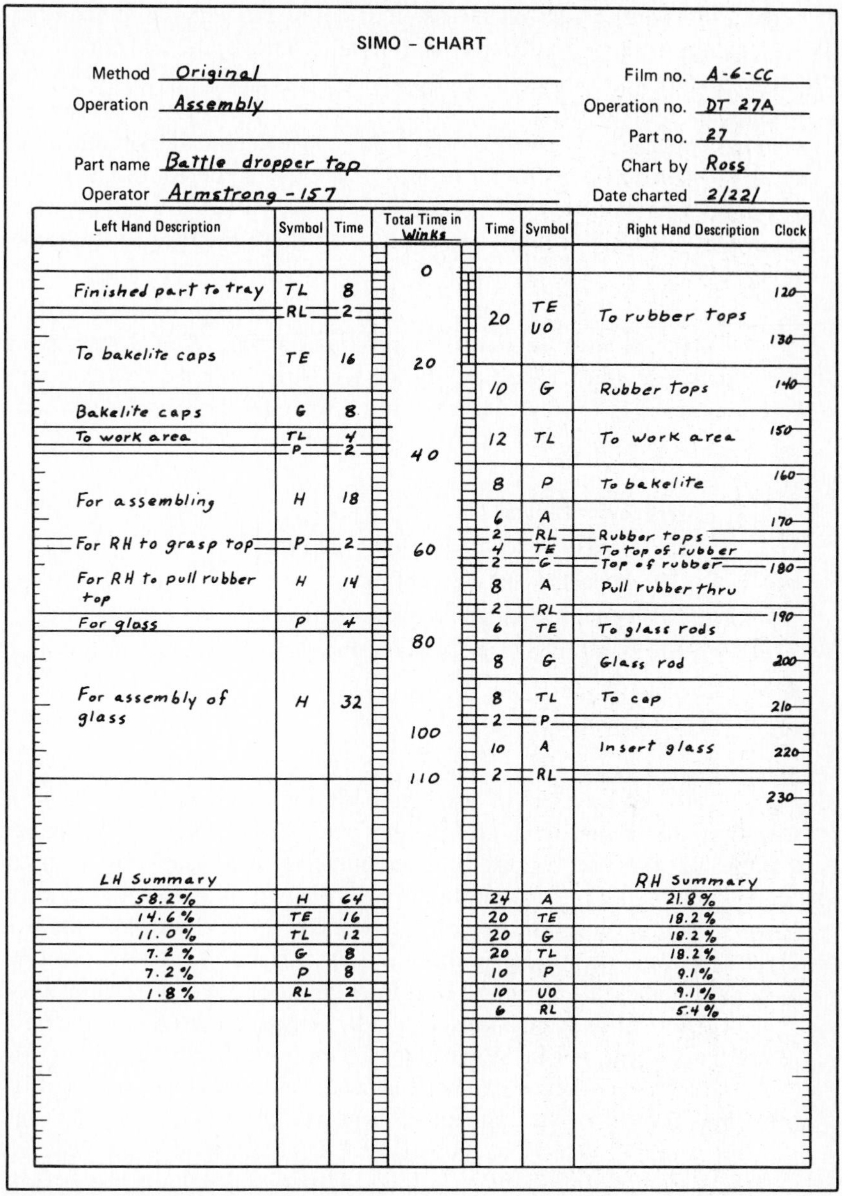

SIMO - CHART

Method *Original*   Film no. *A-6-CC*

Operation *Assembly*   Operation no. *DT 27A*

                                        Part no. *27*

Part name *Battle dropper top*   Chart by *Ross*

Operator *Armstrong - 157*   Date charted *2/22/*

Left Hand Description	Symbol	Time	Total Time in Winks	Time	Symbol	Right Hand Description	Clock
Finished part to tray	TL	8	0				120
	RL	2		20	TE / UO	To rubber tops	
To bakelite caps	TE	16	20				130
				10	G	Rubber Tops	140
Bakelite caps	G	8		12	TL	To work area	150
To work area	TL	4	40				
	P	2		8	P	To bakelite	160
For assembling	H	18		6	A		170
				2	RL	Rubber tops	
For RH to grasp top	P	2	60	4	TE	To top of rubber	
				2	G	Top of rubber	180
For RH to pull rubber top	H	14		8	A	Pull rubber thru	
				2	RL		190
For glass	P	4	80	6	TE	To glass rods	
				8	G	Glass rod	200
For assembly of glass	H	32		8	TL	To cap	210
				2	P		
			100	10	A	Insert glass	220
			110	2	RL		
							230

LH Summary						RH Summary	
58.2%	H	64		24	A	21.8%	
14.6%	TE	16		20	TE	18.2%	
11.0%	TL	12		20	G	18.2%	
7.2%	G	8		20	TL	18.2%	
7.2%	P	8		10	P	9.1%	
1.8%	RL	2		10	UO	9.1%	
				6	RL	5.4%	

FIGURE 6-8   Example of a Simo Chart

SOURCE: Marvin E. Mundel, *Motion and Time Study*, 4th edition (Englewood Cliffs, New Jersey: Prentice-Hall, Inc., 1970).

tool. Like the one shown in Figure 6-9, these reflect each job element and depict what the machine part of the system is doing and what the human part of the system is doing at all times. Therefore, human idleness and machine idleness are readily discernable and rational decisions based on resource cost can be made concerning methods design. Obviously, if a machine cost five times per hour more than the human operating it, operator idle time is far less critical than machine idle time.

When the transformation process involves the coordinated efforts of a team, activity charts or multiman process charts are useful in documenting the activities of each team member on a time scale. See Figure 6-10 for an example of an activity chart.

Steps in work methods improvement study.　The first step in any methods improvement study is to identify the job to be improved. Monks suggests that jobs that have the following characteristics often offer more potential than others for cost reduction or improved industrial relations:

- High labor content
- Large demand and are frequently occurring
- Present quality control problems
- Are bottlenecks in the productive system
- Are unsafe, unpleasant, or fatiguing
- Offer excessively low or high earnings
- Have never been studied before[2]

The second step in any methods improvement study is to document and analyze the present method. This step can take advantage of the principles of motion economy and the various charting methods discussed earlier in this chapter. In documenting and analyzing the present system, it is essential to obtain input from those who are closest to the job, the workers themselves. Not only will involving the workers result in a better understanding and analysis of the present system, but it will aid immeasurably in the implementation of the new work methods.

After the present system or work method has been documented and analyzed, alternative designs can be developed. Once a discrete number of alternatives have been identified, they must be analyzed and measured against the present work method and each other. Based on measures of efficiency such as time, cost, output, quality, and/or social benefits, a method for performing the task must be selected. Again, when defining and selecting alternatives to the present work method, it is important to continue worker involvement in the process. Having a number of workers involved could be achieved through assigning some representative worker to the methods improvement team and through an employee suggestion system.

---

[2]Joseph G. Monks, *Operations Management: Theory and Problems* (New York: McGraw-Hill, 1977).

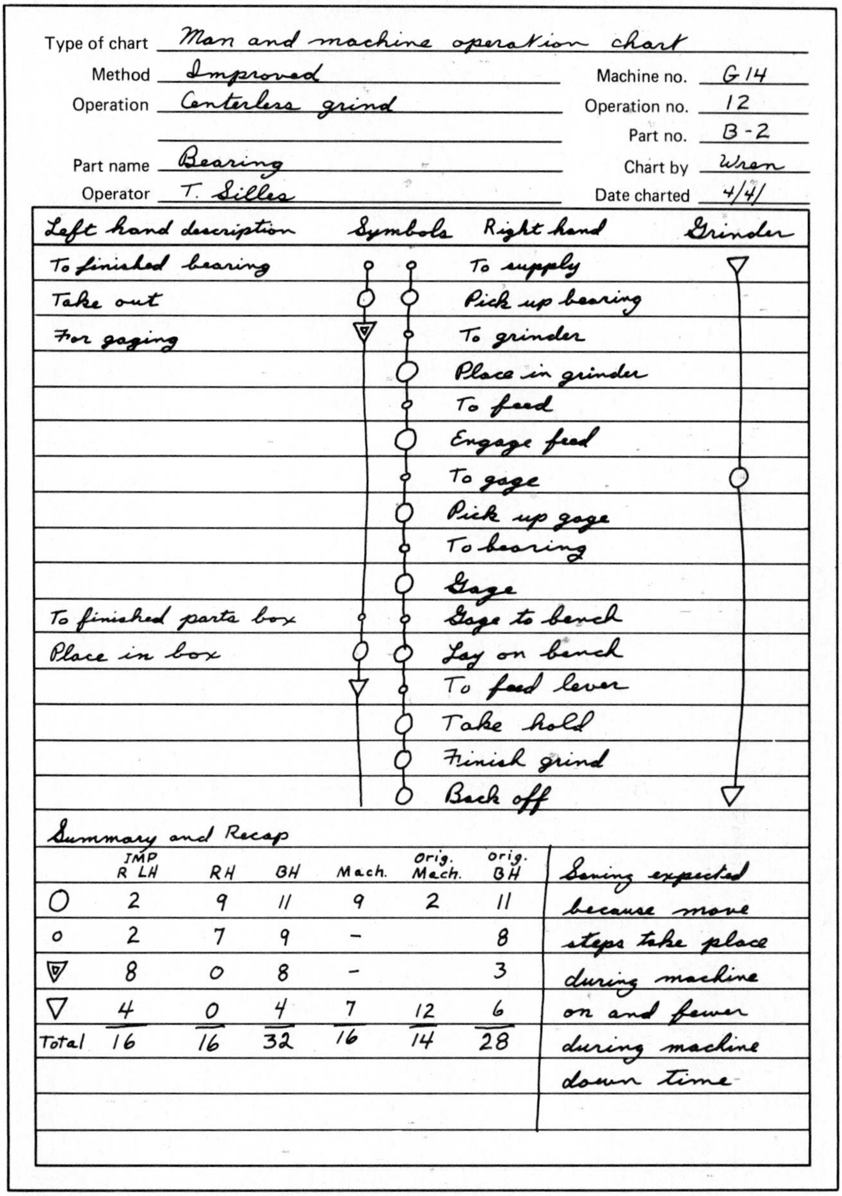

Type of chart   Man and machine operation chart

Method   Improved   Machine no.   G 14

Operation   Centerless grind   Operation no.   12

Part no.   B - 2

Part name   Bearing   Chart by   Wren

Operator   T. Silles   Date charted   4/4/

Left hand description	Symbols	Right hand	Grinder
To finished bearing		To supply	▽
Take out		Pick up bearing	
For gaging		To grinder	
		Place in grinder	
		To feed	
		Engage feed	
		To gage	○
		Pick up gage	
		To bearing	
		Gage	
To finished parts box		Gage to bench	
Place in box		Lay on bench	
		To feed lever	
		Take hold	
		Finish grind	
		Back off	▽

Summary and Recap

	IMP R LH	RH	BH	Mach.	Orig. Mach.	Orig. BH	
○	2	9	11	9	2	11	Saving expected
○	2	7	9	—		8	because move
▽	8	0	8	—		3	steps take place
▽	4	0	4	7	12	6	during machine
Total	16	16	32	16	14	28	on and fewer
							during machine
							down time

FIGURE 6-9   Example of a Man–Machine Chart

SOURCE: Marvin E. Mundel, *Motion and Time Study*, 4th edition (Englewood Cliffs, New Jersey: Prentice-Hall, Inc., 1970).

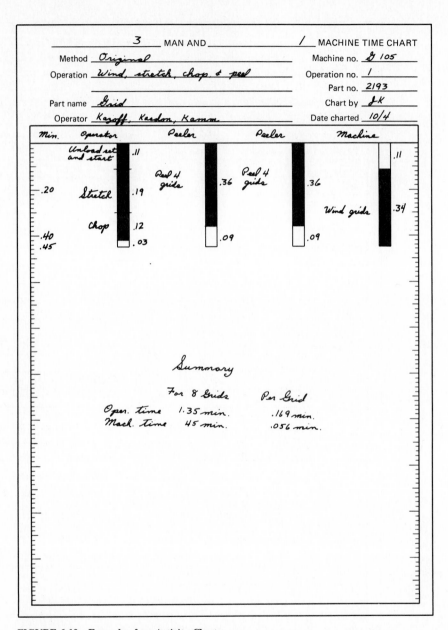

FIGURE 6-10 Example of an Activity Chart

SOURCE: Marvin E. Mundel, *Motion and Time Study*, 4th edition (Englewood Cliffs, New Jersey: Prentice-Hall, Inc., 1970).

Once the improved method has been selected for implementation, it is necessary to convince line management that there is a better way than the way they have been performing a given task. In addition, it is important to sell the idea to the individual workers. If either line supervision or the workers themselves oppose the change, there is little hope for an effective transition, and it is quite possible that the entire methods improvement study could fail in its goal of increased efficiency through improved work methods.

It is important to realize that no job or work method has been designed optimally and that all jobs can be improved. Consequently, once a job has been redesigned or improved, it is necessary to allow work methods to evolve by analyzing and implementing small changes. It is also important to maintain control over a redesigned job to ensure that workers do not regress to the original work methods.

To summarize, there are five basic steps in any methods improvement study:

1. Identify the job to be studied.
2. Document and analyze the existing work method.
3. Develop alternative work methods and choose the best.
4. Implement the new method.
5. Maintain control and supervise additional change of the improved work method.

WORK MEASUREMENT

The output resulting from a work measurement study is in the form of labor standards that seek to establish norm production rates for workers or standard times required to complete a given job. All organizations need labor standards in one form or another. Often, these standards have been derived in a very informal way, owing to the type of job or perhaps the type of organization. Some jobs do not lend themselves to strict standards because of the variable nature of the work activity; and in some very small organizations, even though formal labor standards could be derived, they haven't been, owing simply to the size of the firm or relative lack of sophistication on the part of management personnel.

Regardless of whether labor standards have been developed in a scientific way and formally written into the procedures of an organization, or just exist rather vaguely in the mind of supervisory personnel, they are often necessary raw data that management must use in making a variety of decisions. Decisions upon which labor standards have a direct impact include:

- Pricing decisions
- Budgeting decisions
- Hiring decisions
- Firing decisions
- Wage increase decisions

- Wage incentive plan decisions
- Inventory decisions
- Bidding decisions
- Scheduling decisions

Because of the widespread influence of labor standards, several formal, rather scientific methods of determining labor standards have been developed. The remainder of this chapter consists of a description of these formal work measurement methods.

Time Study

Time-study methods for measuring short, repetitive jobs were first developed by Frederick Taylor in the late nineteenth century. Today, time-study methods are commonly used for deriving labor standards. By analyzing and timing one worker's performance of the task to be measured, the time-study procedure generalizes or infers a standard time for that task for all workers.

To derive a labor standard using time-study methods, the following procedure is followed. First, the worker is selected, and the purpose and procedure of the time study is explained to the worker. The job in question must then be broken into elements or distinct operations, each taking a matter of several minutes or a number of seconds. The next step is to time a number of cycles for each distinct operation. This is done using a stopwatch or, if the cycle time is extremely short, a high-speed camera. The number of cycles that should be timed is a function of the amount of confidence the analyst wishes to have in the mean cycle time and the variance. Rather than devote a great deal of space to sample-size calculation, let us use Table 6-1 as a guide to the number of cycles to be observed. After the appropriate number of cycles has been observed, the average cycle time can be computed as shown in equation 6.1 below:

6.1
$$\bar{t} = \frac{\sum\limits_{i=1}^{N} t_i}{N}$$

where

$\bar{t}$ = average cycle time

t_i = an individual cycle-time observation

N = sample size or number of observations

After all job elements are timed and their respective average times computed, the average time for the job being measured can be computed by merely adding the

Table 6-1   Guide to Number of Cycles to Be Observed in a Time Study

WHEN TIME (HOURS) PER CYCLE IS MORE THAN:	MINIMUM NUMBER OF CYCLES TO STUDY (ACTIVITY)		
	OVER 10,000 PER YEAR	1,000 TO 10,000	UNDER 1,000
8.000	2	1	1
3.000	3	2	1
2.000	4	2	1
1.000	5	3	2
0.800	6	3	2
0.500	8	4	3
0.300	10	5	4
0.200	12	6	5
0.120	15	8	6
0.080	20	10	8
0.050	25	12	10
0.035	30	15	12
0.020	40	20	15
0.012	50	25	20
0.008	60	30	25
0.005	80	40	30
0.003	100	50	40
0.002	120	60	50
under 0.002	140	80	60

From Benjamin W. Niebel, *Motion and Time Study*, 6th ed. (Homewood, Ill.: Richard D. Irwin, 1976), p. 325.

average job-element times. This sum, which is shown in equation 6.2, is known as the observed operator performance time.

6.2
$$PT = \sum_{j=1}^{m} \bar{t}_j$$

where
PT = observed operator performance time

$\bar{t}_j$ = average cycle time for job element j

m = number of job elements

The next step is to modify the observed operator performance time by multiplying it by a subjective estimate of the operator's performance rating. This performance rating represents the analyst's estimate of how much slower or faster the worker is working in relation to a normal pace. If he or she is working 25 percent faster, the performance rating would be 1.25. The modified operator performance time is called normal time and is computed as shown in equation 6.3:

6.3
$$NT = PT \cdot PR$$

where
$$NT = \text{normal time}$$
$$PT = \text{performance time}$$
$$PR = \text{performance rating}$$

The final step is to calculate a standard time for the job by adding an allowance time to the normal time for personal needs of the worker and for unavoidable delays such as machine breakdowns. This allowance for personal time is often included in union contracts and typically varies from 10 to 15 percent. The standard time is calculated using equation 6.4:

6.4
$$ST = NT(1 + A)$$

where
$$ST = \text{standard time}$$
$$NT = \text{normal time}$$
$$A = \text{allowance}$$

To illustrate the procedure just described, let's consider the following example. The operation is to bore a 1.5-centimeter hole in a round metal disk. To perform the operation accurately, it is necessary to place the disk in a jig before drilling. The job can be broken into two elements, positioning the disk in the jig and drilling the hole. The company annually produces more than 10,000 final assemblies for which the disk is a part. Since cycle time for placing the disk in the jig is approximately 3 minutes (.05 hours) and the drilling time is about 1.2 minutes (.02 hours), Table 6-1 indicates sample sizes of 25 and 40 for the two operations respectively. These times are reflected in Tables 6-2 and 6-3 respectively.

The average jig positioning time is:

$$\bar{t}_1 = \frac{2.95 + 2.93 + \cdots + 3.06}{25}$$

$$= \frac{74.47}{25}$$

$$= 2.9788 \text{ minutes}$$

The average drilling time is:

$$\bar{t}_2 = \frac{1.11 + 1.12 + \cdots + 1.17}{40}$$

$$= \frac{47.94}{40}$$

$$= 1.1985 \text{ minutes}$$

Table 6-2 Jig Positioning Times in Minutes

OBSERVATION NO.	TIME	OBSERVATION NO.	TIME
1	2.95	14	3.01
2	2.93	15	2.86
3	3.50	16	3.05
4	2.71	17	3.21
5	2.92	18	3.21
6	3.11	19	2.42
7	3.02	20	2.97
8	3.05	21	2.79
9	2.97	22	3.15
10	2.83	23	3.03
11	2.99	24	2.97
12	2.89	25	3.06
13	2.87		

The performance time of the job is found by adding the two component performance times:

$$PT = 2.9788 + 1.1985$$
$$= 4.1773$$

Let us assume that the analyst's subjective rating was that the worker was working just a little faster than normal pace, let's say 5 percent. Then, the normal

Table 6-3 Drilling Times in Minutes

OBSERVATION NO.	TIME	OBSERVATION NO.	TIME
1	1.11	21	1.20
2	1.12	22	1.22
3	1.21	23	1.12
4	1.09	24	1.09
5	1.31	25	1.31
6	1.21	26	1.22
7	1.22	27	1.21
8	1.40	28	1.20
9	1.15	29	1.19
10	1.11	30	1.17
11	1.13	31	1.23
12	1.21	32	1.15
13	1.20	33	1.14
14	1.23	34	1.24
15	1.21	35	1.27
16	1.18	36	1.26
17	1.25	37	1.30
18	1.27	38	1.10
19	1.17	39	1.21
20	1.16	40	1.17

time for the job could be calculated as follows:

$$NT = (4.1773)(1.05)$$
$$= 4.386$$

The final step is to calculate the standard time for the job using equation 6.4. Let's assume an allowance for personal time of 10 percent.

$$ST = (4.386)(1 + .10)$$
$$= 4.825 \text{ minutes}$$

Predetermined Time Standards

Another way to determine a time standard for a job is to break the job into small elements for which published standards exist. When using predetermined time standards (PTS), the analyst is forced to break the job into very small elementary movements, such as "reach 3 inches," or "grasp," or "handle." Typically, one minute of work is divided into several hundred elementary movements.

Using published time standards offers the following advantages over the time-study methods previously described.

- Predetermined time standards are less subjective than time-study methods because no performance rating is required. Consequently, PTS is widely accepted as being a fair way of determining standards.
- There is no necessity to disrupt operations to time the job.
- Predetermined time standards can be applied to jobs before they are installed in the productive system.
- Developing labor standards using PTS is less expensive than time-study methods.

The major disadvantage to using PTS to set labor standards is theoretical problems that adversely affect the accuracy of the procedure. Much of the accuracy depends on the expertise of the analyst in breaking down the job properly and upon the implicit assumption that the total time for the job is found by merely adding the times required to accomplish the minute elements of the job. Often, if it is cost-effective, a job's standard time is computed using both time-study methods and PTS.

Some companies use the data base they develop by time-study methods to compile their own published or predetermined time standards. The major difference between internally developed and externally published predetermined standards is in the level of detail. Externally published predetermined standards relate to functions taking less than half a second, whereas internally predetermined standards typically relate to job elements taking 20–30 seconds.

Work Sampling

About 50 years after Taylor applied his time-study methods, work sampling was introduced. Work sampling involves drawing a sample of random observations of a particular job to determine what proportion of the worker's time is spent on various job functions. Experience has shown that work sampling is best applied to jobs that have long cycle times or that are infrequent. Repetitive short-interval jobs are still best analyzed using time-study methods or some form of predetermined labor standards.

Work sampling has the following advantages over time-study methods:

- Work sampling is generally less expensive, because the study can be performed by less-skilled and therefore less-expensive personnel.
- Jobs having longer cycle times can be studied economically.
- Work sampling studies are less disruptive to the productive system.
- Since the study period is longer, there is less chance of biasing the results with the effect of short-term variations.

The application of work sampling to the calculation of standard times can be divided into seven steps:

- Identify the job or jobs that are to be the subject of the work sampling study.
- Describe the job in writing by listing the activities of the workers.
- Inform the affected workers.
- Determine the number of observations required. Given a desired degree of accuracy, it is possible to statistically determine the appropriate sample size using equation 6.5 below:

6.5
$$N = \frac{Z_\alpha^2 pq}{a^2}$$

where

N = sample size

Z_α = the standard normal deviate for a given α level

p = value of the sample proportion

$q = 1 - p$

a = absolute error desired

- Prepare a tour schedule that ensures random selection of the sample observations. This can be done using a random-number table to assign observation times.
- Make and record the data necessary to compute standard time.
- Compute the standard time using equation 6.6:

6.6
$$ST = \left(\frac{T \cdot W \cdot I}{P}\right) \cdot \left(\frac{1}{1 - A}\right)$$

where ST = standard time per unit

T = total time spent by the operator (working time and idle time)

W = working time proportion

I = performance index

P = total number of units produced

A = allowances expressed in decimal form

To illustrate the work sampling methodology, let us consider the following example. A large oil company has a credit-card processing center. Gas tickets are

Table 6-4   Standard Normal Deviate

CONFIDENCE LEVEL	Z_α
.99	2.58
.95	1.96
.90	1.64
.85	1.44

mailed into the center, where they are read by optical scanning equipment. Approximately 15 percent of the tickets are rejected and sent to a key-to-disk operation. Trays of tickets are manually keyed into a record stored on a magnetic disk. The job to be studied is the keying of one tray of cards. Specifically, the activities of the operators are idle or busy keying in data. After informing the operators of the study, it is necessary to determine the number of observations. Let us assume we wish to be 95 percent confident that our estimate of busy time will be within ± 3 percent. Suppose we estimate the percentage of time an average operator is busy at 75 percent. Using a confidence level of 95 percent, Table 6-4 shows that Z_α is 1.96.

Using equation 6.5, the number of observations can be calculated in the following manner:

$$N = \frac{(1.96)^2(.75)(.25)}{.03^2}$$
$$= 800.33$$

The next step is to design a random tour schedule. This can be done by dividing the workweek into 2,400 minutes (40 hours × 60 minutes); then, taking a four-digit random-number table and eliminating all numbers greater than 2,400, select 800 random numbers from the shorter list, each of which would represent a time of the week when an observation should be taken.

Once the data have been collected and recorded, it is time to compute the standard time. Assume that the working time percentage of the sample is 80 percent and the subjective estimate of the performance index is 1.05. Also assume that the number of boxes processed in a week by the worker being studied was 48 and that the union contract stipulates an allowance of 15 percent. Standard time is computed using equation 6.6, as shown below:

$$ST = \left(\frac{(2400)(.8)(1.05)}{48} \right) \cdot \left(\frac{1}{1 - .15} \right)$$
$$= 49.41 \text{ minutes/tray}$$

SUMMARY

In this chapter, we have seen that the function of job design and work measurement is an extremely important and demanding function of the manager of a productive system. Extremely complex behavior problems exist that obviously could not be dealt with here. It is safe to say, however, that the job design process should be viewed in terms of the sociotechnical system and that an operations manager who seeks to maximize either the goals of the technical system or those of the social system to the exclusion of the other is ill-advised.

We have attempted here to highlight some of the more commonly used tools for improving work methods. These include the principles of motion study that have evolved over many years and the various charting techniques. The rationale for and the importance of labor standards have been described, and the three most common methods of determining labor standards have been developed. Like all introductory chapters, this chapter should serve as a jumping-off place for further investigations into the area of job design and work measurement.

SOLVED PROBLEMS

Problem Statement

Consider the job of making hot fudge sundaes at the local ice cream parlor. The job can be broken into two elements, filling the dish with ice cream and providing the topping (hot fudge, whipped cream, nuts, and a cherry). Using the time-study technique, develop a standard time for making hot fudge sundaes.

Solution

The first step in the time study is to take the appropriate number of stopwatch measurements. To determine the appropriate number of measurements of each job element, the store manager was asked how many hot fudge sundaes were sold each year and his estimate of cycle times for the two job elements. He said that about 75 hot fudge sundaes were made per day and it took about 30 seconds for each job element. With this information, Table 6-1 indicates that a set of 60 observations is appropriate for each job element. (Use the first column, because 75 sundaes per day is more than 10,000 per year and 30 seconds is approximately .008 hour.)

The next step is to take our time measurements. Let us assume that the average time to put ice cream in the dish was 37 seconds, and average topping time was 29 seconds. Therefore, the operator performance time is:

$$PT = \sum_{i=1}^{2} \bar{t}_i$$

$$= 37 \text{ seconds} + 29 \text{ seconds}$$

$$= 66 \text{ seconds}$$

It was perceived that the worker making the sundae was working about 10 percent faster than normal, and hence the performance rating is 1.10. To calculate normal time, merely multiply the performance time by the performance rating.

$$NT = PT \cdot PR$$
$$= (66 \text{ seconds})(1.1)$$
$$= 72.6 \text{ seconds}$$

Allowance for personal needs is 15 percent. Standard time for making a hot fudge sundae, therefore, is:

$$ST = NT(1 + .15)$$
$$= 72.6(1 + .15)$$
$$= 83.49 \text{ seconds}$$

Problem Statement

The job to be studied is that of a lumberjack team cutting down a tree. The following information must be ascertained.

- Estimate of the proportion of time spent on the task of cutting down a tree. (Assume 70%.)
- The absolute range of error. (Assume 5% absolute error.)
- The confidence level. (Assume 95% confidence level is desired.)
- An allowance for personal time. (Assume 10%.)
- The number of trees cut per day. (Assume 20 trees per day.)
- The performance index. (Estimated to be 1.0.)

Solution

First we must calculate the sample size by using the following formula:

$$N = \frac{Z_\alpha^2 pq}{a^2}$$
$$= \frac{(1.96)^2(.7)(.3)}{.05^2}$$
$$= \frac{.807}{.0025}$$
$$= 322.7$$

If 323 observations are taken randomly and the sample working time percentage was 65, then the standard time can be computed as follows:

$$ST = \left(\frac{T \cdot W \cdot I}{P} \right) \cdot \left(\frac{1}{1 - A} \right)$$

$$= \frac{(8 \text{ hours})(.65)(1.0)}{20} \cdot \frac{1}{1 - .1}$$

$$= .2889 \text{ hour}$$

$$= 17.33 \text{ minutes}$$

REVIEW QUESTIONS

1. What is the major reason that all productive systems of the 1990s will *not* be totally automated?
2. Distinguish between physiological and psychological considerations in job design.
3. Why is work physiology applied more often to strenuous physical tasks than to mental tasks?
4. Briefly describe the methodology of a work physiology study.
5. List four important environmental factors in job design.
6. What relevance does OSHA have to job design?
7. List five major advantages of the division of labor.
8. What is the major premise of the "job enlargement" school of thought?
9. Distinguish between vertical and horizontal job enlargement.
10. List five important advantages of job enlargement accruing to productivity.
11. List four disadvantages of job enlargement with respect to productivity.
12. List five advantages to workers of job enlargement.
13. What is the present consensus regarding job enlargement's effect on productivity?
14. Briefly, what is the major contention of the sociotechnical school of thought?
15. List what you believe to be the five most important motion-study principles described in this chapter.
16. Distinguish between a flow diagram and a process chart.
17. Distinguish between an operations chart and a man–machine chart.
18. What is a simo chart?
19. List five characteristics that could make a job a good candidate for a methods study.

20. What are the basic steps in a work methods study?
21. Give two reasons for involving workers in a methods improvement study.
22. List five decisions for which management needs labor standards data.
23. Distinguish between time-study methods and work sampling.
24. What are predetermined time standards?
25. How does the use of PTS differ from a time study?
26. List two advantages of using published time standards.
27. List two disadvantages of using published standards.
28. List two important advantages of work sampling.
29. To what kind of applications is work sampling best applied?
30. What are the seven steps to setting labor standards through work sampling?

_____ **PROBLEMS** _____

1. The standard time for a particular hospital task was 10 minutes. Owing to a change in the system, unavoidable delays have increased and a new standard must be developed. The appropriate work sampling was performed, with the results reflected below.

Work Sampling Results

ACTIVITY	NUMBER OF OBSERVATIONS	% OF OBSERVATIONS
Working	576	82.3
Idle	124	17.7
Total	700	100.0

Thirty-five patients per 8-hour day are processed. If the union contract has a personal allowance of 10%, what is the new standard time? Assume a performance index of 1.0.

2. The average for the five elementary tasks of a given job were calculated as:

$$\bar{t}_1 = 27 \text{ seconds}$$

$$\bar{t}_2 = 43 \text{ seconds}$$

$$\bar{t}_3 = 15 \text{ seconds}$$

$$\bar{t}_4 = 29 \text{ seconds}$$

$$\bar{t}_5 = 21 \text{ seconds}$$

The worker being timed was judged to be working at a normal pace. What is the difference in the standard time for the job using a 10% allowance for personal time as opposed to a 15% allowance?

3. If α is equal to .05, and the absolute error desired for a work sampling study is $\pm 5\%$, compute the sample size if the proportion of busy time is 70%.

4. If you want to 95% confident in your prediction using work sampling techniques and you can afford to sample only 100 observations, what degree of error must be tolerated if p is 75%?

5. Given the following random numbers, design a tour schedule for taking 25 observations for a work sampling study. Assume an 8-hour observation period.

131	375	124	043	225
311	005	834	621	197
117	152	420	907	527
420	319	254	183	500
817	339	664	298	603
616	153	801	461	721
028	174	395	972	636
306	500	854	386	702
212	054	713	494	190
904	497	154	454	773

6. Make the following charts for jobs of which you have firsthand knowledge:
   a. Flow diagram
   b. Process chart
   c. Operations chart
   d. Simo chart
   e. Man–machine chart
   f. Activity chart

7. Perform a time study for any short-cycle repetitive job to which you have access.

8. Perform a work sampling study of any long-cycle repetitive job to which you have access.

9. If you work, select a job you perform and apply the tools in this chapter to improve that job. Write up a complete report of your study.

10. Do the necessary secondary research and write a report comparing the two most common predetermined time-standard systems.

11. An airline wants to develop a standard time for making an airline reservation so that they can do a better job at personnel planning. For the purpose of this exercise let's assume that making a simple reservation consists of talk time and interaction between the reservation agent and the computer. Average talk time was found to be 3.5 minutes and the mean computer interaction time was .5 minute. If the agent was rated at working 10% faster than the norm and the union contract specifies a 15% allowance for personal time, calculate the standard time for handling a call.

12. A work sampling study is needed to determine the standard time for the baggage loading operation at an airport.
    a. If management wants to 90 percent confident that our estimate will be within $\pm 2\%$ and we estimate the average baggage handler is busy 90% of the time, what is the appropriate sample size?
    b. After making the appropriate number of observations the working time proportion was .95. During 1 week the worker (whose performance index was estimated at 1.20) handled 2000 bags. Given the union contract stipulates a 15% allowance, compute the standard time.

REFERENCES

ABRUZZI, A., *Work Measurement*. New York: Columbia University Press, 1952.

BARNES, RALPH M., *Motion and Time Study: Design and Measurement of Work*, 6th ed. New York: John Wiley, 1968.

BUFFA, ELWOOD SPENCER, *Modern Production/Operations Management*, 6th ed. New York: John Wiley, 1980.

CHAPANIS, ALPHONSE, *Man–Machine Engineering*. Belmont, Calif.: Wadsworth, 1965.

CHASE, RICHARD B., and NICHOLAS J. AQUILANO, *Production and Operations Management*, 3rd ed. Homewood, Ill.: Richard D. Irwin, 1981.

DAVIS, L.E., "Job Satisfaction Research: The Post-Industrial View," *Industrial Relations*, 10 (1971), 176–93.

_____, and A.B. CHERNS, eds., *Quality of Working Life: Cases*, vol. II. New York: Free Press, 1975.

_____, and J.C. TAYLOR, eds., *Design of Jobs*. Middlesex, England: Penguin Books, 1972.

DICKSON, PAUL, *The Future of the Workplace*. New York: Weybright and Talley, 1975.

FOY, N., and H. GORDON, "Worker Participation: Contrasts in Three Countries," *Harvard Business Review*, 54, no. 3 (May–June 1976), 71–83.

HACKMAN, J.R., and E.E. LAWLER III, "Employee Reactions to Job Characteristics," *Journal of Applied Psychology*, 55, (1971), 265–68. Also in Davis and Taylor, *Design of Jobs*.

HERBST, P.G., *Socio-technical Design, Strategies in Multidisciplinary Research*. London: Tavistock, 1974.

HERZBERG, FREDERICK, "One More Time: How Do You Motivate Employees?" *Harvard Business Review*, January–February 1968.

MAYER, RAYMOND R., *Production and Operations Management*, 4th ed. New York: McGraw-Hill, 1982.

MONKS, JOSEPH G., *Operations Management: Theory and Problems*. New York: McGraw-Hill, 1982.

MOORE, FRANKLIN, G., and THOMAS E. HENDRICK, *Production/Operations Management*. Homewood, Ill.: Richard D. Irwin, 1980.

MUNDEL, MARVIN E., *Motion and Time Study*, 5th ed. Englewood Cliffs, N.J.: Prentice-Hall, 1978.

NADLER, G., *Work Design*, rev. ed. Homewood, Ill.: Richard D. Irwin, 1970.

NIEBEL, BENJAMIN W., *Motion and Time Study*, 5th ed. Homewood, Ill.: Richard D. Irwin, 1972.

THORSRUD, E., and F. EMERY, "Industrial Democracy in Norway," *Industrial Relations*, 9, no. 2 (February 1970), 187–96.

7

FACILITY
LOCATION

Capacity planning
    measuring capacity
    capacity and production planning
    long-range capacity planning
Plant location
    factors influencing plant location
    locating a single plant
Multiple warehouse location
    warehouse location example
    extensions
    multiple objectives
    long-range warehouse location analysis
Location models in the public sector
    location of emergency ambulance services
    nuclear power plant location
    cash management
Summary

Two important factors influencing the effectiveness of distribution or services is the sizing and locating of production, warehouse, and service facilities. The capacity and relative location of key facilities has a direct effect on the cost of product distribution and services. In many industries, transportation and distribution costs are one of the largest expenses of doing business. One survey indicated that physical distribution costs absorb between 10 and 25 percent of net sales income.[1]

But although the costs of distributing products and providing services have become increasingly important, only a few companies have been really successful in controlling these costs; these successful companies seem to have in common the fact that they use the available scientific methods and computer technology for analysis of distribution problems and long-range planning of facilities. For example, one U.S. corporation has reduced distribution costs from 9 percent to less than 6 percent of the total cost of goods sold.[2] Standard Oil Company of New Jersey recently saved $5 million through the use of a mathematical model for planning distribution and manufacturing operations.[3]

The rationale for delving into a facility planning analysis is not limited to benefiting only manufacturing-oriented distribution systems. Many benefits have been derived from applying capacity planning and location models to hospitals, ambulances, fire engines, police protection, sewage treatment plants, and nuclear power plants. In this chapter, we first examine some issues in capacity planning. We then look at the locating of manufacturing plants and warehouses followed by examples of locating nonmanufacturing service facilities.

CAPACITY PLANNING

An integral part of facility planning and location analysis involves capacity planning. Forecasting and implementing long-term capacity needs has a direct impact on whether productive facilities should be created, abandoned, or expanded. Capacity planning decisions are especially critical since they can involve long-term commit-

---

[1] R. Shannon and T. Ignizio, "An Heuristic Programming Algorithm for Warehouse Location," *AIIE Transactions*, II, no. 4 (December 1970), 334–39.

[2] R.J. Atkins and R.H. Shriver, "New Approach to Facilities Location," *Harvard Business Review*, May–June 1968, pp. 70–79.

[3] *Ibid.*

ments and affect the overall success of the organization. In facilities planning decisions, the issue of capacity usually involves: how much total capacity to have, when it is needed, and where it should be located.

Measuring Capacity

It is important to be able to assess current capacity and future capacity needs. But what precisely is capacity? Capacity is defined as the maximum rate of productive capability of an organization for a given product mix. If the product mix of an organization changes, so can the productive capacity. There are other factors that make exact calculations of capacity somewhat difficult. Day-to-day variations involving absenteeism, machine maintenance and downtime, vacations, and product changeovers, all contribute to the difficulty of exact determinations of capacity. Thus, measures of capacity are usually estimates and should be interpreted as such.

Capacity for an organization is usually measured in terms of output. For example, an automobile plant might measure capacity in terms of cars per day. Capacity measures are simple for high-volume specialized organizations since the measure is simply the rate of output of a single product. Capacity measures are more difficult for service organizations or organizations with a diverse product mix. In these cases capacity is sometimes measured in terms of the inputs. For example a job shop might measure its capacity in terms of labor or machine hours. We must be careful not to confuse capacity with size. Capacity includes a time dimension and should not be equated with a fixed facility size or volume of output over a limited time period. Thus, a hospital should measure its capacity in terms of patients treated per unit of time rather than number of beds available. Shown below is a list of organizations and some possible measures of capacity.

ORGANIZATION	CAPACITY MEASURE
Steel producer	Tons of steel per year
Oil refinery	Barrels of gasoline per week
Restaurant	People served per day
Airline	Available seat miles per month
Hospital	Patients treated per week
University	Students enrolled per year
Warehouse	Cubic feet of storage space per year
Power company	Megawatts per day

For organizations with a diversified product line, an aggregate unit of capacity must be specified. A firm that produces power drills, lawn edgers, and hedge trimmers might measure capacity as the total number of units produced per day. Organizations with a more diverse product line might have to use a very general measure such as dollars of sales per day.

We should differentiate between peak capacity and normal capacity. Peak capacity can be sustained for only short periods of time through the use of overtime, temporary workers, subcontracting, or other means. Normal capacity can be sustained over long periods of time without extraordinary measures being taken. Normal capacity is most often used for manufacturing-planning purposes, but peak capacity plays a more important role in service industries. This is particularly true for power plants, recreational facilities, and companies such as computer centers.

Capacity and Production Planning

Capacity planning is an integral part of the overall process of production planning for the entire organization. Capacity planning and control is the function of establishing, measuring, monitoring, and adjusting levels of capacity in order to execute all manufacturing plans and schedules. Capacity planning and control is an iterative process that considers capacity on three different time horizons and impacts on three levels of production planning. The three time horizons of capacity planning are:

> Long-range capacity planning
> Medium-range capacity planning
> Short-range capacity control

Long-range capacity planning is concerned with decisions affecting resources that take long periods of time to acquire and that require top management approval. The time period normally associated with this level of planning is six months into the future and longer. Long-range capacity planning is associated with corporate-level production planning. The alternatives used to change long-range capacities are:

1. Change in facilities or capital equipment
2. Change in work force levels or composition

Figure 7-1 illustrates the relationship between the three levels of capacity planning and the primary functions involved in overall production and priority planning.

We will be studying these production planning topics in subsequent chapters. Briefly, corporate production planning involves the setting of directions, goals, product mixes, and budgets for operating departments. Aggregate production planning specifies output requirements for major product families or groups. Requirements are usually specified in labor-hours or units of production. (See Chapter 9.) The master production schedule is derived from the aggregate plans and specific quantities and production dates for individual products and end items. Materials requirements planning (MRP) breaks down the master production schedule into time-phased net requirements of all parts and components that are needed to support the production of the end products. (See Chapter 11.)

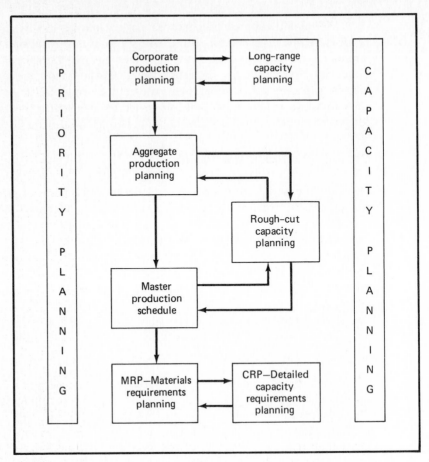

FIGURE 7-1   Relationship Between Capacity and Production Planning

Medium-range or rough-cut capacity planning decisions are concerned with increasing or decreasing capacity over a shorter time frame. The time frame is normally one to twelve months. This level of capacity planning most closely relates to master production scheduling. A rough-cut capacity estimate is accomplished by creating a product profile or bill of labor for each end item specified by the master production schedule. Capacity requirements can be estimated by extending the product profiles to create load profiles for critical work centers. Projected bottlenecks and overloaded work centers can require changes in the proposed master production schedule. The alternatives used to change medium-range capacities are:

1. Change make/buy decisions.
2. Subcontract over long periods.
3. Reallocate work force.

4. Plan alternate production routings.
5. Add additional tooling.

Short-range capacity planning interacts with both MRP (materials requirements planning) and shop-floor control activities. In relation to MRP there is CRP (capacity requirements planning) to derive capacity requirements for specific machine centers by time frame. In the very short time horizons up to four weeks, capacity planning is most related to detailed scheduling and monitoring and controlling of output. The adjustments which can be made in the short term include:

1. Scheduling of overtime
2. Subcontracting over short periods
3. Reallocation of work force
4. Selection of alternate production routings

Long-Range Capacity Planning

Of the three types of capacity planning levels, long-range capacity planning is most related to facility planning which is the main focus of this chapter. Let us look at some of the issues and approaches involved in long-range capacity planning.

Long-range capacity needs are more difficult to assess because of the uncertainties of future market and economic conditions. Top management must attempt to forecast 5 to 15 years into the future in order to decide what products or services will be offered and what the associated levels of demand will be. Additionally, changes in processing technology will have to be anticipated. Productive capacity for a given product can change significantly based just on changes in processing technology. In Chapter 8 we will look at various ways of forecasting future demands and technologies. However, none of the methods for forecasting the future are exact.

Once a measure of capacity has been developed and future demand levels have been forecast, it is necessary to estimate facility and capital equipment needs. These needs will generally vary over time and needed capacity will represent the difference between current available capacity and required capacity in the future. Planned facility capacity levels will also depend on the risk of having too much or too little future capacity. By increasing capacity earlier than needed higher building costs as well as costs of inflation are avoided. Also, the loss of future business because of inadequate capacity is avoided. On the other hand excess expansion or capacity ties up significant capital and can prove disastrous if actual demand levels are lower than expected.

Two important capacity concepts for facility planning include "best operating level" and "economics of scale." The best operating level for a given facility refers to the level of output at which the average unit cost is a minimum. This is illustrated in Figure 7-2.

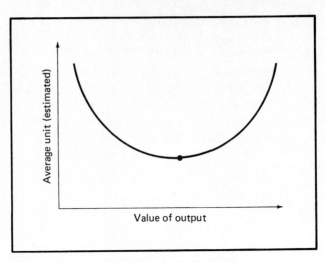

FIGURE 7-2   Illustration of Best Operating Level

The best operating level is not necessarily at the maximum capacity level; this fact should be noted in calculations for future capacity needs. Economies of scale is a vague concept that generally refers to the fact that as a plant gets larger and its volume of output increases, the average cost per unit is reduced since the fixed plant overhead is spread over more units. The conventional wisdom regarding economies of scale is that larger plants are more efficient and therefore desirable. However, as production gets more centrally located, transportation costs increase, deliveries are slower, and flexibility is reduced. Economies of scale should be considered in capacity decisions, but only in conjunction with other factors such as flexibility, responsiveness, distribution costs, and process economics.

Given an estimate of facility capacity needs, the next step is to generate alternatives and to evaluate these alternatives in order to select the best course of action. There are generally many ways to provide a given level of capacity especially if the total capacity is changing over time. Top management preference or certain market conditions can dictate a particular unique solution. If this is not the case, a thorough financial analysis incorporating discounted cash flows or internal rate of return calculations should be done. Computer simulation or decision tree analysis can be helpful in performing a risk analysis of proposed alternatives. Linear programming can also be used to allocate scarce capacity resources in a formal analysis of the problem. In the end, the facilities capacity decision will be made by the chief executive and board of directors in consultation with the operations and financial departments in the firm. The use of effective forecasting and analytical decision methods can certainly aid in the decision process.

We turn now from the capacity planning decision to the facility location decision as the two are closely related.

PLANT LOCATION

A need for locating additional production plants can have several possible causes: Increased product demand may necessitate increased production capacity. Emerging markets or new products may require another production location to facilitate distribution. Changes in the cost or availability of required resources may also precipitate a location analysis.

Many plant location questions are ultimately decided by political factors or the personal preferences of top management. However, it has been demonstrated that the difference in results between a good scientific solution and a manual "seat-of-the-pants" solution can easily be a reduction of at least 5 to 15 percent in total distribution costs. We shall consider some procedures that analytically determine effective locations for reducing relevant costs.

Factors Influencing Plant Location

In actual plant location analysis, many factors other than least-cost distribution influence the final location decision. Since plant and other facility location problems represent large resource commitments; their analysis must be consistent with the long-range goals of the organization. The capital assets that are tied up in plant facilities can be enormous for manufacturing organizations. Furthermore, plant location and capacity decisions can have significant effects on gaining market access, satisfying customer needs, and accruing net revenue for the organization.

Another factor influencing the final location of plants is zoning regulations. Site selection must satisfy city or area zoning regulations with respect to structural characteristics and type of industry.

Technological factors such as availability of power, raw materials, or transportation systems may dictate the unique location of a particular plant. Energy-dependent activities such as aluminum reduction need to be located near relatively inexpensive and plentiful sources of energy. Mining operations have to be located near the origin of the raw resources. Also, the processing plants for these types of resources are generally located near rivers or railway systems for economical transportation.

Intangible factors affecting future costs of a plant can include the tax structure of the local community and the community's attitude toward the type of enterprise. Local land and construction costs are tangible factors that must be compared between communities. Also, the quality and availability of the local labor supply can have significant effects on wage rates and training costs. Some plants have located labor-oriented plants in the southern United States or even foreign countries to take advantage of cheaper labor. However, wage rates can change with unionization, and they are not always commensurate with productivity. The trend of U.S. firms to locate outside this country has lessened with rapidly increasing wages in foreign countries, but some industries with high labor content can still lower costs by locating abroad. The political aspects of such a move should be weighed heavily. The stability of the country and its attitude toward foreign investment are critical factors. In some countries, facilities have been expropriated by the foreign government as a result of political maneuvers.

Development of pollution-control standards has added a new dimension to the location analysis of plants that emit any type of air or water pollution. Standards vary within states or communities and thus can be a decisive factor in choosing a location. Urban areas such as New York and Los Angeles have particularly stringent air-emission standards. In some cases, these standards have not been enforced, in the interest of a productive economy. However, the pollution-control problem is a relatively new one and should continue to pose problems for management not only in location studies, but also in increased plant costs to meet emission standards.

Locating a Single Plant

The decision regarding the location of a plant may be determined by one of the previously discussed factors, such as energy needs or managerial preference. However, even the consideration of these factors alone usually results in several feasible alternatives for plant location. The final decision then is normally based on cost considerations, although other criteria, such as proximity to market and speed of distribution, may be relevant. Once a set of feasible locations has been determined, an optimization model or a heuristic can then be used to find the alternative that results in the minimum production and distribution costs. Assuming that management's objective is to minimize the total cost of production and distribution, let us consider an example problem in locating an additional plant to an existing system. We use the transportation method of linear programming to minimize distribution costs.

Take the Electrovox problem of Chapter 2. We assume that demand for CB radios has increased 20 percent, and this is reflected in increased demand at each warehouse. Let us further assume that management has limited the choice of new plant locations to St. Louis and Atlanta. Figure 7-3 depicts the geographic nature of the distribution problem. Table 7-1 updates the Electrovox problem to include the increase in demand.

The plants at Washington, D.C., Denver, and Los Angeles have monthly production capacities of 50, 80, and 120 respectively. The monthly customer demands at regional warehouses are now 108 at New York, 84 at Chicago, 48 at Dallas, and 60 at San Francisco. The matrix of per-unit shipping costs is presented in Table 7-1.

In Chapter 2, we solved the distribution problem (with reduced demand) by Vogel's Approximation Method. This heuristic reached a final distribution cost of $203,000, an amount only .49 percent more than the optimal cost of $202,000. Let us assume in our analysis that we have an optimization procedure for transportation

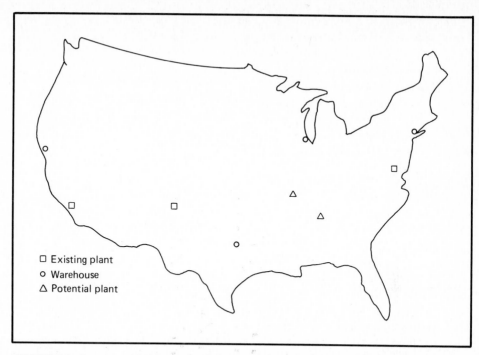

FIGURE 7-3   Locations of Plants and Warehouses, and Potential Plant Locations for Electrovox

Table 7-1   Data for Electrovox Location Problem

	UNIT SHIPPING COSTS				
	TO WAREHOUSE				*PLANT CAPACITY (1,000s)*
FROM PLANT	*NEW YORK*	*CHICAGO*	*DALLAS*	*SAN FRANCISCO*	
Washington, D.C.	.80	.90	1.10	1.60	50
Denver	1.20	.70	.50	.80	80
Los Angeles	1.40	1.00	.60	.70	120
?					100
Demand (1,000s)	108	84	48	60	350
					300

models at our disposal. We can use this procedure to determine the minimum distribution costs when either the St. Louis or Atlanta alternative is considered.

The management at Electrovox has decided that the new plant should have a capacity of 100 per month. This represents 50 units of unused capacity in order to accommodate future demand. Because of differences in local wage rates and overhead, the per-unit production costs of the three existing plants are $9, $10, and $8 respectively, at Washington, D.C., Denver, and Los Angeles. It is estimated that differential production costs would amount to $9 at St. Louis and $8 at Atlanta. The monthly overhead for plant and equipment costs is estimated to be $6,000 at St. Louis and $8,000 at Atlanta over the life of the plant. We are now ready to analyze the location problem on a cost basis. Table 7-2 reflects the combined per-unit shipping and production costs when the St. Louis location is considered; we arrived at the estimated combined costs of shipping and production for St. Louis by adding $9 to each of the shipping costs from St. Louis to New York ($1.00), Chicago ($.50), Dallas ($.60), and San Francisco ($1.10).

Using the MODI method or some other procedure that optimizes standard transportation models, we can determine the optimal production/distribution schedule. In Table 7-3 we present the optimal solution.

The numbers in the upper left-hand corner of the cells in Table 7-3 are the unit production and shipping costs, whereas the numbers in the middle of the cells represent amounts produced and shipped. Thus, the optimal strategy is to produce and ship according to the following plan:

Washington D.C.	to	New York	50
Denver	to	New York	30
Los Angeles	to	New York	12
Los Angeles	to	Dallas	48
Los Angeles	to	San Francisco	60
St. Louis	to	New York	16
St. Louis	to	Chicago	84

Table 7-2   Combined Shipping and Production Costs

	TOTAL COSTS				
	TO WAREHOUSE				PLANT CAPACITY (1,000s)
FROM PLANT	NEW YORK	CHICAGO	DALLAS	SAN FRANCISCO	
Washington, D.C.	9.80	9.90	10.10	10.60	50
Denver	11.20	10.70	10.50	10.80	80
Los Angeles	9.40	9.00	8.60	8.70	120
St. Louis	10.00	9.50	9.60	10.10	100
Demand (1,000s)	108	84	48	60	350 / 300

Table 7-3 Optimal Production / Distribution Strategy for St. Louis Location

FROM \ TO	NEW YORK	CHICAGO	DALLAS	SAN FRANCISCO	PLANT CAPACITY (1,000s)
Washington, D.C.	9.80 / 50	9.90	10.10	10.60	50
Denver	11.20 / 30	10.70	10.50	10.80	80
Los Angeles	9.40 / 12	9.00	8.60 / 48	8.70 / 60	120
St. Louis	10.00 / 16	9.50 / 84	9.60	10.10	100
Demand (1,000s)	108	84	48	60	300 / 350

The total monthly distribution and production cost for this strategy is 50,000(9.80) + 30,000(11.20) + 12,000(9.40) + 48,000(8.60) + 60,000(8.70) + 16,000(10.00) + 84,000(9.50) = \$2,831,600.

To evaluate the Atlanta alternative, we again use a linear programming optimization procedure to determine the best production/distribution strategy. The optimal solution for this alternative is presented in Table 7-4. When the Atlanta location is used, the optimal production/distribution plan is:

Washington D.C.	to	New York	50
Denver	to	Chicago	30
Los Angeles	to	Chicago	12
Los Angeles	to	Dallas	48
Los Angeles	to	San Francisco	60
Atlanta	to	New York	58
Atlanta	to	Chicago	42

The total monthly production/distribution cost for the plan is 50,000(9.80) + 30,000(10.70) + 12,000(9.00) + 48,000(8.60) + 60,000(8.70) + 58,000(9.00) + 42,000 (8.70) = \$2,741,200.

We can now compare the two alternatives on an overall cost basis. We assume here that differences in total cost will result only from differences between distribution, production, and building and equipment costs. For the St. Louis location, the overall costs may be summarized as:

Production costs	\$2,610,000
Distribution costs	221,600
Building and equipment costs	6,000
Total costs	\$2,837,600

Table 7-4   Optimal Production / Distribution Strategy for Atlanta Location

FROM \ TO	NEW YORK	CHICAGO	DALLAS	SAN FRANCISCO	PLANT CAPACITY (1,000s)
Washington, D.C.	9.80 \ 50	9.90	10.10	10.60	50
Denver	11.20	10.70 \ 30	10.50	10.80	80
Los Angeles	9.40	9.00 \ 12	8.60 \ 48	8.70 \ 60	120
Atlanta	9.00 \ 58	8.70 \ 42	8.60	9.30	100
Demand (1,000s)	108	84	48	60	300 / 350

For the Atlanta location, we have:

Production costs	$2,510,000
Distribution costs	231,200
Building and equipment costs	8,000
Total costs	$2,749,200

Based on cost criteria alone, it appears that Atlanta is the more effective location for a new plant.

You may wonder what happened to the additional 50,000 units of production capacity. From Tables 7-3 and 7-4 we can see that the Denver plant absorbed all 50,000 units of slack for either locational alternative. This in reality may not be an acceptable production schedule. To bring the Denver plant down from 80,000 to 30,000 units of production may have negative consequences that are not directly measurable in monetary terms. Later we shall discuss decision making with multiple-criteria objectives.

MULTIPLE WAREHOUSE LOCATION

In the preceding section, we considered the location of an additional plant to meet demand and minimize production/distribution costs. We can generalize that same problem to consider more than one plant. In this section, however, we apply the multiple facility location analysis to warehouses; there are usually more warehouses than plants in a distribution system, and warehouses are less subject to the intangible decision factors often associated with plants.

Many approaches have been developed to solve warehouse location problems. Exact optimization procedures such as branch and bound have been developed by

Effroymson and Ray and Khumawala; these have been successfully applied in actual practice.[4] Computer simulation is a valuable tool in evaluating various warehouse system configurations. However, simulation is not capable of generating solutions; rather, it evaluates them. Simulation is particularly effective in analyzing complex systems in which distribution decisions interact with other operations, such as inventory. Markland used simulation to evaluate field warehouse location configurations and inventory levels for the Ralston Purina Company.[5] Another common approach to warehouse location involves heuristic decision rules. Heuristics are necessary for solving really large-scale problems, since exact optimization techniques are not computationally practical. To give you an idea why less efficient optimization procedures cannot always be used in the analysis of real-world problems, consider a warehouse location problem presented by Khumawala and Whybark.[6] The following characteristics pertain to a medium-sized manufacturing firm that distributes only in the United States:

5,000	customers or demand centers
100	potential warehouse locations
5	producing plants
15	products
4	shipping classes
100	transportation-rate variables

In warehouse location problems, we are usually concerned with how many warehouses to have and where to locate them. Other relevant issues are modes of transportation and appropriate inventory levels to maintain between plant, warehouse, and customer. In our initial analysis here, we will consider the problem of how many warehouses to open and where to locate them. At first we assume that each warehouse has sufficient capacity to serve all customers; thus we have to open only one warehouse. Other warehouses will only be opened in order to further reduce distribution costs. The basic tradeoffs involve variable transportation costs versus fixed costs of operating a warehouse. This particular problem is called the simple warehouse location problem. Let's look at a simple but effective heuristic by Khumawala for solving it.[7]

---

[4]M.A. Effroymson and T.A. Ray, "A Branch-Bound Algorithm for Plant Location," *Operations Research*, 14 (May–June 1966), 361–68; B.M. Khumawala, "An Efficient Branch and Bound Algorithm for the Warehouse Location Problem," *Management Science*, 18 (August 1972), 718–31.

[5]R.E. Markland, "Analyzing Geographically Discrete Warehousing Networks by Computer Simulation," *Decision Sciences*, 4 (April 1973), 216–36.

[6]B.M. Khumawala and D.C. Whybark, "A Comparison of Some Recent Warehouse Location Techniques," *The Logistics Review*, vol. 7 (1971).

[7]B.M. Khumawala, "An Efficient Heuristic Procedure for the Uncapacitated Warehouse Location Problem," *Naval Research Logistics Quarterly*, 20, no. 1 (March 1973), 109–21.

Warehouse Location Example

Consider the Automotive Parts Supply Co., which distributes car parts to five major customer demand centers in Los Angeles, Cleveland, San Antonio, New York, and Atlanta. The firm is considering four potential warehouse locations to facilitate distribution: Salt Lake City, Philadelphia, Chicago, and Dallas. In order to open a warehouse, the company must pay a fixed cost that includes the amortized cost of building the warehouse, inventory, taxes, insurance, and wages. The variable warehouse-to-customer costs include FOB cost at the warehouse, warehouse handling cost, and the warehouse-to-customer transportation costs. Figure 7-4 illustrates the geographical nature of the problems.

In Table 7-5, we present the fixed warehouse costs and distribution costs from warehouse to customer. The distribution costs in the table each represent the total yearly distribution cost if supplied entirely from the warehouse in the particular row. Note that customers will receive all their supply from the single warehouse that is the cheapest open alternative.

The heuristic procedure we consider is called by Khumawala the largest omega rule. The heuristic is based on the concept of opening and closing various warehouses based on some minimum and maximum savings calculations. The heuristic is quite effective, as it often yields the optimal solution. On large, real-world problems, the error (if it exists) is usually no more than 1 or 2 percent.

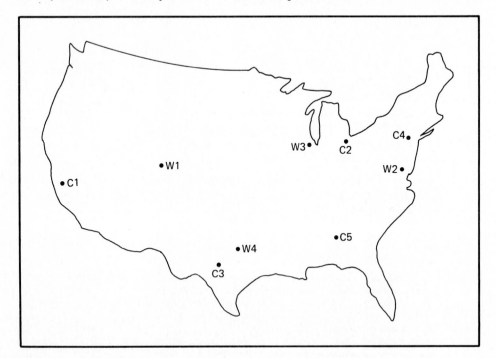

FIGURE 7-4 Automotive Parts Supply Warehouse Location Problem

Table 7-5   Fixed Costs and Warehouse Distribution Costs to Each of 5 Customers

		DISTRIBUTION COSTS FROM WAREHOUSE TO CUSTOMER				
FIXED COSTS PER YEAR		LOS ANGELES	CLEVE-LAND	SAN ANTONIO	NEW YORK	ATLANTA
9,000	Salt Lake City	8,000	20,000	16,000	36,000	28,000
6,000	Philadelphia	24,000	12,000	20,000	8,000	16,000
6,000	Chicago	18,000	8,000	12,000	10,000	10,000
8,000	Dallas	16,000	12,000	10,000	24,000	18,000

Steps of the Heuristic.   First we calculate a lower bound on the savings that could be achieved by opening any single warehouse. If this lower bound is greater than zero, we automatically fix that warehouse open. The minimum distribution savings for opening a warehouse can be calculated by comparing the distribution cost with those of all other warehouses. For the Salt Lake City location, we calculate the minimum savings by looking down each column in Table 7-5 to see how much (if any) the distribution cost to each customer could be reduced if supplied by Salt Lake City. In column 1, we save at least $8,000 ($16,000 − $8,000) if a warehouse at Salt Lake City is opened. In the other four columns, no savings is found above the other best choice for each customer. Thus we may find the net minimum savings by subtracting the fixed costs of operating the warehouse at Salt Lake City. The lower bound or minimum savings is:

$$\text{MINSAV}(1) = [8{,}000 + 0 + 0 + 0 + 0] - \$9{,}000 = -\$1{,}000$$

Calculating the minimum savings for the other three potential warehouses, we obtain:

$$\text{MINSAV}(2) = [0 + 0 + 0 + 2{,}000 + 0] - 6{,}000 = -\$4{,}000$$
$$\text{MINSAV}(3) = [0 + 4{,}000 + 0 + 0 + 6{,}000] - 6{,}000 = \$4{,}000 \quad \text{open}$$
$$\text{MINSAV}(4) = [0 + 0 + 2{,}000 + 0 + 0] - 8{,}000 = -\$6{,}000$$

Since the minimum savings for warehouse 3 is greater than zero, we fix warehouse 3 open. In case all minimum savings are less than zero, we open the one warehouse whose savings is largest.

In step 2, we calculate a maximum savings for these warehouses that have been neither opened nor closed (free). The maximum savings is calculated by comparing the distribution costs of the free warehouse with those of the ones that have been fixed open. Other warehouses that are free or fixed closed are ignored. Thus, the maximum savings for warehouses 1, 2, and 4 are calculated as:

$$\text{MAXSAV}(1) = [10{,}000 + 0 + 0 + 0 + 0] - 9{,}000 = \$1{,}000$$
$$\text{MAXSAV}(2) = [0 + 0 + 0 + 2{,}000 + 0] - 6{,}000 = -\$4{,}000 \quad \text{close}$$
$$\text{MAXSAV}(4) = [2{,}000 + 0 + 2{,}000 + 0 + 0] - 8{,}000 = -\$4{,}000 \quad \text{close}$$

In a MAXSAV calculation we can always close any warehouses whose maximum savings is negative. Thus we should close warehouses 2 and 4. Warehouse 1 has a maximum savings of $1,000 and it is not obvious what we should do. However, Khumawala's heuristic proceeds by opening the warehouse whose MAXSAV calculation yields the highest positive value. (This in fact might not be optimal, but it is usually a good rule of thumb). We therefore open warehouse 1. All warehouses have now been opened or closed and the heuristic procedure is completed. Had some warehouses been left undecided (neither open nor closed) we would repeat the MAXSAV calculation opening or closing additional warehouses. The MINSAV calculation is used only on the first iteration; subsequent calculations involve repeated use of the MAXSAV rule.

The final solution is to open the Salt Lake City and Chicago warehouses. Los Angeles is supplied by Salt Lake City; all other customers are supplied by the Chicago warehouse. The minimum annual cost is $63,000 and is broken down as:

Fixed costs	9,000 + 6,000	= 15,000
Transportation costs	8,000 + 8,000 + 12,000 + 10,000 + 10,000	= 48,000
Total costs		$63,000

Extensions

The simple plant location model has several applications, especially when fixed costs and distribution costs are the main concerns. However, many real-world location problems require generalizations of the model. The most obvious generalization is the case where the warehouses actually have limited capacity and cannot uniquely satisfy all customer demand. The problem is known as the capacitated warehouse-location problem and has been studied by Khumawala and others.[8] The solution procedures are in most cases adaptations of the procedures for the simple plant location problem.

Multiple Objectives

So far, we have assumed that managerial objectives were to minimize costs. In actual location problems, however, cost minimization is usually not the only objective sought by management. Other objectives may include stabilized employment at plants, contract requirements, minimizing inventories, balanced workloads at plants or warehouses, and special treatment of particular customers.

Research is in progress to develop methods that will help achieve multiple and, in some cases, conflicting objectives. One successful approach has been *goal pro-*

---

[8]See G. Sã, "Branch-and-Bound and Approximate Solutions to the Capacitated Plant-Location Problem," *Operations Research*, 17, no. 6 (November–December 1969), 1005–15.

Table 7-6   Demand Forecasts

		PERIOD			
CUSTOMER ZONE	1	2	3	4	5
Milwaukee, Wisc.	0.0	433,235	866,471	1,299,710	1,732,940
Chicago, Ill.	0.0	2,145,070	4,290,140	6,435,200	8,580,270
Bloomington, Ill.	0.0	35,074	70,148	105,223	140,297
Detroit, Mich.	4,459,800	4,459,800	4,459,800	4,459,800	4,459,800
Lansing, Mich.	353,426	353,426	353,426	353,426	353,426
Kalamazoo, Mich.	283,870	283,870	283,870	283,870	283,870
Cleveland, Ohio	2,756,360	2,756,360	2,756,360	2,756,360	2,756,360
Columbus, Ohio	1,142,360	1,142,360	1,142,360	1,142,360	1,142,360
Toledo, Ohio	1,264,290	1,264,290	1,264,290	1,264,290	1,264,290
Cincinnati, Ohio	1,445,380	1,589,920	1,734,450	1,878,990	2,023,530
Dayton, Ohio	881,624	969,786	1,057,950	1,146,110	1,234,270
Akron, Ohio	859,025	859,025	859,025	859,025	859,025
Benton Harbor, Mich.	0.0	62,668	125,337	188,005	250,673
Indianapolis, Ind.	1,166,790	1,283,470	1,400,150	1,156,830	1,633,510
Ft. Wayne, Ind.	388,384	388,384	388,384	388,384	388,384

SOURCE: D. Sweeney and R. Tatham, "An Improved Long-Run Model for Multiple Warehouse Location," *Management Science*, 22, no. 7 (March 1976), 748–58.

gramming. Goal programming is a type of mathematical programming in which constraints are defined and various goals are stated and ranked according to priority. Keeping within the constraints, highest-priority goals are satisfied first. Lower-priority goals are satisfied only if higher-priority goals are not sacrificed. Thus, in location problems, we may first attempt to achieve stable employment, second cost minimization, and third minimal inventories. Lee and Moore have developed a goal programming model for distribution problems.[9]

Long-Range Warehouse Location Analysis

We have thus far considered the location of plants or warehouses under static conditions. That is, we have determined the best locations at a given point in time. Since plants and warehouses represent a long-term commitment, it would be helpful to analyze locations over extended periods of time. Emerging markets and changing demand patterns can cause shifts in the desired locations of warehouses. Sweeney and Tatham have developed a computerized procedure that uses mixed integer programming combined with dynamic programming to determine the optimal sequence of warehouse configurations over multiple periods.[10]

---

[9]S.M. Lee and L.J. Moore, "Optimizing Transportation Problems with Multiple Objectives," *AIIE Transactions*, 5 (December 1973), 333–38.

[10]D. Sweeney and R. Tatham, "An Improved Long-Run Model for Multiple Warehouse Location," *Management Science*, 22, no. 7 (March 1976), 748–58.

Table 7-7   Warehouse and Plant Capacities (lbs. × 1,000)

WAREHOUSE		PERIOD				
LOCATION	NO.	1	2	3	4	5
Toledo	1	10,000	10,000	10,000	10,000	10,000
Chicago	2	7,000	7,000	10,000	10,000	10,000
Detroit	3	8,500	8,500	8,500	8,500	8,500
Cleveland	4	7,500	7,500	7,500	7,500	7,500
Cincinnati	5	12,000	12,000	12,000	12,000	12,000
PLANT						
LOCATION	NO.					
Akron	1	12,000	12,000	—	—	—
Indianapolis	2	18,000	18,000	18,000	18,000	18,000
Toledo	3	—	—	12,000	12,000	12,000

Let us examine an example problem from Sweeney and Tatham, which consists of two plants, five possible warehouse locations, 15 customer zones, and a five-year planning horizon. The demand forecasts for the customer zones are presented in Table 7-6. These demand forecasts reflect the company plans to begin marketing its product in the northern and western regions at the beginning of period 2. Throughout the planning horizon, demand is expected to increase slightly in the southern regions and heavily in the new market areas of Chicago and Milwaukee. The warehouse and plant capacities are shown in Table 7-7, and warehouse fixed costs in Table 7-8. The variable shipping costs were taken to be $.006 per mile between plant and warehouse, and $.01 per mile between warehouse and customer. The variable costs of storing and handling goods were taken to be constant and equal for all warehouses, and thus were not included in the analysis.

Assuming it costs $100,000 to close a warehouse and $200,000 to open a new site, the Sweeney and Tatham model produces the following solution over the five

Table 7-8   Fixed Costs for Warehouses

WAREHOUSE LOCATION NO./ YEAR		FIXED COST (× 1,000)				
		1	2	3	4	5
Toledo	1	300	300	300	300	300
Chicago	2	300	300	300	400	400
Detroit	3	300	300	300	300	300
Cleveland	4	320	320	320	320	320
Cincinnati	5	360	360	360	360	360

years:

YEAR	CONFIGURATION
1	(1, 5)
2	(1, 5)
3	(1, 2, 5)
4	(1, 2, 5)
5	(1, 2, 5)
Total cost	$10,569,000

Thus, the optimal configuration consists of warehouses at Toledo and Cincinnati for the first two years, with the Chicago warehouse being opened for the last three. The analysis in the problem was for a single product, but the general methodology can be extended to include multiple products.

LOCATION MODELS IN THE PUBLIC SECTOR

Location models in the public sector are mainly based on providing services rather than distributing a physical product. Some of the techniques for locating service facilities are similar to distributional location methods but focus more on the geographic concentration of users and their needs.

The location of service-oriented facilities has been much discussed in the literature. The location of hospitals and regional health services has been studied by several researchers, including Abernathy and Hershey.[11] Kolesar and Walker have studied the dynamic relocation of fire companies in New York City in order to provide fire protection to each region at all times.[12] Other public location models include the locating of police protection, sewage treatment plants, and public parks and recreation facilities.[13] These types of location models can be more difficult to analyze in many cases, since multiple objectives and political constraints exist. Optimal location of public facilities depends on several demographic characteristics as well as required response times and priorities of service. In order to demonstrate the nature of locating service facilities, we take a brief look at applications involving ambulance services, nuclear power plants, and cash management services.

---

[11]W.J. Abernathy and J.C. Hershey, "A Spatial-Allocation Model for Regional Health-Services Planning," *Operations Research*, 20 (May–June 1972), 629–42.

[12]P. Kolesar and W.E. Walker, "An Algorithm for the Dynamic Relocation of Fire Companies," *Operations Research*, 22 (March–April 1974), 249–74.

[13]C. Revelle, D. Marks, and J. Liebman, "An Analysis of Private and Public Sector Location Models," *Management Science*, 16, no. 11 (July 1970), 692–707.

Location of Emergency Ambulance Services

The location of ambulances has been studied in major U.S. cities such as Los Angeles (Fitzsimmons)[14] and New York (Savas).[15] Let's consider the problem of improving ambulance service in New York City. Prior to the Savas study, New York's policy had been to station 109 ambulances at a total of 49 hospitals. Each hospital was in a designated district and sent out ambulances in response to requests only from within that district. In order to improve the ambulance response times, the city decided to try satellite garages for the ambulances. Any analytical procedure had to consider where the ambulance satellite garages should be located, the locations of hospitals, the geographic distribution and frequency of calls within each district, and finally, the number of ambulances.

In order to analyze this complex problem the city used a computer simulation model to estimate actual response times and thus the performance of various location alternatives. The analysis was restricted to the Kings County Hospital district in Brooklyn, as shown in Figure 7-5. The average response time with the old system (housing ambulances at the hospital) was 13.5 minutes. Various location alternatives were designed and simulated. Finally, the analysts tried an entirely new approach, in which the hospital districts were ignored. Ambulances located at satellite garages would simply proceed to the nearest available hospital after picking up a patient. This system required a central dispatch facility to coordinate the status of requests with each ambulance and hospital. The simulation model predicted the best overall results from the system. If ten ambulances were located at demand centers in the Kings County district, response times were shown to drop 30 percent.

Nuclear Power Plant Location

Nuclear power plant location differs significantly from manufacturing plant location in that the main objective is to provide energy for nearby users. Decisions as to where to build nuclear power plants are to a large extent determined by political realities and the willingness of a community to accept such a plant. However, the state of Washington, through its Energy Research Group, wanted to determine the most economically viable alternatives for nuclear plant location.

By 1981, available hydropower resources in the Pacific Northwest and all known area resources for coal-fired thermal plants would have been developed. Historical growth in demand for power in the Pacific Northwest has occurred at rates of 6 to 7 percent annually, and it appears that the incremental demand growth arising between 1981 and 1992 would have to be met by nuclear thermal plants.

---

[14]J.A. Fitzsimmons, "A Methodology for Emergency Ambulance Deployment," *Management Science*, 19 (February 1973), 627–36.

[15]E. Savas, "Simulation and Cost-Effectiveness Analysis of New York's Emergency Ambulance Service," *Management Science*, 15 (August 1969), B608–27.

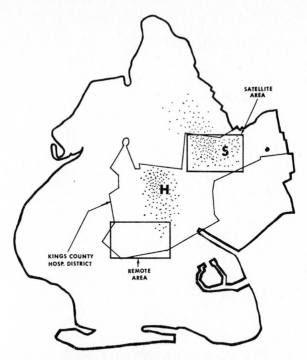

FIGURE 7-5   Map of Brooklyn, Showing Hospital District and Areas near Hospital and Satellite

SOURCE: E. Savas, "Simulation and Cost-Effectiveness Analysis of New York's Emergency Ambulance Service," *Management Science*, 15 (August 1969), B608–27.

Dutton, Hinman, and Millham have developed a model that optimizes nuclear power plant location with respect to capital-construction, operating, and transmission costs.[16] Their procedure uses the simplex method in conjunction with a branch-and-bound process to ensure integer solutions. In Figure 7-6, the layout of the problem studied is presented. The squares designate current power sources, the large circles are demand centers, and the small numbered circles represent potential 1,000-megawatt nuclear plant locations. In analyzing the problem, starting and construction costs were annualized at 14 percent; variable operating costs are measured in mills per kilowatt hour. The model is essentially a two-product model, as peak and average annual power requirements are model constraints. Optimal plant locations are developed for future demand growth rates of 4, 5, 6, and 7 percent. For the 6 percent growth rate, the projected optimal solution is to build plants at all 13 locations except number 4. The combined annual site-dependent

---

[16]R. Dutton, G. Hinman, and C.B. Millham, "The Optimal Location of Nuclear-Power Facilities in the Pacific Northwest," *Operations Research*, 22, no. 3 (May–June 1974), 478–87.

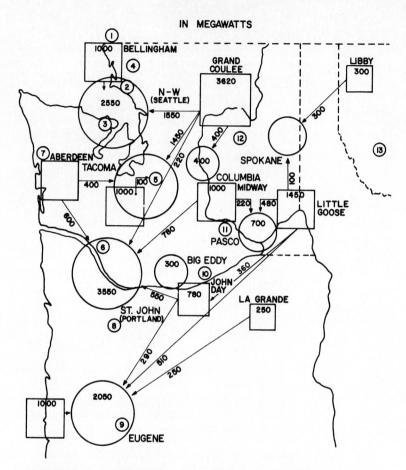

FIGURE 7-6 The Projected Power–Supply Demand–Distribution Pattern for 1981, and the Locations of 13 Proposed 1,000-Megawatt Power Plants

SOURCE: R. Dutton, G. Hinman, and C.B. Millham, "The Optimal Location of Nuclear-Power Facilities in the Pacific Northwest," *Operations Research*, 22, no. 3 (May–June 1974), 478–87.

operating, transmission, and amortized capital-construction costs amounted to $75,700,000.

Cash Management

Our last location example applies location theory to making the best use of monetary resources. The first problem we consider is called the lockbox problem and involves the effective placement of receiving locations for large payments received. Consider a large firm that receives large payments from customers on a monthly basis. The checks are normally mailed by a given deadline. However, several days can elapse before the U.S. mail system and bank clearing system bring the check to be deposited in the recipient's account. Several days of interest on millions of dollars represents a significant amount of lost interest. The question then becomes where to locate lockboxes throughout banks in the United States in order to credit payments to the receiver's accounts as quickly as possible. Relevant data include the speed of the U.S. mail, cost of maintaining a lockbox, check-clearing times, and total dollars involved.

Diametrically opposed to the lockbox problem is the cash disbursement problem.[17] Here, it is the objective of the payee to get his payment postmarked by the deadline but then take the maximum amount of time to clear his account. Maximizing day-dollar float requires data pertaining to check-clearing times between major U.S. banks. Such data are available from certain cash management services. These commercial services also perform a location analysis for clients. The costs for considering 100 potential bank account locations runs as high as $5,000; interestingly, one of the authors has performed a similar analysis with a heuristic, resulting in a total computer cost of less than $2. Some of the quantitative techniques used in solving these cash management problems are very similar to uncapacitated warehouse location problems, as any single account can handle all transactions. The cash disbursement location analysis offers a sophisticated way to generate more revenue for the firm, but only as long as the Federal Reserve System continues to absorb the float.

SUMMARY

In this chapter we have considered the facility planning problems of capacity planning and facility location. Capacity planning was related to priority production planning tasks such as corporate planning, aggregate planning, master production scheduling and materials requirements planning. Issues in measuring capacity were presented as well as capacity concepts such as best operating level and economies of scale. Long-range capacity planning was found to be an integral part of facility location and expansion decisions.

We have considered location models for a wide variety of applications. In the addition of a single manufacturing plant, we found the transportation method of linear programming to be useful in determining minimal distribution costs. Combining distribution costs with plant fixed and operating costs and subjective factors, we can select the best plant location.

For locating multiple plants or warehouses, several optimization procedures exist. We studied an effective heuristic for solving the uncapacitated warehouse location problem. Generalizations of the problem include the capacitated warehouse location problem and location problems with multiple objectives. We also consid-

---

[17]G. Cornuejols, M. Fisher, and G.M. Nemhauser, "Location of Bank Accounts to Optimize Float: An Analytic Study of Exact and Approximate Algorithms," *Management Science*, 23 (April 1977), 789–810.

ered a model that determines the optimal warehouse system configuration over a long-range period of time.

Location theory has many uses in the location of services or public facilities; health services, public parks, and recreation areas are prime examples. We examined three widely diverse applications in ambulance location, nuclear power plant location, and cash management.

All models and procedures studied require accurate data, which are often difficult to obtain. Finally, these procedures provide a rational basis from which to make location decisions; the final location decisions incorporate not only these results but extraneous factors and the subjectivity of the decision maker.

_____ **SOLVED PROBLEMS** _____

Problem Statement

The Zoro Lawn Mower Co. is planning to build a new plant to manufacture a new type of weed trimmer. Potential plant sites have been narrowed down to Oklahoma City and Mobile. The fixed costs of debt, utilities, and taxes are $275,000 for the Oklahoma City site and $255,000 for the Mobile location. The variable costs, which involve labor, materials, and transportation, are $16 and $18 per unit respectively.

1. If the Zoro Co. anticipates sales of 15,000 units, which location should it choose?
2. Suppose that the marketing department projects the following probabilities for annual sales:

SALES VOLUME	PROBABILITY
12,000	.10
15,000	.40
20,000	.30
25,000	.20

Which site would you select?

Solution

1. At a volume of 15,000 units, the annual costs are:

$$\text{Oklahoma City:} \quad \$275,000 + 16(15,000) = \$515,000$$

$$\text{Mobile:} \quad \$255,000 + 18(15,000) = \$525,000$$

Choose Oklahoma City based on cost criteria alone.

2. The solution to part 2 depends upon the company's attitude toward risk. However, calculating the expected volume yields:

$$\text{Expected volume} = .10(12,000) + .40(15,000) + .30(20,000) + .20(25,000)$$
$$= 1,200 + 6,000 + 6,000 + 5,000$$
$$= 18,200 \text{ units}$$

Probabilistically, 18,200 units are expected to sell. Based on this figure, the Oklahoma City site should be selected.

Problem Statement

A firm is considering the establishment of some warehouses to reduce distribution costs and time delays in getting its products from a central plant to their four primary markets. Questions arise as to how many warehouses to establish and where to locate them. The table below reflects fixed annual operating costs and total transportation costs for supplying a given customer entirely from a given warehouse. Which warehouses should be established?

POTENTIAL WAREHOUSES	FIXED COSTS	CUSTOMERS			
		A	B	C	D
St. Louis	50,000	75,000	50,000	55,000	20,000
Memphis	45,000	80,000	45,000	60,000	30,000
Jacksonville	48,000	100,000	35,000	70,000	40,000

Solution

Using the savings calculations of Khumawala's heuristic, we find:

MINSAV (St. Louis) $= [5,000 + 0 + 5,000 + 10,000] - 50,000 = -\$30,000$

MINSAV (Memphis) $= [0 + 0 + 0 + 0] - 45,000 = -\$45,000$

MINSAV (Jacksonville) $= [0 + 10,000 + 0 + 0] - 48,000 = -\$38,000$

Since the St. Louis warehouse yields the largest MINSAV value, we open it.

Next we calculate maximum savings of the Memphis and Jacksonville warehouses, given that the St. Louis warehouse is open:

MAXSAV (Memphis) $= [0 + 5,000 + 0 + 0] - 45,000 = -\$40,000$

MAXSAV (Jacksonville) $= [0 + 15,000 + 0 + 0] - 48,000 = -\$33,000$

Since both remaining warehouses have maximum benefits less than zero, both are closed, and the best solution is to open only the St. Louis warehouse at an annual cost of $250,000.

REVIEW QUESTIONS

1. What is capacity?
2. How might capacity be measured for the following enterprises?
   a. Consulting firm
   b. Electronic calculator plant
   c. Nuclear plant
   d. Public high school
3. What are some factors that should be considered in capacity planning in addition to economies of scale?
4. Relate the three levels of capacity planning to three levels of priority planning.
5. What is the main purpose of using the transportation method of linear programming in locating a simple plant?
6. Besides distribution and fixed and operating costs, what other factors should be considered in locating plants?
7. Computer simulation can be useful in analyzing location problems, but what must you provide the simulator?
8. In multiple-objective problems, what are some of the more likely managerial objectives in addition to cost minimization?
9. How is goal programming useful in facility location?
10. When might it be advantageous for a firm to locate a plant in a foreign country?
11. In what ways does warehouse location differ from plant location?
12. In what ways does the location of service facilities differ from the location of manufacturing facilities?
13. Explain how the MINSAV and MAXSAV calculations of Khumawala's heuristic can be used to open and close warehouses.
14. What is the difference between static and dynamic plant location problems?
15. List the quantitative techniques (those we have mentioned in this chapter) that apply in analyzing location problems.
16. Sometimes the most rational or economical location as calculated by a quantitative model is not chosen. Explain.
17. Discuss the advantages of locating a large, centralized manufacturing facility as opposed to several decentralized facilities. Discuss the disadvantages.
18. Which factors do you think would play a prominent role in the location of each of the following?

a. A large plant for the manufacture of washers and dryers
b. Nuclear power plants
c. Oil company headquarters
d. A retail outlet for exclusive men's clothing

PROBLEMS

---

1. Southwest Metals is concerned about the future capacity in three of its
   departments. Current capacities in the turning, milling, and grinding areas are:

DEPARTMENT	CAPACITY HOURS / MO.
Turning	800
Milling	950
Grinding	1,000

   Annual demand averages 750 hours per month, and has been growing at a rate
   of 12 percent per year. There is a one-year lead time required to add capacity
   to any department.
   a. In how many months will each department reach its capacity limit? Assume
      a demand of 750 in month 1, and a constant rate of growth in each month
      of a given year.
   b. Assuming that this is Janauary 1984, how much additional capacity will be
      required in 1990?
   c. How should management time-phase capacity additions so that there are no
      shortages in any department through 1990?

2. Precision Manufacturing Co. has developed a tentative master production
   schedule for their primary families of products. They want to do a rough-cut
   capacity analysis for all work centers in order to plan any required changes in
   the master production schedule. Shown below is the load profile for the work
   centers in standard hours for next week.

FAMILY OF PRODUCTS	SAW	FORGE	WELD	MACHINE	LATHE	HEAT-TREAT
Mfg. tools	30	42	18	76	114	10
Shop presses	44	2	26	84	72	4
Cylinders	14	4	6	98	238	4
Pumps	6	1	1	200	110	1
TOTAL	94	49	51	458	534	19

Given weekly capacities of 120, 80, 80, 400, 480, and 40 hours respectively for the saw, forge, weld, machine, lathe, and heat-treat work centers respectively, what does rough-cut capacity planning indicate about the master schedule?

3. A curve-fit analysis has yielded the following relationship between average cost per unit of output and volume of output.

$$C(V) = .25(V - 5000)^2 + 75V$$

In the above nonlinear function, V represents volume and $C(V)$ the resulting cost per unit. Determine the volume V that will minimize per unit cost of output.

4. A company is trying to decide how much capacity their new plant should have. Demand is uncertain and the annual cost of providing capacity is $100,000 per each 100 units of monthly output capacity. Assume that there is a $200 cost for each unit of lost sales due to insufficient capacity. Assuming that sales occur in multiples of 100, the probability distribution reflecting the likelihood of monthly sales levels is:

MONTHLY DEMAND	PROBABILITY OF DEMAND
0	.05
100	.10
200	.15
300	.20
400	.25
500	.15
600	.07
700	.03

How much capacity should the new plant have in order to minimize the costs of providing capacity and lost sales?

5. Annual demand for a manufacturing company is expected to be at one of 4 possible levels. The forecasted probabilities are:

DEMAND	PROBABILITY
4,000	.25
5,000	.40
7,000	.20
10,000	.15

Revenues are $30 per unit. The existing manufacturing facility has annual fixed operating costs of $100,000. Variable manufacturing costs are $4.00, $2.50, $2.70, and $3.50 for the 4,000, 5,000, 7,000, and 10,000 output levels, respectively. Management is considering expanding the existing facility. The expanded facility would incur fixed operating costs of $125,000 annually. Variable costs would average $4.50, $2.60, $2.00, and $2.40 for the 4,000, 5,000, 7,000, and 10,000 output levels, respectively.

Should the facility be expanded if management's objective is to maximize net earnings?

6. The Continental Co. currently has three production plants, which ship to its three regional warehouses monthly. Increased demand necessitates a new plant. Given the following data, use a rational means to determine whether the firm should open plant 4 or plant 5.

Distribution Costs

PLANT	WAREHOUSE A	B	C	PRODUCTION CAPACITY
1	10	18	4	45
2	6	14	2	30
3	4	12	8	50
Demand	40	55	80	

The variable per-unit production costs at all plants are approximately the same, but plant 4 would have an estimated per-year building and equipment cost of $23,000, whereas plant 5 would have a $25,000 cost. The two new plants would have capacities of 80 and transportation costs to the warehouses as follows:

PLANT	WAREHOUSE A	B	C
4	11	10	7
5	12	8	5

7. The Parker Co. specializes in the manufacture of oil-rig equipment. It is considering three potential locations for a single new plant. The new plant will have the capacity to produce 5,000 units annually, and is expected to operate at 85 percent capacity. The north, west, and south plants would have annual fixed costs of $480,000, $430,000, and $400,000 respectively. Their variable production costs in the same order would be $100, $110, and $120 per unit. Based on economic criteria, would you select the north, west, or south plant site?

8. Using Khumawala's heuristic, determine which of the following potential warehouses should be opened. The costs under the customer represent per-unit transportation costs times total units demanded.

Total Costs of Supplying Customers

POTENTIAL WAREHOUSES	FIXED COSTS	CUSTOMERS				
		A	B	C	D	E
1	70	5	300	100	20	6
2	130	10	150	300	120	11
3	165	15	120	60	90	45
4	100	20	45	360	100	35

9. Consider a public-park location problem in which it is desired to locate exactly three parks among five communities. The state budget has appropriated money for three similar facilities, and fixed costs are not considered. In the first table below, we have distances from proposed park areas to communities, along with community population sizes.

PARK AREA	COMMUNITY				
	A	B	C	D	E
1	1	10	16	20	24
2	9	2	8	12	16
3	17	8	2	4	10
4	24	15	11	5	1
Population (1,000s)	75	171	153	137	805

When the population factors are used as weights, we obtain the following weighted table of distances:

PARK AREA	COMMUNITY				
	A	*B*	*C*	*D*	*E*
1	75	1,710	2,448	2,740	19,320
2	675	342	1,224	1,644	12,880
3	1,275	1,368	306	548	8,050
4	1,800	2,565	1,683	685	805

Which three areas should be opened to minimize the total weighted distance from park to community?

10. Suppose that a company is planning to expand its warehouse capacity. The company can either build a new warehouse or expand its current facility. Adding a new warehouse will reduce transportation costs by bringing the distribution point closer to the western market. However, the new warehouse will cost $1,000,000 to build, whereas expanding the old one will cost $600,000. Transportation optimization models indicate that the company will save $100,000 per year in distribution costs if the new warehouse is built. Given a 5-year planning horizon and a 10% cost of capital, which alternative should be undertaken? Does the decision change with a 10-year planning horizon?

11. The Smelly Oil Company pays $1 million monthly to suppliers in five major cities. Smelly would like to select cash disbursement points so as to maximize the float times on clearing checks. Below is a table reflecting three of their best options and the check-clearing times between the banks in each city.

DISBURSING BANKS	AVERAGE CLEARING TIMES IN DAYS				
	HOUS-TON	LOS ANGELES	NEW YORK	WICHITA	CHI-CAGO
Phoenix	2.7	3.1	4.2	2.9	3.3
Tucson	3.2	2.9	4.1	2.6	3.4
Helena	4.5	3.3	4.9	3.8	3.0
Payments	$200,000	$200,000	$400,000	$100,000	$100,000

At a 10% cost of capital, the interest on $1 million is about $275 per day. To maintain an account at any of the three banks costs $150 per month. In which of the three cities should disbursing accounts be established?

12. The management of Ancient Times Production Company prefers to solve plant location problems subjectively. One of the firm's new managers has suggested coming up with a single quantified measure for each of the two plant locations

the company is considering. The following table reflects the decision factors and importance weighting factors. Each location is ranked on a scale from 1 to 10 with respect to each factor. Ten is a perfect rating.

Rating of Alternatives

FACTOR	% WEIGHTING	LOCATION 1 RATING	LOCATION 2 RATING
1. Transportation cost	40	8	7
2. Labor cost	15	6	6
3. Building cost	20	5	6
4. Cost of utilities	10	6	5
5. Community attitude	10	7	9
6. Labor attitude	5	6	7

What is your final rating for locations 1 and 2?

13. In problem 8, suppose that location 3 is an already-existing warehouse. Determine the best warehouse configuration with warehouse 3 in the solution. Is it a different solution?

14. A & T Food Distributors currently has warehouses in Chicago and Dallas. It plans to expand from two to four warehouses and to select two new sites out of three possibilities. The potential locations include Salt Lake City, Atlanta, and Philadelphia. The table below reflects fixed operating costs and variable transportation costs to A & T's five main distribution centers. Which two sites should be selected?

	WARE-HOUSES	FIXED COSTS	AVERAGE PER-UNIT TRANSPORTATION COSTS TO DISTRIBUTION CENTERS				
			A	B	C	D	E
Established	Chicago	200,000	5	7	4	3	1
	Dallas	190,000	4	6	7	1	5
Potential	Salt Lake City	200,000	2	9	9	5	8
	Atlanta	180,000	6	3	6	4	7
	Philadelphia	210,000	8	4	2	6	5
	Regional Demand		90,000	70,000	100,000	50,000	80,000

15. Suppose that in problem 7, the new plant may not necessarily operate at 85 percent efficiency. In fact, the marketing department has developed the following annual market volume forecast:

SALES	PROBABILITY
3,500	.20
4,000	.25
4,250	.35
4,750	.20

In view of the uncertainty, which plant would you open?

16. The Radex Company is interested in locating not only two new plants but also three new warehouses. The company would like to design an integrated distribution system that minimizes distribution and fixed and operating costs. It is considering three possible plant locations and five possible warehouse locations. Outline a systematic approach for solving this problem.

REFERENCES

ABERNATHY, W.J., and J.C. HERSHEY, "A Spatial-Allocation Model for Regional Health-Services Planning," *Operations Research*, 20 (May–June 1972), 629–42.

ATKINS, R.J., and R.H. SHRIVER, "New Approach to Facilities Location," *Harvard Business Review*, May–June 1968, pp. 70–79.

CORNUEJOLS, G., M. FISHER, and G.L. NEMHAUSER, "Location of Bank Accounts to Optimize Float: An Analytic Study of Exact and Approximate Algorithms," *Management Science*, 23 (April 1977), 789–810.

DUTTON, R., G. HINMAN, and C.B. MILLHAM, "The Optimal Location of Nuclear-Power Facilities in the Pacific Northwest," *Operations Research*, 22, no. 3 (May–June 1974), 478–87.

EFFROYMSON, M.A., and T.A. RAY, "A Branch-Bound Algorithm for Plant Location," *Operations Research*, 14 (May–June 1966), 361–68.

FITZSIMMONS, J.A., "A Methodology for Emergency Ambulance Deployment," *Management Science*, 19 (February 1973), 627–36.

FRANCIS, R., and J. WHITE, *Facility Layout and Location: An Analytical Approach*. Englewood Cliffs, N.J.: Prentice-Hall, 1974.

KEUHN, A.A., and M.J. HAMBURGER, "A Heuristic Program for Locating Warehouses," *Management Science*, 19 (July 1963), 643–66.

KHUMAWALA, B.M. "An Efficient Branch and Bound Algorithm for the Warehouse Location Problem," *Management Science*, 18 (August 1972), 718–31.

————, "An Efficient Heuristic Procedure for the Uncapacitated Warehouse Location Problem," *Naval Research Logistics Quarterly*, 20, no. 1 (March 1973), 109–21.

_____, and D.C. WHYBARK, "A Comparison of Some Recent Warehouse Location Techniques," *The Logistics Review*, vol. 7 (1971).

KOLESAR, P., and W.E. WALKER, "An Algorithm for the Dynamic Relocation of Fire Companies," *Operations Research*, 22 (March–April 1974), 249–74.

LEE, S.M., and L.J. MOORE, "Optimizing Transportation Problems with Multiple Objectives," *AIIE Transactions*, 5 (December 1973), 333–38.

MARKLAND, R.E., "Analyzing Geographically Discrete Warehousing Networks by Computer Simulation," *Decision Sciences*, 4 (April 1973), 216–36.

REVELLE, C., D. MARKS, and J. LIEBMAN, "An Analysis of Private and Public Sector Location Models," *Management Science*, 16, no. 11 (July 1970), 692–707.

SÃ, G., "Branch-and-Bound and Approximate Solutions to the Capacitated Plant-Location Problem," *Operations Research*, 17, no. 6 (November–December 1969), 1005–15.

SAVAS, E., "Simulation and Cost-Effectiveness Analysis of New York's Emergency Ambulance Service," *Management Science*, 15 (August 1969), B608–27.

SHANNON, R., and T. IGNIZIO, "An Heuristic Programming Algorithm for Warehouse Location," *AIIE Transactions*, II, no. 4 (December 1970), 334–39.

SWEENEY, D., and R. TATHAM, "An Improved Long-Run Model for Multiple Warehouse Location," *Management Science*, 22, no. 7 (March 1976), 748–58.

8

FORECASTING

INTRODUCTION

Regardless of whether an organization's role in society is to provide medical care, police protection, safe streets, consumer goods, or consumer services, it needs accurate and timely forecasts. Hospitals need to predict the demand for resources such as X-ray facilities, surgical rooms, and special nursing stations. Computer organizations must predict demand so that the appropriate hardware and software can be acquired. Farmers need weather forecasts for making planting and harvesting decisions. Automobile manufacturers need demand forecasts to develop the master schedules that are a necessary input to materials requirements planning and aggregate scheduling. In short, many of the planning decisions the operations manager must make are based on forecasts.

Consequently, it is becoming increasingly important for the competitive firm to perform the forecasting function accurately and efficiently.

To emphasize this point, let us demonstrate the effect of a 10 percent error in the demand forecast for automobiles. Let us assume that demand for September is estimated at 100,000 automobiles. Based on this forecast, manpower planning, production schedules, inventory policies, and many other important planning decisions are made. Now assume that sales for September are 90,000 units rather than the 100,000 projected. If we oversimplify the consequences of the forecasting error by using the cost of holding additional inventory to measure the cost of that error, we can compute it in the following manner:

$$\text{Cost of forecast error} = (\text{Cost of auto})(\text{No. of excess autos produced})(\text{Cost of capital})$$

For illustrative purposes, let the per-unit cost of the automobile be $5,000 and the cost of capital be 12 percent per year, or 1 percent per month. Then, the cost of the forecast error for September is:

$$(\$5,000)(10,000)(.01) = \$500,000$$

It ought to be obvious from this oversimplified example that accurate demand forecasts are not only important to the typical organization but are possibly the difference between surviving and not surviving in a competitive marketplace.

Regardless of whether the subject of the forecast is sales, cash flow, GNP, or the weather, forecasts can be categorized by their time horizon. As depicted in Figure 8-1, short-range forecasts (up to one year, but typically a quarter) help the

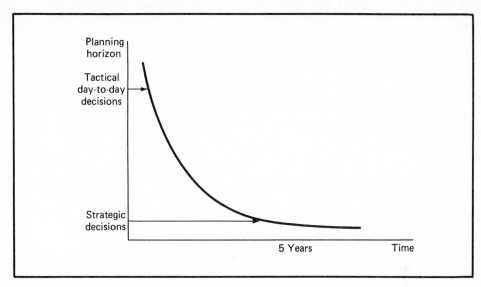

FIGURE 8-1   Forecasting Time Horizon

operations manager make current operational decisions such as production scheduling and short-term financing. Medium-range forecasts (one to three years) aid in making planning decisions that have a longer lead time. For example, a computer installation may use a three-year forecast of demand in order to make decisions concerning hardware acquisitions necessary to satisfy that demand. Long-range forecasts (three or more years) are used to make decisions that affect the organization further in the future. A utility company must make long-range forecasts concerning both its demand and the availability and cost of various fuels, in order to make decisions concerning a new plant and equipment.

Forecasting techniques can be grouped into one of three categories: qualitative techniques, time series analysis, and causal methods. Qualitative techniques use qualitative data such as the aggregate opinion of the sales force to forecast the future. Time series analysis relies entirely on historical data, focusing on seasonal and cyclical variations and trend extrapolations. Causal methods attempt to define relationships between independent and dependent variables in a system of related equations. Each of these three general categories can be further subdivided into individual forecasting techniques. See Figure 8-2 for a breakdown of commonly used forecasting methods. Obviously, the decision of which technique to use is dependent on the parameters of the individual forecasting problem. In this chapter, however, we will attempt to indicate the comparative advantages, costs, and logical applications of the various techniques.

When selecting a forecast technique, a decision maker must keep two types of costs in mind; cost of inaccuracy and cost of the forecast itself. The objective should be to minimize the total costs. In other words, it makes little sense to spend a large amount for a forecast of little significance to the organization. A "gut-feel" forecast

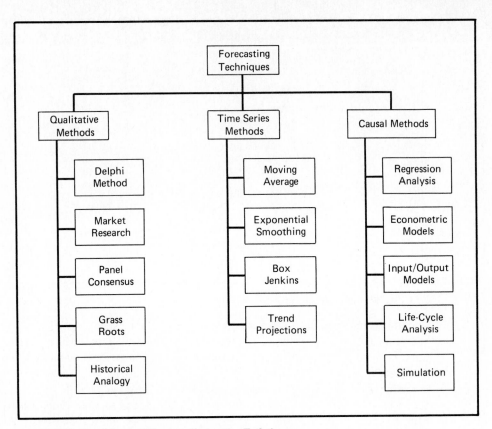

FIGURE 8-2 Breakdown of Common Forecasting Techniques

from the sales manager might be adequate. Alternatively, an important decision that is very sensitive to future conditions may warrant the expenditure of thousands of dollars to improve the forecast by only a small amount.

The selection of a forecasting technique depends on a multitude of factors. Many techniques require a substantial amount of historical data. If adequate and relevant historical data do not exist or are prohibitively expensive to accumulate, then many techniques can be automatically ruled out. Another factor to be considered is the planning horizon. Some techniques are more suited to short-term forecasts and some to long-term forecasts. The time available to make the forecast is another important consideration. If a manager needs a forecast for a current decision, he may not be able to wait six months to get it. Forecasting techniques vary as to cost and accuracy, and therefore it is is important to identify the accuracy needed in the forecast and a reasonable cost for a given level of accuracy. Figure 8-3 gives some logical structure for deciding which forecasting technique is appropriate.

The first question to be asked concerns the availability of historical data. All quantitative forecasting techniques depend upon the existence of adequate and accurate historical data. Therefore, if adequate data do not exist, causal methods and

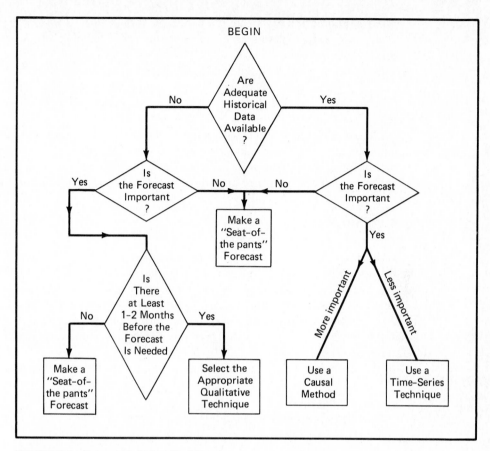

FIGURE 8-3   Forecast Technique Decision

time series analysis techniques are not feasible alternatives. However, even if adequate data do not exist, if the forecast is important, there are qualitative techniques that can be employed that generally yield better results than a judgmental or "seat-of-the-pants" forecast. The more sophisticated qualitative techniques, however, usually take several months to implement, and therefore, if the decision maker cannot wait several months, a judgmental forecast is the forecaster's only alternative.

If adequate historical data do exist, a wide variety of forecasting techniques are available. These methods range from quick-and-dirty time series techniques to very sophisticated econometric models containing hundreds of equations and hundreds of variables. The cruder and simpler methods require very little time and involve little cost. The more commonly used time series techniques are described later in this chapter. Some causal methods can require months and even years of development and thousands of dollars. The automobile demand forecast mentioned earlier in this chapter would be a likely candidate for a causal forecasting method such as multiple regression or econometric modeling.

The responsibility for demand forecasting is delegated to different functional areas depending on the nature of the organization. For example, forecasting the number of patients that are expected to be admitted to a hospital is usually the responsibility of the hospital administrator. Forecasting airline passengers by flight and by day of the week is usually done by the marketing department. In a manufacturing company, the demand forecasting function is often divided between the marketing department and the operations department. The marketing department is often better able to forecast demand for product groups, promotional items, and new products. Production and inventory control personnel can usually do a better job of forecasting demand for most inventory items when the number of items in inventory is large, because they have the necessary experience and historical data.

QUALITATIVE TECHNIQUES

Often, data necessary to generate a forecast using either time series analysis or some type of causal model are not available, and the manager is forced to use some kind of qualitative technique that substitutes human judgment for historical data. This situation frequently arises with the introduction of new products or services. The qualitative forecasting methods to be discussed in this chapter can be and often are formalized, technical procedures designed to incorporate human judgment in the forecasting process.

In this chapter, we describe five commonly used qualitative techniques:

- The Delphi method
- Market research
- Panel consensus
- Grass-roots forecasting
- Historical analogy

The *Delphi method* establishes a panel of experts. This panel is interrogated, using a series of questionnaires in which the answers to each questionnaire are used as input to designing the next. In this way, information is shared among the experts without the disadvantage of having individual experts influencing each other; in other words, the bandwagon effect of majority opinion is eliminated. As indicated in Table 8-1, the Delphi method can be effective regardless of the forecast's horizon. The cost, however, can be rather high.

Market research is probably the most sophisticated of the qualitative techniques and also the most quantitative. Market research encompasses an entire family of techniques that are helpful in revealing predictions about the size, structure, and configuration of markets for various goods and services. Market researchers obtain information about markets of interest through the use of mail questionnaires, telephone surveys, panels, and personal interviews. The data obtained are then subjected to various statistical tests so that hypotheses about the market can be

Table 8-1   Qualitative Forecasting Methods

	DELPHI METHOD	MARKET RESEARCH	PANEL CON-SENSUS	GRASS ROOTS	HISTOR-ICAL ANALOGY
Accuracy					
Short-term	Fair to very good	Excellent	Poor to fair	Fair	Poor
Medium-term	Fair to very good	Good	Poor to fair	Poor to fair	Good to fair
Long-term	Fair to very good	Fair to good	Poor	Poor	Good to fair
Cost	$4,000 +	$10,000 +	$2,000 +	$2,000 +	$2,000 +
Time required	2 months +	3 months +	2 weeks +	2 months +	1 month +

SOURCE: Adapted from J.S. Chambers, S.K. Mullich, and D.D. Smith, "How to Choose the Right Forecasting Technique," *Harvard Business Review*, July–August 1971. Cost figures have been arbitrarily adjusted for inflation.

tested. Market research techniques are generally the most expensive form of qualitative forecasting, take the longest to implement, and if properly applied are often the most accurate.

Panel consensus is a technique based on the assumption that several heads are better than one. With this technique, a panel of experts is assembled for the purpose of jointly developing a forecast. Free communication is encouraged, and the job is finished when a consensus opinion is arrived at. Obviously, the relative merit of this approach depends heavily on the configuration of the panel of experts, but it is generally considered inferior to most other qualitative methods with respect to accuracy. It can, however, be accomplished in a relatively short amount of time at a modest cost.

Grass-roots forecasting refers to asking the people closest to the problem to make individual forecasts for their territory. These individual forecasts are then aggregated to form the overall forecast. Sales forecasts are frequently accomplished in this way. This type of approach depends on the quality of the individual forecasts coming from the field. If done conscientiously, grass-roots forecasting can be very effective.

There are several weaknesses associated with grass-roots forecasting. These weaknesses include:

- Opportunity cost—It is often argued that the sales force should spend its time selling and administrative duties should be minimized. The cost of the forecast could be lost sales.
- Lack of motivation—If salespeople are working on a commission basis, many will lack the motivation necessary to develop a thoughtful forecast.
- Lack of forecasting expertise—Accurate forecasting often requires market information and specialized educational training that many salesmen lack.

The final qualitative forecasting tool to be discussed is the *historical analogy* approach. Like other qualitative methods, this approach is used when specific data are scarce. For example, if a firm is introducing a new product that has strong similarities to an established product, it may use sales data relevant to the established product to predict the relative success or failure of the new product for which no data exist. This technique, while having a modest cost, is dependent on the availability of several years of data on the model product or service. Historical analogy forecasts seem to perform better for medium- and long-range planning horizons than for short-range.

TIME SERIES ANALYSIS

A time series is a set of raw data arranged chronologically; monthly sales is a good example. Time series analysis is used when several years of data exist and when trends are both clear and relatively stable. Because time series analysis is totally dependent upon historical data, its implicit assumption is that the past is a good guide to the future. Consequently, time series analysis performs better in the short-term than in the long-term forecast. In addition, time series analysis cannot predict turning points in trend. For example, typical seasonally adjusted sales for a textbook like this one over a four-year period might behave as shown in Figure 8-4. If our historical data were limited to 1981 and 1982 sales data, we might project sales to be 8,000 copies by 1984, when in fact sales dropped to 1,000. A turning point in sales was caused by the existence of the used-book market, and mere time series analysis does an extremely poor job of predicting turning points in trend. If the data exist, however, most time series analysis techniques are extremely inexpensive, and projections can be produced on a computer in a matter of seconds.

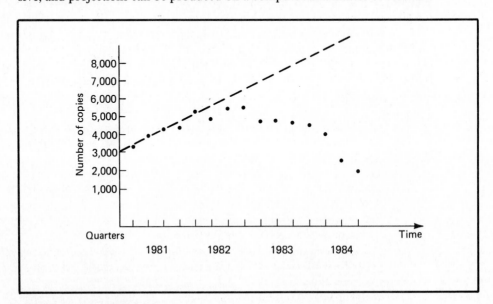

FIGURE 8-4   Sales Time Series

A time series is composed of four basic elements:

- A trend component—Trend refers to long-term growth or decay. Until recently, demand for petroleum products had a history of long-term growth or a postive trend.
- A seasonal component—A seasonal fluctuation in the forecasted variable recurs regularly at periodic intervals. The airline industry is a good example of an industry whose product is subject to fluctuations in demand due to seasonality.
- A cyclical component—Cyclical fluctuations about trend are explainable fluctuations but differ from seasonal fluctuations in that their length of time and amplitude are not constant. Demand for automobiles is highly dependent on the state of the economy which in turn experiences cyclical fluctuations.
- A random component—If a forecaster could precisely measure trend, seasonability, and the cyclical factor, there would still be an unexplained variation between the forecast and reality. This unexplained variation is usually referred to as the erratic or random component in a time series.

In this chapter, we describe three common types of time series forecasting techniques:

- Moving average
- Exponential smoothing
- Trend projection

Simple Moving Average

The simple moving average forecasting method simply eliminates the effects of seasonal, cyclical, and erratic fluctuations by averaging the historical data points. Therefore, if seasonality, trend, and cyclical factors are not critical in the variable being forecast, the moving average method is of some value. The smoothing effect of the simple moving average technique can be seen in Figure 8-5.

To compute a simple moving average, simply choose the number of points in the time series data to include in the average. Then, as each time period evolves, add the new time period data and subtract the oldest time period data, and calculate a new average.

Mathematically, then:

8.1
$$F_t = \frac{\sum_{i=1}^{N} S_{t-i}}{N}$$

where F_t = forecast for time period t

S_{t-i} = actual sales for period $t - i$

N = the number of time periods used in the averaging process

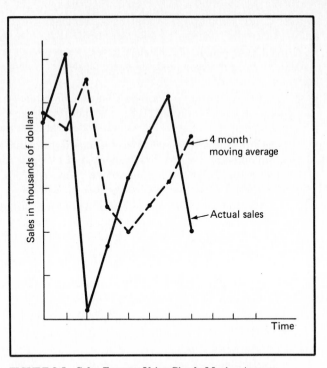

FIGURE 8-5   Sales Forecast Using Simple Moving Average

For example, let us calculate the moving average for the sales data contained in Table 8-2, using a four-month moving average. Since our data go back only to January 1982, our first possible sales forecast using a four-month moving average is for May 1982. The forecast for May 1982 can be computed as follows:

$$F_5 = \frac{S_1 + S_2 + S_3 + S_4}{4}$$

$$= \$238{,}250$$

Once May sales data are available, the forecast for June can be computed:

$$F_6 = \frac{S_2 + S_3 + S_4 + S_5}{4}$$

$$= \$237{,}000$$

It is obvious from Figure 8-6 that the longer the period over which the averaging takes place, the smoother the forecast function.

Table 8-2   Sales Data for Time Series Analysis

YEAR	MONTH	SALES (DOLLARS)	SIMPLE 4-MONTH MOVING AVERAGE FORECAST
1982	January	250,000	
	February	210,000	
	March	223,000	
	April	270,000	
	May	245,000	238,250
	June	261,000	237,000
	July	212,000	249,750
	August	226,000	247,000
	September	241,000	236,000
	October	252,000	235,000
	November	261,000	232,750
	December	229,000	245,000
1983	January	247,000	245,750
	February	255,000	247,250
	March	271,000	248,000
	April	261,000	250,500
	May	258,000	258,500
	June	265,000	261,250
	July	250,000	263,750
	August	275,000	258,500
	September	245,000	262,000
	October	260,000	258,750
	November	255,000	257,500
	December	263,000	258,750

Weighted Moving Average

Often, it is desirable to vary the weights given to historical data in order to forecast future demand or sales. Past history may show that a significantly better forecast is computed when the more recent data are given heavier weight. Mathematically, the weighted moving average is computed as follows:

8.2
$$F_t = \frac{\sum_{i=1}^{N} W_{t-i}S_{t-i}}{\sum_{i=1}^{N} W_{t-i}}$$

where F_t = forecast for time period t

S_{t-i} = actual sales for time period $t - i$

N = the number of time periods used the the averaging process

W_{t-i} = the weight given to the $t - i^{th}$ period in the averaging process

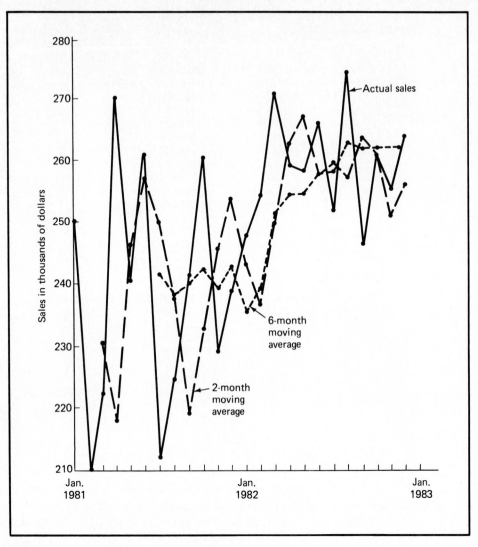

FIGURE 8-6 Sales Forecast Using Simple Moving Average

For example, assume that a weight of 50 is assigned to the most recent month, a weight of 25 to the next most recent month, and weights of 15 and 10 to the next two months respectively. Using the data in Table 8-2, the four-month weighted moving average for May 1982 is computed as follows:

$$F_5 = \frac{(50)(270,000) + (25)(223,000) + (15)(210,000) + (10)(250,000)}{100}$$

$$= \$247,250$$

Table 8-3   Four-Month Weighted Moving Average

YEAR	MONTH	ACTUAL SALES	4-MONTH WEIGHTED MOVING AVERAGE
1982	January	$250,000	
	February	210,000	
	March	223,000	
	April	270,000	
	May	245,000	$247,250
	June	261,000	244,450
	July	212,000	254,550
	August	226,000	235,000
	September	241,000	229,650
	October	252,000	234,900
	November	261,000	241,350
	December	229,000	252,250
1983	January	247,000	241,650
	February	255,000	245,100
	March	271,000	249,700
	April	261,000	259,200
	May	258,000	261,200
	June	265,000	260,400
	July	250,000	263,250
	August	275,000	256,050
	September	245,000	265,550
	October	260,000	255,250
	November	255,000	257,500
	December	263,000	256,750

The data shown in Table 8-3 are plotted in Figure 8-7.

The major advantage of the moving average technique is its simplicity, low cost, and little time necessary to implement. In general, however, the moving average technique does a poor job for long-range and medium-range forecasts. For quick-and-dirty short-term forecasts that don't require a great deal of accuracy, a moving average forecast may be a viable alternative to other forecasting methods.

Exponential Smoothing

Exponential smoothing refers to a family of forecasting models that are very similar to the weighted moving average. The simplest exponential smoothing model is of the following form:

8.3
$$F_t = F_{t-1} + \alpha(A_{t-1} - F_{t-1})$$

where F_t = forecast for time period t

A_{t-1} = actual value of variable being forecast in period $t-1$

α = smoothing constant

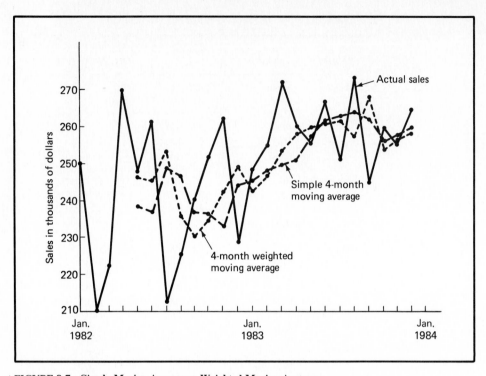

FIGURE 8-7 **Simple Moving Average vs Weighted Moving Average**

The value of α, which can range from 0 to 1, determines the degree of smoothing that takes place and how responsive the model is to fluctuation in the forecast variable. The setting of α is not a scientific process and is usually done by trial and error. Let us assume an α of .15 and a January 1983 forecast of 250 units. The actual January demand turned out to be 260 units. The forecast for February could be computed as follows:

$$F_t = 250 + (.15)(260 - 250)$$
$$= 250 + 1.5$$
$$= 251.5 \text{ units}$$

Given the forecasts in Table 8-4, let us compare the effect of different smoothing constants by looking at Figure 8-8.

Other exponential smoothing models exist that compensate for the various components of a time series such as the seasonal or trend component. To illustrate more complex exponential smoothing models, let us consider a model that has an adjustment for trend built into it. If trend exists in either a positive or a negative form, there will be a lag using the simple exponential smoothing model just described. See Figure 8-9. The basic idea behind the trend-adjusted model is to

Table 8-4   Effects of Various Smoothing Constants

	ACTUAL DEMAND	FORECAST $\alpha = .05$	FORECAST $\alpha = .25$	FORECAST $\alpha = .4$
January	260	250.0	250.0	250.0
February	210	250.5	252.5	254.0
March	223	248.5	241.9	236.4
April	270	247.2	237.2	231.0
May	245	248.3	245.4	246.6
June	261	248.2	245.3	246.0
July	212	248.8	249.2	252.0
August	226	247.0	239.9	236.0
September	241	245.9	236.4	232.0
October	252	245.7	237.6	235.6
November	261	246.0	241.2	242.2
December	249	246.7	246.1	249.7

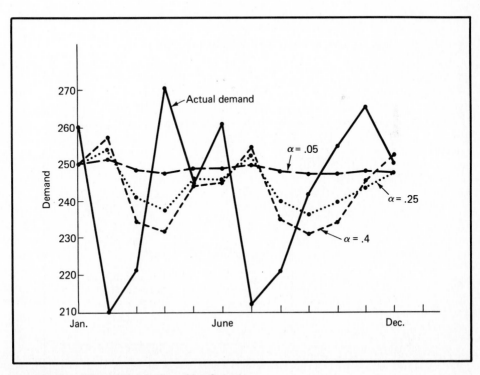

FIGURE 8-8   Effect of Various Smoothing Constants

calculate a simple, exponentially smoothed forecast as described above and adjust the forecast for a trend lag.

Mathematically, the trend-adjusted model can be described as follows:

8.4
$$F'_t = F_t + \frac{1 - \beta}{\beta} T_t$$

where F'_t = trend-adjusted forecast for time period t

F_t = simple exponential smoothing forecast for time period t

β = trend smoothing factor

T_t = exponentially smoothed trend for time period t

T_t is computed using the following formula:

8.5
$$T_t = T_{t-1} + \beta(t_t - T_{t-1})$$
where
$$t_t = F_t - F_{t-1}$$

To compute a trend-adjusted forecast is a four-step process:

Step 1:   Compute a simple forecast (F_t) for time period t.

Step 2:   Compute t_t by finding the difference between F_t and F_{t-1}.

$$t_t = F_t - F_{t-1}$$

Step 3:   Calculate the exponentially smoothed trend.

$$T_t = T_{t-1} + \beta(t_t - T_{t-1})$$

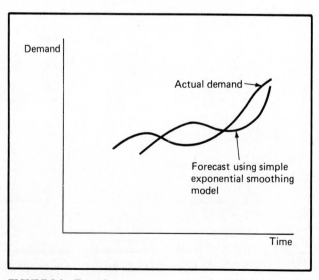

FIGURE 8-9   Trend Lag

Table 8-5 Time Series Data
in Which Trend Is Present

PERIOD	DEMAND
1	12
2	17
3	19
4	16
5	22
6	24
7	30
8	29
9	33
10	34
11	37
12	38

Step 4: Finally, calculate a trend-adjusted forecast by using the formula:

8.6
$$F_t' = F_t + \frac{1 - \beta}{\beta} T_t$$

Let us illustrate how to compute a trend-adjusted, exponentially smoothed forecast using the demand data in Table 8-5 and smoothing constants α and β, equal to .3 and .25 respectively. Let the initial forecast be 11.5. The trend-adjusted forecast for period 2 is computed as follows:

The first step is to compute F_2:

$$F_2 = F_1 + \alpha(A_1 - F_1)$$
$$= 11.5 + .3(12 - 11.5)$$
$$= 11.65$$

The next step is to calculate t_2:

$$t_2 = F_2 - F_1$$
$$= 11.65 - 11.50$$
$$= .15$$

T_2 can now be calculated, assuming the initial trend adjustment is 0:

$$T_2 = T_1 + \beta(t_2 - T_1)$$
$$= 0 + .25(.15)$$
$$= .0375$$

Table 8-6   Trend-Adjusted Forecasts

TIME PERIOD	ACTUAL DEMAND	F_t	t_t	T_t	F_t'
1	12	11.5000	0	0	11.5000
2	17	11.6500	.15000	.03750	11.7625
3	19	13.2550	1.60500	.42937	14.5431
4	16	14.9785	1.72350	.75290	17.2372
5	22	15.2849	3.06450	.64129	17.2088
6	24	17.2995	2.01451	.98459	20.2533
7	30	19.3096	2.01016	1.24099	23.0326
8	29	22.5167	3.20711	1.73252	27.7143
9	33	24.4617	1.94498	1.78563	29.8186
10	34	27.0232	2.56149	1.97960	32.9620
11	37	29.1162	2.09304	2.00796	35.1401
12	38	31.4814	2.36513	2.09725	37.7731

Finally, the trend-adjusted forecast for time period 2 can be computed:

$$F_2' = F_2 + \frac{1 - .25}{.25} T_2$$

$$= 11.65 + 3(.0375)$$

$$= 11.7625$$

Doing the same calculations for the remaining time periods for the time series data shown in Table 8-5 results in the trend-adjusted forecasts reflected in Table 8-6. Figure 8-10, on the following page, graphically contrasts the unadjusted and adjusted forecasts for the time series in Table 8-6.

In addition to providing a more accurate forecast when trend exists in the data, the trend adjusted exponential smoothing model has the advantage of providing a forecast for more than 1 time period into the future. To calculate a forecast for n periods into the future use the following formula.

8.7 $$F_{t+n}' = F_t + nT_t$$

To illustrate, let us calculate a demand for time period 18 using the data in Table 8-6,

$$F_{18}' = F_{12} + nT_{12} = 31.4814 + 6(2.09725)$$

$$= 44.0649$$

Generally, exponential smoothing models are considered superior to the moving average methods previously discussed. Its cost is equivalent and its accuracy especially in the short term is usually better. In addition, because only the smoothing

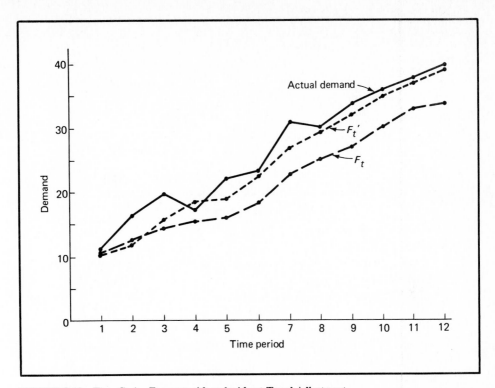

FIGURE 8-10   **Time Series Forecast with and without Trend Adjustment**

constant and the previous forecast need to be stored, exponential smoothing requires considerably less computer storage than moving average methods.

Owing to their relatively small computational cost and computer storage requirement, exponential smoothing models are probably the most widely used of the time series techniques. For longer-term forecasts, however, exponential smoothing is also considered a poor technique.

Trend Projection

Trend projection using a technique called least squares is a special case of a category of causal forecasting methods called regression analysis. The basic idea in trend projection using least squares is to fit a function to a set of time series data in which the independent variable is time and the dependent variable is the variable to be forecasted, such as demand. This function can be linear or nonlinear and the basic idea and methodology are the same. In this chapter, however, we consider only linear trend projection.

Consider the scatter diagram in Figure 8-11. It is easy to imagine a straight line running through the data such that the sum of the differences between the data

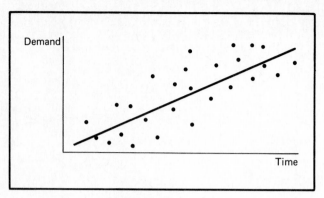

FIGURE 8-11   Scatter Diagram

points and the trend line is minimized. If the equation of the trend line is a function of time then it is a simple matter to "plug" a future time period into the function and calculate a forecast.

Remember, the general equation for a straight line is:

8.8
$$y = mx + b$$

where
y = the dependent variable

b = the y intercept

m = the slope of the line

x = the independent variable

See Figure 8-12 for a graphical interpretation of a straight line.

Now, if we define x as time and y as demand, and b (the y intercept) and m (slope of the line) are known, then demand can be computed by merely letting x

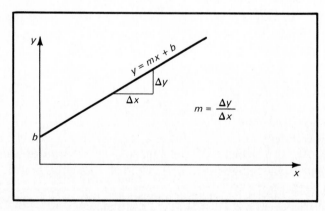

FIGURE 8-12   Graph of Linear Equation

assume a value. For example, assume that the linear function is:

$$y = 150x + 5,000$$

If 1984 is the tenth time period in the time series, the demand forecast for 1984 can be forecast, substituting 10 into the equation:

$$y = 150(10) + 5,000$$
$$= 6,500 \text{ units}$$

Now let us turn to the method of deriving the "best fit" linear equation for a set of time series data. It is possible to find a line that provides a good fit of the data by merely "eyeballing" the scatter diagram and superimposing a line on it. Then, relying on the accuracy of the graph, a y intercept (b) can be read, and the slope of the line can be calculated as $\Delta y/\Delta x$. A more accurate way to find the linear equation that best fits the data is to solve the following equations simultaneously for b and m:

8.9
$$\sum_{i=1}^{n} y_i = nb + m \sum_{i=1}^{n} x_i$$

8.10
$$\sum_{i=1}^{n} x_i y_i = b \sum_{i=1}^{n} x_i + m \sum_{i=1}^{n} x_i^2$$

where
$$y_i = \text{dependent variable for the } i^{\text{th}} \text{ time period}$$
$$n = \text{number of historical time periods}$$
$$x_i = \text{independent variable for the } i^{\text{th}} \text{ time period}$$

Equations 8.9 and 8.10 are called normal equations and are derived using the differential calculus. To illustrate how the simple linear regression equation is found, let us use the data in Table 8-7. The dependent variable (y) is demand, whereas the time period is the independent variable. Looking at normal equations 8.9 and 8.10, it is clear that several sums are required. These values are computed in Table 8-8. Substituting the appropriate sums into the two normal equations, we have the following two equations with two unknowns, b and m:

8.11 $\qquad\qquad\qquad 31,100 = 12b + 78m$

8.12 $\qquad\qquad\qquad 236,300 = 78b + 650m$

If we multiply both sides of equation 8.11 by 6.5 and subtract it from equation 8.12, the b terms will fall out:

$$
\begin{aligned}
236,300 &= 78b + 650m \\
-202,150 &= -78b - 507m \\
\hline
34,150 &= 143m \\
m &= 238.811
\end{aligned}
$$

Table 8-7   Historical Demand Data

TIME PERIOD	DEMAND
1	1200
2	1700
3	1900
4	1600
5	2200
6	2400
7	3000
8	2900
9	3300
10	3400
11	3700
12	3800

Solving for b by substituting m into equation 8.11, we find:

$$31,100 = 12b + 78(238.811)$$
$$b = 1,039.4$$

Therefore, the "best fit" linear forecasting equation is:

8.13 $y = 238.811x + 1,039.4$

Once this equation has been derived, trend extrapolation is simply a mechanical procedure. If a prediction for the fourteenth time period is desired, simply set x

Table 8-8   Least Squares Calculations

x_i	y_i	x_iy_i	x_i^2
1	1,200	1,200	1
2	1,700	3,400	4
3	1,900	5,700	9
4	1,600	6,400	16
5	2,200	11,000	25
6	2,400	14,400	36
7	3,000	21,000	49
8	2,900	23,200	64
9	3,300	29,700	81
10	3,400	34,000	100
11	3,700	40,700	121
12	3,800	45,600	144
$\sum_{i=1}^{12} x_i = 78$	$\sum_{i=1}^{12} y_i = 31,100$	$\sum_{i=1}^{12} x_iy_i = 236,300$	$\sum_{i=1}^{12} x_i^2 = 650$

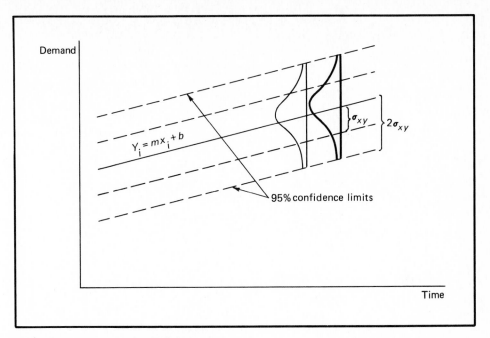

FIGURE 8-13   Least Squares Differences

equal to 14 and solve for y using equation 8.13. The forecast for time period 14 is therefore:

$$y_{14} = 238.811(14) + 1,039.4$$
$$= 4,382.754$$

If we compute a standard error of estimate to determine how well the regression line fits the data, it is possible that more information about a forecast can be obtained. See Figure 8-13. The standard error can be defined mathematically as

$$s_{yx} = \sqrt{\frac{\sum_{i=1}^{n} (y_i - Y_i)^2}{n - 2}}$$

where
y_i = the dependent variable for time period i
  (in our example demand)
Y_i = value for the dependent variable obtained
  from the regression equation
n = the number of historical time periods

To compute the standard error of estimate, we merely do the computation necessary to complete Table 8-9 using the data in Table 8-7 and the regression

Table 8-9   Standard Error Computation

x_i	y_i	Y_i	$y_i - Y_i$	$(y_i - Y_i)^2$
1	1200	1278.21	−78.211	6116.96
2	1700	1517.02	182.978	33480.90
3	1900	1755.83	144.167	20784.10
4	1600	1994.64	−394.644	15574.40
5	2200	2233.45	−33.455	1119.24
6	2400	2472.27	−72.266	5222.37
7	3000	2711.08	288.923	83476.50
8	2900	2949.89	−49.888	2488.81
9	3300	3188.70	111.301	12387.90
10	3400	3427.51	−27.510	756.80
11	3700	3666.32	33.679	1134.28
12	3800	3905.13	−105.132	11052.70
				333,765.00

$$s_{yx} = \sqrt{\frac{333,765}{10}}$$
$$= 182.692$$

equation 8.13. If we assume that demand is normally distributed around the regression line as depicted in Figure 8-13 and want 95.5 percent of the demand values to fall within our prediction interval, the prediction interval can be calculated as follows:

$$\text{Prediction interval for } Y_i = Y_i \pm 2s_{yx}$$

where Y_i = the regression equation value

s_{yx} = standard error of estimate

In our example:

$$\text{Prediction interval for } Y_{14} = 4,382.754 \pm 2(182.692)$$
$$= 4,382.754 \pm 365.384$$

or

$$4,017.37 \leq Y_{14} \leq 4,748.14$$

Remember that we calculated Y_i and s_{yx} using historical data, and to say we are 95.5 percent confident that demand for time period 14 will fall between 4,017 and 4,748 units is to assume that the future is going to behave like the past. Also, a sample size of 12 is too small to assume normality, and a student's t distribution should be used when the sample size is small.

Simple linear regression using time period as the independent variable generally outperforms both moving average and exponential smoothing techniques with regard to forecast accuracy. Usually, very good short-term forecasts can be derived using trend projections, and often, good long-term forecasts can be based on least-squares trend projections. If the historical data are available, the cost of the forecast is minimal and the time lapse required to derive the forecast is often less than one day.

In general, time series methods such as those discussed in this section provide fairly accurate and very inexpensive short-term forecasts. It is therefore very common for one or more of these techniques to be integrated into computerized multiproduct inventory systems such as IBM's IMPACT system. In automated multiproduct inventory systems in which forecasts are automatically generated using a time series technique such as exponential smoothing, it is necessary to consistently monitor the forecasting process to report to management when the forecast and actual demand for a time period differ significantly. This discrepancy may be due to keypunch errors, extraordinary market conditions, or the unsatisfactory performance of the forecasting technique. Whatever the reason, management must be alerted through some type of exception reporting that there is a need to investigate a product's forecast versus its demand and take the appropriate corrective action. Later in this chapter we will describe the measurement of forecast error and the commonly used methods for tracking the forecast accuracy so that management can be notified when the forecast error for a particular item exceeds specified limits.

CAUSAL METHODS

When a particular forecast is of vital importance to an organization and adequate historical data exist, it is often advisable to develop a causal forecasting model in which the variable to be forecast is a function of several or many causal variables. Sales may be a function of price, advertising budget, competitors' actions, quality control budget, disposable personal income, or other independent variables. If the relationship between these independent variables can be adequately defined mathematically, superior forecasts can result. Causal models are the most sophisticated type of forecasting model and generally require more data, more development, more time, and more cost than the time series approaches discussed earlier.

There are two predominant causal forecasting methods:

Multiple regression models
Econometric models

Multiple Regression Models

Multiple regression analysis is a simple extension of simple linear regression. The difference is that instead of one independent variable in the regression equation, there are several or many independent variables. The general form of a multiple linear regression equation is:

8.14
$$Y = \sum_{i=1}^{n} a_i x_i + b$$

where

a_i = coefficient of independent variable x_i

b = constant

x_i = independent variable

Y = forecast variable

n = number of independent variables

The method for deriving a multiple regression equation is analogous to the simple linear case and will not be described in this text. Instead, let us look at the following example.

A typewriter manufacturing firm wishes to forecast demand for two years' maintenance contracts for its most popular typewriter. It is felt that demand is a function of the advertising budget, the premium for a one-year contract, the premium for a two-year contract, and trend. Historical data for the last ten years are available; they are shown in Table 8-10.

These data were used to derive the following regression equation:

$$Y = .05085x_1 + 4.01746x_2 - 7.26361x_3 + 433.175784x_4 + 5,226.50$$

where

Y = demand for two-year maintenance contracts

x_1 = annual advertising budget

x_2 = premium for one-year contract

x_3 = premium for two-year contract

x_4 = time period, using 1973 as time period 1

Table 8-10   Maintenance Contracts Sales Data

YEAR	NUMBER OF 2-YEAR CONTRACTS SOLD	ANNUAL ADVERTISING BUDGET	PREMIUM FOR 1-YEAR CONTRACT	PREMIUM FOR 2-YEAR CONTRACT
1973	5,000	50,000	250	550
1974	6,000	50,000	250	500
1975	6,500	55,000	250	550
1976	7,000	55,000	300	600
1977	6,000	45,000	300	650
1978	7,500	60,000	350	650
1979	8,000	60,000	300	650
1980	9,000	70,000	300	600
1981	10,000	75,000	325	550
1982	10,500	75,000	325	550
1983	12,000	80,000	325	500

In order to calculate a forecast for 1984, values of x_1, x_2, x_3, and x_4 must be set. If the advertising budget for 1984 is set at \$90,000, the premium for a one-year contract at \$325, and the premium for a two-year contract at \$550, then forecast demand can be calculated as:

$$D = (.05085)(90,000) + (4.01746)(325) - (7.26361)(550) + (433.17578)(12)$$
$$+ 5,226.50$$
$$= 12,311.80 \text{ contracts}$$

The calculations necessary to create a multiple regression equation and all the statistical measures needed to evaluate the validity of that equation, are extremely tedious. Fortunately, there are a number of "user-friendly" computer software packages, available at little or no cost. Examples of statistical software that have excellent regression routings include SPSS, SAS, and BMD.

Generally multiple regression is less time consuming and less expensive, but often less accurate than econometric models. Choosing between these two widely used techniques depends on the importance of the forecast, the data available, and the time available to develop the forecasting model.

Econometric Models

An econometric model is a system of interdependent equations that describe some real phenomenon. For example, consider the following three-equation, eight-variable macroeconomic model:

$$C_t = x_1 I_t + x_3 Y_t + x_4 C_{t-1} + x_5 R_t + U_1$$
$$I_t = \beta_1 + \beta_2 Y_t + \beta_3 R_t + U_2$$
$$Y_t = C_t + I_t + G_t$$

where
C_t = aggregate consumption in time period t

I_t = gross investment in time period t

Y_t = gross national product in time period t

G_t = government spending in time period t

R_t = short-term interest rate

U_i = error terms

x_i = parameter estimates for first equation

β_i = parameter estimates for second equation

These equations are solved simultaneously to find the values for unknown variables C_t, I_t, and Y_t.

Econometric models are used extensively in economic forecasting, and some of the models are very complex, with hundreds of variables and hundreds of simultaneous equations. These models often provide superior forecasts but are very costly and time consuming to build and to maintain. The Wharton School econometric model, for example, has over 200 equations and 80 exogenous variables and costs thousands of dollars to develop and more thousands to maintain.

FORECAST ERROR

By their inherent nature all forecasts are wrong and it should be obvious that building a forecast model devoid of error is impossible regardless of the sophistication of the technique being used. The objective of any forecasting activity should be to provide a forecast with a sufficient degree of accuracy at the least possible cost. It is often more important to measure and track the forecast error than to maximize the accuracy of the forecast. This section describes the most commonly used methods for measuring and tracking forecast error.

Measurement of Forecast Error

Probably the most common method used for measuring the error in a forecast is the calculation of the mean absolute deviation (MAD). The mean absolute deviation is simply the average of the absolute differences between the forecasted variable and the actual variable. Mathematically,

8.15
$$MAD = \frac{\sum_{t=1}^{n} |A_t - F_t|}{n}$$

where
$$A_t = \text{actual for time period } t$$
$$F_t = \text{forecast for time period } t$$
$$n = \text{number of time periods}$$

Let us illustrate how to calculate the MAD using the data in Table 8-11. The MAD for Table 8-11 data is:

$$MAD = 2452/6$$
$$= 408.7$$

If we assume that the MAD of a forecast is normally distributed, then we can estimate the probability that the MAD will fall within a specific confidence interval. It can be shown that 1 MAD = .8 standard deviations. Using the above relationship, we can compute the relative frequency of MADS falling within specified ranges. See Table 8-12.

Table 8-11   MAD Calculation

MONTH	ACTUAL DEMAND	FORECAST DEMAND	$|A_t - F_t|$
1	2150	2500	350
2	3210	2465	745
3	2622	2540	82
4	2475	2548	73
5	2910	2541	369
6	3412	2579	833
			2452

Tracking of Forecast Error

A tracking signal is often used to identify those inventory items which are failing to keep pace with either a positive or negative trend. The tracking signal is defined mathematically in equation 8.16.

8.16
$$TS_n = \frac{\sum\limits_{t=1}^{n} d_t}{\text{MAD}_n}$$

where

TS_n = tracking signal for time period

d_t = forecast error $(A_t - F_t)$ in time period t

MAD_n = mean absolute deviation as of time period n

To illustrate the calculation of the tracking signal, let us calculate the tracking signal for the fifth month in Table 8-13.

$$TS_5 = (-350 + 745 + 82 + -73 + 369)/323.8$$
$$= 2.39$$

Most automated demand forecasting systems for multiproduct inventories have a

Table 8-12   Confidence Interval for MADS

RANGE OF MAD	RELATIVE FREQUENCY OF MADS FALLING WITHIN THE RANGE
± 1	.5705
± 2	.8895
± 3	.9833
± 4	.9986

Table 8-13   Tracking Signal Calculation

MONTH	ACTUAL DEMAND	FORECAST DEMAND	ACTUAL DEVIATION $A_t - F_t$	ABSOLUTE DEVIATION $|A_t - F_t|$	MAD	TRACKING SIGNAL
1	2150	2500	−350	350	350.0	−1.00
2	3210	2465	745	745	547.5	.72
3	2622	2540	82	82	392.3	1.22
4	2475	2548	−73	73	312.5	1.29
5	2910	2541	369	369	323.8	2.39
6	3412	2579	833	833	408.7	3.93
7	3310	2662	648	648	442.9	5.09
8	3570	2727	843	843	492.9	6.28
9	3771	2811	960	960	544.8	7.45
10	3621	2907	714	714	561.7	8.49
11	3924	2978	946	946	596.6	9.58
12	4150	3073	1077	1077	636.7	10.67

tracking signal designed into the system. This tracking signal is used by those responsible for the forecast to signal when the forecasting technique is not keeping up with growth or delay in demand. If management were to choose a critical level of 3.0 for the tracking signal, then the system would flag the item in Table 8-13 in June (month 6). If the critical value were set at 4.0, then the item would be included in an exception report for the month of July. Where to set the critical value for a tracking signal depends on the importance of the inventory item. If the item is a class A item, management may want to establish a fairly low critical level (i.e., 2 or 3). Whereas if the item is of little importance a low critical level would be inappropriate because it would indicate a need for investigation and corrective action which may not be cost-justified.

SUMMARY

A good forecast is the primary input to the planning process. If an aggregate plan for use of labor, facilities, and inventory is to be of any value, the forecast or forecasts on which the aggregate plan is based must be accurate. The master schedule on which all automated production/inventory systems depend is based on the sales forecast for end items, and therefore the quality of any production/inventory system depends on the quality of end-item sales forecasts.

In this chapter we have attempted to describe the major forecasting methods and indicate areas of applicability. We have divided forecasting methods into three categories: qualitative methods, time series analysis techniques, and causal methods. In general, qualitative techniques are used when quantitative historical data are not available. Time series analysis techniques are used when the importance of the forecast is not great enough to justify the use of more expensive causal methods.

Time series techniques have found wide usage in automated multiproduct inventory systems. Causal methods are used when their extra cost and time of implementation can be justified by the importance to the organization of the forecast accuracy. To be effective, a forecasting system needs a way to track forecast errors so that management can be alerted when a forecast error starts to exceed acceptable limits. In automated systems, this tracking signal is usually calculated using the MAD.

---------------------------------- **SOLVED PROBLEMS** ----------------------------------

Problem Statement

For the demand data in Table 8-14, calculate the four-quarter moving average for the fourth quarter of 1983 and the first quarter of 1984.

Table 8-14 Calculator Demand

TIME PERIOD	TI-53 CALCULATOR DEMAND
1st Quarter 1980	1,000 units
2nd Quarter 1980	2,500 units
3rd Quarter 1980	3,000 units
4th Quarter 1980	4,000 units
1st Quarter 1981	10,000 units
2nd Quarter 1981	12,000 units
3rd Quarter 1981	15,000 units
4th Quarter 1981	14,000 units
1st Quarter 1982	20,000 units
2nd Quarter 1982	25,000 units
3rd Quarter 1982	40,000 units
4th Quarter 1982	50,000 units
1st Quarter 1983	65,000 units
2nd Quarter 1983	75,000 units
3rd Quarter 1983	80,000 units
4th Quarter 1983	100,000 units

Solution

$$\text{Forecast for the 4th quarter of 1983} = \frac{50,000 + 65,000 + 75,000 + 80,000}{4}$$

$$= 67,500 \text{ units}$$

$$\text{Forecast for the 1st quarter of 1984} = \frac{65,000 + 75,000 + 80,000 + 100,000}{4}$$

$$= 80,000 \text{ units}$$

Problem Statement

Using a weighted five-quarter moving average with the weights as described below, calculate the forecast for the first quarter of 1984 for Table 8-14 data.

	PERIOD	WEIGHT
Oldest data	1	.05
	2	.10
	3	.15
	4	.25
Most recent data	5	.45

Solution

The forecast for the first quarter of 1984 is computed as shown below:

$$F = \frac{(.05)(50{,}000) + (.1)(65{,}000) + (.15)(75{,}000) + (.25)(80{,}000) + (.45)(100{,}000)}{1.00}$$

$$= 85{,}250 \text{ units}$$

Problem Statement

Using a simple exponential smoothing model, calculate the forecast for the first quarter of 1984, given that the forecast for the last quarter of 1983 was 80,250 units. Use $\alpha = .15$. Use Table 8-14 data.

Solution

The exponentially smoothed forecast for the first quarter of 1984 is computed as follows:

$$F_t = F_{t-1} + \alpha(A_{t-1} - F_{t-1})$$
$$= 80{,}250 + .15(100{,}000 - 80{,}250)$$
$$= 83{,}212.5 \text{ units}$$

Problem Statement

Using a trend-adjusted exponential smoothing model, calculate the forecast for the first quarter of 1984. Use a smoothing factor of .15 for the simple model forecast and a smoothing factor of .1 for the trend-smoothing factor. Use Table 8-14 data.

Solution

The first step is to calculate the simple exponential smoothing forecast for the first quarter of 1984. This was accomplished in the preceding example:

$$F_t = 80,250 + .15(100,000 - 80,250)$$
$$= 83,212.5 \text{ units}$$

The next step is to calculate t_t:

$$t_t = F_t - F_{t-1}$$
$$t_t = 83,212.5 - 80,250$$
$$= 2,962.5$$

Now we must calculate T_t, assuming the initial trend adjustment is 0.

$$T_t = T_{t-1} + \beta(t_t - T_{t-1})$$
$$= 0 + .1(2,962.5)$$
$$= 296.25$$

Finally, the trend-adjusted forecast for the first quarter of 1984 can be computed as shown below:

$$F_t' = F_t + \frac{1 - \beta}{\beta} T_t$$

$$= 83,212.5 + \left(\frac{1 - .1}{.1}\right) 296.25$$

$$= 83,212.5 + 2,666.25$$

$$= 85,878.75 \text{ units}$$

Problem Statement

Using the least squares method, find the regression line for the data in Table 8-14 and calculate the forecast for the first quarter of 1984.

Solution

In order to derive the regression equation, it is necessary to solve the following two normal equations simultaneously:

$$\sum_{i=1}^{n} y_i = nb + m \sum_{i=1}^{n} x_i$$

$$\sum_{i=1}^{n} x_i y_i = b \sum_{i=1}^{n} x_i + m \sum_{i=1}^{n} x_i^2$$

Table 8-15

x_i	y_i	$x_i y_i$	x_i^2
1	1,000	1,000	1
2	2,500	5,000	4
3	3,000	9,000	9
4	4,000	16,000	16
5	10,000	50,000	25
6	12,000	72,000	36
7	15,000	105,000	49
8	14,000	112,000	64
9	20,000	180,000	81
10	25,000	250,000	100
11	40,000	440,000	121
12	50,000	600,000	144
13	65,000	845,000	169
14	75,000	1,050,000	196
15	80,000	1,200,000	225
16	100,000	1,600,000	256
136	516,500	6,535,000	1,496

In order to solve the two equations simultaneously, the four sums in the two equations must first be found. This is done in Table 8-15.

Substituting these sums into the two normal equations, we get:

$$516,500 = 16b + 136m$$
$$6,535,000 = 136b + 1,496m$$

To find what factor to multiply the first equation by to add it to the second to eliminate the b terms, we divide 136 by 16, getting 8.5. Therefore, if we multiply the first equation by -8.5 and add it to the second equation, we get:

$$6,535,000 = \quad 136b + 1,496m$$
$$-4,390,250 = -136b - 1,156m$$
$$\overline{ }$$
$$2,144,750 = 340m$$

Therefore:

$$m = \frac{2,144,750}{340}$$
$$= 6,308.0882$$

Once we have the value of one unknown, we can simply substitute it into either normal equation to find the other unknown. Hence:

$$6,535,000 = 136b + (1,496)(6,308.0882)$$
$$6,535,000 = 136b + 9,436,900$$
$$136b = -2,901,900$$
$$b = -21,337.5$$

We can now write the regression equation:

$$Y = 6,308.0882x - 21,337.5$$

To calculate first quarter 1984 demand, we merely substitute the x value corresponding to the first quarter 1984, which is 17.

$$\text{Demand for 1st quarter 1984} = Y = (6,308.0882)(17) - 2,133.75$$
$$= 105,103.75 \text{ units}$$

Problem Statement

Management of the calculator manufacturing firm feels that in addition to time period, the demand for calculators is also a function of price. After price data for the 16 time periods were fed into a multiple regression software package on the company computer, the following regression equation was produced for the firms Model TI-53 calculator.

$$Y = 8121x_1 - 1,045x_2 - 5,525$$

where
$$x_1 = \text{time period}$$
$$x_2 = \text{price}$$
$$Y = \text{demand}$$

What is the forecast for the first quarter of 1984 if the price of the TI-53 calculator is $14.95?

Solution

Forecasting demand for first quarter 1984 is a mechanical procedure of substituting values of the independent variables into the regression equation.

$$Y = 8,121(17) - 1,045(14.95) - 5,525$$
$$= 116,909.25 \text{ units}$$

REVIEW QUESTIONS

1. Define the three basic time horizons for forecasts.
2. List the three categories of forecasting techniques described in this chapter.
3. When are qualitative forecasting techniques most useful?
4. What is the major advantage of time series analysis?
5. How do causal methods differ from time series analysis?
6. What is the major disadvantage of time series analysis?
7. Which category of forecasting technique performs best for long-term forecasts?
8. List four factors to consider in selecting the proper forecasting techniques.
9. List five commonly used qualitative forecasting techniques.
10. Define the Delphi method.
11. Which of the qualitative forecasting techniques discussed in this chapter is the most sophisticated and the most expensive?
12. Which qualitative forecasting technique is generally considered to yield the most accurate forecasts?
13. How does panel consensus differ from a grass-roots approach?
14. Using a historical analogy approach depends on what?
15. What is a time series?
16. What are the four major components of a time series?
17. To what planning horizon is time series analysis best suited?
18. Distinguish between moving average, exponential smoothing, and trend projection.
19. What is the effect of changing the smoothing constant?
20. Why is simple exponential smoothing inadequate when trend exists in time series data?
21. Write the equation of a straight line and define each parameter and variable.
22. Why is it desirable to calculate the standard error of estimate?
23. Distinguish between simple linear regression and multiple linear regression.
24. List three weaknesses of grass-roots forecasting.
25. What is the most common measure of forecast error?
26. What is the basic purpose of a tracking signal?

PROBLEMS

1. Calculate the 4-year simple moving average for 1984, using the time series data in Table 8-16.

Table 8-16   Time Series Data

YEAR	SALES
1965	$250,000
1966	262,000
1967	300,000
1968	351,000
1969	364,000
1970	365,000
1971	377,000
1972	402,000
1973	393,000
1974	400,000
1975	425,000
1976	415,000
1977	430,000
1978	440,000
1979	455,000
1980	457,000
1981	481,000
1982	492,000
1983	505,000

2. For the data in Table 8-16, calculate a 6-year weighted moving average for 1984, using the following weights: .1, .1, .1, .2, .2, and .3 from the oldest to the most recent year.

3. Using an α of .25, calculate the 1984 forecast using the simple exponential smoothing model. Use the data in Table 8-16 and assume a 1983 forecast of $500,000.

4. Using trial-and-error techniques, determine the best α, .10 or .25, for the data in Table 8-16. Assume a 1965 forecast of $250,000.

5. Again using Table 8-16 data, calculate the 1984 forecast using the trend-adjusted exponential smoothing model. Assume $\alpha = .15$, $\beta = .20$, and a 1983 forecast of $500,000.

6. For problem 5, find an α and β that you think do a good job of forecasting sales by writing and running a computer search program.

7. Draw a scatter diagram for the time series data of Table 8-16.

8. Using the method of least squares, find the regression equation for the time series data in Table 8-16. Use the regression equation to forecast sales for 1985.

9. Find the interval estimate for the regression equation derived in problem 8 corresponding to a 95.5% confidence level. Assume normality.

10. Using the regression equation found in problem 8, calculate the MAD for each year and the tracking signal for the last 5 years.

11. Given the data in Table 8-17, compare a 6-month moving average forecast and a 3-month moving average forecast for the 12 months of 1983.

12. Choose weights for a 6-month moving average that do a better job of forecasting demand than the simple 6-month moving average calculated in problem 11.

13. Which is the better smoothing constant for the 1983 data in Table 8-17, $\alpha = .05$, or $\alpha = .25$? Justify your answer.

14. By a limited search procedure, define a good trend-adjusted exponential smoothing model for the 1983 time series data in Table 8-17.

Table 8-17   Time Series Data for Part No. 215-22000

YEAR	MONTH	DEMAND
1982	January	25,450
	February	25,000
	March	25,150
	April	24,950
	May	24,500
	June	24,600
	July	24,250
	August	23,000
	September	23,100
	October	22,900
	November	22,000
	December	19,500
1983	January	19,750
	February	18,950
	March	19,150
	April	18,740
	May	18,500
	June	18,250
	July	17,475
	August	17,500
	September	17,650
	October	17,250
	November	17,100
	December	16,550

15. Write a computer program that will accomplish the search required by problem 14.

16. Draw a scatter diagram of the time series data of Table 8-17 on graph paper and "eyeball" a regression line. Read the slope and intercept off the graph to construct the regression equation.

17. Find the simple linear regression equation for the Table 8-17 data using the least-squares method.

18. How do the January 1984 demand forecasts differ using the "eyeballed" equation and the least-squares equation derived in problem 17?

19. Given a confidence level of 90%, what is the prediction interval for demand for February 1984? Use the regression equation developed in problem 17.

20. Calculate a MAD for each month in Table 8-17 using a simple exponential smoothing model with an α of .25. Which months during 1983 would the tracking signal alert management if the critical level were set at 3.0?

21. The number of pediatric admissions for one month can be forecasted using the following regression equation:

$$Y = 5.1 + 5.72x_1 + .002x_2 + 4.16x_3$$

where

Y = number of pediatric admissions for one month

x_1 = number of pediatricians on the hospital staff

x_2 = city population of people under 20

x_3 = number of obstetricians on the hospital staff

If the hospital has 7 pediatricians and 9 obstetricians and the under-20 population is 14,000, what is the monthly forecast for pediatrics admissions?

22. The ACME Corporation has experienced steady growth in annual sales in its 19-year history. The firm has traditionally used a 4-year moving average to predict sales for the coming year. The new vice-president of marketing feels that a simple 4-year moving average is too "simple minded" and results in extremely poor sales forecasts. Because these inaccuracies affect many important managerial decisions, the vice-president of marketing has asked you to determine the best time series technique for estimating sales by comparing
   a. The 4-year moving average.
   b. A weighted 6-year moving average using the following weights: .1, .1, .1, .2, .2, .3 from the oldest to the most recent year.
   c. A simple exponential smoothing model using an α of .25. Assume a 1966 forecast of $247,000.

    d. A trend-adjusted exponential smoothing model using an $\alpha = .15$ and $\beta = .20$.

    e. A least-squares regression equation.

Acme Corporation Annual Sales

1966	$247,000
1967	251,000
1968	257,000
1969	259,000
1970	271,000
1971	275,000
1972	295,000
1973	289,000
1974	287,000
1975	305,000
1976	328,000
1977	345,000
1978	370,000
1979	387,000
1980	404,000
1981	405,000
1982	419,000
1983	417,000

23. The price of BIM Corporation stock has varied over the past year. The price at the end of each month is reflected in the table.

MONTH	PRICE PER SHARE	MONTH	PRICE PER SHARE
1	$55\frac{1}{8}$	7	$68\frac{3}{4}$
2	$57\frac{1}{4}$	8	$69\frac{1}{8}$
3	$57\frac{1}{2}$	9	$72\frac{1}{8}$
4	$59\frac{3}{8}$	10	$72\frac{3}{8}$
5	65	11	$72\frac{1}{8}$
6	$63\frac{1}{4}$	12	$75\frac{1}{5}$

    a. Draw a scatter diagram for these data.

    b. Forecast the next month's price per share using simple linear regression.

    c. Forecast next month's price per share using a trend-adjusted exponential smoothing model with $\alpha = .2$ and $\beta = .3$. Assume $F_{12} = \$74.00$ per share and $T_{12} = 0$.

    d. Forecast price per share for month 16 using the trend-adjusted model used in part c.

24. The small computer service bureau business is a very volatile and risk-ridden sector of the economy. In a large southwestern city the number of service bureaus going out of business in the last 3 years has been extremely high. The number of failures for each quarter of the previous 3 years is reflected in the following table.

| | 1981 | | 1982 | | 1983 |
QUARTER	NUMBER OF FAILURES	QUARTER	NUMBER OF FAILURES	QUARTER	NUMBER OF FAILURES
1	27	1	30	1	35
2	29	2	35	2	42
3	40	3	49	3	57
4	35	4	40	4	47

a. What is your forecast for each quarter of 1984 using only the time series data given and a trend-adjusted exponential smoothing model with an $\alpha = .25$ and a $\beta = .15$.

b. If the data were available, what other factors do you think would have an effect on service bureau bankruptcies?

25. Crime in the streets has been increasing in the last 3 years at a dramatic rate, and the mayor and the city council are trying to decide on what action to take to alleviate the situation. The police chief contends that if something isn't done soon, the number of violent crimes reported in a month will reach epidemic proportions. Using simple linear regression, predict the number of violent crimes that will be committed for January, June, and December of 1984.

| | NUMBER OF VIOLENT CRIMES | | |
MONTH	1981	1982	1983
January	12	19	35
February	11	22	32
March	14	21	37
April	13	25	38
May	13	23	41
June	15	25	40
July	16	24	45
August	15	27	38
September	18	26	47
October	17	18	49
November	18	23	48
December	20	30	55

26. ZUKON manufacturing company held a patent on their number 1 selling product until 2 years ago. Since that time, demand has been decreasing.

Monthly demand for the last 2 years is reflected in the table.

| | DEMAND (UNITS) | |
MONTH	1982	1983
January	12,150	10,002
February	12,043	10,041
March	12,220	9,679
April	11,980	9,683
May	11,570	9,555
June	11,245	9,145
July	11,247	8,512
August	11,050	8,672
September	10,550	8,444
October	10,600	8,554
November	10,243	8,312
December	10,076	8,001

a. Use the least-squares method to develop a simple linear regression equation.
b. Draw a scatter diagram and visually fit a straight line to the data.
c. Using the regression equation in part a, forecast demand for April 1984.
d. What is your forecast for the total demand for 1984.
e. Calculate the MAD for all months and the tracking signal for the 6 months of 1983. Use the regression equation developed in part a.
f. Fit a trend-adjusted exponential smoothing model to the data and project June 1984 demand.
g. Compare the accuracy of the trend projection model (part a) and the smoothing model (part f) using the MAD.

27. Imagine that the unemployment rate in the United States for the years 1981, 1982, and 1983 has fluctuated as shown in the table. Which, if any, time series techniques would you apply to the data to predict unemployment levels for 1984? How would you improve your forecast?

| HYPOTHETICAL UNEMPLOYMENT RATES IN THE UNITED STATES | | | |
QUARTER	1981	1982	1983
1st	7.46	6.2	5.73
2nd	7.1	6.0	5.73
3rd	6.9	5.96	6.10
4th	6.63	5.83	6.21

28. Enrollment in the College of Business Administration at State University has been increasing in the last few years. The dean of the college is preparing a

5-year plan in which he is asking the university's central administration for significant increases in human and financial resources. These requested resources are based on the dean's forecast of future enrollments in the College of Business. Given semester enrollment for the last 5 years, what is your best estimate of full-time equivalent (FTE) enrollment at the end of the next 5 years? Use simple linear regression. What is wrong with using a simple time series forecast to predict enrollment at the end of 1988?

FULL-TIME EQUIVALENT ENROLLMENT		
YEAR	SEMESTER 1	SEMESTER 2
1979	1,077	998
1980	1,117	1,103
1981	1,353	1,297
1982	1,471	1,419
1983	1,503	1,475

REFERENCES

ADAM, EVERETT E., and RONALD J. EBERT, *Production and Operations Management*, 2nd ed. Englewood Cliffs, N.J.: Prentice-Hall, 1982.

CHAMBERS, I.S., S.K. MULLICH, and D.D. SMITH, "How to Choose the Right Forecasting Technique," *Harvard Business Review*, July–August 1971.

CHASE, RICHARD B., and NICHOLAS J. AQUILANO, *Production and Operations Management*. Homewood, Ill.: Richard D. Irwin, 1981.

CHOW, WEN M., "Adaptive Control of the Exponential Smoothing Constant," *Journal of Industrial Engineering*, 16, no. 5 (September–October 1965), 314–17.

CLARK, CHARLES T., and LAWRENCE L. SCHKADE, *Statistical Methods for Business and Economics*. Cincinnati, O.: South-Western Publishing Company, 1977.

HOEL, PAUL G., and RAYMOND J. JESSEN, *Basic Statistics for Business and Economics*. New York: John Wiley, 1981.

PARKER, G.C., and EDELBERTO L. SEGURA, "How to Get a Better Forecast," *Harvard Business Review*, 49, no. 2 (March–April 1971), 99–109.

MONKS, JOSEPH G., *Operations Management: Theory and Problems*. New York: McGraw-Hill, 1982.

SULLIVAN, WILLIAM G., and W. WAYNE CLAYCOMBE, *Fundamentals of Forecasting*. Reston, Va.: Reston Publishing Company, 1977.

9

AGGREGATE PLANNING

Definition and requirements of aggregate planning
Strategies for aggregate planning
    active strategies
    passive strategies
Methods for aggregate planning
    graphical method
    mathematical and computer techniques
    heuristic methods
    comparison of methods
Learning-curve effects on production
Disaggregation
    master scheduling
    hierarchical planning for aggregate planning and disaggregation
Summary
Supplement to chapter 9
    LP formulation of aggregate planning

Planning is one of the primary functions of a manager. It is through proper planning that an organization can hope to achieve its objectives. Along the dimension of time, planning breaks naturally into three phases: long-range, intermediate-range, and short-range.

Long-range or strategic planning typically involves the formulation of organizational objectives (and strategies for obtaining those objectives) for a planning horizon of several years. Long-range planning is the responsibility of top management and also includes growth policies, establishment of total budgets, and long-range capital investments such as building new facilities. In long-range planning, management has a great deal of flexibility in choosing courses of action. It may order new equipment, change products or services, select new management, or train a new labor force. The duration of the long-range planning horizon can vary from one to more than five years; it depends on the organization and how long it takes to respond to changes. For example, an electrical power company may need five years or more to plan and build a new plant to meet increasing demand, whereas a service company such as an engineering consulting firm can get into a new line of expertise in a year or two.

Intermediate-range planning usually involves from one month to a year or more. This type of planning is usually the function of middle management and involves tactical decisions such as quarterly plans, subdivisions of budgets, and arrangements to meet fluctuations in demand. Aggregate planning is the essence of intermediate-range planning, and that is what we shall study in this chapter. This type of planning has received significant attention, and several methods have been used for it. In intermediate-range planning, management must work within the limitations established in long-range planning, but still has some flexibility in selecting courses of action.

The short-range planning horizon is from a day up to possibly a month. The focus is on operational considerations such as schedules, short-run budgets, and daily or weekly plans. The objective is to meet planned production as economically as possible. Management participating directly in short-range planning is usually at the first level and involves supervisors and foremen. Their decisions must fit within the constraints imposed by the intermediate-planning decisions. In short-run planning, the details of scheduling particular jobs and implementing special projects must be carried out. The aggregate or general plans of intermediate planning must be disaggregated to specify the production or operation plan into time-phased weekly, daily, or hourly activities. Little flexibility exists to achieve these short-range objectives. In a later chapter, we shall turn to the specific methods of scheduling.

See Figure 9-1 for a graphical illustration of the time planning horizons of long-, intermediate-, and short-range planning.

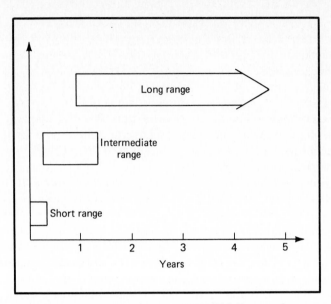

FIGURE 9-1   Planning Horizons of Types of Planning

DEFINITION AND REQUIREMENTS OF AGGREGATE PLANNING

Aggregate planning is intermediate-range planning in which strategies are devised to economically absorb demand fluctuations. The output of aggregate planning should specify values for monthly manpower levels, output levels, inventory levels, overtime commitments, subcontracting needs, vacation plans, undertime levels, and hiring quantities. The objective is to minimize future operating costs over a particular planning horizon.

As the name implies, aggregate planning involves combining the relevant resources into general terms or an overall aggregate. Thus, an organization needs an overall measure of output in aggregate planning. These gross amounts include total demand, inventory, work force, or production capacity requirements—for example, barrels of oil in the oil industry, machine- or man-hours in a manufacturing plant, or beds in a hospital. Consider a paint company whose product line consists of many different types and colors of paint. The aggregate plan for this company might look like the following specification of total gallons of paint (in 1000s) for each month for the upcoming year:

JAN.	FEB.	MAR.	APR.	MAY	JUN.	JUL.	AUG.	SEP.	OCT.	NOV.	DEC.
22	25	30	35	36	38	34	30	25	22	20	20

Aggregate planning also requires some means of forecasting these aggregate levels for the planning horizon. Data pertaining to past sales, trends, and seasonal components are necessary, as well as an effective forecasting technique. See Chapter 8 for a thorough discussion of forecasting.

Successful aggregate planning requires a systems approach. Not only must the aggregate planner have forecasting input from the marketing function, but aggregate strategies must fall within the cash-flow constraints set by finance. Making intermediate operations plans without the input and cooperation of other functions of the organization can result in unworkable or, at least, suboptimal strategies.

In order to be useful, aggregate plans must be translatable into planned production levels for individual products in each month, and assignments of personnel to specific work groups and operations. Additionally productive capacity must be available to accommodate the desired level of production of individual products. The determination of planned production levels and schedules for individual products is called master production scheduling. The master schedule is derived from the aggregate production plan and provides input to MRP (materials requirements planning), which plans the needed coverage of parts and components needed to support the production of end items. Figure 9-2 illustrates the relationship of aggregate planning to master scheduling and MRP. Notice the tie-in with capacity planning and the iterative nature of the information feedback process which insures that planned production is indeed feasible.

STRATEGIES FOR AGGREGATE PLANNING

In planning the future use of operations capacity, the organization can assume an active or a passive role. In the passive role, the planner tries to respond to demand fluctuations but not to affect the rate of demand itself. In the active role, the firm tries to influence or in some way change the demand pattern.

Active Strategies

The objective of active strategies is to smooth out the peaks and valleys of demand during the planning horizon. The goal is to obtain a smoother load on the productive facilities. During periods of low demand, increased sales of goods or services can be encouraged through price cuts. Thus, lawn and garden tools are sometimes cheaper during the off season, telephone calls are cheaper at night, and Miami Beach hotel rooms are most expensive during the winter months. Periods of low demand can also be tackled through expenditures on special advertising programs or promotional gimmicks.

During periods of high demand, management can choose simply to not meet all demand requirements. However this approach is not usually taken as it purposely ignores opportunities for increased revenue. A more reasonable alternative during high demand periods is to incur order backlogs. Backlogs, however, may be acceptable only for certain types of goods or services. The success of backlogging demand certainly depends upon the customer's willingness to wait. In some cases

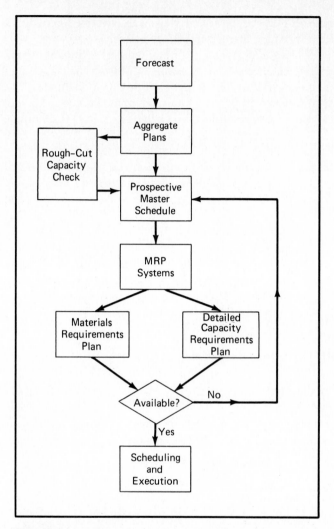

FIGURE 9-2   Relationship of Aggregate Planning to Master Scheduling and MRP

backlogs may result in customer ill will or losses of future sales; customers may be willing to wait for automobiles, but probably not airline tickets.

Another active approach to smoothing demand for productive resources is to select a product mix which consists of counterseasonal products. For example, a firm might manufacture air conditioners during the warm months and heat pumps or furnaces during the winter, another company might maintain a product mix of snow skiis and tennis rackets. Vergin found that the counterseasonal product line was by far the most widely used smoothing strategy among eight manufacturing firms with seasonal demand.

Passive Strategies

The objective of passive strategies is not to change demand but to absorb somehow the fluctuations in demand. The alternatives for passive responses include work-force size, work rate, inventory, subcontracting, and capacity utilization. Varying any one of these factors while holding all others constant is called a pure strategy. Thus, absorbing demand by increasing the size of the work force is a pure strategy. A mixed strategy involves the use of two or more pure strategies—for example, a buildup of inventory and subcontracting of work in order to meet peak demand levels.

The first passive strategy is to vary the size of the work force in accordance with fluctuations in demand. Thus, hiring would be used to absorb high demand, and laying off workers would be used to absorb low demand. From a behavioral and legal standpoint, this strategy has some obvious limitations in terms of morale and labor unions. It could be used to some extent, however, in labor-intensive industries. The strategy of varying the size of the work force requires cost data pertaining to hiring and laying off, but these costs are not always easy to determine. The hiring process would include time spent interviewing, testing, and training. Additionally, the learning-curve phenomenon would require that the typical worker be at his job a while to achieve full productivity. Layoff costs include severance pay, insurance, unemployment compensation, and unmeasurable ill will on the part of the worker and possibly the community.

A strategy that can be used to vary the output rate while keeping the work force constant in size is the use of overtime and undertime. Undertime implies that the workers are receiving full pay, whereas a shorter-workweek policy implies less than full-time pay. The costs of an overtime strategy can be directly measured in terms of increased wages; however, undertime involves opportunity costs, and shorter workweeks involve intangibles such as worker dissatisfaction.

Inventory can be used to absorb demand even when the work force or work rate remains constant. The basic idea is to produce inventory during periods of low demand so that this inventory can be used to meet high demand in other periods. This strategy is usually limited to manufacturing firms, as most service-oriented organizations do not deal with inventoriable items. Maintaining an inventory, however, requires storage space and incurs costs involving capital opportunity cost, taxes, insurance, handling, and possibly obsolescence.

Subcontracting work is another pure strategy that can be used during periods of high demand. Usually, the per-unit production costs are higher when subcontracted rather than produced "in-house," so the benefits must be weighed against the costs. And in subcontracting, the firm also loses some control over the quality of the final product.

A final pure strategy, which is more common to service industries, is the utilization of capacity. Organizations that cannot store their product or service must plan for a capacity to meet peak demand. Examples include electric power companies, telephone companies, computer time-sharing companies, and even airlines. In this approach, all the available capacity is used only during periods of highest demand.

In summary, the pure strategies for absorbing fluctuating demand are:

1. Varying work-force size
2. Varying production rate
3. Increasing inventory
4. Subcontracting
5. Capacity utilization

Even though each of the pure strategies can effectively aid in absorbing demand, it is usually some combination or mixed strategy that works best. The problem of finding the best overall strategy has been approached by several methods, some of them quite simple and some quite sophisticated. In the next section, we first consider a simple graphical approach to aggregate planning and then look at some more effective mathematical and computerized approaches.

METHODS FOR AGGREGATE PLANNING

Graphical Method

Our first approach to aggregate planning is one of the most widely used and offers the advantage of enabling the decision maker to visualize the plans being considered. To illustrate the graphical method, we present an example.

Consider the Braden Company, which has developed monthly forecasts for its leading product. The expected monthly demand for the upcoming year is presented in Table 9-1. The Braden Company assumes that safety stock is 20 percent of monthly demand for planning purposes. (Safety stock is the amount of inventory that is stored in excess of expected demand.) In Table 9-1, we also see the calculated safety stock and number of working days per month. The number of working days in July is low because of vacation time. The implied production rate per day in the last column of the table is calculated by dividing the production requirements by the working days in the month. Figure 9-3 graphically depicts the implied production rate per day for each month, and Table 9-2 presents the costs needed to assess any proposed aggregate plan.

If we assume a starting inventory of 1,000 units at the beginning of the year, we can now compare three proposed plans for absorbing demand fluctuations. In Plan 1, let's consider an approach that maintains a constant work force throughout the year. From Table 9-1 we can see that 111,000 units required and 242 working days yields $111,000/242 = 458.67$ units per working day as an average. Considering that each man works eight hours and each unit requires four hours for production, we see that we need $458.67/2 = 230$ full-time workers. In the first month, January,

Aggregate Planning

Table 9-1   Demand and Safety Stock Forecasts

MONTH	EXPECTED DEMAND	DESIRED SAFETY STOCK	BEGINNING INVENTORY	PRODUCTION REQUIREMENTS	WORKING DAYS	IMPLIED PRODUC- TION RATE PER DAY
Jan.	9,000	1,800	1,000	9,800	22	445
Feb.	8,000	1,600	1,800	7,800	19	411
Mar.	7,000	1,400	1,600	6,800	21	324
Apr.	6,000	1,200	1,400	5,800	21	276
May	5,000	1,000	1,200	4,800	22	218
June	6,000	1,200	1,000	6,200	20	310
July	8,000	1,600	1,200	8,400	12	700
Aug.	10,000	2,000	1,600	10,400	22	473
Sept.	14,000	2,800	2,000	14,800	20	740
Oct.	15,000	3,000	2,800	15,200	23	661
Nov.	12,000	2,400	3,000	11,400	19	600
Dec.	10,000	2,000	2,400	9,600	21	457
	110,000	22,000		111,000	242	

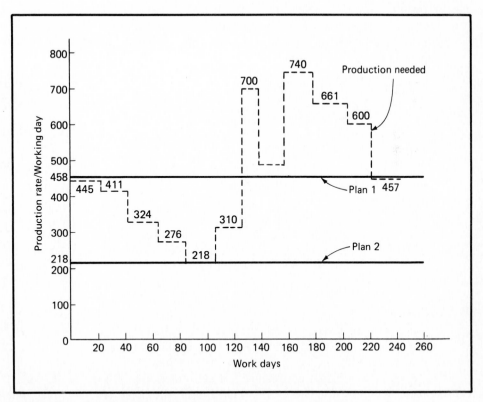

FIGURE 9-3   Production Rates for Various Plans

Table 9-2 Cost Information

Manufacturing cost	=	$30 per unit (excluding labor)
Inventory carrying cost	=	$2 per unit / month
Stockout cost	=	$6 per unit / month
Subcontracting cost	=	$65 per unit ($35 marginal increase)
Average pay rate	=	$5 per hour
Overtime pay rate	=	$7.50 per hour (maximum 25% per month)
Hiring costs	=	$220 per man
Layoff costs	=	$270 per man
Man-hours per unit	=	4

we have 1,000 units on hand, estimated demand of 9,000, and a desired safety stock of 1,800. This yields a needed production of 9,800 units. However, 230 full-time workers will produce 10,120 units in a 22-day work month, and the 320 excess units, along with 1,800 units of safety stock, push the inventory level to 2,120 in January. The various monthly production outputs, resulting inventories, and associated costs are shown in Table 9-4.

In Plan 1, labor costs are relatively high since the work force maintains 230 full-time workers. Inventory costs are higher than the other plans since units are stored early in the year to meet demand later in the year. Notice in Table 9-4 that inventory builds to a peak of 15,140 units in August. Figure 9-3 illustrates the constant daily production rate of Plan 1.

In Plan 2, we investigate another pure strategy, in which a constant work force is maintained at a level necessary only for the lowest month, May; all demand above this level is met by subcontracting. During May, we have a forecasted demand of 5,000 units + 1,000 safety stock − April's safety stock of 1,200 = 4,800, and 22 workdays. Thus, we need 109 full-time workers. Under this plan, subcontracting is required in every month except May. No inventory costs (except for safety stocks) are incurred under Plan 2, as only subcontracting costs apply. The daily production rate of Plan 2 is shown in Figure 9-3. The associated cost calculations are shown in Table 9-5.

In Plan 3, we consider a mixed strategy in which overtime and subcontracting are used to absorb demand. We assume that overtime is limited to 10 hours per week, or two hours per day for each employee. In Plan 3, we maintain a constant work force of 109 workers and subcontract work whenever demand exceeds regular plus overtime production capacity. The cost calculations are shown in Table 9-6.

In Table 9-3, we see the costs broken down for each of the three plans. The costs in Table 9-3 accurately reflect the cost differences between the three plans. The labor costs are total costs, but the inventory costs only reflect inventory levels above the desired safety stock levels. Also, since manufacturing costs of $30 per unit were not included in the cost comparisons, the subcontracting cost used in Tables 9-5 and 9-6 was the marginal cost increase of subcontracting or $65 − $30 = $35 per unit. From Table 9-3 you can see that Plan 1 offers the cheapest alternative for absorbing demand. In this problem, the labor cost was a dominant factor, but subcontracting

Table 9-3   Cost Comparison of the Three Plans

| | PLAN 1 (INVENTORY) | PLAN 2 (SUBCONTRACTING) | PLAN 3 (OVERTIME AND SUBCONTRACTING) |
COST	WORK FORCE = 230	WORK FORCE = 109	WORK FORCE = 109
Regular labor	$2,226,400	$1,055,120	$1,055,120
Overtime labor	0	0	359,700
Inventory	205,760	0	0
Subcontracting	0	2,038,540	1,618,855
TOTAL COST	$2,432,160	$3,093,660	$3,033,675

proved more expensive. In some companies, management may be unable or unwilling to resort to two hours of overtime each working day or to subcontract over 30 percent of the units demanded. Of course, other plans involving other pure or mixed strategies could be considered; we have examined only three possibilities.

Even though the charting method is widely used and useful, it is more helpful in evaluating strategies than in generating or constructing them. The graphical method does not guarantee an optimal or even a near-optimal solution. What is needed is a systematic method that will consider all costs and generate an effective solution. We now turn to some mathematical and computer models for aggregate planning problems.

Mathematical and Computer Techniques

Useful mathematical optimization models have been developed for various cases of aggregate planning problems. All these models, however, make certain assumptions about the cost structure or basic nature of the problem; for this reason, they are not always answers to the general aggregate planning problem. Each model we shall discuss is a useful planning tool for certain types of problems.

Transportation Model. The transportation model that was presented in the supplement to Chapter 2 is useful not only for distributing a product from plant to market, but also for planning production. The transportation model is applicable whenever the costs of production, inventory, and subcontracting are approximately linear in nature. Its most serious limitation for planning purposes is that it does not account for changeover costs, such as hiring and laying off workers from one period to the next. Thus, it would be most useful when management was exploring aggregate plans having a relatively stable work force over time.

The transportation model will determine an optimal aggregate plan assuming linear costs, and demand fluctuations that are to be absorbed only through overtime, undertime, inventory, subcontracting, and backorders. In the transportation model, the destinations or columns will represent product demand and the origins or rows

Table 9-4 Aggregate Planning Cost Calculations — Plan 1

INVENTORY	JAN.	FEB.	MAR.	APR.	MAY	JUN.	JUL.	AUG.	SEP.	OCT.	NOV.	DEC.	TOTAL
RESOURCES													
Regular workers	230	230	230	230	230	230	230	230	230	230	230	230	
Overtime percent	—	—	—	—	—	—	—	—	—	—	—	—	
Working days	22	19	21	21	22	20	12	22	20	23	19	21	242
Units produced	10,120	8,740	9,660	9,660	10,120	9,200	5,520	10,120	9,200	10,580	8,740	9,660	111,320
Demand forecast	9,000	8,000	7,000	6,000	5,000	6,000	8,000	10,000	14,000	15,000	12,000	10,000	110,000
Inventory	2,120	2,860	5,520	9,180	14,300	17,500	15,020	15,140	10,340	5,920	2,660	2,320	
Subcontracted units	—	—	—	—	—	—	—	—	—	—	—	—	
COSTS													
Regular time	202,400	174,800	193,200	193,200	202,400	184,000	110,400	202,400	184,000	211,600	174,800	193,200	2,226,400
Overtime	—	—	—	—	—	—	—	—	—	—	—	—	
Inventory	4,240	5,720	11,040	18,360	28,600	35,000	30,040	30,280	20,680	11,840	5,320	4,640	205,760
Subcontracting	—	—	—	—	—	—	—	—	—	—	—	—	
	$206,640	$180,520	$204,240	$211,560	$231,000	$219,000	$140,440	$232,680	$204,680	$223,440	$180,120	$197,840	$2,432,160

Table 9-5 Aggregate Planning Cost Calculations — Plan 2

SUBCONTRACTING	JAN.	FEB.	MAR.	APR.	MAY	JUN.	JUL.	AUG.	SEP.	OCT.	NOV.	DEC.	TOTAL
RESOURCES													
Regular workers	109	109	109	109	109	109	109	109	109	109	109	109	
Overtime percent	—	—	—	—	—	—	—	—	—	—	—	—	—
Working days	22	19	21	21	22	20	12	22	20	23	19	21	242
Units produced	4,796	4,142	4,578	4,578	4,796	4,360	2,616	4,796	4,630	5,014	4,142	4,578	52,756
Production requirements	9,800	7,800	6,800	5,800	4,800	6,200	8,400	10,400	14,800	15,200	11,400	9,600	111,000
Inventory	—	—	—	—	—	—	—	—	—	—	—	—	—
Subcontracted units	5,004	3,658	2,222	1,222	4	1,840	5,784	5,604	10,440	10,186	7,258	5,022	58,244
COSTS													
Regular time	95,920	82,840	91,560	91,560	95,920	87,200	52,320	95,920	87,200	100,280	82,840	91,560	1,055,120
Overtime	—	—	—	—	—	—	—	—	—	—	—	—	—
Inventory	—	—	—	—	—	—	—	—	—	—	—	—	—
Subcontracting	175,140	128,030	77,770	42,770	140	64,400	202,440	196,140	365,400	356,510	254,030	175,770	2,038,540
TOTAL COST	$271,060	$210,870	$169,330	$134,330	$96,060	$151,600	$254,760	$292,060	$452,600	$456,790	$336,870	$267,330	$3,093,660

Table 9-6 Aggregate Planning Cost Calculations — Plan 3

OVERTIME AND SUBCONTRACTING	JAN.	FEB.	MAR.	APR.	MAY	JUN.	JUL.	AUG.	SEP.	OCT.	NOV.	DEC.	TOTAL
RESOURCES													
Regular workers	109	109	109	109	109	109	109	109	109	109	109	109	
Overtime percent	25	25	25	25	0	25	25	25	25	25	25	25	
Working days	22	19	21	21	22	20	12	22	20	23	19	21	242
Units													
produced	5,995	5,177	5,722	5,722	4,800	5,450	3,270	5,995	5,450	6,267	5,177	5,722	64,747
Production requirements	9,800	7,800	6,800	5,800	4,800	6,200	8,400	10,400	14,800	15,200	11,400	9,600	111,000
Inventory	—	—	—	—	—	—	—	—	—	—	—	—	
Subcontracted units	3,805	2,623	1,078	78	—	750	5,130	4,405	9,350	8,933	6,223	38,782	46,253
COSTS													
Regular time	95,920	82,840	91,560	91,560	95,920	87,200	52,320	95,920	87,200	100,280	82,840	91,560	1,055,120
Overtime	35,970	31,065	34,355	34,335	0	32,700	19,620	35,970	32,700	37,605	31,065	34,355	359,700
Inventory	—	—	—	—	—	—	—	—	—	—	—	—	
Subcontracting	135,175	91,805	37,730	2,730	—	26,250	179,550	154,175	327,250	312,655	217,805	135,730	1,618,855
TOTAL COST	$265,065	$205,710	$163,625	$128,625	$ 95,920	$146,150	$251,490	$286,065	$447,150	$450,540	$331,710	$261,625	$3,033,675

Table 9-7 General Form of Transportation Tableau for Three-Period Model

		PERIOD 1	PERIOD 2	PERIOD 3	FINAL INVENTORY	UNUSED CAPACITY	AVAILABLE CAPACITY
	Beginning inventory	0	c	$2c$	$3c$	$4c$	I_b
Period 1	Regular time	r	$r+c$	$r+2c$	$r+3c$	w	R_1
	Overtime	t	$t+c$	$t+2c$	$t+3c$	0	O_1
	Subcontracted	s	$s+c$	$s+2c$	$s+3c$	0	S_1
Period 2	Regular time	$r+b$	r	$r+c$	$r+2c$	w	R_2
	Overtime	$t+b$	t	$t+c$	$t+2c$	0	O_2
	Subcontracted	$s+b$	s	$s+c$	$s+2c$	0	S_2
Period 3	Regular time	$r+2b$	$r+b$	r	$r+c$	w	R_3
	Overtime	$t+2b$	$t+b$	t	$t+c$	0	O_3
	Subcontracted	$s+2b$	$s+b$	s	$s+c$	0	S_3
	Demand requirement	D_1	D_2	D_3	I_f		

will represent the means and their capacities to absorb demand. For example, Table 9-7 shows the general form of a transportation model for three planning periods. The R_i, O_i, and S_i represent regular time, overtime, and subcontracting capacities respectively in period i. The D_i represent product demand in period i, and I_b and I_f represent beginning and ending inventories. In the cells of the tableau, the costs in the upper left-hand corners are represented by c = inventory carrying cost, r = regular-time production cost, t = overtime production cost, s = subcontracting cost, b = backorder cost, and w = wage cost per idle employee on regular time. The squares or cells of the tableau represent a means of absorbing demand in a particular period by a particular resource. For example, cell 2, 1 (second row, first column) represents the means of satisfying period 1 demand with regular production in period 1.

Let's apply the transportation model to the previous example of the Braden Company. To keep the model conveniently small, we will consider only the third quarter of the year. Assuming that the beginning inventory for July will be the safety stock of June, we have the associated transportation tableau for the Braden Company in Table 9-8. The available capacity is figured on the basis of 109 workers, each of whom is able to produce two units each working day; overtime capacity is assumed to be 25 percent of regular capacity, and subcontracting is limited to 9,000 units per month. Demand requirements are calculated as forecasted demand minus the preceding month's safety stock plus the current month's safety stock. From Table 9-2 we obtain the following cost information:

Table 9-8   Transportation Tableau and Solution for Braden Company

		JULY	AUG.	SEPT.	FINAL INVENTORY	UNUSED CAPACITY	AVAILABLE CAPACITY
	Beginning inventory	0 — 1,200	2	4	6	8	1,200
July	Regular time	50 — 2,616	52	54	56	20	2,616
	Overtime	60 — 654	62	64	66	0	654
	Subcontracted	65 — 3,930	67	69	71	0 — 5,070	9,000
Aug.	Regular time	56	50 — 4,796	52	54	20	4,796
	Overtime	66	60 — 1,199	62	64	0	1,199
	Subcontracted	71	65 — 4,405	67 — 350	69 — 3,000	0 — 1,245	9,000
Sept.	Regular time	62	56	50 — 4,360	52	20	4,360
	Overtime	72	66	60 — 1,090	62	0	1,090
	Subcontracted	77	71	65 — 9,000	67	0	9,000
	Demand requirement	8,400	10,400	14,800	3,000	6,315	

Manufacturing cost = \$50 per unit on regular time

Regular-time labor = \$5 per hour $\times$ 4 hours per unit = \$20

$w = 20$

$r = 30 + 20 = 50$

Overtime labor = \$7.50 per hour $\times$ 4 hours per unit = \$30

$t = 30 + 30 = 60$

Inventory carrying cost = \$2 per unit per month

$c = 2$

Subcontracting cost = \$65 per unit including outside materials, labor, etc.

$s = 65$

Backorder cost = \$6 per unit per month

$b = 6$

The solution to the three-month planning problem is also shown in Table 9-8. The solution represents a mixed strategy; regular time, overtime, subcontracting, and inventory are used to absorb demand. Inventory is stored in August to cover September demand and the desired 3,000 units of final inventory for the safety stock in October. Looking at September demand of 14,800, for example, we can see that 350 units are met by subcontracting and inventory from August; 4,360 units from regular time; 1,090 units from overtime; and 9,000 units for subcontracting in September.

We could have solved the aggregate planning problem for twelve months, but this would have required a larger, 37 × 14 transportation tableau. The transportation-model approach to aggregate planning has been around since 1956, when Bowman first suggested its use in aggregate planning.[1] It isn't widely used because it does not account for costs of production-level changes.

Linear and Goal Programming.   The transportation model is a special type of linear programming model. In general linear programming, the models developed do not have to fit a special form, as transportation models do. Thus, in linear programming models it is possible to account for the costs associated with hiring, firing, and other production change costs. (Refer to the supplement to Chapter 2 for more material on linear programming.) In 1960, Hanssmann and Hess proposed a linear programming approach to production and employment scheduling.[2]

Since general linear models vary from problem to problem, the user must develop his own model for his special application; this requires insight and a certain amount of time spent creating and then solving the model. Fortunately, linear programming models are efficiently solved by the simplex method on a computer. Many computer manufacturers offer standard LP software packages to their users. The potential drawback of linear programming for aggregate planning is the linearity assumptions. In linear programming, the objective function and all constraints must be linear. If production change costs, inventory costs, or problem relationships are not approximately linear, then linear programming would not be an appropriate tool.

Linear programming models also seek to optimize a simple objective such as cost minimization. Many decision problems, including aggregate planning, strive to meet several objectives. For instance, management may want to minimize costs but also maintain a relatively stable work force and keep inventory and overtime at acceptable levels. *Goal programming* is a recent mathematical programming method that attempts to handle multiple incompatible goals. Since it may be impossible to meet all goals, the goals are ranked and highest priority goals are met first. The final solution may result in "satisficing," or only getting as close as possible to some

---

[1]E.H. Bowman, "Production Planning by the Transportation Method of Linear Programming," *Journal of the Operations Research Society*, February 1956.

[2]F. Hanssmann and S.W. Hess, "A Linear Programming Approach to Production and Employment Scheduling," *Management Technology*, 1 (January 1960), 46–52.

goals. Goal programming is an effective tool for multiple-criteria decision making, but most of the work on these models has been linear in nature. Thus, linearity assumptions can be a pitfall just as in linear programming. Some research is being done on nonlinear goal programming models, but these tend to be much more difficult to solve. Further research may enable goal programming to be a highly effective tool for aggregate planning.

Linear Decision Rule.   Another aggregate planning method that attempts to optimize decisions for the intermediate planning horizon is the Linear Decision Rule (LDR). It was developed by Holt, Modigliani, and Simon in 1955.[3] It is possibly the best-known analytical method for aggregate planning, and a classical approach against which others have continued to compare their results.

Unlike the implication of the name, the LDR is actually based on a nonlinear cost function. However, the decision rules for production and work-force levels resulting from the LDR analysis are linear. The LDR minimizes the combined costs of regular payroll, hiring and layoff, overtime, and inventory.

A unique feature of the LDR is that it assumes that each of these four cost functions can be approximated by a quadratic cost curve. A quadratic function is a nonlinear function of the second degree containing products of variables or variables squared. Figure 9-4 illustrates the quadratic cost assumptions and their comparisons with the assumed actual costs.

In Figure 9-4(a), it is assumed that payroll costs rise proportionately with work-force size. The hiring and layoff costs vary with changes in the work force. Assuming linear increases for hiring and linear increases for firing, the V-shaped graph in Figure 9-4(b) is obtained. The hiring and layoff cost curve can be approximated by a second-degree parabola, as shown by the dashed line. In Figure 9-4(c), the overtime costs are assumed to rise at a nonlinear rate, since overtime productivity decreases but production bottlenecks tend to increase as the production rate increases. The inventory costs depicted in Figure 9-4(d) increase with high inventory or low inventory. High inventory levels increase carrying costs, whereas low inventory levels incur shortage costs and possibly more frequent setup costs.

The exact nature of the approximating quadratic curves in Figure 9-4 must be determined by careful data collection and subsequent curve fit analysis to fit the data. The linear decision rules are then obtained by using calculus to differentiate the overall quadratic cost function and solving for the values that achieve the minimum cost.

Example: The authors of the LDR applied their model to data collected from a paint factory for the years 1949 to 1954. The quadratic cost function was determined from actual accounting data, along with subjective estimates of intangible costs. Their analysis yielded two equations or linear decision rules that specify work-force level and production rate for each month *t*. To interpret the decision rules, let us

---

[3]C.C. Holt, F. Modigliani, and H.A. Simon, "A Linear Decision Rule for Production and Employment Scheduling," *Management Science*, 2, no. 2 (October 1955), 1–30.

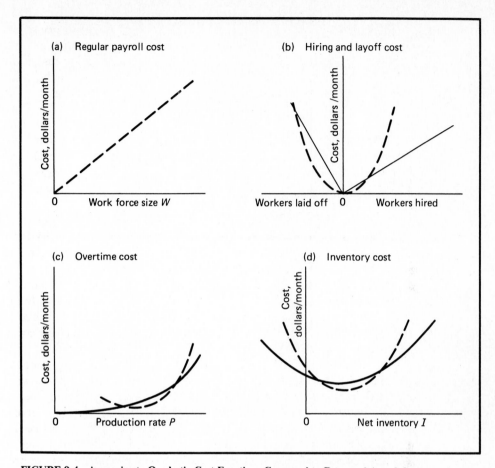

FIGURE 9-4   Approximate Quadratic Cost Functions Compared to Presumed Actual Costs

define the following decision variables:

W_t = number of employees required during month t

W_{t-1} = number of employees in work force at end of preceding month, $t - 1$

P_t = number of units that should be produced in month t

I_{t-1} = number of units in inventory less backorders at beginning of month t

F_t = forecast of number of units to be shipped in month t

F_{t+i} = forecast of number of units to be shipped in month $t + i$

The linear decision rules for the paint factory were calculated as:

$$P_t = \begin{cases} + .463F_t \\ + .234F_{t+1} \\ + .111F_{t+2} \\ + .046F_{t+3} \\ + .013F_{t+4} \\ - .002F_{t+5} \\ - .008F_{t+6} \\ - .010F_{t+7} \\ - .009F_{t+8} \\ - .008F_{t+9} \\ - .007F_{t+10} \\ - .005F_{t+11} \end{cases} + .993W_{t-1} + (153 - .464I_{t-1})$$

$$W_t = .743W_{t-1} + (2.09 - .010I_{t-1}) + \begin{cases} + .0101F_t \\ + .0088F_{t+1} \\ + .0071F_{t+2} \\ + .0054F_{t+3} \\ + .0042F_{t+4} \\ + .0031F_{t+5} \\ + .0023F_{t+6} \\ + .0016F_{t+7} \\ + .0012F_{t+8} \\ + .0009F_{t+9} \\ + .0006F_{t+10} \\ + .0005F_{t+11} \end{cases}$$

The first decision rule for number of units to be produced in time period t, P_t, incorporates a weighted average of forecasts extending 11 months into the future, the heaviest weights being on the most recent months. The value of P_t also depends on employment level in the preceding month and the preceding month's inventory. The second decision rule, for W_t, depends on the same variables.

The authors compared the performance of the LDR with that of the paint company's actual aggregate plans for the six-year period. Using a simple moving average forecast to calculate P_t and W_t, the LDR bettered the actual company performance by $173,000 per year.

Applying the LDR method to other companies would require new data collection and the derivation of the new decision rules. However, to illustrate how simple it is to plug into the LDR equation, let's apply the LDR to the month of January in our previous Braden Company example. We assume that in the preceding month, 109 workers were employed.

$$P_1 = \begin{cases} +.463(9{,}000) \\ +.234(8{,}000) \\ +.111(7{,}000) \\ +.046(6{,}000) \\ +.013(5{,}000) \\ -.002(6{,}000) \\ -.008(8{,}000) \\ -.010(10{,}000) \\ -.009(14{,}000) \\ -.008(15{,}000) \\ -.007(12{,}000) \\ -.005(10{,}000) \end{cases} +.993(109) + 153 - .464(1{,}000)$$

$$W_1 = .743(109) + 2.09 - .010(1{,}000) + \begin{cases} +.0101(9{,}000) \\ +.0088(8{,}000) \\ +.0071(7{,}000) \\ +.0054(6{,}000) \\ +.0042(5{,}000) \\ +.0031(6{,}000) \\ +.0023(8{,}000) \\ +.0016(10{,}000) \\ +.0012(14{,}000) \\ +.0009(15{,}000) \\ +.0006(12{,}000) \\ +.0005(10{,}000) \end{cases}$$

Performing the calculations, we obtain:

$$P_1 = 6{,}398$$
$$W_1 = 432$$

Thus, the LDR recommends the production of 6,398 units in January for the Braden

Company, with an increase in the work force from 109 to 432 workers. This unreasonably high addition to the work force can be explained by noting that the Braden Company is not the paint company for which these specific linear decision rules were developed. The example further illustrates the need to develop unique decision rules for each individual problem.

The LDR approach is limited, much like the linear programming approach, in that it assumes a specific type of cost function. If payroll, hiring and layoff, production, and inventory costs are not approximately quadratic in nature, then the LDR is not applicable. Second, the method requires significant data collection and curve-fit analysis. Finally, the method imposes no constraints on the final values of the decision variables; this can possibly result in solutions that are negative in sign or otherwise unacceptable to management.

Heuristic Methods

The shortcomings of linear programming and the LDR are that they restrict the nature of the costs relevant to aggregate planning. These restrictions have caused aggregate planners to utilize heuristics in order to handle a wider variety of cost functions. Even though heuristics cannot guarantee an optimal solution, they allow us to drop the restrictive assumptions often required by optimization procedures. VAM, for example, is a heuristic that we used to obtain good solutions to transportation problems in the supplement to Chapter 2 and the transportation models in this chapter.

Search Decision Rule. One of the most successful and widely used heuristics is the Search Decision Rule (SDR) developed by Taubert.[4] It is a computerized approximation procedure that uses a direct-search method to find the decision variable values that minimize the total cost function. A high-speed computer is required to systematically search for points that yield a cost reduction. Thousands or even millions of points may be explored by this computerized trial-and-error process. Taubert used the Hooke-Jeeves method of direct search.[5] This type is called pattern search and requires a starting solution as a base point. From the base point, exploratory moves are made to see if improvements can be found. If a better point is found, then it becomes the new base point. From the new base point, a larger pattern move is made, followed by smaller exploratory searches. The procedure terminates when no improvements can be found within a given tolerance—say, .00001. See Figure 9-5 for an illustration of a two-dimensional pattern search.

Other types of direct-search methods can be used, but all have in common that they do not guarantee an optimal solution. They are optimal seeking procedures and

[4]W.H. Taubert, "Search Decision Rule for the Aggregate Scheduling Problem," *Management Science*, 14, no. 6 (February 1968), 343–59.

[5]R. Hooke and T.A. Jeeves, "A 'Direct Search' Solution of Numerical Statistical Problems," *Journal of the Association for Computing Machinery*, April 1961.

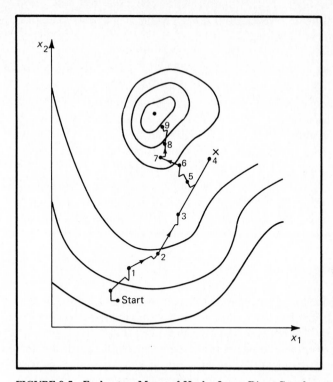

FIGURE 9-5   Exploratory Moves of Hooke-Jeeves Direct Search

often find the optimal solution, but since they employ heuristic search rules, they may not; the direct-search procedures terminate whenever no improvement can be found or a predetermined time limit is exceeded. The strength of the direct-search procedures is that they can be applied to virtually any cost function and will yield good results. This kind of flexibility is important in real-world decision making.

Other Heuristics.   Heuristics usually have the property of being able to find a good solution to one class of problems but not necessarily others. The SDR is fairly robust, in that many cost functions can be used. However, other heuristics have also been found to perform well under various problem types and managerial assumptions. Three heuristics that have found some degree of acceptance are the following:

1. *Parametric production planning model.* This approach was developed by Jones,[6] and like the LDR it assumes a quadratic cost function for the same costs of work force, overtime, production rate, and inventory. Jones uses a heuristic search procedure to develop the coefficients for two decision rules for production

---

[6]C.H. Jones, "Parametric Production Planning," *Management Science*, 13, no. 11 (July 1967), 843–66.

rate and work size. Like the SDR, this approach can be applied to virtually any cost function.

2. *Management coefficients model.* This approach is unique in that it attempts to incorporate the manager's own performance and experience into a formal decision model. Developed by Bowman,[7] the procedure use regression analysis of management's past behavior in similar decisions. The procedure incorporates management's bias (which is favored anyway) and attempts to minimize variance or deviations from this bias or average behavior. The regression coefficients form the basis of an equation from which future decisions can be made that will supposedly be acceptable to management.

3. *Simulation and search.* Vergin developed an approach that incorporates linear, quadratic, and step costs.[8] A heuristic is used to select various aggregate schedules, and simulation is used to evaluate the best alternative.

Comparison of Methods

We have considered several quantitative models for aggregate planning at this point, and each has its advantages and disadvantages. We would expect certain models to do well whenever their assumptions hold true. Thus, we would expect linear programming to perform well when all relationships are linear and the parameters of the model are deterministic. But how do these various methods perform under the true test of real-world experience? Some research has been done in this area. Eilon has considered five approaches to aggregate production planning; he thoroughly examines the limiting assumptions of each approach and the basic shortcomings of each method.[9]

In one interesting study, Lee and Khumawala compared the performance of four aggregate planning models on a firm in the capital-goods industry.[10] A computer simulation model was developed to simulate the aggregate operation of the firm. Past data pertaining to actual demand were used so that comparisons could be made between performance on demand forecasts (implied) and performance on known demand or perfect forecasts.

The four methods tested were the Linear Decision Rule, Search Decision Rule, management coefficients model, and the parametric production planning model. Compared with actual company decisions, all four methods resulted in increased profits. Figure 9-6 illustrates the profit increase for each method. Under perfect

---

[7]E.H. Bowman, "Consistency and Optimality in Managerial Decision Making," *Management Science*, 4 (January 1963), 100–103.

[8]R.C. Vergin, "Production Scheduling under Seasonal Demand," *Journal of Industrial Engineering*, vol. 17, no. 5 (May 1966).

[9]Samuel Eilon, "Five Approaches to Aggregate Production Planning," *AIIE Transactions*, June 1975.

[10]W.B. Lee and B.M. Khumawala, "Simulation Testing of Aggregate Production Planning Models in an Implementation Methodology," *Management Science*, 20, no. 6 (February 1974), 903–11.

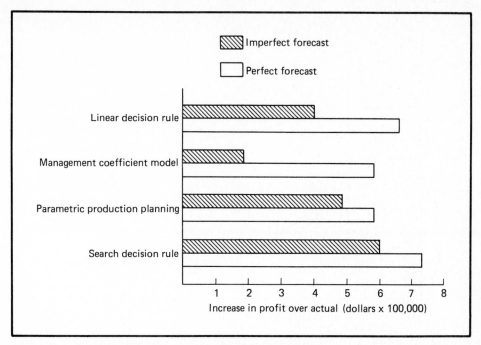

FIGURE 9-6   Profit Comparison of Four Aggregate Planning Models

SOURCE: W.B. Lee and B.M. Khumawala, "Simulation Testing of Aggregate Production Planning Models in an Implementation Methodology," *Management Science*, 20, no. 6 (February 1974), 903–11.

forecasts, all four methods performed well, with the Search Decision Rule being slightly better than the Linear Decision Rule. A more realistic comparison is obtained under imperfect forecasts, which is the usual operating state of a firm. In this case, a wider variation among the four methods occurs. The Search Decision Rule performed best, followed by parametric production planning, Linear Decision Rule, and the management coefficients model. The results of this study, together with the flexibility of the Search Decision Rule, suggest that it is currently the most effective quantitive approach to the aggregate planning problem.

LEARNING-CURVE EFFECTS ON PRODUCTION

Thus far we have assumed that productivity has remained constant. In many productive activities, however, the learning process results in improved efficiency as a function of output. You might expect this phenomenon more in labor-intensive industries, but wherever methods improve or work becomes more organized, you could expect productivity to increase with output. The *learning-curve phenomenon* has been recognized in machine shops and aircraft assembly plants. The Boeing Company, for example, has developed specified rates that decrease with increased

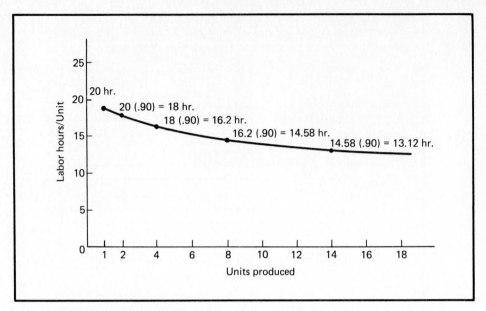

FIGURE 9-7   **Ninety Percent Learning Curve**

output of various aircraft components. The Boeing formula states that each time the production quantity doubles, the number of unit worker-hours is reduced at a constant rate.

A 90 percent learning curve is illustrated in Figure 9-7. Assuming that an activity required 20 hours for the first unit, the second would take 18, the fourth 16.2, and the eighth 14.58. Other learning-curve formulas exist that yield similar but slightly different curves.

If the learning-curve phenomenon applies to a given product or service, then aggregate planners need to consider the learning-curve effect in production planning. Other functions of an organization, including marketing, purchasing, and scheduling, should also consider learning-curve effects; variable production costs will decrease over time, as well as per-piece average processing time. If the learning phenomenon exerts a significant effect, it should be incorporated into aggregate plans.

Traditional approaches to aggregate planning have assumed a constant workforce productivity factor. However, several factors can cause changes in work output capabilities over time. Ebert cites examples involving (1) changes in work methods, (2) product engineering modifications, (3) facilities relocation, (4) facilities layout, (5) equipment redesign, and (6) changes in employee skills or training.[11] Some of the resulting work output effects can be explained in terms of learning-curve phenomena.

---

[11]R.J. Ebert, "Aggregate Planning with Learning Curve Productivity," *Management Science*, 23, no. 2 (October 1976), 171–82.

Recently, Ebert has proposed a method for aggregate planning with learning-curve effects. His model uses the Holt et al. basic cost structure and various manufacturing progress function parameters.[12] A Hooke-Jeeves direct-search computer program is used to obtain approximate solutions that indicate work force and production rate for each time period. The method is capable of incorporating into the scheduling aspects of aggregate planning such established learning-curve applications as (1) cash-flow planning, (2) product pricing, and (3) manpower planning. Cash flows associated with production scheduling can be combined with other cash flows to estimate total cash flow over the life of the product. Future manpower needs can be estimated with respect to various learning-curve rates by examining the output of the computer program. Pricing strategies are aided by a breakdown of the costs into scheduling and nonscheduling costs. For example, Ebert presents product pricing output for a hypothetical company, Dynapro Corp., in Table 9-9. From the total cost figures in the table, we can see that lower-percentage learning curves can really lower total costs by decreasing scheduling costs through greater production efficiency. It is also worthwhile to note that small percentage changes in the learning-curve rate can have significant effect on total costs and selling price. This indicates the importance of estimating learning-curve parameters accurately.

Ebert's methodology is important in that it allows the aggregate planner to use a systematic procedure for incorporating learning-curve phenomena. Equally important is the inclusion of decision factors from the financial and marketing functions of the firm. This wider approach to the aggregate planning function represents a significant step toward a true systems approach to intermediate-range planning.

DISAGGREGATION

The output of the aggregate planning process typically specifies a general schedule for aggregate units for families or product groups. These schedules should have passed rough-cut production capacity checks and should have allowed for vacations and holidays.

The process of breaking the aggregate production plan into greater levels of detail is called disaggregation. Figure 9-8 illustrates the various levels of disaggregation that succeed the aggregate plans. Disaggregation is a topic in the operations management literature that has recently received increased attention in terms of research activities.[13]

Krajewski and Ritzman[14] have delineated the three levels at which disaggregation takes place in both manufacturing and service organizations. The disaggregation

---

[12] Holt, Modigliani, and Simon, "A Linear Decision Rule."

[13] L. Ritzman, L. Krajewski, W. Bervy, S. Goodman, S. Hardy, and L. Vitt, *Disaggregation: Problems in Manufacturing and Service Organizations*, Collection of papers presented at conference held at Ohio State University, March 1977, (Boston: Martinus Nijhoff, 1977).

[14] L.J. Krajewski and L.B. Ritzman, "Disaggregation in Manufacturing and Service Organizations: Survey of Problems and Research," *Decision Sciences*, 8, no. 1 (Jan. 1977), 1–18.

Table 9-9 Cost Estimates for Product Pricing

COST CATEGORY	LEARNING CURVE						CONSTANT PRODUCTIVITY
	70%	75%	80%	85%	90%	95%	100%
Scheduling Costs:							
Overtime	$ 17,790.9	18,824.9	12,221.8	25,458.1	16,516.5	19,117.7	21,433.2
Hiring	6,326.9	7,409.7	7,410.3	12,052.1	17,569.3	26,595.1	37,178.4
Layoff	25,074.7	32,341.7	40,248.0	51,702.2	67,799.6	79,990.6	103,977.7
Inventory carrying	3,532.5	4,960.0	6,570.0	8,787.5	12,087.5	14,030.0	17,085.0
Inventory shortage	806.5	830.5	3,985.9	953.1	7,692.6	4,983.6	5,577.4
TOTAL	$ 53,531.5	64,366.2	72,436.0	98,952.0	121,565.5	144,717.6	185,251.7
Cost / unit	$ 2.723	3.274	3.684	5.033	6.183	7.361	9.422
Nonscheduling Costs:							
Development	$ 250,000.	250,000.	250,000.	250,000.	250,000.	250,000.	250,000.
Direct materials	1,572,880.	1,572,880.	1,572,880.	1,572,880.	1,572,880.	1,572,880.	1,572,880.
Variable materials overhead	314,576.	314,576.	314,576.	314,576.	314,576.	314,576.	314,576.
Administrative	430,000.	430,000.	430,000.	430,000.	430,000.	430,000.	430,000.
Direct labor	369,322.	521,721.	741,890.	1,039,531.	1,458,758.	2,018,561.	2,765,225.
Variable labor overhead	181,583.	256,512.	364,762.	511,102.	717,224.	992,462.	1,359,566.
TOTAL	$3,118,361.	3,345,689.	3,673,108.	4,118,089	4,743,438	5,578,479.	6,692,247.
TOTAL COST	$3,171,893.	3,410,055.	3,746,544.	4,217,041.	4,865,003.	5,723,197.	6,877,498.7
Selling Price (per unit)	$ 179.254	192.713	211.730	238.319	274.938	323.437	349.802

SOURCE: R.J. Ebert, "Aggregate Planning with Learning Curve Productivity," *Management Science*, 23, no. 2 (October 1976), 171–82.

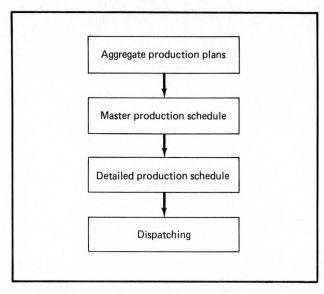

FIGURE 9-8   Levels of Disaggregation in Manufacturing

levels in manufacturing parallel the last three boxes in Figure 9-8 and are described as:

1. Given aggregate decisions on output and capacity, determine the timing and sizing of specific final product production quantities over the time horizon (i.e., master scheduling).
2. Given the timing and sizing of final product production quantities, determine the timing and sizing of manufactured or purchased component quantities.
3. Given the timing and sizing of component quantities, determine the short-term sequences and priorities of the job (orders) and the resource allocations to individual operations.

Disaggregation problems in service organizations possess the complicating characteristics of stringent response-time requirements, time-dependent demand rates, and the inability to use finished goods inventories to smooth production rates. Disaggregation decisions in service organizations also exist at these levels:

1. Given aggregate decisions on output and capacity, allocate manpower and other resources to specific operations over the time horizon (i.e., the staff sizing problem).
2. Given the allocation of resources to specific operations, determine the shift schedules and new assignments of employees.
3. Given the shift schedule assignments, determine short-term adaptations, reallocations between operations, and priorities of the service requirements.

Although similarities exist between disaggregation in manufacturing and service organizations, manufacturing organizations are primarily concerned with scheduling productive resources and physical components whereas service organizations are primarily concerned with scheduling resources and personnel.

Master Scheduling

The master production schedule is the next level of disaggregation that follows the aggregate plan for manufacturing. It breaks the aggregate plan into scheduled production levels of individual end products. The master schedule is the master plan for manufacturing. It provides the end-item production quantities and dates of production that are used to generate planned orders and requirements for piece parts, subassemblies, and raw materials. Even though the master schedule is a manufacturing plan, it is not frozen or inflexible. It can be changed whenever resources can be made available to accommodate the desired changes. The master schedule must be kept current by updating it with actual orders rather than with quantities that were originally forecasted. On the production side, the master schedule must continually incorporate actual production output rather than production levels that had merely been planned.

There are two main demand inputs to the master schedule. Customer order backlogs reflect orders that have been accepted but not shipped. Product sales forecasts reflect anticipated (but uncertain) future demand. Actual customer orders generate input to the "firm" portion of the master schedule. The firm part of the schedule refers to the time periods for which production-level decisions have been made. Sales forecasts are the inputs to the "tentative" portion of the master schedule. The tentative portion of the schedule refers to the future time periods for which production is planned but not yet definite.

For an example of a master production schedule (MPS) let us reconsider the paint company mentioned at the beginning of this chapter. Suppose that this company manufactures three types of paint, interior latex, exterior latex, and enamel. These paints are typically a white-base paint which is custom tinted at the retail paint stores. The MPS would then break the aggregate plans into time-phased output levels for the three individual types of paint. Figure 9-9 illustrates the MPS for this example.

END PRODUCT	JAN.	FEB.	MAR.	APR.	MAY	JUN.	JUL.	AUG.	SEP.	OCT.	NOV.	DEC.
Interior latex	12	10	10	10	10	10	10	10	10	10	12	14
Exterior latex	8	10	16	20	20	20	21	18	9	7	5	3
Enamel	2	5	4	5	5	6	7	6	6	5	3	3
	← Firm →			←			Tentative					→

FIGURE 9-9   Master Production Schedule for Paint Company

In addition to the major inputs of external customer orders and forecasted demand, the master schedule must include input for all required production including spare parts, backlogs, and interplant transfers.

The accuracy and realism of the MPS is essential for smooth production. We have already mentioned the importance of rough-cut capacity planning to assure a feasible production schedule at the major work centers (see Figure 9-2). There are three other common errors in addition to capacity overloading that are frequently made in master-schedule development. One of these errors is the incomplete schedule which considers all standard products but omits special feature items. This type of error can lead to capacity or material availability constraints in subsequent time periods. Another problem is encountered by computerized systems which can dictate MPS changes in a matter of seconds. An unstable MPS can evolve if too many changes are called for that lead to material availability constraints and chaotic scheduling on the shop floor. Lastly, another common error is the short-horizon syndrome in which the MPS is stated for a shorter period of time than is required for the purchase and manufacture of materials. A short horizon is usually caused by sales uncertainty beyond the immediate future. However, at least tentative schedules must be made to plan production into the future.

After the master production schedule has been developed, it is necessary to develop a detailed production schedule. This next step of disaggregation (see Figure 9-8) breaks the MPS down from monthly output levels for end products to weekly or daily schedules for end-item production. At this level MRP or materials requirements planning can also be used to time-phase and schedule the subassemblies and parts needed to support end-item production. The final step in the disaggregation process is to dispatch the work to be done at various work centers. We will look at detailed scheduling and dispatching in Chapter 12. After a look at inventory control methods for end items in the next chapter, we will turn to MRP and planning the coverage of dependent demand items in Chapter 11.

Hierarchical Planning for Aggregate Planning and Disaggregation

Many approaches to aggregate planning have ignored the subsequent problems which follow in the disaggregation process. Models which attempt to incorporate all aspects of aggregate planning and disaggregation tend to be too complex and cumbersome to use.

A hierarchical planning system for aggregate planning and disaggregation has been proposed by Bitran and Hax.[15] Hierarchical planning systems are becoming increasingly popular for multilevel decision problems. In a hierarchical planning system, the set of decisions is partitioned into a hierarchy that corresponds to the

---

[15]G.R. Bitran and A.C. Hax, "On the Design of Hierarchical Production Planning Systems," *Decision Sciences*, 8, no. 1 (January 1977), 28–55.

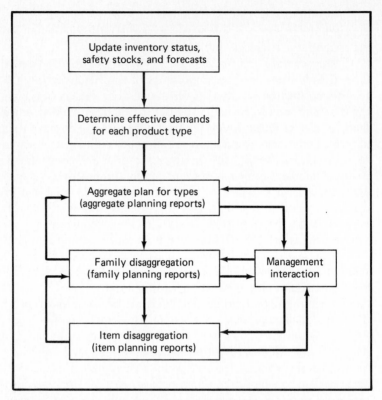

FIGURE 9-10   Hierarchical Process for Aggregate Planning and Disaggregation

levels of managerial decision making involved. There are usually three levels corresponding to the strategic, tactical, and operational levels of managerial decision making. In this type of system no attempt is made to optimize or solve all aspects of a complex decision problem such as aggregate planning and disaggregation "all at once." Rather the decisions are made sequentially starting at the highest level. The higher-level decisions impose constraints on the lower-level actions and lower-level decisions provide the necessary feedback to reevaluate higher-level actions.

Hierarchical production planning as applied to aggregate planning and disaggregation identifies three increasingly aggregated product units: end items, families, and types. At the type level, a linear program is used to set long-range target production levels that minimize production, overtime, and inventory carrying costs. At the family level, the production target for a type is allocated to families within that type, considering setup costs. At the end-item level, item production is planned over a short planning horizon using recent demand data. Figure 9-10 illustrates the hierarchical process.

There are three advantages to the hierarchical approach. Breaking a large decision problem into subproblems simplifies the solution process at each stage. Second, it helps to reduce uncertainty. The hierarchical approach postpones the detailed decisions as long as possible so that more accurate and timely data can be obtained from the previous hierarchical level. Finally, hierarchical systems parallel the hierarchical organization of most firms and hence fit naturally into the managerial decision process. Hierarchical production planning systems will most likely be used increasingly for future aggregate planning and disaggregation problems.

SUMMARY

Aggregate planning is concerned with the development of plans and strategies for utilizing capacity and absorbing demand fluctuations. It is intermediate-range planning, usually the longest-range plans that are dealt with by the operations manager; long-range or strategic plans are the concerns of top management.

The aggregate plans are key to a smooth production and operating system. They must be feasible in terms of men and machine capacities and they must include estimated work shifts, vacations, inventories, and subcontracts. The general information of the aggregate plans are input to a more detailed master production schedule. The master schedule breaks the aggregate plan into greater details and is the basis for disaggregation, scheduling, and computerized MRP (materials requirements planning) systems. The master schedule is updated by actual demand and production figures throughout the year and serves as a means for adjusting general aggregate plans. The successful implementation of aggregate plans requires an information feedback loop between the planning stages and the plant first-line scheduling and operational stages.

Aggregate planning for service and nonmanufacturing organizations can utilize many of the procedures presented in the chapter. The utilization of capacity and planning for personnel are the primary objectives. The main difference between service-oriented and manufacturing organizations is that service industries cannot use inventory as a strategy for demand absorption. The useful strategies include the variation of work force, hours worked, overtime, and capacity utilization.

In actual practice, the trial-and-error graphical methods and the counterseasonal-products methods seem to be the most widely used in service and manufacturing organizations. In addition to the active and passive strategies mentioned in this chapter, some firms may engage in bargaining with suppliers and customers or coalition with other organizations. For example, electric power companies sometimes borrow power from each other during periods of peak demand.

Mathematical and computer techniques are used to a limited extent for aggregate planning. Not only do these methods have their limitations, but management is sometimes skeptical or uneducated in using them. In spite of their shortcomings, the quantitative methods can be useful planning tools; when used properly, they have outperformed "seat-of-the-pants" planning methods in real applications. The most promising approach appears to be the Search Decision Rule coupled with computer simulation to evaluate various aggregate plans.

Aggregate planning is an important part of operations management, and research continues to explore new and better ways of developing effective aggregate plans. Recently, the learning-curve phenomenon has been incorporated in an aggregate planning model. Also, hierarchical planning procedures are being developed to address the combined problems of aggregate planning and disaggregation. Future research should yield new methods for making more realistic aggregate plans. However, effective aggregate planning can be achieved now by making use of forecasting techniques and the tools that are currently available.

SOLVED PROBLEMS

Problem Statement

The Hafler Co. utilizes the counterseasonal-product strategy to smooth production resource requirements. It manufactures its spring product line during the first four months of the year and would like to employ a strategy that minimizes production costs while meeting demand during these four months. Hafler currently employs 30 workers at an average wage of $1,000 per month. Each unit requires eight man-hours to produce, or one full day per worker. Hiring costs are estimated at $400, and layoff costs are $500 per person. Inventory carrying costs are $5/unit/month, and shortage costs are $100/unit/month. Given the forecasted demand figures below, determine the more effective of the proposed pure strategies:

Plan A: Vary work-force levels to meet demand.

Plan B: Maintain 30 employees and use inventory plus stockouts to absorb demand fluctuations.

MONTH	DEMAND	WORKING DAYS
Jan.	500	22
Feb.	600	19
Mar.	800	21
Apr.	400	21

Solution

Assuming that no inventory is available at the beginning of the year, and that safety stock (if used at all) is built into the monthly demand figures, we can compare the overall costs of both strategies.

Plan A

	JAN.	FEB.	MAR.	APR.	TOTAL
1. Workers required	$\frac{500}{22} = 23$	$\frac{600}{19} = 32$	$\frac{300}{21} = 38$	$\frac{400}{21} = 19$	
2. Labor	$23,000	$32,000	$38,000	$19,000	$112,000
3. Hiring		9(400) = 3,600	6(400) = 2,400		6,000
4. Layoff	7(500) = 3,500			19(500) = 9,500	13,000
					$131,000

Plan B

	JAN.	FEB.	MAR.	APR.	TOTAL
1. Workers used	30	30	30	30	
2. Labor	$30,000	$30,000	$30,000	$30,000	$120,000
3. Units produced	660	570	630	630	
4. Inventory	5(160)	5(130)		5(190)	2,400
5. Shortage			100(40)		4,000
					$126,400

Plan B, using inventory and shortages, appears to be the best plan economically, with a total cost of $126,400 versus $131,000 for Plan A. Additionally, Plan B would result in higher worker morale, smoother production, and a higher-quality product.

Problem Statement

Suppose that the Hafler Co. of the problem above has decided to maintain a steady work force of 30 people per month. However, the company wants to analyze the cost of a mixed strategy employing overtime and inventory as means to absorb demand. Inventory costs remain at $5/unit/month, and per-unit labor costs are $50 on regular time and $75 on overtime.

Solution

Given that work-force levels will remain constant, we can use the transportation model of linear programming to solve this problem. Setting up regular time and overtime options for each month and assuming backordering is not allowed, we obtain the following 8 × 5 transportation tableau:

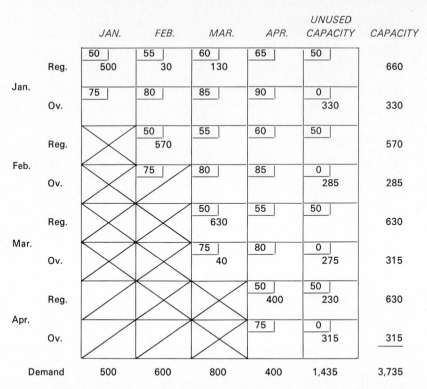

		JAN.	FEB.	MAR.	APR.	UNUSED CAPACITY	CAPACITY
Jan.	Reg.	50 / 500	55 / 30	60 / 130	65	50	660
	Ov.	75	80	85	90	0 / 330	330
Feb.	Reg.		50 / 570	55	60	50	570
	Ov.		75	80	85	0 / 285	285
Mar.	Reg.			50 / 630	55	50	630
	Ov.			75 / 40	80	0 / 275	315
Apr.	Reg.				50 / 400	50 / 230	630
	Ov.				75	0 / 315	315
Demand		500	600	800	400	1,435	3,735

The costs in the cells of the tableau reflect only direct labor costs. This enables us to compare the transportation mixed strategy with the pure inventory strategy. A solution derived by inspection is presented in the tableau. Notice that certain cells are inadmissible, since backordering is not allowed. The final solution differs from Plan B only in that the firm satisfies the peak demand of March through overtime rather than choosing to only partially fulfill demand as in Plan B.

Problem Statement

Cornwell Design Corporation has recently received a contract to manufacture chair frames for a large furniture company. The production process is labor-intensive and a 95 percent learning curve applies. If it takes eight hours for a craftsman to make the first chair, how long will it take to produce the 128th unit?

Solution

The 128th unit represents the seventh doubling of the original output of one unit. Thus, the total time for the 128th unit will be:

$$8 \text{ hours} \times (.95)^7 \times 8 \times .6983 = 5.58 \text{ hours}$$

REVIEW QUESTIONS

1. What is the approximate length of the planning horizon for aggregate planning?
2. What is the objective of aggregate planning, and what are the active and passive strategies for implementing aggregate plans?
3. What are some constraints that the aggregate planner must consider?
4. Which methods are primarily used today by managers to absorb demand fluctuations?
5. Comment on the main shortcoming of the graphical method for aggregate planning.
6. Give some explanations of why mathematical or quantitative models aren't used more in actual aggregate planning.
7. Contrast aggregate planning alternatives for an aircraft manufacturing plant with those of a public accounting firm.
8. How can the following organizations employ active strategies—retail department store, savings and loan, electric power company?
9. What is the main difference between linear programming for aggregate planning and the Linear Decision Rule?
10. Why is the Search Decision Rule probably the best current approach to aggregate planning?
11. Explain how the estimated needs for aggregate capacity get refined through the production planning process.
12. Would you prefer to own a manufacturing company whose production rate was constant, or one that showed an 80% learning-curve rate? Why?
13. Explain the relationship between aggregate planning and master scheduling.
14. What is management concerned with in the disaggregation problem?
15. In what sense does Ebert's learning-curve approach to aggregate planning represent a systems approach?
16. Briefly explain the hierarchical production planning approach to aggregate and disaggregate planning.
17. List four common mistakes in master production scheduling.
18. What are the advantages and disadvantages of the following aggregate planning methods?
    a. graphing and charting
    b. transportation method
    c. linear programming
    d. linear decision rule
    e. search decision rule
    f. management coefficient method
19. Contrast the levels and associated decisions made in disaggregation for manufacturing organizations versus service organizations.

PROBLEMS

1. The forecasted demand for the last six months of the year is shown below. Develop a production requirement graph (like Figure 9-3) in which the implied production rate per day is plotted versus the working days each month. Assume a beginning inventory of 800 units.

MONTH	EXPECTED DEMAND	DESIRED SAFETY STOCK	WORKING DAYS
July	5,000	1,000	21
August	6,000	1,200	13
September	10,000	2,000	20
October	8,000	1,600	23
November	8,000	1,600	21
December	6,000	1,200	20

2. Using the 6-month data in problem 1, evaluate two pure strategies involving variation of work force and subcontracting. To hire and train a worker costs $220, and layoff costs are $240 per worker. Each worker can produce four units per working day, and subcontracting costs are $20 per unit above manufacturing cost. Assume a beginning inventory of 800 units, and a wage rate of $8/hr.

3. Can you improve upon the Plan 1 pure strategy of inventory for the data in Table 9-1? (Costs are given in Table 9-3.) You may use any strategy, pure or mixed.

4. Nickelson Tool and Die Co. has undertaken a new contract. Production of the first unit has required 40 hours. Assuming a 90% production learning curve, how long will it take to produce the second unit? the eighth unit?

5. American Products Corporation experiences a cyclical demand pattern, which they forecast as $y = 500 + 1,000x + (-1)^x 600$, where y = units of demand and x = quarter of the year.
   a. What is the forecasted demand for each of the four quarters of this year?
   b. What must be the level quarterly production rate to meet demand over the year?
   c. What types of demand absorption strategies would the level production plan entail?

6. Consider the following aggregate planning problem for one quarter:

	REGULAR TIME	OVERTIME	SUBCON- TRACTING
Production capacity / month	9,000 units	2,250 units	4,000 units
Production cost / unit	$8	$10	$13

Assume no initial inventory and a forecasted demand of 12,000, 16,000, and 17,000 in the three months of the quarter. Carrying cost is $1.50/unit/mo., backorder cost is $2/unit/mo., and unused regular time costs $5 per unit. Set up the problem in a transportation tableau.

7. Solve problem 6 using Vogel's Approximation Method, which is a heuristic described in the supplement to Chapter 2.

8. Develop a general linear programming model for the aggregate planning problem in problem 6. Take into consideration work-force-level changes by letting the cost of increasing output from one month to the next be $40 per unit, and the decrease cost be $50 per unit.

9. Suppose the following data apply to the paint company mentioned in the chapter. The beginning work force $w_{t-1} = 200$, beginning inventory is 500 gallons of paint, and the company has the following forecast for the year:

MONTH	GALLONS	MONTH	GALLONS
January	300	July	850
February	300	August	900
March	500	September	600
April	500	October	550
May	650	November	300
June	800	December	200

Calculate work and production levels for January using the Holt et al. Linear Decision Rules.

10. Rockwood International has contracted with the federal government to build solar energy panels for orbital space stations. Work on the first panel took 120 worker hours, and estimates are that an 88% learning curve applies to this type of work. Assuming that Rockwood wants to build one panel per 8-hour workday, how many workers should they schedule for the 64th unit?

11. Refer to the Hafler Co. in the first Solved Problem, and evaluate the strategy of employing the minimum number of 19 workers and absorbing demand with overtime (cost = 1.5 × regular time) and inventory (cost = $5 per unit).

12. Refer to the Hafler Co. in the second Solved Problem. Consider the additional strategy of subcontracting for a unit cost of $70. Set up a transportation tableau for this problem and find the new solution.

13. A city administrator is trying to plan personnel requirements for city firemen in the upcoming year. Past years' demand and growth trends suggest the following needs:

January	27,000 man-hours	July	30,000 man-hours
February	22,000	August	32,000
March	23,000	September	28,000
April	24,000	October	21,000
May	25,000	November	19,000
June	29,000	December	26,000

Current work-force levels can provide 25,000 man-hours per month on a regular-time basis. Regular-time costs are $6.00 per hour, and overtime is $9.00 per hour; overtime can furnish only 10%, or 2,500 additional man-hours per month. Part-time firemen can be used, but they are usually not as well qualified and cost $7.00 per hour regular time and $10.50 on overtime. Training costs for firemen are $500 per man, and laying-off costs are $300 per full-time employee. (No cost for laying off part-time firemen.)
   a. What should the monthly personnel levels be for the city firemen? What is the yearly cost?
   b. What pure or mixed strategies did you use?
   c. If you had access to a computer, what method might you prefer to use in solving this problem?

14. A company has used the Linear Decision Rule (LDR) methodology to obtain the following decision rules:

$$P_t = 1.4F_t + .8W_{t-1} - .3I_{t-1}$$

$$W_t = .7W_{t-1} + .1F_t - .05I_{t-1} + 2$$

The company currently has 150 workers and an inventory of 900 units. What are the projected production and work-force levels using the LDR for the next three months, given forecast sales of 1200, 1500, and 1300?

15. The Down Stream Beer Co. has developed the following aggregate plan for beer production in the next six months:

MONTH	JAN.	FEB.	MAR.	APR.	MAY	JUN.
Production	10,000	11,000	11,000	12,000	13,000	16,000

The production quantities are in barrels and include the aggregate of the company's two beer products, lite and heavy beer. Heavy beer normally comprises 60% of Down Stream's total sales. Disaggregate the aggregate plan to create a 6-month master production schedule for lite and heavy beer.

16. Southwest Cube Co. is developing an aggregate plan for the last six months of the year. Listed below is their monthly forecasted demand:

MONTH	JUL.	AUG.	SEP.	OCT.	NOV.	DEC.
Forecasted demand	1,100	1,000	1,200	1,100	1,200	1,300

Assume a beginning inventory of 100 units and 22 work days per month. The current work force consists of 10 workers. The remaining cost information is:

Inventory carrying cost	$8 per unit/month
Stockout cost	$20 per unit/month
Subcontracting cost	$80 per unit
Labor cost per hour regular	$12 per hour
Labor cost per hour overtime	$18 per hour
Hiring cost per worker	$200/worker
Layoff cost per worker	$300/worker
Man-hours per unit	2 hours

Compare the costs of the following two strategies:
a. Vary work force to produce exact demand each month.
b. Maintain a constant work force of 10, vary overtime up to 25% per month, and use subcontracting.

17. Devise the best plan that you can for problem 16.

18. Set up the following three-period aggregate planning problem as an LP model. Assume a beginning inventory level of zero.

PERIOD	1	2	3
Forecast demand	150	200	175
Maximum regular-time production	175	175	175
Maximum overtime production	40	40	40
Maximum subcontracted units	100	100	100

c_1 = cost per unit on regular time = \$6

c_2 = cost per unit on overtime = \$9

c_3 = cost per unit subcontracted = \$15

c_4 = inventory carrying cost per period = \$3

c_5 = cost of increasing production per unit = \$2

c_6 = cost of decreasing production per unit = \$4

Production output in previous period = 120 units

SUPPLEMENT TO CHAPTER 9

LP FORMULATION OF AGGREGATE PLANNING

In this supplement we present a linear programming formulation of the aggregate planning problem. This model will directly extend the linear transportation model by allowing hiring and firing; it will also incorporate the costs of these associated production-level changes. In addition to hiring and layoff costs, the model will minimize the sum of regular production costs, overtime costs, subcontracting costs, and inventory carrying costs. The model constraints will consist of regular time, overtime, and subcontracting capacities, as well as constraints that require that demand be satisfied.

The LP model presented here does not permit backorders and stockouts. A more complex LP model that does incorporate undertime and shortages has been developed by Haussmann and Hess.*

The LP model without backorders and stockouts has the following parameters:

d_t = forecasted demand units during period t

R_t = regular-time production capacity in period t

O_t = overtime production capacity in period t

S_t = subcontracting capacity in period t

c_1 = cost per unit produced on regular time

---

*F. Hanssmann and S.W. Hess, "A Linear Programming Approach to Production and Employment Scheduling," *Management Technology*, vol. 1 (January 1960), 46–52.

c_2 = cost per unit produced on overtime

c_3 = cost per unit subcontracted

c_4 = inventory carrying cost per period

c_5 = cost of increasing the regular production level per unit (hiring)

c_6 = cost of reducing the regular production level per unit (firing)

The variables in the LP model are:

x_t = regular-time production in period t (in units)

y_t = overtime production in period t (in units)

z_t = units subcontracted in period t

i_t = inventory at the end of period t

h_t = increase in units of regular production in period t (hiring)

f_t = reduction in units of regular production in period t (firing)

We can now develop the relevant constraints and associated objective function. We assume that the aggregate planning time horizon consists of n time periods.

Production Capacity Constraints

Each of the regular time, overtime, and subcontracting quantities will have an upper limit on total output in each of the n time periods. These constraints can be written as:

$$x_t \leq R_t \qquad t = 1, \ldots, n$$
$$y_t \leq O_t \qquad t = 1, \ldots, n$$
$$z_t \leq S_t \qquad t = 1, \ldots, n$$

Inventory and Demand Constraints

We need to ensure that demand is met and that the inventory at the end of period t is equal to the inventory in period $t - 1$ plus total production minus demand in period t. This can be written as:

$$i_t = i_{t-1} + x_t + y_t + z_t - d_t, \qquad t = 1, \ldots, n$$

Hiring and Firing Constraints

This last set of constraints defines the change in regular production from one period to the next. The resulting change in units of production is assumed to be directly related to hiring and firing. This is expressed as:

$$x_t = x_{t-1} + h_t - f_t, \qquad t = 1, \ldots, n$$

Variables h_t and f_t will not be in solution at the same time. That is, in any period we could hire or fire but not both; one of the two variables h_t or f_t will be zero for any period t.

Finally, the nonnegativity conditions are required:

$$x_t, y_t, z_t, i_t, h_t, f_t \geq 0, \qquad t = 1, \ldots, n$$

Objective Function

The objective function is a linear expression which sums up all of the costs, times their respective decision variables. The costs consist of various types of production (regular time, overtime, subcontracting), inventory carrying costs, and the costs of changing regular production levels (hiring and firing).

$$\text{Minimize} \sum_{t=1}^{n} c_1 x_t + c_2 y_t + c_3 z_t + c_4 i_t + c_5 h_t + c_6 f_t$$

For a 12-month planning horizon, the LP model would consist of 72 variables and 60 constraints. This is a relatively small model in the realm of real-world applications. The most limiting aspect of the model is its assumption of a linear cost structure. However, LP is a powerful means to derive an effective solution to aggregate planning problems, and could be used to derive an approximate or starting point solution even when some nonlinear cost relationships do exist.

_____ REFERENCES _____

BITRAN, G.R., and A.C. HAX, "On the Design of Hierarchical Production Planning Systems," *Decision Sciences*, 8 (January 1977), 28–55.

BOWMAN, E.H., "Consistence and Optimality in Managerial Decision Making," *Management Science*, 4 (January 1963), 100–103.

_____, "Production Planning by the Transportation Method of Linear Programming," *Journal of the Operations Research Society*, February 1956.

EBERT, R.J., "Aggregate Planning with Learning Curve Productivity," *Management Science*, 23, no. 2 (October 1976), 171–82.

EILON, SAMUEL, "Five Approaches to Aggregate Production Planning," *AIIE Transactions*, June 1975.

HANSSMANN, F., and S.W. HESS, "A Linear Programming Approach to Production and Employment Scheduling," *Management Technology*, vol. 1 (January 1960), 46–52.

HOLT, C.C., F. MODIGLIANI, and H.A. SIMON, "A Linear Decision Rule for Production and Employment Scheduling," *Management Science*, 2, no. 2 (October 19555), 1–30.

HOOKE, R., and T.A. JEEVES, "A 'Direct Search' Solution of Numerical Statistical Problems," *Journal of the Association for Computing Machinery*, April 1961.

JONES, C.H., "Parametric Production Planning," *Management Science*, 13, no. 11 (July 1967), 843–66.

LEE, W.B., and B.M. KHUMAWALA, "Simulation Testing of Aggregate Production Planning Models in an Implementation Methodology," *Management Science*, 20, no. 6 (February 1974), 903–11.

KRAJEWSKI, L.J., and L.B. RITZMAN, "Disaggregation in Manufacturing and Service Organizations: Survey of Problems and Research," *Decision Sciences*, 8, no. 1 (January 1977), 1–18.

ORLICKY, JOSEPH, *Materials Requirements Planning*. New York: McGraw-Hill, 1975.

TAUBERT, W.H., "Search Decision Rule for the Aggregate Scheduling Problem," *Management Science*, 14, no. 6 (February 1968), 343–59.

VERGIN, R.C., "Production Scheduling under Seasonal Demand," *Journal of Industrial Engineering*, 17, no. 5 (May 1966).

WIGHT, OLIVER W., *Production and Inventory Management in the Computer Age*. Boston: Cahners Books, 1974.

10

INVENTORY CONTROL SYSTEMS

INTRODUCTION

An *inventory* is a stock of goods that is held for the purpose of future production or sales. Raw materials, work in progress, and finished goods can all be classified as inventory items, and the decisions about them as inventory are similar. Obviously, such decisions often have a critical effect on the health of an organization.

Organizations carry inventories for a number of the following reasons:

- *Smooth production*. Often, the demand for an item fluctuates widely, owing to a number of factors, such as seasonality and production schedules. For example, 50 percent of all the toys manufactured in one year may be sold in the three weeks before Christmas. If toy manufacturers were to try to produce 50 percent of a year's output in three weeks, they would need a tremendous influx of labor as well as huge manufacturing facilities. Instead, firms find it more economical to produce goods over a longer, slower schedule and store them as inventory. Thus, they keep the labor force fairly stable, and expenditures for capital equipment are lower.
- *Product availability*. Most retail goods and many industrial goods are carried in inventory to ensure prompt delivery to customers. Not only does a good inventory provide a competitive edge, it often means the difference between success and failure. If a firm gains a reputation for constantly being out of stock, it may lose a significant number of customers.
- *Advantages of producing or buying in large quantities*. Most production runs involve machine setup time as well as production time. If setup time is significant, real savings can be achieved by producing in large lots. In addition, most firms offer quantity discounts for buying in large quantities.
- *Hedge against long or uncertain lead times*. The time between ordering and receiving goods is known as lead time. Because firms do not want to stop manufacturing or selling goods during lead time, it is necessary to carry inventory.

Gene Woolsey, writing for *Interfaces*, emphasizes the importance of controlling inventories:

> The second stop on the required tour is the production line of machinists making part X. We proceed as follows. First look for a 5 by 5 by 3 foot bin of gears or parts that looks like it has been there awhile. Pick up a gear and ask, casually, "How much is this worth?" You then ask, "How many of these are in the bin?" followed by, "How long has this bin been here?" and, "What's your cost of money for this company?" I recall one case in a nameless South American country where the unit cost times the number of parts times the time it had been there times the interest rate resulted in a

cost per day figure that would insure a comfortable retirement for the plant manager on the bank of the Rio de la Plata at one of the better resorts to be found there. The plant manager suddenly realized that what he was holding was not just a chunk of high-test steel, but was *real money*. He then pointed out that *he* now understood the value of the inventory but could I suggest a way to drive the point home to upper management? I suggested that he go to the accounting department and borrow enough money to be equal to the bin's value for as long as it had been sitting there, and pile it on the top of the bin. I further suggested that he do that for every bin on the production line. We rapidly figured out that by the time we had the money piled up on the bin, you would not even be able to *see* the bin. My opinion was that if the upper managers were given a tour of the line with the money piled up, they would *never forget it*.[1]

These are two basic functions that must be performed in order to effectively control an organization's inventory. First, management must have a system for accounting or keeping track of inventory. This system can be either a periodic series of physical numerations or a continuous inventory system in which quantities in inventory are calculated each time units are added to or drawn from inventory. The second function that must be performed for effective inventory control is the decision-making function. Decisions must be made regarding how much to order and when to order. In order for him to make intelligent inventory decisions, accurate information about demand and the inventory status for each item must be available to the decision maker.

Demand for inventory items can be classified as dependent or independent. *Dependent demand* is demand for those items in inventory that is determined ultimately by the demand for an end item or final product for which the inventory items are components. An example would be the demand for engine pistons; if the demand for each type of automobile is forecasted, then the demand for engine pistons can be calculated directly based on the number of pistons required for each automobile. The demand for automobiles is an example of *independent demand*. Although dependent-demand items are very common to the manufacturing sector of the economy, the service sector is concerned almost exclusively with independent-demand items. Because the problems associated with each type of demand are essentially different, we treat the problems of independent demand in this chapter and those of dependent demand in the next chapter, on materials requirements planning.

Fortunately, a large number of optimization models have been developed for independent-demand inventories, to aid the decision maker in making good inventory decisions. Therefore, the organization that effectively and efficiently controls inventory has an effective inventory information system and makes use of appropriate mathematical models in making inventory decisions.

Obviously, using a computer-based inventory information system and sophisticated operations research techniques to control the paper-clip inventory

---

[1] Gene Woolsey, "On Doing Good Things and Dumb Things in Production and Inventory Control," *Interfaces*, 5, no. 5 (May 1975), 66–67.

Table 10-1   Annual Dollar-Volume Usage

ITEM NO.	ANNUAL DEMAND	PER-UNIT COST	TOTAL ANNUAL DOLLAR VALUE
22213	100	10,000	1,000,000
22157	2,000	500	1,000,000
22545	200	1,500	300,000
22432	400	500	200,000
22511	150	700	105,000
22457	240	100	24,000
22111	300	50	15,000
22331	10	100	1,000
22471	10	100	1,000
22512	25	25	625
25531	30	20	600
22122	50	10	500
			2,647,725

would be absurd. For this reason, many organizations choose to classify inventory items into three basic categories, usually according to annual dollar volume. The logic of this classification scheme (ABC classification) is to spend money and time controlling only important inventory items, in the realization that the cost of closely controlling relatively unimportant inventory items cannot be justified. To give you an idea how this classification is effected, let us assume that a firm has only twelve individual inventory items. These items and their annual dollar volume are shown in Table 10-1.

The ABC classification typically seeks to put approximately 15 percent of the items in category A, 35 percent in category B, and 50 percent in category C. There is nothing sacred about these percentages, but these are the the ones often used. Since in our example we have twelve items, two would make up 16.6 percent and four would be 35.3 percent. Therefore, you might put items 22213 and 22157 in category A, and 22545, 22432, 22511, and 22457 in category B, with the remaining items in category C. Table 10-2 shows that if we closely controlled only two items, we would be controlling 75.5 percent of the annual inventory dollar volume.

It is possible, of course, that an item that is placed in category C because of its low annual dollar volume may be of a critical nature and therefore deserves greater

Table 10-2   ABC Analysis

CATEGORY	TOTAL ANNUAL DOLLAR VOLUME	PERCENT OF TOTAL
A	2,000,000	75.5
B	629,000	23.8
C	18,725	.7
	2,647,725	100.0

control. A simple solution is to arbitrarily place that item in category A.

INVENTORY ACCOUNTING SYSTEMS

Inventory accounting systems can be classified as physical or continuous. A *physical inventory system* is a system in which management periodically reviews inventory levels of the various items in order to make inventory decisions. A common example of this type of system might be in the small grocery store. Each day, various delivery men stop at the store to replenish inventory. For example, the milkman may come daily, take a physical inventory, and decide what he needs to leave in the dairy case. Each week it may be necessary to order canned goods and other relatively nonperishable items. In order to do this, the manager must look at each item and make a decision on whether to order the item and how much to order.

An alternate way of manually managing a physical inventory system is known as the *two-bin system*, in which each inventory item has two storage bins. As shown in Figure 10-1, Bin 1 contains the inventory on hand when an order is placed to replenish inventory. When an order is received, Bin 1 is filled to the reorder point level and the remainder is placed in Bin 2. When Bin 2 is emptied, a new order is placed. Many firms use this type of two-bin system to control category C inventory items.

Continuous inventory systems are typically more sophisticated than periodic ordering systems. They keep track of the inventory level of each item on a continuous basis. In other words, as items are added to or drawn from inventory, these events are recorded and the new inventory level is computed.

Continuous inventory accounting systems can range from the extremely simple manual system to very sophisticated computer-based systems. An example of a manual but continuous inventory system might be the local blood bank. For each type of blood, there might be a card on which is recorded the number of units in

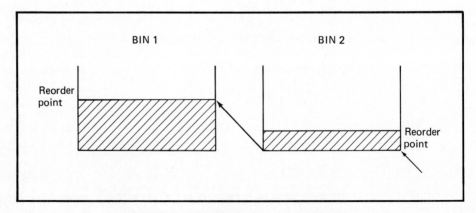

FIGURE 10-1   Two-Bin Inventory Control System

inventory. As units are demanded or added to inventory, a clerk merely makes the appropriate notation on the card. Hence, there is a permanent record of the inventory status of each blood type at all times.

Computerized inventory accounting systems can be classified as batch-processing systems or real-time systems. A *batch-processing inventory system* is a system in which inventory transactions (additions to and withdrawals from inventory) are collected periodically, batched together, and processed to update the current inventory master file. In the simplified example, graphically represented in Figure 10-2, an inventory control clerk creates a transaction document each time an item is drawn from inventory and each time an order is received. Periodically, these documents are "batched" together and sent to data processing, where the information is transcribed into machine-readable form. These data are then processed against the current inventory master file to create an updated master file. Output from this processing could include a list of items that need to be ordered, a list of the status of all inventory items, purchase orders, a value-of-inventory report, suggested order quantities, and so on. Therefore, in a batch-processing environment, the inventory master file is only as current as the data of the last update.

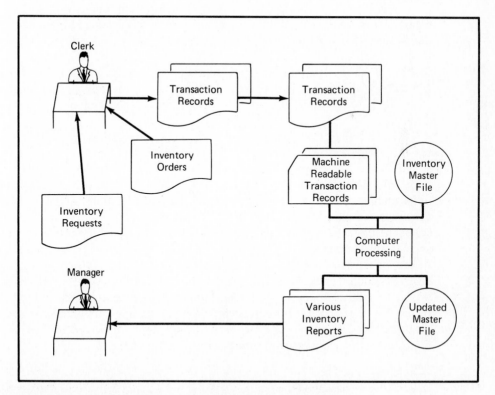

FIGURE 10-2   Simplified Example of Batch Inventory Accounting System

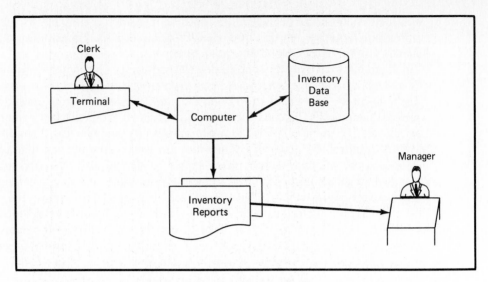

FIGURE 10-3   Simplified Real-Time Inventory Accounting System

Real-time systems keep the inventory master file continuously up to date. When a unit is drawn out of or added to inventory, that event is recorded immediately and the master file reflects the change immediately. Figure 10-3 graphically depicts this process. Typically, real-time systems are more costly than batch systems, but as the cost of computing continues to decrease, the number of real-time inventory systems will inevitably increase. A good example of a real-time inventory system is an airline reservation system where the inventory items being controlled are the seats on the airplane.

Regardless of the mode of processing, a computer-based inventory system can vary according to the amount of inventory decision making that is delegated to the system. Some systems provide only information and all ordering decisions are made by people, whereas with some systems, the computer calculates reorder points and order quantities, and even writes the purchase order or shop order. These are two extremes, and many systems fall somewhere in between. Jack Bishop, Jr., reports a system he designed that calculated order quantities based on the information system and the appropriate inventory models.[2] He emphasizes, however, that the key to the success of the system was that order quantities were not dictated by the computer-based system but rather were just suggestions to operating personnel. His experience was that a system characterized by this kind of man–computer partnership has a far better chance of success. Initially, people were overriding computer-generated order quantities 80 percent of the time. A year later, only 10 percent of the inventory decisions made by the computer were manually overridden.

[2]Jack L. Bishop, Jr., "Experience with a Successful System for Forecasting and Inventory Control," *Operations Research*, 22, no. 6, (November–December 1974), 1224–31.

MODELS FOR INVENTORY DECISION MAKING

As mentioned earlier in this chapter, there are two basic functions necessary to effectively control inventory. In this section, we deal with a scientific approach to performing one of those functions: namely, inventory decision making for independent-demand items.

The objective of any inventory model is to minimize total inventory cost. Minimizing just one of the three components of inventory cost is easy, and of little value. For example, to minimize carrying cost, a firm can simply stop carrying any inventory. This action, however, can be expected to create unreasonable stockout costs. The actual process for minimizing total inventory costs entails two basic decisions: how much and when to order. Understandably, these are the two decision variables that inventory models use in optimizing an inventory system.

In this section, we discuss the five essential steps in analyzing inventory problems:

- Determining inventory properties
- Formulating the appropriate inventory model
- Solving or manipulating the model
- Performing sensitivity analysis on the model
- Incorporating the model into the inventory control system

Determining System Properties

Inventory properties can be classified in four categories: demand properties, replenishment properties, cost properties, and constraints. In order to prevent the misapplication of an inventory model, it is extremely important to identify and consider each property of an inventory system properly.

Demand Properties. These characteristics include the size, and rate, of demand. The size of demand can be constant or variable, depending on the nature of the good. A constant demand merely means that for each time period, the quantity of goods demanded is constant. The size of demand for a good can be deterministic or stochastic. Given a production schedule, for example, it may be a simple calculation to determine demand for a particular period of time. However, the demand of many inventory items cannot be predicted with any degree of certainty; hence, the problem is a stochastic or probabilistic problem rather than a deterministic one.

The rate of demand is the size of demand over a particular unit of time. For example, Vulcan Valve Company has a total demand for the year of 600 valves, and its records verify that the monthly demand rate is 600/12, or 50 units per month. Clearly, demand rate can be variable or constant, deterministic or stochastic.

Replenishment Properties.   When you analyze replenishment properties, it is necessary to define the *scheduling period*. The scheduling period is the length of time between decisions concerning replenishments. This time period can be prescribed or variable. For example, the local supermarket orders fresh lettuce twice a week (prescribed), whereas canned kidney beans are ordered when the inventory reaches a certain reorder point (variable). Variable scheduling periods require a continuous accounting for inventory. In most medium and large firms, an inventory accounting system is, or should be, computerized.

Lead time, you will recall, is the time between ordering a replenishment of inventory and actually receiving the goods into inventory. Lead time can be either a deterministic constant or variable, or a stochastic variable. If lead time is known with a high degree of certainty, its existence is easily treated in inventory modeling. On the other hand, if lead time is stochastic with a large variance, the difficulty in finding an appropriate inventory model is greatly increased.

Like demand, the *size of replenishment* can also be stochastic. In other words, the quantity ordered may not be the same as the quantity received, owing to undershipments, or quality rejections. Replenishment size is often called *lot size*.

The *replenishment period* is the time during which units of a particular order are added to inventory. In a purchasing situation, the replenishment period may be insignificant; but in a production environment, units are added to inventory over a period of time (that is, as they are produced).

Often, instead of specifying the lot size, an inventory policy specifies an *order level*. An order level is the quantity that will be in inventory after replenishment.

Cost Properties.   The costs associated with inventory are traditionally classified into three basic categories: ordering costs, carrying costs, and shortage costs.

Ordering costs are the costs involved in ordering and receiving inventory. These costs consist largely of salaries in the purchasing and accounting departments and wages in the receiving area; they also include purchase and transportation charges. If a firm produces its own inventory instead of purchasing from an outside source, production setup costs are analogous to ordering costs. Ordering costs are usually expressed by a dollar amount per order.

Carrying costs, also referred to as *holding costs*, are the costs that holding inventory entails. Components of carrying costs are both direct and indirect, and they include:

- Interest on the money invested in inventory
- Storage or warehousing costs, including rent, electricity, wages, insurance, security, data processing, and so on
- Obsolescence (If the good is held too long in inventory, its value may decrease substantially.)

Carrying costs are typically calculated as a percentage of inventory value or a dollar value per unit of inventory.

The third category of inventory costs is *shortage* or *stockout costs*. If demand for an off-the-shelf good exists and a firm does not have the good in inventory, there is an inevitable loss of customer goodwill as well as loss of the profit from the sale. The dollar value of this loss of goodwill is, at best, difficult to measure. If you had to assess it, relevant questions would include: Will the firm lose the sale? Will the firm lose the customer? What are the probabilities of these losses? What is the dollar value of that particular customer?

If the inventory is being carried for internal use (that is, production), a stockout can have very serious effects. It can shut down an assembly line, and to shut down a typical automobile assembly line, for example, can cost as much as tens of thousands of dollars per minute.

Cost parameters of an inventory model are rarely known with certainty. Consequently, the inventory manager usually should determine the sensitivity of the optimal solution to small and reasonable changes in these parameters.

Inventory Constraints.   In addition to determining inventory properties, before you can decide on solution methodology you must analyze inventory constraints. For example, if the inventory storage area holds only 100 units, an optimal order quantity of 1,000 units is irrelevant. Similarly, if working capital is severely limited and the optimal inventory policy calls for carrying a high inventory, the optimal policy may not be feasible. Typical inventory constraints include:

- *Capital.* A firm may not have the necessary working capital to carry large inventories.
- *Space.* The amount of storage space may put limits on the order quantity.
- *Scheduling period.* If the scheduling period is prescribed, many inventory models cannot be used.
- *Shortage.* Management may make a decision that stockouts cannot be allowed. On the other hand, shortages may be allowed and may or may not result in lost sales.
- *Dependent demand.* In most inventory models, demand is considered independent of the demand of the preceding period.

Determining inventory properties is crucial to analyzing inventory problems. If we expect to find or develop an appropriate model for the inventory item in question, we must analyze the item's properties and characteristics in depth.

Formulating the Model

The second step in analyzing inventory problems is to discover or derive the appropriate inventory model to solve the particular problem. Basically, there are two types of inventory models: deterministic models and stochastic models. The parameters of deterministic inventory models are assumed to be known with certainty. For example, demand is assumed to be perfectly predictable. Stochastic inventory models contain uncontrollable variables, such as demand or lead time, that are probabilistic in nature. Generally, stochastic inventory models are mathematically more difficult to derive and solve. As the number of stochastic variables increases, it becomes more difficult to derive an analytical optimization model. In addition, if a stochastic variable is not distributed according to a known probability density function, the likelihood of finding or deriving an analytical inventory model is drastically reduced. When an analytical model cannot be developed to model a particular inventory system adequately, simulation can usually be used to determine a good inventory policy. The decision of whether to simulate an inventory system hinges on the cost/benefit of the simulation. This is one area in which ABC analysis can be used.

Solving the Model

The third step in the analysis of inventory systems is to solve the analytical model or run the simulation model. This is typically the easiest part of the process if the first two steps have been performed properly. Because the solution of analytical inventory models is not an iterative process, a computer is not considered an absolute necessity. If a computer is used, very few computer resources (memory and time) are necessary to solve analytic inventory models.

An analytical model is preferable to a simulation model for two reasons. First, the cost in computer resources is considerably less. Second, an analytical model yields an optimal solution, whereas a simulation model can only search for a good solution. In short, analytical inventory models cost *much* less than simulation models to find the *best* answer. This is not to say, however, that a real system should be modeled using an analytical model whose assumptions do not adequately fit the real-system properties. This is a common error in practice, and it is for this reason that we explicitly state the assumptions of each model we present in this chapter.

Performing Sensitivity Analysis

Some models yield order quantities that are extremely sensitive. In other words, slight changes in the order quantity cause significant changes in the total cost of the inventory system. In addition, it is usually helpful to the decision maker to know the relative sensitivity of such inventory variables as demand, lead time, and replenishment quantity. Unlike LP, inventory models cannot easily determine the sensitivity of the system's various parameters and decision variables. Instead, the parameter or variable in question is perturbed, and the effect of the change is observed.

Integrating the Model into the Inventory Control System

Once a model has been found that makes good inventory decisions, it must be integrated into the inventory control system. For example, let us assume Model A calculates an order quantity for a particular item that minimizes cost. If that model is programmed into the software of the inventory system, then any time that item reaches its reorder point, an order quantity can be calculated and suggested to management.

ANALYTICAL MODELS

In this chapter, we are going to consider several deterministic models and one stochastic model. These represent only a small sampling of the inventory models that have been developed and used since the first one was introduced in 1915.

Basic Economic Order Quantity Model (EOQ)

Before examining it, we must identify the assumptions of the basic EOQ model so that you will know under what conditions to apply it. If the following assumptions cannot be accepted, thereby indicating that the real-world inventory problem may not be adequately represented by the basic EOQ model, it is inappropriate to use it.

- *Deterministic demand*. It must be possible to predict demand with a high degree of confidence.
- *Constant rate of demand*. Not only must the total demand be known, but units must be drawn from inventory at a uniform rate. For example, if 365 units are used each year, these items must be drawn one per day during the year to strictly satisfy this assumption.
- *No shortages*. Inventory replenishments are made whenever the inventory level reaches zero. Shortages are not allowed to occur. This assumption implies that one of the three costs involved in an inventory system, stockout cost, does not exist in the basic EOQ model.
- *Constant replenishment size*. The replenishment size, denoted by q, is the only decision variable in the basic EOQ model. The other decision variable—when to reorder—is fixed, because demand is at a constant rate and replenishments occur when the inventory level reaches zero.
- *Zero lead time*. It is assumed that no appreciable time elapses between placing an order and receiving that order. This assumption can be relaxed, as we shall explain later.
- *Infinite replenishment rate*. Replenishment rate is defined as the rate at which units are added to inventory. An infinite replenishment rate implies that inventory replenishment occurs instantaneously. In other words, it takes zero time to receive an order. This assumption is reasonable for most purchased goods but is often unreasonable for manufactured goods. Typically, manufactured goods are added to inventory at some finite rate.
- *Constant inventory costs*. Both costs in the basic EOQ model are constant. Ordering cost is expressed as dollars per order, and holding cost is expressed as dollars per unit per time period.

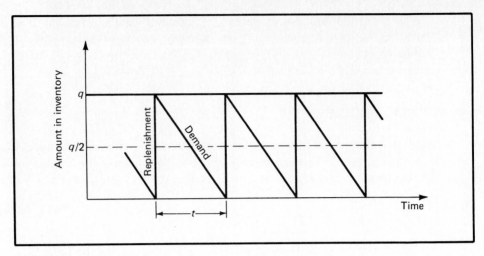

FIGURE 10-4   Graphic Representation of the Basic EOQ Model

These assumptions for the basic EOQ model determine the graph in Figure 10-4.

It would be the rare inventory item for which all the assumptions above could be accepted without reservation. The key point is that you should be aware of these assumptions, and if your inventory problem violates one of them significantly, another inventory model may be more appropriate.

Inventory problems in which the decision variable is the order quantity have the objective function in equation 10.1:

10.1   Min $C(q) = A(q) + B(q) + D(q)$

where $C(q)$ = the total cost function

$A(q)$ = a function of q that defines the holding cost

$B(q)$ = a function of q that represents the shortage cost

$D(q)$ = a function of q that defines the ordering cost

In order to determine the optimal value of q, it is necessary to develop the functions $A(q)$, $B(q)$, and $D(q)$ for the basic EOQ model. For holding cost we have

$$A(q) = C_1(q/2)$$

where C_1 = holding cost per unit of inventory

A look at Figure 10-4 will reveal to you that $q/2$ represents the average number of units in inventory. In other words, half the time there are more than $q/2$ units in inventory, and half the time the amount in inventory is less than $q/2$ units. Therefore, if we multiply a per-unit holding cost by the average number of units in inventory, that product is the holding cost. Since no shortages are allowed in the basic EOQ model, owing to the zero lead-time and zero reorder-point assumptions, $B(q)$ is not present in the total cost function. Ordering cost can be thought of as the cost of placing an order multiplied by the number of orders placed in a particular time period. More specifically:

$$D(q) = C_3(r/q)$$

where C_3 = the cost of processing one order

r = total demand for a given period of time

r/q = number of orders

Given the preceding defined functions, the total cost function can be written as shown in equation 10.2:

10.2
$$C(q) = A(q) + D(q)$$
$$C(q) = C_1(q/2) + C_3(r/q)$$

Remember, the question is to determine the value of q that minimizes the objective function $C(q)$. Figure 10-5 graphs the three functions $A(q)$, $C(q)$, and $D(q)$. From Figure 10-5, it is apparent that the minimum of $C(q)$ occurs at the same level of q where functions $A(q)$ and $D(q)$ intersect. It is possible, therefore, to set $A(q)$ equal

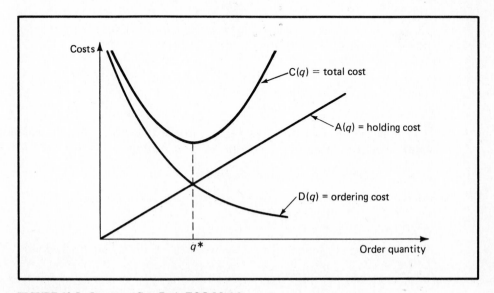

FIGURE 10-5   Inventory Cost Basic EOQ Model

to $D(q)$ and solve for q to find q^*, the optimal value of q. It must be noted that this relationship between ordering cost and carrying cost is not universally true.

$$A(q) = D(q)$$
$$C_1(q/2) = C_3(r/q)$$
$$C_1(q^2/2) = C_3 r$$
10.3
$$q^2/2 = C_3 r/C_1$$
$$q^2 = 2C_3 r/C_1$$
$$q^* = \sqrt{2C_3 r/C_1}$$

Now, let's look at an example of how to use the basic EOQ model. The Ace Aerospace Company uses 10,000 special bolts per year. Each bolt costs \$1. The Materials Department estimates that it costs \$25 to order a shipment of bolts, and the Accounting Department estimates the holding cost is 12.5 percent. All the assumptions of the basic EOQ model are valid.

$$C_1 = \$.125 \text{ per bolt per year}$$
$$C_3 = \$25 \text{ per order}$$
$$r = 10{,}000 \text{ bolts}$$
$$q^* = \sqrt{2C_3 r/C_1}$$
$$= \sqrt{2(25)10{,}000/.125}$$
$$= \sqrt{4{,}000{,}000}$$
$$= 2{,}000 \text{ bolts}$$

If the Ace Aerospace Company buys 2,000 bolts every time inventory reaches zero, the total annual cost of this policy is:

$$C(q^*) = .125(2{,}000/2) + 25(10{,}000/2{,}000)$$
$$= 125 + 125$$
$$= \$250$$

Once q^* is calculated, it is a simple matter to calculate the optimal number of orders per year and the time between each two orders:

$$N^* = \text{optimal number of orders}$$
$$= r/q^*$$
$$= 10{,}000/2{,}000$$
$$= 5$$
$$t^* = \text{optimal time between orders (optimal reorder schedule)}$$
$$= \text{Planning period}/N^*$$
$$= 365/5 = 73 \text{ days}$$

Sensitivity of the Basic EOQ Model

As indicated in Figure 10-5, the typical shape of the total cost curve, $C(q)$, is relatively flat. Consequently, $C(q)$ is often not very sensitive to small changes in q. To illustrate this fact, let us assume that the Ace Aerospace Company orders 1,000 bolts in each order instead of the optimal 2,000 bolts. The annual inventory cost for ordering 1,000 bolts each order is calculated below.

$$C(1,000) = .125(1,000/2) + 25(10,000/1,000)$$
$$= 62.50 + 250$$
$$= \$312.50$$

Hence, a change of 50 percent in q resulted in only a 25 percent increase in the total inventory cost. (See Table 10-3 for a more complete sensitivity analysis.) This means that if total demand, r, is incorrectly estimated, thus causing a suboptimal q to be calculated, the consequences are not as critical as they would be if the shape of the total cost curve were more peaked.

Basic EOQ System with Finite Replenishment Rate

Often, it is unrealistic to assume an infinite replenishment rate. If a firm is purchasing off-the-shelf items for its inventory, then typically, when an order is delivered, the entire replenishment quantity is delivered at one time; hence, an infinite replenishment rate. If, however, a company is producing for inventory, units are added to inventory over a finite period of time. Therefore, the inventory system has a finite replenishment rate. If it can be assumed that this replenishment rate is

Table 10-3   Sensitivity Analysis of Order Quantity

ORDER QUANTITY	ORDER COST ($)	CARRYING COST ($)	TOTAL COST ($)
100	2,500.00	6.25	2,506.25
500	500.00	31.25	531.25
750	333.33	46.88	380.21
1,000	250.00	62.50	312.50
1,250	200.00	78.13	278.13
1,500	166.65	93.75	260.40
1,750	142.85	109.38	252.23
2,000	125.00	125.00	250.00
2,250	111.11	140.63	251.73
2,500	100.00	156.25	256.25
3,000	83.33	187.50	270.83
4,000	62.50	250.00	312.50
10,000	25.00	625.00	650.00

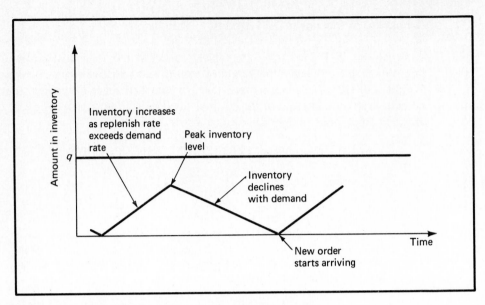

FIGURE 10-6   Basic EOQ System with Uniform Replenishment Rate

uniform and all other assumptions of the basic EOQ model hold, the appropriate model is the basic EOQ system with a finite replenishment rate. The graphic representation of the model is given in Figure 10-6.

The total cost function of the inventory system depicted in Figure 10-6 is:

10.4
$$C(q) = \frac{C_1 q(1 - r/p)}{2} + \frac{C_3 r}{q}$$

The expression for the optimal order quantity is shown in equation 10.5:

10.5
$$q^* = \frac{\sqrt{2rC_3/C_1}}{\sqrt{1 - r/p}}$$

where r = the total demand for a given period of time

C_3 = the setup cost per setup

C_1 = the carrying cost per unit

p = uniform replenishment rate expressed in units per time period

The minimum total inventory cost is given by the following function:

10.6
$$C^* = \sqrt{2rC_1C_3}\sqrt{1 - r/p}$$

where C^* = the minimum inventory cost

Let's alter our previous example just slightly so that the replenishment rate changes from infinite to a uniform 500 bolts per day. To restate, the Ace Aerospace Company uses 10,000 bolts per year. Each bolt costs $1. The Production Engineering Department estimates setup costs at $25, and the Accounting Department estimates that the holding cost is 12.5 percent of the value of inventory.

$$r = 10,000 \text{ bolts}$$

$$C_3 = \$25 \text{ per order}$$

$$C_1 = \$.125 \text{ per bolt per year}$$

$$p = 125,000 \text{ bolts per year}^3$$

$$q^* = \sqrt{\frac{2rC_3/C_1}{1-(r/p)}}$$

$$= \sqrt{\frac{2(10,000)25/.125}{1-(10,000/125,000)}}$$

$$= \sqrt{4,000,000/.92}$$

$$= \sqrt{4,350,000}$$

$$= 2,086$$

Therefore, the Ace Aerospace Company should order 2,086 bolts every time inventory for the bolts reaches zero. The total inventory cost of this ordering policy is calculated below:

$$C^* = \sqrt{2rC_1C_3}\sqrt{1-(r/p)}$$

$$= \sqrt{2(10,000).125(25)}\sqrt{1-(10,000)/125,000}$$

$$= \sqrt{62,500}\sqrt{.92}$$

$$\cong \$239.75$$

Therefore, if the Ace Aerospace Company orders 2,086 bolts approximately five times a year, inventory cost related to this particular bolt is minimized at about $240 per year.

Basic Order-Level System

The basic order-level system is very similar to the basic lot-size system previously described. In fact, all properties are the same except that shortages are allowed and

---

[3] It was necessary to convert the per-day production of bolts to per-year production of bolts because the time units must be compatible; that is, r was expressed in units per year. (250 workdays $\times$ 500 = 125,000 bolts per year.)

backordered and the scheduling period is prescribed. This type of system is very common in the real world when an organization places orders for certain inventory items on a regularly scheduled basis, such as once a month. An advantage of a prescribed scheduling period is that it does *not* necessitate continuous monitoring of inventory levels.

The basic order-level system has the following properties:

· Demand is deterministic.
· The rate of demand is constant; that is, it is a linear demand function.
· The scheduling period is prescribed.
· The lead time is zero.
· The replenishment rate is infinite.
· Shortages are made up; that is, there are no lost sales.
· The decision variable is the order level, S; that is, the decision variable is the amount of inventory after replenishment.
· Holding cost is constant and is expressed as dollars per unit per time period.
· Shortage cost is constant and expressed as dollars per unit per time period.

The basic order-level system is depicted in Figure 10-7.

Since the scheduling period is prescribed, the only controllable inventory costs are the carrying and shortage costs. Since order level is the decision variable in this inventory model, the total cost function is a function of order level, S.

It can be shown geometrically, using similar triangles, that the total cost function is:

10.7 $$C(S) = C_1 S^2/2q_p + C_2(q_p - S)^2/2q_p$$

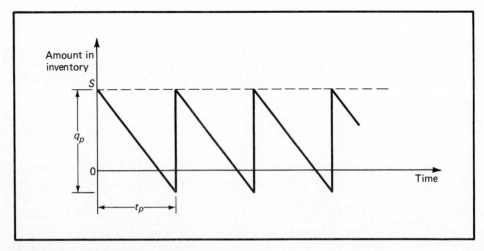

FIGURE 10-7   Basic Order-Level System

where C_1 = carrying cost per unit per time period

   S = order level

   q_p = prescribed lot size (rate of demand multiplied by the prescribed time period)

   C_2 = shortage cost per unit per time period

Minimizing this total cost function using classical optimization procedures of the differential calculus, the optimal order level is:

10.8 $S^* = q_pC_2/(C_1 + C_2)$

Example: A local stereo store reviews its stock of Dynamo preamps every month, then orders for the next month. Last year, it sold 120 Dynamo preamps, and sales were spread evenly throughout the year. Predictions are that this year's sales will be approximately the same. Lead time is effectively zero, and shortages are made up. The holding cost is $80 per preamp per year, and shortage cost has been determined to be $10 per preamp per month ($10 per preamp per month × 12 months equals $120 per preamp per year). The optimal order level, therefore, is:

$$S^* = 10(120)/(80 + 120)$$
$$= 6 \text{ preamps}$$

To find the minimum cost of this solution, merely substitute S^* into the cost function:

$$C(6) = (80 \cdot 6^2)/(2 \cdot 10) + \left[120(10 - 6)^2\right]/20$$
$$= \$240$$

In summary, the inventory policy of the local stereo store is to order ten Dynamo preamps whenever backorders reach four.

This inventory policy costs $240 per year in inventory cost; any other policy would cost the stereo store more. The graph of this inventory policy is shown in Figure 10-8 on the following page.

Basic EOQ Model with Discrete Price Breaks

It is often advantageous to procure inventory items in large quantities in order to get quantity discounts. A supplier often sells a product at a price that fluctuates with the quantity purchased. Usually, the price-break scheme is discrete in nature. For example, the per-unit cost of an item might be $25 for quantities of 50 or less; $22 for quantities of less than 100 but more than 50; and $20 per unit for more than 100 units. As reflected in Table 10-4, buying in large quantities has several advantages and disadvantages.

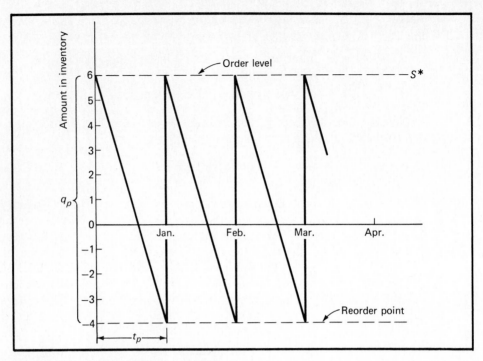

FIGURE 10-8   Order-Level System with Stockouts

Buying large quantities has advantages other than merely lowering the per-unit cost of the particular inventory item. Obviously, because fewer orders are placed, ordering costs are reduced when an organization takes advantage of quantity discounts and buys in larger quantities. Transportation costs, also, are usually lower for a few large shipments rather than many small shipments. If demand is stochastic and lead time is not zero, buying in larger quantities results in fewer stockouts.

Table 10-4   Quantity Buying Advantages and Disadvantages

ADVANTAGES	DISADVANTAGES
Lower unit cost	Higher holding cost
Lower ordering cost	Higher capital requirements
Fewer stockouts	Increased risk of deterioration
Preferential treatment by suppliers	and obsolescence
Lower transportation cost	Older stock on hand
Increase uniformity in goods	
(coming from the same shipment)	
Security (against such factors as	
strikes and price increases)	

As you have probably realized, buying in large quantities has some very important disadvantages, too. The most obvious is that, because the average amount in inventory is increased with large orders, the carrying cost of the inventory item is increased. In addition to increased carrying cost, more capital is required to buy larger quantities. For firms with limited capital, this can be a critical drawback, one that sometimes prevents taking advantage of quantity discounts. If the inventory item is perishable or has an otherwise limited life, buying in larger quantities may also be disadvantageous to a firm. High-fashion, ready-to-wear clothing is an example of such an inventory item. Even if a manufacturer is willing to give a quantity discount that would ordinarily minimize the retailer's total inventory cost, it may be wiser to buy the smaller quantity due to the potential obsolescence of the article.

The model we describe in this section is a simple, discrete price-break model. The assumptions concerning demand and replenishment properties are the same as the basic EOQ model except that in this model there exists the condition of discrete prices based on the quantity ordered. Since the cost of goods purchased is no longer constant but is a function of the price, the objective function is composed of ordering cost, carrying cost, and the cost of goods. More specifically,

10.9 $$C(q_i) = fq_i b_i / 2 + (C_3 r / q_i) + rb_i$$

where
f = carrying cost function
q_i = order quantity for price break i
b_i = unit cost for price break i
C_3 = ordering cost per order
r = total demand

If you look carefully at the objective function in equation 10.9, you can see that it closely resembles the total cost function of the basic EOQ model. In fact, the first two terms are identical if you realize that the carrying cost (C_1) in dollars per unit per time period is simply the cost fraction (f) multiplied by the unit cost (b_i). The only difference is the existence of more than one price level and the addition of the cost of goods.

As depicted in Figure 10-9, the total cost function for the price-break model is not continuous. Therefore, it is not possible to use the calculus to derive a simple formula to compute the optimal order quantity.

Instead, we need an algorithm. The algorithm for the discrete price-break model is presented in flow-chart form in Figure 10-10. The first step in the algorithm is to compute the EOQ for each price level, starting at the price level that has the lowest cost per unit, until an EOQ fits in the relevant range of its price level. In other words, let q_0 be the largest EOQ for which $q_i \leq q_0 < q_{i+1}$, where q_i = minimum order quantity for price level i. The next step is to compare the total cost of q_0 with the total cost of all minimum quantities for orders larger than q_0. In other words, compare $C(q_0)$ to $C(q_j)$ for $j > i$, where q_j = the minimum order quantity for price level j and i = the price level for q_0.

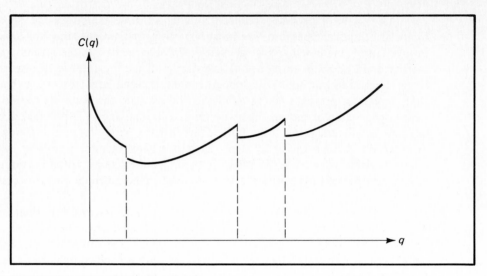

FIGURE 10-9   **Discontinuous Cost Function**

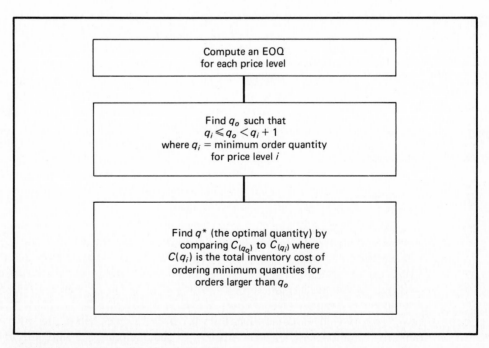

FIGURE 10-10   **Discrete Price-Break Algorithm**

Table 10-5   Victor Pumps Inc., Price Schedule

QUANTITY ORDERED	UNIT PRICE
1 – 1,999	$15.00
2,000 – 4,999	13.50
5,000 – 7,999	12.50
8,000 – 19,999	12.00
20,000 and over	11.50

Example: A manufacturing company has planned its production schedule for the coming year based on forecast demand, back orders, and plant capacity. Instead of making a particular hydraulic pump that goes into the final product, the company has decided to buy the pump. There are two such pumps in the end product, and the production schedule calls for producing 10,000 units of the end product. Therefore, 20,000 pumps will be needed next year. Ordering costs are estimated at $50 per order, and the carrying cost fraction for the firm is .20. A request for bids has yielded only one supplier, Victor Pumps Inc., who is approved by the Engineering Department; hence, the Purchasing Department has only one basic decision. That decision concerns the quantity to be ordered. Victor Pumps Inc., has submitted the price schedule shown in Table 10-5 together with its technical proposal.

The first step is to compute the EOQ for each price break.

$$EOQ_5 = \sqrt{\frac{2(20,000)50}{.2(11.50)}} \qquad b_5 = 11.50$$

$$\cong 933$$

$$EOQ_4 = \sqrt{\frac{2(20,000)50}{.2(12)}} \qquad b_4 = 12.00$$

$$\cong 913$$

$$EOQ_3 = \sqrt{\frac{2(20,000)50}{.2(12.50)}} \qquad b_3 = 12.50$$

$$\cong 894$$

$$EOQ_2 = \sqrt{\frac{2(20,000)50}{.2(13.50)}} \qquad b_2 = 13.50$$

$$\cong 861$$

$$EOQ_1 = \sqrt{\frac{2(20,000)50}{.2(15)}} \qquad b_1 = 15.00$$

$$\cong 816$$

The largest EOQ that falls in the relevant range of order quantities is $q_0 = 816$, falling between 1 and 1,999. What remains to be done is to compare the total cost of $q_0 = 816$ to order quantities equal to the minimum levels of the different price breaks. This is done by substituting the various order quantities into equation 10.9.

$$C(816) = \frac{.2(816)15}{2} + 50\left(\frac{20{,}000}{816}\right) + 20{,}000(15)$$

$$= \$302{,}449.45$$

$$C(2{,}000) = \frac{.2(2{,}000)13.50}{2} + 50\left(\frac{20{,}000}{2{,}000}\right) + 20{,}000(13.50)$$

$$= \$273{,}200$$

$$C(5{,}000) = \frac{.2(5{,}000)12.50}{2} + 50\left(\frac{20{,}000}{5{,}000}\right) + 20{,}000(12.50)$$

$$= \$256{,}450$$

$$C(8{,}000) = \frac{.2(8{,}000)12}{2} + 50\left(\frac{20{,}000}{8{,}000}\right) + 20{,}000(12)$$

$$= \$249{,}725$$

$$C(20{,}000) = \frac{.2(20{,}000)11.50}{2} + 50\left(\frac{20{,}000}{20{,}000}\right) + 20{,}000(11.50)$$

$$= \$253{,}050$$

According to the foregoing analysis, the manufacturing company should order 8,000 pumps in order to minimize total inventory cost for the pump. In addition to the assumptions described for this simple price-break model, it must be noted that buying in quantities of 8,000 is going to require significantly more capital investment in inventory and, consequently, may not be the wisest choice if money is tight for the firm.

A Stochastic Demand Model

Until now, we have assumed that all demand parameters of an inventory system are known with certainty. In addition, we have assumed that lead time is zero. If we loosen only this latter assumption, very little has to change except that we must order prior to running out of inventory to prevent stockouts. Figure 10-11 illustrates the basic EOQ system with nonzero lead time. In this situation, assume that demand is ten units per day and lead time is known to be five days; then the reorder point, s, is equal to 50 units. Therefore, whenever inventory reaches 50 units, an order for q units should be processed.

If we loosen the assumption of known or certain demand, then the problem of when to order becomes more complicated. As you can see in Figure 10-12, there is now the danger of stockouts.

If an inventory system has all the properties of the basic EOQ system except that lead time is not zero and demand is not deterministic and constant, we can proceed in the following manner. The problem is still how much and when to order.

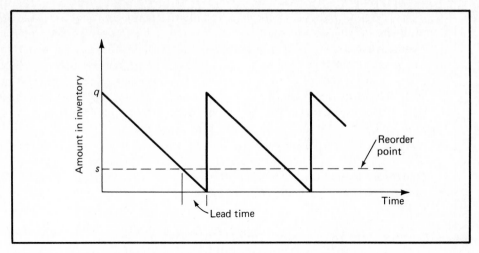

FIGURE 10-11   Basic EOQ with Nonzero Lead Time, Deterministic Demand

If we assume that a reasonable estimate of the optimal order quantity can be calculated using the basic EOQ formula, then the problem reduces to merely determining the reorder point. In many real situations, using the EOQ formula when demand is not known with certainty has little effect on total inventory costs because of the relative insensitivity of total costs to moderate changes in the order quantity.

Since the order quantity is given, ordering costs should not be affected by changes in the reorder point. The inventory costs affected by changes in the reorder point are the carrying costs and the stockout costs. The problem, however, is that when stockout costs are lowered by increasing the safety stock, carrying costs are increased because the average value of inventory is increased.

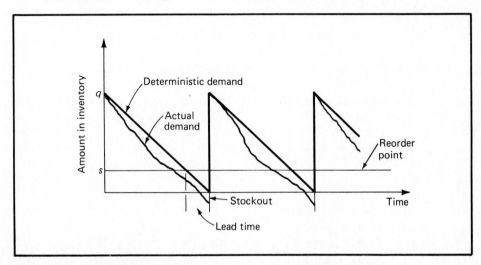

FIGURE 10-12   Stochastic Demand

To illustrate how to determine the reorder point, let us consider the following problem. A camera store wants to determine the proper reorder point for its Instamatic 2 camera. Annual demand is for 1,000 Instamatic 2 cameras, sold at a rate of approximately four per day. It takes five days between the day the order is placed and the receipt of the shipment from the manufacturer. The question is: At what point does the camera store order Instamatic 2 cameras? In order to answer the question, it is necessary to have some idea of the probability distribution of the number of cameras demanded in any five-day period. This information is summarized in Table 10-6. In order to determine a good reorder point, it is possible to look at six reorder points and calculate the expected cost of each, then simply choose the reorder level with the smallest total cost. Let us assume stockout cost is $10 per camera, and carrying cost is $5 per camera per year, and ordering cost is $25 per order.

$$q = \sqrt{[2(1,000)(25)/5]}$$
$$= \sqrt{10,000}$$
$$= 100$$

If the camera store reorders when inventory hits ten cameras, there is a high probability (90 percent) of having a shortage before the shipment is received. The shortage cost associated with this policy can be calculated in the following way:

10.10
$$C_2 = \left[\sum_{i=1}^{n} x_i P(x_i) c_2 \right] (r/q)$$

where
C_2 = shortage cost for year

x_i = number short during lead time

$P(x_i)$ = probability of being short x_i units

c_2 = per-unit shortage costs

r = total annual demand

q = order quantity

n = number of 5-day demand levels

Table 10-6   Frequency Distribution of 5-Day Demand for Instamatic 2 Cameras

DEMAND FOR 5-DAY PERIODS	FREQUENCY OF SPECIFIED DEMAND	RELATIVE FREQUENCY	CUMULATIVE RELATIVE FREQUENCY
10	5	.10	.10
15	15	.30	.40
20	20	.40	.80
25	5	.10	.90
30	4	.08	.98
35	1	.02	1.00
	50	1.00	

Given that the reorder point is 10:

$$C_2 = [0(.1)10 + 5(.3)10 + 10(.4)10 + 15(.10)10 + 20(.08)10 + 25(.02)10]$$
$$\times (1,000/100)$$
$$= \$910$$

Stockout costs for other reorder points are shown in Table 10-7:

Table 10-7 Stockout Costs

REORDER POINT	STOCKOUT COSTS ($)
10	910
15	460
20	160
25	60
30	10
35	0

The incremental carrying costs for the various reorder points under consideration are represented by:

10.11
$$\Delta C_1 = \sum_{i=1}^{n} y_i P(y_i) c_1$$

where y_i = number of units in inventory at the time of replenishment

ΔC_1 = incremental carrying cost

$P(y_i)$ = probability of y_i units in inventory at the time of replenishment

c_1 = per-unit carrying cost

n = number of 5-day demand levels

Given a reorder point of 10:

$$\Delta C_1 = 0(.1)5 + 0(.3)5 + 0(.4)5 + 0(.1)5 + 0(.08)5 + 0(.02)5 = 0$$

For a reorder point of 25:

$$\Delta C_1 = 15(.1)5 + 10(.3)5 + 5(.4)5 + 0(.1)5 + 0(.08)5 + 0(.02)5 = \$32.50$$

Table 10-8 shows total incremental costs per year based on reorder point. Since
the total incremental cost of the various reorder-point policies is minimized when the
reorder point is 30, the optimal inventory policy for the camera store is to order 100
cameras ten times a year, whenever the inventory level reaches 30 cameras.

Table 10-8   Cost of Reorder-Point Policies

REORDER POINT	EXPECTED STOCKOUT COSTS ($) C_2	EXPECTED INCREMENTAL CARRYING COSTS ($) ΔC_1	TOTAL INCREMENTAL COSTS ($) $C_2 + \Delta C_1$
10	910.00	0	910.00
15	460.00	2.50	462.50
20	160.00	12.50	162.50
25	60.00	32.50	92.50
30	10.00	55.00	65.00
35	0	79.50	79.50

The reorder-point analysis described above is appropriate when historical demand data exists for a particular inventory item. However, when historical data do not exist and the probability distribution of lead-time demand cannot be estimated, the inventory manager should consider the following factors when he or she subjectively sets reorder points:

- Expected demand per day for material during lead time
- Variability or uncertainty of the demand per day
- Expected lead time for the materials
- Variability of lead time
- Relative undesirability of stockouts

SIMULATION APPROACH

Although there are many more inventory models than the few we have discussed in this chapter, it is very common for a real inventory problem not to have an analytical counterpart. In other words, a model may not exist or be derivable mathematically that adequately describes a real inventory problem. This is especially true when several properties are stochastic in nature. For example, many systems with stochastic demand, stochastic lead time, and nonconstant cost parameters, have no mathematical model that can be solved analytically. As in the case of complex queuing systems, simulation can usually be applied when inventory systems become too complex to be optimized analytically. The trouble with simulation as a means for solving inventory replenishment problems is that it is a descriptive technique, not an optimization technique. Simulation can answer questions regarding the desirability of various inventory policies; but it cannot, by itself, assign values to the various decision variables.

You can gain specific insight into how simulation is used to answer inventory questions by working through a simple inventory simulation. An industrial equip-

Table 10-9   Historical Frequency of Demand

DEMAND PER DAY	NUMBER OF OBSERVATIONS	RELATIVE FREQUENCY
0	19	.095
1	27	.135
2	42	.210
3	49	.245
4	34	.170
5	17	.085
6	9	.045
7	2	.010
8	1	.005
	200	1.000

ment company carries a particularly popular skill saw that sells for $120 and wishes to know how much and when to order. Because demand is not known with certainty (see Table 10-9) and lead time is not known with certainty (see Table 10-10), simulation appears to be a proper approach to the problem. The cost of the saws, which depends on the quantity ordered, is shown in Table 10-11. Ordering cost is estimated at $25 per order, and the carrying cost fraction is .2. Stockout cost is assumed to be $25 per unit.

In order to utilize simulation to solve this inventory problem, we must develop functions that can be used to generate the two stochastic variables in the

Table 10-10   Historical Frequency of Lead Time

LEAD TIME IN DAYS	NUMBER OF OBSERVATIONS	RELATIVE FREQUENCY
4	11	.22
5	7	.14
6	3	.06
7	21	.42
8	5	.10
9	2	.04
10	1	.02
	50	1.00

Table 10-11   Price Schedule

ORDER	PRICE PER SAW
Less than 25	$100
25 or more	95
50 or more	90
100 or more	80

Table 10-12   Demand-Generating Function

RANDOM NUMBER RANGE	DEMAND PER DAY
0 – .095	0
.095 – .230	1
.230 – .440	2
.440 – .685	3
.685 – .855	4
.855 – .940	5
.940 – .985	6
.985 – .995	7
.995 – 1.00	8

problem—namely, demand and lead time. Let's assume that no known probability distribution can be fitted to the two sets of historical data and that we are forced to use these empirical distributions. Hence, the generating functions we need can be found merely by using the cumulative frequency distribution of the two stochastic variables. (See Tables 10-12 and 10-13 for these distributions.) You can refer back to Chapter 3, if necessary, for an explanation of how these types of generating functions are derived.

Once we have the generating functions, the next step is to experiment with a particular inventory policy. For example, let's compare two inventory policies:

- Order 25 saws when inventory reaches 10 saws.
- Order 25 saws when inventory reaches 15 saws.

For illustrative purposes, we shall simulate one month manually. Then, using a computer, we'll simulate a number of different policies to determine a good inventory policy. Tables 10-14 and 10-15 reflect the results of the manual simulation for both inventory policies we established. Look at the carrying cost and the stockout costs for the two policies simulated in Tables 10-14 and 10-15. (Ordering costs and the cost of goods are constant for the two policies.) You can see that, by

Table 10-13   Lead-Time-Generating Function

RANDOM NUMBER RANGE	LEAD TIME IN DAYS
0 – .22	4
.22 – .36	5
.36 – .42	6
.42 – .84	7
.84 – .94	8
.94 – .98	9
.98 – 1.0	10

Table 10-14 Simulation: Reorder Point = 10, Order Quantity = 25

DAY	RANDOM NUMBER	DEMAND	AMOUNT ORDERED	RANDOM NUMBER	LEAD TIME (DAYS)	AMOUNT RECEIVED	ENDING INVENTORY	CARRYING COST ($)	STOCK-OUT COST ($)	COST OF GOODS ($)	ORDER COST ($)	TOTAL COST ($)
1	.134	1					14	1.06	0	0	0	1.06
2	.909	5	25	.344	5		9	.69	0	2,375	25	2,400.69
3	.204	1					8	.61	0	0	0	.61
4	.906	5					3	.23	0	0	0	.23
5	.387	2					1	.08	0	0	0	.08
6	.045	0					1	.08	0	0	0	.08
7	.894	5					0	0	100	0	0	100.00
8	.172	1				25	24	1.82	0	0	0	1.82
9	.380	2					22	1.67	0	0	0	1.67
10	.390	2					20	1.52	0	0	0	1.52
11	.513	3					17	1.29	0	0	0	1.29
12	.563	3					14	1.06	0	0	0	1.06
13	.670	3					11	.84	0	0	0	.84
14	.428	2	25	.633	7		9	.68	0	0	0	.68
15	.589	3					6	.46	0	0	0	.46
16	.040	0					6	.46	0	0	0	.46
17	.738	4					2	.15	0	0	0	.15
18	.460	3					0	0	25	0	0	25.00
19	.007	0					0	0	0	0	0	0.00
20	.775	4					0	0	100	0	0	100.00
21	.421	2				25	23	1.78	0	2,375	25	2,401.78
22	.072	0					23	1.78	0	0	0	1.78
							Totals	$16.26	$225	$4,750	$50	$5,041.26

Table 10-15 Simulation: Reorder Point = 15, Order Quantity = 25

DAY	RANDOM NUMBER DEMAND	DEMAND	AMOUNT ORDERED	RANDOM NUMBER	LEAD TIME (DAYS)	AMOUNT RECEIVED	ENDING INVENTORY	CARRYING COST ($)	STOCK-OUT COST ($)	COST OF GOODS ($)	ORDER COST ($)	TOTAL COST ($)
1	.134	1	25	.344	5		14	1.06	0	2,375	25	2,401.06
2	.909	5					9	.69	0	0	0	.69
3	.204	1					8	.61	0	0	0	.61
4	.906	5					3	.23	0	0	0	.23
5	.387	2					1	.08	0	0	0	.08
6	.045	0					1	.08	0	0	0	.08
7	.894	5				25	20	1.52	0	0	0	1.52
8	.172	1					19	1.44	0	0	0	1.44
9	.380	2					17	1.29	0	0	0	1.29
10	.390	2	25	.633	7		15	1.14	0	2,375	25	2,401.14
11	.513	3					12	.91	0	0	0	.91
12	.563	3					9	.68	0	0	0	.68
13	.670	3					6	.46	0	0	0	.46
14	.428	2					4	.30	0	0	0	.30
15	.589	3					1	.08	0	0	0	.08
16	.040	0					1	.08	0	0	0	.08
17	.738	4					0	0	75	0	0	75.00
18	.460	3				25	22	1.67	0	0	0	1.67
19	.007	0					22	1.67	0	0	0	1.67
20	.775	4					18	1.37	0	0	0	1.37
21	.421	2					16	1.22	0	0	0	1.22
22	.072	0					16	1.22	0	0	0	1.22
							Totals	$17.80	$75	$4,750	$50	$4,892.80

increasing the reorder level five units, the stockout cost is decreased by $150 with only a $1.50 increase in the month's carrying cost.

Obviously, other inventory policies need to be examined, and the number of days simulated must be significantly increased before we can have much faith in the results of the simulation experiments. To give you some idea of what it costs to "solve" the saw inventory problem using computer simulation, we wrote and ran a simulation program to determine the effects of various inventory policies. The program, Figure 10-13, was written in GPSS, a special-purpose simulation language. It took approximately two hours to write and debug. One experiment simulated four years and took .1214 minutes to run on a Xerox Sigma 6 computer. In all, 15 experiments were run, at a total computer cost of less than $10. As you can see in Table 10-16, the best inventory policy of those simulated is to order 100 saws whenever inventory level reaches 25 saws.

Table 10-16   Simulation Results, Average Annual Inventory Costs

ORDER QUANTITY	REORDER LEVEL				
	10	15	20	25	30
25	$70,814	$69,184	$67,966	$67,403	$67,264
50	$65,897	$64,832	$64,068	$64,092	$63,734
100	$58,140	$57,349	$57,132	$56,944	$56,957

SUMMARY

In order to implement truly effective inventory management, an organization must have an integrated management information system for the purpose of inventory control. In most organizations, inventory control is nothing more than an inventory accounting system. In other words, whether the system is computer-based or not, it merely keeps track of inventory items and alerts management when inventory levels get low. Typically, the system has little capacity for making decisions about when and how much to order. Some progressive organizations, however, are developing or using systems that actually integrate inventory models like the ones described in this chapter into their management information systems. These more progressive systems may be real-time or batch-oriented systems. What distinguishes the progressive information system from the more common inventory accounting system is its decision-making capabilities of MIS.

Management's primary challenge in relation to inventory problems is to use the systems approach for the successful application of existing theory and technology. More theory is potentially useful, but unless organizations can be persuaded to

```
            REALLOCATE DLO,50,XAC,50,FAC,1,STO,1,QUE,1
            REALLOCATE LOG,5,TAB,1,FUM,3,VAR,30,BVR,1,FSV,15
            REALLOCATE HOV,10,BUR,1,FMS,1,HMS,1,CHA,5,COM,5000
            SIMULATE
* X1 = CARRYING COST
* X2 = STOCKOUT COST
* X3 = COST OF GOODS
* X4 = ORDER COST
* X5 = TOTAL COST
* X6 = ENDING INVENTORY
* X7 = REORDER POINT
* X8 = ORDER QUANTITY
* X9 = COST PER UNIT
            INITIAL    X6,30
            INITIAL    X9,8000
            INITIAL    X7,10
            INITIAL    X8,100
  1         VARIABLE   X9*X6*2/2500  CARRYING COST
  2         VARIABLE   X6*(-2500)  STOCKOUT COST
  3         VARIABLE   X9*X8  COST OF GOODS
  4         VARIABLE   X1+X2+X3+X4  TOTAL COST
  1         FUNCTION   RN2,D9 DEMAND FUNCTION
.095,0/.23,1/.44,2/.685,3/.855,4/.94,5/.985,6/.995,7/1,8
  2         FUNCTION   RN3,D7  LEAD TIME FUNCTION
.22,4/.36,5/.42,6/.84,7/.94,8/.98,9/1,10
            GENERATE   1,0,,1000  GENERATE 1 DAY
            SAVEVALUE  6-,FN1  ADJUST ENDING INVENTORY
            TEST GE    X6,0,NEG  CHECK FOR STOCKOUT
            TEST GE    X6,X7,ORDER  CHECK FOR REORDER LEVEL
            SAVEVALUE  1+V1  ACCUMULATE CARRYING COST
            TERMINATE  1
  MEG       SAVEVALUE  2+,V2  ACCUMULATE STOCKOUT COST
            SAVEVALUE  6,0  ZERO ENDING INVENTORY
  TEM       TERMINATE  1  END THE DAY
  ORDER GATE LR   1,TEM  HAS ORDER BEEN MADE??
            LOGIC S    1  SET THE ORDER SWITCH
            SAVEVALUE  4+,2500  ACCUMULATE ORDERING COST
            SAVEVALUE  3+,V3  ACCUMULATE COST OF GOODS
            SAVEVALUE  1+,V1  ACCUMULATE CARRYING COST
            PRIORITY   10  SET PRIORITY OF AN INCOMING ORDER
            ADVANCE    FN2  LEAD TIME
            SAVEVALUE  6+,X8  INCREMENT ENDING INVENTORY
            LOGIC R    1  RESET ORDER SWITCH
            TERMINATE  1
            GENERATE   1001  GENERATE TIMER TRANSACTION
            SAVEVALUE  5,V4  ACCUMULATE TOTAL COST
            TERMINATE  1
            START      1001
```

FIGURE 10-13   GPSS Program

apply the inventory theory thus far developed, the marginal utility of new theory is questionable.

To apply existing inventory theory successfully, you must beware of two pitfalls. First, you must avoid the misapplication of various inventory models by carefully examining the properties of an existing inventory system and making sure system properties adequately match model assumptions. Too many firms are using the basic EOQ model when it is inappropriate. Second, to implement a decision-making management information system, many human factors must be dealt with carefully. People naturally resist change, especially when it threatens their security or self-image. Many times, it is more effective, for example, to have the inventory system suggest an order quantity than to automatically print the purchase or production order. A major reason why models such as those presented in this chapter have not been accepted by many organizations is a failure to take into consideration the human factors connected with organizational change. Unless the people in an organization are in favor of a change, that change, regardless of its merits, will not succeed.

SOLVED PROBLEMS

Problem Statement

A local TV distributor has found from experience that demand for a certain TV model is fairly constant at a rate of 50 sets per month. Lead time is effectively zero and no shortages are to be allowed. If the sets cost \$300, the carrying-cost fraction is 20 percent per year, and ordering cost is estimated to be \$50, how many sets should be ordered, and how many orders must be processed per year?

Solution

Using the basic EOQ model, the optimal order quantity is:

$$q^* = \sqrt{\frac{2C_3 r}{C_1}}$$

where
$$C_3 = \$50 \text{ per order}$$
$$r = (12)(50) = 600 \text{ sets per year}$$
$$C_1 = (.2)(300) = \$60 \text{ per set per year}$$
$$q^* = \sqrt{\frac{(2)(50)(600)}{60}}$$
$$= 31.62 \text{ sets per order}$$

Owing to the relative insensitivity of q^*, we can round q^* up or down with little effect. Let $q^* = 32$ sets per order. This means that the number of orders processed per year is:

$$N = 600/32 = 18.75 \text{ orders}$$

Problem Statement

A basket factory has decided to try and apply an inventory model to its most popular item. Demand is fairly deterministic at a rate of 5,000 baskets per month. Lead time is zero and no shortages are allowed by management. The factory can produce the baskets at a rate of 15,000 per month. Carrying costs are $.20 per basket per year, and setup costs are $100. What is the optimal lot size?

Solution

Using the finite replenishment-rate model:

$$q^* = \frac{\sqrt{2rC_3/C_1}}{\sqrt{1 - r/p}}$$

where r = annual demand = (5,000 baskets per mo.)(12) = 60,000 baskets
   C_3 = setup cost = $100
   C_1 = per-basket carrying cost per year = $.20
   p = replenishment rate = 15,000 baskets/mo.

$$q^* = \frac{\sqrt{(2)(60,000)(100)/.2}}{\sqrt{1 - (5,000/15,000)}}$$

$$\cong 948.7 \text{ baskets}$$

The minimum cost of implementing an order quantity of 949 is:

$$C^* = \sqrt{2rC_1C_3}\sqrt{1 - r/p}$$

$$= \$1264.94$$

Problem Statement

A glass company has patented an extra-strength glass and currently sells it in 25-square-foot sheets. Because the product is patented, being out of stock does not result in a lost sale. A stockout, however, is bad for customer goodwill, and management has assigned a stockout cost of $50 per sheet per month. The sheets cost $1,000 to make, but because of the unusual process, orders can be filled in less than one day. Demand for the glass has averaged 150 sheets per month. Annual holding costs for the company are assumed to be 15 percent of the value of inventory. Lot sizes are 150 sheets (owing to production scheduling, the hi-test glass can be produced only once monthly). The pertinent question is: What is the optimal order level?

$$S^* = \frac{q_p C_2}{C_1 + C2}$$

where

$$q_p = 150 \text{ sheets}$$

$$C_2 = (50)(12) = \$600$$

$$C_1 = (1,000)(.15) = \$150$$

$$S^* = \frac{(150)(600)}{150 + 600}$$

$$= 120$$

In other words, backorders would reach 30 sheets of glass before inventory was replenished.

The cost of the above inventory policy is:

$$C^* = \frac{C_1 S^2}{2q_p} + \frac{C_2(q_p - S)^2}{2q_p}$$

$$= \frac{(150)(120)^2}{2(150)} + \frac{600(150 - 120)^2}{2(150)}$$

$$= \$9,000$$

_____ **REVIEW QUESTIONS** _____

1. List four reasons for carrying inventory.
2. Why is it critical to manage an organization's inventory effectively?
3. What are the two major functions that must be performed in order to effectively control an organization's inventory?
4. In your own words, explain the rationale behind ABC analysis.
5. Classify inventory accounting systems into two categories.
6. Distinguish between real-time inventory control systems and batch-processing systems.
7. Why is it likely that the number of real-time inventory systems will increase in the future?
8. What is the object of inventory models?
9. What are the two major decision variables in inventory models?
10. Describe the three components of inventory cost.
11. Briefly explain the five basic steps in analyzing an inventory system.
12. Why is the determination of system properties so important?

13. What is meant by demand patterns?
14. Define *lead time*.
15. Distinguish between stochastic demand and deterministic demand.
16. Define *replenishment period*.
17. Distinguish between order level and reorder level.
18. Why is it sometimes necessary to simulate an inventory system?
19. Why is sensitivity analysis an important step in analyzing inventory systems?
20. List the assumptions of the basic EOQ model.
21. Distinguish between finite and infinite replenishment rate.
22. What is the major difference between the basic EOQ model and the basic order-level model?
23. Why is simulation often used for inventory problems?
24. Explain the two-bin system.
25. List the factors that should be considered when determining reorder points.
26. What are two major disadvantages of using a simulation approach to inventory problems?
27. What distinguishes a management information system from an inventory accounting system?
28. Why haven't inventory models been more widely applied?

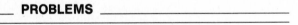

PROBLEMS

1. Given the following information, perform an ABC analysis on the data. Discuss your results.

ITEM NO.	ANNUAL DEMAND	COST PER UNIT IN DOLLARS
157	100	25
222	50	30
315	1,000	50
719	250	15
244	300	20
367	400	25
219	2,000	20
234	345	20
577	500	25
619	750	10
621	1,000	35
322	900	5
357	432	10
192	150	15
334	225	30

2. You are asked by the manager of a blood bank to study its inventory problem and make recommendations for optimizing costs. The manager has been taking some night courses; he has been taught the following formula and wonders if it might be applied to the problem:

$$q^* = \sqrt{2C_3 r / C_1}$$

Specifically, do the following:
a. Indicate to the manager what an inventory model is meant to do.
b. Discuss properties of this inventory problem.
c. Recommend use of the aforementioned formula or state specific reasons why it shouldn't be used.

3. A drill-rig company has a contract with Saudi Arabia to produce 60 drill rigs during the next year. The plan is to produce these rigs at a rate of five per month. A valve used in the drill rig is purchased off the shelf from a nearby supplier; no lead time is required. Each drill rig requires four valves. The valves cost $100 each. Holding cost for the valves is $10 per year per valve. In addition, it costs $75 to order these valves and receive them from the vendor.
a. What is the optimal order quantity?
b. What is the optimal number of orders per year?
c. How frequent should the orders be?
d. What is the total inventory cost of ordering the optimal order quantity?
e. Perform a limited amount of sensitivity analysis on the order quantity.

4. An automobile manufacturer plans to produce 30,000 cars in the next month. All cars planned for production use the same headlamps; therefore, demand for the headlights for the next month is known to be 60,000. The purchasing agent wants to know how many headlamps to buy at one time. Historically, headlamps have been received on the same day they were ordered. It costs $35 to order headlamps, and the carrying-cost fraction used by the auto company is 15% per year. The lamps cost $.87 each.
a. What is the optimal order quantity?
b. What is the optimal number of orders per year?
c. What is the frequency of orders? Assume 22 working days.
d. What is the total inventory cost of ordering the optimal order quantity?
e. Show the inventory cost of q's of 10,000, 20,000, 25,000, 30,000, and 40,000 units.

5. a. Referring to problem 3, what should the drill-rig company do if lead time is one month rather than zero? In other words, what should the inventory policy be?
b. Does the existence of lead time change the total inventory cost of the valves? If so, what is the total cost of the new inventory policy?

6. Management has decided to make the valves in problem 3 rather than buy them from an outside vendor. The demand is for 240 valves for the next year, or 20 valves per month. To make the valves costs the company $90 each, and setup time amounts to $100 per setup. Holding cost remains at $10 per valve. Since these valves are not being bought off the shelf, replenishment of inventory is not simultaneous. In fact, the production department says it can produce 200 valves per month given present human and capital resources.
   a. What is the optimal order quantity?
   b. What is the optimal number of setups per year?
   c. What is the optimal time between orders? Assume 250 working days.
   d. What is the total inventory cost of the optimal order policy?

7. The automobile manufacturer in problem 4 has decided to make the head-lamps. It has been determined that 150,000 headlamps per month can be produced; but owing to various resource constraints, management has decided to buy half the necessary quantity of headlamps and make the other half. It costs the company $.75 to make each headlamp, and setup costs are $50 per setup. Refer to problem 4 for the parameters of the purchasing decision.
   a. What is the optimal order quantity to be purchased from the outside supplier?
   b. What is the EOQ for in-house production?
   c. What is the total inventory cost for the headlamps?
   d. What is the optimal number of purchase orders per month?
   e. What is the optimal number of production runs per month?

8. A mail-order stereo firm reviews its stock of amplifiers each month and orders for the next month. Its most popular amp last year was the SEA-700. Last year, 600 amps were sold; these sales were spread evenly throughout the year. Predictions are that this year's sales will be approximately the same. Lead time from the manufacturer is effectively zero, and no sales are lost owing to shortages; instead, the amps are merely delivered one month later. A recent market survey revealed that 60 percent of the customers surveyed would not buy amps again from this firm if they were made to wait an extra month. Profit on an SEA-700 amp is $50. Management, therefore, has estimated stockout cost to be .6 (profit on two future sales), or $60, or $720 per amp per year. Holding cost per amp is $75 per year.
   a. What is the optimal order level?
   b. What is the minimum inventory cost for the SEA-700 amp?
   c. What is the order-level sensitivity?

9. A deluxe bicycle store sells a particular model men's bike for $200. The bike costs the store $150, including selling cost. The wholesale cost of the bike is $125. Demand for the bike is stochastic; past demand is reflected in the

following table:

MONTHLY DEMAND	FREQUENCY
0	1
1	3
2	6
3	7
4	8
5	11
6	7
7	5
8	2
	$\overline{50}$

Total demand for one year is forecast to be 52 units. Stockout cost is assumed to be the profit lost, or $50. Lead time is one month. Ordering costs are $50 per order. Carrying cost is 20% per year of the inventory value.

a. What is the best inventory policy for the bicycle in this problem?

b. What are the expected stockout and incremental carrying costs of the selected inventory policy?

10. Given the policy you recommended in problem 9, simulate manually one year's activity. Interpret your simulation results. Assume a beginning inventory of ten units.

11. A small charter airline company wants to know how much aviation fuel to buy. Demand for flight fuel has been somewhat constant at 50,000 gallons per month. Fuel costs are $.75 per gallon, and the company's annual carrying-cost fraction is .10. If it costs $100 to get a delivery with no lead time required:

a. What is the optimal order quantity?

b. What assumption did you make in answering *a* above?

c. If storage capacity for the fuel were limited to 10,000 gallons, how would you analyze the problem?

12. Demand for pacemakers has been running at a rate of ten per month. The cost of a pacemaker to the hospital is $1,000. It costs $50 to place an order, and the hospital's annual carrying cost is 12% of inventory value.

a. What information would you need to determine the optimal order quantity?

b. Assuming the basic EOQ model, what are q^* and the minimum inventory cost?

c. If lead time were seven days, what is the proper reorder point, assuming a constant rate of demand?

13. If lead time for the pacemakers in problem 12 is one day and daily demand is distributed according to the following table, what is the reorder point if stockouts are not allowed?

DAILY DEMAND	PROBABILITY
0	.30
1	.40
2	.15
3	.10
4	.05
	1.00

14. A sawmill has been operating at peak capacity for several years. To keep the mill running takes 2,000 trees per day. The supplier of raw material (trees) can deliver only 10,000 trees per day. Trees cost an average of $100. Ordering costs are extremely high at $5,000 per order. The annual carrying cost fraction is 12%. Assume a 365-day operation of the mill.
a. What is the optimal order quantity?
b. What is the total inventory cost?
c. What assumption about system properties did you make in calculating the optimal order quantity?

15. An aerospace company has a contract with the U.S. Navy to produce 120 airplanes during the next year. The plan is to produce these airplanes at a rate of 10 per month. An actuating cylinder used to move the wing flap is purchased off the shelf from a nearby supplier; no lead time is required. Since there are 2 wings, 2 cylinders are needed per airplane. The actuating cylinders cost $200. Holding cost for the cylinders is $20 per year per cylinder. In addition, it costs $75 to order these cylinders and receive them from the vendor.
a. What is the optimal quantity?
b. What is the optimal number of orders per year?
c. What is the optimal time between orders?
d. What is the total inventory cost of ordering the optimal order quantity?
e. Perform a limited amount of sensitivity analysis on the order quantity.

16. Referring to Problem 15,
a. What should the aerospace company do if lead time is 1 month rather than zero? In other words, what should the inventory policy be?
b. Does the existence of lead time change the total inventory cost of the actuating cylinders? If so, what is the total cost of the new inventory policy?

17. A mail-order auto supply firm reviews its stock of tires each month and orders for the next month. Its most popular tire last year was the XR-100 radial. Last year, 1,600 sets were sold; these sales were spread evenly throughout the year. Predictions are that this year's sales will be approximately the same. Lead time from the manufacturer is effectively zero, and no sales are lost due to shortages. Instead, the tires are merely delivered 1 month later. A recent market survey revealed that 50 percent of the customers surveyed would not buy tires again from this firm if they were made to wait an extra month. Profit on a set of tires is $70. Management, therefore, has estimated stockout cost to be .5 (profit on two future sales), or $70, or $840 per set per year. Holding cost per set of tires is $75 per year.

a. What is the optimal order level?
b. What is the minimum inventory cost for the XR-100 radial tire?
c. What is the order level sensitivity?

18. An automobile dealer has the exclusive rights to market a foreign car. For this reason, no sales are lost if he is out of stock when a customer wants to buy. Demand for the car has been running at 20 units per month. The dealer orders one time per month and receives the order within a day or two. The dealer's subjective estimate of the cost of the loss of customer good will is $100 per month. The dealer cost on the cars is $4,000 and his carrying cost fraction is approximately 15% per year.

a. What is the optimal order level?
b. What is the minimum inventory cost for the foreign car?
c. What is the sensitivity of the order level?

19. A large hospital's nursery uses disposable diapers for its newborn babies at a rate of 60 cases per day. Ordering costs have been estimated at $50 per order. The hospital's Accounting Department has assigned an annual carrying-cost fraction of .15 to the nursery supplies. All the assumptions of the basic EOQ model, such as zero lead time, are applicable. The purchasing agent for the hospital has an opportunity to take advantage of one of several quantity discounts. The pricing schedule is listed in the table.

QUANTITY ORDERED (CASES)	UNIT PRICE
0 – 1,999	$2.50
2,000 – 4,999	2.45
5,000 – 9,999	2.40
10,000 and over	2.35

a. What is the optimal order quantity?
b. What is the minimum inventory cost?

20. A large restaurant sells 600 16-ounce strip steaks each week. It costs the restaurant $25 to order steaks from a local meat packer, and since the meat packer is close there is effectively no lead time involved. The restaurant's accountant has estimated the annual carrying cost fraction to be .2. The local meat packer has submitted the price schedule listed in the table. Assume that the restaurant has ample freezing capacity.

a. What is the optimal order quantity?

b. What is the minimum total cost?

c. How much initial investment capital would it require to implement the optimal inventory policy?

d. What policy would you recommend to the restaurant manager?

QUANTITY ORDERED	PRICE PER POUND
Less than 500	$2.00
500 – 999	1.90
1,000 – 1,999	1.85
2,000 – 3,999	1.80
4,000 – 6,999	1.75
7,000 – 9,999	1.73
10,000 and over	1.70

21. A large retail chain store sells a vacuum cleaner for $150. The cost of the vacuum cleaner, including selling cost, is $120. Cost of goods is $100. Demand for this vacuum cleaner model is stochastic; past demand is reflected in the following table. Total demand for 1 year is forecast to be 260 units. Stockout cost is assumed to be the profit lost, or $30. Lead time is 7 days. Ordering costs are $40 per order. Carrying cost is 23% of the inventory value.

WEEKLY DEMAND	FREQUENCY
0	2
1	7
2	10
3	7
4	12
5	20
6	14
7	10
8	9
9	7
10	2
	100

REFERENCES

BERRY, W.L., "Lot Sizing Procedures for Requirements Planning Systems: A Framework for Analysis," *Production and Inventory Management*, 2nd Quarter 1972, pp. 19–34.

BIERMAN, HAROLD, JR., CHARLES P. BONINI, and WARREN H. HAUSMAN, *Quantitative Analysis for Business Decisions*, 4th ed. Homewood, Ill.: Richard D. Irwin, 1973.

BISHOP, JACK L., JR., "Experience with a Successful System for Forecasting and Inventory Control," *Operations Research*, 22, no. 6, 1224–31.

BUFFA, ELWOOD S., *Operations Management: The Management of Productive Systems*. New York: Wiley Hamilton, 1976.

_____, and JEFFERY G. MILLER, *Production Inventory Systems: Planning and Control*. Homewood, Ill.: Richard D. Irwin, 1979.

CHASE, RICHARD B., and NICHOLAS J. AQUILANO, *Production and Operations Management: A Life Cycle Approach*. Homewood, Ill.: Richard D. Irwin, 1981.

HADLEY, GEORGE, and T.M. WHITIN, *Analysis of Inventory Systems*. Englewood Cliffs, N.J.: Prentice-Hall, 1963.

LEE, W.B., and C.P. McLAUGHLIN, "Corporate Simulation Models for Aggregate Materials Management," *Production and Inventory Management*, 1st Quarter 1974, pp. 55–67.

LEVIN, RICHARD I., CHARLES A. KIRKPATRICK, and DAVID S. RUBIN, *Quantitative Approaches to Management*, 5th ed. New York: McGraw-Hill, 1982.

NADDOR, ELIEZER, *Inventory Systems*, New York: John Wiley, 1966.

SCHMIDT, J.W., and R.E. TAYLOR, *Simulation and Analysis of Industrial Systems*. Homewood, Ill.: Richard D. Irwin, 1970.

WAGNER, HARVEY M., *Principles of Operations Research*, 2nd ed. Englewood Cliffs, N.J.: Prentice-Hall, 1975.

WOOLSEY, GENE, "On Doing Good Things and Dumb Things in Production and Inventory Control," *Interfaces*, 5, no. 3 (May 1975), 66–67.

11

MATERIALS REQUIREMENTS PLANNING

In the preceding chapter, we examined classical statistical inventory methods. These methods are useful for managing distribution inventories or items subject to independent demand. Demand for a given inventory item is independent when it is unrelated to demand for other items. Thus, end products and items stocked to meet customer demand are subject to independent demand. Since independent demand is not known exactly, it must be forecasted, and statistical order-point or EOQ methods are appropriate.

In this chapter, we shall study the *materials requirements planning (MRP)* approach to dependent-demand items. An item has *dependent demand* whenever its demand depends on the demand for another item or product. For example, the demand for automobile engines or transmissions depends directly on the demand for the final product, automobiles. The MRP approach is particularly appropriate for manufacturing operations in which the demand for subassemblies, component parts, and raw materials is dependent upon an end product. These dependent-demand items have a demand pattern that is not smooth over time, but lumpy. Demand that is lumpy occurs in discrete batches at different points in time. This type of pattern is very unlike the steady-demand-rate assumption of the basic EOQ models. Thus, MRP was developed to better cope with the lumpy demand patterns of dependent-demand items.

THE DEVELOPMENT OF MRP

MRP has the distinction of being hailed by many as a new way of life in production and inventory management. It is a methodology that has been developed "on the firing line" in industry rather than by academicians or theoreticians. It has been in use by some companies for many years, and is now finding its way into academic courses. MRP has been successful largely because it addresses some of the basic time-phasing problems that confront the inventory manager. It is concerned with that all-important problem we mentioned in the first chapter: getting the right materials to the right place at the right time.

MRP has grown out of a certain disenchantment of practitioners with classical inventory methods for dependent-demand items. Some practitioners felt a need for better data processing and timing rather than better statistical or mathematical methods. MRP has experienced a very rapid growth and level of acceptance since 1970. Its adoption rate among practitioners is growing faster than that of any other inventory control method. This growth is partly attributed to the "MRP crusade" carried out by the APICS (American Production and Inventory Control Society).

APICS is a 12,000-member professional society for the advancement of the practice of production and inventory management. The APICS effort to promote the utility of MRP was spearheaded by such professionals as Dr. Joseph Orlicky of IBM, Oliver Wight, George Plossl, and Walter Goddard. The list of firms using MRP has grown rapidly from 150 in 1971 to 700 by 1975, and over 2,000 in 1982; all indications are that the list will continue to grow.

THE NATURE OF MRP

MRP is a technique for determining when to order dependent-demand items and how to replan and reschedule orders to adjust for changes in demand estimates from the master production schedule. The MRP system consists of inventory records, bills of material, and usually computer programs that translate the master production schedule into time-phased net requirements and planned coverage of these requirements for each component item needed. Because of the large amounts of data that usually need to be manipulated, MRP systems are computerized; they are, in a sense, a data-processing approach to dependent-demand inventory control. Successful MRP systems are taking the systems approach to inventory; they coordinate not only inventory, but purchasing, manufacturing, scheduling, and planning.

MRP avoids the "averaging process" of statistical inventory methods in managing inventory and calculates a specific quantity of what parts to order and when. Thus, an essential feature of MRP is the *calculation* of exact inventory needs rather than a statistical estimation. The calculation is based on a planned production quantity of an end item and the bill of materials (BOM) for that item, which specifies a list of all subassemblies and parts required to produce the end item. The MRP system interacts with production scheduling to correctly time the release orders for all required items.

The purpose of an MRP system is more than to maintain inventory levels by ordering the right quantities of items at the right time. A properly functioning MRP system aids in priority and capacity planning. It helps to establish valid order due dates and order priorities; it also maintains order priority by revising due dates that have been invalidated. An MRP system is an integral part of the priority planning system. It provides valuable information for both purchasing and production operations. However, it cannot cause due dates for purchasing or operations to be met. Thus, MRP must be supplemented by a priority control system in the factory. The control system provides the means to enforce adherence to plans.

A primary tool of priority control is the dispatching list or departmental schedule, which indicates the relative priorities of jobs. The list is based on operations priorities, which are closely tied to the order priorities. Thus, the priority control systems for both dispatching and purchasing cannot function effectively without an information base that maintains timely and valid due dates. MRP can provide this information and the key to a systems approach to manufacturing operations.

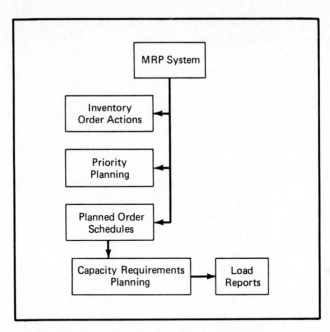

FIGURE 11-1   Priority and Capacity Planning in MRP

MRP, in conjunction with disaggregation and master scheduling has already been mentioned in Chapter 9 on aggregate planning. By utilizing future tentative production quantities as specified by the master schedule, MRP systems can generate load reports for production work centers by period of time. These load reports are more accurate than the rough-cut capacity plans that were generated in aggregate planning. Details concerning not only the end items but all subassemblies and parts are utilized by the MRP system to calculate work-center loads. This process is called *capacity requirements planning* and is based not only on open orders but also planned order receipts to determine time-phased capacity required.

Capacity requirements planning is accomplished by calculating the standard hours required for an order by dividing the order quantity by the pieces per hour specified by each operation on the standard work-flow routing. By using the standard hours required in conjunction with the routing and predefined scheduling rules, each operation can be backward scheduled from the order due date to determine time-phased hours required by the work center for the order. This information is accumulated for all order receipts into the total projected capacity requirements by work center. Figure 11-1 illustrates the MRP system in relation to priority and capacity planning.

Prerequisites and Assumptions of MRP

MRP is primarily intended for manufacturing operations and has been used in such general applications as assembly operations, general machine shops, and fabrication assembly operations. It can be applied to any operation provided that certain assumptions or prerequisites are satisfied. The following conditions are the primary prerequisites for using MRP:

1. The existence of a realistic master production schedule that can be stated in bill-of-material terms.
2. An accurate bill of material for each product that not only lists all components of the product, but also reflects how the product is actually made in steps.
3. Having each inventory item identified with a unique code or part number.
4. Data-file integrity pertaining to inventory status data and bill-of-material data. The system will not function properly without accurate input data.
5. Known lead times on all inventory items.

Benefits and Costs of MRP

The benefits and costs of using an MRP system will vary with individual companies, and efficiency increases will depend on how well the company was doing with its previous inventory system. However, successful adopters of MRP have noted the following potential benefits:

1. Lower inventories. The ability to plan ahead and the flexibility to reschedule rather than maintain large safety stocks allows significant reduction in inventory levels; reductions of up to 50% are not unusual.
2. Improved customer service. The percentage of late orders and stockouts is reduced, sometimes up to 75%.
3. Reduced overtime and idle time—the result of smoother and better planned production.
4. Reduced sales price and improved response to market demands.
5. Ability to modify the master schedule and respond to unanticipated changes in demand.
6. Ability to aid in capacity and priority planning. MRP not only aids the expediting of "hot orders," but also helps in de-expediting orders that must be delayed.
7. Reduced subcontracting and purchasing costs.

The largest cost or disadvantage of any MRP system is the cost of purchasing or leasing a computer system to support the function. However, with increasing inventory and production costs, along with decreasing computation costs, an MRP system is getting easier to justify. An MRP system will also require personnel with MRP expertise and computer programmers to interact with the system, although the actual MRP system software is usually purchased from major computer manufacturers. Additional costs include system maintenance costs and the trials and tribulations of a system changeover. A survey of midwestern APICS members by Schroeder et al.[1] provides cost information for the 422 respondents. Companies reported that they have spent an average of $375,000 on MRP installation to date, and that this figure will rise to $618,000 before the system is fully installed. The cost of installation ranged from a low of $93,000 for smaller companies in the 0–$10 million sales range, to a high of $1,633,000 for large companies with over $500 million a year in sales.

But once functioning smoothly, the MRP system offers really significant advantages to weigh against the costs. The actual benefits depend upon how bad the performance of the current system really is. For example, one company that had some serious inventory problems installed an MRP system and achieved a 12 percent reduction in finished inventories, a work-in-process inventory reduction of 30 percent, and a 35 percent increase in the number of on-time deliveries.[2]

Illustration of Lumpy Demand

Having briefly discussed the nature of MRP and its potential benefits, let's look at an example of dependent or lumpy demand (requirements) to demonstrate the superiority of MRP in handling this type of inventory problem. Let us assume we are to produce a final product A whose demand is uniform at the rate of four units per week. From Figure 11-2, which illustrates the product structure tree for product A, we can see that it takes one unit of component B and two units of component C to make one unit of A. Also, each B requires three Ds, and each C requires one D. Even though demand for product A is uniform, the production of A occurs in lot sizes of 20 units every five weeks. This is shown in Figure 11-3.

Given that 20 units of A take one week to produce and that parts B, C, and D have lead times (for internal production or external ordering) of two, four, and one week respectively, when should we release orders so that 20 units of A can be ready for distribution in week 7? We are faced with the basic problem of time phasing and getting the right parts to the right place at the right time.

In order to have 20 units of product A ready at the end of week 7 (we are concentrating only on these 20 units in week 7), we will have to issue a planned order release for product A in week 6. We can also reason from the product structure in Figure 11-2 that we will need 20 units of B and 2 × 20 = 40 units of C at the beginning of week 6. These gross requirement dates for B and C assume that

---

[1] R.G. Schroeder, J.C. Anderson, S.E. Tupy, and E.M. White, "A Study of MRP Benefits and Costs," *Journal of Operations Management*, October 1981, pp. 1–9.

[2] Jeffrey G. Miller and Linda G. Sprague, "Behind the Growth in Materials Requirements Planning," *Harvard Business Review*, September–October 1975, pp. 83–91.

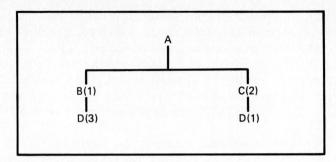

FIGURE 11-2   Product Structure for A

the planned order releases for parent item A are not made until all supporting components are available. Given the lead times of B and C, we should place orders for 20 units of B at the beginning of week 4 and 40 units of C at the beginning of week 2. This in turn would require 60 units of D to be ordered (for the assembly of B) at the beginning of week 3 and 40 units of D to be ordered at the beginning of week 1. These order release dates are summarized in Figure 11-4. Looking at the gross requirements for part D in that figure, we see that the requirements follow a "lumpy pattern" of 0 40 0 60 0 0. In spite of the fact that the demand for the end product A is uniform at four per week, the resulting dependent demand for part D is quite lumpy.

Figure 11-5 illustrates the large amount of error that can result in trying to statistically forecast demand when in fact you can calculate it after end-item production quantities have been established. The forecast in Figure 11-5 is based on exponential smoothing, where Forecast = Previous period forecast + α(Previous demand − Previous forecast), and α = the smoothing constant. For example, using an α of .2, and assuming a previous period forecast of 10 units and demand of 0

		Week					
		1	2	3	4	5	6	7
Demand for product A		4	4	4	4	4	4	4
Gross requirements			20					20
Planned order releases		20					20	

FIGURE 11-3   Master Production Schedule for Product A

Item B Lead time 2 weeks	Week					
	1	2	3	4	5	6
Gross requirements						20
Planned order releases				20		

Item C Lead time 4 weeks	1	2	3	4	5	6
Gross requirements						40
Planned order releases		40				

Item D Lead time 1 week	1	2	3	4	5	6
Gross requirements		40		60		
Planned order releases	40		60			

FIGURE 11-4   Illustration of Lumpy Demand

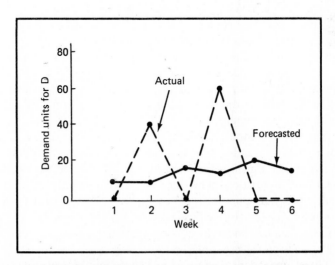

FIGURE 11-5   MRP Calculated Demand versus Statistically Forecasted Demand for Item D

units, we obtain:

$$\text{Forecast in period } 1 = 10 + .2(0 - 10) = 8$$
$$\text{Forecast in period } 2 = 8 + .2(0 - 8) = 6.4$$
$$\text{Forecast in period } 3 = 6.4 + .2(40 - 6.4) = 14.12$$
$$\text{Forecast in period } 4 = 14.12 + .2(0 - 14.12) = 11.3$$
$$\text{Forecast in period } 5 = 11.3 + .2(60 - 11.3) = 21.04$$
$$\text{Forecast in period } 6 = 21.04 + .2(0 - 21.04) = 16.83$$

It is clear from the figure that dependent-demand quantities should be calculated once firm production quantities have been determined from the master production schedule.

PRINCIPLES OF MRP

The example above dealing with lumpy demand illustrates the basic process in MRP —working backward from the scheduled completion dates of end products to determine the dates when the various component parts and materials are to be ordered, and the quantities to be ordered. Of course, the example was a simple one, but the basic process is the same for large-scale real-world manufacturing operations.

The calculations of dependent-demand quantities and order dates are performed by the MRP computer program. The computer program is but one aspect of the overall MRP system, whose structure Figure 11-6 depicts. Chronologically, the MRP system begins with the aggregate production plans, which are refined into a master production schedule. Forecasts of independent-demand items such as end products serve as input to aggregate plans and the master schedule. The master schedule is broken into firm and tentative plans. Firm production schedules are needed for short-range time frames covering up to a month or two; tentative production plans may range from a month up to a year. Tentative plans are sometimes revised according to market reactions, new forecasts, and capacity output reports of the MRP computer program.

The MRP computer program has three major sources of input—the master production schedule, the inventory records file, and the product structure or bill-of-materials file. Using these three inputs, the MRP computer program schedules order releases and production dates for the entire manufacturing operation. The MRP computer program must schedule not only orders for regular customer demand, but also random orders or orders external to the planned master schedule. These external orders can include service and repair parts, interplant orders, and items specially selected for experimentation or testing.

Given dependent demand, the MRP computer program schedules orders by combining information from the master schedule, the bill-of-materials file, and the

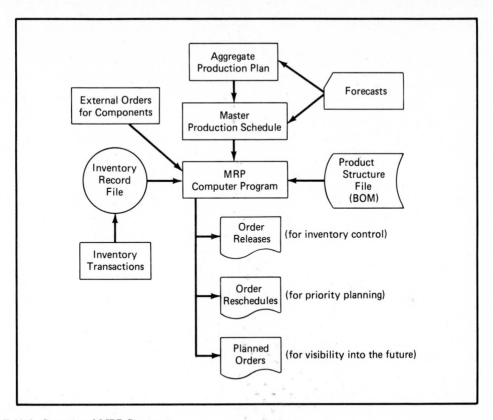

FIGURE 11-6 Structure of MRP System

inventory record file. The master schedule specifies production quantities and due dates, the inventory record file states the number of units on hand and an order for each item, and the bill-of-materials file lists all the items needed to produce a given end product. The logic processor within the MRP computer program then "explodes" the net requirements for the production of the end product and schedules order releases, taking into account any lead times of items.

As can be seen in Figure 11-6, there are three important output reports from the MRP computer program. Order release reports are the principal output, and they represent planned orders in the current period. They form the basis for new shop orders, new purchase requisitions, and due dates for production scheduling. The order reschedule reports call for changes in due dates for open orders. These reports are major input for priority planning and rescheduling, and they also provide expediting information. The planned order reports tentatively schedule orders for release in future periods. These provide information in forecasting inventory and future work-center loads. This visibility into the future is very helpful in capacity planning and the development of realistic master schedules. Other, secondary reports not shown in Figure 11-6 can include performance reports for forecasted usages and costs, and exception reports, which signal errors such as late orders, nonexistent parts numbers, or a due date of an open order outside the planning horizon.

Master Production Schedule

The *master production schedule* is the hub of the MRP system, since it essentially "drives" the system. We have already studied master production scheduling in the disaggregation section of Chapter 9 on aggregate planning. However, since the master production schedule (MPS) is such an important input to MRP systems, we will review its function and relationship to MRP.

The MPS is a refinement of the rougher aggregate plan and it specifies what manufacturing actually plans to produce, not just sales forecasts. The master schedule specifies a time-phased schedule of production quantities of end items. The initial production quantities for end items serve as the first stage of capacity planning. The MRP computer program can "run" on the tentative master schedule production quantities to generate order releases and estimated demands upon plant capacity and various work centers. Revisions may be necessary to reach an authorized master schedule. Figure 11-7 shows the development of an authorized master production schedule.

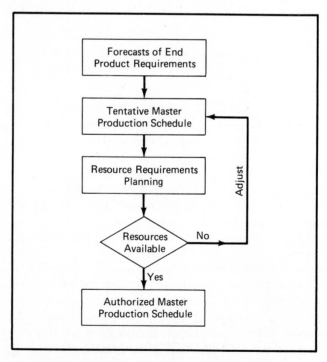

FIGURE 11-7 Development of a Master Production Schedule

The authorized master schedule is a flexible plan that must be able to incorporate changes as they occur. It also serves as the basis for making decisions whenever due dates, capacity, or lead time cannot be satisfied. It is essential that the master schedule be realistic, and hence its development should include input and shared responsibility from not only manufacturing, but also marketing and finance. Marketing is usually responsible for forecasts of demand, product mix, and storage and distribution. Finance must be able to cover the cash flows required in manufacturing operations and finished-goods inventory.

The master production schedule serves two major functions. It is the basis for materials planning, priority planning, and capacity planning over the cumulative production lead time; it is also the basis for estimating long-term resource requirements beyond the cumulative production lead time. The master schedule is usually broken down into a firm and a tentative portion of the planning horizon. Even though last-minute changes can cause the firm schedule to differ slightly from the final assembly schedule, it is usually representative of the scheduled production.

Inventory Record File

The inventory record file serves as a main source of inventory information for the MRP computer program. The inventory record file consists of the following three data segments:

1. Item Master Data Segment
2. Inventory Status Segment
3. Subsidiary Data Segment

These three data segments are called the logical record, since they are related to each other. Each of them may exist for thousands of items, and each segment can contain a significant amount of information. The resulting need to access and move large amounts of data rapidly necessitates a high-speed computer and an efficient information system.

The Item Master Data Segment includes information on item identity, characteristics, and planning factors such as lot size, lead times, safety stock, and scrap allowances. The Inventory Status Segment contains current information on gross requirements, scheduled receipts, on-hand quantities, and planned order releases. The Subsidiary Data Segment includes four types of data: (1) order details, such as open orders and released portions of blanket orders; (2) records of pending action, such as purchase requisitions outstanding and order changes; (3) counters and accumulators that indicate usage to date, demand-history details, and forecast errors; and (4) keeping-track records, which indicate firm planned orders and unused scrap allowance.

These three inventory data segments must be kept up to date in order to be useful. Status data are kept up to date by noting inventory transactions as they

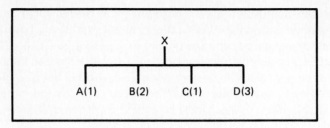

FIGURE 11-8 Product Structure for Product X

occur; these transactions may include stock receipt, disbursements, and scrap losses. The status data are updated frequently—say, daily—whereas planning factors are changed at the user's discretion. The inventory transactions are initially stored on the inventory transactions file (Figure 11-6) and can subsequently be used to update the Status Data Segment.

Bill-of-Materials File

The bill-of-materials file (BOM), or product structure file, represents the way a product is manufactured. It is in a sense a directory for visiting item record files of a "parent's" components. Consider, for example, the product tree structure for product X shown in Figure 11-8.

There are two standard methods for structuring a BOM, the indented file and the single-level file. The single-level file is much more convenient for computer representation, so let's consider it. The single-level bill of material specifies the immediate component items for a given parent item, as well as specific usage quantities of each component. The single-level bill also provides a "pointer" to facilitate retrieval of the bills of material for the components. Figure 11-9 illustrates the single-level BOM for product X.

With the aid of the pointers, the computer can move from one storage location to another to find the appropriate BOM for particular components. This is particu-

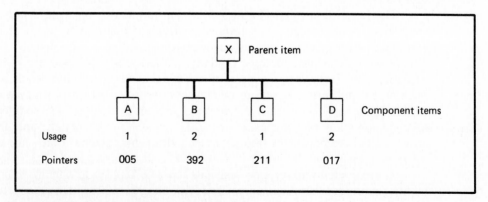

FIGURE 11-9 Single-Level Bill of Material for X

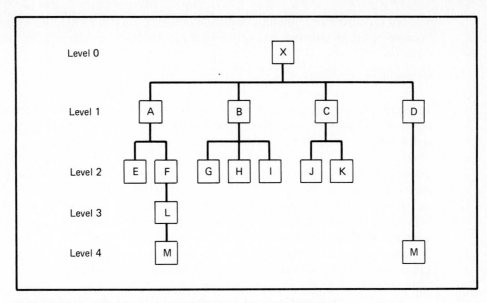

FIGURE 11-10   BOM Hierarchy for Product X and Low-Level Coding

larly helpful, since a component can exist in its own right or as a subassembly or part of another parent item. Through the use of pointers, the computer can move from one single-level BOM to another in order to determine net requirements for order releases.

When the individual single-level bills of material are grouped together graphically, they form a hierarchical, pyramidlike structure. This defines the hierarchy in the BOM of the end product. Figure 11-10 shows the hierarchy and resulting levels in the BOM for product X.

By convention, we keep all identical components at the same level relative to the same parent end item. This is referred to as low-level coding. For example, look at component M in Figure 11-10. It appears at level 4 under components L and D respectively. Component M could have been placed at level 2 under component D, but then it would not have been at the same level as its counterpart under component L. The purpose in keeping all identical components at the same level is to facilitate the computer's calculation of net requirements for parts. If all identical items are on the same level, the computer can scan across a single level of the BOM to summarize all requirements for the components at that level.

PROCESSING LOGIC

We have examined the basic structure of the MRP system and seen how the master schedule, inventory records file, and BOM file are the main input to the MRP computer program. We are now ready to study the logic behind the MRP computer program as it explodes item requirements from the BOM file and time-phases planned order releases. The basic logic is the same as that presented in the previous example of lumpy demand, but we formalize and extend the concepts involved.

Netting Requirements

The materials requirements planning process takes the end-item production quantities as specified by the master schedule and uses the BOM file as well as inventory status data to determine component material needs and their planned order releases. This explosion process is logically simple but can involve hundreds or thousands of calculations for complex products or for determining simultaneously the requirements of many end items.

Two primary concepts needed to accurately calculate the number of subassemblies and parts needed are those of gross and net requirements. The *gross requirement* for an inventory item equals the quantity of the item that will have to be disbursed to support a parent order; it is not necessarily the number of units that will be used by the end product, since there may be hidden inventories of the item in higher-level items in the product structure tree.

Consider, for example, the data in Figure 11-11 pertaining to the manufacture of heavy-duty electrical motors. What are the gross requirements for item D in order to produce 100 units of motor X? The figure is not 100. There are already 20 units of D in any finished subassembly A. Therefore, only 80 units of D need to be disbursed to produce 100 motors, and the gross requirement is 80. The gross requirement is equivalent to demand at item level rather than at product or master production schedule level.

The *net requirements* of an item represent how many additional units must be procured to support the parent item. A formula for net requirements is:

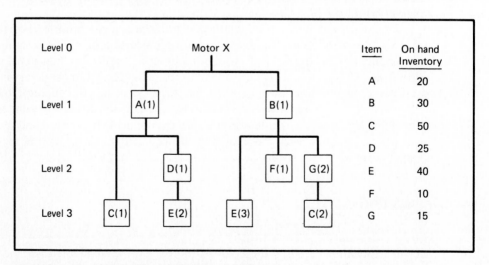

FIGURE 11-11   BOM Levels and Quantities for Motor X

Table 11-1   Gross and Net Requirements to Produce 100 Motors

LEVEL			INVENTORY	GROSS REQUIREMENT	NET REQUIREMENT
1	2	3			
A(1)			20	100	100 − 20 = 80
	D(1)		25	100 − 20 = 80	80 − 25 = 55
		C(1)	50	100 − 20 = 80	80 − 50 = 30
		E(2)	40	(100 − 45) × 2 = 110	110 − 40 = 70
B(1)			30	100	100 − 30 = 70
	F(1)		10	100 − 30 = 70	70 − 10 = 60
	G(2)		15	(100 − 30) × 2 = 140	140 − 15 = 125
		E(3)	—	(100 − 30) × 3 = 210	210 − 0 = 210
		C(2)	—	(140 − 15) × 2 = 250	250 − 0 = 250

New requirements

$$= \begin{cases} \text{Gross requirements} - \text{Scheduled receipts} - \text{Inventory on hand} \\ 0 \text{ if quantity above is negative} \end{cases}$$

In our example of the motor X, we have no scheduled receipts, so the net requirement for item D is gross requirements minus inventory on hand, or $80 - 25 = 55$ units. Table 11-1 summarizes the gross and net requirements for all items.

Time-Phasing

In calculating the net requirements of items, we have basically answered the question of how much. The *time-phasing* aspect of MRP is a key feature distinguishing it from classical inventory methods; it enables us to answer the all-important question of *when*.

There are two basic approaches for relating time to inventory status data, the date/quantity approach and the time-bucket approach. The time-bucket approach is more popular and more widely used; it is the approach we shall study here. A time bucket is a discrete segment of time, usually representing more than one day. It is a coarse division of time that can span five workdays, a week, or a month. Normally a time bucket corresponds to one week.

To illustrate the logic of time phasing, let's consider component F (a coil), which is used in the manufacture of motor X. Suppose the production schedule of the end item, motor X, calls for gross requirements in the amounts indicated in Figure 11-12. The figure shows the time buckets in which component F is needed and receipts are expected. From this information, we can calculate time-phased net requirements. Using abbreviations, the formula for net requirements becomes:

$$NR = \begin{cases} GR - SR - OH \\ 0 \text{ if } (GR - SR - OH) < 0 \end{cases}$$

		Week								Total
		1	2	3	4	5	6	7	8	
Gross requirements			16		22		30	12		80
Schedule receipts				30						30
On hand	20									

FIGURE 11-12 **Time-Phased Status of Component F before Net Requirements Computation**

Incorporating the time-phased net requirements in the time-phased display, we have Figure 11-13. Notice that it is not until the sixth and seventh weeks that additional units of component F are needed, and that the on hand (OH) quantity refers to the amount of inventory available at the beginning of the time period before gross requirements have been deducted.

The next logical concept involves the timing of planned order releases to ensure that 18 and 12 units are available in the sixth and seventh weeks respectively.

In an MRP system, net requirements are covered by *planned orders*, i.e. new orders for the respective items scheduled for release in the future. If no lead time exists, then planned orders can be released in the same period that net requirements occur; however, some lead time usually exists. The timing of planned order releases can be expressed as:

$$\text{Release date} = \text{Due date} - \text{Planned lead time}$$

If we assume a two-week lead time for component F, then the schedule of planned order releases is as shown in Figure 11-14.

		Week								Total
		1	2	3	4	5	6	7	8	
Gross requirements			16		22		30	12		80
Schedule receipts				30						30
On hand	20	20	20	34	34	12	12	0	0	0
Net requirements							18	12		30

FIGURE 11-13 **Time-Phased Status after Net Requirements Computation**

				Week						Total
		1	2	3	4	5	6	7	8	
Gross requirements			16		22		30	12		80
Schedule Receipts				30						30
On hand	20	20	20	34	34	12	12	0	0	0
Net requirements							(18)	(12)		30
Planned order releases					(18)	(12)				

FIGURE 11-14   Time-Phasing Planned Order Releases with Lead Time of 2 Weeks

Lot Sizing

Lot sizing is usually associated with classical inventory control, but it can also be used in MRP to economize on the setup and inventory carrying charges associated with an inventory item. There are several lot-sizing methods to choose from, including the EOQ method that was covered in the previous chapter. In the example shown in Figure 11-14, the order quantities equaled the net requirements exactly. This type of ordering policy is generally referred to as a "lot for lot" policy. It is often used for expensive items or items that are high in the product structure tree.

Suppose that a lot size of 50 units has been calculated for component F using the standard EOQ formula. Figure 11-15 shows the effect on planned order releases.

				Week						Total
		1	2	3	4	5	6	7	8	
Gross requirements			16		22		30	12		80
Scheduled receipts				30						30
On hand	20	20	20	34	34	12	12	0	0	
Net requirements							(18)	(12)		30
Planned order releases					(50)					50

FIGURE 11-15   Time-Phasing with a Lot Size of 50

In this case, the lot size exceeds the net requirements for the eight-week planning horizon by 20 units. This may not pose a problem in this case, but it can where the item is located at a high level near the end item in the product structure tree. An error in the order quantity filters down, becoming more and more exaggerated at the lower levels. Thus, lot sizing can be economical but is generally used for lower-level items in the product structure tree.

An alternative to the EOQ lot size is the *period order quantity* or POQ. The POQ retains the EOQ advantage of low combined setup and inventory carrying costs and it eliminates the EOQ disadvantage of orders which exceed net requirements for the planning period. The POQ is based on the EOQ, but never orders more than is needed for a specified number of time periods. The calculation of the POQ is described in the context of the data of Figure 11-15.

1. Calculate or obtain the EOQ. EOQ = 50
2. Calculate x, the mean gross requirements per period

$$x = \text{total gross requirements/total number of time periods}$$

$$x = \frac{80 \text{ units}}{8 \text{ weeks}} = 10 \text{ units per week}$$

3. Calculate y, the mean number of periods per EOQ order

$$y = \frac{\text{EOQ}}{x} = \frac{50}{10} = 5 \text{ weeks}$$

4. POQ = order y weeks of the net requirements
   = 5 weeks worth of net requirements

In this example, the POQ = 5 weeks worth of net requirements. Normally, successive POQ orders will vary in size. In Figure 11-16 we see that 5 weeks worth of

			Week							
		1	2	3	4	5	6	7	8	Total
Gross requirements			16		22		30	12		80
Scheduled receipts				30						30
On hand	20	20	20	34	34	12	12	0	0	
Net requirements							18	12		30
Planned order releases					30					30

FIGURE 11-16   Illustration of Lot Sizing with POQ

net requirements yields a total of 18 + 12 = 0 = 30. (Only 3 weeks of the planning horizon remain from week 6.)

Time-Phased Order Point (TPOP)

We have examined the basic system structure and processing logic for MRP systems applied to dependent demand. The time-phased order point (TPOP) allows the MRP methodology to be applied to distribution or independent-demand items. Of course, MRP logic can be applied by simply including provisions for safety stock in the scheduling of planned order releases.

Let's consider an example of an end item whose demand is independent. Suppose the following inventory factors apply to the item:

$$
\begin{aligned}
\text{Lead time} &= \text{2 weeks} \\
\text{Safety stock} &= \text{100 units} \\
\text{Lot size} &= 40 \\
\text{Forecasted demand} &= \text{19 per week}
\end{aligned}
$$

Using a statistical order-point approach, the order point would be calculated as:

$$\text{Safety stock} + \text{Period demand} \times \text{Lead time} = 100 + 19 \times 2 = 138$$

The TPOP approach is shown in Figure 11-17. The results of the TPOP approach are similar to those of the order-point approach, but planned order releases are triggered not by an order point but rather by the end of period on-hand quantity dropping down to the safety-stock level (100 in this case).

The MRP system requires no modifications to handle the independent-demand case and has the advantages of offering the same approach for both independent-

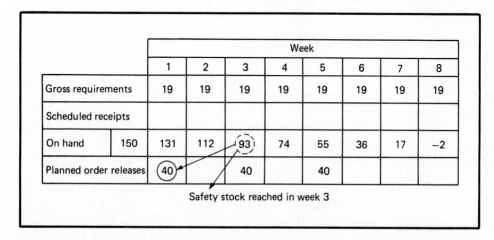

FIGURE 11-17 Time-Phased Order Point

and dependent-demand cases. Additional advantages include the ability to:

1. Plan gross requirements for subparts of the item
2. Develop full schedule of planned orders
3. Keep open order due dates valid
4. Provide an input to capacity planning
5. Plan the priority of dependent and independent items jointly

Regenerative and Net-Change Systems

All MRP systems are executed as either regenerative or net-change systems. The conventional and most commonly used approach is the schedule regeneration implementation, in which the system is run every week or two. This method affords high data-processing efficiency but is not always up to date. The regenerative approach breaks down the new master schedule every week or two into detailed time-phased requirements for each item. This periodic batch-processing approach entails massive data-handling tasks in retrieving BOMs, exploding requirements, and computing the inventory status of all items. The process is executed level by level, starting with end items and proceeding down the levels of the BOM tree structure. Typically, volumes of output are generated pertaining to inventory and requirements data.

Net-change systems allow the user to monitor or replan the MRP system more frequently. In this approach, partial explosions of items that undergo status change are performed. Thus, only part of the master schedule is exploded at any one time and the volume of output is reduced. The approach is analogous to the periodic review system. Few MRP adopters are using the net-change approach even though it offers the capability to keep closer tabs on the system. Some may feel that the more timely information is not worth the additional frequency of computer runs.

MANUFACTURING RESOURCE PLANNING (MRP II)

Materials requirements planning has evolved from a method for managing materials requirements to one that involves both priority and capacity planning in inventory control and production planning. Typically MRP involves planning and scheduling activities applicable to bills of material, purchasing, production scheduling, inventory control, shop-floor control, and deliveries to manufacturing operations. However, some companies have chosen to extend MRP to a highly integrated system for simulating overall company operations.

This extension of MRP is called *manufacturing resource planning* and is often referred to as MRP II. Manufacturing resource planning includes all the above listed activities associated with MRP and also interlocks them with the business and financial planning functions as well as to material and labor costs, and the entire range of plant accounting functions. These include accounts payable, sales analysis, accounts receivable, order-entry invoicing, payroll and general ledger as well as various marketing, administration, and support systems. MRP II thus becomes the nucleus for the "game plan" of the entire business operation. As such, it can represent a true coordinated systems approach to business decision making.

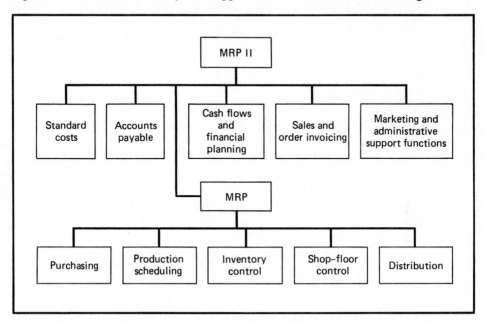

FIGURE 11-18   Business Functions Involved with MRP and MRP II

TOWARD SUCCESSFUL IMPLEMENTATION

MRP is not a panacea for all inventory problems; people still make errors, and unexpected changes in the master schedule can occur. A properly functioning MRP system can, however, aid in time-phasing decisions and planning for the future. It is safe to say that MRP is currently revolutionizing the management of production and inventory control in the United States.

Since all real-world MRP systems entail the use of a computer and massive amounts of data manipulation, they need to function in a highly controlled environment. As in any computer system, the slogan "GIGO" (garbage in, garbage out) applies. An MRP system will fail if the input data is full of errors. It is not possible to prevent input errors entirely, but it is extremely important to minimize them. It is possible to incorporate a variety of internal checks in the MRP system to prevent and correct errors. Three types of preventive measures are (1) barriers to prevent errors from entering the system, (2) detectors to find errors in the input data, and (3) eradicators to eliminate undetected errors.

Barriers can consist of input audits, diagnostic computer routines, and rigid control on external factors such as stockrooms or warehouses. Internal detection routines can be programmed to check against the file being updated; tests of reasonableness can also be employed. Errors that escape barriers and detectors can be tolerated if they are low in percentage and do not accumulate. Error accumulation can be minimized by periodically reconciling differences in planned versus actual requirements and by file purging.

The accuracy of input data, BOM files, and master schedules is necessary, but just as important are the human factors in an MRP system. The people primarily concerned with the system, such as inventory managers, foremen, buyers, and clerks, must be educated as to the basic functioning of MRP systems. Top management must be committed to implementing the system, and sometimes a new attitude toward computers is needed by all concerned, especially during the installation of a new system.

MRP systems can be developed internally, but many commercial MRP software packages are available for mini as well as main-frame computers. Major computer manufacturers such as IBM and Honeywell offer packages, as do companies such as Software International, Arista, and Comserv.

The time required to get an MRP system on line varies with different companies. For example, one $5 million fabrication/assembly company implemented a simple MRP system in six months, whereas a similar $20 million company began to reap benefits only after five years of stop-and-start evolutionary effort on MRP, a larger computer, and a great deal of data-processing support.[3]

Some efforts have been made to implement MRP systems within a broader-reaching control system that performs additional functions. One such system is the Production and Information Control System (PICS) developed by IBM. PICS was developed to aid in the management of dependent demand for fabrication and assembly types of manufacturing. It includes such functions as forecasting, purchasing, scheduling, and shop loading, as well as materials requirements planning.

An even broader-range system that IBM is still developing is called the Communication Oriented Production Information and Control System (COPICS). This computerized system will integrate functions ranging from forecasting, inventory management, and processing control to plant maintenance. Parts of the COPICS system are available, such as programs for forecasting, inventory control, and engineering data management. COPICS will be a dynamic on-line system linked to computer terminals and will provide capabilities for management to test alternate decision strategies. Capacity planning and MRP, along with bill-of-materials files, inventory files, and master production schedules will eventually become integrated parts of the COPICS system. When completed, COPICS is expected to be a comprehensive system for faster information processing and more effective manufacturing planning and control.

SUMMARY

MRP is a systems approach to the management of items subject to dependent demand. It has evolved through the practice of the art in industry and is gaining

---

[3]Miller and Sprague, "Behind the Growth."

acceptance rapidly, although a few firms used similar approaches many years ago.

The basic idea in MRP is to calculate component requirements and then time-phase order releases in order to have needed materials available on time. The MRP computer program takes input from the master production schedule, the inventory records file, and the BOM file. The logic processor then explodes the net requirements for the production of end items and the scheduling of order releases.

MRP systems also provide visibility into the future and the ability to do priority and capacity planning. Other benefits include reduced inventories, fewer late orders, and the ability to adapt to changes in a systematic manner. The only disadvantages pertain to the costs associated with implementing a computerized inventory system. These costs range from around $200,000 to $500,000 for the average company. However, the resulting savings can often recover the initial cost in one to three years.

MRP is most useful for assembly-type manufacturing operations, but it is applicable to any operation involving dependent inventoriable items. MRP has been applied very little (if at all) to service-oriented operations. However, just as the time-phased order point (TPOP) extended MRP methodology to independent-demand items, it does seem conceivable that MRP could be applied to allocating and time-phasing service resources. Only time will tell if this systems approach will be utilized in nonmanufacturing. However, MRP has been extended in some cases to include manufacturing resource planning (MRP II). This extension has carried MRP-type planning activities to the areas of accounting, financial planning, purchasing, and other business planning functions.

Meanwhile, the usage continues among manufacturing firms. MRP is not yet the most widely used inventory technique—ABC analysis and the EOQ model are used more[4]—but its rate of growth is the greatest, and if it continues, MRP will be the dominant dependent-demand inventory method in the near future.

_____ **SOLVED PROBLEMS** _____

Problem Statement

An end item X is assembled from three main subassemblies: A, B, and C. Subassembly A requires two units of part D and three of part E. Subassembly C requires one unit each of components F and G. Furthermore, component G requires four of part H. Given that there are 30, 70 and 90 units on hand of D, G and H, what are the net requirements of A, B, C, D, E, F, G, and H in order to produce 400 units of end item X?

---

[4]Edward W. Davis, "A Look at the Use of Production-Inventory Techniques: Past and Present," *Production and Inventory Management*, 16, no. 4 (December 1975), 1–19.

Solution

In determining net requirements, it is helpful to look at the product structure tree.

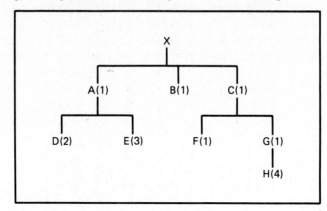

Using the formula $NR = GR - OH$ (in this case, there are no scheduled receipts), we can calculate net requirements as follows:

ITEM	INVENTORY	GROSS REQUIREMENT	NEW REQUIREMENT
A	0	400	400 − 0 = 400
B	0	400	400 − 0 = 400
C	0	400	400 − 0 = 400
D	30	2 × 400 = 800	800 − 30 = 770
E	0	3 × 400 = 1,200	1,200 − 0 = 1,200
F	0	400	400 − 0 = 400
G	70	400	400 − 70 = 330
H	90	4 × (400 − 70) = 1,320	1,320 − 90 = 1,230

Problem Statement

The table below shows the scheduled receipts, current inventory, and gross requirements of component E. Given a lead time of one week and a lot size of 100, determine the timing of planned order releases.

		Week							
		1	2	3	4	5	6	7	8
Gross requirements		100		300	75		200		
Scheduled receipts		100				100			
On hand	90	190	90	90	0	100	100	0	0

Solution

First we must calculate net requirements and then adjust for lot sizes and lead time.

		Week							
		1	2	3	4	5	6	7	8
Gross requirements		100		300	75		200		
Scheduled receipts		100				100			
On hand	90	190	90	90	0	100	100	0	0
Net requirements (cumulative)				210	75		100		

Assuming that all production runs for component E must be in lot-size multiples of 100 or more, we obtain the following planned order releases:

		Week							
		1	2	3	4	5	6	7	8
Gross requirements		100		300	75		200		
Scheduled receipts		100				100			
On hand	90	190	90	90	0	100	100	0	0
Net requirements				210	75		100		
Planned order releases			300			100			

The planned order release of 300 in week 2 will cover gross requirements through week 4. Only 85 more units of component E are required for week 6, but the minimum lot size of 100 requires an order release of size 100 in week 5.

_____ **REVIEW QUESTIONS** _____

1. What is the difference between dependent and independent demand?
2. Explain how errors can arise in applying statistical order-point procedures to lumpy demand.
3. Where did MRP originate?

4. Explain what additional capabilities an MRP system offers besides the time-phasing of order releases.

5. What are the three main inputs to any MRP computer program?

6. How often are most MRP systems run?

7. What kind of information is held in the BOM file? the inventory records file?

8. Explain the TPOP, or how MRP is applied to independent-demand situations.

9. How can the ability to de-expedite be almost as helpful as the ability to expedite?

10. For what types of items should the use of EOQ lot sizing be considered when generating planned order releases?

11. Characterize regenerative and net-change systems.

12. What steps can be taken to prevent input errors from entering the MRP input data?

13. What is the COPICS system?

14. Describe the process by which a tentative master schedule becomes an authorized master schedule.

15. Discuss the relative difficulties in managing manufacturing priorities in businesses that manufacture:
    a. A one-piece product made to order
    b. A one-piece product made to stock
    c. An assembled product made to order
    d. An assembled product made to stock

16. What is capacity requirements planning?

17. How does MRP II relate to MRP?

PROBLEMS

1. Compute the net requirements for items A, B, and C if we want to produce 40 units of X.

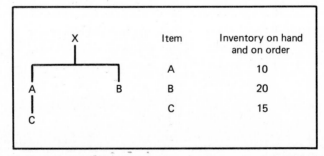

2. Statistical order-level systems sometimes try to store enough safety stock so there is no stockout over a specified percentage of the time. Suppose that enough safety is maintained so that subassemblies A, B, C, and D below will

not stockout over 90% of the time. What is the actual probability that you will be able to produce end item X?

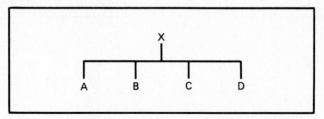

3. Given the following product structure tree, design the associated BOM, showing the hierarchy and components at the correct levels. Use low level coding.

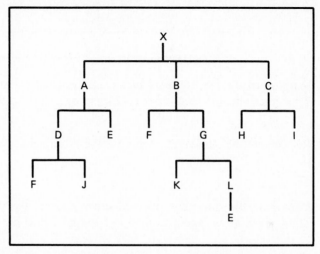

4. Calculate the gross and net requirements for the following BOM and quantities. Assume that you want to produce 50 end items.

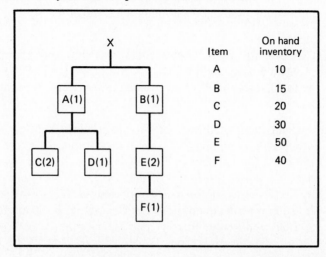

Item	On hand inventory
A	10
B	15
C	20
D	30
E	50
F	40

5. Time-phase the net requirements for component C below by placing the appropriate net requirements in the correct time buckets.

		Week					
		1	2	3	4	5	6
Gross requirements			40		55		70
Scheduled receipts		30		10		30	
On hand	25						
Net requirements							

6. Suppose that a lead time of two weeks applies to the orders in problem 5. Time-phase the planned order releases in order to satisfy net requirements.

7. Recalculate the net requirements for the example in Figure 11-13, given that the on-hand inventory is 35 rather than 20.

8. Determine the timing of planned order releases for the example in Figure 11-14, given an on-hand inventory of 35 and a lead time of three weeks.

9. Suppose that component C of problems 5 and 6 is a lower-level item, and a lot size of 40 units is to be used as the order quantity. Specify the planned order releases for problem 6 assuming a lot size of 40.

10. Calculate the period order quantity (POQ) and planned order releases for problem 6 assuming an EOQ lot size of 40. If the EOQ lot size changes from 40 to 60, does the POQ or planned order release schedule change?

11. An end item Y consists of two main subassemblies, A and B. In order to produce A, components C, D, and two units of E are required. In order to make one B, component F and two units of G are required. Finally, component F requires three units of part H.
    a. Construct the product structure tree for Y.
    b. Determine the quantities of A, B, C, D, E, F, G, and H required to produce 1,000 end items.

12. Advanced Audio Systems is a company specializing in state-of-the-art electronic equipment. It has recently pioneered a new class D amplifier (D for digital), and demand of 52,000 units is expected for the upcoming year. The amplifier is simple in design, consisting externally of only a metal case plus an LED peak-overload indicator. Internally, the amp contains a separate power supply for each of the two channels. Each channel contains a digital processor, which in turn consists of an IC bias regulator, a positive and a negative Darlington driver, and a DC servo control.
   a. Develop your own master production schedule for a planning horizon of eight weeks.
   b. Specify the product structure tree.
   c. Given a lead time of two weeks on power supplies and three weeks on all other components, develop an MRP plan for production, including gross and net requirements and planned order releases (assume no on-hand inventories.)

13. Product A consists of two units of subassembly B, three units of C, and one unit of D. B is composed of five units of E and three units of F. C is made of two units of H and three units of D. D is made of three units of G and one of I.
   a. Construct the product structure tree using low-level coding.
   b. In order to produce 100 units of A, determine the number of units of B, C, D, E, F, G, H, and I required.

14. Product X is made of three units of W and two units of Y. Annual demand for X is uniform at 2400 units, i.e. 48 per week (50 weeks per year). There is a $40 production setup cost. Product X costs $24 each and the inventory carrying cost fraction is 20% of the product cost.
   a. Determine the optimal production run size (EOQ) for X.
   b. Assuming a lead time of one week for X, two weeks for W, and three weeks for Y, create the complete MRP schedule for X, W, and Y for an eight-week period. Assume no on-hand inventory for X, W, or Y.

15. The master scheduler for APEX Co. would like to determine the amount and date of planned order releases for all components including end item 413 shown below. (Lead times specified are in weeks.) The company has contracted to supply 200 units of product 413 in eight weeks. Assuming that there are no on-hand inventories or scheduled receipts, the master scheduler would also like to know if product 413 can be shipped at the end of eight weeks. What would happen if the lead time of component 944 extended to two weeks instead of one?

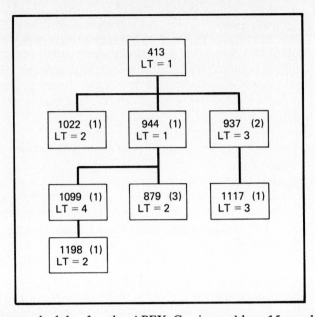

16. The master scheduler for the APEX Co. in problem 15 would also like to determine the capacity requirements in each of four departments that are involved in the production of product 413. Shown in the table are the time requirements in weeks of each component in each of the four departments. Given your dates and quantities of order releases developed in problem 15, determine the total requirements (in weeks) for each of the four departments over the eight-week planning horizon. Assume for simplicity that departmental loads are calculated during the single week in which a planned order release for a given component is executed.

COMPONENT	DEPARTMENT			
	1	2	3	4
1022	0	.005	0	.001
944	.001	0	0	0
937	.001	.0007	.002	.0001
1099	.001	.0005	.0008	.0002
879	.0004	.0006	.0002	.0005
1117	.0008	.002	.001	.0025
1198	.001	.001	.002	.001

17. The Speedy Skate Board Company produces skate boards consisting of the following subassemblies:

$$A001 = \text{completed skate board}$$
$$021 = \text{board (1)}$$
$$035 = \text{wheel assembly (2)}$$
$$049 = \text{axle assembly (2)}$$

Each wheel assembly consists of two components, namely two wheels and two bearing housings. Each wheel contains a locknut and each bearing housing contains two bearings. Each axle assembly consists of an axle and a mounting bracket. Each mounting bracket contains four mounting bolts and nuts.

a. Draw a product structure tree for the Speedy skate board.
b. Assuming that Speedy has an order for 100 skate boards in week 10, use MRP to determine net requirements and the timing of planned order releases for all components. Assume a lead time of two weeks for all materials and no beginning inventory.

_____ **REFERENCES** _____

AMERICAN PRODUCTION and INVENTORY CONTROL SOCIETY, *APICS Special Report: Materials Requirement Planning by Computer*. Washington, D.C., American Production and Inventory Control Society, 1971.

_____, *APICS Training Aid*, "*Materials Requirements Planning*." Washington, D.C., American Production and Inventory Control Society.

CHASE, R.B., and NICHOLAS T. AQUILANO, *Production and Operations Management*. Homewood, Ill.: Richard D. Irwin, 1977.

DAVIS, EDWARD W., "A Look at the Use of Production-Inventory Techniques: Past and Present," *Production and Inventory Management*, 16, no. 4 (December 1975), 1–19.

EVERDELL, ROMEYN, "Master Production Scheduling," *APICS Training Aid*. Washington, D.C.: APICS, 1974.

INTERNATIONAL BUSINESS MACHINES CORPORATION, *Communications Oriented Production Information and Control System*, Publications G320–1974 through G320–1981.

MILLER, JEFFREY G., and LINDA G. SPRAGUE, "Behind the Growth in Materials Requirements Planning," *Harvard Business Review*, 53, no. 5 (September–October 1975), 83–91.

ORLICKY, JOSPEH, *Materials Requirements Planning.* New York: McGraw-Hill, 1975.

PLOSSL, G.W., and O.W. WIGHT, "Materials Requirement Planning by Computer," APICS, Washington, D.C., 1971.

_____, *Production and Inventory Control.* Englewood Cliffs, N.J.: Prentice-Hall, 1967.

SCHROEDER, R.G., J.C. ANDERSON, S.E. TUPY, and E.M. WHITE, "A Study of MRP Benefits and Costs," *Journal of Operations Management*, October 1981, 1–9.

THURSTON, PHILLIP H., "Requirements Planning for Inventory Control," *Harvard Business Review*, May–June 1972, pp. 67–71.

WIGHT, OLIVER W., *Production and Inventory Management in the Computer Age.* Boston: Cahners Books, 1974.

12

SCHEDULING

INTRODUCTION

Regardless of what kind of activity an organization is involved in, scheduling plays an important role. A hospital must schedule operations, admissions, and personnel. Local, state, and federal governments must schedule court cases, transportation systems, a wide variety of projects, mail systems, and a host of other activities. Manufacturing organizations must schedule production, the engineering effort, and materials acquisition. Educational institutions have to schedule classes, buses, and classrooms. The list could go on indefinitely.

Most scheduling problems can be classified into one of three different categories: (1) project scheduling, (2) production scheduling, and (3) scheduling of services. We could further categorize scheduling problems by the type of system being scheduled. In Chapter 1 we said there were basically three types of transformation systems: one-shot systems, intermittent-flow systems, and continuous-flow systems. This relationship between system type and scheduling problems is depicted in Figure 12-1.

Project scheduling refers to the scheduling of unique, one-shot projects. Projects are major tasks that require a significant amount of time to accomplish. The

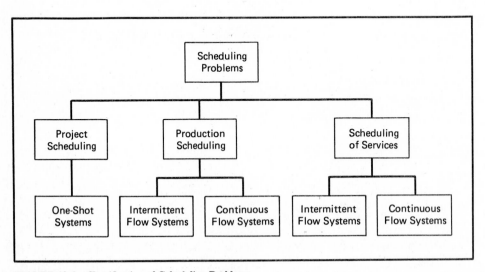

FIGURE 12-1   Classification of Scheduling Problems

construction of a building, the design of a computer-based information system, and the development of a weapons system are all examples. It is obvious that these large projects require a great deal of detailed scheduling in order to complete them in a reasonable length of time. Fortunately, several quantitative techniques have been developed that significantly aid in the project-scheduling process. These techniques are described later in this chapter.

Production scheduling refers to the scheduling of any productive process, but for our purposes, we shall exclude project scheduling from production scheduling. The scheduling of jobs in a computer center, the scheduling of an automotive plant, and the scheduling of a refinery are all examples of production scheduling.

The methods and techniques used to schedule production depend primarily on the production process itself. Scheduling a job-shop or intermittent system is a totally different task from scheduling a continuous system or an assembly-line type of production. Therefore, we shall break production scheduling into two categories, the scheduling of intermittent systems and the scheduling of continuous systems.

The final type of scheduling to be discussed in this chapter is the *scheduling of services*. Provision of services accounts for an increasingly large proportion of our gross national product, and hence the proper scheduling of these services is of no little consequence. Again, scheduling methodology depends on system type. Obvious examples of services that must be scheduled are medical services, legal services, banking services, transportation services, and police protection.

PROJECT SCHEDULING

Project managers must know how long a specific project will take to finish, what the critical tasks are, and, very often, what the probability is of completing the project within a given time span. In addition, it is often important to know the effect on the total project of delays at individual stages. For these and other reasons, several techniques have been created upon which project managers rely. This section examines how the manager can integrate the use of a *work-breakdown structure* (WBS), *Gantt charts*, *project evaluation and review technique* (PERT), and the *critical path method* (CPM) to solve the problems of scheduling and controlling projects.

The scheduling techniques we discuss in this chapter can be applied to a wide variety of projects. Government contractors are almost always required to use scheduling techniques such as PERT for projects of even moderate size. Construction companies often use these techniques for scheduling moderate to large-scale projects. Designers of computerized information systems are using analytical scheduling techniques more and more. In short, almost any large project is a likely candidate, because the cost of using these techniques is usually outweighed by the benefit.

Work-Breakdown Structure

When confronted with the task of scheduling and controlling a project of significant size and scope, you must identify each of the tasks involved. In addition, time estimates for each task must be developed, and the necessary resources, both human and nonhuman, must be identified. In order to accomplish this primary task, it is often desirable to use a WBS. WBS is a graphical representation of the tasks involved in a particular project; it is a way of classifying individual tasks by a natural breakdown of the project in a manner analogous to an organization chart. (See Figure 12-2.) Indeed, WBS is the organizational structure of the project. It starts with a word description of the project and then breaks down the project into major tasks. These major tasks are reduced to tasks, then to minor tasks, and so on. Finally, the smallest element in the WBS, the *work package*, is defined in detail. Each work package identifies the resources and time it requires, all important precedent relationships, and the person who is responsible for it. When all work packages are completed, the project is complete.

Let us use the construction of an apartment building to illustrate the use of WBS. As you can see in Figure 12-3, the entire project can be broken down into six major tasks. These major tasks can then be broken into subtasks, as shown in Figure 12-4. Finally, the subtasks can be broken into work packages, as in Figure 12-5. It

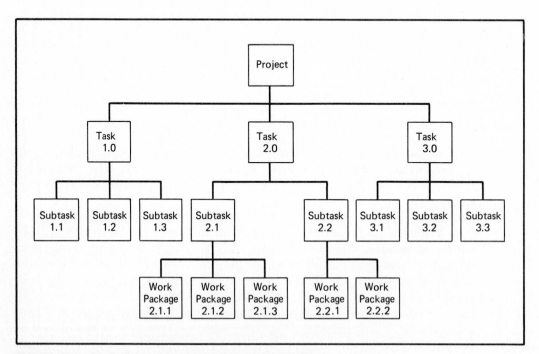

FIGURE 12-2 General Form of Work-Breakdown Structure (WBS)

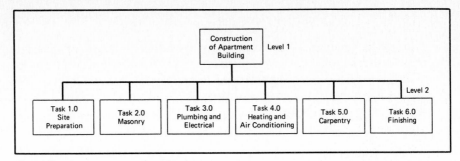

FIGURE 12-3   Second Level, WBS

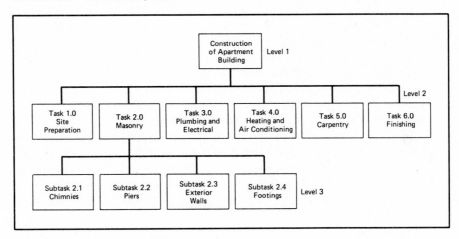

FIGURE 12-4   Third Level, WBS

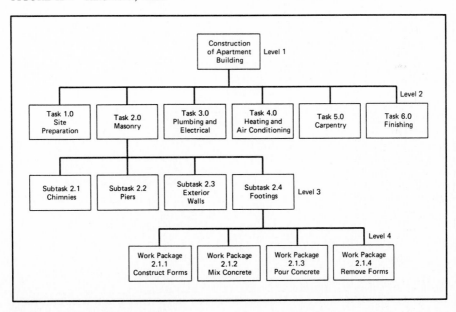

FIGURE 12-5   Fourth Level, WBS

should be emphasized that WBS is not a solution to the project-scheduling problem but rather a preliminary, structured approach to collecting the data necessary for use with one of the more sophisticated techniques, such as PERT or CPM. Once the project has been broken down using WBS, the next step is to choose a way to schedule and control the project.

Gantt Charts

For relatively small projects, a simple Gantt milestone chart, or a series of them, may be the best scheduling tool. A Gantt chart is simply a bar chart that plots tasks against time. Once the project manager has created the WBS for a project, the *Begin* and *Finish* dates for the various tasks, subtasks, and work packages can be scheduled. A single Gantt chart for major tasks and subtasks might be designed for management review, but any real scheduling must be done at the lowest level in the WBS. Each work package must have beginning and ending dates.

A relatively small project, such as building a house, might be effectively scheduled and controlled by means of a Gantt chart. Ordinarily, however, Gantt charts are primarily record-keeping tools used for monitoring projects. They are limited, in that they cannot generate information about the interrelationships among various tasks or about the minimum possible completion times for various tasks. Figure 12-6 shows a typical Gantt chart for an apartment construction project at the major-task level.

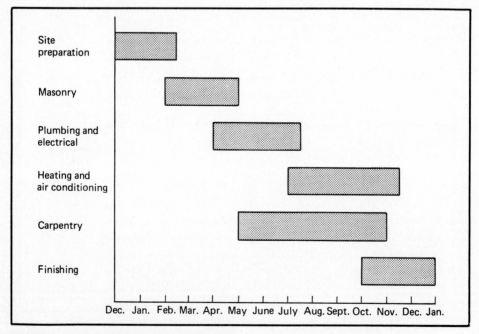

FIGURE 12-6   Gantt Chart for Construction Project

Deterministic PERT

PERT (project evaluation and review technique) evolved from Gantt charts in the late 1950s and was first applied to the U.S. Navy's Polaris submarine project. This project was so large that it actually necessitated the creation of a planning and control technique such as PERT. The project had more than 3,000 contractors, many of whom were performing multiple functions. Because of PERT's success in this and subsequent programs, major federal contracting agencies, such as the Department of Defense and NASA, require many contractors to utilize PERT in scheduling and controlling their projects.

What, specifically, can PERT do for the project manager? PERT can be used as a planning tool as well as a controlling tool. In its planning function, PERT can be used to compute the total expected time needed to complete a project, and it can identify "bottleneck" activities that have a critical effect on the project-completion date. Stochastic PERT, to be discussed later in this chapter, allows the project manager to estimate the probability of meeting project deadlines. One of PERT's greatest benefits is that it forces the project manager to plan the project in explicit detail.

Once a project has been scheduled using PERT, you might think that the technique is of no further use. This is not the case; PERT is typically used throughout the project as a control technique. Used periodically, PERT monitors progress and calls attention to any delays that threaten the success of the project as a whole. In addition, PERT and similar techniques, such as the critical path method (CPM), can be used to evaluate and make decisions concerning time and cost tradeoffs of specific project activities.

Before we examine PERT as a methodology for scheduling and controlling a project, it is important for you to know certain terminology that we shall relate to a specific example.

An *activity* is a task the project requires. Because of the nature of PERT, an activity corresponds to the smallest task in the WBS—namely, the work package. Each activity must have associated with it a *time estimate*, and any *precedence relationships* must be defined. Table 12-1 depicts this pertinent information for a small project.

As these data show, work on activities A and E can begin immediately. Activities B and C cannot be started until activity A has been completed. Activities B, C, and F must be completed before activity D can be started.

One of the problems that PERT addresses is the determination of the minimum time required to complete the project. In order to analyze our project more completely, a *network diagram*, or *PERT chart*, is introduced.

The PERT chart is a graphical representation of the entire project. An arrow represents an activity and a circle represents an *event*, which is defined as the completion of an activity.

Table 12-1   Project Table

ACTIVITY	IMMEDIATE PREDECESSOR	TIME ESTIMATE (IN DAYS)
A	—	3
B	A	4
C	A	5
D	B, C, F	7
E	—	3
F	E	6

The network depicts the precedence relationships involved in the project. As the project table states, the PERT chart shows graphically that is is necessary to finish activity A before beginning activities B and C. The *dummy activity* depicted in the PERT chart, Figure 12-7, is a way to indicate diagrammatically that both B and C must be finished before D can be started. A *path* through a PERT network is a sequence of connected activities. In our example, there are three paths, A-B-D, A-C-D, and E-F-D. The length of each path can be computed by adding the times for each activity on the path. Thus, the length of path A-B-D is 3 + 4 + 7 = 14 days, and the lengths of paths A-C-D and E-F-D are 15 and 16 days, respectively.

The longest path through the network is called the *critical path*. The length of the critical path corresponds to the minimum time required to complete the project; thus, the critical nature of the longest path. The activities on the critical path are *critical activities*, because a delay in any of them results in a delay of the entire project. In other words, there is no slack time in the activities on the critical path. *Slack time* is defined as the latest time an activity can be completed without delaying the project minus the earliest time the activity can be completed. In other words,

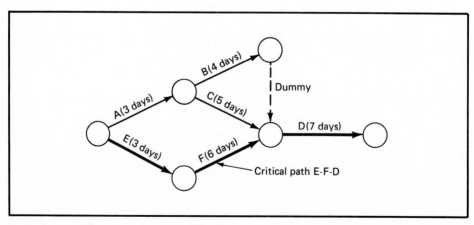

FIGURE 12-7   PERT Chart Showing Critical Path E-F-D

slack time is the amount of time an activity can be delayed without delaying the entire project.

Returning to our example, it is a simple process to identify the critical path by comparing the lengths of each path. Path E-F-D can be completed in 16 days from the start of the project; delay of activities E, F, or D will delay the entire project. Path A-B-D has a total of two days slack time, and path A-C-D has one day of slack time.

As the number of activities increases, drawing a chart and finding the critical path by inspection or complete enumeration becomes more and more impractical. Therefore, we need an algorithm (a systematic approach) to find the critical path. To explain the algorithm, four variables must be defined. Let:

ES_i = the earliest start time for activity i, assuming all predecessor activities
        started at their earliest start time

EF_i = the earliest finish time for activity i

    = $ES_i + t_i$, where t_i is the time estimated for activity i

LF_i = the latest finish time for activity i without delaying the project

LS_i = the latest start time for activity i without delaying the project
    = $LF_i - t_i$

Let us return to our example to illustrate how these four variables are calculated and how the critical path is identified. The algorithm to find the critical path is basically a three-step process. The first step is to calculate the earliest starting time (ES_i) and the earliest finish time (EF_i) for each activity. The second step is to calculate the latest start time (LS_i) and the latest finish time (LF_i). Finally, the slack time is calculated for each activity, and the critical path is the sequence of activities that has zero slack time.

To calculate the earliest start time, let all activities that have no predecessors start at time zero. To calculate the earliest finish time for these initial activities, merely add the time it takes to complete the activities. Hence, the earliest start time for activities A and E of our example is zero, and the earliest finish time for both activities is $LS_i + t_i$, or $0 + 3$. The earliest start time for the other activities is the largest earliest finish time of all immediate predecessor activities for that activity. In our example, activity A has to be finished before B and C are started. Therefore, the earliest start time for activities B and C is 3 (which is the earliest finish time for predecessor A). The earliest finish time for B is $ES_B + t_B$, or $3 + 4 = 7$. Similarly, the earliest finish time for C is 8, and the earliest finish time for F is 9. Consequently, because activity D cannot be started until B, C, and F are finished, the earliest start time for D is 9 (the largest earliest finish time of all immediate predecessors).

Calculating the latest finish times and latest start times is a similar procedure, but to do it, we must start at the other end of the PERT network. For all ending activities, set the latest finish time equal to the largest earliest finish time. In our example, there is only one ending activity; hence, the latest finish time is equal to the earliest finish time for activity D. Subtracting the end activity's time from its latest finish time yields the latest start time. The latest finish time for the other activities is equal to the smallest latest start time for all immediate successor activities. Therefore, the latest finish time for activities B, C, and F is 9. The latest start time for activity B is 9 − 4 = 5.

The latest start time for activity C is 9 − 5 = 4. Activity A has two successor activities, B and C. Remember, activity A's latest finish time is the minimum latest start time for its successor activities. Hence, the latest time activity A can finish is 4. If activity A finishes after the fourth day, the project will be delayed.

Once the four times have been calculated for each activity, it is a simple procedure to identify the critical path. Slack time is calculated by subtracting the earliest finish time from the latest finish time. Activities with zero slack time are on the critical path. In other words, a delay in any activity on the critical path results in a delay of the entire project. Table 12-2 indicates that the critical path is made up of activities E-F-D. (See Figure 12-8 for the graphical representation of this situation.) Any activity that has a nonzero slack time is not critical and can be delayed as much as the slack time without delaying the project.

Stochastic PERT

Until now, we have treated PERT as a deterministic technique in which all activity times are known with certainty. It is obvious that for most projects, these activity times are random variables. If these random times take on values significantly different from those point estimates used in the PERT analysis, the output from PERT (that is, the critical path, project completion time, and so on) is rendered invalid. To compensate for the lack of certainty in many of the time estimates, the project manager is often asked to give three subjective time estimates for each activity. These time estimates are:

a_i = the most optimistic time required for activity i

m_i = the most likely time required for activity i

b_i = the most pessimistic time required for activity i

Table 12-2   Data for PERT Algorithm

ACTIVITY	IMMEDIATE PREDECESSOR	TIME	ES	EF	LS	LF	SLACK
A	—	3	0	3	1	4	1
B	A	4	3	7	5	9	2
C	A	5	3	8	4	9	1
D	B, C, F	7	9	16	9	16	0
E	—	3	0	3	0	3	0
F	E	6	3	9	3	9	0

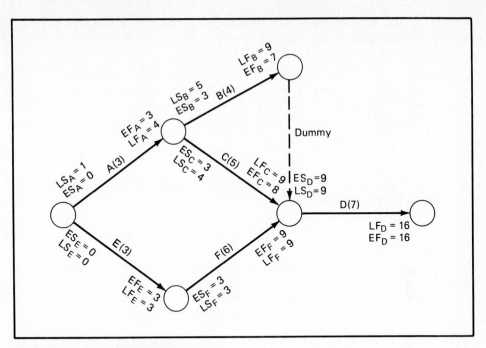

FIGURE 12-8   Evaluated PERT Chart

These three time estimates are used to define a probability distribution of time for each activity. The distribution used almost exclusively is the *beta distribution*. There is no rigorous mathematical proof that the beta distribution is most appropriate, but three properties make it a logical choice. First, it is a continuous probability distribution; second, it is not necessarily symmetrical; and finally, it has a bounded range of values. In addition, empirical investigations support the use of the beta distribution for PERT times. Figure 12-9 depicts a beta-distributed activity time.

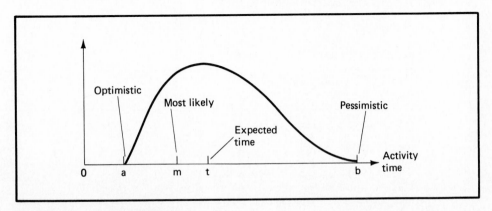

FIGURE 12-9   The Beta Distribution

The mean of the distribution, the expected time for an activity, is calculated using the following function:

$$\bar{t}_i = (a_i + 4m_i + b_i)/6$$

where $\qquad\qquad \bar{t}_i$ = the expected time for activity i

The standard deviation of the beta distribution can be approximated using:

$$\sigma_i = (b_i - a_i)/6$$

Suppose, for example, the three times estimates for activity 5 are $a_5 = 2$ days, $m_5 = 6$ days, and $b_5 = 10$ days. The expected time and standard deviation for activity 5 is achieved as follows:

$$\bar{t}_5 = (2 + 24 + 10)/6$$
$$= 6 \text{ days}$$
$$\sigma_5 = (10 - 2)/6$$
$$= 1.33 \text{ days}$$

The reason for calculating the standard deviation is to provide a means of computing the probability of completing the project on or before the scheduled completion date. To explain how this probability is computed, let's look at a stochastic version of our original problem. The first step is to calculate the expected time and standard deviation for each activity using the formulas specified by the beta distribution. This is done in Table 12-3 below. The next step is to find the *expected critical path*. (Since the calculated critical path may not, in fact, be the actual critical path, we can only refer to it as an expected critical path.) The expected critical path is found by using the algorithm previously developed for deterministic PERT. The only difference is that in this situation, you use the expected activity time instead of the single time estimate. As you can see in Table 12-4 on the following page, the expected critical path is E-F-D.

Table 12-3   Stochastic PERT Table

ACTIVITY	IMMEDIATE PREDECESSOR	a_i	m_i	b_i	$\bar{t}_i$	σ_i	σ_i^2
A	—	1	3	5	3.00	.67	.45
B	A	1	4	5	3.67	.67	.45
C	A	3	5	7	5.00	.67	.45
D	B, C, F	3	7	12	7.16	1.50	2.25
E	—	2	3	4	3.00	.33	.11
F	E	2	6	9	5.83	1.17	1.37

Table 12-4   Data for Stochastic PERT Algorithm

ACTIVITY	IMMEDIATE PREDECESSOR	EXPECTED TIME	ES	EF	LS	LF	SLACK
A	—	3.00	0.00	3.00	.83	3.83	.83
B	A	3.67	3.00	6.67	5.16	8.83	2.16
C	A	5.00	3.00	8.00	3.83	8.83	.83
D	B, C, F	7.16	8.83	15.99	8.83	15.99	0.00
E	—	3.00	0.00	3.00	0.00	3.00	0.00
F	E	5.83	3.00	8.83	3.00	8.83	0.00

Once the expected critical path has been identified, it is often useful to know the probability of completing it within a given length of time. For example, what is the probability that the tasks on the expected critical path will all be complete by the end of the project's seventeenth day? In order to compute a probability of this type, it is necessary to calculate the variance (σ_i^2) for each activity's time. This is done by simply squaring the standard deviation. If we assume that the activities on a given path are independent (that is, that the duration of one task has no effect on the length of time necessary to complete another task), then the variance related to an entire path's length is the sum of the variances of the individual activities on that path. Therefore, assuming independence, the variance for path E-F-D is .11 + 1.37 + 2.25 = 3.73. In addition, if there are many activities on a given path (that is, more than 30), the distribution of the total time of the path is often assumed to be normally distributed.

Given the mean and variance of a normally distributed random variable (path length), it is possible to determine the probability of completing that path within a certain length of time. For example, what is the probability of completing path E-F-D within 17 days? The standard deviation of the total time that it takes to complete path E-F-D is $\sqrt{3.73}$, or 1.93, and the mean is 15.99. Given these facts, the distribution of times necessary to complete path E-F-D is shown in Figure 12-10. The probability of completing path E-F-D within 17 days is represented by the shaded portion of the normal curve in Figure 12-11.

To compute this probability, it is necessary to transform our normal distribution into the standard normal with a mean of 0 and a standard deviation of 1. This is done by using the following Z transformation:

$$Z = \frac{x - \mu}{\sigma}$$

where μ = the mean of the nonstandard normal

σ = the standard deviation of the nonstandard normal

x = the nonstandardized normal variate

Therefore, the probability of completing path E-F-D is calculated by first calculating Z. Thus, $Z = (17 - 15.99)/1.93 = .5233$.

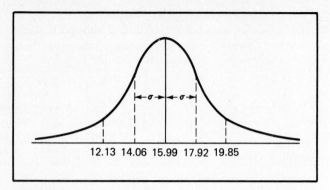

FIGURE 12-10 **Normal Distribution of Days Necessary to Complete Path E-F-D**

Once Z has been computed, the probability of $Z \leq .5233$ is found by using a standard normal table such as the one in Appendix B at the back of this book. The probability that path E-F-D will be finished within 17 days is approximately .699. (To find this, look up $Z \leq .5233$ in the table. Be sure to verify it for yourself.) In other words, $P(x \leq 17) = P(Z \leq .5233) = .699$. It is important to remember that the normality assumption postulates the existence of a large number of random variables (that is, activities on a path). For rough approximations, 30 random variables is usually acceptable; for more rigorous applications, however, an n closer to 100 is preferable.

Having computed the probability of completing the expected critical path within 17 days, can you then conclude that this is the probability of completing the project in 17 days or less? The answer is no. Since activity times are random variables, it is possible that a path different from the expected critical path might cause the project to last longer than 17 days. To illustrate this idea, let's consider path A-C-D. The expected time for path A-C-D ($t_{A\text{-}C\text{-}D}$) is $3 + 5 + 7.16 = 15.16$, and the standard deviation for path A-C-D is $\sqrt{.45 + .45 + 2.25} = 1.775$. Thus,

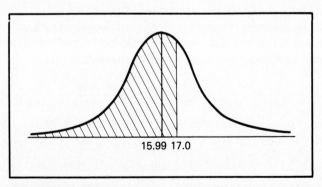

FIGURE 12-11 **Normal Distribution Showing Probability of Completing E-F-D within 17 Days**

$Z = (17 - 15.16)/1.775 = 1.037$. Therefore, $P(t_{\text{A-C-D}} \leq 17) = P(Z \leq 1.037) \cong$ .849. Similarly, the probability of completing path A-B-D within 17 days is approximately .963. Now, if we assume that the lengths of the paths are independent random variables, we can compute the probability of completing the project within 17 days as the joint probability of completing each path within 17 days. In other words, P(Project time $\leq$ 17 days) $= P$(Path A-B-D $\leq$ 17 and Path A-C-D $\leq$ 17 and Path E-F-D $\leq$ 17). If independence is assumed, P(Project time $\leq$ 17) $=$ (.963)(.849)(.699) = .5715.

If the various assumptions necessary to compute the probability of project completion cannot be made (that is, if the individual paths are not independent or do not have a large number of activities), *computer simulation* can be used to estimate the probability of project completion within a specific time period. For each activity, the computer merely samples from a beta distribution for which the parameters have been established as previously described. On each iteration, a project completion time is computed and is added to a frequency distribution of project lengths. Given enough iterations, it is reasonable to use this frequency distribution to describe the probabilities of various project durations.

Evaluating Time – Cost Tradeoffs

So far, we have discussed two variations of PERT that emphasize time factors in project evaluation. *Deterministic PERT* is useful when a project's time parameters are known with a good degree of certainty. *Stochastic PERT*, on the other hand, allows uncertain times to be estimated so that probabilities concerning such activities' duration and completion can be computed. In a third technique, the critical path method (CPM), cost was introduced as a companion factor to time for project evaluation.

In their early use, PERT and CPM actually differed in two ways. First, PERT allowed for stochastic times, using the three-point estimate discussed in the preceding section. CPM, however, assumed that times are known with certainty. This distinction is still valid to some extent. When a project is rather uncertain in nature (as, for example, a research project or an out-of-the-ordinary undertaking), PERT is the logical technique to use for planning and control. For more common projects, such as certain construction projects in which the times necessary to complete individual tasks can be closely estimated, deterministic PERT or CPM may be more desirable.

As we have mentioned, the second distinction between PERT and CPM lay in the area of project costs. CPM made use of a dual perspective—namely, time and cost. You should realize, however, that this difference between PERT and CPM has faded as both techniques have evolved. In fact, most PERT software packages now include provisions for evaluating time–cost tradeoffs. For that reason, the discussion of time and cost factors that follows refers to using "versions of PERT and CPM," because, in fact, both methods have been used to make valid analyses of the kind to be discussed.

Table 12-5   Time – Cost Tradeoff Data

ACTIVITY	NORMAL TIME ESTIMATE	CRASH TIME ESTIMATE	INCREMENTAL COST OF CRASH TIME ($)
A	3	2	150
B	4	$3\frac{1}{2}$	100
C	5	4	200
D	7	5	300
E	3	3	—
F	6	5	75

Until now, we have talked about these project-evaluating techniques primarily as descriptive and predictive tools. Versions of PERT and CPM, however, are used to make decisions concerning how best to shorten a project's completion time. A project manager often has the prerogative of increasing resource allocation to specific tasks so that the project can be finished at an earlier date. In other words, a project manager may have such options as hiring additional workers or working personnel overtime to expedite the completion of a task. To give you an idea of how these time–cost tradeoff decisions are made, let's consider our previous deterministic example. Table 12-5 reflects the costs of feasible reductions in each activity's completion time.

The crash time estimate in Table 12-5 represents the amount of time it would take to complete an activity if management wished to allocate additional resources to that activity. The incremental cost of crashing an activity is also reflected in the table. Remember that there were three paths in the PERT network of our original problem. These paths are summarized in Table 12-6.

In terms of shortening the total project, it is clear that to shorten paths A-B-D or A-C-D without shortening path E-F-D does no good. Remember, the minimum length of the project is the length of the longest individual path. Therefore, we must look at path E-F-D to determine how to expedite the completion of the total project. Table 12-7 indicates that we have two alternatives for shortening path E-F-D. Because of the lower per-day cost, it seems logical to add resources to activity F (that is, activity F is crashed) so that the length of the project is reduced from 16 days to 15 days at a cost of $75.

Table 12-6   PERT Paths

PATH	LENGTH
A – B – D	14 days
A – C – D	15 days
E – F – D	16 days

Table 12-7   Alternatives for Shortening E – F – D

ACTIVITY	EFFECT OF CRASH	COST OF CRASH	COST PER DAY OF CRASH
E	—		—
F	1 day		$75 per day
D	2 days		$150 per day

In order to shorten the project further, both paths A-C-D and E-F-D must be shortened. Since D is the only activity that can still be shortened on path E-F-D, there is no alternative. Fortunately, D is common to all three paths, and a reduction in D results in shortening all three. For $300, D can be reduced from seven days to five days, and each path can be reduced two days. Therefore, paths E-F-D and A-C-D would take 13 days, and path A-B-D would take 12 days. Further reduction in paths A-B-D or A-C-D would not be fruitful, because the length of path E-F-D cannot be reduced. To summarize, we can reduce the project schedule from 16 days to 13 days at a cost of $375.

PERT / Cost

Every project manager has two major problems when managing a large project. First, he or she must be concerned with the time and schedule aspect of the project. We have seen that PERT/CPM can be a very useful tool for scheduling the project and continually monitoring the schedule. A second major problem the project manager is concerned with is that of cost budgets. PERT/Cost can be used to aid in planning, scheduling, and controlling the cost of the project. Specifically, once the various work packages have been identified in the WBS and their costs have been estimated, the project manager must predict the cash flow for the project. In addition, the project manager must periodically review expenditures to determine if actual costs are exceeding budgeted cost so that he or she can take the necessary corrective action to reduce or eliminate cost overruns. Our discussion of PERT/Cost is divided into two sections, the prediction of cash flows and the monitoring and control of project costs.

The estimation of a project's cash flow using PERT/Cost is a five-step process. This five-step process is depicted in the flow chart in Figure 12-12.

Let us illustrate how PERT/Cost estimates monthly cash flows by using the example shown in Table 12-8. The first step in the cash flow analysis is to estimate or budget each activity. In many applications, the cost of a work package or individual task is assumed to be linear (constant). Thus, if activity A is estimated to cost $10,000, the per-month cost is assumed to be $5,000 ($10,000/2 months). With many PERT/Cost software packages, however, this simplifying assumption is not necessary. In our example, however, costs are assumed to be linear. The estimated costs for each activity are shown in Table 12-9.

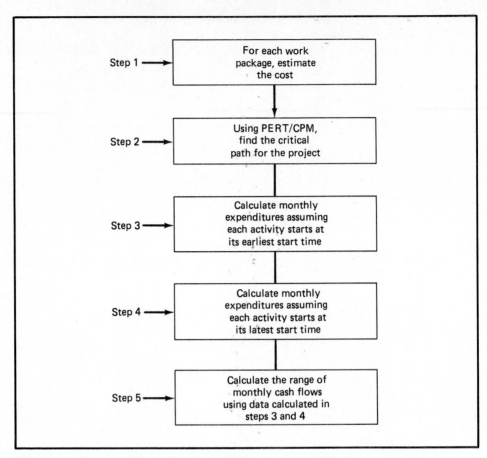

FIGURE 12-12 Steps in Project Cash-Flow Analysis

Table 12-8   Project Table

ACTIVITY	TIME (MONTHS)	IMMEDIATE PREDECESSORS
A	2	—
B	3	—
C	3	A
D	2	A
E	2	B
F	7	B
G	4	C
H	3	D, E
I	2	H
J	4	G, I

Table 12-9   Project Budget

ACTIVITY	TOTAL ESTIMATED COST	ESTIMATED MONTHLY COST
A	$ 10,000	$ 5,000
B	24,000	8,000
C	30,000	10,000
D	20,000	10,000
E	40,000	20,000
F	140,000	20,000
G	160,000	40,000
H	90,000	30,000
I	100,000	50,000
J	100,000	25,000
	$714,000	

Table 12-10   Data for the PERT Algorithm

ACTIVITY	TIME	ES_i	EF_i	LS_i	LF_i	SLACK
A	2	0	2	1	3	1
B	3	0	3	0	3	0
C	3	2	5	3	6	1
D	2	2	4	3	5	1
E	2	3	5	3	5	0
F	7	3	10	7	14	4
G	4	5	9	6	10	1
H	3	5	8	5	8	0
I	2	8	10	8	10	0
J	4	10	14	10	14	0

The next step is to find the critical path for the network in Figure 12-13. Using the PERT algorithm, we can identify the critical path as B-E-H-I-J. See Table 12-10 for the necessary calculations.

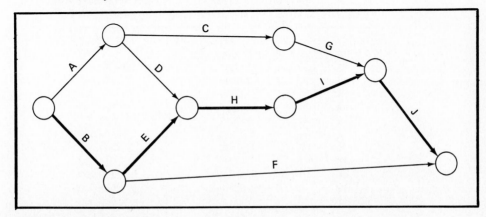

FIGURE 12-13   PERT Network

Step 3 says to calculate expected monthly expenditures based on the assumptions that each activity starts as soon as possible and that cost expenditures are at a uniform rate. Given these two assumptions, the monthly expenditures are calculated in Table 12-11.

The next step is to calculate the expected monthly cash outflows based on the assumption that activities start at their latest starting times. These outflows are calculated in Table 12-12.

The final step in predicting the monthly cumulative cash requirements for a project is to examine the range between the expected monthly cumulative cash outflow assuming an earliest start time and the expected cumulative cash outflow assuming a latest start time. This information is summarized below in Table 12-13. The feasible region of cumulative expected cash outflows is graphed in Figure 12-14 on page 435.

From our example, it should be obvious that the project manager faces a dilemma in scheduling activity starting times when he or she considers project costs as well as project schedules. If activity times are not known with certainty, then starting at the earliest possible times provides the project manager with a hedge. This hedge, however, is not without a cost. The cost is obviously derived from the time value of money. In other words, in addition to the direct budgeted cost of the project, the cost of financing the project must be considered. This cost of financing can be a significant factor in persuading a project manager to delay the start of a task as long as is possible.

In addition to predicting the monthly cash needs for a project, a primary responsibility of the project manager is to monitor and control costs. It is extremely

Table 12-13   Range of Expected Cash Requirements by Month

MONTH	CUMULATIVE EXPECTED CASH OUTFLOWS ASSUMING LS_i	CUMULATIVE EXPECTED CASH OUTFLOWS ASSUMING ES_i
1	$ 8,000	$ 13,000
2	21,000	26,000
3	34,000	54,000
4	74,000	114,000
5	114,000	164,000
6	154,000	254,000
7	224,000	344,000
8	314,000	434,000
9	424,000	544,000
10	534,000	614,000
11	579,000	639,000
12	624,000	664,000
13	669,000	689,000
14	714,000	714,000

Table 12-11 Budgeted Monthly Cash Expenditures Assuming Earliest Start Time

								MONTH						
ACTIVITY	1	2	3	4	5	6	7	8	9	10	11	12	13	14
A	5,000	5,000												
B	8,000	8,000	8,000											
C			10,000	10,000	10,000									
D			10,000	10,000										
E				20,000	20,000									
F				20,000	20,000	20,000	20,000	20,000	20,000	20,000				
G						40,000	40,000	40,000	40,000					
H						30,000	30,000	30,000						
I									50,000	50,000				
J											25,000	25,000	25,000	25,000
Monthly cost	13,000	13,000	28,000	60,000	50,000	90,000	90,000	90,000	110,000	70,000	25,000	25,000	25,000	25,000
Accumulated project cost	13,000	26,000	54,000	114,000	164,000	254,000	344,000	434,000	544,000	614,000	639,000	664,000	689,000	714,000

Table 12-12 Budgeted Monthly Cash Expenditures Outflows Assuming Latest Start Time

ACTIVITY	1	2	3	4	5	6	7	8	9	10	11	12	13	14
										MONTH				
A	8,000	5,000	5,000											
B		8,000	8,000											
C				10,000	10,000	10,000								
D				10,000	10,000									
E				20,000	20,000									
F								20,000	20,000	20,000	20,000	20,000	20,000	20,000
G							40,000	40,000	40,000	40,000				
H						30,000	30,000	30,000						
I									50,000	50,000				
J											25,000	25,000	25,000	25,000
Monthly cost	8,000	13,000	13,000	40,000	40,000	40,000	70,000	90,000	110,000	110,000	45,000	45,000	45,000	45,000
Accumulated project cost	8,000	21,000	34,000	74,000	114,000	154,000	224,000	314,000	424,000	534,000	579,000	624,000	669,000	714,000

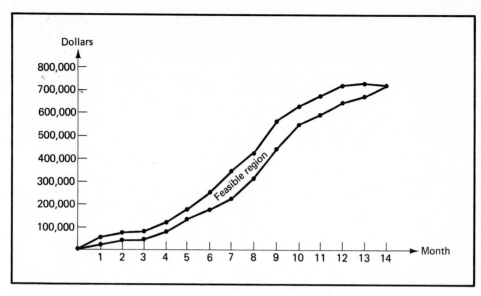

FIGURE 12-14 Feasible Region for Cumulative Expected Cash Outflows

important for a project manager to identify cost overruns and cost underruns so that appropriate action can be taken. Typically, monitoring of project costs is facilitated by a PERT/Cost report produced periodically (monthly or biweekly), which identifies activities that are projected to have a cost overrun or underrun. Let us examine how this critical report is produced. Periodically, a project manager reviews the status of the various work packages to ascertain the actual expenditure to date and the work package's percentage completion. This information, together with the original detailed budget for the project, allows the project manager to identify cost overruns and underruns. Let us illustrate the process of producing a PERT/Cost report by using our previous example. If we assume that we are at the end of the sixth month and the expenditures and activity completion percentages are as shown in Table 12-14, it is possible to calculate a value of work completed for each activity using the formula

$$V_i = \frac{P_i}{100} B_i$$

where

V_i = value of the work completed

P_i = percentage of work completed for activity i

B_i = budget for activity i

Once V_i has been calculated for each activity, it is possible to calculate the amount of the cost overrun or underrun by subtracting the value of the work completed from

Table 12-14   Activity Cost and Completion Data after 6 Months

ACTIVITY	EXPENDITURES TO DATE	PERCENT COMPLETION
A	$12,000	100
B	24,000	100
C	30,000	80
D	18,000	100
E	45,000	95
F	60,000	50
G	40,000	25
H	30,000	25
I	0	0
J	0	0

the actual cost of the work completed using the formula

$$D_i = C_i - V_i$$

where D_i = difference between the actual cost and the value of the work
on activity i; if this difference is positive we have a cost overrun,
and if it is negative we have a cost underrun

C_i = actual cost of activity i

It is apparent from the PERT/Cost report in Table 12-15 that several activities have overruns and several have underruns, and that these overruns and underruns nearly balance each other. The prudent project manager, however, would look closely at activities C, E, and H to determine the cause of the overrun and see if some type of corrective action might be appropriate.

A major advantage of WBS, Gantt charts, PERT, and CPM is that each of these techniques forces the project manager to explicitly plan and schedule the

Table 12-15   PERT / Cost Report

ACTIVITY	BUDGET B_i	EXPENDITURES TO DATE C_i	VALUE V_i	DIFFERENCES D_i
A	$ 10,000	$12,000	$10,000	$ 2,000
B	24,000	24,000	24,000	0
C	30,000	30,000	24,000	6,000
D	20,000	18,000	20,000	−2,000
E	40,000	45,000	38,000	7,000
F	140,000	60,000	70,000	−10,000
G	160,000	40,000	40,000	0
H	90,000	30,000	22,500	7,500
I	100,000	0	0	0
J	100,000	0	0	0

project in great detail. WBS is a necessary first step in planning a project, in that the output from the WBS analysis is the input for any utilization of PERT or CPM. PERT or CPM can then be used to identify critical tasks and to estimate project-completion times with various degrees of confidence. If the normality and independence assumptions of stochastic PERT cannot be accepted, the project manager can always use computer simulation to find the probabilities associated with various completion deadlines. Keep in mind also that more sophisticated versions of PERT exist that can answer such questions as how to shorten the project schedule with the least additional cost, and what to do about various resource constraints.

PRODUCTION SCHEDULING

The way in which production scheduling is approached by an organization depends on many factors. In a firm that produces highly standardized products, such as automobiles, boxes of detergent, children's toys, or the like, the scheduling function is more a function of process design than day-to-day scheduling. In other words, if an assembly line or continuous system has been designed and balanced, then the rate of production has been set, and the only scheduling decision that can be made in the short term is how long the assembly line should operate (that is, whether the workday should be shortened or lengthened). In the longer term, however, the assembly line could be redesigned or rebalanced to alter the output schedule. How to design and balance a continuous-flow system was discussed in Chapter 5 on process design. If the assembly line is to move smoothly, then raw materials and subassemblies must be available on a timely basis or the assembly line will be interrupted. The avoidance of this type of costly interruption is the function of the inventory control system or the materials requirements planning system.

Scheduling intermittent-flow productive systems that are not assembly-line-type systems is difficult and has received a great deal of attention in the operations management literature. Before describing how firms actually accomplish the production scheduling of intermittent systems, it is helpful to list the objectives of a good production-scheduling system. First, firms seek to maximize labor utilization. Idle workers obviously have a negative effect on profitability. Machine utilization is also important and should be used as a criterion to determine the utility of the production-scheduling system. A third objective is to minimize the number of tardy jobs and their degree of tardiness. Minimizing in-process inventory costs and average waiting time for jobs is also an important objective of any production-scheduling system.

With these major objectives in mind, we will examine the ways in which organizations schedule their productive systems. A productive system can be categorized as a flow shop or a job shop. A *flow shop* is a production facility in which each job flows through the same sequence of processing (that is, from one work center to the next). Figure 12-15 depicts the pure flow shop. A *job shop* is one in which each job has to be processed by a different sequence of work centers. If there

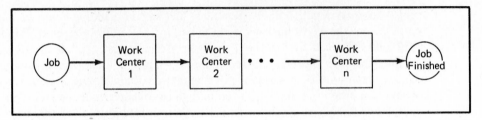

FIGURE 12-15   Flow-Shop Schematic

were three work centers in a job shop, a random job could take one of the many paths indicated in Figure 12-16.

The ways organizations use to schedule flow-shop and job-shop production can be grouped into two major categories, *work-center loading* and *detailed scheduling*. Loading schemes typically take the form of a queue discipline that is used at the various work centers to determine which job is processed next. Detailed scheduling systems compute an operational schedule that defines for each job when processing is to begin and end at each work center.

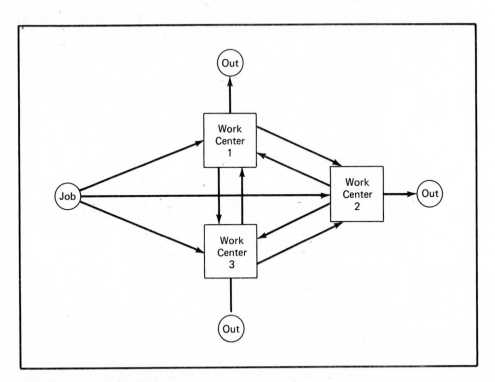

FIGURE 12-16   Job-Shop Schematic

Work-Center Loading

Work-center or machine-loading schemes have received a large amount of attention by researchers in the area of operations management. The job-shop scheduling research was initiated in the late 1950s when it was recognized that a job shop is merely a complex queuing system. Since that time, much has been done to evaluate various scheduling rules under various conditions. (Many of the references at the end of this chapter contain such evaluation. For a concise description of the job-shop scheduling research, see Buffa and Taubert.)[1] More than 100 rules have been tested by researchers operating in different environments, using queuing theory and computer simulation. Some of the queue disciplines or scheduling rules tend to minimize job lateness, some seek to minimize in-process inventory costs, and others seek to maximize the number of jobs that flow through the shop. Some scheduling rules perform better in machine-limited systems (where ample labor is always available), and some perform better in labor-limited systems (where machines are always in ample supply). You should be aware that much has been accomplished in job-shop scheduling research, and that most job shops could benefit from using this research to improve their scheduling function.

To illustrate the use of simple dispatching or machine-loading schemes, let us look at four commonly used scheduling rules in a two-work-center job shop. The dispatching rules to be examined are:

- First come, first served.
- Least slack time. (This rule gives priority to jobs whose due date minus processing time is least.)
- Shortest processing time. (This rule gives priority to jobs with the least remaining processing time.)
- Critical ratio. Sequencing priorities are calculated as follows:

$$\text{Critical ratio} = \frac{\text{Due date} - \text{Today's date}}{\text{Lead time for the balance of the work}}$$

Table 12-16 reflects job-processing characteristics for five jobs to be used in illustrating the four dispatching rules. If we assume that jobs A through E are released to the shop by manufacturing day 210, that there are eight hours available each day, and that work proceeds on all jobs from machine center 1 to machine center 2, Tables 12-17, 12-18, 12-19, and 12-20 summarize the results of using three dispatching rules.

---

[1]E.S. Buffa and William H. Taubert, *Production-Inventory Systems: Planning and Control*, rev. ed. (Homewood, Ill.: Richard D. Irwin), 1972.

Table 12-16   Dispatching-Rules Illustration

JOB	DUE DATE IN MANUFACTURING DAY	TIME REQUIRED IN MACHINE CENTER 1 (IN HOURS)	TIME REQUIRED IN MACHINE CENTER 2 (IN HOURS)
A	213	8	6
B	212	15	5
C	225	40	40
D	214	5	10
E	214	4	9

To illustrate how the machine on and off times are calculated, let's look at job A. Job A arrives on M-day 210 ahead of jobs B, C, D, and E. Therefore, according to the FCFS rule, job A is put on machine center 1 at the beginning of the first hour of M-day 210. Since processing time is eight hours, job A is finished after the eighth hour of M-day 210. Therefore, the next job in line, job B, can begin at the beginning of M-day 211. Since job A is finished at the end of M day 210 on machine center 1, it can begin processing on machine center 2 the following day.

The priority for the least-slack-time heuristic is calculated in the following manner:

$$\text{Priority} = (\text{M-day due date})(8) - \text{Time required for processing}$$

Using the expression above for job A, the priority is:

$$(213)(8) - 14 = 1{,}690$$

Table 12-17   First Come, First Served

JOB	PRIORITY	DATE ON MACHINE CENTER 1	HOUR ON MACHINE CENTER 1	DATE OFF MACHINE CENTER 1	HOUR OFF MACHINE CENTER 1
A	1	210	1	210	8
B	2	211	1	212	7
C	3	212	8	217	7
D	4	217	8	218	4
E	5	218	5	218	8

JOB	DATE ON MACHINE CENTER 2	HOUR ON MACHINE CENTER 2	DATE OFF MACHINE CENTER 2	HOUR OFF MACHINE CENTER 2	HOURS LATE
A	211	1	211	6	0
B	212	8	213	4	4
C	217	8	222	7	0
D	222	8	224	1	73
E	224	2	225	2	82

Table 12-18   Least Slack Time

JOB	PRIORITY	DATE ON MACHINE CENTER 1	TIME ON MACHINE CENTER 1	DATE OFF MACHINE CENTER 1	HOUR OFF MACHINE CENTER 1
A	1,690	211	8	212	7
B	1,676	210	1	211	7
C	1,720	214	1	218	8
D	1,697	212	8	213	4
E	1,699	213	5	213	8

JOB	DATE ON MACHINE CENTER 2	TIME ON MACHINE CENTER 2	DATE OFF MACHINE CENTER 2	HOUR OFF MACHINE CENTER 2	HOURS LATE
A	212	8	213	5	0
B	211	8	212	4	0
C	219	1	223	8	0
D	213	6	214	7	0
E	214	8	215	8	8

For job B, the priority is:

$$(212)(8) - 20 = 1,676$$

Therefore, job B has the highest priority and is loaded on machine center 1 at the beginning of M-day 210, and job A is loaded on machine center 1 as soon as job B is finished.

Table 12-19   Shortest Processing Time

JOB	PRIORITY	DATE ON MACHINE CENTER 1	TIME ON MACHINE CENTER 1	DATE OFF MACHINE CENTER 1	TIME OFF MACHINE CENTER 1
A	2	210	5	211	4
B	4	212	2	213	8
C	5	214	1	219	1
D	3	211	5	212	1
E	1	210	1	210	4

JOB	DATE ON MACHINE CENTER 2	TIME ON MACHINE CENTER 2	DATE OFF MACHINE CENTER 2	TIME OFF MACHINE CENTER 2	HOURS LATE
A	211	6	212	3	0
B	213	6	214	2	10
C	219	2	224	1	0
D	212	4	213	5	0
E	210	5	211	5	0

Table 12-20   Critical Ratio

JOB	PRIORITY	DATE ON MACHINE CENTER 1	HOUR ON MACHINE CENTER 1	DATE OFF MACHINE CENTER 1	HOUR OFF MACHINE CENTER 1
A	1.71	216	8	217	7
B	.80	210	1	211	7
C	1.50	211	8	216	7
D	2.13	217	8	218	4
E	2.46	218	5	218	8

JOB	DATE ON MACHINE CENTER 2	HOUR ON MACHINE CENTER 2	DATE OFF MACHINE CENTER 2	HOUR OFF MACHINE CENTER 2	HOURS LATE
A	221	8	222	5	77
B	211	8	212	4	0
C	216	8	221	7	0
D	222	6	223	7	79
E	223	8	224	8	88

The shortest-processing-time priorities are calculated by simply adding the processing times for each job, with the highest priority (lowest number) being the smallest combined processing time. The combined processing times for jobs A through E are 14, 20, 80, 15, and 13 hours respectively. Therefore, the priorities are 2, 4, 5, 3, and 1 respectively.

The critical ratio for job A is calculated as follows:

$$\frac{(213) \cdot (8) - (210) \cdot (8)}{8 + 6} = 1.71$$

It was necessary to multiply the M-days by eight hours so that both numerator and denominator of the critical ratio would be expressed in consistent units of measurement.

A review of Tables 12-17, 12-18, 12-19, and 12-20 reveals that FCFS and critical ratio rules performed poorly with respect to minimizing job tardiness. You should not generalize from these results. In fact, the critical ratio is one of the most widely used methods for establishing sequencing priorities for operations.

As expected, the least-slack-time heuristic did the best job of minimizing job tardiness. Research has shown that the shortest-processing-time rule typically yields the lowest average flow time, which results in a low in-process inventory cost.

Once an organization has decided on a proper scheduling rule or queue discipline, a decision must be made concerning who is going to actually administer the rule. Should the chore of dictating which job is to be processed next at a particular work center or machine be delegated to the person operating the machine or manning the work center? Or should a foreman determine the sequencing? Or should machine loading be more centralized by letting a computer handle it?

Obviously, the answer to the question of who is going to determine job sequencing depends on many things. First, the size of the organization has much to do with the decision. Second, the nature of the work force would have an influence; if your work force is reliable and mature, there would be more of a tendency to let the individual worker make sequencing decisions. Third, management philosophy concerning job design and job enrichment might dictate that job sequencing be totally decentralized.

Detailed Scheduling

Detailed scheduling of job shops is not widespread in today's manufacturing firm. Only a small percentage of firms produce detailed schedules for each job released to the shop. However, the technical feasibility exists, and the economic feasibility of scheduling each job in the shop will be a reality for most firms in the very near future.

Earlier attempts at detailed job scheduling failed because the technology necessary to do the job just didn't exist. Gantt charts attempted to model a dynamic problem with a basically static model. In other words, as each job is released to manufacturing, production planning dictates the operations to be performed and the sequence of those operations. Variables connected with each job, such as machine time and transportation time, are typically stochastic in nature, whereas Gantt charts assume deterministic times. Therefore, Gantt charts were always out of date, costly to maintain, and generally a total failure at performing the detailed-scheduling function. However, with the advent of computers, the major disadvantage of Gantt charts as a production scheduling tool, lack of timeliness, was eliminated, and detailed scheduling is now technically feasible.

The first attempts at computer-based systems to compute operational shop schedules prescribing starting and finishing times for each job and each operation were batch-oriented systems. Today, most firms using computer-based detailed shop scheduling use real-time systems, which can better cope with the dynamic nature of the job shop. The major advantage of computer-based detailed shop scheduling systems is that the criteria and decision rules used to determine the detailed schedule for a job can be much more complex than simple queue discipline and can use an integrative approach that considers the entire productive system of job shop rather than just a local work center.

Figure 12-17 is a schematic representation or system flow chart of a simplified detailed-scheduling system. As the diagram shows, there are two basic inputs to the detailed-scheduling system. First, work orders are released to the shop from production planning or another automated system such as an MRP system. This work-order file includes all pertinent information regarding processing requirements, such as sequence of operations, setup and processing time required at each operational step, resources required, due dates, and so on. Second, the work-center description file contains pertinent information concerning capacities and capabilities of each functional area in the shop. These data would include hours available each day, maintenance schedules, and other pertinent parameters. These two files, the work-order file and work-center file, provide the raw data that the computer system uses to produce various scheduling reports. The computer system itself can vary through a wide range of complexity. The computer can be programmed to produce schedules based on simple dispatching heuristics like those previously mentioned, or it can be programmed to use more sophisticated techniques, such as simulation, linear programming, and dynamic programming, to derive detailed schedules. These more sophisticated techniques, which typically yield better results, are precluded from a manual system for two reasons. First, the more sophisticated techniques require more timely, accurate, and complete information, and second, the computation can be accomplished only by using a computer.

Figure 12-17 shows four outputs from the computer system. Obviously, these four reports are only representative of those reports being produced by ongoing detailed-scheduling systems. The work-center schedule is a report dictating or suggesting the production schedule to each work center. The work-center load report tells each work center by M day how many hours that work center is scheduled to work. The job schedule reflects the detailed schedule for each job or work order (that is, when the job is to be loaded on a work center and when it is to be finished). The late job report is an example of the exception reporting that is possible with a computerized system. It merely lists jobs that are scheduled to be finished after the due date on the work order.

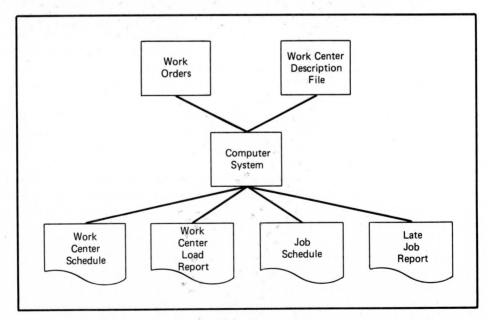

FIGURE 12-17   Simplified Detailed-Scheduling System Flow Chart

The issue of whether the system depicted in Figure 12-17 is a real-time or batch system must be decided by the individual firm. It is generally conceded that because of the rapidly changing nature of the work-order file, this system is a strong candidate for real-time processing. If a firm does not have real-time capability or isn't able to pay the extra cost of a real-time system, detailed-scheduling systems can be batch-oriented if the system is updated frequently to incorporate changes such as changes in processing times, new work orders, and changes in shop capacities.

SCHEDULING OF SERVICES

Although the services sector is an increasingly significant sector in the American economy, the majority of work done in rationalizing the scheduling function pertains to project scheduling and production scheduling. Today, most organizations that provide services schedule them without the aid of any quantitative technique. More often than not, doctors schedule patients, universities schedule classes, and cities schedule buses without any sophisticated techniques to aid in the process.

There is a trend, however, toward improving the scheduling function in the service sector by using queuing models and computer simulation. Examples of this type of research appear often in the literature. The following examples are representative of the kinds of research on the scheduling of services that are currently being reported. (See the references at the end of this chapter for other successful approaches to scheduling services.)

Practically every community in the United States has problems of scheduling school buses. In the majority of school districts, this scheduling is done manually, without the aid of any quantitative techniques. A school district in Tennessee, however, saved approximately a quarter of a million dollars per year by scheduling the school buses using quantitative techniques. The number of buses was reduced from 13 to 9, and the total distance traveled by the buses was nearly cut in half.[2] A similar application involved the scheduling of commercial garbage trucks. By changing the schedule of pickups, a firm was able to reduce the distance traveled by the trucks by approximately 25 percent, and the payback period for the cost of the study was less than two weeks.[3]

Simulation was used by Kwak, Kuzdrall, and Schmitz to investigate scheduling policies for surgical patients in a St. Louis hospital. It was found that just by changing the scheduling strategy, significant manpower reductions could be made, or alternatively, more surgeries could be undertaken using existing facilities and human resources.[4]

---

[2] P. Krolak, "Empirical and Theoretical Bounds on Generalized Vehicle Scheduling," paper presented at the ORSA/TIMS meeting, Las Vegas, Nevada, November 1975.

[3] Thomas M. Cook and Robert A. Russell, "A Simulation and Statistical Analysis of Stochastic Vehicle Routing with Timing Constraints" *Decision Sciences*, 9, no. 4 (October 1978), 673–87.

[4] N.K. Kwak, P.J. Kuzdrall, and Homer H. Schmitz, "The GPSS Simulation of Scheduling Policies for Surgical Patients," *Management Science*, 22, no. 9 (May 1976), 982–89.

Integer programming is being used to assign (schedule) aircraft to a commercial schedule and simulation is being used to evaluate the effect of proposed airline schedule changes on market share. In addition, most large and progressive airlines use models to schedule aircraft maintenance and flight crews.

SUMMARY

In this chapter, we have tried to emphasize the importance of the scheduling function in all organizations. We have seen that the scheduling task can be classified into one of three different categories—project scheduling, production scheduling, and the scheduling of services. To help the project manager schedule and control a project of considerable size, several widely used techniques such as PERT and CPM are available. By now, you should understand the basic steps involved in applying PERT/CPM to scheduling a large project.

As with project scheduling, much work has been done in the area of scheduling the productive process. This work can be categorized as either working-center loading or computer-based detailed scheduling. It should be noted that as the cost of computing continues to decrease, the economic feasibility of timely detailed scheduling will increase, and more and more firms will turn to the computer to schedule their productive systems.

The scheduling of services has received the least amount of attention from researchers and practitioners; the most room for improvement is in this area. It is highly likely that scheduling in the service sector will enjoy increased attention as that sector of the economy continues to grow in absolute and relative terms.

_____ SOLVED PROBLEMS _____

Problem Statement

Consider the project information in the table below.

TASK	IMMEDIATE PREDECESSOR	TIME ESTIMATE (DAYS)
A	—	5
B	—	4
C	A	6
D	A	3
E	B	3
F	B	6
G	E	2
H	F	5
I	C, D	8
J	G, H	5

1. Draw the PERT network for the project.

2. Use the PERT algorithm to find the critical path.

3. What is the minimum project-completion time?

Solution

1. The PERT chart is:

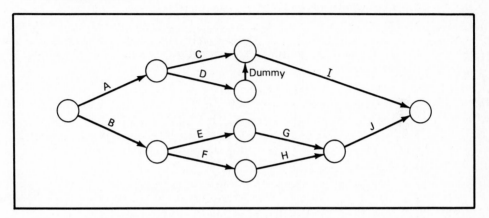

2. To find the critical path, it is necessary to compute the slack time for each task. This is done below using the PERT algorithm.

TASK	TIME	ES	EF	LS	LF	SLACK TIME
A	5	0	5	1	6	1
B	4	0	4	0	4	0
C	6	5	11	6	12	1
D	3	5	8	9	12	4
E	3	4	7	10	13	6
F	6	4	10	4	10	0
G	2	7	9	13	15	6
H	5	10	15	10	15	0
I	8	11	19	12	20	1
J	5	15	20	15	20	0

The critical path consists of those activities that have zero slack time. Therefore, the critical path is B-F-H-J.

3. The minimum project-completion time is the length of the critical path. The length of the critical path is the latest finish time for activity J, which is 20 days.

Problem Statement

Consider the project information in the table below.

1. Draw the PERT network for this project.
2. Compute the mean and variance in time for each activity.
3. Find the expected critical path.
4. What is the expected length of the critical path?
5. Assuming normality and path independence, what is the probability of completing the project in less than 22 days?

TASK	IMMEDIATE PREDECESSOR	TIME ESTIMATES a_i	m_i	b_i
A	—	4	5	7
B	A	2	3	5
C	A	5	7	11
D	B	2	2	2
E	B	3	4	6
F	D	3	5	6
G	C	3	3	3
H	C	2	2	2
I	G, H	3	4	6
J	E, F	4	6	7

Solution

1. The PERT network is:

2. The mean time for task A is computed as follows:

$$\bar{t}_A = \frac{4 + 4(5) + 7}{6}$$

$$= \frac{31}{6} = 5.167$$

The standard deviation for task A is computed:

$$\sigma_A = \frac{7 - 4}{6} = \frac{3}{6} = \frac{1}{2}$$

Therefore, the variance for task A is:

$$\sigma_A^2 = \left(\frac{1}{2}\right)^2 = \frac{1}{4} = .25$$

The mean time and variances for the remaining tasks are shown below.

TASK	MEAN TIME	VARIANCE
A	5.167	.25
B	3.167	.25
C	7.333	1.00
D	2.000	0.00
E	4.167	.25
F	4.833	.25
G	3.000	0.00
H	2.000	0.00
I	4.167	.25
J	5.833	.25

3. The expected critical path is composed of all those activities whose slack time is zero. Slack times are computed below.

TASK	EXPECTED TIME	ES	EF	LS	LF	SLACK TIME
A	5.167	0.000	5.167	0.000	5.167	0.000
B	3.167	5.167	8.333	5.167	8.333	0.000
C	7.333	5.167	12.500	6.500	13.833	1.333
D	2.000	8.333	10.333	8.333	10.333	0.000
E	4.167	8.333	12.500	11.000	15.167	2.667
F	4.833	10.333	15.167	10.333	15.167	0.000
G	3.000	12.500	15.500	13.833	16.833	1.333
H	2.000	12.500	14.500	14.833	16.833	2.333
I	4.167	15.500	19.667	16.833	21.000	1.333
J	5.833	15.167	21.000	15.167	21.000	0.000

Therefore, the expected critical path is A-B-D-F-J.

4. The expected length of the critical path is the latest finish time of the ending activity (activity J), which is 21 days.

5. The probability of completing the project in 22 days is the probability of completing all paths within 22 days. If we make the necessary assumptions, the probability of completing path A-B-D-F-J in 22 days is found as follows:

$$Z = \frac{X - \mu}{\sigma}$$

$$= \frac{22 - 21}{\sqrt{.25 + .25 + 0 + .25 + .25}}$$

$$= \frac{1}{1} = 1$$

$$P(\text{Path A-B-D-F-J} \leq 22) = P(Z \leq 1) = .8413$$

Similarly, P(Path A-B-E-J) is computed:

$$Z = \frac{22 - 18.334}{\sqrt{.25 + .25 + .25 + .25}} = 3.667$$

$$P(\text{Path A-B-E-J} \leq 22) \cong 1.0$$

P(A-C-G-I $\leq$ 22) is:

$$Z = \frac{22 - 19.667}{\sqrt{.25 + 1.0 + 0 + .25}}$$

$$= 1.905$$

$$P(\text{A-C-G-I} \leq 22) = P(Z \leq 1.905)$$

$$= .9713$$

P(A-C-H-I $\leq$ 22) is:

$$Z = \frac{22 - 18.667}{\sqrt{.25 + 1.0 + 0 + .25}}$$

$$= 2.72$$

$$P(\text{A-C-H-I} \leq 22) = P(Z \leq 2.72)$$

$$= .9967$$

The probability of all paths being complete in 22 days, assuming independence of paths and normality, is the product of the individual probabilities, or:

$$P(\text{Project time} \leq 22) = (.8413)(1)(.9713)(.9967)$$

$$= .814$$

_____ **REVIEW QUESTIONS** _____

1. Classify scheduling problems into three categories.
2. Distinguish between project scheduling and production scheduling.
3. Distinguish between Gantt charts and PERT.
4. What are the basic elements in a work package?
5. What is the basic purpose of using WBS?
6. On what type of projects would you use deterministic PERT rather than stochastic PERT?
7. What can PERT do for the project manager?
8. Define *critical path*.
9. How is slack time computed?
10. Why is the beta distribution used for PERT times?
11. Why compute σ_i?
12. What are the assumptions made in order to make probabilistic statements about project-completion schedules?
13. Distinguish between PERT and CPM.
14. What does PERT/Cost do for the project manager?
15. Distinguish between critical-ratio, least-slack-time, and shortest-processing-time dispatching rules.
16. How is the scheduling function accomplished in an assembly-line type of production system?
17. List four objectives of production scheduling.
18. Distinguish between a flow shop and a job shop.
19. Distinguish between the two major methodologies used by job shops to schedule production.
20. Why is detailed job scheduling not widespread in today's job shop?
21. Why did Gantt charts fail as a job-shop scheduling tool?
22. Why is detailed job scheduling likely to become more common in the future?

_____ **PROBLEMS** _____

1. Prepare the WBS for a project with which you are familiar. In addition to identifying each task and subtask, prepare the necessary work packages.

2. Draw Gantt charts for the various task levels of the WBS prepared for problem 1.

3. Consider the information in the following table.

TASK	IMMEDIATE PREDECESSOR	ESTIMATED TIME (DAYS)
A	—	4
B	—	3
C	A	7
D	B	5
E	B, C	6
F	E	4

a. Draw the PERT network diagram for this project.
b. Use the PERT algorithm for finding the critical path.
c. What is the minimum project-completion time?
d. Would the critical path change if F were to take 5 days rather than 4? Explain.

4. Consider the project information in the table below.

TASK	IMMEDIATE PREDECESSOR	ESTIMATED TIME (DAYS)
A	—	5
B	—	6
C	A	3
D	A	5
E	B	4
F	C, D	2
G	E	1
H	G	4
I	F, G	3
J	H	1
K	I, J	7

a. Draw the PERT network diagram for the project.
b. Use the PERT algorithm for finding the critical path.
c. What is the minimum project-completion time?

5. Consider the project information in the table below.

TASK	IMMEDIATE PREDECESSOR	a_i	m_i	b_i
A	—	2	4	7
B	A	3	5	8
C	B	1	3	6
D	B	2	3	7
E	C	2	5	9
F	D	1	2	4
G	E	2	2	4

Note: columns a_i, m_i, b_i are under the heading TIME ESTIMATE IN DAYS.

a. Draw the PERT network diagram for this project.
b. Compute the mean and variance in time for each activity.
c. Find the critical path by inspection.
d. What is the expected length of the expected critical path?
e. Assuming the time required to complete a path is normally distributed, what is the probability of completing the critical path in 15 days or less?
f. Again assuming normality and path independence, what is the probability of completing the entire project in 15 days or less?
g. If you wanted to be at least 95% sure of completing the project on time, what schedule would you quote?

6. Consider the information in the table below.

TASK	IMMEDIATE PREDECESSOR	TIME ESTIMATES a_i	m_i	b_i
A	—	3	4	7
B	—	4	9	12
C	A	5	11	15
D	A	3	5	8
E	B	5	7	12
F	D, C	3	4	7
G	D, C	2	3	4
H	E	7	11	18
I	E	7	10	14
J	F	4	6	9
K	G	5	7	9
L	H, I	2	3	5
M	J, K	7	8	9
N	L	1	3	4
O	M, N	14	17	23

a. Draw the PERT network diagram for this project.
b. Compute the mean and variance in time for each activity.
c. Find the critical path using the PERT algorithm.
d. What is the expected length of the expected critical path?
e. Assuming the time required to complete a path is normally distributed, what is the probability of completing the critical path in 50 days or less?
f. Again assuming normality and path independence, what is the probability of completing the entire project in 50 days or less?
g. If you wanted to be at least 95% sure of completing the project on time, what schedule would you quote?

7. State University is planning a holiday basketball tournament and has decided to use PERT to schedule the project. The following tasks and time estimates

have been identified:

TASK	DESCRIPTION	IMMEDIATE PREDECESSORS	a_i	m_i	b_i
A	Team selection	—	1	3	5
B	Mail out invitations & receive acceptances	A	4	5	10
C	Arrange accommodations	—	8	10	15
D	Plan promotional strategy	B	2	3	5
E	Print tickets	B	4	5	8
F	Sell tickets	E	15	15	15
G	Complete arrangements	B, C	7	8	10
H	Develop practice schedules	C	2	3	4
I	Practice sessions	H	2	2	2
J	Conduct tournament	F, I	3	3	3

a. Draw the PERT diagram and identify the expected critical path.
b. If the tournament is to be held starting December 27, when should team selection begin if we want to be 98% confident that the tournament will be held as scheduled?

8. Consider the project in problem 3. Assume crash times and crash costs as set forth in the table below.

ACTIVITY	NORMAL TIME ESTIMATE	CRASH TIME ESTIMATE	INCREMENTAL COST OF CRASH TIME
A	4	3.0	100
B	3	2.5	100
C	7	5.0	150
D	5	3.0	400
E	6	6.0	—
F	4	4.0	—

a. What is the shortest time in which the project can be completed?
b. What is the total incremental cost of part *a* above?
c. What is the minimum incremental cost of completing the project in 19 days?

9. Consider the project in problem 4, assuming the crash times set forth in the following table.

ACTIVITY	NORMAL TIME ESTIMATE	CRASH TIME ESTIMATE	INCREMENTAL COST OF CRASH TIME
A	5	4.0	100
B	6	4.0	400
C	3	2.5	100
D	5	5.0	—
E	4	3.0	100
F	2	1.5	150
G	1	1.0	—
H	4	3.0	175
I	3	2.0	125
J	1	1.0	—
K	7	4.0	500

a. What is the shortest time in which the project can be completed?
b. What is the total incremental cost of part *a* above?
c. What is the incremental cost of completing the project in 18 days?

10. Apply PERT to the project described in your WBS for problem 1.

11. Consider the project in problem 4. The budgeted costs for the various activities are shown in the table. Develop a total cost budget based on both an earliest start time and a latest start time schedule.

ACTIVITY	BUDGETED COST
A	$70,000
B	85,000
C	27,000
D	43,000
E	45,000
F	50,000
G	15,000
H	25,000
I	32,000
J	48,000
K	79,000

12. Again using the project in problem 4, prepare a cost report that reflects overruns and underruns at the end of 6 weeks. Progress on the project and actual costs incurred through 6 weeks are shown in the table.

ACTIVITY	COST INCURRED	PERCENTAGE COMPLETE
A	$75,000	100
B	77,000	90
C	20,000	100
D	10,000	5
E	0	0
F	0	0
G	0	0
H	0	0
I	0	0
J	0	0
K	0	0

13. Consider the project in problem 6. After 6 weeks of working on the project, top management has requested a detailed cost report that would reflect total cost overruns and cost overruns by various tasks or work packages. To comply, the data shown in the table have been collected. You are to prepare a report that reflects the total cost overruns or underruns and the individual work package overruns and underruns.

ACTIVITY	COST INCURRED TO DATE	BUDGET	PERCENTAGE COMPLETE
A	$ 22,000	$ 25,000	100
B	48,000	45,000	90
C	75,000	100,000	100
D	20,000	20,000	95
E	14,000	20,000	50
F	94,000	85,000	100
G	47,000	40,000	100
H	125,000	120,000	100
I	109,000	100,000	100
J	97,000	100,000	100
K	87,000	100,000	70
L	0	25,000	0
M	0	75,000	0
N	0	73,000	0
O	0	197,000	0

14. Describe what you think would be reasonable criteria in evaluating dispatching rules or the effectiveness of a detailed-scheduling system.

15. Develop two dispatching rules and evaluate them using the following produc-

tive system and work orders:

JOB	DUE DATE M DAY	TIME REQUIRED ON MACHINE CENTER 1	TIME REQUIRED ON MACHINE CENTER 2
A	173	15	7
B	180	20	10
C	175	10	5
D	177	8	9
E	171	12	6
F	182	4	4

Assume all jobs arrive on M day 165 and the factory works 8-hour days. In answering this problem, first list any additional assumptions you are making and then define your dispatching rule explicitly. Finally, specifically define the measures of effectiveness you think are appropriate when comparing the two rules. *Note:* If your are unable to think of alternative dispatching rules yourself, consult the references for Buffa and Taubert, or Conway and Maxwell, for ideas.

16. Compare your results in problem 15 with results you would get in using FCFS, least-slack-time, critical-ratio, and shortest-processing-time rules illustrated in this chapter.

17. Using critical ratio and least slack time, establish the scheduling priorities of the following four jobs. Assume that today is day number 50.

JOB	DUE DATE	REMAINING WORK TIME IN DAYS
W	51	1.0
X	49	.5
Y	52	1.0
Z	50	3.0

18. Using critical ratio and least slack time, prepare two dispatch lists for the following five jobs. That is, list the jobs according to their scheduling priorities. Assume that today is March 1 (8:00 A.M.) and each workday is eight hours.

JOB NO.	DUE DATE	OPERATION TIME REMAINING IN HOURS
1253	3-2	7
1729	3-1	8
5623	3-3	28
2011	2-28	2
4192	3-3	15

————————————— **REFERENCES** —————————————

ABERNATHY, W.J., N. BALOFF, J.C. HERSHEY, and S. WANDEL, "A Three-Stage Manpower Planning and Scheduling Model—A Service Sector Example," *Operations Research*, 22, no. 3 (May–June 1973), 693–711.

ALLEN, M., "The Efficient Utilization of Labor under Conditions of Fluctuating Demand," Chap. 16 in *Industrial Scheduling*, eds. J.F. Muth and G.L. Thompson, Englewood Cliffs, N.J.: Prentice-Hall, 1963.

BAKER, C.T., and P.B. DZIELINSKI, "Simulation of a Simplified Job Shop," *Management Science*, 6, no. 3 (April 1960), 311–23.

BAKER, K.L., "Scheduling Full-Time and Part-Time Staff to Meet Cyclical Requirements," *Operational Research Quarterly*, vol. 25 (March 1974).

BIERMAN, HAROLD, JR., CHARLES P. BONINI, and WARREN H. HAUSMAN, *Quantitative Analysis for Business Decisions*, 4th ed. Homewood, Ill.: Richard D. Irwin, 1973.

BOWMAN, E.H., "The Schedule Sequence Problem," *Operations Research*, 7 (September 1959), 621–24.

BUFFA, ELWOOD S., *Operations Management: The Management of Productive Systems*. New York: John Wiley, 1976.

————, and WILLIAM H. TAUBERT, *Production-Inventory System: Planning and Control*, rev. ed. Homewood, Ill.: Richard D. Irwin, 1972.

CARROLL, D.C., "Heuristic Sequencing of Single and Multiple Component Jobs," unpublished Ph.D. dissertation, Sloan School of Management, M.I.T., 1965.

CHASE, RICHARD B., and NICHOLAS J. AQUILANO, *Production and Operations Management*. Homewood, Ill.: Richard D. Irwin, 1973.

CONWAY, R.W.., and W.L. MAXWELL, "Network Scheduling by the Shortest Operation Discipline," *Operations Research*, 10, no. 1 (1962), 51–73.

COOK, THOMAS M., "Schedule-Constrained Job Scheduling in a Multiprogrammed Computer," *Proceedings of the 1974 Winter Simulation Conference*, 2, 675–87.

COOK, THOMAS M., and ROBERT A. RUSSELL, "A Simulation and Statistical Analysis of Stochastic Vehicle Routing with Timing Constraints," *Decision Sciences*, 9, no. 4, October 1978, 673–687.

COOK, THOMAS M., and ROBERT H. JENNINGS, "Estimating a Project's Completion Time Distribution Using Intelligent Simulation Methods," *Journal of the Operational Research Society*, 50, no. 12, December 1979, 1103–09.

ELMAGHRABY, S.E., and R.T. COLE, "On the Control of Production in Small Job Shops," *Journal of Industrial Engineering*, 14, no. 4 (July–August 1963), 186–96.

EMERY, J., "An Approach to Job Shop Scheduling Using a Large-Scale Computer,"

Industrial Management Review, 3 (Fall 1961), 78–96.

EVARTS, HARRY F., *Introduction to PERT*. Boston: Allyn & Bacon, 1964.

GERE, W.S., JR., "Heuristics in Job Shop Scheduling," *Management Science*, 13, no. 3 (November 1966), 167–90.

HARRIS, R.D., "An Empirical Investigation of a Job Shop as a Network of Queueing Systems," unpublished Ph.D. dissertation, UCLA, 1965.

HEALY, W.C., "Shift Scheduling Made Easy," *Factory*, 117, no. 10 (October 1969).

HELLER, N.B., J.T. MCEWEN, and W.W. STENZEL, *Police Manpower Scheduling*. St. Louis: Board of Police Commissioners, St. Louis Police Department, 1972.

HOLSTEIN, W.K., and W.L. BERRY, "Work Flow Structure: An Analysis for Planning and Control," *Management Science*, 16, no. 6 (February 1970), 324–36.

JACKSON, J.R., "Job Shop-Like Queueing Systems," *Management Science*, 10, no. 1 (October 1963), 131–42.

————, "Networks of Waiting Lines," *Operations Research*, 5 (August 1957), 518–21.

LeGRANDE, E., "The Development of a Factory Simulation System Using Actual Operating Data," *Management Technology*, 3, no. 1 (May 1963). Reprinted as Chap. 9 in *Readings in Production and Operations Management*, ed. E.S. Buffa. New York: John Wiley, 1966.

LEVIN, RICHARD I., and CHARLES A. KIRKPATRICK, *Planning and Control with PERT/CPM*. New York: McGraw-Hill, 1966.

MANN, A.S., "On the Job Shop Scheduling Problem," *Operations Research*, 8 (October 1960), 219–23.

MONROE, G., "Scheduling Manpower for Service Operations," *Industrial Engineering*, 2, no. 28 (August 1970), 10–17.

MURDICK, ROBERT G., and JOEL E. ROSS, *Information Systems for Modern Management*. Englewood Cliffs, N.J.: Prentice-Hall, 1975.

NANOT, Y.R., "An Experimental Investigation and Comparative Evaluation of Priority Disciplines in Job Shop-Like Queueing Networks," unpublished Ph.D. dissertation, UCLA, 1963. Also Management Sciences Research Project, Research Report No. 87, UCLA, 1963.

NELSON, R.T., "Labor and Machine Limited Production Systems," *Management Science*, 13, no. 9 (May 1967), 648–71.

————, "A Simulation Study of Labor Efficiency and Centralized Labor Assignment Control in a Production System Model," *Management Science*, 17, no. 2 (October 1970), 97–106.

REITER, S., "A System for Managing Job-Shop Production," *Journal of Business*, 39, no. 3 (July 1966), 371–93.

ROTHSTEIN, M., "Hospital Manpower Staff Scheduling by Mathematical Programming," *Health Services Research*, 8 (Spring 1973), 60–66.

SMITH, LARRY A., and PETER MAHLER, "Comparing Commercially Available CPM/PERT Computer Programs," *Industrial Engineering*, April 1978, 37–39.

WARNER, D.M., and J. PRAWDA, "A Mathematical Programming Model for Scheduling Nursing Personnel in a Hospital," *Management Science*, 19, no. 4 (1972), 411–22.

WIEST, J., and F.K. LEVY, *Management Guide to PERT/CPM*, 2nd ed. Englewood Cliffs, N.J.: Prentice-Hall, 1977.

13

QUALITY ASSURANCE

Introduction
Determinants of product / service quality
The quality assurance system
Statistical quality control
   process control
   acceptance sampling
Quality control in service industries
Summary

INTRODUCTION

It is difficult to pick up the newspaper today without reading about Japanese competition and superior Japanese quality. It is true that the Japanese have caught up to and passed the United States in the area of quality in many industrial products. Robert E. Cole states "There is no question that the Japanese have set new world standards" in the area of quality control.

For example, *Consumer Reports* contend that Toyotas, Datsuns, Hondas, Mazdas, and Subarus need repairs far less frequently than American-made automobiles. American TV sets are reported to require repairs 50 percent more often than Japanese sets. The list could go on.

The encouraging news for American industry is that in many industries where Japan enjoys a quality advantage, the quality gap is beginning to narrow. Hewlett-Packard ran tests on semiconductors in March 1980 and found the failure rate was five to six times that of the Japanese. The results apparently shocked Hewlett-Packard into action. Similar tests were run eight months later and the Japanese advantage had been cut to three to one. In 1975, American TVs failed 300 percent more often and in 1980 only 50 percent more often. The trend has been the same in the auto industry with major auto manufacturers putting an increased emphasis on product quality.

Two major reasons American companies have been able to narrow the gap are:

- Recognizing the importance of producing a quality product, management has increased its emphasis on quality assurance.
- Recognizing the Japanese lead, management of many companies are willing to emulate the Japanese and use some of their best ideas, such as quality circles.

In this chapter, we will discuss the determinants of product quality, the elements of a quality assurance system, and some of the more widely used statistical quality control techniques.

DETERMINANTS OF PRODUCT / SERVICE QUALITY

There are four major determinants of the quality of a product or service:

- Policy decisions
- Engineering/Design
- Manufacturing/Operational process
- Field support

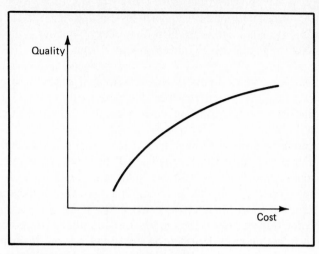

FIGURE 13-1   Quality Cost Relationship

Policy decisions concerning product quality must be made by management. In making these decisions, management must consider several factors. The primary factor to be considered is the market, or target market, for which the product is aimed. Obviously, Volkswagen and Mercedes auto makers are aiming at totally different markets, and hence, quality policy decisions affecting the final products are different. The target market and the price customers are willing to pay determine to some extent the money that can be spent to enhance the product's quality. There is generally a strong relationship between quality level and product price. Typically, as the level of quality increases, so must the price increase. As shown in Figure 13-1, the level of product quality typically reaches a point where additional cost buys little or no additional increase in quality.

In addition to considering the target market and the price customers are willing to pay, management must be conscious of the organization's image. It might not be in the best interests of the firm to produce a product of a quality inconsistent with the firm's image, even though a market exists. Another factor affecting quality policy decisions is management's duty to act in a socially responsible manner. The administration of a ghetto hospital, for example, cannot afford to run a hospital with quality control to match its target customers' ability to pay. A minimum level of quality is dictated by society.

Once policy decisions concerning quality have been made, it is the designer's job to translate those decisions into the design of the product or service—for instance, what materials should be used in making the product, and what tolerances are acceptable. These decisions have an important impact on the variable cost of the product as well as the overall level of its quality. In a nonmanufacturing environment, these same kinds of decisions must be made. For example, after a patient is admitted to the hospital, a doctor must decide on the type of care, the length of stay, and often what tests are to be run on the patient. Again, these decisions affect both quality of health care and cost of health care.

A third determinant of quality level is the input made during the operational process. In a manufacturing firm, a product's quality is largely a function of the manufacturing process. Engineering can design a truly high-quality product, but unless manufacturing builds it as it was designed, the resultant product can be of poor quality. The same dependent relationship exists in service organizations. The owners of a fine restaurant may have decided to serve the best food in town regardless of cost, and they may have hired the best chef in the city to carry out their policy decision, but if the people actually preparing and serving the food don't perform up to these high standards, the product's quality will suffer.

Sometimes a product's quality will be determined by the support it receives from the supplier after it has been sold. It is well known in the computer industry that IBM doesn't have the best computer hardware for the money. However, IBM has captured more than 60 percent of the computer hardware market, and one reason for this success is the quality level of the firm's customer support function. Therefore, although its finished product may not be of higher quality than others, many organizations select IBM because its overall quality, including field service, is perceived to be superior.

THE QUALITY ASSURANCE SYSTEM

As depicted in Figure 13-2, the quality system in any organization combines people with information for the purpose of ensuring that the quality of the organization's product conforms to the quality desired by those making policy decisions about it.

The people working for the quality assurance department of an organization are responsible for ensuring that product quality conforms to the quality decisions of

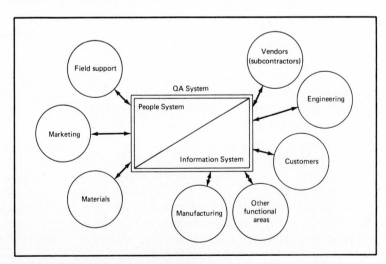

FIGURE 13-2 Quality Assurance System

management. These people must interact with virtually all functional departments, as well as organizations outside the firm, such as vendors and customers. In addition to the human subsystem, there exists an information subsystem that provides the communication link between the quality assurance department and other organizations. As with any information system, the quality assurance system has a formal and an informal component.

In describing a quality assurance system, we are going to define a typical organizational structure of a large manufacturing firm and discuss the informational needs of any quality control system.

Because a product's quality should be the concern of virtually every employee in an organization, it makes good sense that the quality function be placed high in the organizational hierarchy. Therefore, many large firms place it on the same level as marketing, finance, engineering, and manufacturing. Many manufacturing firms, however, leave quality control reporting to the manufacturing vice-president. This can be injurious to overall quality, if manufacturing personnel are allowed to dictate to quality inspectors. Many small firms don't even have a formal quality control department. In most of these firms, quality control is the responsibility of the worker or foreman. Obviously, where the quality function fits in an organization depends on the nature and size of the firm.

The nature and size of the firm also determine the scope of the information system that is part of any quality control system. As the size of a firm increases, the need for a very formal and comprehensive computer-based information system increases. Also, the scope of the information system is highly correlated with the importance of quality control to the success of the firm. Therefore, a quality control information system can fall anywhere in a continuum between a very informal, word-of-mouth system and a real-time computer-based system.

In order to give you more insight into what a quality control system is in today's large manufacturing firm, let us describe the system of a large hypothetical aerospace firm. Remember that the quality control system is composed of basically two parts—people and information. Therefore, this description will consist of a description of the organizational structure of the people in the system and the structure of the information system contained in the total quality control system.

The organizational structure of Aerospace Inc. is shown in Figure 13-3. Notice that the vice-president of quality assurance reports directly to the president of Aerospace Inc., and consequently manufacturing or engineering is not asked to police its own operation. This does not mean, however, that the functional areas such as manufacturing have no responsibility for quality. It merely means that the job of ensuring quality conformity falls on the quality assurance department. The job of producing quality products still rests with each of the functional areas.

There are five major divisions of responsibility within the quality assurance department at Aerospace Inc., as depicted in Figure 13-3. First, a group is charged with ensuring quality and reliability in design. Typically, the Department of Defense invites proposals on aerospace contracts. These invitations define in considerable detail the specifications to which the product must conform. Specifications concern-

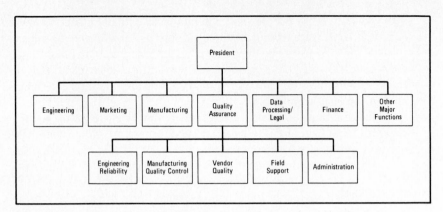

FIGURE 13-3   **Organizational Structure of a Hypothetical Aerospace Company**

ing mean time between failure (MTBF), weight, strength of components, and so on, are all included. The aerospace firm responds to a request for proposal (RFP) with a design proposal and a cost proposal. The design proposal defines how the firm is going to meet the specifications spelled out in the RFP. It is the job of engineering reliability to ensure that the product that is designed conforms to the specifications of the design proposal. In other words, if the technical proposal says that the MTBF of the forward-looking radar would be greater than 50 flight hours, it is the job of engineering reliability to ensure that the forward-looking radar has an MTBF in excess of 50 flight hours.

Manufacturing quality control must perform several functions. First, it must plan the "in-shop" quality control system. This includes participating in decisions concerning the choice of machines and processes, the design of tools, the choice of inspection criteria, and the planning of process quality control.

Two recent developments that have impacted manufacturing quality in recent years are robotics and the development of quality circles. As discussed in Chapter 5, robotics are revolutionizing manufacturing in several key industries. Part of the reason Japan has held a quality lead in autos and electronics is their willingness to invest huge amounts of capital in robotics. Good quality requires good tools. American industry is going to have to make the necessary investment to remain competitive. The five-year, $75-billion retooling of the U.S. auto industry is evidence that we can catch up.

Another important development has been the creation of quality circles. A quality circle is a voluntary group of approximately 10 workers who have a shared responsibility. They meet together on company time for about one hour per week to discuss, analyze, and propose solutions to quality problems. The quality circle movement came to the U.S. during the early seventies after having become a way of life in Japanese industry. Although quality circles are not as common in the U.S. (approximately 25 percent of all hourly Japanese employees are voluntary members of a quality circle), many have been instituted and the literature testifies to their effectiveness and suggests that the number of companies developing quality circles is on a steep growth curve.

In addition to designing the in-shop quality assurance system, manufacturing quality control must be responsible for inspection and testing of parts in the manufacturing process and the investigation of why parts are being rejected and what the appropriate corrective action is. The design and acquisition of test equipment is also a function of manufacturing quality control.

Vendor quality assurance is an important functional area in any aerospace firm. Typically, outside vendors furnish at least half the components of an end item such as an airplane. Consequently, Aerospace Inc. cannot possibly build a high-quality, reliable product if subcontractors are supplying low-quality components. The vendor quality department is charged with the responsibility of ensuring the quality of vendor parts and components. It does this in several ways. Quality control engineers from the vendor quality department visit major subcontractors to see that proper quality assurance systems are being used. Parts and components are inspected and tested upon receipt from a vendor, and if they are rejected for poor quality, it is the responsibility of the vendor quality department to ensure that the vendor takes appropriate corrective action.

The field support unit has responsibility for ensuring quality performance after the product has been sold or delivered to the customer. At Aerospace Inc., the field support unit includes a field engineering staff to investigate problems occurring after delivery. Data collection concerning performance and field failures is performed by the customer, the Department of Defense. In many industries, this type of data collection is the responsibility of a field support unit within the quality assurance department.

The final organizational unit in the quality assurance department is administration. This unit is responsible for several staff functions. Preparing and controlling the departmental budget is one. Another is the responsibility for planning and evaluating the entire quality program at Aerospace Inc. Two technical functions are also performed: statistical services such as sampling plans and the establishment of control charts and operating characteristic curves (statistical quality control is described later in this chapter), and the design and maintenance of the formal computer-based quality assurance information system.

This system of data collection and information dissemination is crucial to the success of the quality assurance program, so we shall describe in some detail the computer-based information system at Aerospace Inc. The quality assurance information system is composed of five essential modules (see Figure 13-4) that produce more than 100 different reports using more than 70 computer programs. Reports produced by this system vary in level of detail, depending on their use. Some reports are distributed to the vice-presidential level and some to individual machine operators.

The in-house rejection module consists of rejection reports written up by inspectors in the manufacturing area for each part or component that is rejected. A copy of each report, which reflects the corrective action that was taken, is forwarded

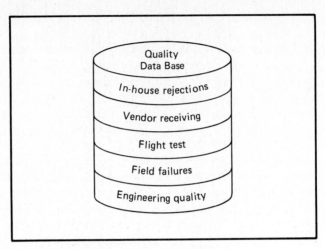

FIGURE 13-4   Quality Assurance Data Base

to data processing, where it is entered into the quality data base. Monthly, more than 30 reports are produced from this module and distributed to various interested departments in Aerospace Inc.

In the receiving area, as shipments are received, they are inspected using various sampling plans. A source document is created at that time that is used as input to the vendor receiving module. Reports are produced monthly that reflect vendor component quality as well as rating the suppliers of various components.

Each time an airplane rolls off the assembly line, it is towed to flight operations for a series of flight tests. After each flight test, the test pilot fills out a source document, called a pilot's crab sheet, reflecting areas of dissatisfaction with the airplane. The data contained on these crab sheets are input to the flight test module, and reports are generated periodically for distribution within Aerospace Inc.

Every time a part or component of an airplane fails in the field after it has been delivered to either the U.S. Navy or the U.S. Air Force, a record is created describing the failure. These records, made worldwide, are mailed monthly to a central processing center and loaded on magnetic tape. These tapes are sent to major DOD contractors. Once received by Aerospace Inc., the field failure tapes are used to update the field failure module of the quality assurance data base, and from it, more than 30 reports are generated to be used internally to improve the reliability of the airplanes produced by the company.

Finally, engineering has its own data-base module that aids in the control of engineering design quality. Designs are reviewed by quality control engineers, design errors are input to the data base, and necessary corrective action is taken.

The quality assurance system that has been described is not meant to be a model to be followed by every firm. It is only one company's approach to the job of ensuring quality conformity. The organizational structure of people and information in a quality assurance system is a function of the type and size of the organization.

STATISTICAL QUALITY CONTROL

There are very few environments in which a firm can afford to inspect the entire population of goods and services. With certain products, in which quality is a matter of life and death, the high cost of total inspection can be rationalized. Most firms, however, rely for inspection purposes on statistical sampling procedures, in which inferences are made about the population based on sample statistics. As seen in Figure 13-5, statistical quality control can be divided into two broad categories, *process control* and *acceptance sampling.*

The objective of process control is to determine when the productive process needs to be investigated in order to determine if corrective action must be taken. For example, a machine that produces valve housings may produce them satisfactorily for a number of weeks and then start violating engineering specifications. This change from satisfactory performance to unsatisfactory performance may be caused by any of a number of factors, such as a change in machine operators or variation in machine adjustments. It is important for management to know as soon as possible that the process, or a portion of the process, is out of control, so that necessary corrective action can be taken. Therefore, process control necessitates a continuous monitoring of each process in the system through sampling. Samples are taken, and attributes and measurements are compared to an acceptable range of variation. If the sample indicates that the process is out of control, the process is usually interrupted so that the problem causing the excessive variance can be found and corrected.

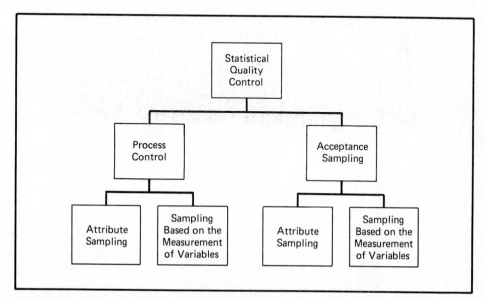

FIGURE 13-5 Classification Scheme for Statistical Quality

The other broad category of quality control, acceptance sampling, occurs after a "lot" of goods has been produced or received. A sample of the lot is taken to determine the overall quality of the total population. If the sample has more unacceptable components than specified in the sampling plan, either the shipment is rejected or a more complete inspection is necessitated.

Both process control and acceptance sampling can be broken into two subcategories, depending on what determines the quality of the product. The quality of a product is determined either by some qualitative attribute that dictates an accept or reject decision, or by the measurement of some variable. An example of attribute sampling might be the case of an electrical switch, where the attribute being examined is whether or not the switch works. Another example might be whether the color of the product is acceptable or not. Examples of sampling based on the measurement of some variable include measuring the diameter of a piston head or the harmonic distortion curve of a stereo amplifier.

Process Control

The purpose of process control is to determine as soon as possible when the process is out of control. The variations in a given characteristic of a manufacturing product can be attributed to one of two classes of causes, assignable and random. *Assignable variations* are those that can be attributed to specific causes. If the quality of a product decreases significantly, the cause may be a degradation in human expertise or motivation, or a deterioration in the machine side of the man–machine system—perhaps the machine is out of adjustment or needs maintenance. Another possible assignable cause may lie in the raw material going into the production process. Whatever the cause, it must be identified and the necessary corrective action taken. The object is to keep the transformation process, as described in Figure 13-6, under control. Given a steady-state man–machine system and uniform raw-material quality, *random variations* in the finished product will still occur. The magnitude of these variations depends on the design of the man-machine system and the specifications placed on the raw material. If the random fluctuations in the end product are too large, then changes must be made in the transformation process or raw material to tighten the range of those fluctuations.

For example, let us look at a hypothetical transformation process.

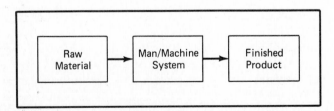

FIGURE 13-6 Transformation Process

The raw material of this process is square steel stock. The man–machine system consists of a lathe and an operator that transform the square raw stock into a cam shaft, as pictured in Figure 13-7. The cam shaft has four critical dimensions, as shown in the figure. If random fluctuations in dimension A, B, or C are too large, it may be necessary to buy a more expensive lathe or hire a better operator. If, however, the random fluctuation in dimension D is too large, the source of raw material might have to be changed.

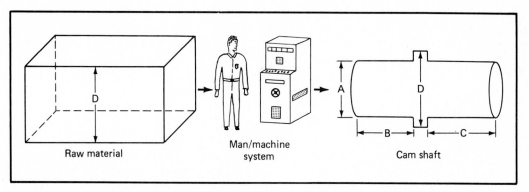

FIGURE 13-7   Example of Transformation Process

Once the random fluctuations are within a tolerable range, it is the function of the quality assurance department to ensure that the transformation process stays under control and to identify problems as soon as they arise. In order to ensure timely notice when the process goes out of control, continuous sampling or surveillance is necessary. With each sample, a test of significance must be made to decide whether or not to reject the hypothesis that variations in the population are due to random causes (that is, the process is still in control). For the continuous monitoring of a process and to perform the numerous tests of hypotheses, control charts are frequently used. Two types of control charts are described in this chapter, one for attribute testing and the other for variable testing.

Control Chart for $\bar{x}$.   Let us return to the transformation process described in Figure 13-7 above. Let us assume that the variable to be measured is the diameter of the cam shaft. Every two hours, a sample of four cam shafts is taken so that quality personnel can see whether the process is still under control. Table 13-1 reflects two days of sampling. During this two-day period, special precautions were taken to ensure that all variations in shaft diameter were due to random causes and not to assignable causes. The first step in developing a control chart for the mean cam-shaft diameter is to estimate the parameters of the population probability distribution.

Table 13-1   Measurement of Cam-Shaft Diameters

SAMPLE NO.	SAMPLE POINTS					
	1	*2*	*3*	*4*	$\bar{x}$	s^2
1	2.15	3.46	3.40	2.32	2.83	.36
2	3.20	2.47	3.53	3.27	3.12	.15
3	2.72	2.80	3.18	2.68	2.84	.04
4	2.30	2.87	3.73	2.52	2.86	.29
5	3.16	2.73	3.18	1.89	2.74	.27
6	3.07	2.50	4.11	3.96	3.41	.44
7	2.42	2.41	3.22	3.50	2.89	.23
8	2.20	2.76	3.28	2.36	2.65	.17
9	3.47	3.47	3.16	3.01	3.28	.04
10	2.41	2.53	2.81	3.99	2.94	.39
11	3.27	2.55	2.30	2.44	2.64	.14
12	2.90	3.22	3.28	3.61	3.25	.06
13	3.26	3.32	3.50	2.32	3.10	.21
14	2.29	3.72	3.28	2.50	3.22	.20
15	2.91	3.40	3.07	4.17	3.39	.23
16	3.56	2.92	2.39	3.43	3.07	.21
17	2.67	2.94	2.86	2.99	2.86	.02
18	3.14	3.22	2.69	3.16	3.05	.04
19	2.50	2.59	2.19	3.32	2.65	.17
20	2.84	3.01	2.76	3.47	3.02	.08
21	3.35	3.50	2.39	2.17	2.85	.33
22	3.35	2.68	2.18	3.12	2.83	.20
23	3.20	2.80	2.81	3.07	2.97	.03
24	3.38	3.14	2.54	3.39	3.11	.12
					71.57	4.42

The mean of the universe can be estimated directly by using the mean of the aggregate sample, $\bar{x}$.

$$\bar{\bar{x}} = \frac{\sum\limits_{i=1}^{24} \bar{x}_i}{24} = \frac{71.57}{24}$$

$$= 2.98$$

In our example, the standard deviation of the population can be estimated using the following function:

$$\hat{\sigma} = \sqrt{\frac{\sum\limits_{i=1}^{n} s_i^2}{N} \frac{N}{n-1}}$$

where $\hat{\sigma}$ = unbiased estimator of the standard deviation

n = sample size for each sample

N = number of samples

$$s_i^2 = \text{variance for sample } i = \frac{\sum\limits_{j=1}^{n} (x_j - \bar{x})^2}{n}$$

In our example, we obtain the following result:

$$\hat{\sigma} = \sqrt{\frac{4.42}{24} \frac{4}{4-1}}$$

$$= \sqrt{.24}$$

$$= .49$$

The next step is to compute the standard error of the mean, using the following function:

$$\hat{\sigma}_{\hat{x}} = \frac{\hat{\sigma}}{\sqrt{n}}$$

In our example, we obtain the following result:

$$\hat{\sigma}_{\hat{x}} = \frac{.49}{\sqrt{4}} = .245$$

Once the standard error of the mean has been computed, it is a fairly simple procedure to define the confidence interval, which is the essence of the control chart. It is common if not almost universal to use a confidence interval of three standard errors; using a range of $\pm 3\sigma_{\bar{x}}$ almost ensures that the process is out of control if a sample mean falls outside the confidence interval. In other words, the probability of rejecting the hypothesis that the process is in control incorrectly is equal to .0027. This type of error, you might remember, is a Type I error. The reason for using a confidence interval that yields such a low probability of a Type I error is that management typically wants to avoid unnecessary interruption of the production process if in fact the process is not out of control. In other words, the wider the confidence interval, the lower the probability of false alarms. Obviously, a small probability of a Type I error means that the probability of a Type II error is large. That is, although the probability of a "false alarm" is small, there is a high probability of accepting the false hypothesis that the process is in control. If it is more important to identify an out-of-control condition early than to avoid unnecessary disruption, a narrower confidence interval could be chosen. This condition might exist when the cost of the part or component being measured is high in relation to the cost of stopping the operation for investigation into the cause of the variation.

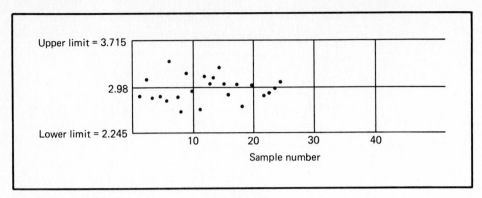

FIGURE 13-8   Control Chart for $\bar{x}$ of Cam-Shaft Diameter

The control chart for the cam-shaft diameter is shown in Figure 13-8. The upper limit is calculated as follows:

$$UL = \bar{\bar{x}} + 3\sigma_{\bar{x}} = 2.98 + (3)(.245) = 3.715$$

The lower limit is:

$$LL = \bar{\bar{x}} - 3\sigma_{\bar{x}} = 2.98 - (3)(.245) = 2.245$$

Control Chart for Fraction Defective.   As mentioned earlier in this chapter, controlling the transformation process statistically may mean measuring a critical variable or testing an attribute in order to make an accept or reject decision. If an item is rejected or accepted on the basis of some test, than a control chart for fraction defective can be used in the same manner as a control chart for $\bar{x}$. Because the statistic being measured is p (fraction defective), this type of control chart is often called a p chart. Because of the nature of the statistic, small sample sizes, which are common with control charts for $\bar{x}$, are not acceptable for p charts. Sample sizes of 100 or larger are common. A p chart can be used to test the hypothesis as to whether the process remains in control. The basic steps in the construction of a p chart are the same as those in the construction of any control chart. The difference is the sampling distribution and how the standard error is calculated.

To illustrate the use of a p chart, let us consider the following example. Metal tennis rackets are welded in several places. Daily, a sample of 100 rackets is taken off the assembly line for the purpose of X-raying the welds. The data contained in Table 13-2 were collected for the purpose of defining a p chart for the tennis-racket welds.

The first step in constructing the p chart is to estimate the population fraction defective. This can be done using the sample fraction defective. Therefore:

$$\hat{p} = \frac{\sum\limits_{i=1}^{n} x_i}{N}$$

Table 13-2   Fraction Defective for Tennis-Racket Welds

SAMPLE NO.	SAMPLE SIZE	NUMBER DEFECTIVE	FRACTION DEFECTIVE
1	100	5	.05
2	100	4	.04
3	100	3	.03
4	100	4	.04
5	100	5	.05
6	100	6	.06
7	100	5	.05
8	100	4	.04
9	100	3	.03
10	100	7	.07
11	100	6	.06
12	100	5	.05
13	100	6	.06
14	100	4	.04
15	100	3	.03
16	100	4	.04
17	100	5	.05
18	100	3	.03
19	100	6	.06
20	100	3	.03
21	100	7	.07
22	100	12	.12
		$\overline{110}$	

where

$\hat{p}$ = estimate of population fraction defective

x_i = number of defective parts in sample i

n = number of samples

N = total sample size

$$\hat{p} = \frac{110}{2,200}$$

$$= .05$$

In order to find the confidence interval for the sample fraction defective, we can use the following function to calculate the standard error:

$$\hat{\sigma}_p = \sqrt{\frac{pq}{n}}$$

where

$\hat{\sigma}_p$ = standard error of p

p = population fraction defective

$q = 1 - p$

n = sample size

For our example:

$$\hat{\sigma}_p = \sqrt{\frac{(.05)(.95)}{100}}$$

$$= .02179$$

Therefore, the range of the confidence interval at the 3σ level is $.05 \pm 3(.02179)$, or $0 < p < .11537$. According to this confidence interval, the last sample shown in Table 13-2 indicates that the welding process is out of control. In other words, that hypothesis that the fraction defective in the population is .05 must be rejected for the 22nd sample. The line must be stopped, the cause of the defective welds found, and the appropriate corrective action taken. Since sample 22 is not representative of the "in-control" process, the p chart should be constructed using only samples 1 through 21 to estimate p. Therefore:

$$\hat{p} = \frac{98}{2,100}$$

$$= .04667$$

and

$$\hat{\sigma}_p = \sqrt{\frac{(.04667)(.95333)}{100}}$$

$$= .02109$$

The range of the new confidence interval at the 3σ level is $.04667 \pm 3(.02109)$, or $0 < p < .10995$. Figure 13-9 shows the original and revised limits for the p chart for the welding process.

Acceptance Sampling

Acceptance sampling is done to determine whether to accept or reject a "lot" of goods that has been produced. The most common use of acceptance sampling is in the receiving department of a firm. As orders are received from various suppliers, a decision must be made of whether or not to accept each shipment. This decision can be made by inspecting each item received or by inspecting a sample. Typically, when a shipment is received, a sample is taken, the appropriate inspection or testing procedure is performed, and a decision based on the sample is made. This decision, as depicted in Figure 13-10, can be to accept the shipment, reject the shipment, or take another sample because the first did not yield enough information to make an accept/reject decision. If the sample results dictate rejection, a firm can elect to return the entire shipment to the supplier or to inspect or test each component and send back only defective units. The latter course of action is common when the shipment is critically needed by the receiving firm.

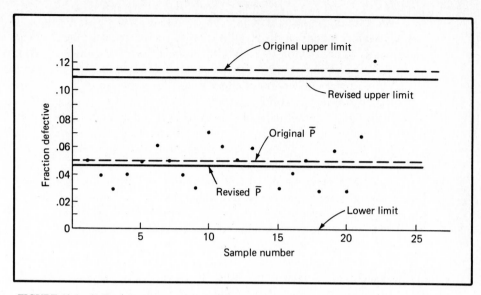

FIGURE 13-9 *P* **Chart for Tennis-Racket Welds**

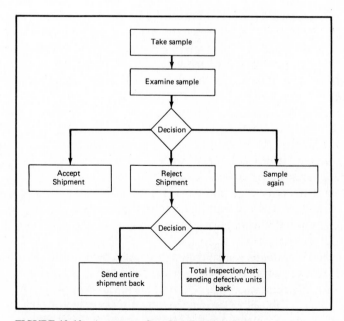

FIGURE 13-10 **Acceptance Sampling Decision Process**

Acceptance sampling schemes can be classified as single, multiple, or sequential. With single sampling plans, a decision to accept or reject the shipment is made on the basis of one sample. With multiple plans, additional samples are taken if an accept/reject decision cannot be made based on a single sample. In other words, if a sample gives a clear indication of either good quality or bad, it is not necessary to go to the expense of testing another sample. For example, if a supplier and its customer have agreed to 2 percent defective items as acceptable, and a sample of 100 items from a shipment is tested and none is defective, additional sampling may not be necessary. If ten out of 100 were found defective, a decision to reject could be made without additional sample information.

Sequential sampling plans call for testing or inspecting smaller samples and accumulating results until a decision can be made. As soon as a decision can be made, sampling is terminated. Sequential sampling plans are generally more powerful, in that the accept/reject decision can be based on a smaller total sample size.

Single-Sample Acceptance Plan.   To give you an idea of some of the issues and techniques in acceptance sampling, let us consider a single-sample acceptance plan for a large data-processing firm. Universal Computing Inc. (UCI) subcontracts a considerable amount of data transcription to smaller service-bureau companies. It has been generally agreed upon that 1 percent error in the keyed data is acceptable. Universal Computing Inc. wants to devise a single-sample acceptance plan that will fairly discriminate between "good" and "bad" batches of data. As with all tests of hypotheses, there is danger of making two different kinds of errors based on sample results. First, UCI could reject a batch of data that in fact is of acceptable (errors < 1%) quality. This type of error is known as a Type I error. The probability of a Type I error is usually denoted by the Greek letter α. In a sense, α defines the producer's risk. The second type, a Type II error, occurs when a bad hypothesis is accepted or not rejected. In UCI's case, this would mean that a batch of data containing in excess of 1 percent errors was accepted as a good shipment. The probability of a Type II error is referred to as the consumer's risk and denoted by the Greek letter β.

Ideally, it would be nice if α and β (the probability of a Type I error and a Type II error) could both equal zero. This ideal situation is not possible if UCI does not want to verify each data card upon receipt. Let's look at a proposed sampling plan for UCI. Upon receipt of a batch of data, let a random sample of 100 records be selected and checked for errors. If more than two errors are found, reject the entire batch (in other words, the acceptance number is 2). Because each card verification could be considered a Bernoulli trial, the appropriate distribution for describing the probability of x errors in n trials, given a percent defective, is the binomial distribution, which for large n can be approximated using the Poisson distribution. Table 13-3 relates the actual percentage of error to the probability of accepting the shipment, using a sample size of 100 and an acceptance number of 2. The information in Table 13-3 is graphed in Figure 13-11. The curve in the figure is known as an operating characteristic curve, or simply an OC curve.

Table 13-3   Probability of Accepting Shipments with Various
Percentages of Errors

N = 100		ACCEPTANCE NUMBER = 2
p (TRUE PROPORTION OF ERRORS)	λ = np	PROBABILITY OF ACCEPTING THE SHIPMENT GIVEN p
.01	1	.920
.02	2	.677
.03	3	.423
.04	4	.238
.05	5	.125
.06	6	.062
.07	7	.030
.08	8	.014
.09	9	.006
.10	10	.003

*λ = the parameter of the Poisson distribution.

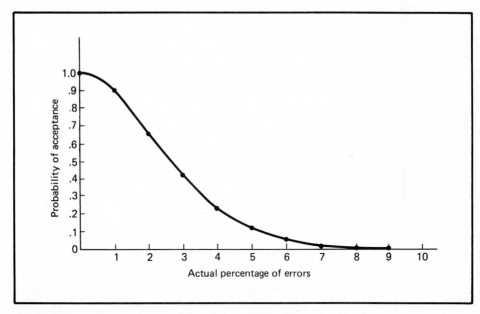

FIGURE 13-11   OC Curve for a Sample of 100 and an Acceptance Number of 2

Looking at Table 13-3 or Figure 13-11, it is apparent that the probability of making a Type I error is $1 - .920$, or .08. If the actual percentage of errors is 2 precent, the probability of accepting the batch is 67.7 percent, which may be much too high. Consequently, it is necessary to balance the probability of making Type I and Type II errors. In other words, the consumer's risk must be balanced against the producer's risk, and if an imbalance exists in an acceptance sampling plan, either the acceptance number or the sample size, or both, can be changed.

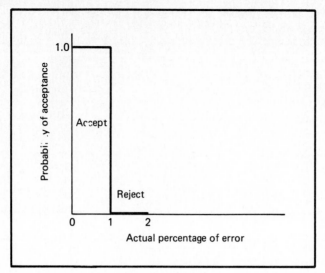

**FIGURE 13-12   OC Curve
with Exhaustive Verification**

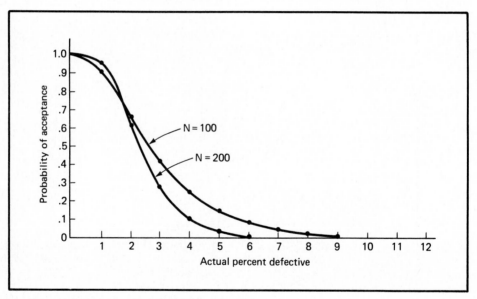

FIGURE 13-13   Effect of Sample Size on an OC Curve

Figure 13-12 shows an OC curve for UCI if all cards in the batch of 10,000 were verified. Notice that α and β are both equal to 0. Figure 13-13 shows the effect on the OC curve if the sample size were doubled. Comparing Table 13-4 to Table 13-3, you can see that the probability of rejecting an acceptable shipment is .08 $(1 - .92)$ for $n = 100$, and .053 for $n = 200$. In addition, the β error or consumer's risk decreased with an increase in sample size. If the actual percentage error was 2 percent, the probability of accepting the shipment was decreased from .677 to .629

Table 13-4   Probability of Accepting Shipments with Various Percentage Errors and a Sample Size of 200 and Acceptance Number of 4

p	$\lambda = np$	PROBABILITY OF ACCEPTING SHIPMENT GIVEN p
.01	2	.9470
.02	4	.6290
.03	6	.2850
.04	8	.1000
.05	10	.0290
.06	12	.0080
.07	14	.0020
.08	16	.0004

Table 13-5   Probability of Accepting Shipments with Various Percentages of Errors

SAMPLE SIZE = 100		ACCEPTANCE NUMBER = 3
p	$\lambda = np$	PROBABILITY OF ACCEPTING THE SHIPMENT GIVEN p
.01	1	.981
.02	2	.857
.03	3	.647
.04	4	.433
.05	5	.265
.06	6	.151
.07	7	.082
.08	8	.042
.09	9	.021
.10	10	.010
.11	11	.005
.12	12	.002

with a doubling of sample size. Figure 13-14 shows the changes in the OC curve if the acceptance number were changed.

As reflected in Tables 13-5 and 13-6, increasing the acceptance number reduces the probability of rejecting a good shipment (producer's risk) but at the same time increases the probability of accepting a bad shipment (consumer's risk). Consequently, it should be clear that the only way of reducing both producer's risk and consumer's risk simultaneously is to increase the sample size. As with all inspection and test procedures, an increase in sample size usually results in an increase in the cost of quality control. A decision about the cost/benefit of increasing the sample size is a subjective decision, but one that must be made.

Table 13-6   Probability of Accepting Shipments with Various
Percentages of Errors

SAMPLE SIZE = 100	ACCEPTANCE NUMBER = 4	
p	*λ = np*	PROBABILITY OF ACCEPTING THE SHIPMENT GIVEN *p*
.01	1	.996
.02	2	.947
.03	3	.815
.04	4	.629
.05	5	.440
.06	6	.285
.07	7	.173
.08	8	.100
.09	9	.055
.10	10	.029
.11	11	.015
.12	12	.008

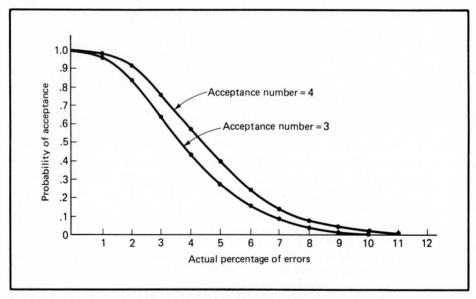

FIGURE 13-14   The Effect of the Acceptance Number on an OC Curve

QUALITY CONTROL IN SERVICE INDUSTRIES

Up until this point, you may have thought that quality control is a subject relevant primarily to manufacturing firms. This is simply not the case. Quality assurance is equally important in the service sector of our economy. The difference between quality assurance programs in manufacturing and nonmanufacturing organizations is not one of necessity but typically one of structure. Quality assurance in a hospital is no less important than in a large manufacturing company, and it is for this reason that considerable human and informational resources are committed to the assurance of quality health care. In order to gain an appreciation for quality control in nonmanufacturing environments, let us describe a quality assurance system of a typical hospital.

In the early 1970s, two key court cases, *Darling v. Charlston* and *Gonzales v. Mercy General Hospital*, resulted in something of a quality assurance revolution in hospitals. Essentially, the decisions in these two cases held that a hospital's board of trustees is legally responsible for ensuring quality health care to patients. Today's hospital is required to have an established and formal mechanism or system to ensure quality health care. In order to give you an understanding of quality assurance programs in hospitals, let us describe in general terms the quality system in a 600-bed midwestern hospital. Figure 13-15 shows a representative organizational structure for the quality assurance system in today's hospital. As seen in Figure 13-15, responsibility for quality health care ultimately rests with the hospital's board of trustees. The board relies on the medical staff through an extensive committee structure to ensure quality health care. Our representative hospital has a standing quality care committee staffed by doctors reporting to the medical executive committee, which in turn reports to the hospital's medical director, who is responsible to the board of trustees. The many quality care standing subcommittees composed of doctors range from a committee that investigates each surgical mortality to one that seeks to ensure that proper medical records are kept on each patient. In addition to these standing committees, each medical section—such as pediatrics, internal medicine, and general surgery—has a special committee dedicated to ensuring quality care in its specialty. These section committees establish criteria for quality care for various types of ailments. For example, if a patient is admitted to the coronary care unit with a suspected heart attack, certain tests should be given and procedures followed. The necessary tests and procedures are determined by the appropriate section QA committee. Periodically, in order to ensure that a coronary patient receives proper care, the medical charts of a sample number of coronary patients are pulled and compared to the criteria for quality care established by the section committee. Those cases that do not meet the criteria are reviewed on an individual basis by the section quality care committee. If adequate explanations exist for individual variances from established criteria, it is the responsibility of the committee to ascertain those explanations. If the variance is due to either physician negligence or other assignable causes, the necessary corrective action is taken by the committee.

SUMMARY

As has been seen during the recent decade, a product's quality is a major determinant of its competitiveness and thus its profitability. Consequently, management of many firms are becoming increasingly quality conscious, willing to invest in the tools

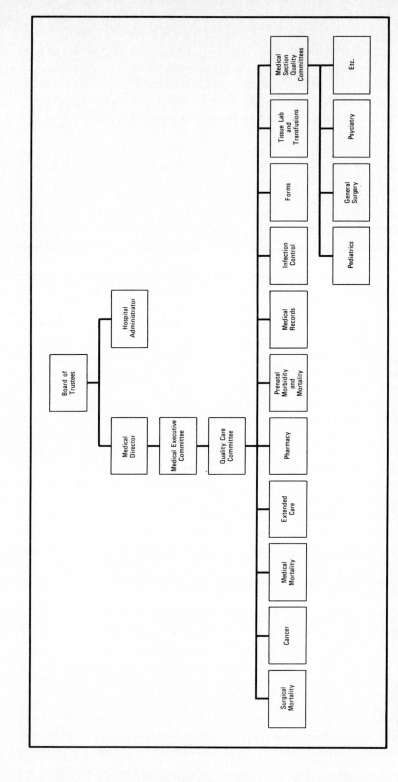

FIGURE 13-15 Organizational Structure for Quality Assurance in Today's Hospital

necessary, and make the necessary organizational changes to promote better quality. In this chapter we have identified the major determinants of product quality and have described the quality assurance system. We have discussed the emerging role of quality circles and the traditional role of statistical quality control.

SOLVED PROBLEMS

Problem Statement

Construct a control chart for the thickness of sheets of plywood for ± 3 standard errors based on the data below. All samples contain five sheets of plywood.

SAMPLE NO.	THICKNESS IN CENTIMETERS				
1	2.111	2.101	2.115	2.015	2.213
2	2.011	2.059	2.143	2.114	2.221
3	2.125	2.215	2.114	2.141	2.321
4	2.055	2.043	2.100	2.097	2.189
5	2.210	2.120	2.012	2.099	2.177
6	2.178	2.213	2.014	2.019	2.191
7	2.189	2.187	2.217	2.143	2.154
8	2.212	2.125	2.200	2.099	2.117
9	2.194	2.087	2.094	2.049	2.196
10	2.287	2.097	2.189	2.205	2.111

Solution

The first step is to calculate an estimate of the mean. This can be done by calculating each sample's mean and then finding the mean of these sample means.

SAMPLE NO.	$\bar{x}_i$	SAMPLE NO.	$\bar{x}_i$
1	2.111	6	2.123
2	2.109	7	2.178
3	2.183	8	2.151
4	2.097	9	2.124
5	2.124	10	2.178

$$\bar{\bar{x}} = \frac{\sum_{i=1}^{10} \bar{x}_i}{10} = 2.138$$

The next step is to estimate the standard error, using the following formula:

$$\hat{\sigma}_{\bar{x}} = \frac{\hat{\sigma}}{\sqrt{n}}$$

In order to solve for $\hat{\sigma}_{\bar{x}}$, it is necessary to calculate an estimate of the population standard deviation ($\hat{\sigma}$). This is done using:

$$\hat{\sigma} = \sqrt{\frac{\sum_{i=1}^{N} s^2}{N} \frac{n}{n-1}}$$

where $\qquad s^2 = \dfrac{\sum_{i=1}^{N} (x_i - \bar{x})^2}{n}$

N = number of samples
n = sample size

SAMPLE NO.	s^2	SAMPLE NO.	s^2
1	.0039	6	.0077
2	.0052	7	.0007
3	.0060	8	.0021
4	.0026	9	.0036
5	.0047	10	.0048

$$\hat{\sigma} = \sqrt{\frac{.0413}{10} \frac{5}{4}}$$

$$= .07185$$

$$\hat{\sigma}_{\bar{x}} = \frac{.07185}{\sqrt{5}}$$

$$= .03213$$

$$\text{UL} = 2.138 + 3(.03213)$$

$$= 2.234 \text{ centimeters}$$

$$\text{LL} = 2.042 \text{ centimeters}$$

Control Chart for $\bar{x}$

2.234

2.138

2.042

Problem Statement

Switches manufactured by a small manufacturing company are tested in batches of 50. Historically, 3 percent of the switches have failed to pass the test. Construct a control chart for testing the switches.

Solution

Since p historically has been .03, it is possible to use p as the estimate of the true population proportion defective. Therefore, the standard error of estimate is:

$$\sigma_p = \sqrt{\frac{pq}{n}}$$

$$= \sqrt{\frac{(.03)(.97)}{50}}$$

$$= .024$$

If we use a range of three standard errors, then the upper limit of the p chart is:

$$UL = .03 + (3)(.024)$$

$$= .03 + .072 = .102$$

The lower limit would normally be calculated as follows:

$$LL = .03 - (3)(.024)$$

$$= -.042$$

Since negative values have no meaning, the lower limit would default to zero.

REVIEW QUESTIONS

1. List four major determinants of product quality.
2. How does the law of diminishing returns relate to quality assurance?

3. What are the two major components of a quality assurance system?
4. Discuss where the quality department should be placed organizationally.
5. What are the two major determinants of the type of quality information system needed in an organization?
6. What is a quality circle?
7. What is the expected impact that the increasing use of robotics will have on product quality?
8. Why is there a need for statistical inference in quality control?
9. What are the two broad categories of statistical quality control?
10. What is the object of process control?
11. Distinguish between attribute sampling and sampling based on measurement of variables.
12. Define what is meant by acceptance sampling.
13. What are the two classes of causes of product variation?
14. Give three examples of assignable causes for product variation.
15. Briefly explain the purpose of a control chart.
16. Distinguish between a Type I error and a Type II error.
17. Why is a $\pm 3\sigma$ range standard for control charts?
18. What is the difference between a p chart and an $\bar{x}$ control chart?
19. What is the basic purpose of acceptance sampling?
20. What quality options does a company have when receiving a shipment from a vendor?
21. Distinguish between sequential sampling and a single-sample acceptance plan.
22. What is the purpose of an OC curve?
23. Distinguish between consumer's risk and producer's risk.
24. Define *acceptance number*.
25. How can α and β be reduced simultaneously?
26. Why is the Poisson distribution used in constructing OC curves?

PROBLEMS

1. Visit one of the types of organizations listed below and investigate its quality assurance system. Specifically, define the organization structure of the human resources committed to quality control and also define the information system used by people in the quality assurance system.

   Police department
   Street-maintenance department
   Fire department
   Hospital

Manufacturing firm
Airline
Zoo
Supermarket
Restaurant
Utility company
Computer firm
Other

2. Construct a control chart for a machine that produces bearings that have a mean diameter of 1.5 centimeters and a standard deviation of .005 centimeters. Construct a control chart for this machine. The table below shows the diameters of samples taken every four hours. Determine when the machine is out of adjustment at the 3σ level.

Bearing Table

SAMPLE NO.	BEARING 1	BEARING 2	BEARING 3	BEARING 4
1	1.501	1.505	1.502	1.501
2	1.493	1.495	1.501	1.502
3	1.505	1.502	1.503	1.501
4	1.493	1.497	1.503	1.502
5	1.505	1.499	1.505	1.500
6	1.515	1.511	1.514	1.520

3. As tennis balls roll off the assembly line, samples of three are taken to test inside air pressure. Construct a control chart for the mean pounds per square inch (psi) for tennis balls, using the following data:

SAMPLE NO.	PSI OF TENNIS BALL 1	PSI OF TENNIS BALL 2	PSI OF TENNIS BALL 3
1	26.1	27.2	24.4
2	25.4	27.1	26.1
3	25.5	25.5	27.0
4	26.1	26.7	25.8
5	25.9	25.6	26.1
6	25.1	24.9	25.0
7	26.0	25.5	25.3
8	25.4	24.8	25.1
9	27.5	28.5	29.0
10	26.0	25.5	24.3

4. In an attempt to control the process of a medical laboratory, the following sampling plan has been instituted for a particular urine test in which human life is not involved. The results of tests are classified as either positive or negative, and it is known that the national average of positive results is 10%. Five samples of 100 tests each have yielded the following results:

SAMPLE NO.	SAMPLE SIZE	FRACTION POSITIVE
1	100	.11
2	100	.09
3	100	.12
4	100	.13
5	100	.07

Construct a *p* chart and determine if the urine test process is under control or not.

5. Emergency calls coming to a central ambulance dispatcher result in some unnecessary ambulance responses; in other words, sometimes ambulances are dispatched when not needed. It is the dispatcher's responsibility to ascertain the presence of a real need for the emergency care. Each day, 50 emergency dispatches are used to determine whether or not the dispatcher is doing an adequate job in screening emergency calls. Use the following data to construct a *p* chart for the process described above.

SAMPLE NO.	SAMPLE SIZE	NUMBER OF FALSE ALARMS
1	50	5
2	50	6
3	50	7
4	50	4
5	50	7
6	50	6
7	50	5
8	50	3
9	50	2
10	50	3

6. At the beginning of each soccer season, a local sports store orders 5,000 soccer balls. For the balls to be tested, they must be inflated, tested, and then deflated.
   a. Construct an OC curve for a sample size of 50 and an acceptance number of 1.

b. Using $\alpha \le .10$ as a guide, examine several different sample sizes and acceptance numbers in an effort to reduce the probability of accepting a shipment with 5% defective. Define a good shipment as 2% defective. Discuss your results.

7. A professor has been teaching for a long time, and over the years, he would like to know when his grading standards deteriorate. Using the last ten semesters as a control group, he calculates the following means and variances based on samples of 15 students:

SEMESTER NO.	$\bar{x}_i$	s_i^2
1	77.1	11.1
2	75.2	9.5
3	73.1	11.9
4	75.7	10.7
5	74.2	12.0
6	79.1	14.0
7	77.1	21.6
8	74.3	10.8
9	78.1	17.2
10	72.9	15.3

Construct a control chart at ± 2 standard errors for the professor.

8. The professor in problem 7 prides himself on the proportion of students he sends on to graduate school. For the last ten years, the proportion has been 60%. Construct a *p* chart that will alert the professor when his process is deviating from the historical 60%. Assume a sample size of 50 students.

REFERENCES

BESTERFIELD, DALE H., *Quality Control*. Englewood Cliffs, N.J.: Prentice-Hall, 1979.

CHASE, RICHARD B., and NICHOLAS J. AQUILANO, *Production and Operations Management: A Life Cycle Approach*, 3rd ed. Homewood, Ill.: Richard D. Irwin, 1981.

COWDEN, D.J., *Statistical Methods in Quality Control*. Englewood Cliffs, N.J.: Prentice-Hall, 1957.

DUNCAN, ACHESON J., *Quality Control and Industrial Statistics*, 3rd ed. Homewood, Ill.: Richard D. Irwin, 1965.

FETTER, ROBERT B., *The Quality Control System*. Homewood, Ill.: Richard D. Irwin, 1967.

HAGEN, J.T., *A Management Role for Quality Control*. New York: American Management Association, 1968.

JURAN, JOSEPH M., *Quality Control Handbook*, 2nd ed. New York: McGraw-Hill, 1967.

_____, and F.M. GRYNA, JR., *Quality Planning and Analysis*. New York: McGraw-Hill, 1962.

KIRKPATRICK, ELWOOD G., *Quality Control for Managers and Engineers*. New York: John Wiley, 1970.

SMITH, C.S., *Quality and Reliability: An Integrated Approach*. New York: Pitman, 1969.

STOCKTON, JOHN R., and CHARLES T. CLARK, *Introduction to Business & Economic Statistics*, 4th ed. Cincinnati, Ohio: South-Western Publishing Co., 1971.

CASES

Case 1
BUSHRANGER SUPPLY PTY. LTD.*

      Bushranger Supply is a tube and pipe manufacturer in Perth (Western Australia). Bushranger was organized ten years after Australia achieved Commonwealth status in 1901 and began operations as a job shop steel fabricator. Subsequent to World War II Bushranger began supplying pipe and tubing as a broker to the new oil refinery complex at Kwinana in Western Australia. Pipe and tubing was purchased from various foreign sources in mill quantities and then sorted, recut, remarked, and rebundled into job size quantities for specific customers. This proved to be an extremely lucrative business and as a natural extension, the management of Bushranger decided in the early 1950's to install their own redraw capabilities.

      Redrawing in the tube and pipe industry consists of buying what are termed "hollows" and, after certain chemical treatments, reducing the O.D. (outside diameter) and wall thickness of the hollows to a different size on machines called drawbenches.

---

*This case was prepared by Thomas M. Box of the University of Tulsa, Tulsa, Oklahoma. Reprinted with permission.

The redraw business in the late 50's and early 60's became the principal business of Bushranger and in the early 1970's extensive capital expenditures were made to provide for an expanded product range and enlarged product capabilities in redraw. The present plant (in December 1982) consists of the following operations:

1. *Pickling*—At this station, redraw hollows purchased from NKQ (a large Japanese trading company representing an integrated steel mill in Japan) are chemically treated with a caustic solution to remove oil and grease and then pickled (in sulphuric acid) followed by rinsing in a phosphoric acid bath and a stearate (soap) bath to provide lubricity for the drawing operations.

2. *Cold Drawing*—At this station the lubricated tube hollows are "stretched" on a cold draw bench which reduces the O.D. and wall to a specific final size.

3. *Annealing*—The cold drawing process results in dramatic increases in the hardness, tensile and yield strengths of the tube hollows as a result of "cold working" and these properties in many cases exceed the values allowable by the end customers. It is necessary to anneal the drawn hollows in a large roller hearth furnace in a reducing atmosphere under tightly controlled temperature guidelines.

4. *Finishing*—At the finishing station the annealed, reduced hollows are tested for splits, tears, and holes electromagnetically; are straightened on a rotary straightener and finally are cut to finished lengths on an automatic saw.

5. *Stenciling & Packing*—At this final station the finished tubing is stenciled with specification numbers, sizes, and other data required by the customers and is then packed in standard bundles of hexagonal cross section and banded for shipment.

In December of 1982 the Managing Director of Bushranger, Lloyd Jones, was wrestling with two serious business problems. The first problem was the maximization of profit as a function of the product mix and manufacturing capabilities of the existing plant. Restrictions on output on each of the five operating stations are in terms of maximum tons which can be produced per equipment hour and are also a function of the grade (metallurgical) of material being processed. This data is shown in Exhibit 1.

Exhibit 1

PROCESS	HRS AVAIL / WK	TONS PER EQUIPMENT HOUR			
		1010	1020	T22	4140
(1) Pickling	80	6.25	6.25	4	7
(2) Cold Drawing	80	7	5	3	2
(3) Annealing	80	9	7	4	4
(4) Finishing	120	3	3	3	3
(5) Stencil & Pack	80	6	6	5	4

The gross profit contribution by item is as follows:

1. 1010   Grade Material = $20/Ton
2. 1020   Grade Material = $25/Ton
3. T22   Grade Material = $75/Ton
4. 4140   Grade Material = $90/Ton

Additional operating constraints are:

1. A maximum of 50 tons of 4140 and 40 tons of T22 is available each week from NKQ.
2. Bobby Morgan, a member of the Board of Directors of Bushranger and a major stockholder is also owner of Shelby Steel (an important, long-term customer). Morgan, who is an influential member of the Labour Party, needed at least 35 tons/wk of 1010 material for Shelby.

In the calendar year 1982, the production volume per week of each grade had averaged as follows:

1010 − 50 tons/wk
1020 − 40 tons/wk
T22 − 20 tons/wk
4140 − 20 tons/wk

This operating plan had been developed by the Plant Superintendent on the basis of his experience and judgment.

Fortunately Bushranger is able to sell (within very wide bounds) every ton of any grade it can produce. This extremely fortuitous marketing situation is as a direct result of being the only supplier in Western Australia of redrawn pipe and tubing. Competitors of a minor nature are located at Newcastle and Port Kemble near the coal fields in eastern New South Wales and to a very limited degree, in Tokyo. The dramatic growth of the oil refinery complex at Kwinana provides and should provide in the near future sufficient market demand such that all products can be sold which can be produced. Given that the product mix can be optimized so as to optimize gross profit contribution, an additional problem presents itself to the management of Bushranger. This problem involves the additional capacity which would be economically justified as a function of resource constraints at the individual operating stations. Jones must determine the maximum amount he would be willing to pay per ton of additional capacity at each of his five operating stations so as to determine which operation or operations should be expanded. Clearly this cannot be done until an optimum strategy (in terms of product mix) has been developed.

_____ CASE DISCUSSION QUESTIONS _____

1. Connie Jackson, a young American immigrant, with a Masters in Mineral Economics from Colorado School of Mines had recently been hired as Assistant to the Managing

Director. Jones assigned the optimization and investment problem to Jackson and asked her to also evaluate any extrinsic factors that she thought might be of significant importance. Put yourself in Ms. Jackson's place and prepare a report for Mr. Jones.

Case 2
TRANSCONTINENTAL AIRWAYS*

Steven Gorman, the Baltimore Washington International (BWI) Airport Station Manager for Transcontinental Airways (TA), has just received the following corporate memo.

---

15 April, 1980

TO: All Station Managers

FROM: J. P. Morganstein, President TA

SUBJECT: Special Flight Sale Inauguration

As you know, first-quarter profits this year ran well below our expectations. TA's corporate financial analyst has attributed this not to any dramatic increases in operating costs but to an overall decrease in ridership. In an effort to reverse this trend, beginning June 1, we are initiating a one-half price sale on all flights originating between the hours of 12:00 A.M. and 6:00 A.M. Our economist and marketing experts feel that such a pricing policy will increase load factors, on the flights involved, from their current level of 60 percent to 97.5 percent.

Since TA pays a hefty commission to agents other than our own who issue TA flights coupons, we have decided that to take full advantage of this increase, the special fare tickets must be issued no sooner than three hours prior to the flight's departure, by agents at our airport ticket counter only.

We recognize that due to differences in the seating capacities of the various aircraft we operate, this type of ticket sales policy may present special staffing problems at a few of our stations. Hence, to help analyze the impact of this policy on your station's operation, I have included data pertinent to the flights involved. I urge you to review it immediately. If you feel that a staffing problem may arise at your station, I will consider proposals submitted no later than April 30, through our corporate Human Resource Management Officer, Bob Hayden.

---

*Based on a case written by John C. Hannon, a DBA student at Nova University, Fort Lauderdale, Fla.

BWI Station Analysis (Data Assembled: April 10, 1980)

FLIGHT NO.	DEPARTURE TIME	SEATING CAPACITY	AVERAGE NO. OF SEATS SOLD PRIOR YEAR	EXPECTED NO. OF SEATS TO BE SOLD WITH SPECIAL FARE
769	1:00 a.m.	200	120	195
478	4:00 a.m.	200	120	195

Due to the currently low ridership, Steven has assigned only one agent to the BWI ticket counter during the hours of 10:00 P.M. and 4:00 A.M. Admittedly, the agent is underutilized, as he normally only processes 12 customers in the three-hour period prior to each flight.[1] Steve is concerned that if this new special fare brings the estimated increases in ridership, this lone BWI agent may not be able to keep up. He has observed all of his agents working each BWI TA flight and theorized that an agent of average ability can write tickets for 36 customers an hour by utilizing the new TA flight inquiry computer. Analyzing this service rate, he discovered that the distribution of its service time closely approximates a negative exponential distribution (due to the different methods of payment). He also noted that customers tend to arrive at the ticket counter in a random fashion. In plotting the frequency distribution of arrival times, he found that its general shape reminded him of the theoretical Poisson distribution discussed in one of his Baltimore University business courses. The average arrival rate of customers during each hour of the day was observed to be constant.

Steven runs a tight ship. His agents appear to be following his policies to the letter. During the graveyard shift he is especially insistent that customers be served only on a first-come–first-serve basis. He is worried now, however, that with the increased demands on this lone agent during the special sale fare hours, policies alone may not be enough to prevent excessively long counter lines.

Within the next two weeks Steven must decide how his station can best handle the projected increase in workload. Unfortunately, there are some factors which limit his alternatives. They are:

1. The airport management will not allow TA to set up a multichannel single-line facility due to space limitations.

2. TA's flight inquiry computer system can only be operated by one agent at a time. Additional terminal costs $12 per hour.

---

[1] The special fare is not applicable to passengers transferring from other airlines, special group flights, and other special fares. Consequently, Steven estimates that 108 of the 120 passengers currently riding flights 769 and 478 will not require ticketing.

3. Corporate studies show that the cost of ill will and lost ticket sales amounts to $260 per customer hour of waiting in the line. This cost occurs mainly because of the stiff competition due to the availability of other airlines' flights to the same destinations.

4. Corporate pay policies forbid the disbursement of incentive pay to any agents when more than one agent is on duty.

Due mainly to these limitations, Steven reasons that he must choose only one from the following three alternatives:

1. Utilize the lone ticket agent.

2. Utilize the lone ticket agent and, in addition to his base pay of $10 per hour, provide a bonus if the agent handles more than 36 customers per hour. The industrial engineering department has estimated that via this type of incentive plan a ticket agent could process 38 per hour. The bonus is $5 each for the 37th and the 38th customer.

3. Hire more agents for the graveyard shift.

_____ **CASE DISCUSSION QUESTIONS** _____

1. Analyze Steven's problem, examining the cost of all alternatives.

2. A consultant suggested to Steven that TA pay the airport $30 per hour of operation for a space increase that will allow multiple channels with a single line. Should TA accept this suggestion? Why or why not?

Case 3
*OTHELLO PRODUCTS, INCORPORATED**

Othello Products, Incorporated, consisted of a plant and office area of 60,000 square feet and employed 150 hourly and 32 salaried employees. Othello had been primarily a job-shop operation producing various-sized lots of medium- to high-quality precision parts for a large number of local consumer goods manufacturers. For many years, the volume of work in the shop had fluctuated widely from period to period. Consequently, Othello employees were either operating under "make work" or "get it out at any cost" conditions. This constant alternation between feast and famine caused numerous supervisory and managerial problems. To combat high costs and excessive employee turnover, the management of Othello initiated two new major programs. The first of these was a work standards program, and the second a

*Meier, et al, *Cases in Production and Operations Management*, © 1982. Reprinted by permission of Prentice-Hall, Inc., Englewood Cliffs, N.J.

program directed toward finding kinds of work that would provide some long-term stability to Othello's volume of business.

The work standards program was designed to provide a method for placing valid production rates on every operation of every work order issued to Othello's manufacturing organization. As an initial step, stopwatch time studies of over 800 basic operations performed on Othello's facilities were made. After the task of collecting the time studies was completed, the individual operational elements from these studies were sorted, classified, and cross-referenced. The final step was to develop a set of predetermined standard times particularly applicable to Othello's operation. It was hoped that this information would provide a means for making economical and accurate cost estimates, for setting shop production standards, and for controlling overall manufacturing costs.

The second program consisted of an all-out effort to find one or more long-term products or contracts. An ideal product was believed to be one that was compact, easy to store, labor-intensive, and yet relatively simple to manufacture. It was felt that if the product could be manufactured for inventory during slack periods, it could provide one means of leveling the overall production rate and labor force required by the firm. After approximately a year, one such product was identified. A sketch of this product is shown in Figure 1.

The product was a compact, variable-speed gear reducer used by a large manufacturer for whom Othello had previously made numerous experimental parts. The reducer appeared ideal in that the components required a considerable amount of medium-precision machining using equipment that Othello currently had avail-

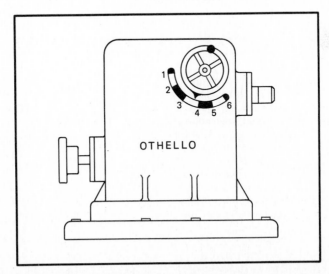

FIGURE 1   Sketch of Proposed Reducer (Overall Dimensions 18 × 18 × 16 Inches High)

able. Over 85 percent of the reducer's finished cost (excluding overhead and profit) consisted of direct labor. The manufacturer had issued an invitation for bids for the first production lot to a group of selected suppliers who were known to be competent in this kind of work.

Since Othello had made most of the parts for the experimental model, it had relatively complete information regarding the raw material cost and machining requirements of the component parts. Actual stopwatch time studies on many of the machine operations required had been made. It was believed that it would be easy to obtain accurate estimates of the remaining machining operations by applying the standard time data, which were scheduled to be available well ahead of the final date for submitting the bid. The major unsolved problem was to determine the assembly costs.

To obtain accurate assembly costs, several workers and a process engineer were assigned the task of devising an appropriate assembly procedure. Data in Table 1 are the result of these efforts. To obtain these data, each worker was allowed, uninstructed but under the surveillance of the process engineer, to assemble and disassemble a reducer. The experience gained was pooled, and from the best method used by the various workers, 34 basic assembly operations were defined. Each of these operations was then time-studied using stopwatch techniques. The times shown in Table 1 represent the standard unit times.

The time-study standards were based on 100 percent performance, this being the output that was expected from an average experienced worker having reasonable

Table 1 Gear Reducer Assembly Requirements

ACTIVITY CODE	ACTIVITY	QUANTITY[1]	UNIT TIME[2]	HANDLING TIME[3]	CANNOT PRECEDE	TOOLING COST[4]
a[5]	Start	..	.00	.00	....	$ 0
b	Press main bearings	2	.59	.21	a	3,500
c	Press grease seals	2	.32	.15	a	1,500[6]
d	Insert welsh plugs	4	.13	.08	a	375(ab)[9]
e	Mount on chain conveyor	1	.17	....	b, c, d	......
f	Assemble main drive gear	1	1.19	.17	e	1,250(k)[9](q)[9]
g	Insert main drive gear assembly	1	.63	.07	f	......
h	Position main drive gear bearing block	1	.30	.07	g	75
i	Insert and engage bolts	4	.04	.02[7]	h	......
j	Tighten bolts with torque wrench	4	.06	.04[8]	i	225
k	Assemble reduction gear	1	.63	.17	e	(f)[9]
l	Insert reduction gear	1	.33	.09	k	......
m	Position reduction gear bearing block	1	.16	.07	l	25
n	Insert and engage bolts	4	.04	.02[7]	m	......

		1	2	3		4
o	Shim for end play	1	.18	.06	m	85
p	Tighten bolts with torque wrench	4	.06	.04[8]	n, o	(j)[9]
q	Assemble idler shaft	1	.23	.17	e	(f)[9]
r	Insert idler shaft	1	.49	....	q	......
s	Position idler shaft bearing block	1	.20	.05	r	95
t	Insert and engage bolts	4	.04	.02[7]	s	......
u	Tighten bolts with torque wrench	4	.06	.04[8]	t	(j)[9]
v	Place gasket	1	.08	.02	e	......
w	Place base plate	1	.29	....	j, p, u, v	......
x	Insert and engage bolts	12	.04	.02[7]	w	......
y	Tighten bolts with torque wrench	12	.05	.04	x	(j)[9]
z	Insert pressure and lubricant fittings	4	.15	.04	e	35
aa	Fill lubricant	1	.51[10]	....	y, z	3,800
ab	Plug lubricant holes	2	.10	.05	aa	(d)[9]
ac	Pressure test	1	3.80[11]	....	ab	1,800
ad	Remove pressure fittings and plug holes	2	.29	.04	ac	60
ae	Dynamometer test	1	1.87[12]	....	ab	4,800
af	Attach name and instruction plate	1	.30	.08	e	900
ag	Wipe clean	1	.26	.03	ad, ae	......
ah	Attach test results	1	.08	....	af, ag	......
ai	Release from conveyor	1	.08	....	ah	......

[1] Number of cycles or repetitions of basic operation to complete the specified activity for each unit.

[2] Time in minutes to complete a single cycle of operation included in the specified activity.

[3] Time in minutes to pick up, position, lay aside tools, etc., if more than one activity is assigned to a specific work station. For example, if activities "b" and "c" are assigned to independent work stations, the performance time is 1.18 and .64 minutes, respectively. If they are assigned to a single work station, the performance time is 2.18 minutes (1.18 + .64 + .21 + .15 = 2.18).

[4] Cost of company-supplied tools and special equipment to perform specified activity. Must be included for every work station at which all or any part of the specified activity is performed.

[5] Dummy operation. Requires no time or manpower. Assumes main castings are positioned on belt conveyor.

[6] Can substitute tool use for operation "b." Can use common tool if this operation is performed at the same work station as operation "b."

[7] Activities "i," "n," "t," and "x" can be combined without incurring handling time, since they contain identical elements and require common tools.

[8] Activities "j," "p," and "u" can be combined without incurring handling time, since they contain identical elements and require common tools.

[9] Requires identical tooling as activity shown in parentheses. Can use common set of tooling if operations are performed at the same work station.

[10] Activity completely automatic, no operator required.

[11] Activity completely automatic except for operator who must visually check for leaks. One operator can oversee the testing of up to four units simultaneously. Operator cannot perform any other function regardless of how many units he oversees.

[12] Activity completely automatic except for operator who connects hydraulic dynamometer coupling, records test results, and shuts down test equipment in case of an emergency. One operator can process up to two units simultaneously. Operator cannot perform any other function regardless of the number of units he oversees.

skill in the type of operation performed and working at a natural rate of speed. Since the time studies were made on employees who were considered to be relatively inexperienced in assembly work, an 85 percent skill rating was assigned to all operations. Because of the highly cooperative spirit of the employees, however, practically all operations were rated for effort at or above 115 percent. Thus, in almost all cases, the stopwatch standards determined were met or exceeded in the actual assembly trials.

The only remaining task with regard to estimating the assembly cost was to lay out the assembly process in terms of specific work stations and determine the equipment and labor costs. It was a company policy to maintain good working conditions, and thus it was felt that the design of work stations should provide each employee with a minimum of 5 linear feet of work space along the assembly line. This was considered possible, since an area 85 feet in length and 25 feet in width was available for the placement of the line and for in-process parts storage areas. It was felt that the entire line should be conveyorized, as this would substantially reduce the problem of maintaining efficient performance. Estimates of conveyor costs indicated that the belt conveyor required for activities "a" through "d" of Table 1 would cost about $6,600, plus $300 per lineal foot of conveyor. This was essentially a belt conveyor from which parts could be removed for processing and replaced for transporting to the next work station.

A chain conveyor was suggested for activities "e" through "ai" of Table 1 and was estimated to cost approximately $9,500 plus $525 per lineal foot. This was a conveyor upon which the housing would be clamped and thus not removable at the work stations. This type of a conveyor would pace the line and allow completely automatic testing of the assembly, as the unit would be accurately and positively located at each work station.

"Banking" facilities capable of holding up to 10 parts at any given work station were available for the belt conveyor at an additional cost of $300 per station. No such facility was available for the chain conveyor. One of the conveyor firms that had been contracted quoted a price of $4,200 plus $175 per lineal foot for small feeder conveyors that could serve as feeders to the main conveyor line for parts or subassemblies.

The contract upon which Othello was bidding was for 1,800 reducers a week for a period of six months. The invitation to bid provided that if the winning bidder wished to absorb all equipment and tooling costs, he would be free to build and sell the reducer in the open market under his own trade name. To Othello management, this appeared to be an excellent opportunity for Othello to develop a new product line, and it was decided that if the contract was received, an initial 8-hour single-shift 5-day-week capacity would be installed that was 10 percent in excess of the contract demand. Since Othello was currently operating on a one-shift 5-day-week basis, this plan would comply with current operations and allow for up to a 200 percent increase in production by going to two shifts of ten hours each on a 6-day-week basis.

_____ **CASE DISCUSSION QUESTIONS** _____

1. Sketch an approximate assembly line designating specific work stations and the operations and activities performed at each work station. At what speed should the conveyor be designed to operate?

2. What are the approximate capital and labor costs per unit associated with the line you sketched? Assume that direct labor costs average $9.65 per hour.

Case 4
YORK CONTAINER COMPANY[*]

The York Container Company was one of the large manufacturers in the container industry. The industry included large, medium, and small companies. Large companies had decentralized their production facilities throughout the country. They engaged in active competition with each other by emphasizing customer service. Smaller manufacturers competed by offering price reductions ranging from 2 to 6 percent, coupled with less service.

John Flint, production planning manager of the Midwest plant of York Container Company, faced a problem involving employment policy, inventory control, and production planning. Early in December, the home office in New York City had dictated a new policy directing all branch plants to stabilize employment of production-line workers to the extent that such a policy was possible without incurring unreasonable cost. During the past year, employment of production-line workers had fluctuated with seasonal requirements from a high of 150 to a low of 30.

The Midwest factory was one of the company's oldest plants and, although unionized, it enjoyed favorable relations with its employees. For years, this plant had followed a policy of hiring and laying off employees as required by market demands. It drew largely upon transient workers and college students to fill manpower needs during the busy summer and fall months. When college students left at the end of summer to go back to school, the factory had to hire and train a new group of employees for one or two months' work. Joe Asplund, the personnel director,

_____

[*]From *Cases in Manufacturing Management* by Schrieber, et al., © 1965 by McGraw Hill, Inc., used with permission of McGraw Hill Book Company.

Meier, et al, *Cases in Production and Operations Management*, © 1982. Reprinted by permission of Prentice-Hall, Inc., Englewood Cliffs, N.J.

estimated that it cost \$425 to hire and train a new employee, and \$175 to terminate one. In contrast to the changes in employment levels of production-line workers, the supervisory, maintenance, lithographing and enameling, and tinplate department employees were hired on a permanent basis, and therefore, the number of people in these categories did not fluctuate with changes in seasonal demand.

The Midwest plant had twelve standard can lines and two frozen-food container lines. Cans manufactured were of several types and sizes. Most cans were classified as open-top cans; that is, the top was not sealed on the can until after the can had been filled. Some cans (such as beer cans) were manufactured differently from the typical fruit or vegetable can; they were sprayed with a protective coating on the inside. Frozen-food containers came in a variety of materials and shapes. For example, the carton for frozen strawberries was made of paper with metal ends. The can lines produced cans at rates varying from 100 to 450 per minute, depending upon the size and complexity of the can. As a general rule, the larger the can, the slower the rate of production. The two frozen-food container lines produced at an average rate of 180 per minute. Standard can lines could be used to produce only beer cans and open-top cans, and frozen-food container lines could be used to produce only frozen-food containers. A list of can sizes produced at this plant, together with production rates, appears in Table 1.

Table 1   Cans Manufactured at Midwest Plant of York Container

		PRODUCTION RATE		
CAN NUMBER[a]	APPROX. SIZE (DIAM. × HEIGHT IN INCHES)	CANS/ LINE-SHIFT[b]	CAR-LOADS/ LINE-MONTH[c]	MANUFAC-TURING COST, \$/CARLOAD
1	$2\frac{3}{4} \times 4\frac{3}{4}$ (beer)	216,000	30	\$5,200
2	$3\frac{1}{4} \times 4\frac{1}{4}$	168,000	30	4,800
3	$4 \times 4\frac{3}{4}$	156,000	45	4,300
4	$3 \times 4\frac{3}{4}$	168,000	25	4,500
5	$3\frac{1}{2} \times 2$	168,000	15	7,000
6	$3 \times 4\frac{1}{2}$	168,000	25	4,800
7	$6\frac{1}{4} \times 7$	48,000	50	3,500
8	$4 \times 5\frac{1}{2}$	139,000	50	4,100
9	Miscellaneous	144,000[d]	25	4,600
10	Frozen-food container	86,000	10	5,500

[a]Can number was a local plant code used for convenient identification. It was not related to the standard can-size number used in the industry. Can numbers 9 and 10 were used to designate groups of special-dimension cans or containers, most of which were infrequently produced and each of which required its own dimension identification.
[b]Line-shift is based on average output per line during eight hours of normal operation.
[c]Line-month is based on a single shift operating 21 days per month.
[d]Average production rate.

A line changeover typically withdrew the line from production for two days and resulted in a cost of $1,100. This cost included wages of two maintenance men who made the mechanical changeover, material scrap, and a charge for lost production capacity. Line operators and supervisors could be reassigned to other jobs during such changeovers. A line that had been idle, however, could be restarted again without any additional setup costs, provided it was used to produce the same-sized can. Machine lines scheduled to be in operating condition on January 1 included two beer lines, two frozen-food lines, and three open-top can lines producing for can numbers 4, 5, and 9.

In past years, the factory had operated two shifts during the peak season, running about ten can lines on the first shift and six on the second shift. In addition, two frozen-food container lines were operated on each shift. The average first-shift hourly pay rate for line operators and supervisors was $6.10 and $9.40, respectively. A 15 percent premium was paid to both line operators and supervisors for second-shift operations. A 50 percent overtime premium was paid for all overtime work not exceeding 20 hours per week per crew (maximum of four hours per day).

Storage space in the factory for finished cans amounted to 50,000 square feet, and when stacked to a height of ten feet (the maximum), 500,000 cubic feet. The empty cans were stored in cardboard cartons that could be used to package the filled cans. A freight car contained approximately 3,200 cubic feet of shipping space.

There was no immediate alternative use for inside storage space; hence depreciation, building taxes, and the like were considered a fixed cost, and no specific charge was levied for the use of this space. A monthly charge, however, equal to 2 percent of the average monthly inventory value, was applied to cover variable costs for capital investment in the inventory, deterioration of inventory, other handling and maintenance costs, and so on, associated with the use of both inside and outside storage space.

Adequate warehouse space was available nearby at a monthly rate of 12 cents per square foot (ten feet high). The rent was determined by the maximum number of square feet used in any single month. To load, transport, and unload a freight car lot of cans from the factory to an outside warehouse cost $300 per car. Shipments were made directly to the customers from the outside warehouses.

Deliveries fluctuated from 30 to more than 300 cars per month. Table 2 shows the sales forecast that Flint intended to use in planning production for the next year. Flint expected to have 83 line operators and 7 supervisors on the payroll as of December 31. Finished-goods inventories as of the same date were estimated to consist of 72 carloads of can number 1, 20 carloads of can number 4, and 12 carloads of can number 5.

Sales forecasts were typically optimistic, but not sufficiently so to justify either specific or general reductions by the production planning group. Production plans were made so that the amount forecast for any given month was planned for production in the same month. Sufficient flexibility existed in delivery dates and production capacity that more specific planning could be delayed until the month

Table 2   Anticipated Inventory and Sales Forecast

| | | | | | | CAN NUMBER | | | | | |
	1	2	3	4	5	6	7	8	9	10	TOTAL
INVENTORY ON HAND (DEC. 31)	72			20	12						*104 CARLOADS*
Sales: Jan.	6			15	9						30 carloads
Feb.	12			25	12			5			54
Mar.	21			55	39			30			145
Apr.	39			55	57			30		5	186
May	36	24		50	42	40		25			217
June	102	90				40	5	20		5	262
July	150	81	18			20		20		28	317
Aug.	111	81	81			20	10			43	346
Sept.	90	42	81				40	25		21	299
Oct.	81	21	81				10	25		33	251
Nov.	15		54	15						17	101
Dec.	27		36	15						41	119
Total	690	339	351	230	159	120	60	75	110	193	2,327 carloads

prior to actual production. Hence, if the sales forecast called for 15 carloads of can number 4, it was sufficient to plan for the production of 15 carloads of can number 4 anytime during the month of January.

Each type of can line required a specific number of workers. Beer cans, open-top cans, and frozen-food containers required thirteen, eleven, and twelve operators, respectively, plus a supervisor for each line. Detailed manpower requirements for each of these lines are shown in Table 3.

Table 3   Workers Required to Operate Lines

JOB TITLE	BEER CAN	OPEN-TOP CAN	FROZEN-FOOD CONTAINER
Slitter operator	1	1	1
Tin and body blank feeder	1	1	1
Spray operator and line tender	1	1	2
Bottom end feeder	1	1	1
Inspector	3	1	2
Packer and sealer	1	4	2
Folder and stitcher	2	0	1
Checker	1	1	1
Car loader	2	1	1
Total	13	11	12

CASE DISCUSSION QUESTIONS

---

1. What kinds of gains may accrue from stabilizing employment?
2. Outline the approach you would take in solving York's labor stabilization problem.
3. Develop a production plan for the operation of the plant during the coming year. (Assume that inventory levels predicted by Flint for December 31 were normal for the end of the year and that there are 21 working days per month.)
4. What are some of the advantages and disadvantages of your solution?

Case 5
SOUTHERN HYDRAULIC
SUPPLIES COMPANY*

The Southern Hydraulic Supplies Company was a distributor of hydraulic supplies in the Gulf states area. Southern handled standard hydraulic fittings, tubing, and similar items. Generally Southern carried an entire line for each manufacturer whose products it handled and provided local stock for rapid delivery to customers. The items that Southern stocked were mainly used in the maintenance, modification, and manufacture of trucks, off-highway construction equipment, and machine tools.

Southern had grown from a small two-person operation to a $75-million-per-year business in a span of 25 years. The growth of its dollar volume was based on an excellent reputation for good service coupled with the general expansion of industry in the Gulf states. From its inception Southern had been a profitable business in sound financial condition.

Despite the continued growth of profits in absolute terms, however, Southern found that profits as a percentage of sales had declined from 11.3 percent of sales to 6.4 percent of sales. When management became aware of the seriousness of the problem, it was decided to undertake a thorough review of policies and procedures in the areas that could have significant influence on costs and profits—namely, product line, sales methods, stock handling and storage methods, billing and record keeping, and inventory replenishment. The last area was included as a major area for

---

*Meier, et al, *Cases in Production and Operations Management*, © 1982. Reprinted by permission of Prentice-Hall, Inc., Englewood Cliffs, N.J.

study because the company had been experiencing increasing difficulty with out-of-stock situations and unbalanced inventories.

Inventory Replenishment Procedures

Up until the time that the review of the inventory replenishment policies and procedures was begun, there had been no formal study of this phase of the company's operations. Since maintaining inventories was one of the company's major functions, Southern had always used experienced personnel to control the placing of orders and had relied on their judgment to make correct decisions. One thing that became immediately apparent as this phase of Southern's operations came under scrutiny was that the inventory replenishment problem had become vastly more complicated in recent years as the variety of items carried had tripled from what it had been five years previously to more than 15,000 separate stock items. Because no formal study had been made previously of the inventory replenishment operations, it was decided as a first step to get some general information about order placement costs and inventory carrying costs and also to analyze in detail several typical items of inventory.

Several years earlier Southern had installed a small computer for maintaining inventory records, writing purchase orders, and other record keeping functions. To use this equipment efficiently, the master inventory records were updated only once weekly. Purchase orders were also prepared on a schedule of once each week. Purchase requisitions were turned in by the supervisors responsible for various types of stock, and these were accumulated until Friday when they were used to initiate purchase orders. In effect this meant that review of the inventory levels occurred once every five days as the supervisors turned in most of their purchase requisitions only once each week immediately before the scheduled machine run. In total, the cost of preparing and processing a requisition, preparing a purchase order, and making necessary record changes was estimated to be $12.50 per order.

Analysis of company records indicated that the following were reasonable estimates of the variable cost per year of carrying inventories (as a percentage of dollar value of average inventory):

COST CATEGORY	% OF TOTAL
Capital cost	18
Obsolescence	5
Insurance	3
Taxes	2
Storage and handling	11
Total	39

One of the typical items of inventory analyzed in detail was a small hydraulic fitting. The fitting was purchased for $14.00 and sold for $19.50. The manufacturer from whom Southern procured the fitting did not offer any quantity discount on the fitting, but it would not fill orders for less than 50 fittings without adding a flat charge of $25.00 to the order. For this particular item, there were other distributors in Southern's immediate vicinity that could supply a comparable fitting made by another manufacturer. Because of this, orders that Southern could not fill immediately were lost.

The fitting was ordered from the manufacturer located about 1,500 miles away and shipped to Southern by truck. An analysis of the time taken to receive the fittings from the day the purchase order was prepared until the fittings were received indicated that this varied between 5 and 14 working days. The historical record of the time between the preparation of the purchase order and receipt of the fittings is shown in Table 1. It was estimated that inspection of the shipments, preparation of receiving reports, and related activities cost Southern $12.25 per order.

Customer orders filled each day for one year (260 working days) were tabulated for this fitting and are shown in Table 2. No record was kept of customer orders that were cancelled because the fitting was out of stock. Further analysis of the records pertaining to this fitting revealed the fact that replenishment orders for

Table 1   Analysis of Procurement
Lead Times*

WORKING DAYS BETWEEN ORDER	
ISSUE AND DELIVERY OF FITTINGS	
8	11
12	14
6	9
5	8
7	9
8	7
8	6
9	8
13	13
9	10
10	7
8	7
11	12
7	10
8	9
5	10
7	7
6	8
9	14
7	6

*Average lead time = 8.7 days.

Table 2   Analysis of Orders for One Year*

ORDERS FILLED PER DAY

35	9	17	16	20	0
0	8	4	0	0	19
0	0	28	11	13	29
17	17	25	16	7	18
36	0	27	0	0	11
6	28	20	13	14	29
0	0	0	24	0	14
5	29	7	11	10	0
11	9	0	0	41	19
18	0	8	27	8	31
0	0	0	26	0	10
4	0	18	0	9	16
16	23	28	6	22	0
25	0	20	0	0	27
0	17	22	26	0	18
19	8	0	13	44	14
14	13	0	0	24	0
32	31	16	21	0	0
15	8	31	17	7	38
0	0	24	22	40	3
17	25	16	0	9	17
18	11	0	10	0	0
10	0	0	42	0	21
30	43	14	0	0	15
15	9	36	18	21	0
0	0	11	0	16	9
12	12	0	12	0	14
21	22	3	27	23	0
23	15	30	4	19	6
15	0	12	19	25	23
12	7	0	17	0	12
0	15	10	0	2	22
19	10	0	34	15	0
37	33	20	17	12	34
0	26	14	21	0	5
13	0	21	0	32	
0	6	0	18	8	
18	20	17	13	0	
20	13	37	24	5	
14	7	19	33	15	
19	0	0	26	20	
18	0	0	0	30	
0	39	35	18	23	
10	19	16	0	0	
15	16	13	16	11	

*Average orders filled per day = 13.1.

the fitting were always for lots of 750 and that the amount of stock on hand averaged about 115 units on the days that purchase orders were issued for replenishment stock.

_____ **CASE DISCUSSION QUESTIONS** _____

1. Analyze the cost of the system currently used for maintaining the inventory of this fitting.
2. What is the minimum cost of maintaining the inventory of the fitting if the once-a-week ordering system is used?
3. What would be the advantage, if any, of revising the computer procedures so that replenishment orders could be placed every day?
4. Based on the analyses in the preceding questions, what possibilities appear to be present for improving the management of inventories?

Case 6
MESA SPORTING GOODS*

Introduction and History

The Mesa Sporting Goods Company was a distributor of over 12,000 items of sporting equipment to small retailers. The company started operations in 1946 from a small warehouse but as the business prospered, it outgrew its facilities and a 50,000-square-foot warehouse was constructed in 1970 near the original facilities. These new facilities were well conceived with ample shelves and a rectangular conveyor system to transport picked orders to the packing and shipping areas. Orders requiring pricing labels attached to the items, a service provided for several select customers, were shunted off to a marking table and then returned to the packing benches.

In 1972 the company purchased a minicomputer system for order entry and to assist in tracking sales and inventory. Until this time, no perpetual inventory records were kept. The buyers, with general forecasts from the sales manager, bought what they believed would sell. Quarterly physicals were taken to monitor inventory investment and for the preparation of financial statements. Thus, there was essentially no sales history maintained nor any stockout data on what could have been sold.

_____

*This case was prepared by J. G. Carlson of the University of Southern California for classroom discussion and is not intended to illustrate either effective or ineffective administrative practice. Reprinted with permission.

The initial perpetual inventory system setup on the computer kept year-to-date sales and balance-on-hand data. Reorder points and reorder quantities provided by the buyers were loaded into the initial data base. Because these parameters were guestimates with no means of updating them, the inventory reports, with special notation of items having reached their reorder point, lacked credibility and were ignored by the buyers.

Early Problems

The initial inventory computer program developed by an outside software house had several errors. For example, it took some months and several spot physicals to discover why some of the inventory balances were incorrect. The error was traced to the programmer's assumption that negative balances "were impossible" and therefore these balances were automatically reset to zero. However, issue transactions might often be processed before receipt transactions thus causing a temporary negative book inventory. If these negative quantities are set to zero, further issues would not be recorded and any subsequent receipt would yield an erroneous balance.

The credibility gap between the computer reports and data kept by the buyers continued for several years. Dan, the senior buyer, continued to keep his own log on what he bought from each vendor for each product for each buying cycle. He and the two assistant buyers appeared to delight in attempting to prove the computer report wrong. An item might show a zero balance on the report but perhaps twenty would be on the shelf. The data entry personnel would try to track down the discrepancy only to discover that the computer had processed the sales order but the physical "pick" had not as yet occurred. Data Processing, defensive at first, tired of these special audit requests and developed a validating system based on periodic cycle counting of each vendor's items.

During the implementation of the system, Mesa discovered that there were dozens of procedural changes that had to be documented and communicated in order to make a computer-based system work even in the simpler distribution environment. Management had failed to foresee the "extra" computer processing required and the necessity for everyone in the system—sales, data entry, and warehouse personnel—to be aware of the sensitivity of the system and the responsibility for its success. For example, Mesa found that order picking time was reduced to one-half if the pick lists were in location sequence. Thus, it was necessary to include the bin location for each item in the Item Master. Items, however, would sometimes be moved from one bin to another without informing the computer. On one occasion, the Sales Department pulled a group of fishing reels and rods into packages and put them in a separate location without notifying the computer. The individual item balances became invalid plus the special packages were essentially "lost."

Turnover vs. Stockouts

Until 1975 management had concentrated on trying to increase the number of inventory turns rather than reducing stockouts. Because demand data were not being accumulated by the minicomputer system, Mesa was not aware that 23 to 27% of total sales were lost due to stockouts ("zeros"). Mr. Kern, the controller and systems designer, believed the stockout problem was much more important than increasing inventory turnover. To assist in analyzing the inventory to prevent stockouts, a consulting firm offered to classify the inventory into A, B, and C and perform a comprehensive inventory analysis on which to base reorder points and reorder quantities. For their proposal, the consultants accumulated some data and performed a sample analysis to show the potential value of developing an inventory profile and computing reorder points and economic reorder quantities from historical data. However, Mr. Kern believed that not only could he perform the complete analysis, but he could write the routines that would maintain a continuous inventory analysis and perform sales and cost analyses as well. The money that would have been spent on the one-time analysis was then committed to upgrading the computer system and adding significant programs to maintain seasonal indexes necessary in managing sporting goods purchases, inventories, and sales.

System Design

The computer system to be installed during 1976 was designed such that as the sales orders were received by phone or mail each day they could be entered directly into the computer via CRTs. As each line entry was made, the inventory level was to be checked by the system. Only the amount available was to be printed on the generated pick list. If there was insufficient stock to fill the order, the amount available was to be shipped and the stockout data stored as a "lost sale," printed out on a daily "zeros" report and included as part of a weekly action report and a monthly sales and inventory analysis.

Forecasting was done in a very aggregate manner by management judgment as to whether the dollar sales of a product group would increase, decrease, or remain the same. The need for a technique that offered more visibility and understanding of probable future demand was apparent. A comprehensive way of viewing individual items as well as item groups for purchasing decisions was needed. Mr. Kern had read a little about MRP (Materials Requirements Planning) and believed that the logic would be appropriate to distribution as well as manufacturing.

However, he was somewhat unsure as to how to gather the necessary data for a complete purchasing, order-entry, and sales information system redesign. The direct involvement of the buyers in the design and how the buyers should be educated in the concepts of Time-Phased Order Planning (TPOP) was a major question. A TPOP system (MRP applied to distribution systems), involves lead time analysis, safety stock decisions, lot sizing, combined purchases, vendor policy interpretation, seasonal indexes, forecasts, demand vs. shipment data, stockouts, carrying costs, provision for deletions, additions, item classification techniques, and many more factors. The buyers should be able to have a projection of their decisions over a 12-month planning horizon. However, this should be in the form of a monthly report or in an inquiry mode on a terminal. With an interactive terminal, the buyers could compose their purchase orders as well.

The Procurement Function

In the past, each of the three buyers was assigned several categories of items and their respective vendors. Because sporting goods is a highly seasonal industry and very volatile in several specific product lines, buying was much more complex than just placing replenishment orders or processing purchase requisitions submitted by others. Fishing tackle is especially variable merchandise at the individual item level. The popularity of a particular lure can change overnight depending on word-of-mouth fishing stories, articles in sports periodicals and newspapers, etc. Sport guns and ammunition are also a difficult category to manage as their demand is a function of hunting seasons, game availability, skeet shooting popularity, and policies of the suppliers.

Categorizing 12,000 items into useful subgroups for analysis is difficult. At present, two groupings are made whereby each item is assigned into one of 77 categories and which can then be summarized into 12 major groups. These groupings do not permit sufficient sensitivity for identifying changes in market demand among items. This is where the years of experience from both selling and buying sporting goods helps Dan. It was his opinion, no computer analysis or report could ever replace human experience in making optimum buying decisions.

In this type of business, no backorders are permitted and substitutions are rare and made only with customer approval. The old monthly summary sales report is shown in Exhibit 1.

The "dated stock" and "early bird" options offered by several vendors was a case in point. It could not be practical to "transfer" all he knew to the computer for critical judgment buying decisions. "Dated stock" plans are those whereby if the distributor orders early and accepts preseason delivery, the manufacturer not only postdates the invoice by several months but also allows a discount of 5%, 10%, or more. "Early Bird" plans are similar to dated stock plans except the invoices are not postdated. The questions which then arise are: how much to order to take advantage of these plans, whether there is sufficient storage space, what will be the total sales, and what will be the sales pattern.

Dan offered the following challenge to the computer: a vendor has announced that next year, whatever Mesa ordered during January would be delivered sometime before April. Payment need not be made until October 1 and a discount of 10% would be allowed on a dated order. For example, footballs cost $10.00 each and total annual sales are about 10,000 units. Though there is sufficient storage space to

Exhibit 1 Year-to-Date Sales, Cogs, & Inventory for 77 Categories

	SALES A	COGS B	INVENTORY C	% B/A
Month 11 1975				
110 01	4,847	2,721	44	.56
111 01	101,665	80,641	36,135	.79
112 01	68,364	45,276	45,371	.66
113 01	470,670	362,718	183,711	.77 ROD
114 01	51,745	29,326	78,059	.57
115 01	815,157	701,720	121,284	.86 REEL
118 02	42,928	28,228	61,459	.66
119 02	479,431	393,001	66,312	.82
120 02	7,321	5,462	4,732	.75
121 02	236,931	187,789	41,580	.79 LURE
122 02	77,138	61,107	29,404	.79
123 02	154,587	129,745	36,421	.84
124 03	66,032	44,811	9,347	.68
125 03	135,745	102,023	35,144	.75
126 03	155,389	103,833	52,362	.67
127 03	224,118	169,200	37,816	.75 LEADER
129 03	126,247	102,545	19,194	.81
131 03	36,673	26,784	8,019	.73
132 03	58,460	32,915	10,091	.56
133 03	148,867	105,218	25,753	.71
135 03	26,001	16,721	19,257	.64
201 11	93,747	67,675	25,823	.72
203 11	67,374	50,701	10,326	.75 JUG
205 11	44,800	33,134	4,043	.74
207 11	18,279	13,045	6,513	.71
209 11	28,256	21,762	8,289	.77
211 11	76,796	54,121	16,872	.70
213 11	17,336	13,324	3,790	.77
215 11	44,351	33,405	6,719	.75
217 11	74,106	55,895	20,032	.75
219 11	7,024	5,324	3,503	.76
301 12	32,020	26,897	16,166	.84
303 12	11,181	8,134	1,394	.73
305 12	38,903	27,123	8,471	.70 VEST
307 12	57,276	41,207	12,367	.72
401 10	35,585	26,312	15,470	.74
403 10	49,076	36,044	7,007	.73 BASKETBALL
405 10	49,908	36,910	8,626	.74
407 10	156,709	107,879	47,006	.69
409 10	86,505	64,665	27,372	.75
411 10	20,376	14,103	7,519	.69
413 10	261,640	193,922	43,605	.74
415 10	214,859	157,555	24,786	.73
417 10	237,509	191,418	31,238	.81

Left margin brackets: TACKLE (110 01 through 135 03), CAMPING (201 11 through 307 12), ATHLETIC (401 10 through 417 10).

accommodate this "dated stock," should Mesa take advantage of this offer? "This can't be solved until you give the computer more data," said the controller. But Dan muttered that he didn't have any more data than this yet he had to make these types of decisions and make them promptly—he couldn't wait for a computer analysis.

An irritating problem arose occasionally with respect to the handling of "freebies" and other promotional and incentive schemes devised by manufacturers. Average costing methods were used which can easily be distorted by large variations in the costs of items purchased. For example, one vendor offered a dozen fishing rods gratis if 24 dozen were ordered. The 24 dozen arrived, were stocked and paid for. A month later, another dozen arrived with no purchase order documentation and no invoice. An accounting clerk suggested several alternatives: (1) enter them as an inventory adjustment rather than a receipt, (2) sent them back for credit, (3) given them to employees or salesmen as a bonus, or (4) pass them on to deserving retailers and have them cope with the accounting headaches.

Some Conversion Problems

The younger buyers seemed more flexible and adaptive to having a computer system help them. It was their understanding that a computer system could tell them when to buy an item by scientifically computing a reorder point which, when reached, could signal a reorder. The computer could certainly compute the most economic quantities to reorder. To reduce ordering and shipping costs, the computer, with its on-line display units, should be able to show other items from a vendor which were approaching reorder points so that consolidated purchase orders could be written. When it was explained that the data for these computerized decisions had to be provided by them, they were very disappointed. Someone, somehow must generate the seasonal indexes for 12,000 items and quantify the complexities of the variety of vendor policies. The computer, it was explained, could only provide signals and guidelines and should never be trusted to make decisions automatically. It appeared as though they would have to continue operating approximately in the same manner which even they perceived as being capricious, unmethodical, uninspiring, and unscientific. They had assumed that the new computer would make many of the decisions they presently must make.

With more computer capacity, the buyers could have much more complete descriptions on the reports of the items which they were buying. However, the buyer who was revising the nomenclature on his own time, abandoned the project because it now appeared as if the computer would not be of much help in identifying what to buy, how much to buy, and when to buy.

For computer-based purchase planning to be performed, each of the 12,000 items needed its own seasonal index table. Seasonal indexes could be developed from history but the data for each month were kept on a separate magnetic tape. To get a perspective of the seasonal indexes, a computer routine was written which computed the indexes from manually prepared data taken from twelve monthly reports of each of the 77 categories. A partial list of these indexes appears in Exhibit 2.

Exhibit 2   Seasonal Indexes by Group

						MONTH						
GROUP	1	2	3	4	5	6	7	8	9	10	11	12
109	147	154	155	158	138	165	85	102	69	54	16	18
110	59	72	93	116	101	156	152	135	116	88	66	37
111	77	68	118	125	110	165	146	115	129	55	31	35
112	190	129	128	128	115	119	118	71	58	31	47	64
113	100	56	111	125	75	106	112	146	95	103	80	85
114	77	64	88	146	114	170	154	108	58	65	43	112
115	79	73	116	121	118	143	128	109	78	74	82	75
116	65	42	42	106	80	94	71	122	58	165	174	177

Based on this output, the controller had to make a decision with respect to generating the individual item indexes. Either the individual item could be represented initially by the index of its category *or* a routine would have to be written to analyze the individual items from the magnetic tapes. Each tape represented one month and the data were in year-to-date format so subtractions would be required and the data accumulated on a temporary file. The history tapes also had items that were added or deleted during the year which would present a serious programming and reconciliation problem. The tapes had only sales data and no stockout data. The existing computer record for each item was also completely full so that any additional item data would have to be stored separately. This separate item data could later be merged with other item master data when the new system was installed, but this appeared to be a very risky procedure. It was also questionable whether the minicomputer had the capacity to process all the data in a reasonable amount of time. Thus, the controller elected to use the category indexes for the initial loading of the data base.

After the indexes for the 77 categories were loaded onto the new system as indexes for the appropriate individual items, an exponential smoothing routine would be needed which would update these initial indexes as each month was closed. The update procedure for each of the 12,000 items would be as follows:

$D(T)$ = Actual demand for Period T

$I(T)$ = Current Seasonal Index (Initially from its category Index)

$C(T)$ = Current Smoothed Deseasonalized Demand

$J(T)$ = Actual Index or Actual Demand/Average Demand = $D(T)/C(T)$

A = Index Smoothing Factor

The computer statement could be:

$$I(T) \text{ Revised} = I(T) + A3[J(T) - I(T)] = I(T) + A3[D(T)/C(T) - I(T)].^{[1]}$$

---

[1] If $T = 3$, (March) $A = .3$, $D(3) = 72$, $C(3) = 100$, and the current index $I(3)$ for March for an item was .6, then the updated index for March of next year for the individual item would be: $I(3) = .6 + .3(.72 - .60) = .64$.

While the controller was trying to get better insight into the buyer's problems and desires, the computer routines from the smaller system were being converted to the new computer system. Although the original routines were written in BASIC computer language, the BASIC of the new computer was slightly different and much more comprehensive. Simultaneously, new routines were being written to make use of an expanded data base which would include each item's seasonal index, its demand in addition to its sales, and other useful statistics.

TPOP Education

To appreciate the ability of the proposed system to help monitor what was happening, the controller developed a TPOP (Time-Phased Order Planning) exercise. Two years of sales data for a picnic jug were collected and seasonal indexes computed and averaged. Using the index, an exponential smoothing factor of .2, and an expected average demand of 100 units, the demand in successive months could be iteratively forecasted.

Index Generation for a Picnic Jug

MONTH	1	2	3	4	5	6	7	8	9	10	11	12	UNITS / MO.
1973	0.9	0.9	0.6	0.6	1.1	1.9	2.0	1.5	0.9	0.5	0.5	0.5	75
1974	0.9	0.7	0.5	0.6	1.2	2.1	1.9	1.5	1.1	0.5	0.4	0.6	100
Average	0.9	0.8	0.5	0.6	1.2	2.0	1.9	1.5	1.0	0.5	0.4	0.7	1.0

With the above data, twelve months of experience could be simulated by operating the TPOP system as if the experimenter was both decision maker and computer. With the actual data for 1975[2] what would be the successive TPOP displays as each month's actuals are revealed one month at a time? The computer routine generated the displays for each month but the buyers used a score sheet shown in Exhibit 3.

TPOP Display — Month 1

ITEM		NAME	COST	PRICE	VEND		SAFETY	ROQ.	LEAD
3008		JUG.	PICNIC	5.00	8.50	1234		25	108	3
Index		0.90	0.80	0.50	0.60	1.20	2.00	1.90	1.50	1.00
Period	0	1	2	3	4	5	6	7	8	9
FCST.DMD		90	80	50	60	120	200	190	150	100
SCHED.RCTS		108	108	0	0	0	0	0	0	0
AVAIL	61	79	107	57	−3	−123	−323	−513	−663	−763
PLND ORDS		108	108	216	108	216	108	0	108	0

2

ACTUAL 1975 DEMAND

	1	2	3	4	5	6	7	8	9	10	11	12
1975	96	97	25	27	84	163	90	68	52	31	22	44

Exhibit 3 Simulation Worksheet

Cost = **$5.00**   LT = 3   Fcst = 1200

$$*W(T) = \text{Exp. Smoothed Avg.,} \quad F(T+1) = \left\{ W(T) - 2\left(\frac{D(T)}{I(T)} - W(T)\right)\right\} I(T-1)$$

	1	2	3	4	5	6	7	8	9	10	11	12
Orig. Fcst. W(1) = 100	90	80	50	60	120	200	190	150	100	50	40	70
Rev. Fcst. W(T)*I(T+1)	90	81										
Period / Index T I(T)	1 0.90	2 0.80	3 0.50	4 0.60	5 1.20	6 2.00	7 1.90	8 1.50	9 1.00	10 0.50	11 0.40	12 0.70
Beg'g OnHand	61											
Receipts (Sched)	108	108		(108)								
Sub-Total	169											
Demand	96											
End'g OnHand	73											
Qty. Ord'd (for T + 3)	(108)											
Holding Cost (2%/Mo)	7											
Ordering Cost ($20/Ord.)	20											
Stockout Cost (50%/Lost Cost)												
Cumulative Costs	27											

This display suggests that the buyer place an order now (Planned Order for Month 1, January) for 108 units for delivery in April. If the Scheduled Receipt of 108 was received and the actual demand for the month of January is simulated as 96 units, the TPOP as of February 1 then would be computed and displayed and the buyer decides how many units to reorder for delivery during May.

TPOP Display — Month 2			REC'D = 108			January Demand = 96			
ITEM	*NAME*		*COST*	*PRICE*		*VEND*	*SAFETY*	*ROQ.*	*LEAD*
nr3008	JUG.	PICNIC	5.00	8.50		1234	25	108	3
Index	0.80	0.50	0.60	1.20	2.00	1.90	1.50	1.00	0.50
Period 1	2	3	4	5	6	7	8	9	10
FCST.DMD	81	51	61	122	203	193	152	101	51
SCHED.RCTS	108	0	108	0	0	0	0	0	0
AVAIL 73	100	49	96	−25	−228	−420	−572	−674	−724
PLND ORDS	108	216	216	108	108	0	108	0	108

This is repeated for a number of months with the separate score sheet tallying the costs of inventory carried, the stockouts incurred, number of orders placed, and the total operating cost (see Exhibit 3). (The reader is invited to complete the exercise by entering decisions and the actuals month-by-month. No cheating.) This "compressed-time" exercise was supposed to help the buyers with their day-to-day decision making.

Present Situation

The simulation was enlightening for the buyers, but they still wanted the computer to tell them the specific quantity to reorder, and when to reorder. Safety stock was still quite arbitrarily determined by such guidelines as one month's supply, one-half of the usage during lead time or by the sales manager's best guess. An ongoing measurement of variability of demand from forecast, or forecast error, was not to be performed. A mean absolute deviation (MAD) statistic could assist in predicting the service level achievable from the safety stock investment but top management was not interested in sophisticated statistics—they wanted results in the form of fewer lost sales and less inventory.

The decision of what to stock, when to reorder, and how much to reorder is very difficult when dealing with 12,000 items. The new computer reports were to keep management generally appraised of stockouts, shipments, and inventory investments. Stockouts, however, still averaged about 24% of sales during 1976 and the inventory was still growing as sales increased. The president upon discovering this, issued an ultimatum that unless inventory was reduced by 10% and stockouts did not exceed 16% by May 1977, there would be some changes in personnel.

The buyers, Mr. Kern noted:

...must get more involved in the system design to communicate and maintain the special categories of information needed. Otherwise the data, reports, and signals will never be valid; nor what the buyers need to help themselves. They are still very reluctant and won't take the time to sit down and discuss their needs and learn about the capabilities of a computerized system. They still view the computer as a threat because it appears to be monitoring more and more of their daily decisions and performance. Computer messages such as STOCKOUT and NOTHING ON ORDER may not help their ego but they should help the buyers reach our mutual objectives.

CASE DISCUSSION QUESTIONS

1. What does a buyer at Mesa really need in the way of a daily, weekly, and monthly report in order to do a better job?
2. Besides avoiding unnecessary inventory checks for the buyers, what does cycle counting do for a company?
3. If Mesa does not have to pay until October for jugs (in the exercise) which they order before April, how many should they order in January, February, and March?
4. How would the controller determine the trade-off between stockouts and overstocking?

Case 7
SOUTHWEST TUBE
MANUFACTURING COMPANY*

History

Southwest Tube, located in Sand Springs, Oklahoma (a Tulsa suburb) was organized in 1969 by F. William Weber, a former regional manager for U.S. Steel. The initial goal of the company was to address an unfilled niche in the southwestern tube and pipe market. Specifically, the company hoped to achieve success by offering special sizes of redraw tube to the fabricators of pressure and processes vessels on a "quick turnaround" basis.

---

*This case was prepared by Thomas M. Box of the University of Tulsa, Tulsa, Oklahoma. Reprinted with permission.

The company achieved dramatic success in the early '70 s due, primarily, to its ability to react very quickly in filling customer orders for special grades and sizes of redrawn tube and a "lean and mean" operating philosophy.

In 1974 the company began a major facility expansion to address an emergent market trend which, if not addressed, would have threatened their viability. The trend was the growing use of electric-resistance welded (ERW) tubing in heat exchangers as a cost-saving replacement for redrawn seamless tubing. ERW tubing costs roughly 1/2 what redrawn seamless tubing costs and is made by entirely different manufacturing processes.

The facility expansion, which included a quadrupling of the plant floor space and the installation of a Yoder slitter, two Yoder ERW rolling mills, a new batch annealing furnace, and a finishing floor, was completed in late 1975.

As a result of the expansion, the company in 1976 had a physical capacity of roughly 1500 tons/month of ERW tubing and 1500 tons/month of redraw seamless tubing. Recognizing that market expansion was required (to fill the redraw capability which had been vacated because of the ERW capability), Weber hired Robert N. Pressly as Senior Vice President–Commercial to enter the mechanical tubing market. Pressly, with many years of high-level sales experience in the specialty (mechanical) tubing market, vigorously moved to capture a significant share of the market.

The years 1976 through 1979 were troublesome for the company from several standpoints. New competitors had built plants in Houston, Gainsville, Texas, and St. Louis. The ERW expansion, although obviously required to remain competitive, had generated a series of technical and manufacturing problems (in terms of product quality and production throughput) that were quite serious. Labor availability became very troublesome during the late '70's as the Tulsa area had one of the lowest unemployment rates in the nation.

EXHIBIT 1   Organizational Structure of Southwest Tube Manufacturing Company

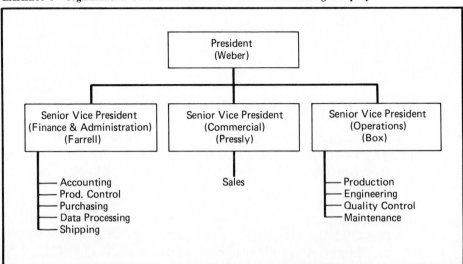

Recognizing a need to get outside, expert advice in redirecting the company on the path of growth and profitability, Weber commissioned an exhaustive review of every facet of company operations and structure by the Management Services Division of Arthur Young and Company.

Among the many changes instituted as a result of the Arthur Young studies was the hiring of two new Senior Vice Presidents and the complete realignment of functional responsibilities.

These changes resulted in the organizational structure shown in Exhibit 1. At the beginning of 1980 the company employed 450 hourly and salaried people.

Manufacturing

Manufacturing operations at Southwest Tube, are divided (physically and logically) between the Weld Mill Department and the Cold Draw Department. The Weld Mill Department is a *batch process* operation with all orders moving sequentially through 4 major work stations.

WORK STATION 1: *Slitter*—At this station, 20-ton master sheet coils (from Inland and Bethlehem Steel) are slit into various "mults" for welding into tube on the Yoder ERW mills.

WORK STATION 2: *Mills*—There are two ERW welding mills which have the capability of forming and welding 5/8" O.D. through $2\frac{1}{2}$" O.D. tube with wall thickness from .060" through .135". Tube is formed, welded, rolled to final size, and cut into 60'–80' lengths.

WORK STATION 3: *Furnace*—All tubing is annealed in a 7,000 lb/hour batch furnace in a reducing (gas) atmosphere at 1700°F. The annealing process reduces hardness and improves such physical properties as elongation and grain structure.

WORK STATION 4: *Finish Floor*—At the finish floor all tubing is rotary straightened, cut to exact length, eddy current tested, stenciled, and banded into bundles of hexagonal cross section. All tube bundles are moved from the finish floor via powered conveyor to the shipping department where they are oil dipped (for rust protection) and stored awaiting shipment.

Individual jobs processed through the Weld Mill Department are in the range of 10,000 to 100,000 linear feet of the same O.D. (outside diameter) and wall. Precise engineered labor standards are available for each operation at each work station. Labor standards are of the form of standard hours per 1000 feet of finished product. The pacing ("bottleneck") operation in the Weld Mill Department is at Work Station 4 (the Finish Floor) which is quite sensitive to product mix. For each combination of O.D. and wall, there is a different labor standard for *each operation*.

The Cold Draw Department is a large *job-shop* operation with six work stations. The controlling ("bottleneck") operation is the annealing furnace. The furnace does not run at constant temperature, but must be "cycled" up and down between 950°F and 1650°F as a function of the specific annealing requirements of the job being run. The furnace has 42 burners which consume natural gas at the rate of 366,000 btu/hr each when "firing". The furnace is 150 feet long, has a 10,000 lb/hr capacity and runs between 1 and 5 ft/min (as a function, again, of product mix).

The Cold Draw Department work stations are as follows:

WORK STATION 1:   *Yard*—Tube "hollows", which are heavy wall, $1\frac{1}{2}''$ to $2\frac{7}{8}''$ O.D. pipe purchased from various foreign and domestic steel mills, are stored in the yard. Yard operations include receiving, storage, initial cutting to length, and sorting by job.

WORK STATION 2:   *Tanks*—At the tanks tube hollows from the yard undergo the following chemical treatment: cleaning, pickling, phosphating, and stearate (soap) coating. The soap coating is used in the drawing operation (Work Station 4) to provide lubricity for the very heavy "cold working" done on the draw benches.

WORK STATION 3:   *Pointer*—At this work station, the tube hollows are reduced in diameter for about 1 foot on one end. The purpose of this operation is to allow the "points" of the tube hollows to pass through the dies on the draw benches without interference.

WORK STATION 4:   *Drawbenches*—There are 3 drawbenches with different capacities. A drawbench is used to change the O.D. and wall size from the starting hollow dimensions to the finished customer size. The grade of steel, the hardness, the percentage reduction of O.D. and wall and other variables determine how many "passes" are required on the benches and whether or not an order must be process annealed (in the annealing furnace) between passes.

WORK STATION 5:   *Annealing Furnace*—The operation of the annealing furnace is as described above. The important characteristic of the furnace is that it literally determines the sequence of jobs going to Work Station 6 regardless of priority. Refer to Exhibit 2 for furnace time/temperature relationships.

WORK STATION 6:   *Finish Floor*—The cold draw finish floor encompasses the same basic operations as the weld mill finish floor.

The Cold Draw Department produces 250–300 jobs per month and 70% of the jobs are less than 5,000 feet. The jobs are much more complex in the Cold Draw Department because any job after lubricating and pointing may make several trips through the draw benches and furnace as a result of metallurgical requirements. Engineered labor standards are available for each operation in the Cold Draw Department.

Production Scheduling.   The overall goal of the production scheduling process (in 1980) was to maximize shipped footage and concurrently to meet customer

EXHIBIT 2   Southwest Tube Manufacturing Company Furnace Scheduling

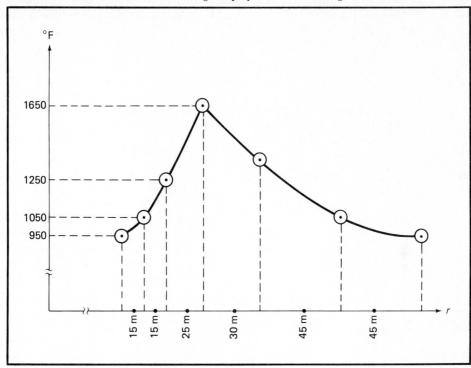

shipping requirements. The production scheduling function was performed by the Production Planning Department under the supervision of a Director of Materials Management reporting to the Senior Vice President–Finance & Administration. The Director of Material Management had limited responsibility for purchasing and inventory control. Inventory Control, in fact, reported to the Controller, who, in turn, reported to the Senior Vice President–Finance & Administration. The inventory control function was one of record-keeping and job costing. Raw material purchasing decisions were made by a committee consisting of the President, the Senior Vice President–Commercial, the Director of Sales, the Senior Vice President–Finance & Administration, and the Director of Purchasing.

Raw material lead times for foreign-produced tube hollows were generally 3–6 months. The reasons for purchasing foreign-produced hollows were lower purchase cost and a reputation for better product quality than domestic. Sheet coil (for the Weld Mill Department) had a 3–4 week lead time.

Customer orders ("jobs") generally had a 2–4 week delivery requirement. Production schedules issued to the shop were hand-written, incomplete, and frequently did not show expected completion times. Production scheduling was hampered by the lack of a job status "tracking" system and frequent sequence changes caused by in-process quality problems and customer priority changes.

The Production Planning Department consisted of 12 employees (and the Director) who were responsible for the following functions:

1. Writing production orders
2. Scheduling manufacturing operations
3. Releasing jobs to ship

In May of 1980 the Senior Staff (consisting of the President and the three Senior Vice Presidents) met to consider what might be done to improve the production scheduling function, which was obviously inadequate from both a manufacturing and a general management perspective.

_____ **CASE DISCUSSION QUESTIONS** _____

1. What specific type of scheduling methods should be employed at Southwest Tube? Should there be any difference between the Cold Draw and Weld Mill method?
2. Does the organizational structure contribute to the goals of the organization or detract from them?
3. Would an MRP System be useful to this organization?
4. What extrinsic factors and influences are important to this organization?

Case 8
AMERICAN CERAMIC
AND GLASS
PRODUCTS CORPORATION*

The American Ceramic and Glass Products Corporation employed a total of approximately 13,000 people, each of its three plants employing between 4,000 and 5,000 of this total. About three quarters of its sales volume came from standard glass containers produced on highly automatic equipment; the balance of the company's sales were of specialized ceramic and glass items produced in batches on much less automated equipment. John Parr, production manager for American Ceramic and

*Meier, et al, *Cases in Production and Operations Management*, © 1982. Reprinted by permission of Prentice-Hall, Inc., Englewood Cliffs, N.J.

Glass Products, had just completed a trip that covered eight states, seven universities, and three major industrial centers. The purpose of his trip was to recruit personnel for American's three plants. He felt that his trip had been extremely successful and that he had made contacts that would, he hoped, result in his firm's acquiring some useful and needed personnel.

Parr was anxious to secure a capable person to head up the inspection and quality control department of the largest of American's plants, located in Denver, Colorado. The position of chief of inspection and quality control had just been vacated by George Downs, who had taken an indefinite leave of absence due to a serious illness. There was little possibility that Downs would be capable of resuming any work duties within a year and a substantial probability that he would never be capable of working on a full-time basis. During the ten years that Downs held the position of chief of inspection and quality control, he had completely modernized the firm's inspection facilities and had developed a training program in the use of the most modern inspection equipment and techniques. The physical facilities of Downs's inspection department were a major attraction for visitors to the plant.

Thomas Calligan

During his trip, Parr interviewed two men whom he felt were qualified to fill Downs's position. Although each appeared more than qualified, Parr felt that a wrong choice could easily be made. Thomas Calligan, the first of the two men, was a graduate of a reputable trade school and had eight years of experience in the inspection department of a moderately large manufacturing firm (approximately 800 employees). He began working as a production inspector and was promoted to group leader within two years and chief inspector two years later. His work record as a production inspector, as a group leader, and as chief inspector was extremely good. His reason for wishing to leave the firm was "to seek better opportunities." He felt that in his present firm he could not expect further promotions in the near future. His firm was known for its stability, low employee turnover, and slow but assured advancement opportunities. His superior, the head of quality control, was recently promoted to this position and was doing a more than satisfactory job. Further, he was a young man, only 32 years old.

James King

James King, the second of the two men being considered by Parr, was a graduate of a major southwestern university and had approximately five years of experience. King was currently employed as head of inspection and quality control in a small manufacturing firm employing approximately 300 people. His abilities exceeded the requirements of his job, and he had made arrangements with his employer to do a limited amount of consulting work for noncompeting firms. His major reason for wanting to secure a different position was a continuing conflict of interests between himself and his employer. King did not wish to make consulting his sole source of income, but he felt that his current position was equally unsatisfactory. He believed that by working for a large firm he would be able to fully utilize his talents within that firm and thus resolve conflict occurring between his professional interests and the interests of his employer.

King's work record appeared to be good. This was evidenced by the fact that he had recently been granted a sizable pay increase. King, like Calligan, began his career as a bench inspector and was rapidly promoted to his current supervisory position. Unlike Calligan, King viewed his initial position of bench inspector primarily as a means of financing his education and not as the beginning of his lifetime career. King was 31 years old.

Role of Inspection and Quality Control

Major differences between these individuals centered on their philosophies regarding the role of inspection and quality control in a manufacturing organization. Calligan's philosophy was:

> Quality is an essential part of every product.... It is the product development engineer's function to specify what constitutes quality and the function of quality control to see that the manufacturing departments maintain these specifications.... Accurate and vigilant inspection is the key to controlled quality.

When asked how important process control was in the manufacture of quality products, he stated,

> Process control is achieved primarily through the worker's attitude. If a firm pays high wages and provides good working conditions, they should be able to acquire highly capable workers.... A well-executed and efficient inspection program will, as it has done in my firm, impress the importance of quality on the employees and motivate high-quality production. In the few cases when quality lapses do occur, an efficient inspection program prevents defective products from leaving the plant.... Any valid quality control program must hold quality equal in importance to quantity.... Quality records must be maintained for each employee and be made known to both the employee and his immediate superiors. Superior quality should be a major consideration in recommending individuals for promotion or merit pay increases.

King's philosophy paralleled that of Calligan only to the extent that "quality was an essential part of every product." King made the following comments regarding his philosophy toward inspection and quality control:

> If quality is properly controlled, inspection becomes a minor function. The more effective a quality control system becomes, the less inspection is required.... The key to quality control is process control, and inspection serves only as a check to assure

that the process controls are being properly administered.... An effective inspection scheme should locate and pinpoint the cause of defects rather than place the blame on an often innocent individual. A good rejection report will include the seeds from which a solution to future rejections can be developed.... One sign of an unsatisfactory quality control system is a large, impressive inspection program.

King was asked what steps he would take to develop such a program if he were to be offered and accept the job of chief of inspection and quality control in the Denver plant. He answered,

I would design and install a completely automatic inspection and process control system throughout the plant. By automatic I do not mean a mechanical or computer-directed system, but rather a completely standardized procedure for making all decisions concerning inspection and process control. The procedures would be based on a theoretically sound statistical foundation translated into laymen's terminology. The core of the program would be a detailed inspection and quality control manual.

When asked how long this might take King continued,

I constructed a similar manual for my present employer in a period of less than twelve months and had the whole process operating smoothly within eighteen months after beginning work on the task. Since your firm is somewhat larger, and accounting for my added experience, I would estimate it to take no longer than two years and hopefully significantly less time.... As previously stated, I would place major emphasis on process control and would minimize inspection by applying appropriate sampling procedures wherever possible.... Employee quality performance should be rated on the basis of process control charts rather than on the basis of final inspection reports. The employee should be trained and encouraged to use these charts as his chief tool toward achieving quality output.

King further stated that one of the reasons for his desire to find a new employer was that he had developed the quality control program in his present firm to the point where it was no longer offering him any challenge. He further stated that he felt this situation would recur at American Ceramic and Glass Products but that, because of the size of the firm, he could direct his attention to bigger and more interesting problems rather than be required to seek outside consulting work to satisfy his need for professional growth.

When asked what his real interests were, King stated, "Application of statistical concepts to the nonroutine activities of a manufacturing organization." He cited worker training, supplier performance, and trouble shooting as areas of interest. King submitted several reports that summarized projects that he had successfully completed in these or related areas.

This was the extent of information that Parr had on each of the two individuals he felt might best fill the position vacated by Downs, the retiring chief of the inspection and quality control department.

CASE DISCUSSION QUESTIONS

1. What is quality, who determines it, how is it described, and how is it attained?
2. What should be the role of the chief of inspection and quality control?
3. What was Calligan's philosophy toward quality control?
4. What was King's philosophy toward quality control?
5. Under what conditions would you expect Calligan and King, respectively, to be most effective?
6. Excluding the differences in philosophies between King and Calligan, what other factors relative to each require consideration?
7. Which of the two candidates, if either, should be selected for the position of chief of the inspection and quality control department?
8. Where could each man be utilized outside of the area of inspection and quality control?

Case 9
AAA FARM EQUIPMENT MANUFACTURING COMPANY

Background

AAA Farm Equipment Manufacturing Company (AAA) has been hard hit by current economic conditions. High interest rates and low farm prices have left the nation's farmer in a extremely poor financial situation with respect to capital investments. AAA manufactures various size augers and elevators that are used to transport grain.

In an effort to survive, AAA has diversified its product line and has entered the oil field equipment market with several new products. In addition to introducing a new product line, AAA's president, John Henderson, has required each department to operate with a minimum of personnel. Although these efforts have succeeded in reducing the magnitude of operating losses, the problem of returning the company to profitability still persists.

Tom Miller, Vice-President of Operations, hopes that the new MRP system AAA is currently implementing will have a material effect on the Company's bottom line.

AAA produces five basic sizes of augers and four types of grain elevators for the Farm Products product line. Each of these nine basic product groups or end items can vary based on customer or distributor specifications. Each end item is assembled from a variety of subassemblies called "bundles". There is wide bundle commonality amongst the various end items. In other words, many of the bundles are used on more than one end item. Because of the variable nature of the final product, the new MRP system will consider bundles as end items when scheduling production.

Tom Miller realizes that the success of the new MRP system will be highly dependent on how well AAA can forecast demand for bundles and major spare parts.

Current Forecasting Methodology

Currently, forecasting responsibility is divided at AAA between the Marketing Department and the Operations Department. Marketing is responsible for developing product group forecasts. Operations takes the product group forecasts and develops a bundle forecast for each bundle. In addition, Operations must predict demand for spare parts so that these items can be integrated into the production schedule.

To develop product group forecasts, Marketing uses a combination of grass roots forecasting (aggregating forecasts from regional sales managers) and subjective forecasting at the corporate level where the two product line managers and the manager of marketing develop a consensus forecast. To aid in developing subjective product group forecasts AAA subscribes to several publications such as *Agricultural Outlook*, *Predicasts*, and *Midwest Unit Buying Intentions* to ascertain farm income, available grain storage capacity, total farm loans (Farm Credit Administration), and other information relevant to demand forecasting.

Operations takes the Product Group Forecast from Marketing and estimates the bundle demand using the estimated number of bundles of each type for each end item or product group. For example, bundle 1235712-12 is used on 2 size augers—2 on the 6-inch auger and 1 on the 8-inch auger. This means that if the 6-inch auger forecast is 75 units and the 8-inch auger forecast is for 50 units, Operations will have to manufacture 200 1235712-12 bundles.

Historically, spare parts forecasting has been a manual "eye ball" estimate. However, the new MRP software has the facility to forecast spare parts by using a simple exponential smoothing model.

Tom Miller has hired you as an external consultant to examine their forecasting procedure and make recommendations. Specifically, he has asked whether:

There is a more scientific way of forecasting product group demand

The new MRP system should use the exponential smoothing model for forecasting spare parts

CASE DISCUSSION QUESTIONS

1. What techniques might apply to the product group forecasting?
2. What steps would you take to develop an alternative to the existing product group forecasting methodology?
3. How would you evaluate your alternative product group forecasting methodology?
4. What models would you apply to the spare parts forecasting?
5. How would you set up a study to choose the best model?

Case 10
AIRLINE TERMINAL DESIGN*

Since the Deregulation Act of 1978, American Airlines (AA) has successfully made a transition from a point-to-point carrier to a hub and spoke carrier. The two major hubs for AA are at Chicago and Dallas/Ft. Worth.

The passenger loads on a nonstop flight from city A to city B on a point-to-point network primarily consists of local passengers wanting to travel from A to B. In a hub and spoke network with city A as the hub, the flight from A to B has, in addition to the local traffic from A to B, traffic from cities C, D, E, F, etc. which feed the hub. The hub and spoke network for DFW is shown in Exhibit 1. American is currently the largest carrier at DFW, accounting for almost two thirds of the traffic.

American's flights at DFW are stacked into "complexes". These complexes are groups of flights which arrive almost simultaneously, stay on the ground for approximately the same time (50 minutes) and depart almost simultaneously. The ground time is used to transfer passengers and baggage from the inbound flight to the outbound flight. This method of complexing has two major advantages—the ground times are relatively small, making the connecting service competitive with nonstop service and giving more connecting opportunities, thereby increasing loads on flights. A complex with 20 flights inbound and 20 flights outbound gives 20 × 20 or 400 connections between 40 origination/destination cities. American's daily operations at DFW consists of more than 260 flights in eleven complexes during 1983. The biggest complex has approximately 30 inbound and outbound flights.

Although substantial progress had been made by American at DFW with respect to developing complexes, it was clear that terminal capacity constraints were

---

*Thomas M. Cook and Prakash Rao. Reprinted with permission.

EXHIBIT 1 American's Dallas/Ft. Worth Complex

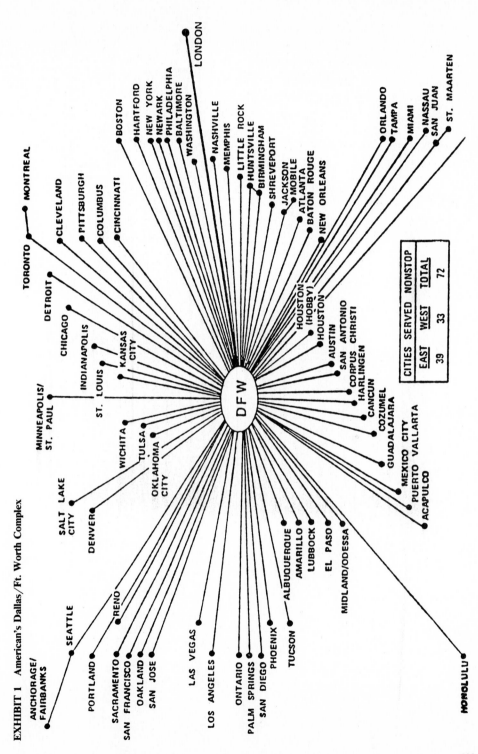

CITIES SERVED NONSTOP		
EAST	WEST	TOTAL
39	33	72

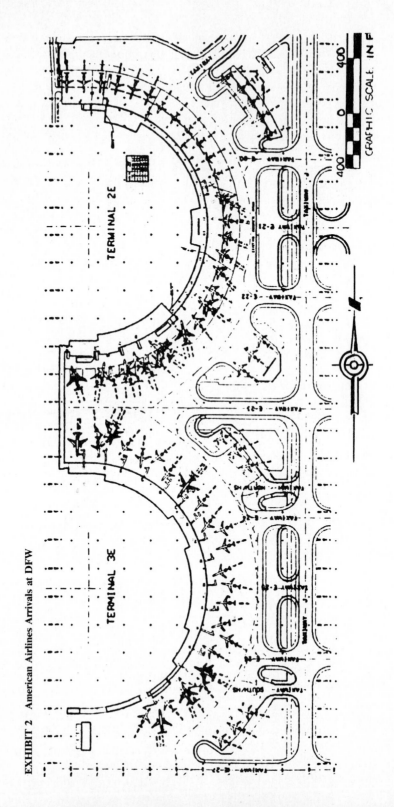

EXHIBIT 2 American Airlines Arrivals at DFW

going to limit the size of the complexes. Consequently, a decision was made to expand DFW facilities substantially. AA terminal facilities at DFW are shown in Exhibit 2. Prior to 1983, AA occupied terminal 3E with 22 gate positions. Seizing an opportunity to acquire additional gates in Terminal 2E, AA set in motion an expansion program that ultimately resulted in 34 gate positions.

The cost of renovating existing facilities and building new facilities, such as parking lots and moving sidewalks, has been estimated to be approximately $80 million.

The Operations Research group at American Airlines was asked by senior management to support the DFW expansion project with a number of analytical studies. These studies included:

> *Dynamic Gate Assignment Model*—The purpose of this model is to assign flights to gates to minimize baggage handling cost and passenger inconvenience.
>
> *Sign Selection and Programming*—The initial study involved a decision of the type of sign to be bought. The purpose of a followup on study was to develop an algorithm for automatically programming signs to direct incoming passengers to the right terminal, thereby minimizing the number of passengers misdirected.
>
> *Short-Term Parking*—The purpose of this study was to determine the number and location of short-term parking spaces needed to accommodate the anticipated expanded schedule.
>
> *Terminal Integrity*—Because the new terminal is only 880 feet from the existing AA terminal, it would be possible to consider the new terminal as part of Terminal 3E. This would afford increased flexibility in assigning gates and coping with problems such as gate holds. However, operating the new terminal as a separate terminal has many other marketing and operational advantages. The purpose of this study was to estimate the effect of operating the terminals separately as opposed to operating them as one larger terminal.
>
> *Spare Gate Analysis*—Experience has demonstrated the need for a number of spare gates to act as a safety stock or buffer to dampen the dependability effects of operational problems. The purpose of this study was to determine the optimal number of spare gates for each terminal and each complex.

Problem Definition

Two extremely important problems associated with American's expansion at DFW were amenable to an analytical approach. First, a policy decision had to be made concerning whether to treat the two terminals as separate and distinct terminals and not allow flights to be dynamically switched from one terminal to the other for a variety of operational or marketing reasons. The problem posed by senior management was to estimate the effect on departure and arrival dependability of splitting the two terminals. The split terminal operation has significant advantages such as:

> Key destinations and international flights can be isolated in the new terminal, thereby reinforcing the association between the terminal and destinations for the frequent

traveler; e.g. flights to/from Los Angeles will always arrive and depart from Terminal 2E, etc.

Splitting the terminals helps to balance the utilization of the facilities such as close-in parking spaces.

There is less likelihood that computer driven signs would misdirect passengers to the wrong terminal.

However, the impact of the split terminal configuration on key operational indicators such as departure dependability and gate holds had to be estimated before decisions could be taken. The loss of flexibility and possible deterioration in performance indicators had to be traded off against passenger convenience and balancing of facilities.

The second question to be answered, once the terminal integrity decision was made, concerned spare gate configuration. Spare gates or buffers are used to accommodate flight overlaps, i.e. a late departure from one complex overlapping with an early arrival from the next complex. Thus, a gate hold occurs when a flight has to wait until its assigned gate becomes available. (Spare gates reduce gate holds and their duration). The spare gate configuration would indicate the number of spares needed in each terminal for each complex.

The issue of spare gates is a classic conflict between airline marketing and operations personnel. Marketing typically wants to fill up each complex to the brim in order to maximize revenue, and Operations wants as many spare gates as possible to minimize the effect of unexpected operational problems. Consequently, an objective study of the spare gate requirements at DFW was important to determine the ultimate limit on the sizes of the complexes.

CASE DISCUSSION QUESTIONS

1. How would you approach the two problems described above?
2. If you would use a modeling approach, what would be the inputs and outputs of the model?
3. Develop a task plan for addressing the two problems.

APPENDIXES

Appendix A
NORMAL CURVE AREAS*

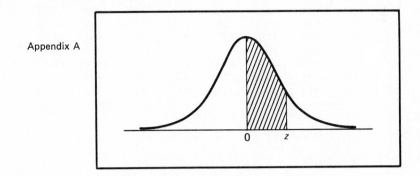

Appendix A

The entries in Table 1 are the probabilities that a random variable having the standard normal distribution assumes a value between 0 and z; they are given by the area of the white region under the curve in the figure shown above.

*John E. Freund, Frank J. Williams, *Elementary Business Statistics: The Modern Approach*, 4th edition. © 1982. Reprinted by permission of Prentice-Hall, Inc., Englewood Cliffs, N.J.

Table 1

z	.00	.01	.02	.03	.04	.05	.06	.07	.08	.09
0.0	.0000	.0040	.0080	.0120	.0160	.0199	.0239	.0279	.0319	.0359
0.1	.0398	.0438	.0478	.0517	.0557	.0596	.0636	.0675	.0714	.0753
0.2	.0793	.0832	.0871	.0910	.0948	.0987	.1026	.1064	.1103	.1141
0.3	.1179	.1217	.1255	.1293	.1331	.1368	.1406	.1443	.1480	.1517
0.4	.1554	.1591	.1628	.1664	.1700	.1736	.1772	.1808	.1844	.1879
0.5	.1915	.1950	.1985	.2019	.2054	.2088	.2123	.2157	.2190	.2224
0.6	.2257	.2291	.2324	.2357	.2389	.2422	.2454	.2486	.2517	.2549
0.7	.2580	.2611	.2642	.2673	.2704	.2734	.2764	.2794	.2823	.2852
0.8	.2881	.2910	.2939	.2967	.2995	.3023	.3051	.3078	.3106	.3133
0.9	.3159	.3186	.3212	.3238	.3264	.3289	.3315	.3340	.3365	.3389
1.0	.3413	.3438	.3461	.3485	.3508	.3531	.3554	.3577	.3599	.3621
1.1	.3643	.3665	.3686	.3708	.3729	.3749	.3770	.3790	.3810	.3830
1.2	.3849	.3869	.3888	.3907	.3925	.3944	.3962	.3980	.3997	.4015
1.3	.4032	.4049	.4066	.4082	.4099	.4115	.4131	.4147	.4162	.4177
1.4	.4192	.4207	.4222	.4236	.4251	.4265	.4279	.4292	.4306	.4319
1.5	.4332	.4345	.4357	.4370	.4382	.4394	.4406	.4418	.4429	.4441
1.6	.4452	.4463	.4474	.4484	.4495	.4505	.4515	.4525	.4535	.4545
1.7	.4554	.4564	.4573	.4582	.4591	.4599	.4608	.4616	.4625	.4633
1.8	.4641	.4649	.4656	.4664	.4671	.4678	.4686	.4693	.4699	.4706
1.9	.4713	.4719	.4726	.4732	.4738	.4744	.4750	.4756	.4761	.4767
2.0	.4772	.4778	.4783	.4788	.4793	.4798	.4803	.4808	.4812	.4817
2.1	.4821	.4826	.4830	.4834	.4838	.4842	.4846	.4850	.4854	.4857
2.2	.4861	.4864	.4868	.4871	.4875	.4878	.4881	.4884	.4887	.4890
2.3	.4893	.4896	.4898	.4901	.4904	.4906	.4909	.4911	.4913	.4916
2.4	.4918	.4920	.4922	.4925	.4927	.4929	.4931	.4932	.4934	.4936
2.5	.4938	.4940	.4941	.4943	.4945	.4946	.4948	.4949	.4951	.4952
2.6	.4953	.4955	.4956	.4957	.4959	.4960	.4961	.4962	.4963	.4964
2.7	.4965	.4966	.4967	.4968	.4969	.4970	.4971	.4972	.4973	.4974
2.8	.4974	.4975	.4976	.4977	.4977	.4978	.4979	.4979	.4980	.4981
2.9	.4981	.4982	.4982	.4983	.4984	.4984	.4985	.4985	.4986	.4986
3.0	.4987	.4987	.4987	.4988	.4988	.4989	.4989	.4989	.4990	.4990

Appendix B
POISSON CUMULATIVE DISTRIBUTION FUNCTION

$$F(k) = \sum_{x=0}^{k} \frac{\lambda^x \theta^{-\lambda}}{x!}$$

k	.5	1.0	1.5	2.0	2.5	3.0	3.5	4.0	4.5	5.0	5.5	6.0	6.5	7.0	7.5	8.0
0	.607	.368	.223	.135	.082	.050	.030	.018	.011	.007	.004	.002	.002	.001	.001	.000
1	.910	.736	.558	.406	.287	.199	.136	.092	.061	.040	.027	.017	.011	.007	.005	.003
2	.986	.920	.809	.677	.544	.423	.321	.238	.174	.125	.088	.062	.043	.030	.020	.014
3	.998	.981	.934	.857	.758	.647	.537	.433	.342	.265	.202	.151	.112	.082	.059	.042
4	1.000	.996	.981	.947	.891	.815	.725	.629	.532	.440	.358	.285	.224	.173	.132	.100
5	1.000	.999	.996	.983	.958	.916	.858	.785	.703	.616	.529	.446	.369	.301	.241	.191
6	1.000	1.000	.999	.995	.986	.966	.935	.889	.831	.762	.686	.606	.527	.450	.378	.313
7	1.000	1.000	1.000	.999	.996	.988	.973	.949	.913	.867	.809	.744	.673	.599	.525	.453
8	1.000	1.000	1.000	1.000	.999	.996	.990	.979	.960	.932	.894	.847	.792	.729	.662	.593
9	1.000	1.000	1.000	1.000	1.000	.999	.997	.992	.983	.968	.946	.916	.877	.830	.776	.717
10	1.000	1.000	1.000	1.000	1.000	1.000	.999	.997	.993	.986	.975	.957	.933	.901	.862	.816
11	1.000	1.000	1.000	1.000	1.000	1.000	1.000	.999	.998	.995	.989	.980	.966	.947	.921	.888
12	1.000	1.000	1.000	1.000	1.000	1.000	1.000	1.000	.999	.998	.996	.991	.984	.973	.957	.936
13	1.000	1.000	1.000	1.000	1.000	1.000	1.000	1.000	1.000	.999	.998	.996	.993	.987	.978	.966
14	1.000	1.000	1.000	1.000	1.000	1.000	1.000	1.000	1.000	1.000	.999	.999	.997	.994	.990	.983
15	1.000	1.000	1.000	1.000	1.000	1.000	1.000	1.000	1.000	1.000	1.000	.999	.999	.998	.995	.992
16	1.000	1.000	1.000	1.000	1.000	1.000	1.000	1.000	1.000	1.000	1.000	1.000	1.000	.999	.998	.996
17	1.000	1.000	1.000	1.000	1.000	1.000	1.000	1.000	1.000	1.000	1.000	1.000	1.000	1.000	.999	.998
18	1.000	1.000	1.000	1.000	1.000	1.000	1.000	1.000	1.000	1.000	1.000	1.000	1.000	1.000	1.000	.999
19	1.000	1.000	1.000	1.000	1.000	1.000	1.000	1.000	1.000	1.000	1.000	1.000	1.000	1.000	1.000	1.000
20	1.000	1.000	1.000	1.000	1.000	1.000	1.000	1.000	1.000	1.000	1.000	1.000	1.000	1.000	1.000	1.000
21	1.000	1.000	1.000	1.000	1.000	1.000	1.000	1.000	1.000	1.000	1.000	1.000	1.000	1.000	1.000	1.000
22	1.000	1.000	1.000	1.000	1.000	1.000	1.000	1.000	1.000	1.000	1.000	1.000	1.000	1.000	1.000	1.000
23	1.000	1.000	1.000	1.000	1.000	1.000	1.000	1.000	1.000	1.000	1.000	1.000	1.000	1.000	1.000	1.000
24	1.000	1.000	1.000	1.000	1.000	1.000	1.000	1.000	1.000	1.000	1.000	1.000	1.000	1.000	1.000	1.000
25	1.000	1.000	1.000	1.000	1.000	1.000	1.000	1.000	1.000	1.000	1.000	1.000	1.000	1.000	1.000	1.000
26	1.000	1.000	1.000	1.000	1.000	1.000	1.000	1.000	1.000	1.000	1.000	1.000	1.000	1.000	1.000	1.000
27	1.000	1.000	1.000	1.000	1.000	1.000	1.000	1.000	1.000	1.000	1.000	1.000	1.000	1.000	1.000	1.000
28	1.000	1.000	1.000	1.000	1.000	1.000	1.000	1.000	1.000	1.000	1.000	1.000	1.000	1.000	1.000	1.000
29	1.000	1.000	1.000	1.000	1.000	1.000	1.000	1.000	1.000	1.000	1.000	1.000	1.000	1.000	1.000	1.000
30	1.000	1.000	1.000	1.000	1.000	1.000	1.000	1.000	1.000	1.000	1.000	1.000	1.000	1.000	1.000	1.000
31	1.000	1.000	1.000	1.000	1.000	1.000	1.000	1.000	1.000	1.000	1.000	1.000	1.000	1.000	1.000	1.000

Appendix B (Continued)

k	8.5	9.0	9.5	10.0	10.5	11.0	11.5	12.0	12.5	13.0	13.5	14.0	14.5	15.0	15.5	16.0
0	.000	.000	.000	.000	.000	.000	.000	.000	.000	.000	.000	.000	.000	.000	.000	.000
1	.002	.001	.001	.000	.000	.000	.000	.000	.000	.000	.000	.000	.000	.000	.000	.000
2	.009	.006	.004	.003	.002	.001	.001	.001	.000	.000	.000	.000	.000	.000	.000	.000
3	.030	.021	.015	.010	.007	.005	.003	.002	.002	.001	.001	.000	.000	.000	.000	.000
4	.074	.055	.040	.029	.021	.015	.011	.008	.005	.004	.003	.002	.001	.001	.001	.000
5	.150	.116	.089	.067	.050	.038	.028	.020	.015	.011	.008	.006	.004	.003	.002	.001
6	.256	.207	.165	.130	.102	.079	.060	.046	.035	.026	.019	.014	.010	.008	.006	.004
7	.386	.324	.269	.220	.179	.143	.114	.090	.070	.054	.041	.032	.024	.018	.013	.010
8	.523	.456	.392	.333	.279	.232	.191	.155	.125	.100	.079	.062	.048	.037	.029	.022
9	.653	.587	.522	.458	.397	.341	.289	.242	.201	.166	.135	.109	.088	.070	.055	.043
10	.763	.706	.645	.583	.521	.460	.402	.347	.297	.252	.211	.176	.145	.118	.096	.077
11	.849	.803	.752	.697	.639	.579	.520	.462	.406	.353	.304	.260	.220	.185	.154	.127
12	.909	.876	.836	.792	.742	.689	.633	.576	.519	.463	.409	.358	.311	.268	.228	.193
13	.949	.926	.898	.864	.825	.781	.733	.682	.628	.573	.518	.464	.413	.363	.317	.275
14	.973	.959	.940	.917	.888	.854	.815	.772	.725	.675	.623	.570	.518	.466	.415	.368
15	.986	.978	.967	.951	.932	.907	.878	.844	.806	.764	.718	.669	.619	.568	.517	.467
16	.993	.989	.982	.973	.960	.944	.924	.899	.869	.836	.798	.756	.711	.664	.615	.566
17	.997	.995	.991	.986	.978	.968	.954	.937	.916	.890	.861	.827	.790	.749	.705	.659
18	.999	.998	.996	.993	.988	.982	.974	.963	.948	.930	.908	.883	.853	.819	.782	.742
19	.999	.999	.998	.997	.994	.991	.986	.979	.969	.957	.942	.923	.901	.875	.846	.812
20	1.000	1.000	.999	.998	.997	.995	.993	.988	.983	.975	.965	.952	.936	.917	.894	.868
21	1.000	1.000	1.000	.999	.999	.998	.996	.994	.991	.986	.980	.971	.960	.947	.930	.911
22	1.000	1.000	1.000	1.000	.999	.999	.998	.997	.995	.992	.989	.983	.976	.967	.956	.942
23	1.000	1.000	1.000	1.000	1.000	1.000	.999	.999	.998	.996	.994	.991	.986	.981	.973	.963
24	1.000	1.000	1.000	1.000	1.000	1.000	1.000	.999	.999	.998	.997	.995	.992	.989	.984	.978
25	1.000	1.000	1.000	1.000	1.000	1.000	1.000	1.000	.999	.999	.998	.997	.996	.994	.991	.987
26	1.000	1.000	1.000	1.000	1.000	1.000	1.000	1.000	1.000	1.000	.999	.999	.998	.997	.995	.993
27	1.000	1.000	1.000	1.000	1.000	1.000	1.000	1.000	1.000	1.000	1.000	.999	.999	.998	.997	.996
28	1.000	1.000	1.000	1.000	1.000	1.000	1.000	1.000	1.000	1.000	1.000	1.000	.999	.999	.999	.998
29	1.000	1.000	1.000	1.000	1.000	1.000	1.000	1.000	1.000	1.000	1.000	1.000	1.000	1.000	.999	.999
30	1.000	1.000	1.000	1.000	1.000	1.000	1.000	1.000	1.000	1.000	1.000	1.000	1.000	1.000	1.000	.999
31	1.000	1.000	1.000	1.000	1.000	1.000	1.000	1.000	1.000	1.000	1.000	1.000	1.000	1.000	1.000	1.000

Appendix C
EXPONENTIAL FUNCTIONS

x	e^{-x}	x	e^{-x}	x	e^{-x}
.0	1.000	2.4	.091	4.9	.007
.1	.905	2.5	.082	5.0	.007
.2	.819	2.6	.074	5.1	.006
.3	.741	2.7	.067	5.2	.006
.4	.670	2.8	.061	5.3	.005
.5	.607	2.9	.055	5.4	.005
.6	.549	3.0	.050	5.5	.004
.7	.497	3.1	.045	5.6	.004
.8	.449	3.2	.041	5.7	.003
.9	.407	3.3	.037	5.8	.003
1.0	.368	3.4	.033	5.9	.003
1.1	.333	3.5	.030	6.0	.002
1.2	.301	3.6	.027	6.1	.002
1.3	.273	3.7	.025	6.2	.002
1.4	.247	3.8	.022	6.3	.002
1.5	.223	3.9	.020	6.4	.002
1.6	.202	4.0	.018	6.5	.002
1.7	.183	4.1	.017	6.6	.001
1.8	.165	4.2	.015	6.7	.001
1.9	.150	4.3	.014	6.8	.001
2.0	.135	4.4	.012	6.9	.001
2.1	.122	4.5	.011	7.0	.001
2.2	.111	4.6	.010		
2.3	.100	4.7	.009		
		4.8	.008		

GLOSSARY

Acceptance sampling—Sampling from a "lot" of goods to determine whether to accept or reject the lot.

Activity—A task to be accomplished in the completion of a project.

Aggregate planning—Intermediate-range planning in which strategies are devised to economically absorb demand fluctuations for the organization's product or service.

Assembly chart—A chart that shows the component parts of a product, the sequence of assembly, and the flow-of-materials pattern.

Assembly-line balancing—The process of smoothing the assembly process and minimizing worker or machine idle time.

Assignable variations—Variations in a given characteristic of a product or service that can be attributed to a specific cause.

Batch-processing system—A data-processing system in which transactions are accumulated and master files are updated periodically.

Beta distribution—A continuous probability distribution often used in stochastic PERT analysis.

Bill of materials (BOM)—A list that specifies all component items that a product comprises.

CAD—Computer-aided design

CAM—Computer-aided manufacturing

Calling population (also called *input source*)—Consists of all customers or calling units that can arrive to a queuing system. When the calling population is finite, it is referred to as a finite calling population or limited-source calling population. An infinite calling population refers to a calling population containing an infinite number of calling units.

Capacity planning—The process of establishing, measuring, and adjusting levels of capacity in order to execute all manufacturing plans and schedules.

Carrying cost (also called *holding cost*)—One of three components of inventory costs. Carrying costs are those costs incurred for holding inventory.

Chi-square test—A nonparametric goodness-of-fit test used to test the hypothesis that a random variable is distributed in a specified manner.

Computer simulation—A numerical technique that involves modeling a stochastic system on a digital computer with the intention of predicting the system's behavior.

Constraints—Mathematical expressions that state resource limitations or other physical restrictions in a particular decision model.

Continuous inventory system—A system of accounting for inventory that updates inventory levels whenever there is an inventory replenishment or decrement.

Critical activities—Activities in a PERT network that are on the critical path and consequently have zero slack time.

Critical path—The longest path through a PERT network. The critical path is composed of activities with zero slack time.

Critical path method—A project scheduling and control method similar to PERT.

Critical ratio—A work center loading rule that assigns priorities based on the ratio of due date minus today's date to time required for the balance of the work.

Cycle time—The length of time between completed products' coming off an assembly line.

Delphi method—A qualitative forecasting technique that utilizes a panel of experts and a series of questionnaires to develop a forecast.

Dependent demand—Demand whose magnitude depends on the demand for another item or product.

Detailed scheduling—A centralized method of scheduling a job shop that outputs a detailed schedule for each job released to the shop.

Deterministic PERT—A project-scheduling technique in which the activity times are assumed to be known with certainty.

Disaggregation—The process by which aggregate plans are broken down into greater details for various work centers and operations.

Event—In PERT analysis, the completion of an activity or task.

Expected critical path—The path in a stochastic PERT network that would be the critical path if length of each activity were the expected time.

Flow shop—A production facility in which each job flows through the same sequence of processing.

Gantt chart—A simple bar chart depicting the starting time and completion time for various project tasks.

Goal programming—A mathematical programming technique that solves optimization problems having multiple and sometimes incompatible goals.

Grass-roots forecasting—A qualitative forecasting technique in which individual forecasts are generated at the end of the distribution channel and are aggregated to generate the total forecast.

Gross requirements—The quantity of an item that will have to be disbursed to support the production of a parent item.

Heuristic—A method or rule of thumb that determines good but not necessarily optimal solutions to a problem.

Hierarchical planning—A type of planning in which the set of decisions is partitioned into a hierarchy that corresponds to the levels of managerial decision making involved.

Historical analogy—A qualitative forecasting technique that forecasts demand based upon past experience with a similar product or service.

Holding costs (see *Carrying costs*)

Independent demand—Demand that is not dependent on the demand for an end item.

Input source (see *Calling population*)

Inventory—A stock of goods that is held for the purpose of future production or sales.

Job shop—A productive system typified by each job's having to be processed by a different sequence of work centers.

Kolmogorov-Smirnov test—A nonparametric goodness-of-fit test.

Lead time—The time between the release of an order and the time the goods start being added to inventory.

Learning-curve phenomenon—A phenomenon by which human productivity and efficiency increase as a function of experience or volume of output.

Least-squares method—A method for deriving a function that best fits a set of data.

Linear programming—A mathematical technique that can be used to maximize or minimize a linear objective function subject to certain linear constraints.

MAD—See Mean Absolute Deviation

Management information system—A system designed to collect, store, and process data so that they are useful for decision making.

Management science—The discipline devoted to studying and developing scientific procedures to help in the process of managerial decision making (see *Operations research*).

Manufacturing resource planning (MRP II)—An extension of MRP that interlocks the scheduling and materials management aspects of MRP with the accounting and financial planning functions of the firm.

Market research—A family of qualitative forecasting techniques that is helpful in revealing predictions about the size, structure, and configuration of markets for various goods and services.

Master production schedule—A refinement of the aggregate plans; it specifies what is to be produced (and in what quantities) for a specified period of time (six months to one year).

Materials requirements planning (MRP)—A system of logically related records, procedures, and decision rules that translate the master schedule into time-phased net requirements and planned coverage of these requirements for all component items needed.

Mean absolute deviation—Average absolute difference between the forecasted demand and the actual demand.

Model—A representation or an abstraction of an object or a particular real-world phenomenon.

Monte Carlo simulation—A simulation using a sampling technique that consists of the generation of random variates from a specified probability distribution.

Net requirements—The quantity of additional component items to procure in order to support the production of a parent item. Net requirements = Gross requirements − Scheduled receipts − Inventory on hand.

Network—A graphical representation of a problem or situation consisting of a collection of nodes connected by links (lines).

Network diagram (see *PERT chart*)

Objective function—A mathematical expression used to represent the goal or objective of a particular decision problem.

Operations management—The discipline devoted to the effective management of productive systems.

Operations research—The discipline devoted to studying and developing scientific procedures to help in the process of making decisions (see *Management science*).

Order costs—The costs incurred when processing an order for inventory.

Order level—The inventory level after replenishment.

Panel consensus—A qualitative forecasting technique that involves assembling a panel of experts for the purpose of jointly developing a forecast.

Path—A sequential series of activities in a PERT network.

PERT (see *Project evaluation and review technique*)

PERT / Cost—A methodology for planning, scheduling and controlling the cost of a project.

PERT chart—A network diagram of a project.

Physical inventory system—An inventory accounting system in which management periodically reviews levels of the various items in inventory in order to make inventory decisions.

Poisson probability density function—A discrete probability function that yields the probability of *n* events occurring in a given time interval.

Poisson process—Usually refers to a random arrival process where the number of arrivals in a time period is distributed according to a Poisson probability distribution.

Process control—A category of statistical quality control whose object is to determine when the productive process needs to be investigated to determine if corrective action must be taken.

Process generator—A function that transforms a uniformly distributed random number into a nonuniform random variate.

Production scheduling—The scheduling of the production process.

Productive system—A system that transforms inputs into outputs for the purpose of creating goods and services.

Productivity—A measure of how effectively labor and materials are converted into finished goods and services.

Project evaluation and review technique (PERT)—A technique for scheduling and controlling large projects.

Project scheduling—The scheduling of major tasks that require a significant amount of time to accomplish.

Quality circle—A voluntary group of workers that meet together on company time to discuss, analyze and prepare solutions to quality problems.

Queue discipline (also called *service discipline*)—The decision rule that determines which calling unit in the queuing system receives service.

Queuing system—Any system that has a waiting line as an element of the system.

Queuing theory—A branch of operations research that through mathematical models describes the behavior of queuing systems.

Random variations—One of four components of a time series. Random variations are fluctuations in the dependent variable of a time series that cannot be assigned to trend, seasonality, or some cyclical component.

Real-time system—A computer-based system that is on-line to the computer. This enables instantaneous response to inquiries and often instantaneous update of a data base.

Regression analysis—A forecasting technique yielding a forecasting equation that defines the dependent variable as a function of one or more independent variables.

Reorder level—The inventory level at the time of placing the order.

Replenishment period—The time it takes to replenish inventory once replenishment has begun.

Robotics—The use of industrial robots or automated manipulator arms.

Sensitivity analysis—The analysis of how an optimal solution and the value of its objective function are affected by changes in the various inputs or components of the decision model.

Service discipline (see **Queue discipline**)

Service facility—The server in a queuing system.

Shadow price—The marginal value of a resource associated with a linear programming constraint at optimality.

Shortage costs (also called *stockout costs*)—Inventory costs associated with being out of stock.

Simplex method—A mathematical procedure for solving linear programming problems.

Slack time—In PERT analysis, the amount of time an activity can be delayed without delaying the entire project.

Steady state—A queuing system is in a steady-state condition when its behavior is not a function of time.

Stochastic PERT—A project-scheduling technique in which the activity times are of a probabilistic nature.

Stockout costs (see **Shortage costs**)

System—A whole comprising interrelated parts intended to accomplish a specific objective.

Systems approach—A modern integrated approach to decision making in which all relevant factors (including intra-organizational and environmental or external factors) are considered in the decision process. The objective is to achieve the goals of the organization as a whole.

Time phasing—The process of timing inventory needs to arrive at the point in time when they are needed.

Tracking signal—The sum of the deviations between the actual demand and the forecasted demand divided by the MAD for that time period.

Work-breakdown structure—The top-down organizational structure of a project.

Work-center loading—One of two major categories of ways to schedule a job shop. Loading schemes typically take the form of a queue discipline, which is employed at each work center.

Work package—The smallest element in the work-breakdown structure.

INDEX